AF725205

The Handbook of Fraud Deterrence

THE HANDBOOK OF FRAUD DETERRENCE

HARRY CENDROWSKI

JAMES P. MARTIN

LOUIS W. PETRO

BICENTENNIAL 1807 WILEY 2007 BICENTENNIAL

John Wiley & Sons, Inc.

This book is printed on acid-free paper. ♾

Copyright © 2007 by John Wiley & Sons, Inc. All rights reserved.

Published by John Wiley & Sons, Inc., Hoboken, New Jersey.

Published simultaneously in Canada.

No part of this publication may be reproduced, stored in a retrieval system, or transmitted in any form or by any means, electronic, mechanical, photocopying, recording, scanning, or otherwise, except as permitted under Section 107 or 108 of the 1976 United States Copyright Act, without either the prior written permission of the Publisher, or authorization through payment of the appropriate per-copy fee to the Copyright Clearance Center, Inc., 222 Rosewood Drive, Danvers, MA 01923, 978-750-8400, fax 978-646-8600, or on the web at www.copyright.com. Requests to the Publisher for permission should be addressed to the Permissions Department, John Wiley & Sons, Inc., 111 River Street, Hoboken, NJ 07030, 201-748-6011, fax 201-748-6008, or online at http://www.wiley.com/go/permissions.

Limit of Liability/Disclaimer of Warranty: While the publisher and author have used their best efforts in preparing this book, they make no representations or warranties with respect to the accuracy or completeness of the contents of this book and specifically disclaim any implied warranties of merchantability or fitness for a particular purpose. No warranty may be created or extended by sales representatives or written sales materials. The advice and strategies contained herein may not be suitable for your situation. You should consult with a professional where appropriate. Neither the publisher nor author shall be liable for any loss of profit or any other commercial damages, including but not limited to special, incidental, consequential, or other damages.

For general information on our other products and services, or technical support, please contact our Customer Care Department within the United States at 800-762-2974, outside the United States at 317-572-3993 or fax 317-572-4002.

Wiley also publishes its books in a variety of electronic formats. Some content that appears in print may not be available in electronic books.

For more information about Wiley products, visit our Web site at http://*www.wiley.com.*

Library of Congress Cataloging-in-Publication Data:

Handbook of fraud deterrence / [edited by] Harry Cendrowski,
James P. Martin, Louis W. Petro.
p. cm.
Includes index.
ISBN-13: 978-0-471-93134-8 (cloth)
ISBN-10: 0-471-93134-9 (cloth)
1. Fraud—prevention. 2. Employee crimes—Prevention. 3. Fraud investigation. 4. Forensic accounting. I. Cendrowski, Harry. II. Martin, James P. III. Petro, Louis W.
HV6691.F74 2007
658.4'73—dc22

2006021643

Printed in the United States of America

10 9 8 7 6 5 4 3 2 1

About the Contributors

Harry Cendrowski, CPA, CFE, CVA, CFD
Cofounder and President, Cendrowski Corporate Advisors and Cendrowski Selecky PC, Bloomfield Hills, MI

Harry Cendrowski has over 25 years of extensive experience in entrepreneurial, personal, and corporate tax matters. His business consulting engagements have included real estate, business valuations, mergers, due diligence, complex commercial and divorce litigation support, forensic accounting, and fraud auditing. Mr. Cendrowski is also President and Managing Director of The Prosperitas Group LLC, an independent multiclient family office providing coordinated planning and administrative management services to individuals and families of significant wealth.

Mr. Cendrowski has been an expert witness at various courts and administrative agencies in the United States and United Kingdom. After receiving his bachelor's degree from University of Detroit, he began his professional career in the audit department of Deloitte & Touche (formerly Touche Ross). He has authored articles in professional publications and has presented to various bar association and business conferences.

James P. Martin, CMA, CIA, CFD
Senior Manager, Cendrowski Corporate Advisors, Bloomfield Hills, MI;
Adjunct Professor, Walsh College, Troy, MI

Jim Martin combines hands-on experience with diverse business processes and a thorough understanding of the associated control objectives and systems to facilitate the review and redesign of organizations and business functions.

Mr. Martin has performed comprehensive risk assessments in a variety of industries focusing on the evaluation of operating effectiveness of business processes and the internal control structure, and the development of recommendations for improvement. In many cases, these services were provided to companies where basic internal control lapses had led to financial reporting and operational issues. Mr. Martin also held various management positions within Chrysler Financial and with the Corporate Treasury unit of Chrysler Corporation. In these management positions, he designed and implemented internal control systems covering basic accounting transactions. Mr. Martin holds a BBA in Accounting and an MS in Accounting Information Systems from Eastern Michigan University.

Louis W. Petro, PhD, CPA, CMA, CFE, CIA, CISA, CFM, CCP, PE
Senior Manager, Cendrowski Corporate Advisors, Bloomfield Hills, MI

Since 1969, Louis Petro has taught auditing, systems, accounting, and finance courses at a number of colleges and universities in Michigan and Ontario, Canada. He was the Dean of the Lawrence Technological University School of Management from 1979 through 1989.

From 1971 through 1979, Dr. Petro held consulting and auditing positions at the CPA firms of Ernst and Young, Plante and Moran, and Grant Thornton. He was a Management Advisory Services (MAS) Manager at Grant Thornton in Chicago immediately prior to becoming the Dean at LTU.

Prior to his auditing and consulting career, Dr. Petro was a manufacturing engineer at the Chevrolet Division of General Motors and the GM Manufacturing Development Staff.

Dr. Petro remains active in providing continuing professional education for certified public accountants, certified internal auditors, and certified management accountants. He regularly conducts classes and seminars for the Michigan Association of CPAs, the Oakland University CPE Program for CPAs, the Institute of Internal Auditors, and the Institute of Management Accountants. In addition, he has been a question writer for the U.S. Certified Management Accountant examination.

Amelia Annette Baldwin, PhD
Professor, University of Alabama in Huntsville

Amelia Annette Baldwin received her PhD from Virginia Tech and earned BS and MS in accounting from Auburn University. She currently teaches and researches accounting and technology issues at the UAH. Previously she has taught and researched at the University of Alabama, Thammasat University (Thailand), Florida International University, University of Queensland (Australia), University of Tasmania (Australia), Oregon State University, and Eastern Michigan University. Her research on accounting and technology issues has been published in numerous U.S. and European journals.

Dr. Baldwin is an active member of the American Accounting Association and its sections, including the Artificial Intelligence/Emerging Technologies section and the Information Systems section. She has won several research and service awards. She also presents workshops and delivers keynote speeches upon request.

Matthew P. Breuer
Consultant, Cendrowski Corporate Advisors, Bloomfield Hills, MI

Mr. Breuer, in addition to his work on this publication, is a contributing author to "The Fraud Files", a current events newsletter published twice per month by Cendrowski Corporate Advisors, and appearing in the bi-monthly *Value Examiner* published by the National Association of Certified Valuation Analysts (NACVA).

Marion E. Briggs, CDE, CFE
President, Briggs & Associates, Inc., Troy, MI

Ms. Briggs has over 25 years experience with the examination of disputed documents for signature authentication and/or writer identification; detection of eradication, alteration, or additions; and decipherment of obliterations and indented writings. She has presented her findings and expert testimony in numerous courts and legal forums.

David J. Brophy, MBA, PhD
Professor, University of Michigan Ross School of Business and Director, Center for Venture Capital and Private Equity Finance, Ann Arbor, MI

David J. Brophy teaches courses in venture capital and private equity finance. He is Director of the UMBS Center for Venture Capital and Private Equity Finance (CVP) and is a member of the executive committee for the Zell-Lurie Institute for Entrepreneurial Studies (ZLI).

He has published extensive research on venture capital and private equity finance and has twice won the National Association of Small Business Investment Companies Research Award. He is the author of a book titled *Finance, Entrepreneurship and Economic Development* and has published a large number of research papers in this and other aspects of finance. He is a founding member of the editorial board of the *Journal of Business Venturing,* the *Journal of Private Equity Finance,* and the *International Venture Capital Journal.*

He has been a director of several public companies and is a director and advisor to a number of banks, money market funds, and financial services firms including Compass Technology Partners (a venture capital firm in Palo Alto, CA), Munder Capital Management (Birmingham, MI), Continental Capital (OH), River Place Holdings (Detroit, MI), and General Motors Acceptance Corporation Wholesale Auto Receivables Corporation. He also is an investor in and an advisor to a number of emerging technology-based firms.

Charles Calio
Associate, Kerr, Russell and Weber, PLC., Detroit, MI

Charles G. Calio practices in the areas of commercial litigation, bankruptcy, and real estate. Mr. Calio is fluent in Spanish and is a First Lieutenant in the Michigan Army National Guard. Mr. Calio earned his law degree at the College of William and Mary Law School and BA degrees in Political Science and History at Michigan State University.

Samuel C. Damren, Esq.
Member, Dykema Gossett, Detroit, MI

Samuel Damren has enjoyed a wide breadth of experience during his professional career. He began his career as a trial prosecutor in Detroit, first with Wayne County and then with the United States Attorney's Office. Since entering private practice in 1981, Mr. Damren has counseled and represented privately and publicly held entities in civil and criminal litigation, business planning, and transactional work. He has served as an arbitrator and court appointed master, mediator and case evaluator, and is the author of a number of scholarly articles.

His experience includes complex business litigation; intra-entity disputes involving shareholders, directors, officers, partners, trustees, beneficiaries, members, and managers; business formation, reorganization, and relations, including acquisitions, contracts, fiduciary obligations, financing and real estate; and corporate governance, internal investigations, audits, and white-collar criminal defense.

Lawrence R. Donaldson, Esq.
Senior Shareholder, Plunkett & Cooney PC, Mount Clemens, MI

Lawrence R. Donaldson holds BBA (1961) and MBA (1963) degrees from the University of Michigan and a JD *cum laude* (1969), from Detroit College of Law. He served as a public/attorney member of the Michigan State Board of Accountancy from 1997 to 2005. He is a member of the firm's Professional Liability Practice Group.

Christopher A. Grosman, Esq.
Associate, Carson Fischer PLC, Bloomfield Hills, MI

Christopher A. Grosman is an associate in the Bloomfield Hills, Michigan law firm of Carson Fischer, P.L.C. He has extensive experience in representing Chapter 11 debtor companies and committees of unsecured creditors in complex bankruptcy litigation. Mr. Grosman received his B.A., with distinction, from Michigan State University and his law degree, cum laude, from the Wayne State University Law School, where he was a member of the Moot Court Team. Mr. Grosman is a member of the Oakland County, Federal and American Bar Associations, and the State Bar of Michigan.

Brieh Guevara, CFE, CFD
Brieh Guevara combines business process and information systems expertise to design and implement data analysis, and content quality management programs. Uses of such information have included analyses of Sarbanes-Oxley compliance data, merger and acquisition integrations, executive information systems, purchase-to-pay leakage, securitization recalculations, data migration efforts, and Web-based security systems.

Mr. Guevara earned a BBA from the University of Michigan Business School, Ann Arbor. He is a member of the National Association of Certified Valuation Analysts and the Data Management Association and has served as a board member for Hope Worldwide—Michigan.

Jeffrey S. Hengeveld, Esq.
Associate, Plunkett & Cooney PC, Bloomfield Hills, MI

Jeffrey S. Hengeveld is a graduate of James Madison College at Michigan State University (1999) and received his JD *magna cum laude* from Michigan State University, Detroit College of Law, in 2003. He is a member of the firm's Professional Liability Practice Group.

Fred K. Herrmann
Member, Kerr, Russell and Weber, PLC., Detroit, MI

Fred K. Herrmann specializes in the areas of commercial and complex litigation, and practices in both state and federal courts. Mr. Herrmann has extensive experience handling disputes involving the Uniform Commercial Code, contracts, insurance coverage, antitrust, intellectual property, securities, class action defense, attorney and accountant liability, and multidistrict litigation. He also practices in the appellate courts at both the state and federal levels.

Mr. Herrmann is a 1996 graduate of the University of Michigan Law School. While there, he was an editor of the *Michigan Journal of International Law*. Mr. Herrmann often serves as a judge for moot court competitions at both Michigan Law School and Wayne State University School of Law.

Mr. Herrmann received his BS in English, with merit, from the United States Naval Academy in 1988. He served as a logistics officer in the United States Marine Corps from 1988 to 1993 (active duty) and from 1993 to 1996 (reserve).

David R. Janis
Associate, Kerr, Russell and Weber, PLC., Detroit, MI

David R. Janis practices in various areas of litigation and is active in the firm's corporate practice. Mr. Janis is a member of the American Bar Association, the Federal Bar Association, and the State Bar of Michigan.

Mr. Janis received his law degree from Wayne State University Law School in 2005, where he was an active member of the Law School's Moot Court team as both an oralist and a coach. While there, Mr. Janis interned with the Honorable Judge Avern Cohn of the United States District Court of the Eastern District of Michigan. Mr. Janis graduated with honors from James Madison College at Michigan State University in 2002, where he earned a BA degree in Political Theory and Constitutional Democracy.

Sandy Kronenberg
Chairman and President, Netarx, Inc.

Sandy is well versed in industry standards and best practices associated with information technology. During his career he has consulted, planned, and implemented IT solutions for countless organizations in North America. Sandy founded Netarx, Inc., to focus on advanced technologies including IP Telephony, Security, Information Life-Cycle Management and Monitoring Services. In addition to his duties at Netarx, Sandy is actively involved in developing new technologies (he currently holds two U.S. Patents issued and has one more pending) and contributing to the IT community via lectures and publications. Sandy holds a BS from the University of Michigan and an MS from Georgetown University.

Patrick J. Kukla, Esq.
Associate, Carson Fischer PLC

Patrick J. Kukla has extensive experience in representing Chapter 11 debtor companies and committees of unsecured creditors in complex bankruptcy litigation. Mr. Kukla received his BA, with honors, from the University of Detroit Mercy and his law degree, cum laude, from the Wayne State University Law School, where he was a member of the Moot Court Team. Mr. Kukla is a member of the Oakland County Bar Association and the State Bar of Michigan.

Lawrence A. Lichtman, Esq.
Partner, Carson Fischer PLC, Bloomfield Hills, MI

Lawrence A. Lichtman has expertise in representing Chapter 11 debtor companies and committees of unsecured creditors in complex bankruptcy litigation, including fraudulent transfer and other avoidance actions. In over 20 years of practice, Mr. Lichtman has presented to various bar association and professional conferences. He is a member of the Detroit Metropolitan, Oakland County, Federal and American Bar Associations, and the State Bar of Michigan.

Mr. Lichtman is a graduate of the University of Michigan and a cum laude graduate of the Detroit College of Law, where he served as a Note & Comment Editor of the *Law Review*. Mr. Lichtman has been very active in civic affairs. He is a former Mayor of the City of Farmington Hills, Michigan, which community he also served, among other capacities, as a member of the City Council, as Chairman of the Board of Zoning Appeals, and as a member of the Planning Commission.

J. Andrew Moss, Esq.
Associate, Sachnoff & Weaver, Ltd., Chicago, IL

J. Andrew Moss is an associate in the Sachnoff & Weaver Insurance Coverage Group; he assists policy holders in negotiating insurance and resolving coverage disputes, and counsels business entities, directors and officers, risk managers, attorneys, and other professionals on insurance coverage and litigation matters throughout the United States and abroad. Prior to joining Sachnoff & Weaver, Mr. Moss served as a Staff Attorney at the United States Court of Appeals for the Seventh Circuit and as a law clerk to Circuit Judge Ilana Diamond Rovner. Mr. Moss earned his J.D. with honors, Order of the Coif, from DePaul University College of Law, and earned undergraduate degrees from Tufts University and the School of the Art Institute of Chicago.

Gregory V. Murray, Esq.
Vice President, Treasurer and Founder, Director and Shareholder, Vercruysse Murray & Calzone, P.C., Bingham Farms, MI

Gregory Murray practices in federal and state courts on behalf of public and private sector employers in the areas of wrongful discharge and employment litigation, civil rights and discrimination litigation. He is a graduate of the University of Michigan (BA, 1971) and the Detroit College of Law (JD, cum laude, 1978), where he served on the Detroit College of Law Review. Mr. Murray has over 25 years of experience in employment litigation and counseling, labor arbitrations, hospital medical staff privilege appeals, and proceedings before administrative agencies such as the Equal Employment Opportunity Commission and the Michigan Department of Civil Rights.

He is a frequent lecturer on employment issues. Mr. Murray has been included in *The Best Lawyers in America* (Management Labor Lawyers) since 2003 and is listed in the 2004 and 2005 editions of *Chambers USA: America's Leading Lawyers for Business* and *Who's Who Legal USA—Management Labor & Employment* (2006). He is also coauthor of *Employment Litigation in Michigan* (ICLE 1999) and *Employment Litigation in Michigan,* 2nd edition (ICLE 2004).

Jagdish Pathak, PhD
Professor, Louise & Edmond Odette School of Business, University of Windsor, Windsor ON, Canada

Jagdish Pathak's principal research activities are in information systems assurance, with special emphasis on information technology auditing in relation to e-commerce, distributed systems, and computer networks. He is currently developing a Center for Applied Research in e-Commerce Assurance in Odette School of Business, Windsor, Ontario, Canada, to take up applied research activities in this area. He has published articles and papers in numerous journals. His research monograph, *Information Technology Auditing—An Evolving Agenda,* was released in March 2005.

James A. Rolfes, Esq.
Member, Sachnoff & Weaver, Ltd., Chicago, IL

James A. Rolfes is a member in the Sachnoff & Weaver Securities Litigation and Regulation Practice Group, holds a Certified Public Accountant license and represents corporations, officers and directors in corporate governance and securities litigation, and SEC investigations.

He also has extensive experience in litigation involving alleged securities violations and malpractice against accountants, underwriters, and attorneys and in providing a defense to class-based and shareholder derivative claims.

Mr. Rolfes graduated magna cum laude from the University of Illinois College of Law (1987) where he was Order of the Coif, and received a BBA from the University of Michigan (1981).

Carolyn H. Rosenberg, Esq.
Member, Sachnoff & Weaver, Ltd., Chicago, IL

Carolyn H. Rosenberg heads the Insurance Coverage Group at the law firm of Sachnoff & Weaver, and provides counsel to business entities, board members, officers, partners and other professionals in the negotiation of insurance coverage and resolution of insurance disputes. Her areas of emphasis include insurance coverage and corporate indemnification and litigation. Ms. Rosenberg assists clients in evaluating insurance coverage and other protections when negotiating transactions and represents them in resolving coverage disputes.

Ms. Rosenberg was confirmed as the nation's top D&O liability insurance lawyer by *Corporate Board Member* magazine in a feature on superstar corporate attorneys (July 2004) and was selected by *Corporate Board Member* magazine as one of the country's 12 legal superstars and the top D&O liability insurance lawyer (August 2001). She is the Chair, S&W Insurance Coverage Group, and the Co-Chair, American Bar Association Corporate Counsel Committee's Subcommittee on Insurance Coverage. She served as a law clerk to the Honorable Frederick H. Weisberg of the Superior Court of the District of Columbia and has contributed to and authored numerous articles on insurance and indemnification issues.

E. Leonard Rubin, Esq.
Of Counsel, Sachnoff & Weaver, Ltd., Chicago, IL

E. Leonard Rubin's areas of emphasis include copyright law, trademark law, trade secret law and entertainment law. He handled numerous transactional and Internet matters involving counseling and transfers of and protection for all forms of intellectual property, and has engaged in a variety of litigation regarding the communications, publishing, recording, television, theatrical, and motion picture industries.

Mr. Rubin has served as an Adjunct Professor at the University of Illinois College of Law, the John Marshall Law School, and the Northwestern University School of Law. He was a Director for CBA-TV Inc. and the President of the Midwest Chapter of Copyright Society of U.S.A. He served as Chair of the Copyright Committee for the Intellectual Property Lawyers Association of Chicago and a member of the Internationale des Avocates, President, Intellectual Property Commission.

Brian Sommariva
Founder and Managing Director, Design Runway, Plymouth, MI

Brian Sommariva advises businesses and consumers on Web site development and usability, including information architecture and security for Internet applications. In addition, he consults with organizations on network and data security best practices including wireless network security. Mr. Sommariva also presents to various professional associations on topics such as identity theft and other computer-related threats.

Robert M. Vercruysse, Esq.
President and Founder, Director and Shareholder, Vercruysse Murray & Calzone, P.C., Bingham Farms, MI

Robert M. Vercruysse is widely recognized as a leading counselor and litigator in all areas of employment, labor, and civil rights law. His clients include manufacturing operations, institutions of higher education, hospitals and physicians, distributors, financial institutions, news organizations, and television stations. He recently represented management in the Detroit newspaper strike.

He is listed in *The Best Lawyers in America, Chambers USA: America's Leading Lawyers for Business,* and *Who's Who Legal USA—Management Labour & Employment* (2006). Mr. Vercruysse is a Fellow of the College of Labor and Employment Lawyers, a Fellow of the American Bar Foundation, and a Charter Member of the American Employment Law Council.

Mr. Vercruysse graduated from Michigan State University with high honors and received his J.D. (cum laude) from the University of Michigan Law School. He served as a law clerk to the Honorable Clifford O'Sullivan of the United States Court of Appeals for the Sixth Circuit. He has also been an adjunct professor at the University of Michigan Law School, and he has authored numerous articles and book chapters.

Adam A. Wadecki
Consultant, Cendrowski Corporate Advisors, Bloomfield Hills, MI

Adam Wadecki is a PhD student at the University of Michigan, concentrating in Financial Engineering and Manufacturing Management.

Mr. Wadecki's research currently focuses on governance structures and financial models that describe the private equity arena. He has presented at national conferences and frequently collaborates with Professor David J. Brophy at the University of Michigan Ross School of Business.

Adam graduated *magna cum laude* with BS degrees in Mechanical and Industrial and Operations Engineering, along with a minor in Mathematics, from the University of Michigan.

Robert A. Weisberg, Esq.
Partner, Carson Fischer PLC, Bloomfield Hills, MI

Robert A. Weisberg concentrates his legal practice in the area of complex financial restructuring and bankruptcy reorganization. For over 25 years, he has represented corporate and business debtors, individual creditors, and creditors' committees in insolvency matters, both in United States bankruptcy courts and in out-of-court proceedings throughout the country. Many of these matters have involved pursuing or defending actions seeking to recover assets fraudulently concealed or transferred.

Mr. Weisberg received his BA, with distinction, from the University of Michigan and his JD from Georgetown University Law Center, where he was a member of the Tax Lawyer Law Review. He has authored articles on a variety of bankruptcy topics. He has also lectured to many business and bar groups on bankruptcy issues.

Mr. Weisberg is a member of the American and Federal Bar Associations and the State Bar of Michigan and a former chair of the Oakland County (Michigan) Bar Association Bankruptcy Committee.

Douglas E. Wicklander, CFE, CFI
Chairman, Wicklander-Zulawski & Associates, Downers Grove, IL

Douglas E. Wicklander has personally conducted over 10,000 investigative interviews in the public and private sectors. He has investigated thousands of employee theft and dishonesty cases over the last 24 years and has personally directed hundreds of investigations. He has testified as an expert in interview and interrogation.

Douglas E. Wicklander is a member of the Advisory Board for the Center for Interviewer Standards and Assessment. He is also an active member of the Item Writing Committee, which develops test questions for the Certified Forensic Interviewer examination.

Mr. Wicklander coauthored, with David E. Zulawski, *Practical Aspects of Interview and Interrogation,* now in its second edition. This text has been used in college and university classes and has been selected as source material for the Certified Forensic Interviewer examination.

Jason C. Yert
Associate, Kerr, Russell and Weber, PLC., Detroit, MI

Jason C. Yert's practice involves a wide range of commercial litigation matters in both state and federal court. He has also been involved in a variety of complex securities and products liability class action matters.

Mr. Yert earned his BA degree from Clemson University in 1999 and his law degree from Suffolk University Law School in 2002.

David E. Zulawski
Senior Partner, Wicklander-Zulawski & Associates, Downers Grove, IL

David E. Zulawski is a 1973 graduate of Knox College from which he received a Bachelor of Arts degree. After college, Mr. Zulawski spent two years with the Chicago & Northwestern Railroad as a special Agent. During this time, he primarily investigated thefts from interstate shipments in transit. Mr. Zulawski then accepted a position with the Barrington, Illinois, Police Department.

Mr. Zulawski is a licensed polygraph examiner and has personally conducted over 9,000 interviews and polygraph examinations. He has provided expert witness testimony on interview and interrogation, and was a subject matter expert during the development of the interactive training program, *The Art of Interviewing.* He has coauthored the text *Practical Aspects of Interview and Interrogation,* 2nd edition, with Douglas E. Wicklander.

Contents

List of Exhibits xxi

Preface xxiii

Acknowledgments xxv

SECTION I
PROFESSIONAL ENVIRONMENT OF FRAUD DETERRENCE 1

1 Fraud Deterrence as a Business Management Tool 3
- Introduction 3
- Motivations for Process Improvement and Monitoring 3
- How the Mighty Have Fallen 5
- Importance of Internal Controls in Dynamic External Environments 6
- Environmental Change and Its Effect on the Fraud Triangle 7
- Where Is Bedrock for Fraud Deterrence? 9
- Conclusion 11

2 Definition of Fraud Deterrence 13
- Overview 13
- Deterrence Activities Will Affect Control Culture 14

3 History of Fraud Deterrence 15
- Introduction 15
- Early Fraud Deterrence 15
- Modern Fraud Deterrence 16

4 The Role of Professional Standards 29
- Introduction 29
- PCAOB Standards 29
- American Institute of Certified Public Accountants Auditing Standards 31
- American Institute of Certified Public Accountants Accounting and Review Standards 38
- Institute of Internal Auditors Standards 38
- Association of Certified Fraud Examiners Standards 39
- Certified Fraud Deterrence Analyst—National Association of Certified Valuation Analysts 40

5 The Fraud Triangle **41**
Overview 41
Elements 41
The Fraud Triangle and Financial Reporting Fraud 45

6 Motivations of Fraud Deterrence and the Transition to Investigation **47**
Introduction 47
Motivations for Deterrence Analysis 48
Transition to Investigation 50
Conclusion 55

7 A Fraud Deterrence Professional's Overview of the Legal Process **57**
Introduction and Objectives 57
Basics of Opinion Testimony and the Role of the Judiciary 57
Expert Qualification Standards: When Is a Witness an "Expert"? 59
Admissibility versus Weight: When Is an Expert's Opinion and/or Testimony Admissible? 60
Limitations on the Scope of Expert Opinion Testimony 63
Reports and Discovery Obligations 64
Conclusion 65

8 Human Resources Concerns **69**
Retaliation: The Newest Wave of Employment Litigation 69
An Ounce of Prevention: Background Checks and Employment Inquiries Under the Fair Credit Reporting Act 79
Checklist for Complying with the FCRA When Using a Third Party to Obtain "Consumer Reports" 83
Conclusion 84
Appendix 8A
Selected Federal Whistleblower Statutes 85
Appendix 8B
The U.S. Equal Employment Opportunity Commission 86
Appendix 8C
Disclosure to Applicant Regarding Consumer Reports 103
Appendix 8D
Disclosure to Employee Regarding Consumer Reports 104
Appendix 8E
Sample Notice of Intent to Obtain an Investigative Consumer Report 105
Appendix 8F
Fair Credit Reporting Act 106
Appendix 8G
Sample Disclosure of Nature and Scope of Investigative Consumer Report 109
Appendix 8H
Sample Pre-Adverse Action Notice 110

Appendix 8I
Sample Adverse Action Notice 111
Appendix 8J
Applicant 112
Appendix 8K
Current Employee 113

SECTION II
TOOLS OF FRAUD DETERRENCE **117**

9 Internal Control and Fraud Deterrence: The COSO Integrated Framework **119**
Background 119
Control Environment 122
Information and Communication 126
Risk Assessment 128
Control Procedures 131
Monitoring 137

10 Recent Corporate Governance Reforms Enacted to Deter Financial Fraud: The Sarbanes-Oxley Act of 2002 and Related Rules and Regulations **143**
Introduction 143
Board of Directors 148
Audit Committee 149
Management 152
Internal Auditors 153
Enforcement 154
Protections for Directors and Officers 154
Conclusion 155

11 Generation-X Technologies and Information Assurance **161**
Overview 161
Do We Need a Paradigm Shift in Systems Assurance and Auditing? 161
Generation X Enterprise Technologies: State of the Art 162
Information Systems Integration: A Challenge 163
Assured Information Emanates from Assured Systems 166
Information Assurance: A Function of Strategic Importance 166
Various Information Assurance and Control Measures 170
British Standards: BS7799 and BS 7799-2:2002 173
System Security Engineering Capability Maturity Model: SSE-CMM 174
Conclusion 174

12 The Impact of Communications Infrastructure on Fraud Detection and Deterrence **177**
Introduction 177
Fraud and Technology 177
Communication Security Solutions 178
Correlation 187

13 Process and Information Validation **189**

Part I: Interview and Interrogation Process **189**
Difference between Interview and Interrogation 190
Preparation and Room Setting 190
Interviewer/Interrogator Demeanor 193
Detecting Deception 195
Conducting the Interview 199
Interrogation 208
Structured Approach to the Interview and Interrogation of a Suspect in a Fraud Investigation 212
Conclusion 215

Part II: Forensic Document and Handwriting Examination **216**
What Is a "Document"? 216
Forgery 217
Red Flags of Document Examination 218
Caution 219
Red Flags of Handwriting Identification 220
Suggested Reading 221

14 Data Analysis and Monitoring: How Effective Data Analysis Can Identify Fraud Risk Indicators and Promote Business Intelligence **223**
Introduction 223
Data Basics 225
Information Systems 237
Generating Business Intelligence 244
What to Look for in Data Analysis Technology 247
Putting It All Together 248

15 Reporting **249**
Introduction 249
Function of Fraud Deterrence Reports 249
Reporting on Internal Control 251
Reporting in an Investigation 254
Importance of Documentation 258
Conclusion 259

SECTION III
APPLICATIONS OF FRAUD DETERRENCE **261**

16 Deterring Fraudulent Financial Reporting and Asset Misappropriation **263**
Introduction 263
Organizational (Corporate) Culture 264
Organizational (Corporate) Governance 266
Internal Controls for Deterrence 268
Deterrence Monitoring 268

17 Fraud and the Bankruptcy Code **271**
Introduction 271
Bankruptcy Refuge for Fraudulent Actors 272
Bankruptcy Fraud 285
Fraudulent Transfer Statutes 296
Intentionally Fraudulent Transfers 302
Constructively Fraudulent Transfers 303
Application of Fraudulent Transfer Laws 306
Remedies for the Recovery of Fraudulent Transfers 311
Corporate Actors/Individual Liability 313
Conclusion 317
Appendix 17A
Uniform Fraudulent Conveyance Act and Uniform Fraudulent Transfer Act 318
Appendix 17B
Uniform Fraudulent Conveyance Act 320
Appendix 17C
Uniform Fraudulent Transfer Act 322
Appendix 17D
18 U.S.C. §§ 152–157 328
Appendix 17E
11 U.S.C. § 548. Fraudulent Transfers and Obligations 330
Appendix 17F
11 U.S.C. § 522 Exemptions 333
Appendix 17G
11 U.S.C. § 101(31). Definitions 336

18 Discovering and Preventing Fraud in Business Formation and Dissolution **351**
Introduction 351
Fundamental Assessments 351
Factors Affecting Whether the Fraud Will Succeed 353
Informational Rights and Fraud 353
Approval Rights and Governance 354
Additional Drafting Solutions 355
Minimizing the Occurrence of Fraud 355
Discovery of Fraud 356
Remedies 356

19 Identity Theft and Privacy Protection **359**
Introduction 359
Definition 360
Development of an Epidemic 361
The Outbreak and Law Enforcement 366
Protecting Personal Information 369
Detect Unauthorized Use 373
Defend and Regain Your Identity 374

Bulk Data Breaches 375
The Online Frontier of Phishing and Spoofing 378
Impact on Fraud Deterrence 380

20 Intellectual Property 383
Introduction 383
How to Tell When Your Company Has Intellectual Property 387
Basic Reasons for Protecting 389
Routine Protection 390
Policing Intellectual Property Rights 394
Possible Recoveries through Litigation 396
Conclusion 397

21 Fraud Deterrence in the U.S. Private Equity Finance System 399
Introduction 399
U.S. Private Equity System and Its Governance Structure 399
Foundations of a Fraud Deterrence System in Private Equity 405
Adoption of Internal Control Systems within the U.S. Private Equity System 408
Conclusions and Recommendations 413

Glossary of Terms 415

Index 423

List of Exhibits

1.1	Maslow's *Hierarchy of Needs*	6
1.2	USDL Manufacturing Multifactor Productivity Index Values from 1970 to 2001	7
6.1	Key Elements of Attest Audits and Assessments of Internal Controls	50
6.2	Pictorial Representation of the Investigation Cycle and Task Detail for Phase 1	53
14.1	Vendor Master Table	228
14.2	Purchasing Discounts Master Table	229
14.3	Purchasing Transaction Table	230
14.4	Purchasing Master Table (Prior to Normalization)	231
14.5	Vendor Table and Product Table (First Normal Form)	232
14.6	Vendor Table, Product Table, and Vendor Product ID Table (Second Normal Form)	233
14.7	Vendor Table (with Key Independent Fields)	234
14.8	Table Structure	236
14.9	Table Relationships	237
14.10	Sample Process and Control Matrix	239
14.11	Sample Process and Control Flow	240
14.12	Sample Process and Control Procedures	241
14.13	Macro and Micro Level Analysis	245
14.14	Systems Migration Criteria and Assessment Model	247
14.15	Sample Project Plan	248
15.1	Sample Information for Inclusion in a Fraud Deterrence Report	252
15.2	Sample Report on Overall Process Internal Control Status	253
21.1	Private Equity Cycle	400
21.2	Private Equity Investment Horizon Performance through December 31, 2005	402
21.3	Sand Hill Index Values, January 1989 to September 2005	404

Preface

The world of fraud deterrence and detection has experienced dramatic change in recent years. While the concept of fraud is as old as history itself, recent accounting scandals have brought the practice of investigating, detecting, and deterring fraud into the limelight. The provisions of the Sarbanes-Oxley Act of 2002 demand increased responsibility by corporate executives to ensure that adequate controls exist within an organization to prevent fraudulent financial reporting. The fraud deterrence professional has an obligation not only to assist management in achieving this objective, but also to facilitate the development of an internal control system that can serve to improve an organization's operational efficiency and effectiveness. Although this text is written primarily as a guide to assist the fraud deterrence practitioner in achieving both of these goals, it can also provide valuable insight to management professionals seeking a holistic understanding of the fraud deterrence discipline.

Included within this book are 21 chapters, organized into three sections that address specific facets of the fraud deterrence practice. While each chapter has been written in a "stand-alone" fashion, we believe the reader will derive the most benefit from the book by reading the chapters sequentially.

Additionally, it is hoped that the format of this text—particularly its inclusion of numerous chapters written by experienced professionals—will provide the reader with a well-rounded, multifaceted perspective of the tenets and applications of fraud deterrence. This approach was employed in order to maximize the diversity of thoughts contained within this single text.

Section I, "Professional Environment of Fraud Deterrence," provides general background information about the development of fraud deterrence techniques and procedures. Here fraud deterrence is examined first from the novel perspective of a business management tool. This section serves to set the tone of the book, explaining motivations of employees and the need for businesses to promote a disciplined corporate culture centered on the use of internal controls.

Section II, "Tools of Fraud Deterrence," explains common tools used in fraud deterrence to implement an effective internal control system. These tools are comprehensive yet flexible enough to be employed in a manner best suited to the needs of a particular fraud deterrence engagement.

Section III, "Applications of Fraud Deterrence," describes real-world applications of the principles set forth in Section II. This section seeks to enhance the tangibility of the fraud deterrence discipline to the reader through complex, well-developed examples.

Although the chapters within this book are intended to provide the reader with a comprehensive view of fraud deterrence, one must keep in mind the enormous scope of the discipline. Fraud deterrence, at its core, is a process improvement tool. As business structures and the laws that govern them continue to evolve, new methods of managing processes will invariably give rise to new perspectives on fraud deterrence: a discipline that is, in every sense of the word, dynamic. It is for this reason that future supplements to this text are already in the works. Nonetheless, after reading this book, a reader should possess significant knowledge of the discipline and the methods employed in applying its principles.

Although members of the Cendrowski Corporate Advisors (CCA) team have written numerous professional articles and classroom materials, coordinating, authoring, and editing this comprehensive, original treatise proved challenging. However, the production of this book also proved the professionalism that pervades the fraud deterrence discipline and underscored the intricacies of the field.

As you will soon experience, this book is unique in its content and novel in its approach. We at CCA believe that our approach to fraud deterrence affords our clients "a different perspective," one that offers a true business-oriented approach to fraud deterrence.

June 2006

HARRY CENDROWSKI
Bloomfield Hills, Michigan

Acknowledgments

I am sincerely grateful to many individuals for their unique contributions to this book as well as their steadfast support and encouragement. First and foremost, I would like to thank John DeRemigis and the staff at John Wiley & Sons for their skillful mentoring throughout the book-writing process. John was instrumental in guiding the book to its final, completed form and helped immensely with the formatting of the text.

I would also like to thank those authors outside of CCA for their contributions; without them the production of this book would not have been possible. These individuals are indisputably professionals of the highest order, a statement that is duly verified by the quality of their work. Their loyalty and dedication to the publication of this book is greatly appreciated.

Section I

Professional Environment of Fraud Deterrence

Chapter 1

Fraud Deterrence as a Business Management Tool

Harry Cendrowski and Louis W. Petro

INTRODUCTION

Many in management today believe that fraud deterrence is not a business management tool but rather an approach that focuses solely on the safeguarding of assets. While such a practice is a key tenet of fraud deterrence, the discipline is not, by nature, simply a tool to assess the security of assets within a firm; rather, it provides a means by which the overall efficiency and effectiveness of the organization can be improved. Fraud deterrence is, at its core, a *process improvement and monitoring tool*. When implemented successfully within a corporation, employees, customers, and shareholders can all reap the benefits that fraud deterrence provides.

Fraud deterrence procedures provide a comprehensive map of the organization's internal control architecture, including an assessment of operating effectiveness. This set of policies, procedures, communication standards, systems, and behavior expectations ensure that processes operate efficiently and effectively within the organization, and that the goals of the organization are accomplished. While safeguarding assets and achieving accurate financial statements are certainly two of the major goals, there is a tremendous amount of additional benefit provided to the organization through the fraud deterrence procedures.

MOTIVATIONS FOR PROCESS IMPROVEMENT AND MONITORING

The message behind fraud deterrence is quite similar to the quality movements popularized in the 1980s, many of which had their roots in Japanese corporate culture. The beginnings of a global economy in the early 1970s required American corporations to move faster than ever in order to keep up with their overseas counterparts and the industry changes that resulted. Firms such as Xerox, General Motors, Ford Motor Company, Chrysler Corporation, and Kodak struggled to adapt to such environmental instability as their corporate bureaucracies had been designed for once-static external environments. These firms, and others, soon found that their current system of corporate control did not provide them with satisfactory financial results, year after year, quarter after quarter, as it had in the past. New methods and tools were required to adapt to suddenly dynamic external environments and to keep businesses on top of their competition.

One of the first quality tools that was brought to the United States from Japan was Total Quality Management (TQM). In the words of the International Standards Organization, TQM is "a management approach of an organization, centered on quality, based on the participation of all its members and aiming at long-term success through customer satisfaction, and benefits to all members of the organization and to society."[1] In essence, TQM seeks to infuse the concept of a rigid quality standard throughout the organization and ensure that it is maintained in all aspects of the business.

While TQM arguably reached its peak in the mid-1990s, remnants still exist in newer business management processes, and the existence of TQM helped to open corporate America's eyes to the effectiveness of Japanese management techniques.

In recent years, another Japanese management tool, lean manufacturing (hereafter "Lean") has grown increasingly popular as once-mature industries have become more highly fragmented, increasing competition and forcing manufacturers to compete on both quality and cost. Lean has brought with it a new way of focusing on achieving goals of efficiency and organizational relevance, primarily through standardization of processes.

Toyota Motor Corporation is world-renowned for its development of Lean and the notable successes it has had in implementing its tenets across the corporation. Numerous publications on the "Toyota Production System" (TPS) have been published in the past 20 years, all attempting to explain how Toyota has been so successful in implementing a process that it has honed over more than 50 years.

While many agree that Lean initiatives are productive for most organizations, implementations have often failed in the past because management has viewed TPS as a *production system* and not a *corporate culture*. In this sense, the name, Toyota Production System is very misleading, as TPS holds the development of a nurturing, people-centric culture as one of its primary tenets. TPS is not a way to run only a manufacturing division, but instead a proven system for developing a corporate culture and achieving business objectives.

In much the same vein as TPS, fraud deterrence not only speaks to the active safeguarding of assets, but also is a method of developing a corporate culture that is centered on efficiency and continuous improvement.

The primary purpose in conducting a fraud deterrence assessment is to study an organization's overall internal control system to identify opportunities for improvement. While some controls may specifically address the security of assets, seeking to ensure that misappropriation does not occur, other controls *should* address operational aspects of the firm and its environment. In this manner, the fraud deterrence engagement is a continuous improvement initiative that evolves to remain current with changes in the business environment. Culturally, one goal of the initiative is to instill a sense that adequate internal controls are essential, and that appropriate behavior on the part of all employees is paramount to the success of the organization.

The quality improvement initiatives of the 1980s demonstrated that no amount of quality inspectors at the end of the assembly line can "inspect" quality into a product; quality must be designed into the product from the beginning, and all employees at each step in production are responsible for ensuring the quality of the product. Fraud deterrence recognizes that similarly, no amount of quality inspectors, also commonly called 'auditors', can inspect "quality" into a financial statement: quality must emanate from appropriate procedures and competent, ethical employees who are responsible for the quality of financial information at every step of the business process.

For these reasons, fraud deterrence engagements are frequently referred to as "operations assessments," "control diagnostics," or "business process improvement initiatives." These titles recognize the organizational improvement achieved beyond the deterrence of fraud, and also avoid the negative stigma associated with the word "fraud."

HOW THE MIGHTY HAVE FALLEN

If one examines the characteristics of once-mighty corporations and their reasons for faltering, it becomes evident that many of these firms fell victim to the "paradox of success." In the words of Anderson and Tushman, firms that succumb to this phenomenon allow themselves to be "out innovated by more nimble, foresightful (though not more resource-rich) competitors."[2]

How do internal controls assist organizations in resisting the "paradox of success"? They do so by helping to standardize processes, "across the organization and fostering a culture of continuous improvement, thus providing benchmarks for operations and also a process for improving them."

Some of today's large corporations are organized in a highly bureaucratic manner, with strict chains of command and little attention paid to the "human aspects" of the company. Employees are expected to arrive at work at a given time, perform a predetermined set of activities, take breaks at specified times, and then go home. Only the employee's need for wealth is satisfied through employment.

Such organizations allow and sometimes foster employee disgruntlement because of their machinelike nature. This practice, in turn, potentially allows one of the key pieces of the fraud triangle to arise in the mind of an employee: "rationalization." (Note: Three pieces make up the fraud triangle: motive, opportunity, and rationalization. For further information on the triangle, see Chapter 5.)

Abraham Maslow, in his 1943 paper, "A Theory of Human Motivation," detailed a *hierarchy of needs* that each human seeks to satisfy over his or her lifetime. Maslow defined a pyramid consisting of five types of needs: (1) physiological, (2) safety, (3) love/being, (4) esteem, and (5) actualization. (See Exhibit 1.1 for a pictorial representation of Maslow's hierarchy.) His key assertion was that as humans meet the lower-level needs (i.e., physiological, safety, etc.), they then seek to satisfy higher needs, occupying a set hierarchy.[3]

In using Maslow's framework to analyze employee motivations behind fraud, one sees that eventually, as lower-level needs are fulfilled, people seek "esteem." Humans crave respect and also desire to respect themselves: They need or require recognition for deeds that they have done in order to promote self-worth. Unfortunately, if one's workplace provides no way of fulfilling this need, as is sometimes the case in highly bureaucratic organizational structures, an employee may turn to fraud, should the opportunity exist to do so. An organization that fails to properly recognize its employees can significantly fuel their rationalization of a fraudulent act.

Employees may also be driven to fraud in such organizations because these firms are often susceptive to problems when the external environment in which they participate changes rapidly. The chain of command associated with bureaucracy often distorts problems as they are passed up, down, and around the organizational structure. Moreover, when new, never-before-seen problems arise, no particular individual specifically knows how to address these issues. An extreme focus has been placed on maximizing *internal* organizational efficiency and effectiveness, without regard to *externalities*.

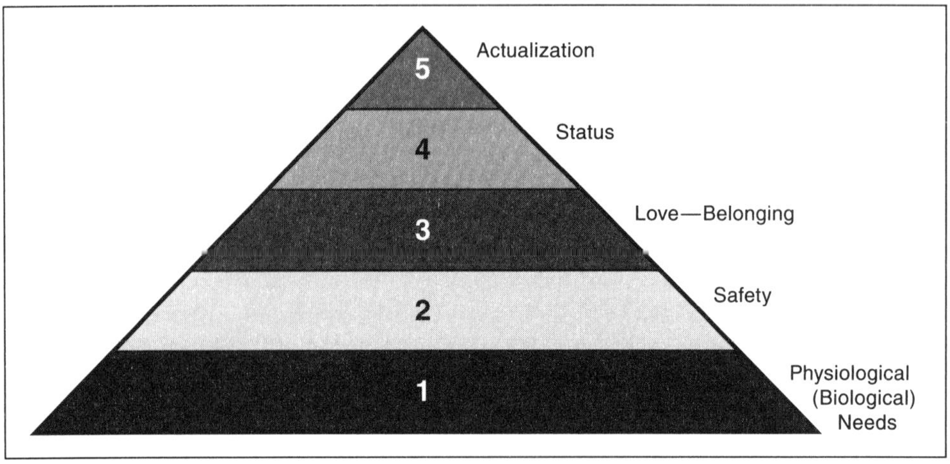

Exhibit 1.1 Maslow's *Hierarchy of Needs*

IMPORTANCE OF INTERNAL CONTROLS IN DYNAMIC EXTERNAL ENVIRONMENTS

While an organization's overall structure can have a significant impact on both the encouragement or suppression of the elements in the fraud triangle, so too can the external environment in which the firm participates.

Recent technological developments have transformed formerly stable external environments into dynamic, competitive marketplaces. Improvements in productivity have culminated in the creation of overcapacity and, hence, the requirement for businesses to exit the industry.

Macroeconomic data from the Bureau of Labor Statistics of the U.S. Department of Labor (USDL) illustrates that manufacturing productivity is currently growing at its fastest rate in 30 years.[4] Consider these facts: The USDL's manufacturing multifactor productivity index posted average gains of 0.5 percent, 1.5 percent, and 1.7 percent per year during the 1970s, 1980s, and 1990s, respectively. In other words, manufacturing productivity improved three times faster in the 1990s than it did in the 1970s. Exhibit 1.2 presents a graph of the multifactor index by year from 1970 to 2001 (the latest data currently available).

As evidenced by the exhibit, productivity growth in the manufacturing sector remained largely stagnant from 1970 to 1980 and began a rapid ascension in approximately 1982.

In this environment, many firms were forced to make major changes in order to survive, given the industry's strides in productivity. At the same time, this rapid change presented tremendous opportunities for growth to those companies with the ability to rapidly adapt. While some firms were able to seize the opportunity presented, others did not. General Motor's board revolt of 1992, IBM's move to a "closed" architecture with the PS/2 personal computer, and Xerox's inability to capitalize on the value of its 8010 Star workstation (featuring one of the first graphical user interfaces) were all results of poor management decisions reinforced by weak internal control systems. The system that each of these companies employed to effectively "sense" and perceive its external environment failed to detect any significant changes that would signify the need for significant organizational changes: In short, internal control evaluation procedures within these organizations were not employed as *process improvement* tools, and instead, while

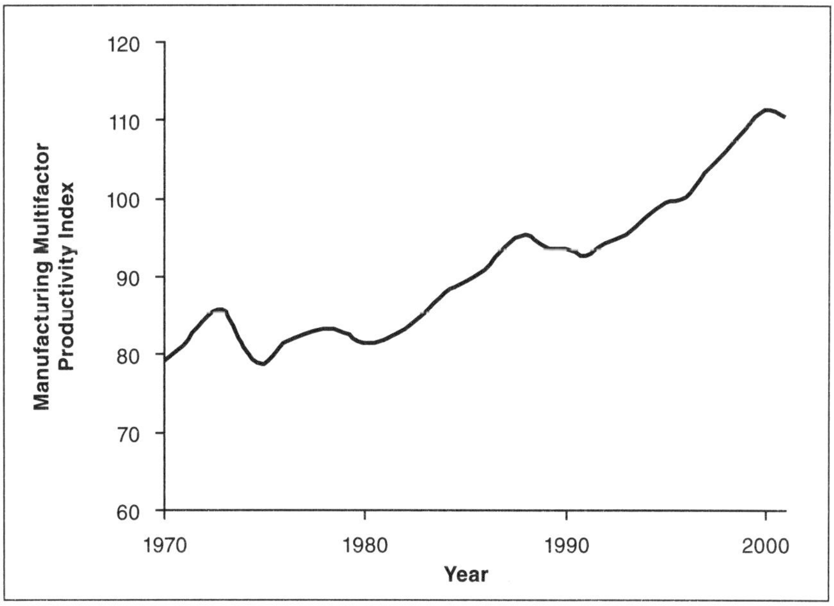

Exhibit 1.2 USDL Manufacturing Multifactor Productivity Index Values from 1970 to 2001

the company was still able to survive, tremendous opportunity for organizational improvement was lost.

ENVIRONMENTAL CHANGE AND ITS EFFECT ON THE FRAUD TRIANGLE

When an organization realizes that it is in a crisis, it may be driven to take desperate measures, and another key element of the fraud triangle soon arises: motive. Organizations of all forms, whether public or private, large or small, ultimately have one primary goal: survival. Members of management and employees alike recognize that should the organization cease to exist, they will lose their jobs, possibly their pensions, and, in a difficult economy, it is uncertain that they will be able to find a similar position in a different organization. Keeping the organization going, therefore, becomes a vital function.

A company on the brink of financial ruin can cause employees and management to make poor or unethical decisions to allow the company to survive, even for a bit longer. For public companies, fraudulent financial reporting may be viewed as a way to temporarily prevent the "ship from sinking" by concealing the true dire situation of the company. The motive of survival is further underscored by the rationalization that such misstatement may be saving the jobs of thousands of employees, and thus the misstatement is an 'ethical' act.

If the opportunity exists to pursue such fraudulent actions, all three pieces of the fraud triangle will coexist, and the opportunity for fraud is ripe. Weak internal control structures could allow management to override financial reporting controls, and misstate the financials. While this might even be helpful in the short term, the long-term effects are most likely going to be far worse. Effective control structures and a strong ethical foundation are essential to ensure that fraudulent acts are not allowed, even in dire economic circumstances.

Internal control, as defined by the Committee of Sponsoring Organizations of the Treadway Commission (COSO) is "a process, effected by an entity's board of directors, management and other personnel, designed to provide reasonable assurance regarding the achievement of objectives in the following categories: effectiveness and efficiency of operations, reliability of financial reporting, and compliance with applicable laws and regulations." Furthermore, internal control is "effected by *people*. It's not merely policy manuals and forms, but people at every level of an organization."[5]

This last quote from the COSO model delineates perhaps the most important aspect of all internal control systems: that they are *people-centric*. Accordingly, organizations that treat employees as cogs in a machine, that do not have opportunities to recognize these individuals properly, open themselves to fraudulent activity. In such organizations, the tone at the top does not communicate the value of employees to the organization. Consequently, employees are more easily able to rationalize fraudulent activity to satisfy their personal vices and need for esteem.

In order for an organization to foster an effective internal control system, it must recognize that employees have complex needs that must be satisfied if they are to lead full and healthy lives and perform effectively in the workplace. Organizations must recognize that they participate in a dynamic environment, both within and external to the brick and mortar of the business. By fulfilling the needs of employees, organizations are largely able to achieve a homeostatic, internal environment, in which workers are able to regulate themselves with minimal input from management. Once such a state is achieved, management can focus on satisfying and balancing the internal needs of the organization with environmental circumstances.

The promotion of the employee self-worth, in turn, leads workers to look out for the well-being of their employer, thus helping to minimize the "rationalization" for fraud. With much regulation being performed by employees themselves, management can turn to addressing the needs of the organization's external environment: anticipating change and proactively addressing foreseen problems by "reading the controls" that are part of an organization's internal control system.

When management is able to recognize the needs of employees, top-down initiatives are regarded with greater respect. If fraud deterrence becomes a "fabric" of management, and this is communicated to the employees, then an effective *control environment*—consisting of an organization's employees, ethical values, competence, and integrity—will be created. Eventually, the importance of fraud deterrence will be ingrained into the mind of each employee, and the organization will work as a whole toward the goal of deterring fraud. Much like the Toyota Production System, fraud deterrence is not simply a way of governing the financial and accounting staffs of a corporation, but a way of fostering a proactive, objective-driven corporate culture.

Furthermore, the adoption of an effective internal control system, together with the fostering of a proactive control environment, will allow the organization to achieve three types of objectives: those associated with operations, financial reporting, and regulatory compliance. (For further detail on these objectives, please refer to the "Risk Assessment" section of Chapter 9.)

Every year, public companies must be certified for compliance with Section 404 of the Sarbanes-Oxley Act (SOX). This certification often generates a plethora of detailed information about how employees conduct their jobs, current gaps in internal control, and recommendations to remediate these gaps. Task-level detail for each job within the organization must be analyzed and used in producing a report used to certify management's opinion on the organization's overall internal control system.

While some chief financial officers scoff at the seemingly unwieldy amount of information produced by this process, it should be noted that Section 404 compliance also produces the opportunity for an organization to standardize job tasks and allow for improved efficiency by ensuring employees use the standards in performing their jobs. In this manner, should an employee be terminated or change positions within the company, the person filling his or her spot would now have a standardized document to work with that details best practices for performing tasks. Such a practice could be realized by making the Section 404 report, in essence, an online employee manual.

Indeed many private equity managers of private portfolio companies are now requiring their entities to be Sarbanes-Oxley compliant not only to ready the entity for a liquidity event (where it may be sold to a public firm), but also to better instill the tenets of fraud deterrence within the organization. For these organizations, the standardization of processes required by Section 404 compliance helps the portfolio companies to follow their own policies more closely, allowing managers to better understand an organization's performance with respect to previously-set goals.[6] (For further information on the Sarbanes-Oxley Act's influence on private equity firms, please see Chapter 21).

WHERE IS BEDROCK FOR FRAUD DETERRENCE?

In 1992, Harvard Business professor Robert S. Kaplan and consultant David Norton first introduced the Balanced Scorecard concept, which provided a revolutionary way of measuring a company's activities and their alignment with the firm's vision and strategies. The Balanced Scorecard was intended to help executives better understand the health of the entire organization, not just the state of its finances. In the years since its introduction, the technique was embraced by the business community, with some research suggesting that up to 64 percent of surveyed businesses employed measures similar to the balanced scorecard to measure overall success.[7]

In essence, the Balanced Scorecard sought to understand and track an organization's progress through the examination of four types of business "perspectives": financial, customer, business process, and learning and growth. Examples of each perspective follow.[8]

- Financial perspective
  - Return on assets
  - Return on equity
  - Earnings per share
- Customer perspective
  - Total process lead time
  - On-time delivery rate
  - Customer satisfaction survey results
- Business perspective
  - Time spent prospecting
  - First-time-through quality rate

  - Process change costs
- Learning and growth perspective
  - Hours of training per employee
  - Number of employee suggestions received
  - Number of employee suggestions implemented

In essence, fraud deterrence is an extension of the Balanced Scorecard concept to today's regulatory environment. In setting up an effective internal control system, each of these four perspectives should be addressed and monitored, and senior management should receive frequent reports of the status of these controls. However, given the current regulatory environment, precipitated by SOX, a fifth perspective should be added to the four just listed: the compliance perspective.

Such an addition would provide business executives with a simple way of understanding the current state of affairs with respect to a firm's compliance with SOX requirements and also a Securities and Exchange Commission investigation, should one ever arise.

The days of management measuring the company purely on financials are over. Moreover, such practices can lead to deleterious conclusions for several reasons. First and foremost, financial figures are historical: They only describe past successes and failures, not the current or future state of the organization. Typical financial metrics also fail to assess the intellectual capital of an organization, a figure that is sometimes calculated by *Tobin's q*.[9] In essence, this metric measures the ratio of the replacement value of a company's assets to its market value. Given the problems associated with measurement based purely on financials, fraud deterrence initiatives provide the organization with a unique approach to tackling tomorrow's tasks and better understanding the current state of the organization.

When a suitable internal control system is developed that addresses these metrics, management can quickly and accurately discern the state of the organization, especially if these metrics are provided in an easily readable format. Such a practice, today called the "Enterprise Dashboard" or "Executive Dashboard," is growing in popularity.

In essence, the Enterprise Dashboard is a series of short, electronic reports that present the current status of vital business controls and metrics to key management officials. It is quite similar to the dashboard of a car in that it is able to quickly provide essential information to employees. (For more information on this reporting technique, see Chapter 15.)

In developing internal controls for an organization, fraud deterrence analysts have the ability to give each employee his/her own Enterprise Dashboard that uniquely specifies controls that this individual should monitor on a frequent basis. For example, such a report could show manufacturing employees the current status of: average die changeover time, average equipment uptime, first-time-through quality rate, and also a goal for each metric. Those in the financial staff could have an Enterprise Dashboard that tracks: inventory turnover, asset turnover, one-year sales growth, and so on. In this manner, internal controls seek to foster an environment of continuous improvement within an organization, providing goals for employees and a way of assessing the current state with respect to this goal.

When fraud deterrence is viewed as a holistic way of measuring the past, current, and future states of the business, companies will have greater incentive to outperform and outpace their competitors. There is already growing evidence that the stock market, at least in the United States, supports better corporate governance through increased security returns. For example, Gompers, Metrick, and Iishi found that the abnormal return—alpha, as many financial managers call it—to a portfolio employing a long strategy in firms with the best corporate governance while short-selling those with the worst corporate governance was about 8 percent per year.[10]

With respect to Section 404 compliance, a recent report by Lord and Benoit stated that firms who reported effective internal controls over the two year period beginning March 31, 2004 experienced 33 percent higher share returns than those companies who reported ineffective internal controls over the same period.[11] This prognosis clearly does not bode well for the nearly 16 percent of SEC companies who received failing grades on their internal controls according to a study performed by AuditAnalytics.com.[12] Moreover, as domestic firms continue to expand and grow overseas, they must remain vigilant of the significant opportunities for fraud abroad. In a recent survey conducted by Ernst and Young, 32 percent of the firms surveyed experienced a fraud in an emerging market, while 20 percent of respondents elected "not to invest in certain emerging markets as a result of fraud risk assessments."[13]

As illustrated by the above studies, a clear focus on fraud deterrence translates into better health and well-being for all participants in an organization: employees, shareholders, and customers.

CONCLUSION

Fraud deterrence is not simply a method of safeguarding assets, but rather a *process improvement* initiative with wide-ranging implications.

Fraud deterrence, and the rigorous adoption of internal controls, is a must for any organization participating in today's global economy. It allows a business to better fulfill the needs of its customers, employees, and shareholders. Adoption of an effective control environment where the tenets of fraud deterrence are ingrained in the minds of each employee serves not only to minimize fraud, but also to assist a business in maintaining its "relevancy" and avoiding the "paradox of success."

When businesses begin to adopt and foster a culture that is acutely focused on the development and monitoring of internal controls, the chance for failure is minimized and the prospect of success is more apparent. In our view, the adoption of a fraud deterrence, *people-centric* culture is essential for achieving continued success in today's global business world.

NOTES

1. International Organization of Standards, ISO 8402, "Quality Management and Quality Assurance—Vocabulary" (1994).
2. P. Anderson and M. Tushman, eds., "Technology Cycles, Innovation Streams, and Ambidextrous Organizations," *Managing Strategic Innovation and Change* (New York: Oxford University Press, 1997).
3. A. H. Maslow, "A Theory of Human Motivation," *Psychological Review* 50 (1943): 370–396.
4. United States Bureau of Labor Statistics. Data available at: http://data.bls.gov/cgi-bin/surveymost?mp.
5. Committee of Sponsoring Organizations of the Treadway Commission. *Internal Control—Integrated Framework*. (AICPA Publications Division, 1994).
6. J. Badal and P. Dvorak. "Sarbanes-Oxley Gains Adherents," *The Wall Street Journal*, August 14, 2006.
7. J. Kurtzman, "Is Your Company Off Course? Now You Can Find Out Why," *Fortune*, February 17 1997, 128–130.
8. R. Kaplan and D. Norton, "The Balanced Scorecard: Measures that Drive Performance," *Harvard Business Review* (January-February 1992): 71–80.

9. J. Tobin, "A General Equilibrium Approach to Monetary Theory," *Journal of Money Credit and Banking* 1, no. 1 (1969): 15–29.
10. P. Gompers, J. Ishii, and A. Metrick, "Corporate Governance and Equity Prices," *Quarterly Journal of Economics* 118, no. 1 (2003): 107–155.
11. "The Lord & Benoit Report: Do the Benefits of 404 Exceed the Cost?" Article available at: http://www.section404.org/resources.html.
12. "Material Weakness Opinions Come In Slightly Above Expectations" *Public Accounting Report*, April 30, 2006, 4–6.
13. Ernst & Young, "Fraud Risk in Emerging Markets." Article available at: http://www.eycom.ch/publications/items/fraud_report_2006/en.pdf.

Chapter 2

Definition of Fraud Deterrence

Harry Cendrowski and James Martin

OVERVIEW

Fraud deterrence is the proactive identification and removal of the causal and enabling factors of fraud.

Fraud deterrence is based on the premise that fraud is not a random occurrence; fraud occurs where the conditions are right for it to occur. Fraud deterrence attacks the root causes and enablers of fraud; this analysis could reveal potential fraud opportunities in the process, but is performed on the premise that improving organizational procedures to reduce or eliminate the causal factors of fraud is the single best defense against fraud. Fraud deterrence involves both short-term (procedural) and long-term (cultural) initiatives.

Fraud deterrence is not earlier fraud detection, and this is often a confusing point. Fraud detection involves a review of historical transactions to identify indicators of a nonconforming transaction. Deterrence involves an analysis of the conditions and procedures that affect fraud enablers, in essence, looking at what could happen in the future given the process definitions in place and the people operating that process. Deterrence is a preventive measure—reducing input factors. An illustrative analogy would be fire prevention and response. For the analogy of a fire, what is a *deterrence* measure?

- Fire Extinguisher = Remediation
  - The event has already happened.
  - Minimize the damage by quickly controlling the fire.
  - The longer the response time, the greater the damage that will occur.
- Smoke Detector = Earlier Detection
  - Designed to be earlier detection, before fumes can even be smelled.
  - Detects nothing until the event actually happens.
  - By the time the detector is activated, there has been a fire.
- Removal of Causal Factors = Deterrence
  - Removal of flammable materials.
  - Removal of sources of ignition (e.g., not allowing smoking, flammables away from a flame source such as a water heater).
  - Increasing awareness of risk of fire (e.g., Smokey the Bear).

In the case of the causal factors that should be removed to deter fraud, this is best defined by the fraud triangle, which describes the three factors present in every situation of fraud:

1. *Motive.* The driving need for misappropriated assets
2. *Rationalization.* The mind-set of the perpetrator that allows him or her to commit a wrongful action
3. *Opportunity.* The situation (typically a control weakness) that allows a fraud to occur

Of course, should the deterrence analysis reveal that conditions are such that a fraud could be perpetrated and not discovered, fraud examination techniques should be applied to the related area to discover if the opportunity for fraud was indeed exploited.

Fraud deterrence and fraud examination procedures are inherently linked; as described, deterrence analysis will lead directly into examination procedures when a fraud opportunity is identified. Likewise, where fraud has been discovered, deterrence procedures are appropriate to identify additional control weaknesses in an organization with a known control failure. In essence, these discrete but related activities answer the questions commonly asked by management when fraud is discovered: "What did the perpetrator get away with [examination], and who else in the organization could do this [deterrence]?" Of course, the fraud deterrence activities will provide a clear organizational map that will prioritize processes for detection activities based on the evaluation of control weakness.

While deterrence is preventive in nature, there are semantic problems with referring to "fraud prevention." "Prevention" can imply complete elimination of a risk, which is not possible in the case of fraud. The risk of fraud can never be completely eliminated; to attempt do so would be cost prohibitive, as the cost of additional internal controls to further reduce the risk of fraud would dramatically outweigh the incremental reduction in potential fraud loss. Also, the imposition of additional internal controls tends to degrade process functioning and efficiency.

DETERRENCE ACTIVITIES WILL AFFECT CONTROL CULTURE

Fraud deterrence activities directly affect internal control procedures, but the fraud deterrence process will indirectly improve the organization's control culture. As actions are taken to identify control weaknesses and the opportunity for fraud, employees of the organization will become less likely to commit fraud. It is harder to rationalize that fraud is "no big deal" when fraud deterrence is clearly a management imperative. Also, the deterrence activities will generate greater awareness that management is looking at business processes to improve the control structures, including process monitoring controls; thus it is likely that any fraudulent activities would be detected.

Chapter 3

History of Fraud Deterrence

Harry Cendrowski and Louis W. Petro

INTRODUCTION

Fraud, the intentional misrepresentation of a material fact to encourage a party to act to its own detriment, is as old as the human race itself. Fraud occurs at least twice in Genesis, the first book of the Bible's Old Testament. Close to the very beginning, there is the story of the serpent tricking Eve in the Garden of Eden. Later, in the same book, Jacob steals Esau's birthright. Greek mythology has many fraud tales. One of the most widely known is the story of the Trojan horse. Because fraud is as old as time, attempts to deter fraud are virtually as old.

Fraud deterrence involves the removal of the causal factors of fraud – the motives and opportunities that allow fraud to occur. Fraud deterrence efforts have evolved over time as fraud methods have evolved. This chapter provides an overview of the evolution of fraud deterrence from the ancient world until the late nineteenth century will be covered. Then the chapter presents the modern history (circa 1892 to date).

EARLY FRAUD DETERRENCE

Early fraud deterrence will be covered in three sections:

1. The Ancient World
2. The Middle Ages
3. The Early Modern Era

The Ancient World

The large organizations in the ancient world were religious, military, or political. Business organizations were predominately small family-owned farms or small commercial enterprises, such as shops or inns. Managers were also owners. Most fraud deterrence in such organizations involved fear of physical punishment or incarceration or threats of religious, political, or social ostracism. Formal internal control systems such as exist today were virtually unknown. Death, dismemberment, whippings, beatings, and other corporal punishments and the fear of them were commonly used to deter criminal behavior, including fraud. Fears of incarceration and banishment from the family, community, or tribe were also used to control behavior.

The Middle Ages

During the period from the fall of Rome in the late fifth century to the late fifteenth century, Christianity, monarchs, and feudal estate lords ruled the western world. Monarchs wielded power under the guise of "the divine right of kings." Authority flowed from the monarchs to the privileged estates: the aristocracy, the clergy, and the military. The three privileged estates controlled behavior in ways quite similar to those used in the ancient world. Business enterprises continued to be small and owner-operated and managed. Formal internal controls to help prevent or detect problems such as fraud were still relatively unknown. Control still consisted primarily of coercion. Formal controls would not come until the early modern era (1500 to 1892).

The Early Modern Era

The early modern period includes the ages of discovery, mercantilism, reason, and enlightenment as well as the industrial revolution and the rise of capitalism. Capitalism brought about the development of the corporate form of organization with its separation of ownership and management, limited liability, and capital-raising ability. In corporations, control shifts from the owner/operator to hired professional managers acting as agents for the shareholders/owners. The advent of the corporate structure brought about an increase in the size and complexity of organizations. The need for formal internal control systems to deter and prevent fraud was beginning to become apparent.

The first auditing text was published in England in the year 1892 by Lawrence R. Dicksee.[1] The American edition was published in 1905. The publishing of the text marked the recognition of the importance of internal controls. Dicksee states, "It is of the highest degree of necessity that the Auditor, before commencing the investigation . . . should thoroughly acquaint himself with the general system upon which the books have been kept . . . . Having thoroughly made himself the master of the system, the Auditor should look for its weakest points."[2] Dicksee lists three internal controls that have become standard. They are:

1. Separation of cash and recording
2. Self-balancing ledgers
3. Rotation of duties[3]

In 1896, the first U.S. Certified Public Accountant act was enacted in New York State. It marked the beginning of public accounting in the United States. Dicksee's text and the rise of the public accounting profession mark the start of the modern era of fraud deterrence.

MODERN FRAUD DETERRENCE

Modern fraud deterrence involves the use of laws, regulations, and formal internal control systems along with the traditional, centuries-old coercive methods. The late 1800s witnessed the start, in the United States, of professional detective agencies. Although such agencies were primarily involved in the apprehension of criminals, including fraud perpetrators, their presence tended to deter criminal acts. The first private agency, the Pinkerton Detective Agency, was started by Alan Pinkerton in 1850. Federal agencies involved in fraud deterrence include:

- Bureau of Alcohol, Tobacco, and Firearms
- Secret Service

- Federal Bureau of Investigation
- Internal Revenue Service Criminal Investigation Division
- Food and Drug Administration
- Federal Trade Commission
- Securities and Exchange Commission

Bureau of Alcohol, Tobacco, and Firearms

The Bureau of Alcohol, Tobacco, and Firearms (ATF), although officially the youngest tax-collecting agency in the United States, can trace its legacy to the United States Constitution (1789). The first U.S. Congress imposed taxes on imported alcoholic beverages. Another tax on domestically produced alcoholic beverages was enacted in 1791. The two taxes began a history of alcohol tax collection that continues into the present. Congress, in July 1862, created the Office of Internal Revenue, responsible for the collection of taxes on tobacco products as well as on alcoholic beverages. The Eighteenth Amendment to the U.S. Constitution (1919) and the 1919 Volstead Prohibition Enforcement Act gave special prominence to the alcohol tax collectors. The most prominent of them, Eliot Ness, was responsible for the tax evasion conviction of Al Capone.

The Twenty-first Amendment to the U.S. Constitution (1933) repealed the prohibition amendment. President Franklin D. Roosevelt, by executive order, created the Federal Alcohol Control Administration (FACA). The FACA, along with the U.S. Department of Agriculture and the U.S. Department of the Treasury, was to create a system of voluntary codes of fair competition among wineries and distilleries. The FACA was supplanted in 1935 by the passage of the Federal Alcohol Administration Act (FAAA). The FAAA continues to guide the ATF's alcohol tax enforcement activities.

The gang-related firearm violence of the prohibition period (1919–1933) and the weaponry used encouraged the U.S. Congress to pass the 1934 National Firearms Act and the 1938 Federal Firearms Act. The Bureau of Internal Revenue Miscellaneous Tax Unit assumed gun tax collection as well as alcohol and tobacco tax collections. In 1952, the Bureau of Internal Revenue became known as the Internal Revenue Service (IRS). The IRS changed the name of the Miscellaneous Tax Unit to the Alcohol and Tobacco Tax Division. In 1968, with the passage of the 1968 Gun Control Act, the name was changed to the Alcohol, Tobacco, and Firearms (ATF) Division. A 1972 U.S. Treasury Department order made ATF a function separate from the IRS. In 2003, the Homeland Security Act transferred the ATF from the Treasury Department to the U.S. Justice Department.

The ATF has an over 200-year history of deterring, preventing, and detecting frauds relating to the production and sale of alcoholic beverages, tobacco products, and firearms.

Secret Service

The Secret Service Division of the United States Treasury Department, whose operation followed the Pinkerton model, was started in July 1865. Its original mandate was to suppress counterfeit currency. The initial use of paper money, or "greenbacks," during the U.S. Civil War created a whole new fraud venue.

In 1984, the United States Congress enacted legislation criminalizing the fraudulent use of credit and debit cards. The law gave investigative jurisdiction to the U.S. Secret Service. The jurisdiction also covered federal-interest fraud and fraudulent identification documents.

Beginning with the 1984 Computer Fraud and Abuse Act (CFAA), the Secret Service has been given jurisdiction to conduct investigations into alleged computer crimes. The act as originally written applied only to federal government and large financial institution computers. The CFAA was amended in 1996 to cover all computers connected to the Internet. The amending act is the National Information Infrastructure Protection Act. The CFAA prohibits:

- Unauthorized access to and transmission of classified government information
- Theft of financial information
- Unauthorized access to any Internet-connected computer
- Using the computer in perpetrating a fraud or extortion
- Transmitting code that damages a computer system
- Trafficking in passwords or access techniques and methods to allow a computer to be accessed without authorization

The 1988 Telemarketing Fraud Protection Act provides for forfeiture of fraud proceeds for convictions of fraud or conspiracy to commit fraud when the fraud involves telecommunications.

There are many other computer crime laws. The Electronic Communications Privacy Act (ECPA) of 1986 amended the Federal Wire Tap Act to cover computer systems. The ECPA was amended in 1994 by the Communications Assistance for Law Enforcement Act (CALEA) requiring telecommunications carriers to update their equipment to comply with authorized surveillance. The 1996 Economic Espionage Act (EEA) covers the protection of trade secrets. The 1998 Identity Theft and Assumption Deterrence Act (ITADA) criminalizes identity theft and provides for the coverage of losses suffered by identity theft. The 2001 Patriot Act enhanced the Secret Service's role in investigating computer frauds. In addition, many states have enacted laws to fight computer crime and abuse.

Federal Bureau of Investigation

The Federal Bureau of Investigation (FBI), originally named the Bureau of Investigation, was started in 1908 by President Theodore Roosevelt and Attorney General Charles Bonaparte. The "Bureau" consisted of a cadre of Special Agents investigating violation of laws regarding national banking, bankruptcy, immigration, antitrust, labor, and land transactions. The 1919 National Motor Vehicle Theft Act gave the FBI the power to investigate and apprehend criminals who previously avoided apprehension by crossing state lines. The FBI is also patterned after the Pinkerton model.

The FBI often works with the Secret Service on the computer crime laws noted earlier. In addition, the FBI is heavily involved in investigations related to the 1996 Health Insurance Portability and Accountability Act and those involving wire and mail fraud. The bureau collaborates with the Federal Communication Commission (FCC) on wire fraud cases and with the United States Postal Service (USPS) on mail fraud cases. Wire fraud goes back to the telegraph (ca. 1844) while mail fraud began as early as 1775 following the appointment of Benjamin Franklin by the Continental Congress as the first Postmaster General.

Internal Revenue Service Criminal Investigation Division

In 1862, the United States Congress created the Office of Internal Revenue, the forerunner of the current Internal Revenue Service. The United States Revenue Act of 1913 changed the name to the Bureau of Internal Revenue. The name was changed again in 1952 to the Internal Revenue Service (IRS). The 1913 act began the history of the IRS Criminal Investigation Division (IRS/CID). The CID was involved in the investigation of alleged tax frauds as early as 1919, when the highest marginal tax rate was 6 percent on incomes exceeding $20,000 annually. Awareness of the IRS Code and Regulations and of the IRS/CID provides additional fraud deterrence.

Food and Drug Administration

The mislabeling and/or adulteration of food and drug products have been concerns since products have been manufactured, packaged, and sold. Such frauds increased dramatically throughout the nineteenth century. Public concern led to the creation of the United States Department of Agriculture's Division of Chemistry in 1862. The division employed one chemist. By 1867, the division was investigating the adulteration of agricultural products. The division's name was changed to the Bureau of Chemistry in 1901. The Food and Drug Administration (FDA) itself, although still called the Bureau of Chemistry, began in 1906 with the passage of the Food and Drugs Act.

The Bureau of Chemistry name was changed to the Food, Drug, and Insecticide Administration in 1927. The current name, the Food and Drug Administration, was adopted in 1930. In 1940, jurisdiction over the FDA was moved from the Department of Agriculture to the new Federal Security Agency. The FDA was moved to the Department of Health, Education, and Welfare (HEW) in 1953. In 1968, the FDA became a part of the Public Health Service within HEW. In 1980, the Department of Education was formed, and HEW became the Department of Health and Human Services (HHS).

The FDA has responsibility for enforcing the 1906 Food and Drugs Act as well as the 1938 Food, Drug, and Cosmetic Act. Its jurisdiction includes food products other than meat, poultry, and fish, therapeutic biological agents, medical devices, radiation-emitting products used by consumers or for medical and/or occupational use, animal feeds, and cosmetics. The FDA evaluates and approves human and animal drugs, medical devices, food additives and colorings, and infant formulas. Its purpose is to deter and prevent manufacture, import, transport, storage, and sale of mislabeled and/or adulterated food and drug products.

Federal Trade Commission

The Federal Trade Commission (FTC) is charged with investigations regarding federal antitrust legislation and investigations involving federal consumer protection legislation.

Federal Antitrust Legislation. The FTC enforces these United States antitrust statutes:

- Sherman Antitrust Act (1890)
- Clayton Antitrust Act (1914)
- Federal Trade Commission Act (1914)
- Robinson-Patman Act (1936)
- Celler-Kefauver Anti-Merger Act (1950)
- Hart-Scoss-Rodino Antitrust Improvement Act (1976)

Sherman Antitrust Act The Sherman Antitrust Act of 1890 was the first U.S. statute passed that deals with business practices used by companies to create monopolies. Several states had already passed similar laws, but such laws are limited to intrastate commerce. A federal law was needed to handle companies engaged in interstate commerce.

The act prohibits actions restraints of trade leading to monopolies. Specifically, it prohibits these acts:

- Vertical price fixing (resale price maintenance). Agreements with customers obligating them to resell at manufacturer mandated prices
- Horizontal price fixing. Agreements among competitors dictating quantities produced, offered for sale, or bought
- Bid rigging by competitors
- Boycotts
- Market allocation by competitors

By raising these fraudulent activities to the federal level, the Sherman Act has added additional deterrent power.

Clayton Antitrust Act The 1890 Sherman Act did not outlaw attempts to limit competition. It focused only on the creation of monopolies. The Clayton Act of 1914 amends and clarifies the Sherman Act by making illegal certain acts that tend to lessen competition. The Clayton Act added these restraints of trade to those enumerated in the Sherman Act:

- Acquisition of a competitor when such acquisition would tend to limit competition
- Interlocking directorates
- Price discrimination
- Tie-in sales agreements unless such an agreement is needed to protect the selling company's goodwill

The Clayton Act focus on limiting competition as well as monopolizing has enhanced the fraud deterrence facets of the 1890 Sherman Act.

Federal Trade Commission Act The 1914 Federal Trade Commission (FTC) Act prohibits certain unfair acts and practices not covered by the Sherman Act and Clayton Act. In addition, the FTC Act created the Federal Trade Commission, a bipartisan commission composed of five presidential appointees, to enforce its provisions as well as those of the Sherman and Clayton acts. The practices prohibited by the FTC Act include:

- Unfair competition, such as price discrimination or using size or market position to coerce suppliers to grant price concessions
- Deceptive practices, such as false or misleading advertising

The FTC Act provisions and the FTC enforcement have increased the fraud deterrence abilities of the first two antitrust acts.

Robinson-Patman Act The purpose of the Robinson-Patman Act of 1936, sometimes referred to as the "Anti-Chain Store Act," is to protect smaller, independent retailers from larger, chain-store pricing practices. The act was supported by wholesalers wanting to stop chain stores from buying directly from manufacturers at prices lower than those charged by the wholesalers. In other words, the wholesalers wanted to lessen competition from the chains.

The Robinson-Patman Act prohibits price discrimination that is not cost justified or that is not based on a response to a competitor's price. The act allegedly deters competitors from using unfair pricing practices.

Celler-Kefauver Anti-Merger Act The 1950 Celler-Kefauver Act closed a loophole in the antimerger provisions of the 1914 Clayton Act. The Clayton Act prohibits stock purchases that result in reduced competition but does not prohibit asset purchases accomplishing the same end. The Celler-Kefauver Act prohibits the acquisition of a competitor's assets that lessens competition.

Federal Consumer Protection Legislation. The Federal Trade Commission is charged with enforcing consumer protection legislation as well as with enforcing antitrust legislation. Consumer protection legislation is directed at deterring business practices aimed at deceiving consumers. There are numerous consumer protection acts. Among them are:

- Wool Products Labeling Act (1939)
- Fur Products Labeling Act (1951)
- Textile Fiber Products Identification Act (1958)
- Federal Cigarette Labeling and Advertising Act (1966)
- Fair Packaging and Labeling Act (1966)
- Truth in Lending Act (1968)
- Fair Credit Reporting Act (1970)
- Postal Reorganization Act (1970)
- Dolphin Protection Consumer Information Act (1972)
- Hobby Protection Act (1973)
- Fair Credit Billing Act (1974)
- Magnuson-Moss Warranty–Federal Trade Commission Improvements Act (1975)
- Consumer Leasing Act (1976)
- Petroleum Marketing Practices Act (1978)
- Drug Price Competition and Patent Term Restoration Act (1984)
- Comprehensive Smokeless Tobacco Health Education Act (1986)
- Fair Credit and Charge Card Disclosure Act (1988)
- Federal Deposit Insurance Corporation Improvement Act (1991)
- Energy Policy Act (1992)
- Telephone Disclosure and Dispute Resolution Act (1992)
- Telemarketing and Consumer Fraud and Abuse Prevention Act (1994)
- Violent Crime Control and Law Enforcement Act (1994)
- Home Ownership and Equity Protection Act (1994)
- Home Equity Loan Consumer Protection Act (1995)
- Electronic Fund Transfer Act (1996)
- Telecommunications Act (1996)

- Credit Repair Organizations Act (1996)
- Identity Theft Assumption and Deterrence Act (1998)
- Equal Credit Opportunity Act (1999)
- Fair Debt Collection Practices Act (1999)
- Gramm-Leach-Bailey Act (1999)
- Children's Online Privacy Protection Act (2000)
- College Scholarship Fraud Protection Act (2000)
- Crimes Against Charitable Americans Act (2001)
- Sports Agent Responsibility and Trust Act (2002)
- Do-Not-Call Registry Act (2003)
- Do-Not-Call Implementation Act (2003)
- Fair and Accurate Credit Transactions Act (2003)
- Controlling the Assault of Non-Solicited Pornography and Marketing Act (2003)

The list of consumer protection acts administered by the FTC is long and quite inclusive. A number of potential frauds directed at the consuming public are covered.

Securities and Exchange Commission

The stock market crash of October 29, 1929, aside from ushering in the Great Depression, encouraged the United States Congress to enact legislation regarding the interstate sale of securities and publicly held company financial reporting. Several federal acts are administered by the SEC. They are:

- Securities Act (1933)
- Securities and Exchange Act (1934)
- Public Utility Holding Company Act (1935)
- Trust Indenture Act (1939)
- Investment Company Act (1940)
- Investment Advisers Act (1940)
- Foreign Corrupt Practices Act (1977)
- Sarbanes-Oxley Act (2002)

Securities Act The 1933 Securities Act, often referred to as the Truth in Securities Law, has two primary fraud deterrence objectives. First, the act prohibits any type of fraud, misrepresentation, and deceit in the interstate sale of securities. Second, the act, through its required registration process, requires that investors be provided with information, both financial and nonfinancial, regarding securities offered for public interstate sale.

The registration process requires that the organization offering the securities for sale provide to investors:

- Descriptions of the corporation and its properties
- Descriptions of the securities being offered for sale

- Information about the corporation's board of directors and management
- Certified financial statements

The purpose of the act is to prevent a recurrence of the fraudulent practices thought to have contributed heavily to the 1929 crash. Later acts have added additional teeth to the deterrence provisions of the 1933 act.

Securities Exchange Act The 1934 Securities Exchange Act, among other things, created the Securities and Exchange Commission. The SEC has regulatory authority over brokerage firms, transfer agents, clearing agencies, security self-regulatory organizations (SROs), and the stock exchanges. The stock exchanges are SROs. The act specifies appropriate conduct in the securities markets and prohibits fraudulent activities, such as insider trading, relating to the offer, purchase, or sale of securities. The act gives the SEC the power to set GAAP (generally accepted accounting principles) for SEC registrants. Periodic, such as quarterly, and annual reporting requirements are also mandated by the 1934 act. Corporate SEC filings are publicly available through the SEC's EDGAR (Electronic Data Gathering and Retrieval System).

SEC filings include significant events (8-K or 8-Q), such as the acquisition or sale of a subsidiary, a change in officers or directors, addition or deletion of a product line, and a change in auditor, as well as annual (10-K) and quarterly financial reports (8-K). The reporting requirements apply to corporations with more than $10 million in assets and more than 500 shareholders.

Last, the 1934 act covers regulations regarding information requirements for proxy solicitations and for tender offers. The 1934 SEC Act is one of the deterrents of corporate financial reporting fraud.

Public Utility Holding Company Act The 1935 Public Utility Holding Company Act has requirements designed to protect utility customers from, among other things, utility company fraudulent behavior. Specifically, the act requires public utilities to be incorporated in the state in which they operate or to be regulated by the SEC if they operate in more than one state. The former requirement allows the individual state to regulate public utilities. In addition, the act prohibits non–public utility companies, such as investment banks or oil companies, to own public utilities.

The 1935 act was repealed by the Energy Policy Act in 2005 and replaced by the Public Utility Holding Company Act of 2005. The Energy Policy Act moved jurisdiction over public utilities from the SEC to the Federal Energy Regulatory Commission (FERC).

Trust Indenture Act The 1939 Trust Indenture Act applies to debt securities, such as bonds and notes, offered for public sale. It requires that registered debt securities be accompanied by a formal indenture agreement between the debtor and the creditor. The agreement, known as the trust indenture, must conform to the provisions of the act. The trust indenture covers the reciprocal rights and duties of the debt security issuer (debtor) and the debt security buyer (creditor) and is publicly available. The act helps to deter the making of fraudulent debt agreements.

Investment Company Act The 1940 Investment Company Act gives the SEC authority to regulate the organization and operation of companies engaging in the trading of publicly traded securities. The act includes mutual funds. A primary purpose of the law is to minimize potential conflicts of interest that might arise in the principal/agent relationship between the trading company and the actual owner(s) of the securities being traded. In addition, the act requires investment companies to disclose their financial condition and investment policies when initially selling securities and thereafter on a regular basis. The act does not give the SEC authority to mandate investment decisions and activities to investment companies.

Investment Advisers Act The 1940 Investment Advisers Act requires investment companies operating as agents for security purchasers and sellers to register with the SEC and to conform to appropriate SEC regulations. The regulations include the provisions of the 1940 Investment Company Act, as well as this act. The Investment Advisers Act was amended in 1996 to cover, in general, only those having over $25 million in assets under management. This act enhances the fraud deterrence capabilities of the Investment Company Act.

Foreign Corrupt Practices Act The 1977 Foreign Corrupt Practices Act (FCPA) was precipitated by the bribery of foreign officials by agents for U.S. companies or their employees, officers, or directors. The bribes were for the purpose of obtaining foreign business. Many of the bribes were made without the authorization or knowledge of the bribing company's officers or directors. The FCPA has two major provisions. First, the FCPA prohibits companies, their subsidiaries, directors, officers, employees, and agents from bribing foreign officials. Second, the act mandates that SEC registrants maintain an adequate internal control system.

The definition of internal used in the FCPA follows the one used in the American Institute of Certified Public Accountants (AICPA) Statement on Auditing Standards Number 1 (SAS 1). The FCPA provisions require the SEC registrants maintain an internal control system that provides reasonable assurance that:

- Transactions are executed in accordance with management's general or specific authorization.
- Transactions are recorded as necessary to:
  - Permit preparation of financial statements in conformity with GAAP or any other criteria applicable to such statements
  - Maintain accountability for assets
- Access to assets is permitted only in accordance with management's general or specific authorization.
- The recorded accountability for assets is compared with the existing assets at reasonable intervals and appropriate action is taken with respect to any differences.[4]

The internal control requirements are to help deter the prohibited bribery of foreign officials. Violations of the FCPA may result in both criminal and civil penalties.

Sarbanes-Oxley Act President George W. Bush, on July 30, 2002, signed into law the United States Company Accounting Reform and Investor Protection Act of 2002. He characterized the act, commonly referred to as the Sarbanes-Oxley Act (or SOX) after its two sponsors, Senator Paul Sarbanes of Maryland and Representative Michael Oxley of Ohio, as "the most far-reaching reforms of American business practices since the time of Franklin Delano Roosevelt."[5] SOX amends the 1934 SEC Act and gives the SEC additional authority and responsibility for the deterrence of management fraud. The enactment of SOX was precipitated primarily by the collapse of Enron. Problems involving corporate governance and/or audit issues at Adelphia Communications, Merrill Lynch, WorldCom, ImClone, Tyco, and Salomon Smith Barney helped encourage the passage.

With Sarbanes-Oxley, Congress recognized that the methods of gathering and evaluating public financial statements required additional procedures to deter financial reporting fraud. The act contained specific requirements to reduce each of the elements of the fraud triangle, for example:

- Motive—Personal liability for misstatement, and increased fines
- Rationalization—Positive certification by management of their responsibility for accurate financial reporting and the internal control environment.
- Opportunity—New rules for interface with external auditors, requirement for an anonymous reporting facility, new rules to improve board oversight.

Despite concerns about the costs associated with additional compliance requirements, the fraud deterrence procedures mandated by the Sarbanes-Oxley Act seem to have restored the faith of the investing public.

SOX covers six areas. They are:

1. The Public Company Accounting Oversight Board (PCAOB)
2. Auditor independence
3. Corporate governance
4. Chief executive officer (CEO)/chief financial officer (CFO) certifications
5. Enhanced financial disclosure
6. Civil and criminal penalties

All of the provisions are designed to improve corporate governance and audits and to deter fraudulent financial reporting.

Public Company Accounting Oversight Board The role of the Public Company Accounting Oversight Board (PCAOB) is to protect the interests of investors in the preparation of accurate and independent audit reports. It has taken over what was the AICPA's role in the setting of auditing standards for public company audits and in the oversight of public company audits. In particular, the PCAOB is responsible for:

- Registering certified public accounting (CPA) firms that audit public companies
- Establishing auditing, quality control, ethical, and independence standards for such CPA firms
- Inspecting such CPA firms
- Conducting investigations of such CPA firms
- Disciplining such CPA firms
- Enforcing CPA firm compliance with the act, with PCAOB rules, with professional standards, and with security laws relating to the preparation of financial statements and audit reports

Auditor Independence The Sarbanes-Oxley Act has provisions to improve the perception of auditor independence as well as the actuality of auditor independence. It intends to do this in four ways.

1. The PCAOB prohibits CPA firms from offering certain services to publicly held audit clients. The prohibited services are:
   - Bookkeeping/accounting
   - Financial information systems design and implementation
   - Appraisal/valuation services
   - Actuarial services
   - Internal auditing outsourcing
   - Management/human resource functions
   - Broker/dealer/investment advisor/investment banker services
   - Legal/expert services unrelated to the audit
   - Other services that the PCAOB proscribes

   The first additional service proscribed by the PCAOB is the advising of a publicly held audit client to engage in "aggressive" tax shelters.
2. SOX requires that all nonaudit services provided to a publicly held audit client be approved by the client's audit committee.
3. SOX requires that the both the audit partner in charge and the review partner on a public company audit be rotated out in five years or less.
4. SOX mandates that a CPA firm may not audit a publicly held company if any of these people worked for the CPA firm on an audit of the client during the past year:
   - CEO
   - CFO
   - Controller
   - Chief accounting officer

Corporate Governance The primary corporate governance provision of SOX is the mandating of a board of directors' level audit committee and the provision of whistleblower protection rules. The audit committee members must not be affiliated with the corporation even as a consultant or an advisor. The members may only receive a normal director's fee. No additional compensation is allowed. At least one of the audit committee members must be a designated financial expert. The expertise areas consist of the understanding:

- GAAP and financial statements
- The preparation and audit of financial statements for a comparable company
- Internal controls
- The role and functions of an audit committee

The mandated duties of the audit committee consist of:

- Approving the selection of the external auditor
- Liaison with the external auditor
- Determining the external auditor's compensation
- Overseeing the external auditor's work
- Resolving auditor disputes and disagreements

In addition, SOX requires CPA firms auditing publicly held clients to report to the client's audit committee.

SOX enhances employee reporting of complaints regarding accounting, audit, and control issues by mandating whistleblower protection and by mandating that publicly held corporations provide confidential, anonymous mechanisms for employee submission of accounting, audit, and control matters. Procedures must be established for receiving, retaining and responding to complaints.

SOX has added provisions banning corporate loans to officers and directors, decreasing the time allowed between the execution of and the reporting to the SEC of insider stock trading, and the disgorgement by recipients of bonuses and other compensation gained by fraudulent behavior.

Last, SOX requires publicly held corporations to have a code of ethics for senior financial officers. The corporation is required to disclose whether, and if not, the reason why not, the corporation has adopted such a code. The act also requires immediate disclosure to the SEC of any change in or waiver of the code of ethics for senior financial officers.

CEO/CFO Certifications SOX requires both the CEO and a CFO of a publicly held company to certify both the company's financial statements and its internal control system. The CEO and CFO have to certify that the financial statements have been reviewed by them and that, to the best of their knowledge, the statements have no material errors or omissions and that the statements fairly present the company's financial position and results of operations in accordance with GAAP or other appropriate reporting criteria.

Regarding the company's internal control, the CEO and CFO certify management's responsibility for establishing and maintaining the internal control system and that the internal control system has been evaluated within 90 days and whether the system is effective. Effectiveness is compromised if there are one or more material weaknesses in the internal control system. A material weakness is defined by the PCAOB as ". . . a significant deficiency or combination of deficiencies that could result in more than a remote likelihood that a material misstatement of the annual or interim financial statements will not be prevented or detected."[6]

Enhanced Financial Disclosure SOX has these enhanced financial statement disclosure requirements:

- An internal control report confirming management's responsibility for the establishing and maintaining of the internal control system and management's evaluation of the effectiveness of the system
- The auditor's opinion on the effectiveness of the internal control system
- Management's statement that no material or immaterial employee and/or management fraud occurred during the period covered by the financial statements
- The reporting of all material audit corrections and all material off–balance sheet financing arrangements in SEC filings
- Enhanced MD&A (management discussion and analysis) disclosures in the company's annual report, and the requirement that the organization implement "disclosure controls and procedures" to identify and evaluate potential disclosures.

The MD&A requirements include disclosure of significant trends, demands, uncertainties, and commitments confronting the corporation.

Civil and Criminal Penalties SOX has amended U.S. federal sentencing guidelines mandating harsher penalties for fraud and for obstruction of justice. Current sentencing guidelines also provide incentive for the organization to demonstrate an intent to be compliant with laws and regulations, and to provide cooperation and open disclosure during an investigation. Such actions can be used to reduce possible sanctions and penalties.

While the regulatory environment currently remains in a state of flux due to the ongoing implementation and interpretation of Sarbanes-Oxley, it is clear that the focus on proactive actions to mitigate potential adverse situations will continue. Additionally, many non-public entities are voluntarily adopting certain requirements of the Sarbanes-Oxley act, even though they are not required to do so. In essence, the Sarbanes-Oxley act has become the new gold standard for governance and control procedures.

NOTES

1. Dicksee, L.R. *Auditing: A Practical Manual of Auditors,* Gee and Company, London, 1892.
2. Ibid, p. 8.
3. Ibid, p. 53.
4. *Anti-Bribery and Books and Records Provisions of the Foreign Corrupt Practices Act.* United States Code, Title 15, Commerce and Trade, Chapter 2B—Securities Exchanges.
5. *The Laws That Govern the Securities Industry,* http://sec.gov/about/laws/.shtml, March 3, 2006.
6. Vorhies, James Brady, "The New Importance of Materiality," *The Journal of Accountancy,* May, 2005, p. 56.

Chapter 4

The Role of Professional Standards

Lawrence R. Donaldson, Jeffrey S. Hengeveld, and Louis W. Petro

INTRODUCTION

Fraud deterrence is a complex process. On one hand, it seems intuitive and easy to accomplish; on the other hand, it may seem impossible. Of course, the application of hindsight always makes it easier to determine how fraud could have been prevented or detected earlier. The difficulty is in identifying those effective measures and procedures ahead of time, and then applying them.

Successful fraud deterrence depends on a combination of the efforts by management, and outside professionals and consultants, such as external and internal auditors (CPAs and CIAs), fraud examiners (CFEs), and fraud deterrence professionals (CFDs). Once management understands its role as the first line of defense against fraud, it is then important for management to have an accurate understanding of the role outside professionals and consultants can play in fraud deterrence. The role of management, as covered in Section 404 of the 2002 Sarbanes-Oxley Act ("Management Assessment of Internal Controls") is discussed later in the chapter after looking at the professional standards applicable to outside professionals.

This chapter covers the professional standards related to fraud deterrence promulgated by the leading professional organizations in this area:

- Public Company Accounting Oversight Board (PCAOB)
- American Institute of Certified Public Accountants Auditing (AICPA) Standards
- American Institute of Certified Public Accountants (AICPA) Accounting and Review Standards
- Institute of Internal Auditors (IIA)
- Association of Certified Fraud Examiners (ACFE)
- National Association of Certified Valuation Analysts (NACVA)

PCAOB STANDARDS

The Public Company Accounting Oversight Board (PCAOB), a provision of the 2002 Sarbanes-Oxley Act, has issued four auditing standards through July 2005. They are:

- Auditing Standard No. 1, "References in Auditors' Reports to the Standards of the Public Company Accounting Oversight Board"

- Auditing Standard No. 2, "An Audit of Internal Control Over Financial Reporting Performed in Conjunction With an Audit of Financial Statements"
- Auditing Standard No. 3, "Audit Documentation"
- Auditing Standard No. 4, "Reporting on Whether a Previously Reported Material Weakness Continue to Exist"

Although the PCAOB auditing standards legally apply only to audits of publicly held companies (Securities and Exchange Commission [SEC] registrants), they provide a benchmark for the audit of any type of organization. They are seen by many as best practices.

PCAOB Auditing Standard No. 1

The first standard released by the PCAOB, "References in Auditors' Reports to the Standards of the Public Company Accounting Oversight Board," has two major provisions. First, the standard states that the PCAOB has adapted as initial standards, on an initial, transitional basis, the generally accepted auditing standards described in the American Institute of Certified Public Accountants' (AICPA) Auditing Standards Board's Statement on Auditing Standards (SAS) No. 95, "Generally Accepted Auditing Standards," in existence on April 16, 2003. Therefore, the PCAOB has adopted SAS No. 82, "Consideration of Fraud in a Financial Statement Audit," which, as superseded by SAS No. 99, will be discussed later.

The second issue in PCAOB No. 1 notes that in the auditor's report on either an audit or a review, the auditor should note that the engagement was conducted "in accordance with the standards of the Public Company Accounting Oversight Board (United States)."

PCAOB Auditing Standard No. 2

PCAOB Auditing Standard No. 2, "An Audit of Internal Control over Financial Reporting Performed in Conjunction with an Audit of Financial Statements," should provide a real assist to fraud deterrence. The PCAOB feels that the standard will "enhance the accuracy, reliability, and fairness of the financial statements, which are such an important element in the success of our financial markets."[i] The standard, effective for all audits of publicly held corporations for fiscal years ending on or after June 15, 2004, requires the external auditor of the corporation to issue two opinions, one on the corporation management's assessment of the organization's internal control system and one on the auditor's assessment of the effectiveness of the corporation's internal control over financial reporting. An effective internal control system is one with *no* material internal control weaknesses existing as of the date of management's assessment.

The PCAOB standard defines a material weakness as "a significant deficiency, or combination of significant deficiencies, that results in more than a remote likelihood that a material misstatement of the annual or interim financial statements will not be prevented or detected."[2] The significance of a deficiency is determined by:[3]

- The likelihood that a deficiency, or combination of deficiencies, could result in a misstatement of an account balance or disclosure.
- The magnitude of the potential misstatement resulting from the deficiency or deficiencies.

The possibility of an adverse opinion on the effectiveness of the internal control system strongly motivates management to develop and implement an effective internal control system. The more effective the control system is, the stronger will be its fraud deterrence capability.

PCAOB Auditing Standard No. 2 has these other provisions:

- The Committee of Sponsoring Organizations of the Treadway Commission (COSO) *Internal Control-Integrated Framework* is recommended as guidance for internal control performance and reporting.
- Auditor independence principles are defined.
- The evaluation of audit committee effectiveness is covered.
- The standard requires the auditor to perform at least one walk-through for each major class of transactions.
- The standard states that the external auditor may use the work of others (e.g., internal auditors, fraud examiners, or consultants) to help determine the nature, extent, and timing of internal control tests.

The COSO internal control framework is covered in Chapter 9. Corporate governance and audit committees are covered in Chapter 10.

PCAOB Auditing Standard No. 3

PCAOB Auditing Standard No. 3, "Audit Documentation," provides guidelines for the documentation of any type of external audit, including an audit of internal controls. The primary purpose of audit documentation is to provide the evidence to support the auditor's opinion. The documentation also provides evidence that the auditor followed generally accepted audit standards (GAAS) in planning, supervising, executing, reporting, and reviewing the engagement. The requirement that audit engagements be documented adequately encourages the auditor to exercise due care in the performance of the engagement.

PCAOB Auditing Standard No. 4

PCAOB Auditing Standard No. 4, "Reporting on Whether a Previously Reported Material Weakness Continues to Exist," applies to engagements geared solely to reporting on whether a previously reported material weakness has not been corrected and, therefore, continues to exist. Such engagements are performed at management's discretion and as of a reasonable date selected by the management. The engagement need not be in conjunction with an audit or review and may cover more than one allegedly corrected material weakness. In order to perform the engagement, the auditor must receive a written statement from management noting that the specified weakness or weaknesses no longer exist as of the date specified by management.

AMERICAN INSTITUTE OF CERTIFIED PUBLIC ACCOUNTANTS AUDITING STANDARDS

The primary AICPA audit standard relating to fraud deterrence is Statement on Auditing Standards No. 99 (SAS 99), "Consideration of Fraud in a Financial Statement Audit." SAS 99, issued in 2002, replaced SAS 82 which had the same title. SAS 99 emphasizes that auditor consider the client's susceptibility to fraud in the planning of an audit of the client's financial statements. Specifically, the standard:

- Replaces SAS 82
- Amends SAS 1, "Codification of Auditing Standards and Procedures"
- Amends SAS 85, "Management Representations"

SAS 99 has been effective for financial statements for periods beginning on or after December 15, 2002. The amendments to SAS 1 and SAS 85 will be discussed first, followed by the replacement provisions to SAS 82.

SAS 1 Amendments

The SAS 99 amendments to SAS 1 add new language regarding due professional care in the performance of work and the concept of reasonable assurance. SAS 99 notes that due professional care in the performance of a financial statement audit should include audit staff discussions regarding the potential for client fraud. The fraud could be either asset misappropriation or fraudulent financial reporting.

SAS 99 requires the auditor to recognize that reasonable assurance is affected by both the characteristics of fraud and the inherent ineffectiveness of audit procedures in detecting fraud. The characteristics of fraud noted in particular are:

- Concealment and/or collusion by management and/or employees
- Documents withheld, misrepresented, altered, or falsified
- The ability of management to override the control system

The characteristics cause the inherent ineffectiveness of audit procedures in the detection of fraud.

SAS 85 Amendments

The amendments to SAS 85, "Management Representations," add new language to the management representation letter and require the auditor to inquire of management regarding fraud and the risk of fraud. Specifically, the new language requires that management acknowledge in the written management representation letter management's:

- Responsibility for fraud prevention and detection
- Knowledge of suspected management and employee frauds
- Knowledge of employee allegations of fraud and the follow-up on the allegations

The amendments should provide additional fraud deterrence motivation to client management.

SAS 82 Replacements

SAS 99 covers these areas relating to fraud:

- Descriptions and characteristics of fraud
- Professional skepticism
- Discussions of fraud with audit engagement personnel
- Fraud risks
- The evaluation of audit evidence
- Auditor communication with client management, the audit committee, and others
- Documenting the auditor's consideration of fraud during the audit engagement

Each of these areas will be discussed.

Description and Characteristics of Fraud. The two basic types of fraud are fraudulent financial reporting (management fraud) and misappropriation of assets (employee fraud). Fraudulent financial reporting involves:

- Manipulation, falsification, or alteration of documents or records
- Misrepresentations
- Omissions
- Misapplication of generally accepted accounting principles (GAAP)

Asset misappropriation involves misstatements arising from employee theft and/or embezzlement. Fraud characteristics should be considered within the fraud triangle framework of incentive, opportunity, and rationalization (attitude). The fraud triangle is covered in Chapter 5.

Professional Skepticism. SAS 99 mandates that the auditor conduct a financial statement audit with an attitude of professional skepticism. Professional skepticism in auditing consists of a questioning mind and the critical assessment of audit evidence. The auditor must recognize that in any audit engagement, the possibility of fraud exists. The possibility is there regardless of the auditor's previous knowledge and beliefs about the client management and employee integrity and honesty. In addition, professional skepticism requires the auditor to extend audit procedures should an indicator of fraud be noticed. Finally, the auditor should not accept less than pervasive evidence about an audit assertion just because he or she believes the management to be honest.

Engagement Team Discussions. SAS 99 requires that there be audit team discussion and communication throughout the engagement. The standard requires brainstorming during the planning phase of the audit. The brainstorming sessions should cover how and where the client's financial statements might be susceptible to fraudulent misstatement. The sessions should reinforce the skeptical mind-set mentioned earlier. The sessions should also encourage effective communication of fraud indicators during the execution and evaluation phases of the audit.

Fraud Risks. SAS 99 requires the auditor to consider these areas regarding fraud risk when conducting a financial statement audit:

- Obtaining information to identify risks
- Identifying risks
- Assessing risks
- Responding to the risk assessment

Obtaining information requires:

- Inquiries of the audit committee management, employees, and the client's in-house legal counsel
- Analytical review procedures designed to indicate possible area of fraud
- Consideration of the three fraud triangle elements (incentive, opportunity, and rationalization)

In addition, the information from the results of certain procedures and reviews may be relevant to the assessment of possible fraud risk:

- Client acceptance and continuance procedures
- Interim financial statement reviews

SAS 99 requires that risks identified by the information gathering procedures covered above be segregated by type (management or employee), significance or materiality, likelihood or probability, and pervasiveness. Pervasiveness relates to whether a fraud misstates only a part of the financial statements or the statements taken as a whole.

SAS 55, "Consideration of Internal Control in a Financial Statement Audit" described procedures for assessing risks associated with an audit, but was subsequently amended by SAS 78, "Consideration of Internal Control in a Financial Statement Audit: An Amendment to SAS No. 55." SAS 55 requires that the auditor obtain an understanding of the three elements of the client's internal control structure sufficient to plan the audit adequately. The three elements are:

1. The control environment
2. The accounting system
3. Control procedures, defined as the following categories
    - Segregation of duties
    - Authorizations
    - Documentation
    - Safeguards
    - Independent checks

SAS 55 also notes that the auditor should recognize that there are two primary inherent internal control limitations: management override of internal control procedures, and the collusion of two or more people. In addition, the standard mandates that the auditor should evaluate whether client controls addressing risks of material misstatements due to fraud have been implemented and are operating effectively. Finally, the auditor should assess the risks of fraud based on the evaluation and respond to the risk.

SAS 78 changed the definition of internal control to be unified with the five elements of internal control as defined in the COSO Internal Control—Integrated Framework.

1. Control environment
2. Risk assessment
3. Control activities
4. Information and communication
5. Monitoring

Additional information about COSO Internal Control—Integrated Framework appears in Chapter 8.

The auditor's response to the risk assessment consists of six activities. They are:

1. Adjusting the planning, staffing, and supervising the audit
2. Modifying the nature of audit tests covered in SAS 31 and SAS 80, "Evidential Matter"

3. Changing the extent of audit tests covered in SAS 39, "Audit Sampling"
4. Moving the timing of audit tests covered in SAS 45, "Substantive Tests Prior to the Balance Sheet Date"
5. Reviewing journal entries and adjustments
6. Reviewing management estimates

The last two are particularly important from a fraud detection standpoint. The review of journal entries, among other things, should focus on:

- Entries to unrelated, unusual, or seldom-used accounts
- Entries made by personnel not usually making journal entries
- End-of-period and/or post-closing entries
- Entries made right before or during financial statement preparation, in particular, any entries to unnumbered accounts
- Entries whose dollar amounts are round or inconsistent with expectations
- Complex journal entries
- Intracompany and related-party transaction journal entries
- Unusual entries involving such things as mergers and acquisitions, impairments, abandonment's, restructurings, extraordinary gains or losses, and discontinued operations

All of these types of entries have been used to cover up fraudulent activities.

The preparation of financial statements requires management to make many accounting estimates. When perpetrating a fraud involving financial statement misstatement, management often accomplishes the fraud by manipulating accounting estimates. SAS 99 requires the external auditor to obtain persuasive evidence to support any significant management estimates. Estimates that should be reviewed include these commonly made ones:

- Actuarial parameters and imputed interest rates used in accounting for pensions and other postretirement benefits
- Imputed interest rates used for lease capitalization
- Contingent liabilities related to environmental and health and safety issues
- Cash flows used for property, plant, and equipment impairment present value calculations
- Fair values for goodwill impairment calculations
- Warranty liabilities
- Uncollectible account expense and the related allowance for doubtful accounts
- Allowances for sales returns, sales allowances, and sales discounts
- Inventory obsolescence values
- Useful lives and residual values for buildings and equipment
- Useful lives for amortizable intangible assets

This list contains the more common management estimates. It is not all-inclusive.

Evaluating Audit Evidence. SAS 99 requires the external auditor to review evidence as it relates to the overall audit and to apply analytical procedures to determine the reasonableness of the financial statements. The evidence review should focus on:

- Discrepancies in accounting records
- Untimely information or data
- Conflicting or missing evidence
- Problematic or unusual auditor/client relationships

Examples of evidence discrepancies are:

- Incomplete data, information, or documentation
- Unsupported entries or management assertions
- Significant last-minute adjusting entries
- Tips from or complaints by employees regarding financial reporting issues

Conflicting or missing evidence includes such things as:

- Missing or altered documents
- Unusual documents
- The use of photocopies of documents when originals would be the norm
- Inconsistent, vague, or implausible auditor inquiry responses made by management or employees
- Missing evidence, such as assets, data in electronic form, program change records, and data destruction inconsistent with client document retention policies

Problematic or unusual auditor/client relationships include, but are not limited to:

- Client denial of access to records, assets, facilities, or personnel
- The unwillingness of the client to assist with or to facilitate the audit
- Client intimidation of the auditor
- Delays in responses to auditor inquiries or requests for access to records, assets, facilities, or employees
- The unwillingness of the client to make auditor requested adjustments to the financial statements
- The unwillingness of the client to make adequate financial statement disclosures

SAS 99 requires the auditor of financial statements to use analytical review procedures, such as financial ratio analysis, to determine the overall reasonableness of the financial statements. In particular, the auditor should look for and follow up on any unusual or unexpected relationships. Relationships to be reviewed would include such things as:

- Current and quick ratios
- Net income to cash flow from operations
- Gross margins on sales
- Margins on sales
- Return on assets
- Inventory and receivables turnovers

- Inventory days on hand and receivables collection periods
- Uncollectible account expense and the allowance for doubtful accounts
- Asset turnovers
- Interest and fixed charge coverages

The ratios should be reviewed over time as well as compared to industry averages and ranges for reasonableness. Significant changes or discrepancies in the ratios indicate the possibility of fraud. The auditor is required by SAS 99 to follow up on the possibilities.

SAS 99 requires the external auditor to evaluate the materiality of any detected misstatements. If any misstatements are material, the auditor must, first, determine the implications regarding the gathering of additional audit evidence. Second, the auditor should advise management of the finding and further investigate the finding. Last, the auditor should advise the client to consult its legal counsel about the matter. If the misstatements are immaterial, the auditor should consider its implications regarding his/her evaluation of management and/or employee integrity.

Auditor Communication. SAS 99 requires the auditor of financial statements to communicate any fraud-related issues to management, the client audit committee, and others. Auditor communications are covered in three other Statements on Auditing Standards. They are:

- SAS 60, "Communication of Internal Control Related Matters Noted in an Audit"
- SAS 61, "Quality of the Entities Accounting Principles"
- SAS 84, "Communications Between Predecessor and Successor Auditors"

In addition, the auditor needs to consider legal and regulatory reporting requirements such as responses to subpoenas or to requests from governmental funding agencies. Government funding agency requests are covered in the Governmental Accountability Office (GAO) Auditing Standards ("The Yellow Book").

Audit Documentation. The standard requires the auditor of financial statements to document fraud issues related to the audit. Specifically, SAS 99 requires the auditor to document:

- Fraud discussions with audit and among the audit engagement personnel
- Risk procedures used during the engagement
- Audit evidence and/or analytical procedures leading to the need for additional audit procedures
- The nature of fraud communication resulting from the audit

The discussion documentation must cover how the discussions were conducted, who was involved, when the discussions occurred, and what was discussed.

Risk procedures documented must include:

- How risk information was obtained
- The identification of specific risks
- The assessment of the risk of material misstatements
- The assessment of the risk of management override of internal controls

All fraud communications with management, the audit committee, or others regarding the audit must be documented.

AMERICAN INSTITUTE OF CERTIFIED PUBLIC ACCOUNTANTS ACCOUNTING AND REVIEW STANDARDS

The AICPA accounting and review standard relevant to fraud deterrence are Statement on Standards for Accounting and Review Services No. 10 (SSARS 10), "Standards for Accounting and Review Services," and SSARS 12, "Omnibus Statement on Standards for Accounting and Review Services—2005." The two SSARS will be discussed separately.

SSARS 10

SSARS 10 amends SSARS 1, "Compilation and Review of Financial Statements." Among other things, SSARS 1 covers the performance and documentation of review engagements. SSARS 10 does not apply to compilations.

Among other things, SSARS 10 provides for inquiries regarding fraud in a review engagement. Under the new standard, accountants performing a review engagement will need to develop an understanding of the client's business, understand the potential for misstatement of the financial statements due to fraud, and be able to apply additional inquiries or analytical procedures to identify any material adjustments needed to bring the financial statements into conformity with GAAP.

The illustrative inquiries in SSARS 10 have been expanded to include questions that seem to assess the operation of the underlying business processes. If the accountant is not prepared to judge the responses to the inquiries, recognize the warning signs of fraud, and develop appropriate communication to company ownership, he or she could be exposed to professional liability.

The risk to the accountant highlighted by the revised standard is that a fraudulent situation could exist within the organization that is not uncovered during the review. SSARS 10 reiterates that an understanding of internal controls is not part of a review engagement. However, fraud studies claim that about 90 percent of fraud would be prevented by appropriate internal controls. This means the single most powerful tool to understand the potential for fraud in the organization is not available to an accountant performing the review. The accountant is left with the responsibility for considering fraud without the ability to identify conditions that present the opportunity for fraud.

SSARS 12

SSARS 12, "Omnibus Statement on Standards for Accounting and Review Services—2005," amends SSARS 1. It requires the external accountant to have an understanding with a compilation or review client regarding the reporting to the client of fraud or illegal acts that come to the accountant's attention during the performance of the compilation or review engagement. The standard recommends, but does not require, that the understanding be in writing. The accountant must report any evidence or information that comes to his or her attention regarding fraud or illegal activities to the appropriate level of management.

INSTITUTE OF INTERNAL AUDITORS STANDARDS

Statement on Internal Auditing Standards 3 (SIAS 3), "Deterrence, Detection, Investigation, and Reporting of Fraud (1985)," provides guidance for the performance of financial, compliance, and operational audits by internal auditors. SIAS 3 requires internal auditors to determine if their organization has fraud deterrence policies and procedures in place. The standard notes:

- Effective internal controls the principal way to deter fraud.
- The control system is management's responsibility.
- The role of the internal auditor is to assist management in deterring fraud.

In fulfilling the role, the internal auditor reviews and evaluates the adequacy and effectiveness of the organization's internal controls.

In determining the effectiveness of the internal control system in deterring fraud, the internal auditor considers:

- Does the organization's management have the proper attitude toward internal controls?
- Does the management set the proper control tone for the organization?
- Does the organization establish realistic goals and objectives for the management and employees?
- Does the organization have a code of conduct?
- Does the code adequately cover prohibited activities and the consequences of code violations?
- Is the code communicated to all employees?
- Do appropriate authorization policies exist, and are they followed?
- Are procedures to monitor activities in place, and are they followed?
- Are asset safeguarding procedures in place, and are they followed?

Last, the internal auditor must make recommendations, as appropriate, to improve fraud deterrence controls.

ASSOCIATION OF CERTIFIED FRAUD EXAMINERS STANDARDS

Certified Fraud Examiner (CFE) is a designation awarded by the Association of Certified Fraud Examiners (ACFE). While many members of that association also happen to be Certified Public Accountants, many of the members come from other backgrounds as well. The association has its own Code of Professional Ethics and Code of Professional Standards. These codes can be found in their entirety through the association's Web site, www.acfe.com.

The association's Code of Professional Ethics requires all of the conduct that management would expect from an outside professional. These include diligence, ethical conduct, the avoidance of conflict of interest, and integrity. The Code of Professional Ethics requires adherence to lawful orders of the court. It also requires obtaining appropriate evidence to support opinions and conclusions reached. It imposes on the CFE an obligation of confidentiality, but requires revealing all the appropriate information that, if omitted, might create a distortion of the facts.

The professional standards, in many regards, read much like the standards for the accounting profession itself. Ethical conduct and integrity are of prime importance. Serving the interest of the clients as well as the public is also recognized. CFEs are admonished to investigate for potential conflicts of interest before accepting an engagement. They are obligated to maintain objectivity in the discharge of their engagement. Of course, members are not to make any knowingly false statements nor violate any lawful orders of a court or other similar body. The association requires certain continuing professional education in order to maintain one's level of competence and effectiveness. Many of the same requirements can be found in the CFE's standards as are found in the accounting standards.

As with the engagement of an outside accountant, the engagement of a CFE should likewise be the matter of a full and complete understanding between client and professional, evidenced by a written engagement letter. CFEs are obligated not to disclose any confidential or privileged information. This can be overcome by express permission of the client or an appropriate order of a court.

The standards speak to how a fraud examination is to be conducted, the nature of the evidence to be obtained and relied on, and the manner in which the reports of the CFE's activities be made.

It is important for management to understand, before engaging a CFE, that the standards and the Code of Professional Ethics for CFE's do not allow the CFE to express an opinion regarding the guilt or innocence of any person or party.

It may be a good idea for management, from time to time, to have a fraud audit or fraud examination conducted by an outside accountant or CFE simply to satisfy management that its internal accounting controls are effective and enforced and that the entity's assets are being appropriately safeguarded.

CERTIFIED FRAUD DETERRENCE ANALYST—NATIONAL ASSOCIATION OF CERTIFIED VALUATION ANALYSTS

The Certified Fraud Deterrence Analyst (CFD) is a certificate awarded by the National Association of Certified Valuation Analysts (NACVA) and sponsored by the Fraud Deterrence Institute to those having demonstrated an appropriate level of fraud deterrence and analytical forensics experience and knowledge. The appropriate level is determined by the Fraud Deterrence Institute. The purpose of the certificate is to provide the public with assurance of the holder's fraud deterrence competence. The program is designed to educate participants on how specifically to enact a proactive fraud deterrence assignment. Earning the CFD requires that the candidate complete a rigorous five-day fraud deterrence program and pass a comprehensive examination. NACVA has issued Guidelines for Fraud Deterrence Engagements and is in the process of drafting comprehensive standards.

Components of the foundation and methodology of the CFD program contain proprietary information that has been licensed by NACVA by Cendrowski Corporate Advisors, LLC and its affiliates.

NOTES

1. Nicholas G. Apostolou and D. Larry Crumbley, "Sarbanes-Oxley Fallout Leads to Auditing Standard No. 2: Importance of Internal Controls," *The Value Examiner* (November/December 2004): 56.
2. Ibid., p. 59.
3. Ibid., p. 59.

Chapter 5

The Fraud Triangle

Harry Cendrowski and James Martin

OVERVIEW

The concept of the fraud triangle was originated by fraud researcher Dr. Donald R. Cressey to explain the three causal factors present in every situation of fraud. The three factors are motive, rationalization, and attitude. The different factors included in the triangle explain why fraud will be perpetrated in some situations where there is an internal control weakness and not others.

The fraud triangle is applicable to financial reporting fraud as well as asset-related fraud. American Institute of Certified Public Accountants (AICPA) guidance for financial reporting fraud, including Statement on Auditing Standards (SAS) Number 99 guidance, refers to the fraud triangle elements but uses different terminology for the elements.

Breaking the fraud triangle is a key to fraud deterrence; if an organization can find a way to break the fraud triangle—in essence, to remove one of the elements—the organization should be able to reduce the potential for fraudulent incidents. Of the three elements, removal of opportunity is most directly affected by the system of internal controls and generally provides the most actionable route to deterrence of fraud.

ELEMENTS

The fraud triangle defines three elements present in every fraud situation. All three elements must be present for the fraud to occur; if one element is removed, the fraud will not be perpetrated or will be prevented by the internal controls of the organization.

Motive

Motive describes the driving need for funds or, alternatively, the reason a person needs to commit a crime. Sometimes referred to as pressure, this element is typically a driving need for additional income for various purposes. When fraud is discovered, the perpetrator can describe the reasons he or she needed to steal, and forensic analysis can reveal where the ill-gotten gains were expended. Cash, of course, can be used for many purposes, some inherently illicit, others not. In any case, even behavior that is not inherently illegal (e.g., gambling at a casino) can create pressures that can cause otherwise law-abiding people to commit fraud.

Fraud usually starts out small and grows over time. Likewise the motives that people have to steal often also will grow over time as their problems worsen or they set their sights on more elaborate purchases.

Lifestyle Needs. Often misappropriated funds are used to purchase goods and services that would otherwise be out of reach of the perpetrator. Many times these purchases are underpinned by a driving need to be viewed as being successful; over time the perpetrator will need to continue to make elaborate purchases to reinforce that illusion. Such goods and services may include:

- Expensive restaurant meals, clothing, jewelry, living beyond legitimate means
- Real estate, vacation homes
- Trips, travel, vacations
- Home improvements
- Boats and other recreational vehicles

Many of these purchases will be visible to the business owner, manager, others within the organization, friends, and neighbors. Purchases clearly in excess of legitimate income levels are a strong red flag of fraud.

Illicit Activities. Many fraud perpetrators state that the pressure in their situation was created by participation in an illicit activity; often these activities are considered addictive.

- Drugs, Often this includes addiction.
- Gambling. While gambling is now legal in many areas, it should be considered entertainment, and gamblers should bet within their means. When people develop a gambling habit, they can be driven to find other funds to support their activities.
- Restitution. Fraud perpetrators, when discovered, often enter into a restitution arrangement with the victim; perpetrators may steal from their current employer to pay back the prior victim

Life Pressures. Often fraud perpetrators explain that they needed extra funds simply because the normal cost of living expenditures exceeded their legitimate income.

- A close relative becomes ill, and medical expenses accumulate.
- Home heating, gas, and other necessary commodities become more expensive.
- Credit card debt becomes unmanageable. (Note, however, that lifestyle issues will often contribute to this.)
- Educational costs for children may increase.
- The perpetrator participates in other legitimate organizations, charities, or church groups that need funds to achieve objectives (i.e., the "Robin Hood" perpetrator).

Many of the motives for fraud involve purchases and expenditures that are not recoverable by the victim if and when the fraud is discovered. Trips and meals are consumed, vehicles depreciate, and real estate purchases are often made in excess of prevailing market values. The 2004 Certified Fraud Examiners' "Report to the Nation" reported that fraud victims see a 20 percent median recovery rate, and in 40 percent of the cases, recover nothing at all.

It is difficult for an organization to manage the motives for fraud as many pressures that employees face are external. The organization could, however, provide counseling programs for employees under pressure before their only alternative would involve turning to fraud.

Organizations can attempt to evaluate candidates for potential fraud motives through public records searches, which reveal items such as vehicle registrations, property and mortgage filings, and tax liens. Obtaining a full credit report for potential employees, however, is generally restricted without the consent of the candidate; organizations are advised to seek competent legal advice for guidance on employee background searches.

Rationalization

Fraud perpetrators describe their actions as something other than committing a crime or taking unfair advantage of a company or another person. They have come to terms with their actions and overcome their apprehensions of breaking the law. Fraud perpetrators rationalize their actions. It is this rationalization that allows them to conduct their fraudulent activities.

The element of rationalization explains why fraud does not occur in every situation where there is a control weakness and a person with a need for funds: The person could believe it would be wrong to take advantage of the company or person who would be harmed by the fraud. In essence, the person would view the fraud as a wrongful act and will not commit it.

Fraud usually starts out small and grows over time. Many perpetrators start out by rationalizing a small amount of misappropriation, in essence, an amount that they consider to be immaterial. They enter a slippery slope of rationalization. As each progressive amount taken falls under the umbrella of acceptability, they become comfortable with greater and more frequent fraudulent acts.

A discussion of frequently cited rationalizations follows.

Not a Crime

- The company has so much money—they won't miss it.
- It's not really stealing—these are small amounts.
- "It's like taking a penny out of the jar at 7-Eleven, except we aren't even taking a whole penny, just part of a penny." From the movie *Office Space*
- My problems outweigh the risk of being caught—there is nowhere else to turn.
- Everyone I know has a nicer car and nicer house. I deserve those things too.

Constructive Income

- They owe me this money, I work hard and haven't gotten a raise.
- I'm just fixing what should have happened anyway.
- It's not fraud—I'm going to put the money back when things turn around.

Vendetta

- The company deserves to lose money; everyone hates working there.
- I'm not a criminal—I'm a hero.
- This can't be inappropriate, I'm sure my boss would do something like this.

The element of rationalization also explains why an organization should not consider a small fraud to be immaterial. Even in a small fraud, perpetrators have rationalized their actions as something other than a crime. It would be much easier for them to expand their activities if future opportunities presented themselves. Even a small fraud indicates a mind-set that is unhealthy to the success of the organization.

Rationalization is managed most effectively through an appropriate control environment. Employees should receive consistent reinforcement of what is considered appropriate conduct, through both written policy and appropriate management behavior.

Management should be aware of the morale of the organization—if the morale is dismal, if the employees truly hate their jobs and hate the company, it is much easier to justify fraudulent actions. Preventing rationalization is strongly related to human resource policies and procedures to assess employee satisfaction and help develop a strong culture.

Opportunity

Opportunity describes the condition that allows the fraud to occur. Typically this is a weakness in the internal control structure that allows an asset to be converted and the act concealed. This weakness typically stems from poorly designed control activities, poorly enforced control activities, or a combination of both.

Fraud usually starts out small and grows over time. Often perpetrators test the internal controls of an organization for weakness with smaller transactions. If discovered, the transaction could be explained away as an error. If not discovered, however, perpetrators have located a control weakness that provides access to funds and a method of concealment that has apparently been successful. Unless there is a change in the control structure to remove the weakness, perpetrators can continue to exploit that weakness for additional gain without detection. Also, as fraud perpetrators continue to test the internal control structure, they may discover additional ways to extract additional funds.

Many internal control breakdowns provide potential perpetrators with an opportunity to commit fraud—in essence, to remove funds from an organization and conceal the act. Fraud perpetrators are extremely creative in identifying ways to defeat internal controls and in finding ways to conceal the act. Critical control weaknesses exist where incompatible duties are not appropriately separated, for example:

- An employee who handles cash payments and can write off receivables has the ability to steal a payment and conceal the theft by writing off the receivable amount.
- An employee who handles cash payments and can apply payments against a customer account (but not necessarily write off the payment) has the ability to steal a payment and conceal the theft for a short time by lapping another payment to cover the receivable.

Critical internal control weakness can exist in an organization without necessarily being exploited for fraud; the control weakness is just an opportunity to do so. The opportunity might not be exploited because:

- A potential fraud perpetrator did not realize it was an opportunity for fraud (lack of recognition of the opportunity).
- The person with knowledge of the control weakness did not think it was right to steal from the organization (lack of rationalization).
- The person with knowledge of the control weakness did not have a driving need for funds (lack of motive).

Of the three elements, removal of opportunity generally provides the most actionable route to fraud deterrence. While an organization should still be mindful of motive and rationalization, opportunity can be lessened through the development and consistent enforcement of an appropriate system of internal controls.

THE FRAUD TRIANGLE AND FINANCIAL REPORTING FRAUD

Asset fraud typically results in a direct reward—the perpetrator directly receives cash or other valuable assets from the organization. For financial reporting fraud, the reward is typically indirect—the perpetrator receives a bonus or pay raise for financial performance or achievement of a measure. To reflect the indirect nature of the reward, discussion of the fraud triangle related to financial reporting fraud uses slightly different terms; these terms are used by the AICPA in its discussion of SAS 99.

Incentive or Pressure

Since the manipulation results in an indirect reward, the motive to misstate the financial statements is referred to as an incentive or pressure: The employee has an incentive to distort the actual financial results.

Organizations should be careful when defining their compensation programs to not define large rewards for a target or hurdle, as this can become an incentive or pressure to distort the financials.

For public companies, new rules require disgorgement of any income received through the manipulation of the financial statements; in essence, this removes the reward for such activities.

Attitude

The mind-set of the person engaged in the manipulation of the financial statements is referred to as attitude. Additionally, this term describes the attitude of the individual for accurate financial reporting. Financial statement manipulation can be accomplished through many techniques, including management judgments:

- Timing differences, accelerating income, or delaying expense recognition
- Changes to estimates or reserves
- Deliberate misapplication of generally accepted accounting principles (GAAP)
- Engaging in transactions simply to manage GAAP application

Management judgments should be founded on an attitude that accurate financial reporting is key to the success of the organization.

Opportunity

The opportunity to distort the financial statements is still referred to as opportunity. Asset-related fraud results in the direct removal of an asset; financial reporting fraud is accomplished by manipulating the accounting system to achieve a certain result. In the case of financial statement fraud, management does not need to conceal an asset removal; it only needs to prevent the discovery that the financials are not correct. This can be accomplished in a variety of ways.

- Management has the opportunity to direct or coerce subordinate employees to make entries to the financial statements.
- Employees often are not comfortable challenging the judgment of management.
- Management can make this discomfort more pronounced by purposefully hiring less than qualified employees.
- Management can control the communication of issues between operating units.

Many of the features of the Sarbanes-Oxley Act are designed to reveal potential manipulations of the financial statements. Even with the new safeguards, however, the most important control remains appropriate behavior of management.

Chapter 6

Motivations of Fraud Deterrence and the Transition to Investigation

Harry Cendrowski and James Martin

INTRODUCTION

Fraud deterrence engagements play a central role in the assessment of internal controls. While many in management believe that such a role is fulfilled by both the internal audit department and third-party audits, fraud deterrence is not the primary goal of either function. Fraud deterrence engagements have a specific place in the organization, above and beyond the functions of internal and external audits. Deterrence and investigation are complimentary processes, and frequently intertwined. Consider the most common questions asked by management if a fraud is suspected:

1. Was there a fraud, who was responsible, what was lost?
2. Could anyone else do the same thing?

The first question is describing an investigation—figure out what happened. The second question describes a fraud deterrence process—find out where there are additional opportunities for fraud. Investigations lead to deterrence activities, and deterrence activities, by revealing opportunities for fraud, frequently lead to investigations.

When performing a fraud deterrence assessment, weaknesses in an organization's internal control system are typically identified in a systematic manner. Where the opportunity for fraud is great, the organization should perform investigative actions to determine if the opportunity was indeed exploited. Given such a broad scope of the deterrence engagements, there is often a gray area between the end of a fraud deterrence engagement and the start of a fraud investigation. Such a period, and the actions taken within it, is crucial to successful fraud litigation.

It is important that when opportunities for fraud are identified, an examiner makes an abrupt shift in course: from performing a *subjective* appraisal of future problems, to an *objective* assessment of past actions. Furthermore, it is crucial that the examiner review evidence by assessing it against past information, thus linking the chain of data as an investigation proceeds.

This chapter details not only the motivation behind fraud deterrence engagements, but also the pitfalls associated with them and methods to ensure success, should an investigation end with a courtroom trail.

MOTIVATIONS FOR DETERRENCE ANALYSIS

According to Statement of Accounting Standards (SAS 99), "Consideration of Fraud in a Financial Statement Audit," there are two overarching categories of fraud: misstatements arising from fraudulent financial reporting and misstatements arising from misappropriation of assets. The former category largely deals with fraud that is committed "on paper." No objects are physically taken from a workplace, nor is there an exchange of physical assets in any way. These misrepresentations are the result of deliberate omissions or falsification "of accounting records...from which financial statements are prepared." Frauds of this type are typically made to achieve a bonus level, increase share price, or obtain access to an equity market; by definition, they are material. The latter category of fraud deals with theft of physical assets where the concealment of such an action results in the preparation of nonconforming financial statements (as governed by Generally Accepted Accounting Principles [GAAP]). Such thefts could include "embezzling receipts, stealing assets, or causing an entity to pay for goods or services that have not been received."[1]

As discussed in Chapter 5, three elements must be present for a fraud to occur: motive, opportunity, and rationalization. Should any one of these elements be removed from the triangle, the likeliness of fraud is significantly reduced. Nonetheless, the American Institute of Certified Public Accountants (AICPA) believes that even "otherwise honest individuals can commit fraud in an environment that imposes sufficient pressure on them."[2] It is important to note that this environment includes not only the workplace environs in which an individual works, but also the individual's personal life as well.

Even an honest man can be brought to his knees when he runs out of money to help fund his wife's cancer treatment. Perhaps more individuals choose to commit fraud to fuel an addictive vice, such as gambling, drug use, or even abnormal avarice. Still more employees resort to fraud because of a pay-for-performance bonus system that may be instituted in their workplace. It is for these reasons that fraud examiners and auditors must always assess a situation while "exercising professional skepticism," no matter whom or what they are investigating.[3]

Given this essential, omnipresent mental state that an examiner must constantly maintain, it is important to address what actions must be taken—and how they must be pursued—when the examiner has determined that an opportunity exists for fraud to occur within an organization.

As mentioned in previous chapters, fraud detection is not a simple issue. Often fraud involves active concealment of actions and trickery on the part of the perpetrator. Those choosing to engage in fraudulent activities typically go to extreme lengths to cover their tracks. For this reason alone, it is essential that business owners understand that a routine external audit cannot be used to ensure that fraud is not occurring within an organization.

One of the largest problems associated with this issue is the conflict of interest between the client and the auditor whom he or she hired. Although the AICPA has long had a SAS document governing the reporting of fraudulent information (SAS 99, 82, 53), there still exists a classic conflict of interest between the client and auditor simply because the client is both the end user of the audit information and the remitter of payment. Gary Zeune nicely addresses this issue: "You cannot be independent of and objective about someone who pays you to do the work." To paraphrase another of Zeune's ideas, 90 percent of drivers believe that they are a "better-than-average driver."[4] One does not have to be a statistician to realize that such a figure is realistically inaccurate.

Furthermore, there ultimately exists another conflict of interest within the auditing firm itself. As a for-profit enterprise, an auditing firm's ultimate responsibility is to its own survival.

If the firm cannot remain profitable and undertake economically lucrative projects, it will soon cease to exist. While such a task appears on the surface to be quite obvious, real-life implementation is hampered by the fact that the audit business, in its current state, is not a growing enterprise.

Section 404 of Sarbanes-Oxley, and indeed the Sarbanes-Oxley Act (SOX) itself created new channels of business for audit firms when they were first introduced. However, now that the industry has swelled to its current, mature size, companies must grow revenues by increasing their market share (i.e., decreasing another firm's share) or investing in noncore industries.

Given the challenging environment in which audit firms practice, it is somewhat disheartening to learn that many of the procedures set forth in SAS 99 are only suggested, not mandatory. For example, it is only suggested that an auditor "*should* inquire of management about . . . management's understanding about the risks of fraud in the entity."

SAS 99 also specifies that "prior to or in conjunction with the information-gathering procedures . . . members of the audit team should discuss the potential for material misstatement due to fraud." Such a discussion should include:

> An exchange of ideas or 'brainstorming" among the audit team members, including the auditor with final responsibility for the audit, about how and where they believe the entity's financial statements might be susceptible to material misstatement due to fraud, how management could perpetrate and conceal fraudulent financial reporting, and how assets of the entity could be misappropriated.

While the brainstorming practice just outlined should serve to assist auditors in perceiving opportunities for fraud, this activity could be significantly augmented by the inclusion of a forensic expert in the process. Such a practice would allow members of the audit team to keep abreast of current developments in the fraud arena and allow auditors to better understand common fraudulent practices. Nonetheless, while SAS 99 encourages auditors to "brainstorm" about opportunities for fraud, business owners should realize that an auditor's primary responsibility is *not* to detect fraud.

Instead, the primary purpose of an external auditor's tests is simply to ensure that transactions are properly recorded and that all financial statements accurately reflect these transactions and the nature of the business. In this manner, external audit engagements are first and foremost responsible for ensuring that financial statements are reasonably free of material misstatement. Internal auditors are principally concerned with operational audits, not financial audits, and are typically responsible for identifying internal control weaknesses that could lead to fraud events. Special audits may be conducted with the internal audit department to review detailed transactions or investigate fraud.

The principal differences between an external attest audit and an internally directed assessment of internal controls are outlined in Exhibit 6.1.

As emphasized by the exhibit, there are large differences between attest audits and internal control assessments, most specifically in their purpose and ultimate deliverable. Both serve a purpose within the organization, but ultimately it is an assessment of internal controls that will successfully lead to fraud detection if implemented correctly. It is important to note that many practitioners in the field (i.e., Certified Fraud Examiners) fail to understand the importance of first assessing internal controls before performing a deep dive on transaction level data. This is an essential starting point for an investigation, primarily so that it eventually does not suffer from, in the words of former International Telephone and Telegraph (ITT) chief executive officer (CEO) Harold Geneen, "paralysis by analysis." If this high-level assessment of controls is not performed first, much time could be wasted simply by checking volumes of transactions in a control-intensive, safe environment.

Exhibit 6.1 Key Elements of Attest Audits and Assessments of Internal Controls

Issue	Attest Audit	Internal Control Assessment
Purpose	Focused on *result* of financial reporting process	Focused on *process* of producing financial reporting results
Judgment standard	Reasonably free of material misstatements	Effective control environment to achieve objectives
Internal Control (IC) Focus	IC environment determines the level of testing for transactions related to detections of erroneous records	IC environment controls the processing of transactions to control and prevent erroneous transactions
Deliverable	Summary opinion on financial statements Opines on internal control structure (for public companies required to comply with Sarbanes-Oxley (§ 464)	Implements, develops, and revises internal control structure

As such, when fraud deterrence evaluations are performed, typically by an external third party, their main focus is to assess an organization against a set of benchmarks on the quality and robustness of their internal controls. There is typically high-level buy-in from management, and the assessment begins with a proactive tone. These fraud deterrence engagements are seen as an overall process improvement initiative.

From a macro level perspective, investigators are principally looking to examine the checks and balances of power within an organization and whether they are appropriate for a business. If these checks and balances are out of place or are inappropriate given a company's business model, the entire organization may be severely hampered. For example, suppose you decide to place self-locking, dead-bolt locks on all doors within your house in order to minimize the chances of theft in a burglary. While this may or may not serve as an adequate deterrent to perpetrators, the system would certainly fail in the event of a serious emergency, such as a fire. Such disaster planning, while seemingly important to an organization, often is not taken into account when an internal control system is developed, and can have serious implications should such an event occur. As companies are continually in either a state of growth or decline, the incorporation of disaster planning into an internal control system is imperative.

TRANSITION TO INVESTIGATION

When performing a deterrence analysis, red flags may arise that point to the possibility for fraud. Should an investigation yield suspicion of fraudulent activity, it is important for the head of such an initiative (hereafter the "examiner") to realize that in order to proceed with an investigation, the rules of engagement much change completely. Specifically, the procedures and cautions for performing a fraud investigation are entirely different from those of a fraud deterrence engagement. However, often actions taken by the professional practitioner at the onset of the investigation will determine the overall success of the engagement. In this manner, there is often a gray area between the time when a fraud deterrence engagement concludes and an investigation begins.

When performing a fraud deterrence assessment, the principal purpose of the investigation is to look for weaknesses in an organization's internal control structure and to assess whether there is/was an opportunity to exploit these weaknesses. By contrast, the overarching purpose of an investigation is simply to examine whether fraudulent activity occurred.

There is also a difference in the focus and scope of each engagement. Fraud deterrence involves a *subjective* assessment of internal control weaknesses complete with an assessment of potentially exploitable opportunities that may be used by employees in the future. Investigations, however, are focused on *objectively* gathering information on historical events and transactions related to fraud.

When a shift occurs in a fraud deterrence engagement from assessment to investigation, it is essential that the examiner shift his or her focus from a *subjective* appraisal of future problems to an *objective* assessment of past actions. This objectivity is inherently important because the occurrence of fraud will ultimately be determined by a court of law.

The U.S. Supreme Court has defined fraud as an action in which there were four elements:

1. Misrepresentation of a material fact.
2. The perpetrator knew that such misrepresentation was false.
3. The misrepresentation was made with the intent that such an action would be relied on.
4. The victim relied on the misrepresentation and suffered damages as a result.

If any one of these four elements is not accurately proven beyond a burden of proof by the plaintiff's attorneys in court, then a case cannot legally be deemed "fraud." Such is the reason that the firm of Arthur Andersen was ultimately acquitted of fraud in its Enron-related trial: The requirement to prove that Andersen *intended* to obstruct justice was improperly deleted from the jury instructions.

Moreover, an examiner's adherence to objectivity will better facilitate proper presentation of results and impartial conclusions in court. When conducting a fraud examination, the examiner should keep in mind the four main functions of expert testimony (which the examiner may provide):

1. To establish the facts of the case
2. To interpret these facts
3. To comment on the opposing expert's facts and opinions
4. To define the professional standards in the area of the opponent's expertise

It is with these four functions in mind that expert testimony may be used in supporting a case for fraud litigated in a court of law.

The first function speaks to the expert's ability to develop a strategy for collecting and critically examining documents that support the case for litigation. Often a fraud investigation will yield an unwieldy amount of data and facts. The expert's function is to probe these documents for relevance and evaluate how each can support the case for or against fraud.

The second function refers to the expert's duty to identify cause-and-effect relationships within the data and provide his or her attorney with concrete facts to support the technical basis of the case.

The third of these four functions speaks to the expert's ability to develop an understanding of the opposition's case by reviewing their expert's background and experience. In serving this role, the expert probes for weaknesses in the opponent's case to be exploited and systematically examines the opposition's report piece by piece for weaknesses. The expert also supports his or her attorney by providing him or her with the most intimate details of the case. This includes prepping the attorney for trial and ensuring that he or she understands all facts of the case.

The fourth function speaks to the expert's ability to define the "standard of care" exercised by fellow professionals in the field. The expert must also comment on the basis of judgment normally exercised by professionals in good standing.

It is important to remember that there are great differences between the requirement or "burden of proof" that the plaintiffs must prove in court, given the nature of the trial. In civil litigation, the burden of proof is governed by a "preponderance of the evidence." Furthermore, civil trials do not require unanimous verdicts to convict. In a criminal case, however, the burden of proof must extend "beyond a reasonable doubt," with a unanimous verdict required in nearly all circumstances.

Investigations are entirely different beasts from fraud deterrence engagements, and require much careful thought and planning in order to be executed properly. With respect to the methodology used by Cendrowski Corporate Advisors, there are five principal phases associated with investigations:

1. Establish your role with the client.
2. Accumulate and assimilate information.
3. Analyze case data.
4. Develop the case.
5. Finalize the case or settlement.

Within each of these five phases, several tasks must be performed in order for the phase to be deemed complete. Exhibit 6.2 presents a pictorial representation of the investigation cycle with task detail for Phase 1.

The first step in the investigation, to "Establish your role with the client," is perhaps the most important in ensuring that successful litigation will result from the examiner's activities. It is during this phase that the examiner discusses with the potential client overarching objectives of the investigation and the current status of the case. "Customer requirements," defined as the needs of the client, are laid forth in a detailed manner. This stage is mostly closely associated with the gray area between a fraud deterrence engagement and an investigation, and it often signifies the passing of the torch between both phases.

A budget and fee schedule are also prepared during this phase, and a detailed schedule (e.g., Gantt chart), showing tasks and milestone dates, is compiled. This phase ends with the examiner's acceptance or rejection of the proposed assignment.

The second phase in the investigation describes the execution of the tasks laid out in the schedule. It is during this phase that the methods used for discovery of evidence must be decided and a detailed work schedule, complete with methods to achieve the work, is created. Information requests must also be prepared. These requests may take the form of interrogatories, subpoenas, depositions, and the like. Interviews with key personnel are executed, and notes from these interviews are transcribed contemporaneously so as not to show any bias either for or against an interviewee.

It is important to note that there are significant differences associated with the interview process in fraud deterrence engagements and formal investigations. In a fraud deterrence engagement, interviews are "passive," meaning that they consist of largely open-ended questions that seek to assess employees' opinions and perceptions of the current internal control system.

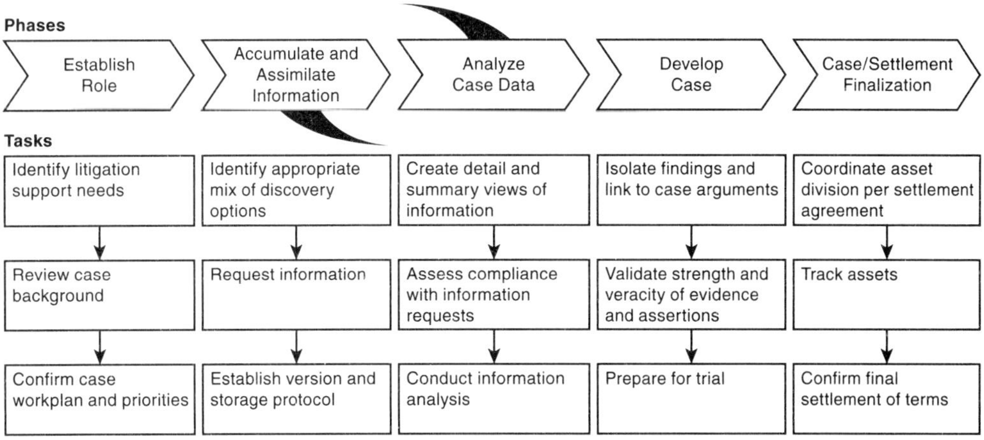

Task Detail:

Identify litigation support needs

1. Debrief parties on case origination and progress.
2. Identify party goals and objectives.
3. Confirm key dates in case life cycle.
4. Establish plan for proceeding as either a consultant or expert.

Review case background

1. Receive initial documentation.
2. Create case timeline and associated milestones.
3. Conduct preliminary related party searches.
4. Maintain running list of questions and open items.
5. Develop logical, physical, and chronological inventory.

Confirm case workplan and priorities

1. Identify potential information sources.
2. Confirm appropriate cut-off dates for analysis.
3. Identify key litigator support and analysis dependencies.
4. Communicate workplan priorities.
5. Confirm deliverable expectations.
6. Establish communications protocol.

Phase Objective
Confirm client objectives, case requirements, and initial course of action

Phase Outputs
- Initial Inventory
- Case Workplan

Source: Cendrowski Corporate Advisors

Exhibit 6.2 Pictorial Representation of the Investigation Cycle and Task Detail for Phase 1

By contrast, interviews in investigatory engagements are focused on obtaining information about historical actions of a given employee or employees.

In the third phase of an investigation, where case data are analyzed, documents are created to summarize all electronic and hard-copy information. Information is probed at a detailed level in order to help the examiner formulate an opinion about the existence or nonexistence of fraud. In this manner, an examiner begins to piece together an opinion on the case, substantiated solely by facts. Often information not amassed in the initial gathering phase will be requested in order to help support the examiner's eventual conclusion with respect to fraud.

In addition, forensic backups are created for sensitive information that is received. These backups are then submitted to subject matter experts for analysis (should the examiner not feel comfortable analyzing this evidence). This step is crucial to ensure that evidence will not be discredited in a deposition or trial based on an expert's lack of knowledge, or perceived lack thereof.

It is important to highlight the inner cycle that takes place within Phases 2 and 3 that is depicted in Exhibit 6.2. As an investigation progresses, reviews of evidence will ultimately fuel requests for further information, which must then be analyzed. Furthermore, over the course of an investigation, an invariably large and seemingly unwieldy amount of evidence will be collected. It is the examiner's responsibility not only to test the relevance and reliability of all such data, but also to ensure that all incoming evidence is viewed synchronously in context with previously gathered data. For this reason, in conducting a fraud investigation, it is essential that the examiner possess intimate knowledge of even the most minute of details.

As data pour in, the examiner must continually inform the team of the relevance of newfound evidence to previously gathered items, continually reviewing the investigatory process and the current state of evidence amalgamation. Once all evidence has been collected, the examiner should have effectively linked all relevant pieces of data with one another, thereby providing his or her attorney with a strong case for trial.

The fourth phase of an investigation centers on developing the case for or against fraud. In this phase the examiner must isolate his or her findings and link these directly to case arguments. Furthermore, the examiner must determine the quantity and quality of trial-related exhibits in order to support his or her conclusions. In doing so, it is crucial that the examiner reassess the evidence and conclusions from the case to ensure that they are indeed veracious.

Reports must be written in a way that the examiner's conclusions are explained in a lay manner. (For more information on proper report etiquette, see Chapter 15.) Such a practice will better allow either judge or jury to understand the intricacies of the fraud case without forcing them to delve deep into the discipline's jargon and practices. As the success of a trial often depends on the ability of an expert witness and his or her attorney to communicate an opinion effectively to a judge or jury, such a practice is tantamount to success.

Throughout an investigation, an examiner must continually remember that his or her advocacy, in conducting an investigation, must always be to the truth, never to the client. Furthermore, any evidence that is gathered within an investigation must be usable in court—meaning that it must be gathered legally with full adherence to an employee's rights and in accordance with the "clean hands doctrine" of common law. An examiner must investigate the case both for and against fraud and use common, accepted techniques to analyze them. In order to prove a fraud has occurred, it is essential that the proof presented in court also show that attempts were made to prove that it had not occurred. If such actions are not taken, a defendant's attorney could well prove that an examiner was biased in his or her process and potentially move to have the examiner thrown out of court.

It is also important for an examiner to recognize his or her own weaknesses when performing an investigation. For example, suppose that an examiner is investigating the case both for and against an individual committing a fraudulent act, and wishes to examine the contents of this particular individual's computer hard drive disk. The best procedure for engaging in such an activity would be to contract an outside, independent firm with prior experience in technology-based fraud investigations to create a backup of this person's hard drive, which can then be investigated. Such an action shows that a qualified expert was the only individual to analyze a suspect's property (or backup of their property).

In addition, throughout the course of an investigation, evidence collection and analysis must always be performed on a forensic backup of the original item. Such a precaution will allow the examiner to establish a firm chain of custody for the object in question and allow assurance in court that the original article had not been touched by anyone except the perpetrator. Should such actions not be taken, attorneys for the defendant could possibly inject "reasonable doubt" into the minds of the judge or jury about the alleged perpetrator's role in the fraud.

Additionally, as fraud investigations will invariably involve interviews with key personnel, it is imperative that notes from such interviews are immediately transcribed. If such an action is not taken, a defendant's attorney may be able to show a judge or jury that the examiner was biased in his or her investigation and that his or her credibility must be questioned.

In short, an examiner must be fully comfortable in performing an investigation—meaning that he or she has intimate knowledge of both the case details and also the methodologies used for examination. If this is not true, then an examiner should relinquish control of the investigation to a more qualified professional in order to better assist the prosecution in preparing an airtight case for trial.

Furthermore, cutting-edge, proprietary techniques developed by the examiner will not hold up in court and will be challenged. This philosophy is exemplified by the 1993 U.S. Supreme Court case of *Daubert v. Merrell Dow Pharmaceuticals*.[5] In the ruling, the Court documented four factors that a trial judge may consider in making a decision on the relevance and reliability of expert testimony:

1. Whether the expert's analysis derives from a scientific method that can be or has been tested
2. Whether the expert's method has been the subject of peer review and testing
3. The actual or potential rate of error in the expert's methodology
4. Whether the relevant scientific community generally accepts the expert's methodology

The *Daubert* decision, as well as subsequent cases, has also provided litigants in a lawsuit with the right to request a pretrial hearing in which the judge can apply the *Daubert* criteria in determining whether to disallow the expert witness's testimony. It is evident that the judge in a case, in addition to ruling on the final verdict, is also a gatekeeper who determines whether an expert's opinion should be admitted.

CONCLUSION

A fraud deterrence engagement, and the investigation that may follow, requires careful supervision and execution by highly qualified personnel. While there is often a gray area between the conclusion of a fraud deterrence engagement and the initiation of a fraud investigation, the success of a fraud litigation often hinges on the actions of examiners throughout this period.

Both a fraud deterrence engagement and subsequent investigation are complex phenomena that require constant monitoring and a commitment to the process to produce satisfactory results. If adherence to these axioms is present, the investigation has a high probability of succeeding in bolstering the case for or against fraud.

NOTES

1. American Institute of Certified Public Accountants, Statements on Auditing Standards 99 (2002). Available at: www.aicpa.org/download/members/div/auditstd/AU-00316.PDF.
2. Id.
3. Id.
4. G. Zeune, "SAS 99—Friend or Foe?" FMN Online, 2003. Available at: www.fmnonline.com/publishing/article.cfm?article_id=759.
5. Daubert v. Merrell Dow Pharmaceuticals. 509 US 579, 1993. Available at: http://caselaw.lp.findlaw.com/scripts/getcase.pl?court=US&vol=509&invol=579.

Chapter 7

A Fraud Deterrence Professional's Overview of the Legal Process

Fred Herrmann, Charles Calio, Jason C. Yert, and David R. Janis

INTRODUCTION AND OBJECTIVES

The legal system plays a critical role in effectively deterring fraud by providing a framework for the government and the public to address possible fraudulent activity and by providing civil and criminal penalties, and other remedies, designed to both deter fraud and compensate its victims. The forensic accountant is a key player in this system, often called on to apply his or her knowledge and experience to aid a judge or jury in reaching critical decisions.

The legal system has its own unique set of procedural and evidentiary rules that govern every facet of an expert's participation in the legal process. Testimony in the federal court system is governed by the Federal Rules of Civil Procedure (FRCP) and the Federal Rules of Evidence (FRE).[1] In the various state courts, an expert's obligations will normally be governed by equivalent state rules of procedure and evidence, which are largely patterned after the federal rules.[2] In any matter involving pending or threatened litigation, it is critical that the fraud deterrence professional work closely with legal counsel in order to ensure compliance with all applicable federal and/or state rules of procedure and evidence. This chapter informs potential expert witnesses regarding:

- Their role in the judicial system
- The criteria courts use to evaluate whether a witness qualifies to testify as an expert
- Facts and evidence experts may use to form the bases of their opinions and testimony
- Proper subject matter of expert opinion testimony
- Ongoing duties and requirements imposed on expert witnesses once they begin providing their services in litigation

BASICS OF OPINION TESTIMONY AND THE ROLE OF THE JUDICIARY

Lay witnesses are called to testify regarding knowledge they have of the events or facts that form the basis of a lawsuit or other legal action. For example, a company employee may testify that the company's chief financial officer directed him to make a series of questionable journal entries. In contrast, expert witnesses are called to testify regarding scientific, technical, or other specialized knowledge they have that will help a trier of fact[3] to understand the evidence presented at trial or determine a fact in issue, leaving the trier of fact to apply the knowledge to the facts.[4] For example, an expert witness may opine that the journal entries in question were not appropriate under generally acceptable accounting principles (GAAP). Or the expert may simply give a dissertation before the court explaining a company's duties under GAAP, without offering an opinion as to whether the defendant company complied with its duties. Expert witnesses are often asked to testify at trial to explain to the jury matters that are complex and/or outside the common knowledge of most laypeople. Used correctly, expert testimony is an effective tool for educating the jury.

A witness may testify as an expert only if:

- The court finds that because of the witness's experience, education or training, the witness is qualified to offer opinions in the relevant field or subject matter.
- The offered testimony is based on sufficient facts or data.
- The expert's conclusions, opinion, and/or testimony is the product of reliable principles and methods.
- The witness has applied the principles and methods reliably to the facts of the case.
- The testimony is relevant to the lawsuit.
- The testimony is not so prejudicial that a party to the legal action is deprived of a fair trial.

In both federal and most state courts, the judge acts as a "gatekeeper."[5] A judge must evaluate each witness offered as an expert to determine whether the opinions, theories, reports, and testimony offered may be admitted into evidence. Judges are given great leeway to determine whether a witness will be allowed to testify as an expert. Absent serious judicial mistakes or a completely erroneous application of the law, appellate courts typically will not countermand a trial court's decision regarding the admissibility of expert testimony.[6] In its role as gatekeeper, a court will analyze the admissibility of the evidence by determining whether the expert is qualified to testify competently on the issues and whether the expert's testimony is reliable and relevant by reviewing:

- His or her underlying methodology
- The underlying facts and data
- Whether the testimony is sufficient to assist the trier of fact in determining an issue in the underlying litigation

A court's determination regarding the qualifications of an expert and the reliability and relevance of his or her testimony is not meant to replace the adversary system. The trier of fact will ultimately decide what "weight" to give to the expert and his or her opinions when determining the underlying issues of the case. In most instances, the trier of fact will weigh an expert's qualifications and the reliability and relevance of the testimony against the qualifications and opinions of an opposing party's expert. Thus, passing the admissibility test is only the first hurdle; convincing the trier of fact is equally important.

EXPERT QUALIFICATION STANDARDS: WHEN IS A WITNESS AN "EXPERT"?

A witness may be deemed an expert witness only if the court finds that the witness possesses the requisite level of "knowledge, skill, experience, training, or education" to make the witness an expert in the area in which he or she is to testify.[7]

Specialized Knowledge: Experience, Education, or Training

A court, in its gatekeeping role, will first determine if a witness is qualified to testify as an expert. FRE 702 requires an expert to have "specialized knowledge" in the areas to which his or her testimony relates. This specialized knowledge may be based on a professional's "knowledge, skill, education, experience or training."[8] Courts have indicated that the "or" conjunction contained in FRE 702 intimates that an expert may be qualified by any one of the five listed qualifications.[9] Although there is no requirement that a professional have a specific degree or certification to be considered an expert in a particular field,[10] if the professional is relying only on his or her experience, the professional must present evidence that his or her experience is a sufficient basis for the opinion and demonstrate that the experience can be applied to the facts in a reliable manner. For example, in the bankruptcy case of *In re Adler,* the court analyzed whether plaintiff's proffered witness was qualified to testify as an expert.[11] The court deemed plaintiff's witness an expert, notwithstanding his lack of a certified public accountant's (CPA) certification, because he had 16 years of accounting experience conducting financial and operational reviews similar to the type he performed in the case, and he also conducted a thorough review of all of the relevant books and records. At a minimum, an expert must have greater skill and knowledge than the average person.[12]

If an expert is opining only on general accounting principles, courts will typically focus their evaluation on the accountant's education, practical experience, and general knowledge of accounting principles. But if the accountant is opining on more specialized accounting principles, or testifying regarding the application of accounting principles to a specific industry, courts will look at the accountant's knowledge of, and breadth of practical experience in, the specialized accounting practice or relevant industry.[13] For example, in *JMJ Enterprises, Inc. v. Via Veneto Italian Ice, Inc.*, the district court held inadmissible a witness's testimony on lost profits, despite the witness having a master's degree in taxation and holding CPA and Fraud Examiner certifications.[14] The court excluded the testimony because it was based on subjective beliefs and unsupported assumptions about an industry the witness knew little about. The more experience accountants have outside the courtroom in handling the issues and matters they intend to opine on, the more likely the court will qualify them as experts.[15] A court may also consider any experience accountants have in testifying as an expert in other complex litigation matters.[16] Therefore, it is important that accountants strive to gain as much educational, professional, and litigation experience as possible if they intend to be an expert witness in litigation matters.

Aura of Reliability: Lay Opinions versus Expert Opinions

Because jurors may afford expert testimony an unwarranted level of credibility due to the expert's training, credentials, and status, courts will consider this "aura of reliability" when determining the admissibility of the expert's opinions. For example, courts have refused to allow proffered experts to testify when their opinions consist of merely "rubber stamping" the conclusions or analysis of lay witnesses. Accordingly, it is critical that experts perform their own independent analysis and testing of the underlying facts, and not blindly accept positions of lay witnesses.

ADMISSIBILITY VERSUS WEIGHT: WHEN IS AN EXPERT'S OPINION AND/OR TESTIMONY ADMISSIBLE?

Expert's Opinions and/or Testimony Must Be Reliable

Under FRE 702, the court, as part of its gatekeeping function, will assess three things:

1. Whether the expert's testimony is based on reliable facts and data
2. Whether the testimony is the product of reliable principles and methods
3. Whether there is a sufficient nexus between the testimony and the facts of the case

Experts should be aware that the more subjective and unsupported their testimony, the more likely it will be deemed unreliable.[17] Therefore, experts must review all of the available facts and data, ensure that their underlying methodology and reasoning is based on generally acceptable principles of forensic accounting, and ensure that their testimony fits the issues in the case. Frequent communication with counsel will facilitate these goals.

Reliability of an Expert's Methodology. A court has considerable leeway in its gatekeeping role when determining the reliability of an expert's testimony. *Daubert v. Merrell Dow Pharmaceuticals,*[18] a landmark case in the analysis and admissibility of expert testimony, provides for a five-prong inquiry when determining the reliability of scientific testimony: acceptance in the relevant professional community, testing, peer review, error rate, and maintenance of standards and controls. No single factor is dispositive of the reliability prong.[19] The *Daubert* factors are simply a guide, not a checklist.[20] For example, the "testing" inquiry would be applicable only in the limited circumstances where scientific approaches, such as statistics, sampling, and probabilities, are used by a forensic accountant.

The *Daubert* factors applicable to forensic accounting experts and other nonscientific experts depend on the facts and circumstances of a particular case. A few courts strictly apply the *Daubert* five-factor analysis to all expert testimony, but most courts look at a variety of additional factors when performing the gatekeeping function. Inquiries forensic accountants may see from a court include:

- Whether an expert's testimony was the result of matters growing naturally or directly from the litigation
- Whether the expert has extrapolated from an acceptable premise to an unfounded conclusion
- Whether the expert has accounted for obvious alternative explanations
- Whether the expert has applied the same standard of care in the litigation as he or she would normally apply outside of the litigation
- Whether the expert's field of expertise is known to reach reliable results on the subject of the proffered testimony

The latest revision of FRE 702 has codified the factors and principles outlined in *Daubert* and *Kumho Tire Co. v. Carmichael,* a case that expanded the principles of *Daubert* to nonscientific experts and that gave courts more flexibility in the conduct of their expert witness analysis.[21]

With respect to forensic accounting experts, courts have looked closely at forensic accountants' breadth of experience and knowledge analyzing issues similar to the ones they are opining on in the litigation. The more "polished" and knowledgeable experts are, the more reliable, credible, and trustworthy their reasoning and methodology will be. But an expert's conclusions should be based on more than just his experience. A court will also look at whether the forensic accounting expert's testimony was the product of the principles and methods used by accountants in performing forensic accounting work. A forensic accountant should use reliable techniques and methods that produce consistent results, not rogue or unsupported techniques or methods. This is not to say that new and innovative techniques or alternative methodologies will be deemed unreliable if they produce consistent results.[22] Therefore, it is important that forensic accountants continue to keep abreast of industry practice and new techniques and methods. Experts should be prepared to support their methodology and techniques as they will be subject to vigorous cross-examination.

Reliability of Facts and Data and the Bases of an Expert's Opinion. Experts' testimony must be based on reliable facts and data that support the conclusions they reach. Expert witnesses typically base their opinions and conclusions on facts or data provided them in one of three ways:

1. Firsthand observation
2. Observations at trial
3. Information presented outside of court that is not within the expert's personal knowledge[23]

For example, a forensic accountant might perceive facts by analyzing the financial records of a company, interviewing lay witnesses, hearing testimony of witnesses in court, or analyzing an audit conducted by a third-party.

Experts must also ensure that they have an adequate, factual foundation for their opinion. It is important that forensic accounting experts take the time to review the relevant documents and records of all the parties involved, and take all of the facts and data into consideration in their analysis. Courts have deemed an expert's testimony unreliable in situations where an accountant has reviewed documents from only one party. Counsel should take the leading role in acquiring a complete set of documents for an expert to review, but if there are gaps in the data or facts, a forensic accounting expert should bring it to counsel's attention immediately so that counsel may make the appropriate inquiry with the opposing side and/or obtain the necessary facts and data from other sources. It is important that an expert remain flexible when forming opinions, as counsel will continue to collect documents and facts that may alter a forensic accountant's analysis.

Under FRE 702, an expert's testimony and opinions may be based on admissible or inadmissible evidence, as long as the evidence is of the type "reasonably relied upon by experts in the particular field in forming opinions or inferences upon the subject."[24] As mentioned previously, however, some states have not adopted the FRE, or have adopted the FRE with certain distinctions. For example, Michigan's version of FRE 702 states that "[t]he facts or data . . . upon which an expert bases an opinion or inference *shall be in evidence*[25] (emphasis added). Whether the underlying facts and data forming the bases of an expert's opinion or testimony is revealed to the jury is determined by the court.[26] This is an issue in jury trials, not bench trials, because a judge sitting as a trier of fact is expected to "ignore" inadmissible evidence when making fact determinations.[27] Under the FRE, if the facts and data in question are reasonably relied upon by experts in a particular field, and the evidence is otherwise admissible in court, an expert may reveal the underlying facts to a jury.[28] An expert may not reveal to a jury inadmissible facts and data, even if reasonably relied upon by experts in the field, ". . . unless the court determines that their probative value in assisting the jury to evaluate the expert's testimony substantially outweighs their prejudicial effect."[29] Where an expert reveals otherwise inadmissible facts to a jury, a court, on request by opposing counsel, must give a limiting instruction to the jury informing them that the underlying information must not be used for substantive purposes.[30]

Sufficient Fit between the Facts of the Case and the Expert's Testimony. Even if an expert's testimony is deemed reliable, the court must still ensure that the testimony is relevant to the dispute. In making this determination, a court will investigate whether the testimony is sufficiently tied to the facts of the case, thereby assisting the trier of fact to better resolve an issue in question. In most cases, a forensic accountant's testimony should make complex issues more understandable to the trier of fact. The accountant's conclusions must be relevant to an issue in dispute in the underlying action or at least educate the jury on an issue before it. A forensic accountant must use caution, as experts may not testify on matters reserved exclusively for the court or the trier of fact, such as the credibility of a witness, the state of mind of the parties, or what law should apply to the case. Counsel should properly advise an expert on the proper scope of his testimony.

A court's determinations that an expert is qualified and that his or her testimony is reliable and relevant does not end the process. Once the expert testimony is admitted by the court, the trier of fact will ultimately decide what weight should be given to an expert's qualifications and to what extent the expert's methodologies, facts and data, techniques, and conclusions will be relied on in determining an issue in the underlying litigation.

Weight: Convincing the Fact Finder

Once expert testimony is admitted by the court, the trier of fact will determine the credibility and trustworthiness of the expert, from the individual's qualifications to his or her conclusions.

The trier of fact's duty is to assess all the facts and circumstances in order to determine how much weight should be given to an expert's conclusions, qualifications, credibility, skill, knowledge, and methodology as well the underlying facts and data. For example, if one party's expert has an advanced degree and the opposing party's expert does not, the trier of fact may properly give more weight to the conclusions of the expert with the advanced degree when making its determination on that particular issue. The trier of fact will be able to consider the cross-examination of the expert, presentation of contrary evidence by opposing counsel, and instructions regarding the burden of proof before making its decision.

Summaries of Evidence and Expert Opinions

FRE 1006 allows summaries, such as charts and graphs, into evidence to summarize voluminous writings, records, and other data that are otherwise admissible but would be too large and burdensome to introduce into evidence during trial. FRE 1006 states:

> The contents of voluminous writings, recordings, or photographs which cannot conveniently be examined in court may be presented in the form of a chart, summary, or calculation. The originals, or duplicates, shall be made available for examination or copying, or both, by other parties at reasonable time and place. The court may order that they be produced in court.

The rules of evidence require that when a witness offers an expert opinion using summary evidence under Rule 1006, the proponent show that the person who prepared the 1006 exhibit is qualified as an expert. In *U.S. v. Gold,* where the defendants were convicted of conspiracy and Medicare fraud, the court admitted into evidence a 40-page chart containing an expert witness's opinions on what Medicare should actually pay in each instance, because the witness was properly qualified as an expert on Medicare coverage.[31]

Alternatively, in *U.S. v. Seelig,* where a pharmacist was prosecuted for the improper sale of controlled substances, a chart summarizing and comparing the sales of two of the defendant's pharmacies with other pharmacies was not allowed into evidence because the witness who prepared the chart was not qualified as an expert.[32] The witness who prepared the chart was a police sergeant who admitted that he was not an economist, statistician, or otherwise qualified as an expert.

The expert should work closely with counsel to ensure that the summary is not in violation of any rules of evidence.

LIMITATIONS ON THE SCOPE OF EXPERT OPINION TESTIMONY

Generally, the Federal Rules of Evidence allow expert witnesses to provide opinion testimony on the ultimate issues to be decided in the case.[33] However, FRE 704(b) provides that an expert witness may not testify to whether or not a criminal defendant had or did not have the requisite mental state or condition constituting an element of the crime. Rule 704(b) states:

> (b) No expert witness testifying with respect to the mental state or condition of a defendant in a criminal case may state an opinion or inference as to whether the defendant did or did not have the mental state or condition constituting an element of the crime charged or of a defense thereto. Such ultimate issues are matters for the trier of fact alone.

Since issues involving fraud arise in both civil and criminal cases, it is important to understand the implications of Rule 704(b). In *U.S. v. Liner,* a criminal case where the defendant was convicted of wire fraud, the court held that while the expert witness implied that the defendant's conduct was fraudulent, the expert did not directly address the defendant's intent to defraud and therefore did not violate Rule 704(b).[34]

In *U.S. v. Suzanne Barbara Schurrer,* the Twelfth Circuit Court of Appeals affirmed the defendant's conviction on multiple counts of mail and wire fraud.[35] On appeal, the defendant argued that the testimony of an expert witness that certain invoices and a contract were not valid violated Rule 704(b). The court disagreed and held that Rule 704 permits an expert witness to provide opinion testimony on the ultimate facts and circumstances of the case. The court stated that whether or not the documents were valid was a question of fact and the expert's opinion, based on her analysis, could be considered by the jury.

These cases and the language of Rule 704 indicate that an expert is free to offer opinion testimony on the ultimate issues of a case, including whether or not a certain document or conduct is fraudulent.[36] Rule 704(b) becomes an issue, however, when the expert testifies directly to the state of mind or intent of a criminal defendant when the defendant's intent or mental state is an element of the crime.

REPORTS AND DISCOVERY OBLIGATIONS

Expert Witnesses Expected to Testify at Trial

If a witness is retained or specially employed to provide expert testimony in a case, or if the witness is an employee who regularly gives expert testimony on behalf of a party, the Federal Rules of Evidence require specific reporting obligations well in advance of trial. It is critical that an expert witness remain in constant communication with counsel to ensure these obligations are met in a timely manner.

Signed Report. The witness must prepare a signed report to be provided to the court and opposing parties. The report must contain:

- A complete statement of all opinions to be expressed and the basis and reasons for such opinions
- The data or other information considered by the witness in forming the opinions
- Any exhibits to be used as a summary of or support for the opinions
- The qualifications of the witness, including a list of all publications authored within the preceding 10 years
- The compensation to be paid for the study and testimony
- A list of any other cases in which the witness has testified as an expert at trial or by deposition within the preceding four years

Timing of Report. The report shall be provided to the court as directed or, in the absence of court direction, at least 90 days before the trial date or the date the case is to be ready for trial.[37] If the evidence is intended solely as rebuttal evidence, the report must be provided within 30 days after disclosures made by the opposing party.[38]

Reports and Other Materials Must Be Updated. The report and any other information provided through interrogatories or depositions must be updated when the witness, or party for whom the witness works, learns that in some material respect the information, documents, or report provided to the court and opposing parties is incomplete or incorrect.[39]

Depositions and Interrogatories. A party may depose any expert witness an opposing party identifies as expected to testify at trial.[40] However, if the expert witness is required to provide a report as just outlined, then the witness's deposition may not be taken until after the report is provided.[41]

Experts Not Expected to Testify at Trial

A "consulting expert," or an expert not expected to testify at trial, may be hired to help an attorney in various ways. For example, a consulting expert may help an attorney develop strategies for proving or disproving the existence of fraud or develop lines of questioning for both direct and cross-examination, or analyze financial data like sales records, invoices, financial statements, competitive pricing data, inventory management reports, and so on.[42] Because a consulting expert is not expected to present his or her opinions at trial, an opposing party's ability to obtain information and opinions from a consulting expert is restricted, and a consulting expert's duties under the Federal Rules of Evidence are not as extensive as those of an expert expected to testify at trial.

Consulting experts may be called on to disclose the facts known or opinions held by them upon a "showing of exceptional circumstances under which it is impracticable for the party seeking discovery to obtain facts or opinions on the same subject by other means."[43] The restriction on discoverability of consulting expert opinions, reports, advice, and so on, exists so that each party "does its own work," and to protect the mental impressions and strategies of the attorney.

Expert Witness Fees

If an expert is required to prepare a report as just outlined, or is deposed, the party seeking discovery must pay the witness a reasonable fee "for time spent in responding to discovery."[44] Experts may be compensated for their time—for example, the time spent going to and from a deposition and for the time spent at the deposition.[45] Experts will normally be compensated at their normal hourly rate, if the court finds it to be reasonable.[46] Parties in litigation often agree, however, to each bear the costs of their own experts.

CONCLUSION

Forensic accountants play a critical role in deterring fraud and assisting the legal system in effectively compensating those parties harmed by fraudulent activity. By utilizing their experience and specialized knowledge, forensic accountants educate the court and the jury as to what conduct constitutes fraud and how damages should appropriately be measured. While this chapter provides an overview of the issues forensic accountants will face while serving as experts during litigation, it is important that any expert work closely with counsel to ensure that all of the applicable statutes and rules are followed.

NOTES

1. In addition to the Federal Rules of Civil Procedure and the Federal Rules of Evidence, an accountant serving as an expert witness may be subject to other federal and state laws as well as any applicable codes of ethics. For example, the National Association of Forensic Economics, the American Academy of Economic and Financial Experts and the American Rehabilitation Economic Association have all adopted codes of ethics that govern their members' expert witness activities. See Francis J. Colella and Thomas R. Ireland, *Neutrality and Advocacy: A Challenge for Forensic Economics,* 8 J. Legal. Econ. 71 (Spring/Summer 1998).
2. For example, the most recent comments to Michigan Rule of Evidence 702, which corresponds to FRE 702, states that "This rule is similar to the corresponding Federal rule" and the 1978 comments state that " MRE 702 is identical with Rule 702 of the Federal Rules of Evidence. . . ." An expert should discuss any relevant rules with counsel, however, before making the assumption that the relevant state rule(s) are identical to their federal counterparts and that the rules have been interpreted in the same manner.
3. "Trier of fact" refers to the entity that will decide the existence of facts as they pertain to the case. For example, in a hit-and-run case, the plaintiff may claim that defendant was driving the car in question, a fact that the defendant may dispute by asserting that it was his friend that was driving the car. The trier of fact may be called on to decide whether defendant was driving the car at the time of the accident. This fact in itself may not determine the defendant's liability in the case, but it is a factual

determination that must be made before legal liability may be attached. In a jury trial, the trier of fact is the jury. In a nonjury, or "bench trial," the trier of fact is a judge.

4. Federal Rule of Evidence 702 (1972 Advisory Committee Note).
5. *See e.g., Gilbert v. Daimler Chrysler Corp.,* 470 Mich. 749, 780-781 (2004) ("In both its former and current incarnations, MRE 702 has imposed an obligation on the trial court to ensure that any expert testimony admitted at trial is reliable. While the exercise of this gatekeeper role is within a court's discretion, a trial judge may neither "abandon" this obligation nor "perform the function inadequately.") (citations omitted).
6. *Hamling v. United States,* 418 U.S. 87, 108 (1974) (". . . [a] District Court has wide discretion in its determination to admit and exclude evidence, and this is particularly true in the case of expert testimony.").
7. Federal Rule of Evidence 702.
8. Id.
9. *Kopf v. Skyrm,* 993 F.2d 374, 377 (4th Cir., 1993) ("Inasmuch as the rule uses the disjunctive, a person may qualify to render expert testimony in any one of the five listed ways . . . ."); *United States v. Paiva,* 892 F.2d 148, 160 (1st Cir., 1989) ("A witness may qualify as an expert on any one of the five listed grounds.").
10. *United States v. Hoffman,* 832 F.2d 1299, 1310 (1st Cir. 1987) ("Expertise is not necessarily synonymous with a string of academic degrees or multiple memberships in learned societies.").
11. *In re Adler,* 1998 Bankr. LEXIS 404 (S.D.N.Y. 1998) (Case No. 95-08203 (JLG), Adv. Proc. No. 97/8423A).
12. *Waldorf v. Shuta,* 142 F.3d. 601, 625 (3rd Cir. 1998).
13. *McCullock v. H.B. Fuller Co.,* 61 F.3d 1038 (2d Cir. 1995).
14. *JMJ Enterprises, Inc. v. Via Veneto Italian Ice, Inc.,* 1998 U.S. Dist. LEXIS 7750 (E.D. Penn. 1998) (Civil Action No. 97-CV-0652).
15. *See In re Adler, Coleman Clearing Corp.,* 1998 Bankr. LEXIS 404 (S.D.N.Y. 1998).
16. *Wechsler v. Hunt Health Systems, Ltd.,* 381 F. Supp. 2d 135, 142–143 (S.D.N.Y. 2003).
17. *See, e.g., 1325 "G" Street Assocs., LP v. Rockwood Pigments NA, Inc.,* 2004 U.S. Dist. LEXIS 19178 at *47–48 (2004).
18. *Daubert v. Merrell Dow Pharmaceuticals, Inc.,* 509 U.S. 579 (1993), dealt somewhat narrowly with the admissibility of scientific evidence, and it was not until *Kuhmo Tire Co., Ltd. v. Carmichael,* 526 U.S. 137 (1999), that the Supreme Court held that courts must conduct a reliability analysis for all expert testimony. *See* Cecil C. Kuhne III, *Excluding Testimony of Financial Experts in Federal Litigation: How Far Do the Daubert Standards Extend,* 18 St. John's J.L. Comm. 525, 527 (Spring 2004) ("Kumho Tire concluded that regardless of the type of knowledge under consideration, Rule 702 requires a judicial inquiry as a precondition to admissibility, and that when the testimony's factual basis, data, principles, methods or application is called into question, the trial judge must determine whether the testimony has a reliable basis in the knowledge and experience of the relevant discipline.").
19. *Kuhmo Tire Co., Ltd. v. Carmichael,* 526 U.S. 137, 141–142 (1999) (". . . a trial court may consider one or more specific factors . . . the test of reliability is 'flexible,' and Daubert's list of specific factors neither necessarily nor exclusively applies to all experts in every case.").
20. *See Travelers Property & Casualty Corp. v. GE,* 150 F. Supp. 2d 360 (D. Conn. 2001) ("The test of reliability . . . is a 'flexible' one, and the . . . factors set forth in Daubert do not constitute a 'definitive checklist or test.' Whether the Daubert factors are pertinent to assessing reliability in a particular case depends on "the nature of the issue, the expert's particular expertise, and the subject of his testimony," and "a trial court should consider the specific factors identified in Daubert where they are reasonable measures of the reliability of expert testimony.") (citations omitted).
21. Federal Rule of Evidence 702 (2000 Advisory Committee Note).
22. Although new methodologies are not dismissed automatically, a new methodology will fair better before a court if it has been subjected to some kind of review. For example, in *G.T. Laboratories, Inc. v. The Cooper Companies, Inc.,* the defendant sought to admit the testimony of its accountant on the

subject of damages and lost profits. 1998 U.S. Dist. LEXIS 15745 (N.D. Ill. 1998) (Case No. 92 C 6647). The court refused to admit the accountant's testimony because the methodology employed was an unsupported alternative methodology to traditional methods, the accountant failed to submit evidence that the methodology had been tested, subjected to peer review or publication, and the accountant did not submit any evidence of any known or potential error rate.

23. Federal Rule of Evidence 703; Charles A.Wright & Arthur R.Miller, 29 Federal Practice and Procedure § 6271, p. 300 (1997, 2005 Supp.).
24. Federal Rule of Evidence 703.
25. Michigan Rule of Evidence 703. Frequent communication with counsel will help ensure that the expert complies with any distinctions between the federal rules and state rules.
26. Federal Rule of Evidence 703.
27. *See e.g., Harris v. Rivera,* 454 U.S. 339, 347; 102 S. Ct. 460 (1981) ("In bench trials, judges routinely hear inadmissible evidence that they are presumed to ignore when making decisions.").
28. *See* Federal Rules of Evidence 703 and 705.
29. Federal Rule of Evidence 703; Joseph M. McLaughlin, 4 *Weinstein's Federal Evidence,* § 703.03, p. 703-8 (2 ed., 2006).
30. Federal Rule of Evidence 703; Federal Rule of Evidence 703 (2000 Committee Note).
31. *United States v. Gold,* 743 F.2d 800 (11th Cir. 1984).
32. *U.S. v. Seelig,* 622 F.2d 207 (6th Cir. 1980).
33. *Beech Aircraft Corp. v. Rainey,* 488 U.S. 153, 169 (1988).
34. *United States v. Liner,* 435 F.3d 920 (8th Cir. 2006).
35. *United States v. Schurrer,* 1998 U.S. App. LEXIS 21009 (10th Cir. 1998).
36. While an expert witness may generally testify to the ultimate issue of a case, the other Federal Rules of Evidence always apply and could potentially preclude testimony on an ultimate issue. For instance, if the Court determines that under Rule 403, an expert witness' testimony would be more prejudicial than probative on an ultimate issue in a case, the expert would be precluded from offering such testimony.
37. Federal Rule of Civil Procedure 26(a)(2)(C).
38. Federal Rule of Civil Procedure 26(a)(2)(C).
39. Federal Rule of Civil Procedure 26(e)(1)-(2).
40. Federal Rule of Civil Procedure 26(2)(b)(4).
41. Federal Rule of Civil Procedure 26(2)(b)(4).
42. Howard Fielstein, *Forensic Accounting in Litigation: Understanding an Important Resource,* New York Law Journal, p. S5 (July 20, 1998). Where financial statement fraud is suspected, Mr. Fielstein suggests that a forensic accountant may help an attorney look for the following red flags: revenue recognition in improper periods; improper asset valuations; inadequate disclosure of related-party transactions; misclassification of gains; and improper treatment of sales transactions. *Id.* Accountants who are also Certified Fraud Examiners are often integral parts of a legal team and may help an attorney obtain evidence, take statements/interview employees, conduct background checks, etc. *See* Mona M. Clayton, *Use Forensic Accounting to Resolve Disputes,* The Indiana Lawyer, p. 11 (December 8, 1999).
43. Federal Rule of Civil Procedure 26(b)(4)(B).
44. Federal Rule of Evidence 26(b)(4)(C).
45. *Haarhuis v. Kunnan Enterprises, Ltd.,* 177 F.3d 1007, 1015-1016 (1999).
46. *Haarhuis* at 1016.

Chapter 8

Human Resources Concerns

Robert M. Vercruysse and Gregory V. Murray

When considering the human resources concerns that arise with regard to fraud deterrence, one logically focuses on the Corporate and Criminal Fraud Accountability Act of 2002, a/k/a the Sarbanes-Oxley Act (Sarbanes-Oxley).[1]

However, to disregard other controlling federal statutes and the plethora of state regulations that also bind employers would be a serious mistake. This chapter addresses both the logical concerns raised by the Sarbanes-Oxley Act and discusses other statutory concerns.

Finally, this chapter contains an overview of the Federal Fair Credit Reporting Act (FCRA).[2] While often overlooked in an employment context, the statute governs procedures required before employers can legally retain certain outside parties to assist in conducting background checks of applicants and current employees.

RETALIATION: THE NEWEST WAVE OF EMPLOYMENT LITIGATION

Sarbanes-Oxley Act

Genesis of the Act. After highly publicized scandals at Enron, Global Crossing, and WorldCom, widespread investor mistrust of corporate management inspired a congressional response: the Sarbanes-Oxley Act. Signed into law by President Bush in July 2002, the act is an attempt to restore public confidence in the U.S. marketplace, reform corporate accounting practices, and provide protection for "whistleblowers" who bring violations of the act to the attention of authorities within or outside of their employers.

Coverage. Entities covered under Sarbanes-Oxley include companies whose stocks trade publicly as well as all registered foreign companies and all no-public companies whose debt securities are publicly traded, whose equity or debt securities are registered under the Securities Exchange Act, who are required to file reports under that act, or who have filed a statement for a public offering under that act. Coverage also extends to any officer, employee, contractor, subcontractor, or agent of a covered entity. As a result, nonpublic companies that are contractors or subcontractors of a public company, such as privately held automotive suppliers to publicly traded automotive companies, are "covered entities" subject to Sarbanes-Oxley obligations and proceedings.

Publicly held companies need to understand that their employment lawyers must gear up for the Sarbanes-Oxley whistleblower provisions and that the companies should provide internal whistleblower procedures to demonstrate good faith to federal agencies. However, companies that mistakenly believe that Sarbanes-Oxley impacts only publicly traded companies or that ethical obligations reach only securities lawyers take false comfort.

The lawyers of covered entities who "appear and practice" before the Securities and Exchange Commission (SEC), as that term is broadly defined in the new SEC Rule 205 interpreting Section 307 of the act, fall subject to Sarbanes-Oxley's ethical obligations. Even the lawyer who does not specialize in or devote substantial amounts of time to securities law can fall within the broad definition. For example, the employment lawyer who may, among other things, negotiate executive compensation packages, advise on employee benefit plan amendment, or navigate employment disputes for higher level managers or employees entrusted with nonpublic information should become familiar with the act's protections, obligations and penalties.

Moreover, employees working for companies that do not fall within the protective umbrella of Sarbanes-Oxley may be protected under other federal or state common law, or statutory whistleblower protection.

Overview of Sarbanes-Oxley's Whistleblower Provisions. Sarbanes-Oxley establishes a private federal whistleblower cause of action for, and prohibits retaliation against, employees and former employees[3] who blow the whistle on covered entities engaged in or planning a violation of federal criminal law prohibiting, mail,[4] wire,[5] bank[6] or securities fraud[7]; any rule or regulation of the Securities and Exchange Commission (SEC); or any provision of federal law relating to fraud against shareholders.[8]

Protected Activities and Penalties An employee of a covered entity engages in protected activity under Sarbanes-Oxley Section 806 if he or she acts in the public interest by providing certain information, causing such information to be provided, or otherwise participating or assisting in a "proceeding" or in an investigation by a federal regulatory or law enforcement agency, by any member or committee of Congress, or by any of the employer's supervising employees, including but not limited to an employee charged with the responsibility of investigating, discovering, or terminating corporate misconduct.[9] While the statute does not define "proceeding," employees will undoubtedly argue that the term embraces both administrative and judicial proceedings. The information provided must involve misconduct that the employee "reasonably believes" constitutes a violation of federal securities law, SEC rules, any federal law relating to securities fraud, or federal criminal law provisions prohibiting mail fraud, bank fraud, or fraud by wire or radio or television.[10] The act does not protect employee complaints to the news media.

Sarbanes-Oxley Section 1107[11] provides criminal penalties of fines, imprisonment up to 10 years, or both for retaliation against a whistleblower who provides truthful information to a law enforcement officer regarding the commission of a federal offense. Section 1107 appears to apply to reports of wrongdoing involving any federal law, not just fraud against shareholders. Furthermore, Section 1107 prohibits any form of intentional retaliation, "including interference with the lawful employment or livelihood of any person." A host of other remedies protecting whistleblowers are described in the sections that follow.

Investigation and Enforcement Sarbanes-Oxley creates a new enforcement scheme for employees alleging violations of the act. An employee who alleges that he or she suffered an adverse employment action as the result of protected whistleblower activity may file a complaint with the secretary of the Department of Labor (DOL).[12] To be timely, the complaint must be filed within 90 days of the alleged adverse employment action.[13]

The DOL has delegated responsibility to investigate whistleblower complaints to the Occupational Safety and Health Administration (OSHA).[14] Within 60 days of the filing of a complaint, OSHA must investigate and issue findings as to whether there is "reasonable cause" to believe that the respondent employer has retaliated against the complainant. If so, then the regulations grant OSHA the extraordinary ability to enter a preliminary order reinstating the employee, to award back pay with interest, and to award special damages.

Following the enforcement procedures set forth in the Whistleblower Protection Program of the Aviation Investment and Reform Act for the 21st Century (AIR21)[15] adopted by Sarbanes-Oxley,[16] OSHA will not conduct an investigation and will dismiss a complaint unless the complainant makes a prima facie showing that the protected conduct was a contributing factor in an adverse employment action.[17] Even if the employee makes such a showing, OSHA will not conduct an investigation if the employer demonstrates, by clear and convincing evidence, that it would have taken the adverse employment action notwithstanding the protected activity.[18]

Parties objecting to the OSHA findings must challenge those findings or preliminary orders by filing written objections with the DOL within 30 days.[19] The objections must identify the findings, the preliminary order, and/or the award of attorneys' fees (if any) to which the party objects. A timely filed objection stays all relief ordered in the preliminary order except for preliminary reinstatement. Upon the timely filing of an objection, a de novo hearing before a DOL Administrative Law Judge (ALJ) (not an OSHA ALJ) must occur "expeditiously."[20] Unless one or more of the parties files a petition for review, articulating specific exceptions taken to specific findings, conclusions, or orders with the DOL Administrative Review Board within 10 business days of the ALJ's decision, that decision becomes the final decision of the Secretary of Labor. The Secretary of Labor must issue a decision within 120 days of the conclusion of the hearing before the ALJ.[21]

If a final agency decision is issued, any person adversely affected or aggrieved by that decision may obtain review in the United States Court of Appeals for the circuit in which the violation, with respect to which the decision was issued, allegedly occurred or in the circuit in which the complainant resided on the date of the alleged violation.[22] The agency's decision may be set aside only if it is found to be arbitrary, capricious, an abuse of discretion, or otherwise not in conformity with the law.

Private Party Litigation If a final decision of the Secretary of Labor is not issued under the DOL administrative procedures within 180 days of the filing of the complaint,[23] an employee may initiate a de novo private cause of action in the appropriate federal district court, without regard to the amount in controversy, so long as the employee's own bad faith did not cause the delay.[24] It is important to note that the clear and convincing standard discussed earlier, by which an employer may preclude an OSHA investigation, serves only as an agency gatekeeping function. Under cases interpreting the analogous Energy Reorganization Act, in private cause of action cases, a plaintiff bears the ultimate burden of proving, by a preponderance of the evidence, that the employer retaliated against him or her for engaging in protected activity.[25]

Arbitration/ADR of Sarbanes-Oxley Claims Some early support exists for arbitration agreements involving Sarbanes-Oxley whistleblower claims. For example, in *Boss v. Salomon Smith Barney, Inc.*,[26] where plaintiff alleged that the company had terminated his employment in violation of Sarbanes-Oxley after he had refused to change his recommendations on a research report, the court enforced plaintiff's Form U-4 application for registration with the National Association of Securities Dealers, in which he had agreed to arbitrate any dispute, claim, or controversy arising out of his employment or its termination. Two other documents supplemented the Form U-4 application and referred to the company's employment arbitration policy. The court rejected Boss's argument that the grant of federal jurisdiction over Sarbanes-Oxley claims demonstrated a congressional intent to disturb the federal presumption in favor of arbitration.

The Solicitor of Labor has issued an advice memorandum on the subject of arbitrating those types of claims that is a mixed blessing. On one hand, it identifies whistleblower cases, among others, as a type of case where, under appropriate circumstances, enforcement agencies, including OSHA, may stay enforcement proceedings, deferring to a private arbitration agreement. The memorandum states, among other things, that:

> deferral should be considered not only when the arbitration agreement covers the same statutory claim that would be brought by the Department, but also when arbitration of a different legal claim is substantially likely to resolve the factual dispute in a way that would dispose of the statutory claim. For example, if an arbitrator determines that a complainant was terminated for legitimate performance reasons and not because of national origin, the award may also resolve the complainant's whistleblower claim . . . . Deferral will be most appropriate in matters involving individual claims for relief in the form of back pay and reinstatement: matters under Section 11(c) of the OSH Act, for example, STAA, other whistleblower statutes . . . .[27]

On a cautionary note, however, the same memorandum points out that where the DOL may seek immediate provisional relief, such as reinstatement provided for in Sarbanes-Oxley, that relief should be sought even if it is decided to defer to arbitration on the ultimate merits.

Available Remedies Employees who prevail in whistleblower cases (whether in an administrative proceeding, arbitration, or trial) are entitled to damages, which may include: reinstatement to the same seniority status that the employee would have had but for the adverse employment action; back pay; interest; all compensatory damages to make the employee whole; and "special damages," including litigation costs, reasonable attorney's fees and costs, expert witness fees, and "all relief necessary to make the employee whole."[28] Sarbanes-Oxley does not provide for punitive damages. The act does, however, expressly provide that the statute does not preempt state and federal law. Therefore, alternate causes of action and remedies provided under other federal statutes as well as various state laws, including those protecting whistleblowers, remain available.

Ethical Concerns and Obligations. Internal or external Sarbanes-Oxley whistleblower investigations may pose questions of conflict of interest among the company, its officers, directors, employees, and shareholders.

When a Sarbanes-Oxley complaint is filed with the DOL, a company may find itself defending not only the Sarbanes-Oxley whistleblower allegations before the DOL or in private litigation, but also the alleged securities violations before the SEC or in private litigation. The company will also likely be engaged in an internal investigation of the alleged securities violations for the corporation or its audit committee in order to determine whether it must restate earnings or correct any other material misstatements of its finances, or whether it must file supplemental SEC disclosures. The investigation may also include inquiries into alleged retaliation in order to maintain the integrity of the company's internal whistleblower procedures and/or codes of conduct. Because of the layered investigation/defense possibilities, a conflict of interest may arise requiring separate and/or external counsel. The SEC and the Department of Justice (DOJ) consider corporate conduct during these investigations as one factor demonstrating the good faith of the entities under scrutiny, and defenses should be geared toward demonstrating that good faith. Companies and their attorneys must also be aware that the SEC and the DOJ often request, as one measure of good faith, a waiver of attorney-client privilege and/or work product doctrine; although the agencies typically agree to "selective waiver" in which privileges remain intact as against third parties.

"Appearing and Practicing" Attorneys. The final SEC rule implementing Sarbanes-Oxley Section 307, effective August 5, 2003, provides that attorneys "appearing or practicing" before the SEC have certain ethical obligations in an ongoing effort to preclude or to stem corporate misconduct harmful to investors and shareholders.

The rule defines "appearing or practicing" to include any attorney who transacts business before or communicates with the SEC; who represents issuers in SEC administrative proceedings or in connection with any SEC investigation, inquiry, information request, or subpoena; who provides advice about securities law or SEC rules or regulations regarding any document that the attorney has notice will be or has been filed with the SEC; or who advises an issuer as to whether information or a statement, opinion, or other writing is required to be filed with or submitted to the SEC.[29]

For example, to the extent that an in-house or outside employment and/or employee benefits lawyer provides advice and counsel on the reporting of executive compensation and benefits on any paper required to be filed with the SEC, that lawyer "appears and practices" before the SEC and is subject to the ethical obligations under Sarbanes-Oxley. The act even reaches the attorney who is retained to investigate corporate misconduct.[30]

Attorneys subject to Sarbanes-Oxley ethical obligations who violate the SEC rule are subject to SEC disciplinary enforcement proceedings may be censured or temporarily or permanently denied the privilege of appearing or practicing before the SEC. They may also be subjected to the civil penalties and remedies for securities laws violations enforceable by the SEC.[31]

Obligation to Report Section 307 and its implementing guidelines establish new rules of conduct for any attorney who appears or practices before the SEC. Under the SEC final rule, effective August 5, 2003, covered attorneys must report "evidence of a material violation of securities law" or "breach(es) of fiduciary dut(ies)" or "similar violation(s)" to a covered entity's chief legal officer (CLO) or to the CLO and the chief executive officer.[32]

The rule defines "evidence of a material violation" as "credible evidence, based upon which it would be unreasonable, under the circumstances, for a prudent and competent attorney not to conclude that it is reasonably likely that a material violation has occurred, is ongoing, or is about to occur." "Material violation" is defined as:

1. A material violation of federal or state securities law
2. A "material breach" of fiduciary duty "arising under United States federal or state law"
3. A similar material violation of any federal or state law

Breach of fiduciary duty, for Sarbanes-Oxley purposes, refers to "any breach of fiduciary or similar duty to the issuer recognized under an applicable Federal or State statute or at common law, including but not limited to misfeasance, nonfeasance, abdication of duty, abuse of trust and approval of unlawful transactions." Given these definitions, it is probable that a Sarbanes-Oxley violation may be pled in certain Employee Retirement Insurance Security Act (ERISA) cases, or in cases like Enron, WorldCom and Global Crossing, where counts alleging securities laws violations are joined with counts alleging breach of fiduciary duty under ERISA.

If an attorney makes a required report,[33] the CLO has a duty to initiate an "inquiry into the evidence of a material violation as he or she reasonably believes is appropriate to determine" whether the violation has occurred, is occurring, or is about to occur.[34] In lieu of doing so, the CLO may refer the matter to a qualified legal compliance committee.

Unless the CLO believes that no material violation has so occurred or is so occurring, the CLO must "cause the issuer to adopt an appropriate response."[35] If the response of the corporate officer does not properly resolve a reporting attorney's concerns, an attorney is required to further report his or her concerns to the company's audit committee, to a committee comprised entirely of outside directors, or to the board of directors.[36]

The SEC is reconsidering whether to issue, as a final rule, a requirement that attorneys who remain unsatisfied with a company's attempts to remediate a problem, engage in "noisy withdrawal" from representation of an offending client, with a requirement that the withdrawal be reported outside the company to the SEC.

Internal Client Procedures. Compliance with the Sarbanes-Oxley Act will require covered employers to establish internal procedures in the following three areas:

1. *Audit committee.* Section 301 of the Sarbanes-Oxley Act mandates that covered companies establish an audit committee responsible for the appointment, compensation, and oversight of the work of the "registered public accounting firm" that is employed on behalf of the company to issue an audit report or related work. The audit committee must establish procedures for the confidential, even anonymous, reporting by employees and individuals outside the company of concerns regarding questionable accounting or auditing matters.[37] Under the whistleblower provisions of Sarbanes-Oxley, internal reports to such committees constitute protected activity subject to the antiretaliation provisions of the act. A covered company that fails to comply with this requirement may be removed from a national exchange.
2. *Code of ethics.* Section 406 of the Act mandates the adoption of a code of ethics for senior financial officers. Each reporting company must also promptly disclose the failure to adopt such rules or any changes in, or waivers from, its code of ethics. Corporate ethics policies typically include:
   (a) The procedures for handling any conflicts between personal and corporate interests
   (b) Corporate theft
   (c) Improper use of confidential or insider information
   (d) Accurate financial and expense reporting
   (e) Falsification of company records and financial statements

   The SEC issued proposed rules under Section 406, which define a code of ethics as standards "reasonably necessary to deter wrongdoing" and to promote honest and ethical conduct, including the ethical handling of actual or apparent conflicts of interest between personal and professional relationships; avoidance of conflicts of interest and potential conflicts of interest and internal disclosure procedures; compliance with applicable governmental laws, rules and regulations; prompt internal reporting of code violations; and accountability for adherence to the code. Significantly, the proposed rules require a public company to report on a current basis amendments to, and waivers from, its code of ethics.

While Sarbanes-Oxley requires only that the procedures relate to complaints of accounting, accounting controls and audit matters, companies may choose to incorporate the statute's reporting procedures into more comprehensive codes of conduct or ethics policies. If these procedures are included in a code of conduct or ethics policy that addresses other ethical standards and areas of conduct, the policy should make clear that the audit committee is specifically responsible for handling and responding to complaints about accounting, accounting controls, and audit matters, whereas company management may have responsibility for compliance with other standards.

3. *Heightened document retention requirements.* Sarbanes-Oxley tightens document retention requirements in a way that reinforces and complements its whistleblowing provisions by targeting acts that are intended to impede, obstruct, or influence other investigations, including acts done in relation to, or contemplation of, any matter or case arising from whistleblowing. Whether document destruction relates to a federal agency investigation or an "official proceeding," the wrongdoer may be fined under Sarbanes-Oxley or imprisoned for up to 20 years or both.

   The act prohibits the knowing alteration, destruction, mutilation, concealment, cover-up, falsification, or making of a false entry in any record, document, or tangible object with the specific intent to impede, obstruct, or influence the investigation or proper administration of any matter within the jurisdiction of any department or agency of the United States or any case filed under Title 11 or in relation to or contemplation of any such matter or case. Whistleblowers will be protected when reporting destruction of documentation arguably relevant to a covered investigation. The prohibition on document destruction "with the intent to obstruct a federal investigation" appears to apply to more than financial or accountancy investigations.

   The second document-retention provision of Sarbanes-Oxley is more limited in scope. The act amends a witness-tampering statute and focuses on the destruction of documents involved in an "official proceeding." An "official proceeding" generally means a proceeding before a judge or court of the United States, a proceeding before Congress, or a proceeding before a federal government agency. Specifically, the act imposes penalties on any person who "corruptly—

   - Alters, destroys, mutilates or conceals a record, document or other object, or attempts to do so, with the intent to impair the object's integrity or availability for use in an official proceeding; or
   - Otherwise obstructs, influences or impedes any official proceeding, or attempts to do so."

   This provision prohibits not only destruction of documents, but also the alteration or concealing of documents. It may also apply to those making false entries in a covered documents.

Multiple-Count Class Actions. Because the act does not preempt other federal or state law, it is probable that claims under Sarbanes-Oxley will be joined with other state and federal claims. For example, the same factual allegations that form the gravamen of the complaints in the Enron and WorldCom cases may now inspire an additional theory of liability under the Sarbanes-Oxley Act, whether in an action brought by an individual complainant who claims to be a whistleblower as well as an injured benefit plan participant and employee stockholder, or in a class action brought by injured internal/employee stockholders, some of whom claim to be whistleblowers. In recent class action litigation, litigants have bootstrapped both ERISA and securities fraud claims on the same factual allegations. In an ERISA claim or a securities fraud claim brought against pension plans, benefits administrators and human resource personnel, corporate officers, directors, and investment advisors, plaintiffs typically allege both breach of fiduciary duty claims, contending that corporate officers and directors made material misrepresentations about the soundness of company stock and the prudence of investing in company stock, as well as a failure to disclose fully and accurately infirmities in the company's stock price.

Courts have consolidated breach of fiduciary class actions governed by ERISA with securities class actions governed by the Private Securities Litigation Reform Act. For example, in *In re: Global Crossing Ltd Securities & ERISA Litigation,*[38] 57 actions against Global Crossing were transferred to a multidistrict panel in the Southern District of New York, which found consolidation based upon common questions of fact in both the securities and the ERISA litigation. In *In re WorldCom, Inc Securities & ERISA Litigation,*[39] a judicial panel on multidistrict litigation consolidated and centralized 42 ERISA and securities claims against WorldCom in New York over plaintiffs' opposition to such consolidation.

The moral of the Sarbanes-Oxley story is that the act is not just for publicly traded companies or securities lawyers who advise public companies. Its whistleblower provisions and its ethical obligations reach nonpublic companies that are covered entities and their lawyers who "appear and practice" before the SEC and are having a spillover effect on other companies. Both public and nonpublic companies should involve employment lawyers in the development of internal whistleblower procedures and in the conduct of Sarbanes-Oxley and Sarbanes-Oxley–like investigations, whether internal or external, so that the integrity of the process, including the preservation of all relevant documents and, to the extent possible, the privilege of the product can be protected.

Other Federal and State Whistleblower Laws

In addition to Sarbanes-Oxley, various other state and federal laws prohibit employers from retaliating against whistleblowing employees who bring complaints of discrimination and other perceived unlawful workplace practices. Lawsuits filed by employees who allege retaliation are often the most difficult to defend for a variety of reasons. First, many employers make the incorrect assumption that they cannot be held liable for retaliation if the underlying claim is proven to be without merit. This simply is not true. Second, retaliation claims are difficult to defeat at the summary disposition/judgment phase of the litigation. An adverse employment action closely following a complaint of unlawful workplace practices is often deemed sufficient to create a question of fact necessary to prevent a case from being summarily dismissed prior to trial. Thus, many retaliation claims reach the courthouse steps if not settled by the parties beforehand. Third, retaliation claims are difficult to defend. Many people are inclined to believe that once you have rocked the boat with your employer, especially if you have made allegations against key members of management, your days are numbered. For these reasons, the problem employee who lodges an unfounded complaint of disparate treatment and is terminated shortly thereafter for legitimate performance issues may find himself losing his disparate treatment claim, but receiving a favorable settlement or jury verdict on a claim of retaliation.

For these reasons, retaliation claims are on the rise, particularly in employment discrimination cases. According to the Equal Employment Opportunity Commission, the number of retaliation charges filed with the federal agency's nationwide field offices increased from 7,900 in fiscal year 1991, to 18,100 in fiscal year 1997. For fiscal year 2003, the number was up to 22,690.[40]

Like Sarbanes-Oxley, many employment-related statutes offer some form of protection against retaliation. In those statutes, the retaliatory action itself is considered a distinct discriminatory practice, such as in cases involving Title VII of the Civil Rights Act of 1964, the Americans with Disabilities Act, the Age Discrimination in Employment Act, and the Family and Medical Leave Act. In addition to federal law, employers need to concern themselves with the myriad of state statutes that also prohibit retaliation. As a general principle, therefore, an employer should refrain from taking any adverse action against an employee who has recently participated in protected activity, without first consulting its in-house legal department or outside counsel.

Proof of Retaliation. What is required to prove an employee's case in a court of law differs depending on which statute's antiretaliation provision is alleged to have been violated. Under federal and most state laws, an employee who files a charge of discrimination, otherwise opposes an unlawful employment practice, or participates in an investigation, proceeding, or hearing regarding an unlawful accounting or employment practice is engaged in protected activity and may not suffer an adverse employment action for doing so. To establish the engagement in a protected activity, however, it is not typically essential that the employee prove that the underlying claim is meritorious. Instead, the employee must simply possess a good faith belief that the unlawful conduct occurred and establish that the belief was subjectively reasonable in light of the facts. Because an employee can win a case where the employer responded improperly to his or her efforts to help enforce the law, even if the underlying complaint is meritless, retaliation can be a challenging concept for employers to understand.

For example, Title VII prohibits retaliation against an employee who challenges conduct as being in violation of that statute. Generally, courts require that the shifting burden of proof analysis must be applied in retaliation actions. To show a prima facie case of retaliation, an employee must prove that (1) he or she engaged in protected activity, (2) the employer knew about the activity, (3) the employer took action that was adverse to the employee, and (4) there was a causal connection between the protected activity and the adverse employment action. There is no requirement that the employee demonstrate that illegal activity, in fact, took place. If the employee proves a prima facie case of discrimination, the employer must set forth a legitimate, nondiscriminatory reason for the adverse action. If the employer succeeds in articulating such a reason, the employee-plaintiff must prove that the employer's reason was a pretext for retaliation.

Questions often arise as to whether an employee has satisfied each of the four prongs of establishing a prima facie case of retaliation. Whether the employee alleges that he or she was retaliated against for opposing a violation of a law or for participating in the enforcement of a law, the employee must show that he or she was engaged in protected activity.

It is often difficult to determine just when an employee is deemed to have participated in an investigation, hearing, or proceeding, and whether an employer's internal investigation falls under this definition. An employee need not always have filed a formal complaint in order to bring a claim of retaliation. If the adverse employment decision is the direct result of an employee's having raised the specter of an accounting violation or discrimination complaint, retaliation may be held to have occurred, regardless of the vagueness of the employee's charge or the lack of a formal invocation of statutory protection.

Similarly, Title VII also protects an employee's participation in an employer's internal investigation into allegations of unlawful discrimination, provided, however, that the investigation occurs pursuant to a charge pending before the Federal Equal Employment Opportunity Commission or similar state agency.[41]

It goes without saying that an employer must have knowledge of the employee's having engaged in protected activity at the time the adverse action was taken in order for that employer to have retaliated against the employee as a result. That causal connection will be found to be lacking when it is undisputed that the employer actually made the decision to terminate the plaintiff's employment before becoming aware of any protected activity.

Under many statutory schemes, in order to sustain a claim of retaliation, the employee must be affected by an adverse employment action, generally defined as a materially adverse change in the terms and conditions of employment. In interpreting what constitutes a materially adverse change in the terms and conditions of employment, courts have repeatedly held that that de minimus employment actions do not constitute adverse actions as a matter of law:

> If every low evaluation or other action by an employer that makes an employee unhappy or resentful were considered an adverse action, Title VII would be triggered by supervisor criticism or even facial expressions indicating displeasure. Paranoia in the workplace would replace the prima facie case as the basis for a Title VII cause of action. The case law supports our view that the employer conduct in this case will not support a Title VII cause of action. *Primes v. Reno,* 190 F.3d 765 (6th Cir. 1999).[42]

However, some courts have held that an increase in an already heavy workload, heightened scrutiny, and/or constructive discharge could be deemed adverse employment actions.[43] Similarly, a supervisor's failure to respond to an employee's complaints of coworker harassment can constitute an adverse employment action for the purposes of a retaliation claim. Thus, it is possible that an employer's failure to act, if it materially changes the terms and conditions of one's employment, can constitute an adverse employment action.

Most litigation surrounding retaliation claims turns on the issue of whether the alleged adverse action was causally related to the protected activity. To establish a causal connection, an employee must demonstrate that participation in the protected activity was a "significant factor" in the employer's adverse employment action, not merely that there was a causal link between the two events.[44] Moreover, a mere discriminatory or adverse action will not suffice as evidence of retaliation unless the employee demonstrates a clear nexus between such action and the protected activity.

To prove that the protected activity was a significant factor, an employee must show that the activity was one of the reasons for the employer's action that made a difference in determining whether the action was to be taken. Put another way, an employee "must produce sufficient evidence from which an inference could be drawn that the adverse action would not have been taken had the plaintiff not filed a . . . claim.[45]

A key factor in determining causation is the proximity in time of the adverse action to the protected activity. Although a causal connection may be established by showing close timing between the adverse action and the protected activity, courts have repeatedly held that "temporal proximity alone will not support an inference of retaliatory discrimination when there is no other compelling evidence."[46]

Some courts have held that where an employee is cited for performance issues or work violations both before and after engaging in protected activity, he or she must come forward with direct evidence linking the employer's actions and the protected activity in order to sustain a claim of retaliation.[47] Similarly, no causal connection has been found in cases where the employer began considering the adverse action prior to the employee's engagement in protected activity.[48] Cases like these have, not surprisingly, led to some strategic thinking on the part of both employees and employers. The retaliation provisions contained in many employment law statutes and similar whistleblowers' protection laws have led some employees to "blow the whistle" as an insurance policy to protect themselves from discharge or other adverse employment actions that they see coming. It is becoming more and more common that the employee who has been warned of performance problems suddenly has a claim of alleged illegal activity, discrimination, harassment, or the like to bring to the attention of his or her employer. By the same token, however, some employers are exercising their patience and waiting the perceived requisite number of months before taking adverse action against an employee who has engaged in protected activity—to avoid the causal inference of a retaliation claim. Although it is still possible to prove a retaliation claim after a significant time gap, more evidence is generally required.

The Sarbanes-Oxley Act's whistleblower protection is patterned on earlier federal statutes. The interpretation of those laws provides guidance with respect to claims brought under Sarbanes-Oxley. For a list of other selected federal whistleblowers' protection statutes, see Appendix 8A. For a detailed explanation of the manner in which the Equal Employment Opportunity Commission (EEOC) evaluates claims of retaliation brought to its attention, see Appendix 8B, the EEOC's Guidance on Retaliation Claims, which contains instructions for investigating and analyzing claims of retaliation under the statutes enforced by the EEOC.

AN OUNCE OF PREVENTION: BACKGROUND CHECKS AND EMPLOYMENT INQUIRIES UNDER THE FAIR CREDIT REPORTING ACT

Amendments to the Fair Credit Reporting Act

The Fair Credit Reporting Act (FCRA)[49] as amended by the Consumer Credit Reporting Reform Act of 1996, PL104-208,[50] governs employers wishing to obtain certain information regarding job applicants. The FCRA, which until 1996 covered credit bureaus dealing with reports concerning an individual's creditworthiness, now covers reports on driving records, criminal conviction histories, school records, and other related information, depending on how the information is obtained by an employer and such other information that is often of interest to employers when making hiring decisions.

The FCRA is designed primarily to protect the privacy of consumer report information and to guarantee that the information supplied by consumer reporting agencies is as accurate as possible. The 1996 amendments significantly increase the legal obligations of employers who use consumer reports. Congress expanded employer responsibilities because of a concern that inaccurate or incomplete consumer reports were unjustly causing applicants to be denied jobs or causing employees to be denied promotions or favorable job reassignments. The amendments ensure that job applicants and employees are aware that consumer reports may be used for employment purposes and agree to such use, and are notified promptly if any information in a consumer report may result in a negative employment decision.

Consumer Reporting Agencies

The FCRA comes into play when an employer obtains covered information, that is, a "consumer report"[51] or a more intrusive form of a consumer report known as an "investigative consumer report"[52] through a "consumer reporting agency."[53] A consumer reporting agency (CRA) is any person or firm that, for monetary fees, dues, or on a cooperative nonprofit basis, regularly engages in whole or in part in the practice of assembling or evaluating consumer credit information or other information on consumers for the purpose of furnishing consumer reports to third parties, and that uses any means or facilities of interstate commerce for the purpose of preparing or furnishing consumer reports.[54] An employer can avoid application of the FCRA when it uses internal sources, instead of third parties, to obtain covered information and to conduct investigations.

Federal Trade Commission (FTC)[55] staff have issued opinion letters stating that public agencies providing consumer information to employers for employment purposes and charging a fee for the reports are not "consumer reporting agencies." Therefore, although a strict interpretation of the term "consumer reporting agency" would include law enforcement agencies, courts, and other agencies, the act does not restrict such public agencies from fulfilling legislatively mandated public policy.[56]

Despite the constraints raised by the FCRA, employers should consider using third parties to conduct background checks in situations in which the employer does not have employees with the experience, training, skills, and knowledge necessary to accomplish effective and lawful investigations; or the investigations may be considered biased or lacking in credibility if conducted in-house.

Types of Reports Covered

Employers often do background checks before extending offers of employment or promotion. Some employers only want an applicant's or employee's credit payment history; others want driving records and criminal histories. In filling particularly sensitive positions, it is not unusual for employers to order reports that include interviews with an applicant's or employee's friends, neighbors, and associates. All of these types of reports are considered consumer reports if they are obtained from a consumer reporting agency. The more intrusive reports are, however, subject to stricter scrutiny under the FCRA. The distinction is important.

Consumer Reports. A consumer report is any written, oral, or other communication of any information by a consumer reporting agency bearing on a consumer's creditworthiness, credit standing, credit capacity, character, general reputation, personal characteristics, or mode of living that is used or expected to be used or collected, in whole or in part, for the purpose of serving as a factor in establishing the consumer's eligibility for purposes of employment.[57] The term "employment purposes," when used in connection with a consumer report, means a report used for the purpose of evaluating a consumer for employment, promotion, reassignment, or retention as an employee.[58]

Investigative Consumer Reports. An investigative consumer report is a consumer report or a portion thereof in which information on a consumer's character, general reputation, personal characteristics, or mode of living is obtained through personal interviews with neighbors, friends, or associates of the consumer, or with others with whom the consumer is acquainted or who may have knowledge concerning any such items of information.[59]

Use of Consumer Reports for Employment Purposes

An employer may procure a consumer report on an employee or applicant only for a purpose permissible under the FCRA[60] and then only after disclosure to and authorization from the employee. An employer must disclose to the employee or applicant that a consumer report may be obtained for employment purposes. This disclosure must be clear and conspicuous, must be in writing, and must be contained in a document that consists solely of the disclosure, without any extraneous information.[61] As discussed in the section that follows, a heightened disclosure request is necessary before securing an investigative consumer report. An employer must also obtain written authorization from the employee or applicant, following disclosure and prior to receiving the report.[62]

The obligation to disclose and obtain authorization can be satisfied as part of a routine procedure at the start of employment.[63] This will relieve the employer from being in the awkward position of having to ask a suspected wrongdoer for permission to allow a third party to provide an investigative or other consumer report to the employer.

Once an employer has received the employee's or applicant's permission to obtain a consumer report, the employer must certify to the consumer reporting agency the permissible purposes for which the report is being obtained and certify that the report will not be used for any other purpose.[64]

Use of Investigative Consumer Reports

Prior to procuring an investigative consumer report, an employer must clearly and accurately disclose to the applicant or employee that such a report, including information as to his or her character, general reputation, personal characteristics, and mode of living, may be made.[65] The disclosure must be in writing and mailed or otherwise delivered to the individual no later than three days after the date on which the report was first requested. It must include a statement informing the individual of his or her right to request additional disclosure of the nature and scope of the investigation and must include a summary of the individual's rights under the FCRA.[66] The employer must certify to the consumer reporting agency that such disclosures have been made.[67] Additionally, upon the request of the consumer within a reasonable time period after receipt of the disclosures, an employer must make a complete disclosure of the nature and scope of the investigation that was requested.[68] This must be made in a written statement, mailed or otherwise delivered to the individual no later than five days after the date on which the request was received from the consumer or the report was first requested, whichever is later.[69]

As is the case with a normal consumer report, the employer must certify to the consumer reporting agency the permissible purposes for which the investigative consumer report is being obtained and certify that the report will not be used for any other purpose.

Adverse Actions Resulting from Information Disclosed in a Consumer Report

If an employer considers taking adverse action either wholly or partly as a result of the information contained in a consumer report, it has additional reporting responsibilities, including providing the employee with a pre–adverse action notice to give him or her an opportunity to correct any errors in the consumer report.[70] The pre–adverse action notice must include a copy of the consumer report as well as a summary of the consumer's rights under FCRA.[71]

An adverse action in the employment setting includes a denial of employment or any other decision for employment purposes that adversely affects any current or prospective employment (e.g., adverse hiring, promotion, demotion, reassignment, and retention decisions).[72]

An employer cannot avoid FCRA compliance by the continuance of not ordering a written report and simply receiving instead only an oral report. The FTC has stated that employers must actually provide "oral copies" of oral information received from CRAs in order to comply with the pre–adverse action notice requirement of the FCRA.[73]

The FCRA does not prescribe a set waiting period between notifying the applicant or employee that adverse action is intended and the action actually taking place. However, FTC attorneys have issued guidance letters suggesting that, at a minimum, a five-day period should elapse.[74] A shorter waiting period may be appropriate under unusual circumstances, such as in cases of sex harassment discipline.[75] This waiting period is intended to provide the applicant or employee with time to address any inaccuracies in the report.

After taking an adverse action, an employer must notify the individual within three days, orally, in writing, or electronically, that the adverse action has been taken.[76] This notice must include:

- The name, address, and phone number of the credit reporting agency that supplied the report (including the toll-free number established by the agency if the agency compiles and maintains files on consumers on a nationwide basis)
- A statement that the credit reporting agency supplying the report did not make the adverse action decision and cannot give specific reasons for it
- A notice of the individual's right to dispute the accuracy or completeness of any information the agency furnished, and his or her right to an additional free consumer report from the agency upon request within 60 days[77]

Medical Information

Special provisions were also established for consumer reports containing medical information. The FCRA prohibits a consumer reporting agency from providing reports that contain medical information to be used for employment purposes without the specific prior consent of the individual who is the subject of the report. In the case of medical information sought for employment purposes, the applicant or employee must explicitly consent to the release of medical information and authorize the obtaining of a general consumer report.[78]

Remedies for Violations of the Act

The FCRA allows individuals to sue employers in federal court for damages where employers fail to get an applicant's permission before requesting a consumer report or fail to provide pre–adverse action disclosure and adverse action notices to unsuccessful job applicants. Potential damages include court costs and reasonable legal fees. The law also allows individuals to seek punitive damages for deliberate violations.[79] In addition, the FTC may sue employers for noncompliance and obtain civil penalties.[80] Related actions under state law are not preempted. The statute of limitations for pursuing such a claim is the later of two years from the date of discovery by the plaintiff of the violation or five years after the date on which the violation occurred.[81]

The FCRA also provides that any person who knowingly and willfully obtains information on a consumer from a consumer reporting agency under false pretenses shall be fined and imprisoned for not more than two years, or both.[82]

CHECKLIST FOR COMPLYING WITH THE FCRA WHEN USING A THIRD PARTY TO OBTAIN "CONSUMER REPORTS"[83]

Certify Compliance with the FCRA

Before obtaining a consumer report, an employer must certify to the outside investigator (background screeners, criminal history providers, private investigator, law firm, etc.):

- The permissible purpose for which the report is being obtained and that the report will not be used for any other purpose.
- That proper, written disclosure was given to any employee affected by the investigation.
- That prior, written authorization was gained from the affected employee.
- That the information being obtained will not be used in violation of any federal or state equal opportunity law or regulation.
- That if any adverse action is to be taken based on the report, a copy of the report and a summary of the employee's rights will be provided to the employee.
- If an "investigative consumer report" is obtained, an employer must also certify that the several additional required disclosures triggered by that subcategory of "consumer report" were made to the employee.

Provide Written Disclosure to and Obtain Written Consent from the Employee

Before obtaining a consumer report, an employer must:

- Give the employee affected by the investigation a clear and conspicuous written disclosure that such a report may be obtained.
- Obtain prior written authorization from the employee to obtain the report.

The FTC suggests that this written disclosure and written consent may be presented in a single document. However, the disclosure must appear conspicuously. The document must consist solely of the disclosure and the authorization; for example, it must not be inserted within the fine print of an employee handbook.

For investigative consumer reports, there are additional disclosure requirements. An employer commissioning an investigative report must:

- Advise the employee that the investigative consumer report is being sought. (This must be done within three days of the date the report is requested.)
- Inform the employee of his or her right to request in writing additional disclosure of the nature and scope of the investigation to be undertaken. (This must be done within three days of the date the report is first requested.) If the employee does request information on the nature and scope of the investigation planned, an employer must provide that additional information to the employee who requests it within five days.
- Provide the employee with "A Summary of Your Rights Under the Fair Credit Reporting Act." (This must be done within three days of the date the report is first requested.)

These time frames effectively prohibit blanket disclosures that would allow an employer to obtain a consumer investigative report at any time during an individual's employment. In effect, this warning serves to "tip off" an employee suspected of wrongdoing that he or she is about to be investigated.

Notify the Employee before Adverse Action Is Taken

If an employer plans to take adverse action (discipline, discharge, denial of promotion, failure to hire, etc.) that is based even in part on information contained in the consumer report, before taking that action an employer must provide to the employee who will be the subject of the adverse action:

- A copy of the consumer report
- A summary of "Your Rights Under the Fair Credit Reporting Act"

The FCRA does not indicate how long an employer must wait between notifying the employee that adverse action is anticipated and actually taking the adverse action. FTC opinion letters suggest that waiting five business days between the notification and the adverse action "appears reasonable." However, the FTC warns that the waiting period could be shorter or longer depending on the facts of a particular employment situation.

Notify the Employee after Adverse Action Is Taken

If an employer takes adverse action against an employee or applicant based at least in part on information contained in the consumer report, it must notify the employee in writing, orally, or electronically. This notification must include:

- The name, address, and telephone number of the consumer reporting agency (including a toll-free telephone number, if it is a nationwide CRA) that provided the report
- A statement that the external investigator did not make the adverse decision and is not able to explain or provide specific reasons why the decision was made
- Notice of the employee's right to obtain a free copy of the consumer report from the external investigator if the employee requests the report within 60 days
- A statement setting forth the employee's right to dispute the accuracy or completeness of any information provided directly with the external investigator

Obviously some of these requirements duplicate those that must be taken before an adverse action occurs. Therefore, an employer may opt to mail a copy of each applicant's or employee's consumer report along with a notice of rights under the FCRA, as soon as it obtains the report.

CONCLUSION

Oftentimes employers involved in the investigation of serious misconduct get sidetracked by the business implications of the alleged wrongdoing. To ensure that all areas of concern are addressed, a team approach is recommended. Whether internal or external to the company, the team should consist of not only experienced forensic investigators but also human resource and legal representatives.

APPENDIX 8A

Selected Federal Whistleblower Statutes

Statute	Citation	Statute of Limitations
Age Discrimination in Employment Act (ADEA)	29 USC § 623(d)	180 – 300 days
Americans with Disabilities Act (ADA)	42 USC § 12203(a)	180 – 300 days
Asbestos Hazard Emergency Response Act	15 USC § 2641 et seq.	90 days
Atomic Energy and Energy Reorganization Acts	42 USC § 5851	180 days
Civil Rights Act of 1964 (Title VII)	42 USC § 2003(a)	180 – 300 days
Clean Air Act	42 USC § 7622	30 days
Commercial Motor Vehicle Safety, Trucking and Transportation	49 USC § 31105	180 days
Comprehensive Environmental Response, Compensation & Liability Act (CERCLA/Superfund)	42 USC § 9610	30 days
Defense Contractor Employees	10 USC § 2409	None stated in statute
Employee Retirement Income Security Act (ERISA)	29 USC § 1132(a), 1140	3 years
Equal Pay Act	29 USC § 206(d)	2 years; 3 years if "willful"
Fair Labor Standards Act (FLSA)	29 USC § 215(a)(3)	2 years; 3 years if "willful"
Family and Medical Leave Act (FMLA)	29 USC § 2615	2 years; 3 years if "willful"
Federal Mine Health and Safety Act	30 USC § 815(c)	60 days
International Safe Container Act	46 USC § 1506	60 days
Longshore and Harbor Workers' Compensation Act	33 USC § 901 et seq.	None stated in statute
Occupational Safety and Health Act	29 USC § 660	30 days
Safe Drinking Water Act	42 USC § 300j-9	30 days
Solid Waste Disposal Act	42 USC § 6971	30 days
Surface Mining Control and Reclamation Act	30 USC § 1293	30 days
Surface Transportation Assistance Act	49 USC § 2305	180 days
Safe Containers for International Cargo Act	46 USC § 1501 et. seq	60 days
Toxic Substances Control Act	15 USC § 2622	30 days
Water Pollution Control Act	33 1367	30 days
Wendell H. Ford Aviation Investment and Reform Act for the 21st Century (AIR 21)	49 USC § 42121	90 days

APPENDIX 8B

The U.S. Equal Employment Opportunity Commission

EEOC DIRECTIVES TRANSMITTAL

Number 915.003

Date 5/20/98

SUBJECT: EEOC COMPLIANCE MANUAL

PURPOSE: This transmittal covers the issuance of Section 8 of the new Compliance Manual on "Retaliation." The section provides guidance and instructions for investigating and analyzing claims of retaliation under the statutes enforced by the EEOC.

EFFECTIVE DATE: Upon receipt

DISTRIBUTION: EEOC Compliance Manual holders

OBSOLETE DATA: Section 614 of Compliance Manual, Volume 2

FILING INSTRUCTIONS: This is the first section issued as part of the new Compliance Manual. Section 614 of the existing Compliance Manual should be discarded.

/s/

Paul M. Igasaki
Chairman

SECTION 8: RETALIATION

TABLE OF CONTENTS

Charge-Processing Outline

8-I. Introduction

- A. Overview
- B. Basis for Filing a Charge

8-II. Elements of a Retaliation Claim

- A. Overview
- B. Protected Activity: Opposition
- C. Protected Activity: Participation
- D. Adverse Action
- E. Proof of Causal Connection

8-III. Special Remedies Issues

- A. Temporary or Preliminary Relief
- B. Compensatory and Punitive Damages

CHARGE-PROCESSING OUTLINE

In processing a charge involving an allegation of retaliation, consider the following issues. There are three essential elements of a retaliation claim:

1. protected activity — opposition to discrimination or participation in the statutory complaint process
2. adverse action
3. causal connection between the protected activity and the adverse action

I. Protected Activity

- a. Did CP oppose discrimination?
  - i. Did the charging party (CP) explicitly or implicitly communicate to the respondent (R) or another covered entity a belief that its activity constituted unlawful discrimination under Title VII, the ADA, the ADEA, or the EPA?
    1. If the protest was broad or ambiguous, would CP's protest reasonably have been interpreted as opposition to such unlawful discrimination?
    2. Did someone closely associated with CP oppose discrimination?
  - ii. Was the manner of opposition reasonable? Was the manner of opposition so disruptive that it significantly interfered with R's legitimate business concerns?
    1. If the manner of opposition was not reasonable, CP is not protected under the anti-retaliation clauses.
  - iii. Did CP have a reasonable and good faith belief that the opposed practice violated the anti-discrimination laws?
    1. If so, CP is protected against retaliation, even if s/he was mistaken about the unlawfulness of the challenged practices.
    2. If not, CP is not protected under the anti-retaliation clauses.
- b. Did CP participate in the statutory complaint process?
  - i. Did CP or someone closely associated with CP file a charge, or testify, assist, or participate in any manner in an investigation, proceeding, hearing, or lawsuit under the statutes enforced by the EEOC?
    1. If so, CP is protected against retaliation regardless of the validity or reasonableness of the original allegation of discrimination.
    2. CP is protected against retaliation by a respondent for participating in statutory complaint proceedings even if that complaint involved a different covered entity.

II. Adverse Action

- a. Did R subject CP to any kind of adverse treatment?
  - i. Adverse actions undertaken after CP's employment relationship with R ended, such as negative job references, can be challenged.
  - ii. Although trivial annoyances are not actionable, more significant retaliatory treatment that is reasonably likely to deter protected activity is unlawful. There is no requirement that the adverse action materially affect the terms, conditions, or privileges of employment.

III. Causal Connection

- a. Is there direct evidence that retaliation was a motive for the adverse action?
  - i. Did R official admit that it undertook the adverse action because of the protected activity?

ii. Did R official express bias against CP based on the protected activity? If so, is there evidence linking that statement of bias to the adverse action?

1. Such a link would be established if, for example, the statement was made by the decision-maker at the time of the challenged action.

iii. If there is direct evidence that retaliation was a motive for the adverse action, "cause" should be found. Evidence as to any additional legitimate motive would be relevant only to relief, under a mixed-motives analysis.

b. Is there circumstantial evidence that retaliation was the true reason for the adverse action?

i. Is there evidence raising an inference that retaliation was the cause of the adverse action?

1. Such an inference is raised if the adverse action took place shortly after the protected activity and if the decision-maker was aware of the protected activity before undertaking the adverse action.

2. If there was a long period of time between the protected activity and the adverse action, determine whether there is other evidence raising an inference that the cause of the adverse action was retaliation.

ii. Has R produced evidence of a legitimate, nondiscriminatory reason for the adverse action?

iii. Is R's explanation a pretext designed to hide retaliation?

1. Did R treat similarly situated employees who did not engage in protected activity differently from CP?

2. Did R subject CP to heightened scrutiny after s/he engaged in protected activity?

iv. If, on the basis of all of the evidence, the investigator is persuaded that retaliation was the true reason for the adverse action, then "cause" should be found.

IV. Special Remedies Issues

a. Is it appropriate to seek temporary or preliminary relief pending final disposition of the charge?

i. Is there a substantial likelihood that the challenged action will be found to constitute unlawful retaliation?

ii. Will the retaliation cause irreparable harm to CP and/or the EEOC?

1. Will CP likely incur irreparable harm beyond financial hardship because of the retaliation?

2. If the retaliation appears to be based on CP's filing of a prior EEOC charge, will that retaliation likely cause irreparable harm to EEOC's ability to investigate CP's original charge of discrimination?

iii. If there is a substantial likelihood that the challenged action will constitute retaliation and if that retaliation will cause irreparable harm to CP and/or the EEOC, contact the Regional Attorney about pursuing temporary or preliminary relief.

b. Are compensatory and punitive damages available and appropriate?

i. Compensatory and punitive damages are available for retaliation claims under all of the statutes enforced by the EEOC, including the ADEA and the EPA. Compensatory and punitive damages for retaliation claims under the ADEA and the EPA are not subject to statutory caps.

ii. Punitive damages often are appropriate in retaliation claims under any of the statutes enforced by the EEOC.

8-I. INTRODUCTION

A. OVERVIEW

Title VII of the Civil Rights Act of 1964,[1] the Age Discrimination in Employment Act,[2] the Americans with Disabilities Act,[3] and the Equal Pay Act[4] prohibit retaliation by an employer, employment agency, or labor organization because an individual has engaged in protected activity.[5]

Protected activity consists of the following:

1. opposing a practice made unlawful by one of the employment discrimination statutes (the "opposition" clause); or
2. filing a charge, testifying, assisting, or participating in any manner in an investigation, proceeding, or hearing under the applicable statute (the "participation" clause).

This chapter reaffirms the Commission's policy of ensuring that individuals who oppose unlawful employment discrimination, participate in employment discrimination proceedings, or otherwise assert their rights under the laws enforced by the Commission are protected against retaliation. Voluntary compliance with and effective enforcement of the anti-discrimination statutes depend in large part on the initiative of individuals to oppose employment practices that they reasonably believe to be unlawful, and to file charges of discrimination. If retaliation for such activities were permitted to go unremedied, it would have a chilling effect upon the willingness of individuals to speak out against employment discrimination or to participate in the EEOC's administrative process or other employment discrimination proceedings.

The Commission can sue for temporary or preliminary relief before completing its processing of a retaliation charge if the charging party or the Commission will likely suffer irreparable harm because of the retaliation. The investigator should contact the Regional Attorney early in the investigation if it appears that it may be appropriate to seek such relief. See Section 8-III A for guidance on the standards for seeking temporary or preliminary relief.

B. BASIS FOR FILING A CHARGE

A charging party who alleges retaliation under Title VII, the ADA, the ADEA, or the EPA need not also allege that he was treated differently because of race, religion, sex, national origin, age, or disability.[6] A charging party who alleges retaliation in violation of the ADA need not be a qualified individual with a disability.[7] Similarly, a charging party who alleges retaliation for protesting discrimination against persons in the protected age group need not be in the protected age group in order to bring an ADEA claim.[8]

A charging party can challenge retaliation by a respondent even if the retaliation occurred after their employment relationship ended.[9] S/he can also challenge retaliation by a respondent based on his/her protected activity involving a different employer, or based on protected activity by someone closely related to or associated with the charging party.[10]

A charging party can bring an ADA retaliation claim against an individual supervisor, as well as an employer. This is because Section 503(a) of the ADA makes it unlawful for a "person" to retaliate against an individual for engaging in protected activity.[11]

8-II. ELEMENTS OF A RETALIATION CLAIM

I. OVERVIEW

a. There are three essential elements of a retaliation claim:

i. opposition to discrimination or participation in covered proceedings

ii. adverse action

iii. causal connection between the protected activity and the adverse action

b. PROTECTED ACTIVITY: OPPOSITION

i. Definition

1. The anti-retaliation provisions make it unlawful to discriminate against an individual because s/he has opposed any practice made unlawful under the employment discrimination statutes.[12] This protection applies if an individual explicitly or implicitly communicates to his or her employer or other covered entity a belief that its activity constitutes a form of employment discrimination that is covered by any of the statutes enforced by the EEOC.
2. While Title VII and the ADEA prohibit retaliation based on opposition to a practice made unlawful by those statutes, the ADA prohibits retaliation based on opposition to "any act or practice made unlawful by this chapter." The referenced chapter prohibits not only disability-based employment discrimination, but also disability discrimination in state and local government services, public accommodations, commercial facilities, and telecommunications. Thus, the ADA prohibits retaliation for opposing not just allegedly discriminatory employment practices but also practices made unlawful by the other titles of the statute.

ii. Examples of Opposition

1. Threatening to file a charge or other formal complaint alleging discrimination
   a. Threatening to file a complaint with the Commission, a state fair employment practices agency, union, court, or any other entity that receives complaints relating to discrimination is a form of opposition.
   b. *Example*—CP tells her manager that if he fails to raise her salary to that of a male coworker who performs the same job, she will file a lawsuit under either the federal Equal Pay Act or under her state's parallel law. This statement constitutes "opposition."
2. Complaining to anyone about alleged discrimination against oneself or others
   a. A complaint or protest about alleged employment discrimination to a manager, union official, co-worker, company EEO official, attorney, newspaper reporter, Congressperson, or anyone else constitutes opposition. Opposition may be nonverbal, such as picketing or engaging in a production slow-down. Furthermore, a complaint on behalf of another, or by an employee's representative, rather than by the employee herself, constitutes protected opposition by both the person who makes the complaint and the person on behalf of whom the complaint is made.
   b. A complaint about an employment practice constitutes protected opposition only if the individual explicitly or implicitly communicates a belief that the practice constitutes unlawful employment discrimination.[13] Because individuals often may not know the specific requirements of the anti-discrimination laws enforced by the EEOC, they may make broad or ambiguous complaints of unfair treatment. Such a protest is protected opposition if the complaint would reasonably have been interpreted as opposition to employment discrimination.
   c. *Example 1*—CP calls the President of R's parent company to protest religious discrimination by R. CP's protest constitutes "opposition."
   d. *Example 2*—CP complains to co-workers about harassment of a disabled employee by a supervisor. This complaint constitutes "opposition."
   e. *Example 3*—CP complains to her foreman about graffiti in her workplace that is derogatory toward women. Although CP does not specify that she believes the graffiti creates a hostile work environment based on sex, her complaint reasonably would have been interpreted by the foreman as opposition to sex discrimination, due to the sex-based content of the graffiti. Her complaint therefore constitutes "opposition."

f. *Example 4*—CP (African-American) requests a wage increase from R, arguing that he deserves to get paid a higher salary. He does not state or suggest a belief that he is being subjected to wage discrimination based on race. There also is no basis to conclude that R would reasonably have interpreted his complaint as opposition to race discrimination because the challenged unfairness could have been based on any of several reasons. CP's protest therefore does not constitute protected "opposition."

3. Refusing to obey an order because of a reasonable belief that it is discriminatory

a. Refusal to obey an order constitutes protected opposition if the individual reasonably believes that the order requires him or her to carry out unlawful employment discrimination.

b. *Example*—CP works for an employment agency. His manager instructs him not to refer any African-Americans to a particular client, based on the client's request. CP refuses to obey the order and refers an African-American applicant to that client. CP's action constitutes "opposition."

c. Refusal to obey an order also constitutes protected opposition if the individual reasonably believes that the order makes discrimination a term or condition of employment. For example, in one case a court recognized that a correction officer's refusal to cooperate with the defendant's practice of allowing white but not black inmates to shower after work shifts constituted protected opposition. Even if the inmates were not "employees," the plaintiff could show that his enforcement of the policy made race discrimination a term or condition of his employment. Thus, his refusal to obey the order constituted opposition to an unlawful employment practice.[14]

4. Requesting reasonable accommodation or religious accommodation

a. A request for reasonable accommodation of a disability constitutes protected activity under Section 503 of the ADA. Although a person making such a request might not literally "oppose" discrimination or "participate" in the administrative or judicial complaint process, s/he is protected against retaliation for making the request.

b. As one court stated, "It would seem anomalous . . . to think Congress intended no retaliation protection for employees who request a reasonable accommodation unless they also file a formal charge. This would leave employees unprotected if an employer granted the accommodation and shortly thereafter terminated the employee in retaliation."[15]

c. By the same rationale, persons requesting religious accommodation under Title VII are protected against retaliation for making such requests.

iii. Standards Governing Application of the Opposition Clause

1. Although the opposition clause in each of the EEO statutes is broad, it does not protect every protest against job discrimination. The following principles apply:

a. Manner of Opposition Must Be Reasonable

i. The manner in which an individual protests perceived employment discrimination must be reasonable in order for the anti-retaliation provisions to apply. In applying a "reasonableness" standard, courts and the Commission balance the right of individuals to oppose employment discrimination and the public's interest in enforcement of the EEO laws against an employer's need for a stable and productive work environment.

ii. Public criticism of alleged discrimination may be a reasonable form of opposition. Courts have protected an employee's right to inform an employer's customers about the employer's alleged discrimination, as well as the right to engage in peaceful picketing to oppose allegedly discriminatory employment practices.[16]

iii. On the other hand, courts have found that the following activities were not reasonable and thus not protected: searching and photocopying confidential documents relating to alleged ADEA discrimination and showing them to co-workers;[17] making an overwhelming number of complaints based on unsupported allegations and bypassing the chain of command in bringing the complaints;[18] and badgering a subordinate employee to give a witness statement in support of an EEOC charge and attempting to coerce her to change her statement.[19] Similarly, unlawful activities, such as acts or threats of violence to life or property, are not protected.

iv. If an employee's protests against allegedly discriminatory employment practices interfere with job performance to the extent that they render him or her ineffective in the job, the retaliation provisions do not immunize the worker from appropriate discipline or discharge.[20] Opposition to perceived discrimination does not serve as license for the employee to neglect job duties.

b. Opposition Need Only Be Based on Reasonable and Good Faith Belief

i. A person is protected against retaliation for opposing perceived discrimination if s/he had a reasonable and good faith belief that the opposed practices were unlawful. Thus, it is well settled that a violation of the retaliation provision can be found whether or not the challenged practice ultimately is found to be unlawful.[21] As one court has stated, requiring a finding of actual illegality would "undermine[] Title VII's central purpose, the elimination of employment discrimination by informal means; destroy[] one of the chief means of achieving that purpose, the frank and non-disruptive exchange of ideas between employers and employees; and serve[] no redeeming statutory or policy purposes of its own."[22]

ii. *Example 1*—CP complains to her office manager that her supervisor failed to promote her because of her gender. (She believes that sex discrimination occurred because she was qualified for the promotion and the supervisor promoted a male instead.) CP has engaged in protected opposition regardless of whether the promotion decision was in fact discriminatory because she had a reasonable and good faith belief that discrimination occurred.

iii. *Example 2*— Same as above, except the job sought by CP was in accounting and required a CPA license, which CP lacked and the selectee had. CP knew that it was necessary to have a CPA license to perform this job. CP has not engaged in protected opposition because she did not have a reasonable and good faith belief that she was rejected because of sex discrimination.

c. Person Claiming Retaliation Need Not Be the Person Who Engaged in Opposition

i. Title VII, the ADEA, the EPA, and the ADA prohibit retaliation against someone so closely related to or associated with the person exercising his or her statutory rights that it would discourage that person from pursuing those rights.[23] For example, it is unlawful to retaliate against an employee because his son, who is also an employee, opposed allegedly unlawful employment practices. Retaliation against a close relative of an individual who opposed discrimination can be challenged by both the individual who engaged in protected activity and the relative, where both are employees. See Section 8-II C.3. for discussion of similar principle under "participation" clause.

d. Practices Opposed Need Not Have Been Engaged in by the Named Respondent

i. There is no requirement that the entity charged with retaliation be the same as the entity whose allegedly discriminatory practices were opposed by the charging party. For example, a violation would be found if a respondent refused to hire the charging party because it was aware that she opposed her previous employer's allegedly discriminatory practices.

c. PROTECTED ACTIVITY: PARTICIPATION

i. Definition

1. The anti-retaliation provisions make it unlawful to discriminate against any individual because s/he has made a charge, testified, assisted, or participated in any manner in an investigation, proceeding, hearing, or litigation under Title VII, the ADEA, the EPA, or the ADA. This protection applies to individuals challenging employment discrimination under the statutes enforced by EEOC in EEOC proceedings, in state administrative or court proceedings, as well as in federal court proceedings, and to individuals who testify or otherwise participate in such proceedings.[24] Protection under the participation clause extends to those who file untimely charges. In the federal sector, once a federal employee initiates contact with an EEO counselor, (s)he is engaging in "participation."[25]

ii. Participation Is Protected Regardless of Whether the Allegations in the Original Charge Were Valid or Reasonable

1. The anti-discrimination statutes do not limit or condition in any way the protection against retaliation for participating in the charge process. While the opposition clause applies only to those who protest practices that they reasonably and in good faith believe are unlawful, the participation clause applies to all individuals who participate in the statutory complaint process. Thus, courts have consistently held that a respondent is liable for retaliating against an individual for filing an EEOC charge regardless of the validity or reasonableness of the charge.[26] To permit an employer to retaliate against a charging party based on its unilateral determination that the charge was unreasonable or otherwise unjustified would chill the rights of all individuals protected by the anti-discrimination statutes.

iii. Person Claiming Retaliation Need Not Be the Person Who Engaged in Participation

1. The retaliation provisions of Title VII, the ADEA, the EPA, and the ADA prohibit retaliation against someone so closely related to or associated with the person exercising his or her statutory rights that it would discourage or prevent the person from pursuing those rights. For example, it would be unlawful for a respondent to retaliate against an employee because his or her spouse, who is also an employee, filed an EEOC charge.[27] Both spouses, in such circumstances, could bring retaliation claims.

iv. The Practices Challenged in Prior or Pending Statutory Proceedings Need Not Have Been Engaged in by the Named Respondent

1. An individual is protected against retaliation for participation in employment discrimination proceedings even if those proceedings involved a different entity.[28] For example, a violation would be found if a respondent refused to hire the charging party because it was aware that she filed an EEOC charge against her former employer.

d. ADVERSE ACTION

i. General Types of Adverse Actions

The most obvious types of retaliation are denial of promotion, refusal to hire, denial of job benefits, demotion, suspension, and discharge. Other types of adverse actions include threats, reprimands, negative evaluations, harassment, or other adverse treatment.

Suspending or limiting access to an internal grievance procedure also constitutes an "adverse action." For example, in EEOC v. Board of Governors of State Colleges & Universities,[29] a university's collective bargaining agreement provided for a specific internal grievance procedure leading to arbitration. The agreement further provided that this procedure could be terminated if the employee sought resolution in any other forum, such as the EEOC. The Seventh Circuit ruled that termination of the grievance process constituted an adverse employment action in violation of the anti-retaliation clause of the ADEA.[30]

ii. Adverse Actions Can Occur After the Employment Relationship Between the Charging Party and Respondent Has Ended

In Robinson v. Shell Oil Company,[31] the Supreme Court unanimously held that Title VII prohibits respondents from retaliating against former employees as well as current employees for participating in any proceeding under Title VII or opposing any practice made unlawful by that Act. The plaintiff in Robinson alleged that his former employer gave him a negative job reference in retaliation for his having filed an EEOC charge against it. Some courts previously had held that former employees could not challenge retaliation that occurred after their employment had ended because Title VII, the ADEA, and the EPA prohibit retaliation against "any employee."[32] However, the Supreme Court stated that coverage of post-employment retaliation is more consistent with the broader context of the statute and with the statutory purpose of maintaining unfettered access to the statute's remedial mechanisms. The Court's holding applies to each of the statutes enforced by the EEOC because of the similar language and common purpose of the anti-retaliation provisions.

Examples of post-employment retaliation include actions that are designed to interfere with the individual's prospects for employment, such as giving an unjustified negative job reference, refusing to provide a job reference, and informing an individual's prospective employer about the individual's protected activity.[33] However, a negative job reference about an individual who engaged in protected activity does not constitute unlawful retaliation unless the reference was based on a retaliatory motive. The truthfulness of the information in the reference may serve as a defense unless there is proof of pretext, such as evidence that the former employer routinely declines to offer information about its former employees' job performance and violated that policy with regard to an individual who engaged in protected activity. See Section 8-II E. below.

Retaliatory acts designed to interfere with an individual's prospects for employment are unlawful regardless of whether they cause a prospective employer to refrain from hiring the individual.[34] As the Third Circuit stated, "an employer who retaliates cannot escape liability merely because the retaliation falls short of its intended result."[35] However, the fact that the reference did not affect the individual's job prospects may affect the relief that is due.

iii. Adverse Actions Need Not Qualify as "Ultimate Employment Actions" or Materially Affect the Terms or Conditions of Employment to Constitute Retaliation.

Some courts have held that the retaliation provisions apply only to retaliation that takes the form of ultimate employment actions.[36] Others have construed the provisions more broadly, but have required that the action materially affect the terms, conditions, or privileges of employment.[37]

The Commission disagrees with those decisions and concludes that such constructions are unduly restrictive. The statutory retaliation clauses prohibit any adverse treatment that is based on a retaliatory motive and is reasonably likely to deter the charging party or others from engaging in protected activity. Of course, petty slights and trivial annoyances are not actionable, as they are not likely to deter protected activity. More significant retaliatory treatment, however, can be challenged regardless of the level of harm. As the Ninth Circuit has stated, the degree of harm suffered by the individual "goes to the issue of damages, not liability."[38]

Example 1—CP filed a charge alleging that he was racially harassed by his supervisor and co-workers. After learning about the charge, CP's manager asked two employees to keep CP under surveillance and report back about his activities. The surveillance constitutes an "adverse action" that is likely to deter protected activity, and is unlawful if it was conducted because of CP's protected activity.

Example 2—CP filed a charge alleging that she was denied a promotion because of her gender. One week later, her supervisor invited a few employees out to lunch. CP believed that the reason he excluded her was because of her EEOC charge. Even if the supervisor chose not to invite CP because of her charge, this would not constitute unlawful retaliation because it is not reasonably likely to deter protected activity.

Example 3—Same as Example 2, except that CP's supervisor invites all employees in CP's unit to regular weekly lunches. The supervisor excluded CP from these lunches after she filed the sex discrimination charge. If CP was excluded because of her charge, this would constitute unlawful retaliation since it could reasonably deter CP or others from engaging in protected activity.

The Commission's position is based on statutory language and policy considerations. The anti-retaliation provisions are exceptionally broad. They make it unlawful "to discriminate" against an individual because of his or her protected activity. This is in contrast to the general anti-discrimination provisions which make it unlawful to discriminate with respect to an individual's "terms, conditions, or privileges of employment." The retaliation provisions set no qualifiers on the term "to discriminate," and therefore prohibit any discrimination that is reasonably likely to deter protected activity.[39] They do not restrict the actions that can be challenged to those that affect the terms and conditions of employment.[40] Thus, a violation will be found if an employer retaliates against a worker for engaging in protected activity through threats,[41] harassment in or out of the workplace, or any other adverse treatment that is reasonably likely to deter protected activity by that individual or other employees.[42]

This broad view of coverage accords with the primary purpose of the anti-retaliation provisions, which is to "[m]aintain[] unfettered access to statutory remedial mechanisms."[43] Regardless of the degree or quality of harm to the particular complainant, retaliation harms the public interest by deterring others from filing a charge.[44] An interpretation of Title VII that permits some forms of retaliation to go unpunished would undermine the effectiveness of the EEO statutes and conflict with the language and purpose of the anti-retaliation provisions.

e. PROOF OF CAUSAL CONNECTION

i. In order to establish unlawful retaliation, there must be proof that the respondent took an adverse action because the charging party engaged in protected activity. Proof of this retaliatory motive can be through direct or circumstantial evidence. The evidentiary framework that applies to other types of discrimination claims also applies to retaliation claims.

ii. Direct Evidence

1. If there is credible direct evidence that retaliation was a motive for the challenged action, "cause" should be found. Evidence as to any legitimate motive for the challenged action would be relevant only to relief, not to liability.[45]

2. Direct evidence of a retaliatory motive is any written or verbal statement by a respondent official that s/he undertook the challenged action because the charging party engaged in protected activity. Such evidence also includes a written or oral statement by a respondent

official that on its face demonstrates a bias toward the charging party based on his or her protected activity, along with evidence linking that bias to the adverse action. Such a link could be shown if the statement was made by the decision-maker at the time of the adverse action.[46] Direct evidence of retaliation is rare.

3. *Example*—CP filed a charge against Respondent A, alleging that her supervisor sexually harassed and constructively discharged her. CP subsequently sued A and reached a settlement. When CP applied for a new job with Respondent B, she received a conditional offer subject to a reference check. When B called CP's former supervisor at A Co. for a reference, the supervisor said that CP was a "troublemaker," started a sex harassment lawsuit, and was not anyone B "would want to get mixed up with." B did not hire CP. She suspected that her former supervisor gave her a negative reference and filed retaliation charges against A and B. The EEOC investigator discovered notes memorializing the phone conversation between A and B. These notes are direct evidence of retaliation by A because they prove on their face that A told B about CP's protected activity and that A gave CP a negative reference because of that protected activity. These notes are not direct evidence of retaliation by B because they do not directly prove that B rejected CP because of her protected activity. However, the fact that B gave CP a conditional job offer and then decided not to hire her after learning about her protected activity is strong circumstantial evidence of B's retaliation. (See Section 8-II E.2. below.)

iii. Circumstantial Evidence

1. The most common method of proving that retaliation was the reason for an adverse action is through circumstantial evidence. A violation is established if there is circumstantial evidence raising an inference of retaliation and if the respondent fails to produce evidence of a legitimate, non-retaliatory reason for the challenged action, or if the reason advanced by the respondent is a pretext to hide the retaliatory motive.

2. Circumstantial Evidence of Retaliation
   a. Evidence raises inference that retaliation was the cause of the challenged action;
   b. Respondent produces evidence of a legitimate, non-retaliatory reason for the challenged action; and
   c. Complainant proves that the reason advanced by the respondent is a pretext to hide the retaliatory motive.

3. An initial inference of retaliation arises where there is proof that the protected activity and the adverse action were related.[47] Typically, the link is demonstrated by evidence that:
   a. the adverse action occurred shortly after the protected activity, and
   b. the person who undertook the adverse action was aware of the complainant's protected activity before taking the action.

4. An inference of retaliation may arise even if the time period between the protected activity and the adverse action was long, if there is other evidence that raises an inference of retaliation. For example, in Shirley v. Chrysler First, Inc.,[48] a 14-month interval between the plaintiff's filing of an EEOC charge and her termination did not conclusively disprove retaliation where the plaintiff's manager mentioned the EEOC charge at least twice a week during the interim and termination occurred just two months after the EOC dismissed her charge.[49]

5. Common non-retaliatory reasons offered by respondents for challenged actions include: poor job performance; inadequate qualifications for the position sought; violation of work rules or insubordination; and, with regard to negative job references, truthfulness of the information in the reference. For example, in one case, the plaintiff claimed that she was

discharged for retaliatory reasons but the employer produced unrebutted evidence that she was discharged because of her excessive absenteeism.[50] In another case, the plaintiff alleged that his former employer's negative job reference was retaliatory, but the defendant established that the evaluation was based on the former supervisor's personal observation of the plaintiff during his employment and contemporary business records documenting those observations.[51]

6. Even if the respondent produces evidence of a legitimate, nondiscriminatory reason for the challenged action, a violation will still be found if this explanation is a pretext designed to hide the true retaliatory motive. Typically, pretext is proved through evidence that the respondent treated the complainant differently from similarly situated employees or that the respondent's explanation for the adverse action is not believable. Pretext can also be shown if the respondent subjected the charging party's work performance to heightened scrutiny after she engaged in protected activity.[52]
7. *Example 1*—CP alleges that R denied her a promotion because she opposed the underrepresentation of women in management jobs and was therefore viewed as a "troublemaker." The promotion went to another female employee. R asserts that the selectee was better qualified for the job because she had a Masters in Business Administration, while CP only had a college degree. The EEOC investigator finds that this explanation is pretextual because CP has significantly greater experience working at R Company and experience has always been the most important criterion for selection for management jobs.
8. *Example 2*—CP alleges that R gave him a negative job reference because he had filed an EEOC charge. R produces evidence that its negative statements to CP's prospective employer were honest assessments of CP's job performance. There is no proof of pretext, and therefore the investigator finds no retaliation.
9. *Example 3*—Same as Example 2, except there is evidence that R routinely declines to offer information about former employees' job performance. R fails to offer a credible explanation for why it violated this policy with regard to CP. Therefore, pretext is found.

8-III. SPECIAL REMEDIES ISSUES

I. TEMPORARY OR PRELIMINARY RELIEF

Section 706(f)(2) of Title VII authorizes the Commission to seek temporary injunctive relief before final disposition of a charge when a preliminary investigation indicates that prompt judicial action is necessary to carry out the purposes of Title VII. Section 107 of the ADA incorporates this provision. The ADEA and the EPA do not authorize a court to give interim relief pending resolution of an EEOC charge. However, the EEOC can seek such relief as part of a lawsuit for permanent relief, pursuant to Rule 65 of the Federal Rules of Civil Procedure.

Temporary or preliminary relief allows a court to stop retaliation before it occurs or continues. Such relief is appropriate if there is a substantial likelihood that the challenged action will be found to constitute unlawful retaliation, and if the charging party and/or the EEOC will likely suffer irreparable harm because of the retaliation. Although courts have ruled that financial hardships are not irreparable, other harms that accompany loss of a job may be irreparable. For example, in one case forced retirees showed irreparable harm and qualified for a preliminary injunction where they lost work and future prospects for work, consequently suffering emotional distress, depression, a contracted social life, and other related harms.[53] A temporary injunction also is appropriate if the respondent's retaliation will likely cause irreparable harm to the Commission's ability to investigate the charging party's original charge of discrimination. For example, the retaliation may discourage others from providing testimony or from filing additional charges based on the same or other alleged unlawful acts.[54]

The intake officer or investigator should notify the Regional Attorney when a charge of retaliation is filed and where temporary or preliminary relief may be appropriate.[55]

II. COMPENSATORY AND PUNITIVE DAMAGES

a. Availability of Damages for Retaliation Under ADEA and EPA

A 1977 amendment to the Fair Labor Standards Act authorizes both legal and equitable relief for retaliation claims under that Act.[56] Compensatory and punitive damages therefore are available for retaliation claims brought under the EPA and the ADEA, as well as under Title VII and the ADA.[57] The compensatory and punitive damages obtained under the EPA and the ADEA are not subject to statutory caps.

b. Appropriateness of Punitive Damages

Proven retaliation frequently constitutes a practice undertaken "with malice or with reckless indifference to the federally protected rights of an aggrieved individual." Therefore, punitive damages often will be appropriate in retaliation claims brought under any of the statutes enforced by the EEOC.[58] Section 503(a) of the ADA, 42 U.S.C. § 12203(a). Section 503 (b) of the ADA, 42 U.S.C.12203(b), further provides that it is unlawful "to coerce, intimidate, threaten, or interfere with any individual in the exercise or enjoyment of, or on account of his or her having exercised or enjoyed, or on account of his or her having aided or encouraged any other individual in the exercise or enjoyment of, any right granted or protected by this chapter."

NOTES

1. Section 704(a) of Title VII, 42 U.S.C. § 2000e-3(a).
2. Section 4(d) of the ADEA, 29 U.S.C. § 623(d).
3. Section 503(a) of the ADA, 42 U.S.C. § 12203(a). Section 503 (b) of the ADA, 42 U.S.C.12203(b), further provides that it is unlawful "to coerce, intimidate, threaten, or interfere with an individual in the exercise or enjoyment of, or on account of his or her having exercised or enjoyed, or on account of his or her having aided or encouraged any other individual in the exercise or enjoyment of, any right granted or protected by this chapter."
4. Section 15(a)(3) of the Fair Labor Standards Act (FLSA), 29 U.S.C. § 215(a)(3).
5. Federal employees are also protected against retaliation under each of the employment discrimination statutes. See, e.g., Hale v. Marsh, 808 F.2d 616, 619 (7th Cir. 1986) (recognizing retaliation cause of action for federal employees under Title VII); Bornholdt v. Brady, 869 F.2d 57, 62 (2d Cir. 1989) (recognizing retaliation cause of action for federal employees under ADEA).
6. Where it appears that a charging party's allegation of unlawful retaliation may also be subject to the jurisdiction of another federal agency or a state or local government, s/he should be referred promptly to the appropriate office. For example, if the charging party is covered by a collective bargaining agreement and is a member of the union, s/he should be referred to the NLRB to be counseled on unlawful retaliation under the National Labor Relations Act. Non-payment of overtime pay should be directed to the Department of Labor, Wage and Hour Division. The EEOC office should proceed with its investigation of allegations under its jurisdiction, and refer to any applicable memorandum of understanding or coordination rule with the agency that also has jurisdiction over the matter.
7. Krouse v. American Sterilizer, 126 F.3d 494 (3d Cir. 1997).
8. Anderson v. Phillips Petroleum, 722 F. Supp. 668, 671-72 (D. Kan. 1989).
9. See Section 8-II D.
10. See Section 8-II B and C.
11. Ostrach v. Regents of University of California, 957 F. Supp. 196 (E.D. Ca. 1997) (individual can be sued for retaliation under section 503 of ADA).

12. The anti-retaliation provision of the Fair Labor Standards Act, which applies to the Equal Pay Act, does not contain a specific "opposition" clause. However, courts have recognized that the statute prohibits retaliation based on opposition to allegedly unlawful practices. See, e.g., EEOC v. Romeo Community Sch., 976 F.2d 985, 989-90 (6th Cir. 1992); EEOC v. White & Son Enterprises, 881 F.2d 1006, 1011 (11th Cir. 1989). Contra Lambert v. Genessee Hospital, 10 F.3d 46, 55 (2d Cir. 1993), cert. denied, 511 U.S. 1052 (1994).
13. See, e.g., Barber v. CSX Distrib. Services, 68 F.3d 694 (3d Cir. 1995) (plaintiff's letter to defendant's human resources department complaining about unfair treatment and expressing dissatisfaction that job he sought went to a less qualified individual did not constitute ADEA opposition because letter did not explicitly or implicitly allege that age was reason for alleged unfairness).
14. Moyo v. Gomez, 40 F.3d 982 (9th Cir. 1994), cert. denied, 513 U.S. 1081 (1995).
15. Soileau v. Guilford of Maine, 105 F.3d 12, 16 (1st Cir. 1997). See also Garza v. Abbott Laboratories, 940 F. Supp. 1227, 1294 (N.D. Ill. 1996) (plaintiff engaged in statutorily protected expression by requesting accommodation for her disability). The courts in Soileau and Garza only considered whether accommodation requests fall within the opposition or participation clause in Section 503(a) of the ADA. Note, however, that Section 503(b) more broadly makes it unlawful to interfere with "the exercise or enjoyment of . . . any right granted or protected" by the statute.
16. See, e.g., Sumner v. United States Postal Service, 899 F.2d 203 (2d Cir. 1990) (practices protected by opposition clause include writing letters to customers criticizing employer's alleged discrimination).
17. O'Day v. McDonnell Douglas Helicopter Co., 79 F.3d 756 (9th Cir. 1996).
18. Rollins v. Florida Dep't of Law Enforcement, 868 F.2d 397 (11th Cir.1989).
19. Jackson v. St. Joseph State Hospital, 840 F.2d 1387 (8th Cir.), cert. denied, 488 U.S. 892 (1988).
20. See, e.g., Coutu v. Martin County Bd. of Comm'rs, 47 F.3d 1068, 1074 (11th Cir. 1995) (no retaliation found where plaintiff was criticized by her supervisor not because she was opposing discrimination but because she was spending an inordinate amount of time in "employee advocacy" activities and was not completing other aspects of her personnel job).
21. This standard has been adopted by every circuit that has considered the issue. See, e.g., Little v. United Technologies, 103 F.3d 956, 960 (11th Cir. 1997), and Trent v. Valley Electric Association, Inc., 41 F.3d 524, 526 (9th Cir. 1994).
22. Berg v. La Crosse Cooler Co., 612 F.2d 1041, 1045 (7th Cir. 1980).
23. See, e.g., Murphy v. Cadillac Rubber & Plastics, Inc., 946 F. Supp. 1108, 1118 (W.D. N.Y. 1996) (plaintiff stated claim of retaliation where he was subjected to adverse action based on his wife's protected activities).
24. The participation clause protects those who testify in an employment discrimination case about their own discriminatory conduct, even if such testimony is involuntary. For example, in Merritt v. Dillard Paper Co. 120 F.3d 1181 (11th Cir.1997), the defendant fired the plaintiff after he reluctantly testified in his co-worker's Title VII case about workplace sexual activities in which he participated. The president of the defendant company told the plaintiff at the time of his termination that his testimony was "the most damning" to the defendant's case. The court found that this comment constituted direct evidence of retaliation.
25. Hashimoto v. Dalton, 118 F.3d 671, 680 (9th Cir. 1997).
26. See, e.g., Wyatt v. Boston, 35 F.3d 13, 15 (1st Cir. 1994).
27. See, e.g., EEOC v. Ohio Edison Co., 7 F.3d 541, 544 (6th Cir. 1993) (agreeing that plaintiff's allegation of reprisal for relative's protected activities states claim under Title VII); Thurman v. Robertshaw Control Co., 869 F. Supp. 934, 941 (N.D. Ga. 1994) (plaintiff could make out first element of prima facie case of retaliation by showing that plaintiff's close relative participated in the complaint process).

    The Commission disagrees with the Fifth Circuit's holding in Holt v. JTM Indus., 89 F.3d 1224 (5th Cir. 1996), cert. denied, 117 S.Ct. 1821 (1997), that there was no unlawful retaliation where the plaintiff was put on paid administrative leave because his wife had filed an age discrimination charge.
28. See, e.g., Christopher v. Stouder Memorial Hosp., 936 F.2d 870, 873-74 (6th Cir.) (defendant's frequent reference to plaintiff's sex discrimination action against prior employer warranted inference that defendant's refusal to hire was retaliatory), cert. denied, 502 U.S. 1013 (1991).

29. 957 F.2d 424 (7th Cir.), cert. denied, 506 U.S. 906 (1992).
30. See also Johnson v. Palma, 931 F.2d 203 (2d Cir. 1991) (union's refusal to proceed with plaintiff's grievance after he filed race discrimination complaint with state agency constituted unlawful retaliation).
31. ___ U.S. ___, 117 S. Ct. 843 (1997).
32. The ADA, unlike the other anti-discrimination statutes, prohibits retaliation against "any individual" who has opposed discrimination based on disability or participated in the charge process. 42 U.S.C. § 12203.
33. See, e.g., EEOC v. L. B. Foster, 123 F.3d 746 (3d Cir. 1997), cert. denied, 66 U.S. L.W. 3388 (U.S. March 2, 1998); Ruedlinger v. Jarrett, 106 F.3d 212 (7th Cir. 1997).
34. Hashimoto v. Dalton, 118 F.3d 671, 676 (9th Cir. 1997).
35. EEOC v. L. B. Foster, 123 F.3d at 754.
36. See Ledergerber v. Stangler, 122 F.3d 1142 (8th Cir. 1997) (reassignment of plaintiff's staff, with attendant loss of status, did not rise to level of ultimate employment decision to constitute actionable retaliation); Mattern v. Eastman Kodak Co.,104 F.3d 702 (5th Cir.) (anti-retaliation provisions only bar "ultimate employment actions" that are retaliatory; harassment, reprimands, and poor evaluation could not be challenged), cert. denied, 118 S. Ct. 336 (1997).
37. See, e.g., Munday v. Waste Management of North America, 126 F.3d 239 (4th Cir. 1997) (employer's instruction to workers to shun plaintiff who had engaged in protected activity, to spy on her, and to report back to management whatever she said to them did not adversely affect plaintiff's terms, condition, or benefits of employment and therefore could not be challenged), cert. denied, 118 S. Ct. 1053 (1998).
38. Hashimoto, 118 F.3d at 676. See also EEOC v. L. B. Foster, 123 F.3d at 754 n.4 (plaintiff need not prove that retaliatory denial of job reference caused prospective employer to reject her; such a showing is relevant only to damages, not liability); Smith v. Secretary of Navy, 659 F.2d 1113, 1120 (D.C. Cir. 1981) ("the questions of statutory violation and appropriate statutory remedy are conceptually distinct. An illegal act of discrimination—whether based on race or some other factor such as a motive of reprisal—is a wrong in itself under Title VII, regardless of whether that wrong would warrant an award of [damages]").
39. See, e.g., Knox v. State of Indiana, 93 F.3d 1327, 1334 (7th Cir. 1996) ("[t]here is nothing in the law of retaliation that restricts the type of retaliatory act that might be visited upon an employee who seeks to invoke her rights by filing a complaint"); Passer v. American Chemical Society, 935 F.2d 322, 331 (D.C. Cir. 1991) (Section 704(a) broadly prohibits an employer from discriminating against its employees in any way for engaging in protected activity and does not "limit its reach only to acts of retaliation that take the form of cognizable employment actions such as discharge, transfer or demotion").
40. Even if there were a requirement that the challenged action affect the terms or conditions of employment, retaliatory acts that create a hostile work environment would meet that standard since, as the Supreme Court has made clear, the terms and condition of employment include the intangible work environment. Meritor Savings Bank v. Vinson, 477 U.S. 57, 64-67 (1986). For examples of cases recognizing that retaliatory harassment is unlawful, see DeAngelis v. El Paso Municipal Police Officers Ass'n., 51 F.3d 591 (5th Cir.), cert. denied, 116 S. Ct. 473 (1995); Davis v. Tri-State Mack Distributor, 981 F.2d 340 (8th Cir. 1992).
41. See McKnight v. General Motors Corp., 908 F.2d 104, 111 (7th Cir. 1990) "[r]etaliation or a threat of retaliation is a common method of deterrence"), cert. denied, 499 U.S. 919 (1991); Garcia v. Lawn, 805 F.2d 1400, 1401-02 (9th Cir. 1986) (threatened transfer to undesirable location); Atkinson v. Oliver T. Carr Co., 40 FEP Cases (BNA) 1041, 1043-44 (D.D.C. 1986) (threat to press criminal complaint).
42. For examples of cases finding unlawful retaliation based on adverse actions that did not affect the terms or conditions of employment, see Hashimoto, 118 F.3d at 675-76 (retaliatory job reference violated Title VII even though it did not cause failure to hire); Berry v. Stevinson Chevrolet, 74 F.3d 980, 986 (10th Cir. 1996) (instigating criminal theft and forgery charges against former employee

who filed EEOC charge found retaliatory); Passer, 935 F.2d at 331 (canceling symposium in honor of retired employee who filed ADEA charge found retaliatory).

43. Robinson v. Shell Oil Co., 117 S. Ct. 843, 848 (1997).
44. Garcia, 805 F.2d at 1405.
45. The basis for finding "cause" whenever there is credible direct evidence of a retaliatory motive is Section 107 of the 1991 Civil Rights Act, 42 U.S.C. §§ 2000e-2(m) and 2000e-5(g)(2)(B). Section 107 provides that an unlawful employment practice is established whenever race, color, religion, sex, or national origin was a motivating factor, even though other factors also motivated the practice. It further provides that a complainant who makes such a showing can obtain declaratory relief, injunctive relief, and attorneys fees but no damages or reinstatement if the respondent proves that it would have taken the same action even absent the discrimination. Section 107 partially overrules Price Waterhouse v. Hopkins, 490 U.S. 228 (1989), which held that a respondent can avoid liability for intentional discrimination in mixed-motives cases if it can prove that it would have made the same decision in the absence of the discrimination.

    Some courts have ruled that Section 107 does not apply to retaliation claims. See, e.g., Woodson v. Scott Paper, 109 F.3d 913 (3d Cir.), cert. denied, 118 S. Ct. 299 (1997). Those courts apply Price Waterhouse v. Hopkins, and therefore absolve the employer of liability for proven retaliation if the establishes that it would have made the same decision in the absence of retaliation. Other courts have applied Section 107 to retaliation claims. See, e.g., Merritt v. Dillard Paper Co., 120 F.3d 1181, 1191 (11th Cir. 1997).

    The Commission concludes that Section 107 applies to retaliation. Courts have long held that the evidentiary framework for proving employment discrimination based on race, sex, or other protected class status also applies to claims of discrimination based on retaliation. Furthermore, an interpretation of Section 107 that permits proven retaliation to go unpunished undermines the purpose of the anti-retaliation provisions of maintaining unfettered access to the statutory remedial mechanism.
46. For example, in Merritt v. Dillard Paper Company, 120 F.3d 1181 (11th Cir. 1997), the plaintiff testified in a co-worker's Title VII action about sexual harassment in the workplace. Shortly after the case was settled, the president of the company fired the plaintiff. The court found direct evidence of retaliation based on the president's statement to the plaintiff, "[y]our deposition was the most damning to Dillard's case, and you no longer have a place here at Dillard Paper Company."
47. Simmons v. Camden County Bd. of Educ., 757 F.2d 1187, 1189 (11th Cir.), cert. denied, 474 U.S. 981 (1985).
48. 970 F.2d 39 (5th Cir. 1992).
49. See Kachmar v. Sunguard Data Systems, 109 F.3d 173 (3d Cir. 1997) (district court erroneously dismissed plaintiff's retaliation claim because termination occurred nearly one year after her protected activity; when there may be reasons why adverse action was not taken immediately, absence of immediacy does not disprove causation).
50. Miller v. Vesta, Inc., 946 F. Supp. 697 (E.D. Wis. 1996).
51. Fields v. Phillips School of Business & Tech., 870 F. Supp. 149 (W.D. Tex.), aff'd mem., 59 F.3d 1242 (5th Cir. 1994).
52. See, e.g., Hossaini v. Western Missouri Medical Center, 97 F.3d 1085 (8th Cir. 1996) (reasonable person could infer that defendant's explanation for plaintiff's discharge was pretextual where defendant launched investigation into allegedly improper conduct by plaintiff shortly after she engaged in protected activity).
53. EEOC v. Chrysler Corp., 733 F.2d 1183, 1186 (6th Cir.), reh'g denied, 738 F.2d 167 (1984). See also EEOC v. City of Bowling Green, Kentucky, 607 F. Supp. 524 (D. Ky. 1985) (granting preliminary injunction preventing defendant from mandatorily retiring policy department employee because of his age; although plaintiff could have collected back pay and been reinstated at later time, he would have suffered from inability to keep up with current matters in police department and would have suffered anxiety or emotional problems due to compulsory retirement).
54. See, e.g., Garcia v. Lawn, 805 F.2d 1400, 1405-06 (9th Cir. 1986) (chilling effect of retaliation on other employee's willingness to exercise their rights or testify for plaintiff constitutes irreparable harm).

55. 29 C.F.R. § 1601.23 sets forth procedures for seeking preliminary or temporary relief. Section 13.1 of Volume I of the EEOC Compliance Manual sets forth procedures for selecting, developing, and obtaining approval of such cases.
56. 29 U.S.C. § 216(b).
57. See Moskowitz v. Trustees of Purdue University, 5 F.3d 279 (7th Cir. 1993) (FLSA amendment allows common law damages in addition to back wages and liquidated damages where plaintiff is retaliated against for exercising his rights under the ADEA); Soto v. Adams Elevator Equip. Co., 941 F.2d 543 (7th Cir. 1991) (FLSA amendment authorizes compensatory and punitive damages for retaliation claims under the EPA, in addition to lost wages and liquidated damages).
58. See Kim v. Nash Finch Co., 123 F.3d 1046 (8th Cir. 1997) (evidence of retaliation supported jury finding of reckless indifference to plaintiff's rights; although $7 million award for punitive damages was excessive, district court's lowered award of $300,000 was not).

Disclosure to Applicant Regarding Consumer Reports

You have applied to [Insert Company Name] (the "Company") for employment. The Company may obtain consumer reports about you from a consumer reporting agency or agencies and may use the reports in deciding whether to hire you.

If you are hired by the Company, the Company may obtain consumer reports about you from time to time. The Company may use the reports in deciding whether to retain you, promote you, reassign you, or for other employment purposes.

AUTHORIZATION

I understand that the Company may not obtain consumer reports about me unless I authorize it to do so.

I also understand that if I refuse to give the Company authorization to obtain consumer reports my application for employment will not be considered.

(Instructions to Applicant: Check one box below.)

❑ I authorize the Company to obtain consumer reports about me.

❑ I do not authorize the Company to obtain consumer reports about me.

Date: ____

Signature of Applicant: ______________________________

Name—Please Print: ________________________________

APPENDIX 8D

Disclosure to Employee Regarding Consumer Reports

From time to time, [Insert Company Name] (the "Company") may obtain consumer reports about employees from a consumer reporting agency or agencies. The Company may use the reports in deciding whether to retain you, promote you, reassign you, or for other employment purposes.

AUTHORIZATION

I understand that the Company may not obtain consumer reports about me unless I authorize it to do so.

I understand that failing to authorize the Company to obtain consumer reports about me may affect my continued or future employment.

(Instructions to Employee: Check one box below.)

❑ I authorize the Company to obtain consumer reports about me.

❑ I do not authorize the Company to obtain consumer reports about me.

Date: ____

Signature of Employee: ________________________________

Name—Please Print: __________________________________

Sample Notice of Intent to Obtain an Investigative Consumer Report

[Letterhead]

Date

Applicant/Employee's Name

Address

RE: Notice of Request for Investigative Consumer Report

Dear ______________________________:

This letter serves as notification that on [Insert date], the Company requested an investigative consumer report regarding you. An investigative consumer report is a consumer report for which the information is gathered through personal interviews of neighbors, friends, or associates of the employee or applicant reported on, or from other personal acquaintances or persons who may have knowledge about information bearing on the employee or applicant's credit worthiness, credit standing, credit capacity, character, general reputation, personal characteristics, or mode of living which is used or expected to be used or collected for employment purposes.

Enclosed is a summary of your rights under the federal Fair Credit Reporting Act, issued by the Federal Trade Commission. You also have a right to submit a written request that the Company disclose the complete and accurate nature and scope of the investigation requested. The Company will respond to your request within five (5) days of receiving it.

Very truly yours,

____

[Company Representative]

APPENDIX 8F

Fair Credit Reporting Act

Para informacion en espanol, visite www.ftc.gov/credit o escribe a la FTC Consumer Response Center, Room 130-A 600 Pennsylvania Ave. N.W., Washington, D.C. 20580.

A Summary of Your Rights Under the Fair Credit Reporting Act

The federal Fair Credit Reporting Act (FCRA) promotes the accuracy, fairness, and privacy of information in the files of consumer reporting agencies. There are many types of consumer reporting agencies, including credit bureaus and specialty agencies (such as agencies that sell information about check writing histories, medical records, and rental history records). Here is a summary of your major rights under the FCRA. **For more information, including information about additional rights, go to www-.ftc.gov/credit or write to: Consumer Response Center, Room 130-A, Federal Trade Commission, 600 Pennsylvania Ave. N.W., Washington, D.C. 20580.**

You must be told if information in your file has been used against you. Anyone who uses a credit report or another type of consumer report to deny your application for credit, insurance, or employment — or to take another adverse action against you — must tell you, and must give you the name, address, and phone number of the agency that provided the information.

You have the right to know what is in your file. You may request and obtain all the information about you in the files of a consumer reporting agency (your "file disclosure"). You will be required to provide proper identification, which may include your Social Security number. In many cases, the disclosure will be free. You are entitled to a free file disclosure if:

> A person has taken adverse action against you because of information in your credit report;
>
> You are the victim of identify theft and place a fraud alert in your file; C your file contains inaccurate information as a result of fraud; C you are on public assistance; C you are unemployed but expect to apply for employment within 60 days. In addition, by September 2005 all consumers will be entitled to one free disclosure every 12 months upon request from each nationwide credit bureau and from nationwide specialty consumer reporting agencies. See www.ftc.gov/credit for additional information.

You have the right to ask for a credit score. Credit scores are numerical summaries of your credit-worthiness based on information from credit bureaus. You may request a credit score from consumer reporting agencies that create scores or distribute scores used in residential real property loans, but you will have to pay for it. In some mortgage transactions, you will receive credit score information for free from the mortgage lender.

You have the right to dispute incomplete or inaccurate information. If you identify information in your file that is incomplete or inaccurate, and report it to the consumer reporting agency, the agency must investigate unless your dispute is frivolous. See www.ftc.gov/credit for an explanation of dispute procedures.

Consumer reporting agencies must correct or delete inaccurate, incomplete, or unverifiable information. Inaccurate, incomplete or unverifiable information must be removed or corrected, usually within 30 days. However, a consumer reporting agency may continue to report information it has verified as accurate.

Consumer reporting agencies may not report outdated negative information. In most cases, a consumer reporting agency may not report negative information that is more than seven years old, or bankruptcies that are more than 10 years old.

Access to your file is limited. A consumer reporting agency may provide information about you only to people with a valid need — usually to consider an application with a creditor, insurer, employer, landlord, or other business. The FCRA specifies those with a valid need for access.

You must give your consent for reports to be provided to employers. A consumer reporting agency may not give out information about you to your employer, or a potential employer, without your written consent given to the employer. Written consent generally is not required in the trucking industry. For more information, go to www.ftc.gov/credit.

You may limit "prescreened" offers of credit and insurance you get based on information in your credit report. Unsolicited "prescreened" offers for credit and insurance must include a toll-free phone number you can call if you choose to remove your name and address from the lists these offers are based on. You may opt-out with the nationwide credit bureaus at 1-888-5-OPTOUT (1-888-567-8688).

You may seek damages from violators. If a consumer reporting agency, or, in some cases, a user of consumer reports or a furnisher of information to a consumer reporting agency violates the FCRA, you may be able to sue in state or federal court.

Identity theft victims and active duty military personnel have additional rights. For more information, visit www.ftc.gov/credit.

States may enforce the FCRA, and many states have their own consumer reporting laws. In some cases, you may have more rights under state law. For more information, contact your state or local consumer protection agency or your state Attorney General. Federal enforcers are:

Type of Business	Contact
Consumer reporting agencies, creditors and others not listed below	Federal Trade Commission: Consumer Response Center — FCRA Washington, DC 20580 1-877-382-4357
National banks, federal branches/agencies of foreign banks (word "National" or initials "N.A." appear in or after bank's name)	Office of the Comptroller of the Currency Compliance Management, Mail Stop 6-6 Washington, DC 20219 800-613-6743
Federal Reserve System member banks (except national banks, and federal branches/agencies of foreign banks)	Federal Reserve Board Division of Consumer & Community Affairs Washington, DC 20551 202-452-3693
Savings associations and federally chartered savings banks (word) "Federal" or initials "F.S.B." appear in federal institution's name)	Office of Thrift Supervision Consumer Complaints Washington, DC 20552 800-842-6929
Federal credit unions (words "Federal Credit Union" appear in institution's name)	National Credit Union Administration 1775 Duke Street Alexandria, VA 22314 703-519-4600
State-chartered banks that are not members of the Federal Reserve System	Federal Deposit Insurance Corporation Consumer Response Center, 2345 Grand Avenue, Suite 100, Kansas City, Missouri 64108-2638 1-877-275-3342

(continues)

Type of Business *(Continued)*	**Contact**
Air, surface, or rail common carriers regulated by former Civil Aeronautics Board or Interstate Commerce Commission	Department of Transportation, Office of Financial Management Washington, DC 20590 202-366-1306
Activities subject to the Packers and Stockyards Act, 1921	Department of Agriculture Office of Deputy Administrator—GIPSA Washington, DC 20250 202-720-7051

Sample Disclosure of Nature and Scope of Investigative Consumer Report

[Letterhead]

Date

Applicant/Employee's Name

Address

RE: Disclosure of Nature and Scope of Investigative Consumer Report

Dear ____:

This letter responds to your request that the Company make a complete and accurate disclosure of the nature and scope of the investigative consumer report requested on [Insert date]. We received your request on [Insert date]. Also enclosed with this letter is a summary of your rights under the Fair Credit Reporting Act, in a form prescribed by the Federal Trade Commission.

The investigative consumer report requested involved interviews with your [Identify the persons interviewed—neighbors, friends, associates, or others with whom the applicant is acquainted or who may have knowledge concerning the applicant's character, general reputation, personal characteristics, or mode of living]. The subject(s) of this investigation was/were [Identify the nature of the investigation—e.g., work performance, starting and ending dates, salary, attitude, honesty, compliance with policies and procedures, tendency toward violence, etc.]. The investigative consumer report was prepared by [Consumer Reporting Agency, Consumer Reporting Agency's address].

Very truly yours,

____

[Company Representative]

Appendix 8H

Sample Pre–Adverse Action Notice

[Letterhead]

Date

Applicant/Employee's Name

Address

Dear ____ :

Enclosed is a copy of a consumer report that was requested by the Company in connection with your [select one—employment/application for employment]. Also enclosed is a summary of your rights provided under the Fair Credit Reporting Act. In the event that any portion of the report is inaccurate, please contact us promptly.

Very truly yours,

____

[Company Representative]

Sample Adverse Action Notice

[Letterhead]

Date

Applicant/Employee's Name

Address

RE: Notice of Adverse Employment Action

Dear ____:

[Describe adverse action taken] This action was taken [choose one—solely because of/or in part based on] information contained in the consumer report that you have previously received.

[Insert name, address, and telephone numbers (including toll-free number of the consumer reporting agency)] (the "Agency") furnished the consumer report. However, the Agency did not have any input with regard to the above-stated employment decision and cannot provide you with any information regarding why the action was taken.

You may obtain another free copy of the consumer report from the Agency if you request a copy from it within sixty (60) days of receipt of this notice. You also have the right to dispute with the Agency the accuracy or completeness of any information in the consumer report furnished by the Agency.

Very truly yours,

____

[Company Representative]

Appendix 8J

Applicant

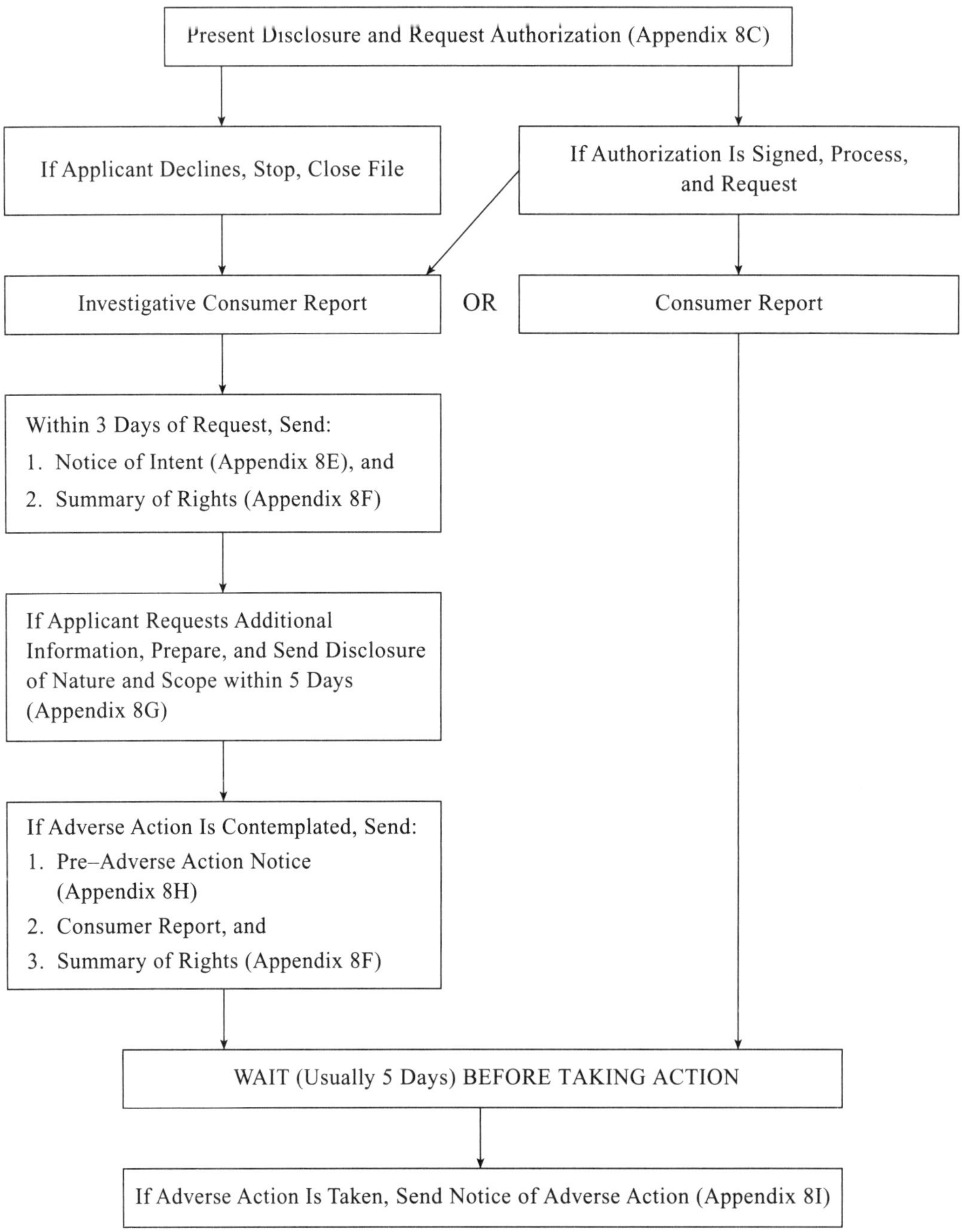

Current Employee

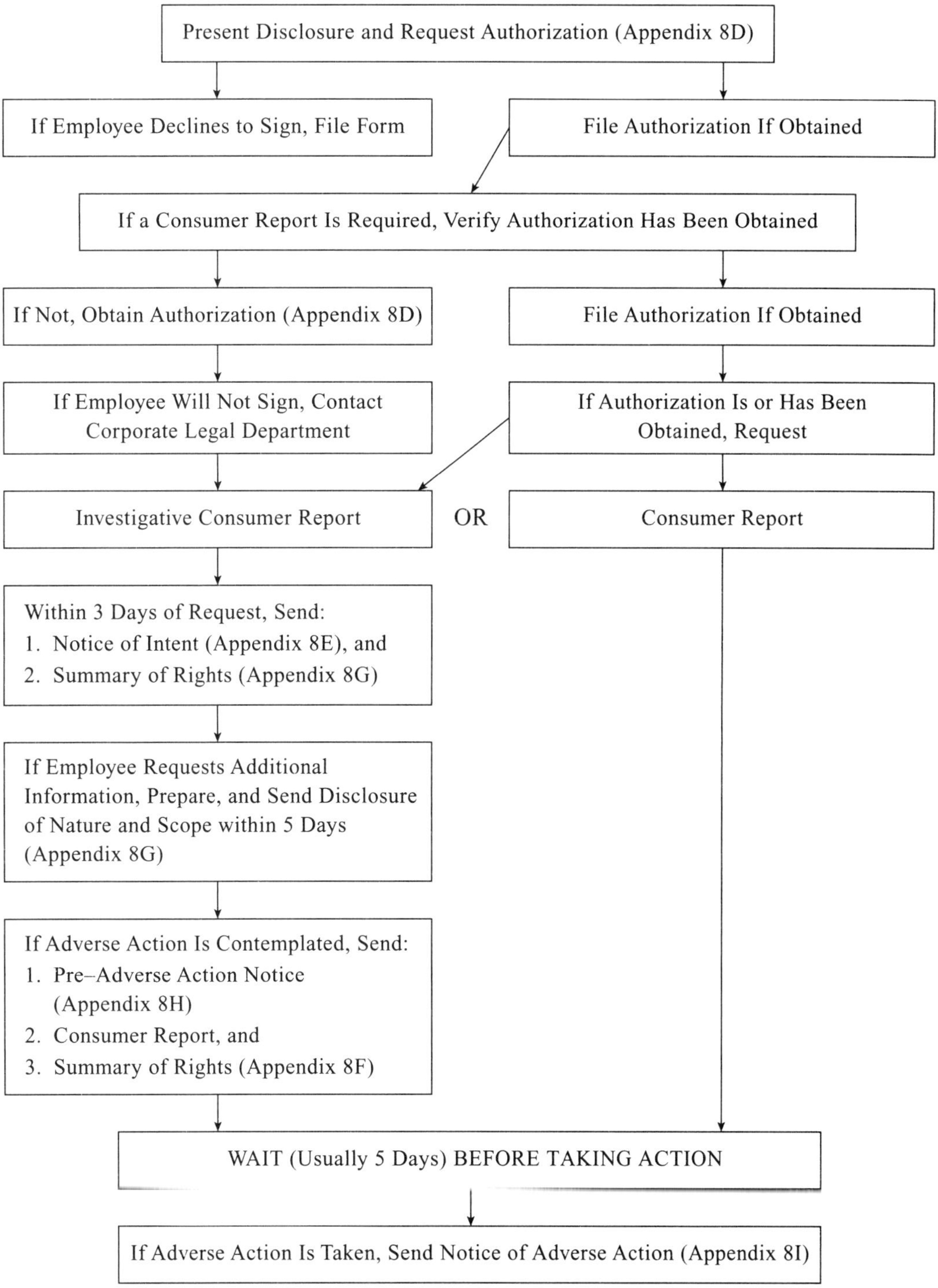

NOTES

1. Pub. L. 107-204, July 30, 2002; 15 U.S.C. 7201 note.
2. 15 U.S.C. 1681–1681y.
3. See 29 C.F.R. 1980.101.
4. 18 U.S.C. 1341.
5. 18 U.S.C. 1343.
6. 18 U.S.C. 1344.
7. 18 U.S.C. 1348.
8. 18 U.S.C. 1514A(a).
9. 18 U.S.C. 1514A.
10. Id.
11. 18 U.S.C. 1513.
12. 18 U.S.C. 1514A(b).
13. Id.
14. 29 C.F.R. 1980.100 et seq.
15. 49 U.S.C. 42121.
16. 18 U.S.C. 1514A(b)(2).
17. 49 U.S.C. 42121(b)(B).
18. Id.
19. 29 C.F.R. 1980.105(c), 106.
20. 29 C.F.R. 1980.107.
21. 49 U.S.C. 42121(b)(3)(A.)
22. 49 U.S.C. 42121(b)(4).
23. While there is not enough anecdotal evidence under the act to suggest whether the DOL will routinely complete the administrative procedures within 180 days, experience with other federal agencies and similar time frames suggests that timely compliance will more likely be the exception rather than the rule.
24. 18 U.S.C. 1514A(b)(1)(B).
25. *See, e.g.,* Hassan v. U. S. Dep't of Labor, 298 F.3d 914 (10th Cir. 2002).
26. C.A. No. 02-7539, 2003 WL 21146653 (SDNY 5/15/03).
27. The memorandum is posted on the Department of Labor Web site and can be accessed at: www.dol-.gov/sol/media/memos/August 9.htm.
28. 15 U.S.C. 1514A(c).
29. 17 C.F.R. 205.2.
30. 17 C.F.R. 205.3(b)(5).
31. 17 C.F.R. 205.6.
32. 17 C.F.R. 205.3(b)(1).
33. Interestingly, the reporting would itself be a protected whistleblowing activity.
34. 17 C.F.R. 205.3(b)(2).
35. Id.
36. 17 C.F.R. 205.3(b)(3).
37. 15 U.S.C. 301(m)(4).
38. 2002 US Dist LEXIS 16863.
39. 2002 US Dist LEXIS 19661 (SDNY 2002).
40. Neil, Martha. "A Trap for Employers" *ABA Journal* August, 2005: 20:21.
41. *See:* Abbott v. Crown Motor Co., 348 F.3d 537 (6th Cir. 2003) ("Today, we hold that Title VII protects an employee's participating in an employer's internal investigation into allegations of unlawful

discrimination where that investigation occurs pursuant to a pending EEOC charge); EEOC v. Total Sys. Serv., Inc., 221 F.3d 1171 (11th Cir. 2000) ("The participation clause protects an employee's activities that 'occur in conjunction with or after the filing of a formal charge with the EEOC,' not an employee's participating 'in an employer's internal, in-house investigation, conducted apart from a formal charge with the EEOC'; at a minimum, an employee must have filed a charge with the EEOC or otherwise instigated proceedings under Title VII'").

42. *See also:* Jones v. City of Jackson, 335 F. Supp. 2d 865 (W.D. Tenn. 2003) (supervisor's negative notations in plaintiff's personnel file, negative evaluations, failure to transfer, and "general unpleasantness" do not constitute materially adverse employment actions sufficient to establish a claim of retaliation); Smart v. Ball State Univ., 89 F.3d 437 (7th Cir. 1996) (". . . [Plaintiff] has not identified, nor have we discovered, a single case where adverse performance ratings alone were found to constitute adverse action"); Hollins v. Atlantic Co., 188 F.3d 652 (6th Cir. 1999) ("[A] materially adverse change in the terms and conditions of employment must be more disruptive than a mere inconvenience or an alteration of job responsibilities"); Watts v. Kroger Co., 170 F.3d 505 (5th Cir. 1999) ("Simply changing one's work schedule is not a change in her employment status" and thus not an adverse employment action.); Benningfield v. City of Houston, 157 F.3d 369 (5th Cir. 1998) (transferring an employee to the night shift does not constitute an adverse action).
43. *See, e.g.,* Ford v. GMC, 305 F.3d 545 (6th Cir. 2002).
44. Booker v. Brown & Williamson Tobacco Co., 879 F.2d 1304 (6th Cir. 1989).
45. Nguyen v. City of Cleveland, 229 F.3d 559 (6th Cir. 2000).
46. Id. *See also:* Hafford v. Seidneri, 183 F.3d 506 (6th Cir. 1999) (finding disciplinary action occurring two to five months after protected activity insufficient to establish a causal connection); Cooper v. City of North Olmstead, 795 F.2d 1265 (6th Cir. 1986) (finding discharge four months after filing of discrimination complaint insufficient to support an inference of retaliation).
47. *See* Cooper v. City of North Olmsted.
48. *See* Culver v. Gorman & Company, 2004 WL 1920220 (W.D. Wis. 2004) (no causal connection established because of the conduct plaintiff displayed at the time of her termination, despite the fact that she received a very favorable performance evaluation three days before her termination; was terminated two days after first complaint of discrimination; and within one hour of her second complaint of discrimination).
49. 15 U.S.C. 1681–1681y.
50. Id.
51. 15 U.S.C. 1681a(d).
52. 15 U.S.C. 1681a(e).
53. 15 U.S.C. 1681a(f).
54. Id.
55. The FTC is responsible for enforcement of the FCRA. Copies of the opinion letters referenced throughout this section as well as additional materials discussing the FCRA can be obtained from the FTC FCRA Web site, www.ftc.gov/os/statutes/fcrajump.htm.
56. *See, e.g.,* Copple Opinion letter, June 10, 1998.
57. 15 U.S.C. 1681a(d).
58. 15 U.S.C. 1681a(h).
59. 15 U.S.C. 1681a(e).
60. 15 U.S.C. 1681b.
61. 15 U.S.C. 1681b(b)(2). See Appendix 8C for an example of a disclosure to a job applicant. Appendix 8D is a similar disclosure directed at current employees.
62. *See* notes 55and 61above.
63. Meisinger Opinion letter, August 31, 1999; See also *Kelchner v. Sycamore Manor Health Center*, 305 F. Supp.2d 429 (M.D. Pa 2004).
64. For examples of impermissible purposes, *see* Zamora v. Valley Federal Saving & Loan Association of Grand Junction, 811 F.2d 1368 (10th Cir. 1987) (the intended and actual use of a credit report on

the spouse of an employee being considered for a security-sensitive position in order to evaluate the employee's trustworthiness does not permit the employer to obtain the credit report of the employee's spouse.); Russell v. Shelter Financial Services, 604 F. Supp. 201 (W.D. Mo. 1984) (A consumer loan company's request for a consumer report about a former employee could not be justified for "employment purposes" where the report was not sought until after the employee had announced his resignation.).

65. 15 U.S.C. 1681d. See, e.g, Appendix 8E.
66. Appendix 8F.
67. 15 U.S.C. 1681d(d)(1).
68. *See, e.g.,* Appendix 8G.
69. 15 U.S.C. 1681d(b)
70. 15 U.S.C. 1861b(b)3. *See, e.g.,* Appendix 8H.
71. Appendix 8F.
72. 15 U.S.C. 1681a(k).
73. Heathers Opinion letter, September 9, 1998.
74. *See, e.g.,* Weisberg Opinion letter, June 27, 1997.
75. See Vail Opinion letter, April 5, 1999. Please note that while useful for the purpose cited, the Vail Opinion letter has been substantially eviscerated by the Fair and Accurate Credit Transaction Act of 2003 (Pub.L. 108-159 Dec. 4, 2003), which amended the FCRA to make it easier for employers to conduct prompt, appropriate investigations of workplace misconduct utilizing third parties for these purposes.
76. *See, e.g.,* Appendix 8I.
77. 15 U.S.C. 1681b(b)3.
78. 15 U.S.C. 1681b(g).
79. 15 U.S.C. 1681n, 1681o.
80. 15 U.S.C. 1681s.
81. 15 U.S.C. 1681p.
82. 15 U.S.C. 1681q.
83. Appendixes 8J and 8K track FCRA compliance for applicants and current employees, respectively.

Section II

Tools of Fraud Deterrence

Chapter 9

Internal Control and Fraud Deterrence: The COSO Integrated Framework

Harry Cendrowski and James Martin

BACKGROUND

The Committee on Sponsoring Organizations of the Treadway Commission (COSO) was formed in 1985, and is an independent private sector initiative that studies the causal factors of fraud and fraudulent financial reporting. COSO continues to define recommendations and best practices for industry; many of these recommendations are implemented and codified by regulators such as the Securities and Exchange Commission (SEC) and Public Companies Accounting Oversight Board (PCAOB).

Originally, the COSO sponsored the National Commission on Financial Reporting, which was chaired by James C. Treadway, Jr., former commissioner of the SEC. Treadway was named to the SEC by President Ronald Reagan in 1982 and served until April 17, 1985; his involvement with the national commission resulted in the popular name the Treadway Commission.

The professional associations that sponsored the Treadway Commission include:

- *American Accounting Association*. Founded in 1916, the American Accounting Association promotes worldwide excellence in accounting education, research. and practice.
- *American Institute of Certified Public Accountants (AICPA)*. The professional association governing the practice of public accountancy. In 1985, the AICPA was responsible for the definition of standards for the audit of public companies; this authority was removed by the Sarbanes-Oxley Act of 2002 and assigned to the Public Company Accounting Oversight Board (PCAOB).
- *Financial Executives International (FEI)*. The preeminent organization for chief financial officers and other senior finance executives.
- *Institute of Internal Auditors (IIA)*. Association that defines professional standards for the practice of internal auditing, risk assessment, and governance.
- *National Association of Accountants (now the Institute of Management Accountants (IMA))*. Provides leadership in the areas of management accounting and financial management.

Since the mid-1980s, COSO has published five major reports:

1. *The National Commission on Fraudulent Financial Reporting*(October 1987)
2. *Internal Control, Integrated Framework* (1992)
3. *Internal Control Issues in Derivatives Usage* (1996)
4. Fraudulent Financial Reporting, 1987–1997: An Analysis of U.S. Public Companies (1999)
5. *Enterprise Risk Management, Integrated Framework* (2004)

Additionally, COSO released an exposure draft of new guidance for the application of the COSO Integrated Framework to smaller public companies. The final version of that work was released in mid-2006.

COSO materials are available for reference on the COSO Web site, www.coso.org.

Relevance

The primary objective of the internal control system is to provide the company, its management, its board and audit committee, and its owners and other stakeholders with a reasonable basis to rely on the company's financial reporting, which includes accurate financial reporting, retention of business records, and the prevention of unauthorized acquisition and removal of assets.[1]

The COSO Integrated Framework is not written as an internal control model for public companies; rather, the concepts of internal control encompassed in the integrated framework are applicable to all companies, large and small, public and private. Recent studies by the Association of Certified Fraud Examiners revealed that 90 percent of the frauds in their study would have been prevented by an appropriate set of internal controls defined for and consistently enforced within an organization.[2]

The COSO model of internal control is considered the gold standard of internal control for organizations. According to COSO chairman Larry E. Rittenberg, the *Internal Control, Integrated Framework* is a breakthrough in thinking because it:

- Is comprehensive. The framework is broader than financial reporting and identifies important control objectives related to operations and to compliance with regulations and company policies.
- Recognizes that internal control is an integrative process that starts with a strong control environment.
- Is conceptual and principles based. It lays out the fundamental characteristics of good internal control without prescribing specific control activities that all companies must perform.[3]

While the Integrated Framework existed for many years as a best practice standard for many organizations, it has become a requirement for many organizations through the implementation of laws and regulations.

FDICIA—The Federal Deposit Insurance Corporation Improvement Act was enacted in 1991 to help the financial institutions industry avoid the problems that plagued the savings and loan industry in the late 1980s. FDICIA requires institutions to maintain adequate internal control systems according to a generally accepted internal control framework; the COSO model was the model considered when the act was enacted.

PCAOB—The Sarbanes-Oxley Act of 2002, Section 404, requires issuers of financial statements to assess their internal control systems against a suitable recognized internal control framework. PCAOB Auditing Standard 2 defines the COSO framework as the standard for control evaluation.

> 14. In the United States, the Committee of Sponsoring Organizations ("COSO") of the Treadway Commission has published Internal Control—Integrated Framework. Known as the COSO report, it provides a suitable and available framework for purposes of management's assessment. For that reason, the performance and reporting directions in this standard are based on the COSO framework.[4]

COSO broadly defines internal control as a process, effected by an entity's board of directors, management, and other personnel, designed to provide reasonable assurance regarding the achievement of objectives in these categories:

- Effectiveness and efficiency of operations
- Reliability of financial reporting
- Compliance with applicable laws and regulations[5]

The comprehensive definition of the Integrated Framework is intended to address asset related fraud, financial misstatement and financial reporting fraud, as well as external fraud (corruption). The COSO Integrated Framework is a unifying model of control that recognizes the role of internal controls in business management. Internal controls are responsible for the allocation of resources, production of products according to quality standards, and the management of employees in addition to the objectives listing above. The COSO framework recognizes that for the organization to achieve maximum value and benefit from the controls architecture, internal controls must be viewed as a holistic and integrated set of polices, procedures, and actions.

While the COSO model provides outstanding guidance for fraud deterrence activities, fraud deterrence is a subset of the goals of the entire internal control structure within an organization and a subset of the COSO model itself. The discussion of the elements that follows focuses on that subset.

Elements

The COSO Integrated Framework identifies five components of internal control. As an *integrated* framework, these procedures are intended to be integrated with ongoing business operations, not just function as a discrete layer on top of the organization. For the organization to achieve effective internal controls, all five layers must be present and functioning. Weakness in one or more of the components will degrade the effectiveness of the system. The five elements of internal control are:

1. Control environment
2. Information and communication
3. Risk assessment
4. Control procedures
5. Monitoring

Note that these components include both hard factors, such as procedures and systems, as well as soft factors, such as culture and communication practices. For these reasons, the implementation of the Integrated Framework into an organization is a lengthy process involving organizational change and redesign.

CONTROL ENVIRONMENT

The control environment is the foundation for the system of internal control in an organization. It is most commonly identified as management's tone at the top, but the control environment also includes factors that reinforce other elements of the internal control system. The control environment also defines the control culture of the organization; this reinforces appropriate behavior in the absence of defined policies and procedures over a specific situation. In essence, the control environment is the living expression of the moral code of the organization.

Many of the major corporate financial reporting failures in the early 2000s were caused by a poor control environment. Management chose to override internal controls, ignore generally accepted accounting principles (GAAP), and violate their duties for accurate financial reporting. These problems were not caused by a lack of documented procedures, lack of communication, or lack of monitoring, although weaknesses in these areas contributed to a delay in the detection of the misstatements. Instead, these failures were the result of the wrong people in charge of a large company at the wrong time.

Even with the new oversight requirements of Sarbanes-Oxley, management override of internal control is still a primary concern of the accounting profession and regulators. In essence, those members of management who design and implement internal control procedures also can choose to bypass or override those controls. The AICPA refers to this situation as the Achilles' heel of financial reporting.[6] This point highlights the importance of the control environment in any organization: Despite all the other internal control systems in place in an organization, at the end of the day, management that truly believes it is important to execute duties with a sense of propriety is often the differentiator between integrity and fraud.

The fraud triangle defines the three factors present in any situation of fraud (motive/incentive, rationalization/attitude, opportunity); a proper control environment and positive control culture is important to help reduce the motive for fraud and deter the rationalization of inappropriate conduct.

Management Tone at the Top

Employees within the organization are keenly aware of the actions of management; even in the face of words to the contrary, inappropriate management behavior sets a bad example for other members of the organization to follow. Owners and management affect the control culture by ensuring the organization implements appropriate policies, procedures, and practices. Equally importantly, they must reinforce these messages by actually following the procedures they set. This tone at the top helps send a clear message, reinforcing the owners' and managers' commitment to integrity and ethical values.

Additionally, management must consistently reinforce, through words and actions, that a properly functioning internal control structure is an imperative of all employees and business processes. This management priority is essential to ensure the development and execution of all the aspects of the internal control system throughout the organization. For example, individual business units must develop and consistently execute internal control procedures; to be successful, doing this must be known as a management imperative. Additionally, the control environment is the reinforcement of the internal control structure by deterring any attempts to override approved control procedures.

Sarbanes-Oxley Section 302 requires that management certify the internal controls of the organization are in place and functioning properly; this certification is made by management with indirect knowledge of the true state. The chief executive officer (CEO) and chief financial officer (CFO) cannot possibly visit every business unit and directly examine the state of internal controls; thus they rely on the competency of others in the organization to report the status of the controls within their domain. Management, therefore, is expressing tremendous trust in the control environment of the organization, assuming that each unit is honestly reporting the true state and not concealing ineffective procedures. Again, management must demonstrate through its actions that its members are truly concerned with the development of adequate controls, not merely looking to report a positive yet overstated status.

Appropriate management behaviors can greatly deter the rationalization of a potential fraud perpetrator. If managers behave in a manner contrary to written policies and procedures, or if they otherwise demonstrate a lack of integrity through their actions, it will be much easier for employees to rationalize that inappropriate behavior on their part is not really a major concern.

Board Considerations

Management is responsible for the definition of the system of internal controls, and the board is responsible to ensure management effectively executes that duty. Sarbanes-Oxley defined new standards for the audit committee of public companies; these standards are rapidly becoming best practice standards for other organizations as well. To be effective, members of the audit committee must be qualified and independent from the organization. Audit committee members should be well versed with industry standards for the organization, GAAP, and organizational objectives and internal procedures. Independence is essential to allow the board members to challenge management and provide appropriate guidance if management presents information that does not conform to the expectations of the board.

The board is also responsible for collecting and resolving any concerns presented by the organization's employees related to potential inappropriate accounting procedures and management actions. In this manner, the employees are monitoring management behaviors, but the control environment must be such that the employees will actually report their findings to the board for action. The board is the top level of the monitoring process and, as such, must be both qualified and independent to monitor organizational concerns, as well as to independently monitor the actions of management.

Elevation of Employee Concerns

A properly functioning control environment should welcome the elevation of employee concerns regarding conduct or financial reporting issues. Management should operate with a culture that recognizes individual employees as a vital resource in the risk assessment and monitoring processes. When risks are identified, they should be freely presented in an environment free of threats, reprisals, or intimidation.

Issuers of financial statements are required under Sarbanes-Oxley Section 301 to establish procedures for the confidential, anonymous submission by employees of the issuer of concerns regarding questionable accounting or auditing matters. While this provision is designed to provide an outlet for reporting a management override of internal control, the need for an anonymous channel is an indicator that the control environment may not be functioning correctly. Management that operates with unquestioned authority can be an indicator of tendencies that could eventually lead to the override of internal controls, and should be of concern to the board or company ownership.

Conflict of Interest and Compliance Programs

Policies and procedures should clearly specify appropriate conduct with trading partners and what is considered a conflict of interest. Not every situation can be addressed by policies and procedures, however; it is hoped the control environment guides individuals to ethical behavior in the absence of clear procedural instruction. In this manner the control environment turns the static policy into an active guideline for appropriate conduct. The control environment consistently reinforces that any actual or apparent conflicts of interest will not be tolerated; this is done by enforcing policies and procedures and defining a standard of high ethical conduct.

A conflict of interest is an agent taking an interest in a transaction that is potentially adverse to the principal without full and timely disclosure to the principal. In other words, it occurs if a person has a duty to two parties and cannot fairly represent the adverse interests of both parties. A conflict of interest could include, for example, a real estate agent receiving a commission from both the buyer and the seller in a real estate transaction, or a purchasing agent who purchases materials from a side company in which she has an ownership interest.

While a conflict of interest can assume many forms, most commonly an organization is concerned about excessive gifts from a vendor to influence a purchase decision. For example, in a kickback scheme, the purchasing agent receives cash or other valuable assets in exchange for paying a higher purchase price or otherwise committing to a purchase that he otherwise would not make. This is harmful to the company (it pays a higher price), and the conflict is not disclosed to the company.

Organizations have taken differing approaches to the definition of a gift level that would constitute a conflict.

- A relative definition of a conflict of interest, such as "no gift or gratuity may be accepted of a value that would be high enough to influence the person." Some feel this is not appropriate guidance, as the "value" of such a gift is undefined and could be subject to wild interpretation. This approach could be successful if the organization has achieved an appropriate control culture; in such an environment employees would actually consider the effects of a gift value and behave appropriately.
- A hard dollar ceiling for gift levels, such as "no gift or gratuity may be accepted where the fair value of that gift exceeds $100." This raises the concern that an ill-willed employee might compromise the dollar limit if the gift was "slightly" over the cap, or might not consider the total value of a package of gifts, or might simply receive a stream of smaller gifts, each of which does not exceed the cap.
- An outright prohibition on gifts. While this sets a clear level of accepted performance, it raises the issue that even insignificant token items (e.g., a cheap plastic pen with a vendor logo) cannot be accepted. In a sense, this is acknowledging that the control environment is not sufficient to cause appropriate behavior and that employees should not be guided by discretionary limits.

Regardless of the ceiling limit set to define a conflict of interest, the organization needs to define a clear penalty for violating the policy and ensure that the policy is consistently monitored and enforced, including violations by senior management. Proactively, this includes requiring an annual declaration of any conflicts of interest by all employees within the organization. Additionally, the conflict of interest policy should be openly disseminated to trading partners, including instructions that any deviations from the policy should be reported to an appropriate authority within the organization, such as internal audit or a compliance office. Many organizations have found success with an annual letter to trading partners reminding them of the policy, especially around the holiday season.

Compensation Programs and Human Resources Polices and Procedures

Compensation programs and human resource policies and procedures should be defined to reinforce appropriate behaviors throughout the organization. Pay increases, commissions, and bonus programs should be aligned with organizational objectives and not suboptimized to individual goals that might be opposed to organizational objectives, including accurate financial reporting. Large compensation levels linked too closely with short term financial results can create an incentive to distort the financial statements, deviate from GAAP, or alter business transactions. For example, if a department head is offered a \$100,000 bonus for achieving a 10 percent increase in sales during the calendar year, and the actual sales are only increased by 9.2 percent as of the beginning of December, he has a tremendous incentive to find additional sales, legitimate or otherwise.

Compensation programs can create a motive for fraud if employees are underpaid; such low compensation can also create a ready rationalization if employees additionally believe they are "owed" more compensation by the organization. Additionally, many of the outside influences that create a motive for fraud are addressed by employee support programs in many organizations (e.g., substance abuse, credit counseling).

Human resource procedures must also instill a commitment to competence through the hiring, training, and retention of adequately qualified employees. Qualified employees are essential to accomplish organizational objectives such as quality, sales, and customer satisfaction. Qualified employees are also essential to adequately implement the internal control structure that allows those objectives to be met; for example, skilled employees in the accounting area should be able to understand the accounting considerations of a transaction and potentially identify and report inappropriate conduct on the part of other employees or management. Employee qualification also means that authority should be assigned to an appropriate level within the organization. Delegation of authority to an inappropriate level in the organization (e.g., authorizing a bookkeeper to meet with the attest accountants or approve major transactions) can introduce the opportunity to override controls, jeopardizing accuracy of financial reporting and the security of assets.

In general, compensation programs and human resource policies and procedures should be defined to adequately reward employees for their efforts, support the positive morale of the organization, and create an environment where the employees strive for the success of the organization through the internal control structure.

Fraud Deterrence

The fact that management is concerned with ethical issues and fraud incidents is, in itself, a tremendous deterrence to fraud: It is more difficult to rationalize inappropriate behavior if management projects continuous, strong signals that such behavior will not be tolerated.

Additionally, the presence of a strong system of internal controls will reinforce the message that any deviation from expected behaviors will be rapidly detected and the perpetrator punished accordingly.

INFORMATION AND COMMUNICATION

Information and communication relates to the flow of information in two directions within the organization. First, information should flow downward to the line functions and provide the best, most accurate information as needed to allow the function to produce the best results possible. Second, information about performance should flow upward through management, through both formal and informal communication channels, providing objective feedback. Both communication channels must function effectively to safeguard the organization.

Accuracy of Information

The availability of accurate information when business transactions are processed is essential for fraud deterrence, both in terms of internal and external fraud. Accurate information facilitated by properly designed and implemented systems information will help prevent the concealment of inappropriate transactions.

In most organizations, information technology (IT) systems are responsible for storing and providing access to operating information. The internal controls over these systems must be properly designed and implemented to provide assurance that the information within these systems is accurate. An understanding of IT controls is essential to understand the effectiveness of the overall control structure. Specific frameworks to guide management through the realm of IT controls have been developed.

COBIT (Control Objectives for Information and Related Technology) is a comprehensive model for IT control; it is published by the Information Systems Audit and Control Association (ISACA).[7] COBIT defines control objectives required to allow IT processes to deliver information that businesses need to achieve their objectives—planning and organization, acquisition and implementation, delivery and support, and monitoring according to several business requirements:

- Effectiveness
- Efficiency
- Confidentiality
- Integrity
- Availability
- Compliance
- Reliability[8]

The COBIT model provides detailed guidance for the implementation and assessment of appropriate control structures to achieve business objectives, and is a tremendous resource for management.

More recently, the Institute of Internal Auditors introduced the Global Technology Audit Guides (GTAG); the primary focus of GTAG is "technology-associated risks and recommended practices."[9] GTAG takes a management approach, describing the needs and key risks associated with the information technology control structure. The IIA has published the first two volumes of the GTAG work. *Guide 1, Information Technology Controls,* describes the view of IT controls from management's perspectives, especially given new corporate compliance requirements. *Guide 2, Change and Patch Management Controls,* describes the importance of adequate controls over software updates. The IIA intends to continue to publish additional volumes of the GTAG work as needed to support the needs of management and the chief audit executive.

Manual (nonautomated) control procedures are also responsible for the flow of accurate information to the business processes; however, in most organizations, weakness in the IT control structure will create pervasive issues that are particularly detrimental. Additionally, many senior executives, including senior finance executives, are not well versed in the detailed technical aspects of information technology and treat the IT environment as something of a "magic box." For these reasons, properly functioning IT controls have significant impact on the information and communication within the organization.

Open Communication

Open communication is one of the hallmarks of an appropriately functioning control environment and is a key driver of employee morale as well. Employees should feel empowered to raise awareness of a risk, report an issue, offer a suggestion to improve process quality (financial process or otherwise), or generally express a concern. If such open communication is suppressed, employees can feel resentment toward management or the company or feel that management truly does not care about the proper operation of business processes.

Under Sarbanes-Oxley Section 301, anonymous reporting is required for issuers of financial statements: "Each audit committee shall establish procedures for . . . the confidential, anonymous submission by employees of the issuer of concerns regarding questionable accounting or auditing matters."[10] The need for *confidential* reporting of issues indicates, however, that open communication is not encouraged within an organization, and the control environment is not functioning as expected. The anonymous reporting facility is required because of the rash of senior officers of public companies that intentionally distorted the financial statements. It is unrealistic to believe that open communication would be welcome in such an environment.

Even beyond the role in public companies, confidential reporting systems reduce fraud losses significantly. A process for the submission and evaluation of confidential reporting should be expanded to include third-party sources such as customers and vendors, especially in small businesses, which are hardest hit by fraud.[11] Tips are a very common way that fraud is eventually discovered, and the anonymous facility is a means to allow management to obtain as many tips as possible. Additionally, the existence of a confidential reporting channel sends a clear message that fraud can easily be reported to management, and thus, a perpetrator runs greater risk of intervention once discovered.

To be successful, the anonymous reporting facility needs to be supported with clear procedures for what types of concerns should be reported and how to report. This guidance should be disseminated both internally for employees and externally to vendors and suppliers. This is further explained in the "Conflict of Interest and Compliance Programs" section earlier in the chapter.

Open employee communication supports other organizational objectives beyond fraud deterrence. For example, a cornerstone of quality theory is that employees are individually responsible for process outputs, and factors that negatively constrain that output should be elevated to management. The Saturn division of General Motors Corporation once featured an ad depicting an employee on his first day of work who located a defect in production and pulled a cord to stop the line and notify management. In the commercial, the employee was praised for his diligence and the behavior was reinforced. The commercial reinforced another key of quality theory: Corrective action is less expensive when detected earlier in the process. This holds true for fraud deterrence as well: Prevention of fraud is much cheaper than remediation; earlier detection is much cheaper than allowing a fraud to continue on a long-term basis. Open communication is an enabler for fraud deterrence as it allows the organization to raise concerns to management more easily.

Fraud Deterrence

Information and communication help with the fraud deterrence function in two ways. First, the flow of complete and accurate information helps remove the concealment aspect of fraud; this reduces the opportunity for a person to commit fraud and conceal the activity for a long period of time. Second, open communication will allow all employees to raise concerns of inappropriate conduct in an environment free of angst or concern that the messenger will be shot. This will facilitate the earlier detection of fraudulent misconduct.

RISK ASSESSMENT

Risk assessment is a forward-looking survey of the business environment to identify anything that could prevent the accomplishment of organizational objectives. As it relates to fraud deterrence, risk assessment involves the identification of internal and external means that could potentially defeat the organization's internal control structure, compromise an asset, and conceal the actions from management. Risk assessment is a creative process; it involves identifying as many potential threats as possible and evaluating them in a way to determine which require action, and the priority for that action.

Ideally, risk assessment activities are performed on a continuous basis, by all employees within the organization. As risks are identified, they are elevated to the appropriate level of management for consideration. This type of risk assessment culture becomes part of the control environment. In most instances, and typically for strategic risks, the risk assessment process is conducted on an interval basis, usually once per year.

Risk Identification

Risk identification seeks to identify as many threats as possible without evaluation of the threat. This will naturally drive the process to include as many individuals from the organization as possible, especially including those with specific detailed information about the particular risk area being considered. For example, a strategic risk assessment would involve senior management, senior finance people, and the strategic planning area. An operational risk assessment would include those from the operating units as they will have tremendous insight into how the business processes actually work and specifically what threats would interrupt the accomplishments of business objectives.

To facilitate the risk identification process, a risk framework can be helpful to provide additional guidance to the risk assessment participants and help organize the identified threats. The framework can organize risk categories and specific risks by structural element (e.g., strategy, people, process, technology, data), or by business process (e.g., revenue cycle, disbursement cycle, cash management and treasury, financial reporting, operations).

The risk framework should consider both internal and external factors; risk assessment participants should be reminded and encouraged to identify threats from both factors.

- Internal factors
  - Communication methods
  - Risk assessment activities
  - Appropriateness of internal control activities
  - Labor relations
  - Training and capability of the employees
  - Degree of supervision of employees
- External factors
  - Regulatory changes
  - Industry competition
  - Relationships with key suppliers
  - Relationships with customers
  - Recruiting and hiring activities
  - International risk

Additionally, it is appropriate to consider a hindsight evaluation of risk assessment activities: examining experienced risks that were not identified in the prior risk assessment. The risk is examined to see if it was not identified, and if not, why not, or if it was indeed identified but evaluated as a lower-risk item. In either case, observations should be made to refine the risk assessment process for future iterations.

Risk Evaluation

The goal of risk evaluation is to provide an objective and independent assessment of the risks facing the organization. Each identified risk item is evaluated, generally by a two-factor scale of impact and likelihood:

- *Impact.* The effect the risk occurrence would have on the organization's objective *if it were to actually occur.*
- *Likelihood.* The chance that the risk will actually occur.

By graphing the evaluation of risk items on this two-factor scale, with the origin of the graph being low-impact and low-likelihood, higher-priority items (i.e., those items with a high impact and high likelihood ratings) will graph in the upper right quadrant.

Risks can be evaluated on the inherent or residual risk level, and this is an item of debate among risk assessment practitioners.

- *Inherent risk* is the risk that exists before any controls are implemented to mitigate such risk.
- *Residual risk* is the risk that still exists after all control activities are executed.

Evaluating on inherent risk will tend to evaluate all items as a high-impact, high-likelihood risk (i.e., because there is no consideration of controls), thus preventing any sort of prioritization of the risk item. Evaluating on residual risk is evaluating on control activities that may or may not be effective; a risk could be overlooked because the evaluator is reliant on internal controls that do not actually function. For this reason, many risk assessment activities evaluate residual risk and identify the key controls to achieve the lower impact and likelihood scores, and then verify that those controls are indeed in place and functioning. Not surprisingly, preventive control activities will tend to reduce the likelihood of a risk occurrence, while detective and corrective controls will tend to reduce the impact of a risk occurrence.

Disclosure Controls and Procedures

Sarbanes-Oxley Section 302 requires a company's CEO and CFO to certify their responsibility for establishing, maintaining and evaluating disclosure controls and procedures; these procedures are used to develop the management discussion and analysis (MD&A) portion of the financial statements.

The SEC defines disclosure controls and procedures as a process to gather, analyze, and report events, uncertainties, conditions, contingencies that could materially affect the operating results of the enterprise. The MD&A should offer the shareholder an internal view of the enterprise, based on the items management believes could have an impact on future operations. Company disclosures present prospective rather than historical information, strategic and operating information rather that transactional, financial information.[12]

Procedures within the organization should capture information that is relevant to an assessment of the need to disclose developments and risks that pertain to the issuer's businesses. For example, for some businesses, an assessment and evaluation of operational and regulatory risks may be necessary.[13] Management ultimately must decide the level of risk they are willing to allow within any process; the risk assessment process, however, can provide a documented structure to facilitate the identification and evaluation of these issues.

Enterprise Risk Management

Enterprise risk management (ERM) is a comprehensive analysis of all risks facing the organization, including financial, operational, and compliance risk. Many organizations implemented an ERM process due to increased regulatory pressures, or to take greater advantage of business opportunities that often were accompanied by greater levels of risk.

In September 2004 COSO issued the Enterprise Risk Management—Integrated Framework. The ERM Framework includes this definition:

> Enterprise risk management is a process, effected by an entity's board of directors, management and other personnel, applied in strategy setting and across the enterprise, designed to identify potential events that may affect the entity, and manage risk to be within its risk appetite, to provide reasonable assurance regarding the achievement of entity objectives.[14]

This definition recognizes that ERM is an ongoing fluid process involving the entire organization. Just as the COSO model of control is intended to be a unifying theory of internal control, the COSO enterprise risk management framework is intended to be a unifying and comprehensive analysis of risk. According to the model, ERM encompasses:

- *Aligning risk appetite and strategy.* Management considers the entity's risk appetite in evaluating strategic alternatives, setting related objectives, and developing mechanisms to manage related risks.

- *Enhancing risk response decisions.* Enterprise risk management provides the rigor to identify and select among alternative risk responses: risk avoidance, reduction, sharing, and acceptance.
- *Reducing operational surprises and losses.* Entities gain enhanced capability to identify potential events and establish responses, reducing surprises and associated costs or losses.
- *Identifying and managing multiple and cross-enterprise risks.* Every enterprise faces a myriad of risks affecting different parts of the organization, and ERM facilitates effective response to the interrelated impacts, and integrated responses to multiple risks.
- *Seizing opportunities.* By considering a full range of potential events, management is positioned to identify and proactively realize opportunities.
- *Improving deployment of capital.* Obtaining robust risk information allows management to effectively assess overall capital needs and enhance capital allocation.

These capabilities inherent in ERM help management achieve the entity's performance and profitability targets and prevent loss of resources. ERM helps ensure effective reporting and compliance with laws and regulations, and helps avoid damage to the entity's reputation and associated consequences. In sum, ERM helps an entity get to where it wants to go and avoid pitfalls and surprises along the way.[15]

The COSO Enterprise Risk Management Integrated Framework provides excellent guidance for management and is available from COSO at www.coso.org.

Fraud Deterrence

Risk assessment activities facilitate the identification of potential fraud schemes based on organizational understanding of the business environment and current control structure. Risk assessment, therefore, is an essential means to challenge the control implementation and discover if any previously unexpected actions could be used to defeat the controls of an organization. Risk assessment also provides a prioritization to understand where additional resources should be deployed to provide additional assurance to the organization.

CONTROL PROCEDURES

Control procedures, although only one of the five elements of internal control defined in the COSO integrated framework, is the element typically identified with "internal control." Control procedures are the documented policies, procedures, and guidance that directs employees through the conduct of their ongoing business processes. Control procedures are also a prime focus area for fraud deterrence engagements; if control procedures are not adequately defined and consistently enforced within the organization, the opportunity for fraud is introduced. They must, however, be considered within the functioning of the entire system of internal controls. For example, it does little good to have a well-defined set of control procedures that provide excellent guidance for employees in the conduct of their work yet lack basic monitoring controls to ensure that guidance is consistently followed.

Control procedures define the business process and reflect management's approved means to accomplish every critical task. Documented procedures are static, yet the business process functions continually, and frequently needs to change to reflect new management objectives, opportunities, and business risks. For this reason, a change management process should be in place to identify and certify required changes and update the documentation of acceptable procedures on a regular, if not continuous, basis. This is an especially critical element of control procedures for those companies required to report on the status of internal controls under Sarbanes-Oxley Section 404. In such companies, informal changes to procedures without updating the approved control procedures can lead to reporting violations.

Control Procedures and Fraud Deterrence

Control procedures must be designed by management, implemented, and consistently enforced to ensure that assets are safeguarded and financial reporting is accurate. For asset protection, this typically involves identifying assets within the organization that would be susceptible to fraud and defining control procedures such that the assets cannot be removed and the removal concealed. Fraud deterrence involves proactively examining these control procedures to verify that they are adequately designed and actually functioning within the organization.

Fraud deterrence also needs to apply a process analysis approach to threats to the organization. Often management considers and appropriately controls a risk area without identifying other risks within the same business process. Consider the example of a hospital with a very well-designed cash count room, with restricted access to the two authorized cashiers. Management believes their cash procedures are in place and functioning. Throughout the hospital, however, cash is collected by various clinical units, the cafeteria, a coffee bar, a gift shop, and a valet parking service, all of which is taken by the person responsible for the collection of cash (e.g., the gift shop clerk) to the cashier window. Management did not consider or approve any control procedures governing how such retail activities are to be performed, and the hospital has the risk that someone could convert cash before it is taken to the cashier window. The fraud deterrence engagement should track valuable assets completely through the business cycle ensuring that assets are continuously safeguarded as they move through the organization.

Removal of assets needs to be prevented whether concealed or not. While fraud involves the element of concealment that allows the theft to continue over a longer period of time, unconcealed larceny is still a problem for the organization in that it creates an asset loss. Control procedures should be designed to limit access to valuable assets to only those approved employees with a legitimate business purpose. A common example of such a control procedure is restricting access to the cash count room. Most organizations recognize the need to have a separate locked room where cash is counted, verified, and prepared for deposit. For the same reason, access to inventory areas, small tools stores, and other valuable items should be restricted as they are inviting targets for theft.

Separation of Duties

The concealment aspect of fraud typically is countered through the assignment of duties to separate the custodianship function (i.e., the person in control of the asset) from the record-keeping function (i.e., the person responsible for the records of the asset). While this is an important aspect of control procedures, it is only one of several elements that should be considered.

More important than the actual separation of procedures is the thought process that management went through to assign the procedures appropriately. It is hoped they identified valuable assets and related record-keeping functions and considered possible schemes that a malicious employee could use to compromise an asset and conceal that act. Then armed with that information, they methodically assigned duties to reduce the risk of loss. This process, however, should not be a one-time event. Fraud perpetrators are incredibly clever when it comes to defeating control procedures, and management needs to remain diligent for new threats and redesign control procedures appropriately. The assignment of duties to separate incompatible functions, while an important aspect of control, has inherent limitations that must be understood in the overall context of the system of internal controls.

Separation of the custodianship and record-keeping function is not generally effective to prevent a collusional fraud. For example, it is common to separate the check production function (custodianship) from the bank reconciliation process (record keeping), but if the two individuals in charge of the functions decide to work together to remove assets and conceal the act, the control structure can be defeated. In many cases such as this, the apparent separation of duties creates a false sense of security that everything must be working correctly. Additional monitoring procedures must be applied to allow management to ensure that all processed transactions are appropriate even if collusional fraud occurs.

Small organizations have a natural limit with the assignment of duties: It could be impossible to separate the custodianship and record-keeping functions due to the limited number of personnel. It is not always possible to simply hire additional personnel to achieve greater control, and the fraud deterrence practitioner should be extremely cautious if making this recommendation to management. In these cases, management should understand the additional potential exposure allowed by the assignment of incompatible duties and develop additional monitoring procedures to ensure transactions are processed correctly. For example, a small organization may have a single bookkeeper responsible for the preparation of checks and the reconciliation of the bank account. No other qualified person is employed that can assume either of these duties. In this case management should understand that it must develop additional control procedures to oversee the situation. For example, management in that case should directly receive the bank statement, review the statement for suspicious items, examine canceled checks or check images, and then give the statement to the bookkeeper for reconciliation. In this case, even though the bookkeeper is performing the reconciliation, management is performing a high-level review to help ensure no inappropriate transactions are made.

In many organizations, computer systems control the actual ability of employees to process transactions despite what is documented in written procedures. In essence, these systems enforce the separation of incompatible duties and must be maintained with appropriate security procedures to ensure the objectives of management are met. For example, if an employee changes positions within the organization, their old authorities should be removed as new authorities are added. Security procedures to ensure authorities are maintained are critical to ensure employees can perform only the procedures management has authorized.

Additionally, the separation of the record-keeping and custodianship function may not result in the optimum control environment. Consider the separation of the check preparation and bank reconciliation function. Management could decide to assign the reconciliation function to a clerk that has nothing to do with check production. However, given this situation, it is likely the reconciliation that would be prepared would simply be a "tick-and-tie" reconciliation as the clerk would have little knowledge to challenge a given transaction. Such reconciliation is produced by automated systems: If the check number and amount is the same, the item will match and automatically reconcile. In certain situations, a more effective control procedure would be to allow the person who prepared the checks to reconcile the account, and provide additional management oversight of the reconciliation process through additional monitoring procedures.

Procedures Appropriate for Level and Personnel

Fraud-related losses are directly related to the position of the perpetrator. Fraud by the owner or senior executive of an organization causes losses 6 times larger than fraud perpetrated by managers, and 14 times larger than fraud perpetrated by employees.[16] This is because more senior people within the organization have the ability to direct subordinates and override internal control procedures; and they also have the ability to control major relationships, such as with the bank and the external accountant. The ability to perpetrate larger amounts of fraud also can occur when management defines control procedures that delegate too much control to lower levels of the organization. Management, especially in small organizations, should be careful to retain control over key processes, including wire transfer authorities, approval of new vendors, bank relationships, and relationships with external advisors, including accountants and lawyers.

Control procedures also need to be defined correctly for the qualifications of employees within the organization. For small companies, if management puts undue reliance on the work of an unqualified accounting staff, poor accounting records, improper reconciliations, and bad business decisions could result. Eventually this could impair tax reporting and relationships with banks or investors, and could prevent appropriate financial planning of the business owners. For public companies, the risks are even greater.

If management expects employees to make decisions related to complex accounting and business issues—for example, GAAP interpretations—it must invest in appropriately qualified individuals. Section 13A of the Exchange Act requires issuers to file annual and quarterly reports with the SEC; this embodies the requirement that the reports are correct. Issuers must devise and implement internal controls to ensure that transactions are recorded as necessary to permit preparation of financial statements in conformity with GAAP and to maintain accountability of assets. This requirement includes maintaining appropriately qualified and trained staff to perform the duties necessary to record such transactions and prepare financial statements. The SEC imposed cease-and-desist proceedings against Cummins, Inc., for financial reporting deficiencies. The findings of the SEC included:

> Among other things, Cummins failed to employ and train qualified personnel in its Fridley and Darlington finance departments and failed to have an internal control system adequate to monitor the accounts reconciliation process.[17]

Maintaining competent and trained employees is also an important part of the monitoring process. Employees must be versed with the approved control procedures and be able to understand the potential effects of deviating from those procedures in order to understand and challenge a potential management override of the internal control system. In many cases where fraud was perpetrated, management deliberately hired unqualified personnel and deliberately failed to document clear control procedures such that it was extremely easy to instruct the employees to perform inappropriate acts, thus facilitating the fraud.

Control Objectives

Business processes vary from organization to organization based on the size, resources, and objectives of that organization. Likewise, the control procedures need to change as well. Control objectives—the goals that the procedures are designed to accomplish—are fairly consistent from organization to organization. For example, an important control objective is ensuring that vendor invoices are only paid once, or, said another way, duplicate invoices are identified and not paid. In many large companies, the accounts payable system is a primary control; the system checks the vendor number, invoice number, invoice date, and invoice amount against the paid history file, and duplicates are identified. In a smaller organization, with a manual accounts payable system, the clerk pulls a paper file containing prior paid invoices and checks the invoice against the prior paid invoice. In each case, the control objective of "duplicate payments are avoided" is met, but by completely different control procedures.

The common layer of control objectives allows professional advisors, including fraud deterrence analysts and attest auditors, to consistently evaluate the control procedures in diverse organizations. Once the advisor becomes familiar with the control objectives for a given process, it is possible to assess the degree to which the implemented control procedures achieve the control objective. For financial statement audit purposes, the auditor specifically focuses on the control objectives that support the management assertions over the financial statements as well as the transaction- and balance-related audit objectives.

Management Assertions

- Existence
- Completeness
- Valuation and allocation
- Obligation and rights
- Presentation and disclosure

Transaction-related Audit Objectives

- Existence
- Completeness
- Accuracy
- Classification
- Timeliness
- Posting
- Summarization

Balance-related Audit Objectives

- Existence
- Completeness
- Accuracy
- Classification
- Cut-off
- Detail tie-in (sub-accounts tie to general ledger)
- Realizable Value (e.g., impairment)
- Rights and obligations
- Presentation and disclosure

Control Evaluation

The objective of control evaluation is to define the optimum level of control procedures required for an organization to ensure the business processes objectives are met, but still allow the processes to function efficiently. Excessive control procedures tend to degrade the efficiency of operation; appropriate control procedures should balance getting things done with getting them done correctly. The correct level of control is a management decision that must be made explicitly, with knowledge of the risks being assumed by the organization. An example would be the level at which a member of management must countersign checks. A low threshold would mean the manager would spend a majority of their day reviewing and signing checks—probably not the best use of time. Too high a level means management oversight of important transactions may not be achieved. The right level balances the risk against the cost of control, all based on management's view of an acceptable level of risk to the organization.

The control evaluation process will document the internal control structure as implemented within the organization to allow for an assessment of the effectiveness of those controls. This is accomplished by documenting the control objectives necessary to produce accurate results for each task within the business process and identifying the control procedure that ensures that each particular control objective is met. In this manner, the process objectives drive the control objectives, which are satisfied by control procedures.

To help manage the assessment, each business process should be disaggregated into any number of subprocesses and tasks. This will help make the assessment more manageable, as each task can be assessed individually and the results aggregated to achieve an organizational view. Also, the process model can be used to ensure no processes, subprocesses, or tasks are missed in the evaluation.

The main goal of such an assessment is to improve the internal control structure within an organization and reduce the opportunity for fraud and financial misstatement. This includes identifying where control procedures are not adequately designed (i.e., the current control procedures will not satisfy the control objectives), as well as where the control procedures are not consistently followed by the organization. At the same time, the efficiency and effectiveness of operations should be assessed as well. Often new control techniques become available that can help improve the efficiency of the operations with similar or improved control. A recent example is the general availability of Internet banking that allows an authorized user to browse check clearings on a daily basis and review check images online. Additionally, the assessment provides the opportunity to question why a control is performed in the first place, potentially identifying where archaic or obsolete controls should be eliminated and freeing resources to perform essential control activities.

The assessment will reveal control gaps where the design, implementation, or efficiency improvements should be made by the organization. These improvement opportunities will provide value to management, and should be ranked to help management focus on the control issues that require priority action. For example, if a control objective is not met by the controls in place in the process, it could present an opportunity to remove an asset or conceal an illicit act (i.e., allow a fraud to occur). This finding should be flagged for immediate action. If a control objective that presents a lesser risk to the organization is not met, it should be flagged for future follow-up. Control gaps and corrective action plans, including additional investigation (for further reference, please see Chapter 6), if needed, should be thoroughly documented to help ensure adequate follow-up by management.

The end goal of the control evaluation process is to provide management with detail to positively conclude that a system is in place to safeguard assets and ensure that accurate financial reporting is achieved. This documentation is helpful to every organization, and is required for those companies that must report the status of their internal control structures to the SEC under Sarbanes-Oxley Section 404.

MONITORING

Monitoring is a process designed to provide independent assurance that internal control procedures are operating effectively and that all transactions processed conform to standards. Ongoing monitoring should be performed at various levels throughout the organization as part of normal business operations.

For information technology controls, many accepted frameworks, such as the COBIT model published by the Information Systems Audit and Control Association, include a monitoring aspect as key to success of the organization. The COBIT framework includes monitoring standards and detailed implementation guidance for management to:

- Monitor the processes
- Assess internal control adequacy
- Obtain independent assurance
- Provide for independent audit[18]

Monitoring involves both fraud deterrence and fraud detection activities. First, management must ensure that all control processes are performed as designed and approved. Control compliance analysis to verify correct performance of procedures could reveal a control that has been inappropriately modified or is not performed as approved; this control weakness could present the opportunity for fraud. Proactively identifying these weaknesses and correcting them is the fraud deterrence aspect of the monitoring process.

Additionally, management should analyze historical transactions independently from the normal reporting process. This is the fraud detection aspect of monitoring, and it is essential to detect if someone has identified a means to defeat the approved control procedures. For example, collusion could defeat standard internal control procedures, and monitoring of control procedure performance might not detect this. Transaction analysis, including detailed tests of electronic data, can often detect these nonconforming transactions. Comprehensive guidance for independent data monitoring techniques is covered in Chapter 14.

The audit committee should specify the scope and frequency of evaluations of the internal control system; for those organizations with an internal audit function, this timeline should be set as part of the annual internal audit planning process. Additionally, the audit committee should define the process to report deficiencies to senior management, including timing and detail to be included in the report.

Performance of Procedures

Management should regularly verify that internal control procedures are performed as intended as part of the monitoring process. For issuers of financial statements that are required to report the status of internal controls under Sarbanes-Oxley Section 404, the verification of the performance of control procedures is part of the required reporting process. For other issuers and nonpublic companies, this verification is still essential to ensure the system of internal control is operating correctly.

Monitoring of control activities should ensure that all employees performing procedures understand the standard of performance for their functions and should obtain positive evidence that the employees consistently execute the procedures according to that standard. Several methods of verification can be applied to obtain this evidence.

- *Interviews.* The employees should be able to clearly articulate how they perform their procedures. Often these interviews will reveal slight variations in process performance due to shortcuts, impromptu process changes, or process changes that have not been communicated to management. For all companies, these should be explored and certified if indeed a process improvement. For issuers reporting under Section 404 of Sarbanes-Oxley, such undocumented process changes can result in financial reporting issues.
- *Process walk-throughs.* Observation of the business process as performed by the employee should match the process descriptions. This validation method is useful as it allows the observation of the source of the transaction (input), the processing of the transaction, and the output of the transaction (i.e., the link to the subsequent business process into which the transaction flows). Often, in a process walk-through, differences are observed for shortcuts, undocumented system changes, or differences in sources of information (e.g., the source of the information used to process the transaction). This can happen because the person executing the process did not describe the actual processing methods in enough detail during the detail or has made changes to the processing that he or she considers insignificant. Careful analysis should be applied to determine how these minor changes affect the overall control system.
- *Corroboration.* Information obtained during interviews and process observations in one process should verify the understanding of the internal control standards obtained in the analysis of related processes. For example, if the payroll accounting supervisor notes that all employee change request forms are processed prior to the pay week cutoff, and the users of the payroll summary report note that changes are often missed or processed late, further investigation of processing procedures in the payroll area is appropriate.
- *External corroboration.* Communications from external parties should corroborate internally generated information about process execution. External parties, such as vendors and customers, will often have tremendous insight into the actual processing methods of the organization; monitoring this information can provide an independent perspective for how the processes actually work.

Transaction Verification

Transaction verification monitors processing integrity through the latent records produced by the transactions processed by the system. These verifications can be based on system data processed or a review of paper based transaction records. Management should develop scenarios to defeat the internal controls to allow a fraud or financial misstatement; tests should monitor for transactions that could indicate the scenario has occurred.

Account reconciliations can provide insight into the appropriateness of transactions; management should ensure that:

- Key reconciliations are assigned to an independent person
- Key accounts for which reconciliations should be performed are cataloged
- Reconciling items are identified, documented, investigated and resolved
- Management is aware of the processing of reconciliations and aware of major reconciling items and unreconciled items and accounts

Management should also develop monitoring methods independent from reports produced as part of the normal business process. Often these reports are developed with inherent extraction limits that could allow transactions to be processed and not detected as part of the normal business process. Chapter 14 includes guidance for the development of independent monitoring activities. A useful monitoring system should provide:

- Independence from the system processing transactions
- Cross-system and cross-functional comparisons of data to the business rules
- Processing of large volumes of data, not just samples
- Notifications to management of potential anomalies for additional follow-up

Internal Audit

An internal audit function serves as a primary monitoring activity of management; an internal audit function is required by many stock exchanges as a condition for being listed. The internal audit profession is guided by professional standards issued by the Institute of Internal Auditors.[19] The IIA definition of internal auditing states:

> Internal auditing is an independent, objective assurance and consulting activity designed to add value and improve an organization's operations.
>
> It helps an organization accomplish its objectives by bringing a systematic, disciplined approach to evaluate and improve the effectiveness of risk management, control, and governance processes.[20]

IIA standards require the audit function to remain independent from operating management, in essence, putting the auditors in a position to provide objective assessments of company operations to the audit committee of the board. The internal audit function assists the audit committee with the implementation and evaluation of corporate governance by communicating values and goals and by monitoring organizational accomplishment of those goals.

Traditionally, internal audit was involved with operational and compliance auditing; however, since the requirements of the Sarbanes-Oxley Act placed particular emphasis on the importance of accurate financial reporting, many internal audit functions increased their involvement in the evaluation of Sarbanes-Oxley compliance initiatives within the organization, including financial reporting procedures and Section 404 internal control documentation efforts.

The audit charter defines the purpose, authority, and responsibility of the internal audit function within the organization. The internal audit function develops the charter with the approval of the audit committee of the board based on their need for oversight within the organization. Once board expectations are identified, the internal audit function can develop a high-level audit budget, often including a mix of compliance auditing, financial reporting oversight, internal consulting activities, and special projects. Many of these activities go beyond traditional "compliance" activities: For internal controls, for example, internal audit can assist with the evaluation of the efficiency and effectiveness of internal control procedures, as well as overall compliance with those procedures.

During the conduct of their work, internal auditors will remain vigilant for significant control weaknesses, and report any such observations to the appropriate level of management.[21] This places the internal audit function on the front lines of fraud deterrence. Significant control weaknesses could present the opportunity for fraud, and such opportunities, depending on the specific situation, should be explored to determine if the opportunity was indeed exploited. Internal audit could perform the fraud investigation; however, this would require a change in scope, qualifications, and budget from the initial audit plan. The examiner performing the fraud audit would need to be qualified; this skill set is usually available in most internal audit functions. If not, the chief audit executive should have the authority and budget to hire an outside expert to assist with the fraud examination.

Fraud Deterrence

Monitoring is inherently a detection activity; however, the fact that management actively monitors internal control performance to ensure compliance with procedures and additionally monitors for nonconforming transactions sends a clear message that any attempts of fraudulent activity will be rapidly detected and remediated. This, in essence, reinforces the control culture and control environment messages that such behavior will not be tolerated. In this manner, organizational knowledge of effective monitoring activities is a strong deterrence to fraud.

NOTES

1. PCAOB Auditing Standard 2, "An Audit of Internal Control over Financial Reporting Performed in Conjunction with an Audit of Financial Statements," March 9, 2004. Available at: http://www.pcaobus.org/Rules/Rules_of_the_Board/Auditing_Standard_2.pdf.
2. Association of Certified Fraud Examiners Report to the Nation, 2002.
3. Letter to SEC Advisory Committee on Smaller Public Companies, September 19, 2005. Available at: http://www.sec.gov/info/smallbus/acspc/coxacspcletter081805.pdf.
4. PCAOB Auditing Standard 2, paragraph 14. Available at: http://www.pcaobus.org/Rules/Rules_of_the_Board/Auditing_Standard_2.pdf.
5. Internal Control, Integrated Framework, "Executive Summary."
6. Management Override of Internal Controls: The Achilles Heel of Financial Reporting, AICPA, 2005. Available at: http://www.aicpa.org/audcommctr/download/achilles_heel.pdf.
7. Additional information on ISACA and the COBIT model of IT control is available at the ISACA Web site" www.isaca.org.
8. COBIT Executive Summary, Information Systems Audit and Control Foundation. Available at: http://www.isaca.org/Template.cfm?Section=COBIT6&Template=/MembersOnly.cfm&ContentID=23325.
9. GTAG Guide 1: Information Technology Controls. Available at: http://www.theiia.org/index.cfm?doc_id=5166.
10. Sarbanes-Oxley Section 301. Available at: http://frwebgate.access.gpo.gov/cgi-bin/getdoc.cgi?dbname=107_cong_bills&docid=f:h3763enr.tst.pdf.
11. Association of Certified Fraud Examiners 2004 Report to the Nation. Available at: http://www.cfenet.com/pdfs/2004RttN.pdf.
12. SEC Statement on Management Discussion and Analysis of Financial Condition and Results of Operations. Available at: www.sec.gov/rules/other/33-8056.htm.
13. Final Rule: Certification of Disclosure in Companies' Quarterly and Annual Reports, available: www.sec.gov/rules/final/33-8124.htm.
14. COSO—Enterprise Risk Management Integrated Framework, © 1992, 2004 AICPA, by the Committee of Sponsoring Organizations of the Treadway Commission. Reproduced with permission from the AICPA acting as authorized copyright administrator for COSO.
15. COSO—Enterprise Risk Management Integrated Framework, © 1992, 2004 AICPA, by the Committee of Sponsoring Organizations of the Treadway Commission. Reproduced with permission from the AICPA acting as authorized copyright administrator for COSO.
16. Certified Fraud Examiners 2004 Report to the Nation. Available at: http://www.cfenet.com/pdfs/2004RttN.pdf.
17. Accounting and Auditing Enforcement Release No. 2370/February 7, 2006, In the Matter of Cummins, Inc. Respondent. Available at: http://www.sec.gov/divisions/enforce/friactions.shtml.

18. COBIT, 4th Edition, COBIT Steering Committee and the IT Governance Institute. Available at: www.isaca.org.
19. For more information about the Institute of Internal Auditors, please visit their Web site: www.theiia.org.
20. Institute of Internal Auditors, IIA Definition of Internal Auditing. Available at: http://www.theiia.org/index.cfm?doc_id=123.
21. Institute of Internal Auditors, IIA Performance Standards. Available at: http://www.theiia.org/?doc_id=1617.

Chapter 10

Recent Corporate Governance Reforms Enacted to Deter Financial Fraud: The Sarbanes-Oxley Act of 2002 and Related Rules and Regulations

Carolyn H. Rosenberg, James A. Rolfes, and J. Andrew Moss

INTRODUCTION

Scope of Chapter

In 2002, Congress said "Enough!" A string of high-profile corporate scandals, often involving egregious financial statement manipulation, had shaken confidence in the U.S. securities markets. Billion-dollar accounting errors had occurred despite the presence of independent directors, duly formed audit committees, and outside auditors. An outcry for reform of corporate governance followed, leading to the July 2002 enactment of the Sarbanes-Oxley Act[1] and the subsequent revision of the New York Stock Exchange (NYSE) and Nasdaq listing standards, all with the goal of enhancing public and investor confidence in the integrity of financial reporting and disclosure.

Believing that the links in the chain of financial statement preparation—from initial bookkeeping through public disclosure of financial results—had failed to assure honest and accurate financial reporting, Congress designed Sarbanes-Oxley to force substantial change. Key provisions of this legislation mandate that: senior management explicitly take responsibility for, and certify the effectiveness of, internal controls over financial reporting; the company's outside auditors examine, and independently assess, management's documentation, testing, and

Note: This synopsis of key provisions of the Sarbanes-Oxley Act of 2002 and related corporate governance rules is informational only and is not intended to provide legal advice nor express the opinions of Sachnoff & Weaver, Ltd., any of its attorneys, or any of its clients, as applied to any particular circumstances. Readers should consult knowledgeable legal counsel to answer questions and obtain advice.

Note: The authors thank Neil Berkowitz, a paralegal in Sachnoff & Weaver's Insurance Coverage Group, for his invaluable assistance in preparing this Chapter.

evaluation of internal control effectiveness; and the company adopt procedures aimed at encouraging individual employees to report accounting and auditing problems. The legislation also establishes more rigorous independence and substantive qualifications for members of a company's audit committee, and requires them to take a proactive role in ensuring the accuracy and integrity of reported financial results.

To further strengthen issuer accountability, integrity and transparency, the NYSE and Nasdaq issued revised corporate governance listing standards in November 2003 that imposed requirements even more expansive than demanded by Sarbanes-Oxley. In general, listed companies must:

1. Have boards composed of a majority of independent directors
2. Establish procedures for communication between nonmanagement parties and nonmanagement directors
3. Adopt and publish an audit committee charter, corporate governance guidelines, and codes of business conduct and ethics
4. Employ internal auditors
5. Put in place nominating and compensation committees composed entirely of independent directors.

The NYSE and Nasdaq governance rules also require the nonmanagement directors to meet in executive session at regular intervals, and for the audit committee to meet separately and periodically with management, internal audit, and the independent auditor.

This chapter explores the reforms brought about by the Sarbanes-Oxley legislation and the related changes to the listing standards of the exchanges, with emphasis on the effect they have on the structure and responsibilities of a company's board, audit committee, and internal audit department.

Efforts to Reform Corporate Governance Prior to the Enactment of the Sarbanes-Oxley Act

In the summer of 1998, Securities and Exchange Commission (SEC) chairman Arthur Levitt sounded an alarm in the face of the growing predilection of companies to employ what he called "hocus-pocus" accounting to achieve desired reported financial results.[2] In remarks intended to signal the need for fundamental change in the conduct in the nation's corporate boardrooms, Levitt stated:

> Too many corporate managers, auditors, and analysts are participants in a game of nods and winks. In the zeal to satisfy consensus earnings estimates and project a smooth earnings path, wishful thinking may be winning the day over faithful representation. As a result, I fear that we are witnessing an erosion in the quality of earnings, and therefore, the quality of financial reporting.[3]

Levitt then lamented that audit committees—which he believed could serve as the most reliable guardians of the public interest—instead rarely met, had allegiances to management, and lacked expertise in the basic principles of financial reporting.[4]

In response to Levitt's call to arms, the NYSE and National Association of Securities Dealers (NASD) Blue Ribbon Committee on Improving the Effectiveness of Corporate Audit Committees issued a 71-page report. Included in the report were 10 recommendations that focused on installing independent and financially literate individuals on a company's audit committee who would inform themselves of both the acceptability and quality of the company's application of accounting principles.[5] The Blue Ribbon Committee Report further suggested a series of guiding principles for audit committee best practices highlighting the audit committee's responsibility to understand and monitor the financial reporting activities of management and the outside auditors, the benefits of having regularly scheduled and probing communications with the internal and outside auditors, and the need to engage independent legal counsel and financial advisors when circumstances dictate.[6]

This emphasis on improving the qualifications for, and the rigor expected of, audit committees represented a sea change in corporate governance. While the Delaware Chancery Court in 1996 emphasized a director's duty to assure that corporate information and reporting systems provided "timely, accurate information sufficient to allow management and the board . . . to reach informed judgments concerning both the corporation's compliance with laws and its business performance,"[7] nothing before had so particularized the criteria for audit committee oversight. To the contrary, academic research identified that some companies populated their audit committees with the least experienced of all board members, either because board members perceived such service as the least desirable of the board committees, or as the result of being bestowed on more senior board members solely because they had a little more time to devote to such matters.[8] Further, in some cases, audit committees failed to hold executive sessions with internal or outside auditors, thus potentially inhibiting the ability of such committees to receive information free from the influence of senior management.[9]

A quick succession of significant corporate failures in 2001—such as Adelphia, Tyco, WorldCom, and Enron—led the market regulators, the president, and Congress to focus on what they perceived as the failure of directors, audit committees, internal auditors, and outside accountants to prevent wrongdoing. From January through June 2002, nine congressional committees announced hearings to investigate the corporate failures; the SEC proposed new corporate disclosure requirements; the president issued a 10-point plan aimed at improving investor information, corporate executive accountability, and independent auditor quality; the NYSE and Nasdaq formed committees to study corporate governance rules; and federal legislators introduced at least 23 reform bills in the House of Representatives and 12 reform bills in the Senate.[10] Then, in July 2002, Congress enacted the Sarbanes-Oxley legislation, which transformed many of the recommendations noted in the 1999 Blue Ribbon Report into explicit statutory requirements for public companies (and followed by many private companies as well). A year and a half later, in November 2003, the NYSE and Nasdaq received SEC approval of their updated, and even more stringent, corporate governance listing requirements.

Key Provisions of Sarbanes-Oxley and Related Rules and Market Regulations

Some commentators have referred to the enactment of the Sarbanes-Oxley Act as the most significant corporate governance legislation since the passage of the federal securities laws in 1933 and 1934.[11] The act's emphasis on identifying the responsibilities of various corporate actors, assuring the independence of audit committee members, and establishing a structure in which an audit committee can conduct its oversight role free from the potential undue influence of senior management signify a marked change in the mandatory measures a corporation must take to monitor the production of its reported financial results. The specific requirements of selected provisions of the Sarbanes-Oxley follow.

Sarbanes-Oxley Section 301—Public Company Audit Committees. Public companies must establish audit committees made up of independent directors and require that such audit committees:

1. Appoint, determine compensation of, oversee, and receive the reports of the company's outside auditors
2. Resolve disputes between management and the outside auditors
3. Establish procedures for the receipt and treatment of complaints regarding the accounting, internal accounting controls, and auditing matters
4. Engage, as necessary, independent counsel and other advisors
5. Receive sufficient funding to employ the outside auditors and audit committee advisors

To meet the independence requirements of the act, a member of the audit committee may not receive consulting, advisory, or other compensatory fees from the company other than compensation as a board member, audit committee member, or other board committee member, and cannot be affiliated with (e.g., in the management of) the company or its subsidiaries.[12]

Sarbanes-Oxley Section 302—Management Attestation to Financial Statements. A company's chief executive officer (CEO) and chief financial officer (CFO) must certify in quarterly and fiscal year-end reports that:

1. The company's financial statements contain no material misstatements.
2. The financial statements fairly present the company's financial position and results of operations.
3. Internal controls have been established to ensure the receipt material information about the company.
4. They have evaluated and opined on the effectiveness of such internal controls.
5. The outside auditors and the audit committee have received disclosure of all significant deficiencies in internal controls and any fraud that involves management or employees with a significant role with the company's internal controls.
6. Significant changes in internal controls, including any corrective actions taken with regard to deficiencies and material weaknesses, have been disclosed.[13]

Sarbanes-Oxley Section 404—Management Assessment of Internal Controls. A report by management on the effectiveness of internal controls must accompany the company's annual report. The company's outside auditors must attest to and report on management's assessment of internal controls.[14]

Sarbanes-Oxley Section 406—Code of Ethics. A company must disclose whether it has adopted a code of ethics for senior financial experts.[15]

Sarbanes-Oxley Section 407—Audit Committee Financial Expert Disclosure. A company must disclose whether at least one member of the audit committee is a financial expert (i.e., that such committee member has an understanding of generally accepted accounting principles and financial statements), and experience in, or understanding of:

1. The preparation or auditing of financial statements
2. The accounting for estimates, accruals and reserves
3. Internal accounting controls
4. Audit committee functions[16]

Sarbanes-Oxley Section 906—Corporate Responsibility for Financial Reports. The CEO and CFO must certify that financial statements issued by the company comply with SEC reporting rules and that the statements fairly present, in all material respects, the financial condition and results of operations of the company.

In November 2003, the NYSE and Nasdaq reformed their respective corporate governance rules, both to conform their rules to the requirements of Sarbanes-Oxley and to impose additional standards on listed companies. Some significant NYSE and Nasdaq requirements follow.

Independent Directors. Both the NYSE and Nasdaq require that the majority of a company's directors be independent and meet in regularly scheduled executive sessions (i.e., without nonindependent directors or management). Additionally, listed companies must establish procedures pursuant to which interested parties can make their concerns known to the independent directors.[17]

Nominating and Compensation Committees. A listed company must establish committees made up of independent directors that determine procedures for nominating persons to serve on the board of directors and for determining the compensation of senior management.[18]

Expanded Role for Audit Committees. Audit committees must consist of at least three directors, all of whom must be independent and financially literate, with at least one member possessing accounting or related financial management expertise. A written audit committee charter must set forth the committee's purpose, which, at minimum, includes oversight of the integrity of the financial statements, compliance with legal and regulatory requirements, qualifications of the independent auditor, and performance of the company's internal audit function. Additionally, the charter must indicate how the audit committee will conduct its annual performance evaluation, and articulate the committee's duties and responsibilities, including:

- Obtaining and reviewing independent auditor report on internal controls
- Discussing with management and independent auditors the annual audited financial statements
- Discussing press releases and financial guidance provided to analysts
- Meeting periodically and regularly with management, internal auditors, and independent auditors[19]

Internal Audit. Listed companies must maintain an internal audit function to provide management and audit committee with ongoing assessments of the company's risk management processes and system of internal control.[20]

Code of Ethics. All listed companies must adopt and publish codes of ethics that are reasonably calculated to deter wrongdoing and promote: honest and ethical conduct; full, fair, accurate, timely, and understandable disclosure; compliance with applicable laws; prompt internal reporting of ethical violations; and accountability for adherence to the ethical code.[21]

BOARD OF DIRECTORS

Much investor attention of late has focused on the asserted failure of some corporate boards to provide adequate oversight and to fulfill their duties to act in the best interests of the company and its shareholders. In addition to calls by public pension funds, such as California Public Employees' Retirement System (CalPERS) and TIAA-CREF, for corporate governance reform and increased board participation in corporate affairs,[22] governmental, regulatory, and investor watchdog groups also have asserted that a passive board, beholden to, or hand picked by senior corporate management, or unduly influenced by pro-management presentations, may create an environment that makes financial statement fraud possible.[23] Government regulation and investor concerns have led companies to take additional measures to increase the independence, competence, and understanding of boards of directors.

Although Sarbanes-Oxley and the NYSE and Nasdaq listing standards focus much attention on auditors, audit committees, and CEO and CFO responsibility, they each contain provisions aimed at increasing the board of directors' oversight effectiveness.

Director independence serves as the touchstone of the regulatory scheme established by corporate governance reform laws and regulation. After setting forth detailed independence criteria aimed at assuring that an "independent director" has neither financial nor material relationships with the corporate entity, or a recent past affiliation with the management of the corporation, the mandated NYSE and Nasdaq governance standards require that independent directors make up the majority of the board members.[24] According to commentary to the NYSE corporate governance rules, "Requiring a majority of independent directors will increase the quality of board oversight and lessen the possibility of damaging conflicts of interest."[25] Additionally, three committees of the board must be comprised solely of independent directors: audit; compensation; and nominating and corporate governance.[26]

The regulations make the board responsible for setting criteria for independence and for deciding on and monitoring annually the independence of its members. Commentary to the NYSE listing standards advises that in doing so, a board must consider all relevant facts and circumstances and must look at the issue from the standpoint of both the director and of persons or organizations with which the director has an affiliation.[27] Material relationships, such as commercial, industrial, banking, consulting, legal, accounting, charitable, and familial, all can affect the independence of a particular director.[28] According to NYSE commentary, by adopting categorical standards to assist its independence determinations and disclosing how directors either meet or do not meet such standards, the board also can give investors a means of assessing the quality of a board's independence.[29]

The NYSE and Nasdaq corporate governance reforms also require enactment of procedures that encourage communication among and with nonmanagement directors as a distinct group. Independent directors must meet regularly in executive session without management directors present. Additionally, the board must either name a presiding independent director or establish procedures so that all independent directors can act as a group, and must further provide a means for interested parties to communicate with independent directors.[30]

The new regulations also express the need to attract qualified individuals for board service. Boards should consist of highly qualified persons who can and will make the substantial commitment of time and effort necessary to take proactive steps rather than passively ratifying management's agenda.[31] The NYSE and various commentators suggest that a company also provide a detailed orientation program for new directors and comprehensive continuing education programs for all directors.[32] Boards also should have the power to consult with independent advisors when business, compensation, or legal issues requiring particularized knowledge arise.[33] To align each director's interest with those of the shareholders, many companies require directors to own a certain minimum amount of stock or to comply with some limitations on their ability to sell stock while on the board.[34] Further, to assure that any particular board member is not overburdened, some companies limit the number of other boards on which their directors may serve.

The NYSE Listed Company Manual and NASD Marketplace Rules provide that the board of directors also must take responsibility for establishing written corporate governance guidelines and a code of ethical conduct.[35] Because the board must rely on financial statements in deciding where and how to allocate corporate resources, it cannot allow a failure in how the company assembles and presents financial information to cause a disconnect between operational reality and the resource planning and control the board oversees.[36] Thus, the Sarbanes-Oxley Act and other recent reforms call for "quality control of not only the financial reports, but also the processes and systems that combine to provide input to those reports,"[37] and focus on establishing the appropriate ethical culture and tone at the top as opposed to a formalized rigid approach on policies and procedures.[38]

The Committee of Sponsoring Organizations of the Treadway Commission (COSO)—a public interest organization organized to suggest a framework to help businesses assess and enhance internal control systems—suggests that undertaking a thorough risk and compliance assessment represents the first step in establishing appropriate corporate and ethical guidelines.[39] From such a review, the board can develop particularized compliance standards and procedures tailored to the organization and that specify the responsibilities of the organization's governing authority and leadership in assuring compliance.[40] The board should give special attention in this regard to fashioning a prominent role for itself in assuring compliance with corporate guidelines, a goal former Federal Reserve chairman Paul Volker believed could more easily be met by separating the chief executive and chairman positions.[41]

Some commentators recommend that boards also should conduct annual reviews of their performance as well as that of board committees.[42] Such reviews should consider not only the entity's progress in complying with the reforms mandated by recent legislation and regulation, but also the substantive commitment individual directors have made to the organization. Commentators urge that by making the personal commitment of time and effort to pursue their role as guardians of shareholder interests, directors can instill the standards of integrity and effectiveness necessary to restore investor confidence.[43]

AUDIT COMMITTEE

Courts and commentators have identified an audit committee's lack of vigilance a key factor for how a substantial financial statement fraud could take place and grow. For instance, both have criticized Enron's audit committee (referred to by the chairman of the NASD as "the worst audit committee I have ever seen") for failing to prevent fraud by taking an overly deferential role to management.[44] Similarly, the court in the WorldCom securities litigation concluded that the WorldCom audit committee likely would have uncovered accounting fraud had it not met for only three to five hours each year, kept almost no records, and abdicated its responsibilities to challenge upper financial management.[45] And recently, the SEC showed its determination to prosecute audit committee members that fail to fulfill oversight duties by citing the Hollinger International audit committee members for allegedly "ignoring clear signs of wrongdoing."[46]

Not surprisingly, therefore, the Sarbanes-Oxley legislation and the NYSE and Nasdaq listing standards mandate specific measures for, and impose weighty responsibilities on, members of audit committees.[47] Referred to as "the most obvious expression of Sarbanes-Oxley interference in corporate governance," the reforms seek to make the audit committee an integral part of corporate accountability and governance. As one commentor said:

> [T]he Audit committee is the lynchpin of reform of accounting, financial statement and auditing matters, and the heart of the corporate governance reforms that are the focus of [Sarbanes-Oxley], regulations promulgated by the SEC under the act, . . . the . . . listing requirements of the New York Stock Exchange and the revised listing standards [of] the Nasdaq Stock market.[48]

As with the board generally, the recent reforms emphasize the independence and qualifications of those who sit on an audit committee. The NYSE and Nasdaq rules require that all members of a company's audit committee (which must consist of at least three individuals) be independent, meaning not part of management; not receiving consulting, advisory, or compensation other than director fees; and not otherwise affiliated with the company or any of its subsidiaries.[49] All must also have financial acumen and at least one must possess financial expertise—that is, understands GAAP and financial statements; has experience with the preparation or auditing of financial statements of comparable companies and the application of principles in connection with accounting of estimates, accruals, and reserves; has experience with internal accounting controls; and understands audit committee functions.[50] Commentators suggest that the intent behind the financial expert requirement is that this person will take a leadership role in spotting issues of importance and explaining financial data to colleagues on the committee.[51] Although not mandated, various commentators also suggest that audit committee members obtain continuing accounting education by scheduling sessions with the CFO, the auditor, and possibly a consultant such as an accounting professor, to ensure that they remain current on the latest accounting pronouncements and industry issues.[52]

Such independence and accounting knowledge are important as the regulatory scheme calls for the audit committee to serve as the central communication hub of financial and internal control information. For instance, the regulations demand that the audit committee meet separately with management, internal audit, and the outside accountants.[53] Various commentators suggest that the committee should use these meetings as opportunities to identify the company's critical accounting policies, discuss the company's risk assessment and risk management policies, evaluate the material financial risks the company faces, understand any off–balance sheet financing the company uses, surface any related party transactions, and judge the abilities of the company's management and auditing personnel.[54] The audit committee must also study the various reports the regulations require management and the outside auditors to prepare. The regulations provide that these reports highlight critical accounting policies and practices, alternative treatments and disclosure of financial information suggested by the outside auditors, and any observed deficiencies with internal controls.[55] The audit committee must also field concerns raised by other interested parties, such as lower-level employees, that identify potentially problematic accounting or internal control issues, as well as any fraud, whether material or not, that involves management or other employees with a significant role in the company's internal controls.[56]

According to the commentators, being the intended recipient of such information implies a responsibility to address any concerns or issues that arise.[57] This may require that from time to time the members of the committee ask probing questions in response to management reports, take positions adversarial to management, and conduct investigations of questionable practices or behavior.[58] Depending on the issues involved, commentators suggest that this may require the committee to engage counsel and investigative personnel and to work directly with internal or outside auditors to gain a sufficient understanding of the problem and devise appropriate corrective actions.[59]

The audit committee should not restrict itself, however, simply to reacting to issues raised affirmatively by management, auditors, or employee complaints, but instead should take a proactive approach to understanding the current issues as they arise.[60] This means seeking input from those outside the senior management ranks. For instance, according to one commentator, interviewing sales personnel can provide insight to the reasonableness of the company's revenue recognition policies.[61] Similarly, discussions with tax managers may identify aggressive tax strategies employed by the company.[62] Audit committees should also consider whether events such as sales of stock by management, transactions creating a conflict of interest for management, or questionable or extravagant personal behavior of senior officers demand further independent analysis.[63] In sum, audit committee members who interact with employees below the CEO and CFO level may gain an understanding of the company's ethical culture and its compliance with laws and regulations.[64]

The audit committee must take care that disclosure provided by the company fairly and accurately reflects the material information the committee obtains as the result of the reports it receives and the investigations it performs, and includes balanced presentation of financial information. The regulations explicitly require that the audit committee review and discuss with management and the outside auditors the company's quarterly and annual financial statements, including the management discussion and analysis (MD&A) sections of such reports, and report they have done so in the company's proxy statements.[65] The committee must also give independent analysis to the company's earnings releases and the financial information and earnings guidance provided to analysts and rating agencies.[66] The company's obligation pursuant to Sarbanes-Oxley Section 404 to produce an annual report on management's assessment of the effectiveness of the company's internal controls also represents an area of required focus for the audit committee.[67] It is incumbent on the audit committee to ensure that management has undertaken the procedures necessary to make such an assessment and that any weakness in internal controls such assessment identifies receives proper disclosure.[68]

The audit committee also has the responsibility for establishing the company's relationship with the outside auditors and overseeing the conduct and scope of company audits.[69] Sarbanes-Oxley mandates that the audit committee employ, and decide the compensation of, the independent auditors.[70] The regulations also task the committee with the review and approval of all audit and nonaudit services the outside auditor provides the company.[71] The committee additionally determines whether the outside auditor meets the independence criteria established by Sarbanes-Oxley and sets hiring policies for employees of the outside auditors who seek positions within the company.[72] From a substantive standpoint, the committee must meet periodically in executive session with the outside auditors, resolve any disagreements the auditors have with management, consider any issues raised by peer reviews of the outsider auditor's performance, and, at least on an annual basis, review and discuss the outside auditor's report on the company's internal quality-control procedures.[73] According to commentators, best practices also dictate that members of the audit committee comment on the audit scope set by the auditors, review results of significant audit tests, and ask the auditors detailed questions about the financial statements, focusing on the quality of earnings as well as the overall quality of financial reporting.[74]

The charter requirements of the corporate governance reforms additionally demand that the audit committee spell out its purpose, duties, and responsibilities.[75] The written charter, which the company must publish, should identify the overall mission of the audit committee including, at a minimum, its obligation to oversee the preparation of annual proxy materials and financial statements, the company's compliance with legal and regulatory requirements, and the independence and quality of the internal and outside audit performance.[76] The committee should also set forth the specific duties and responsibilities taken on by the committee, including those just mentioned, and annually evaluate its own performance in fulfilling its established purpose and responsibilities.[77]

Clearly Sarbanes-Oxley and the NYSE and Nasdaq regulations have ushered in a new era of audit committee rigor and duty. As the commentators summarize, audit committee members must come to the job with significant financial experience, the temperament necessary to challenge management, and the ability to devote significant time and effort.[78] To ensure that it fulfills the responsibilities assigned, the committee should conduct its affairs with a sense of purpose and formality that may have been absent in the past in certain companies.[79]

MANAGEMENT

The Sarbanes-Oxley legislation is explicit in establishing the obligations of a company's CEO and CFO to develop internal controls and to certify the company's financial reports.

Under the Sarbanes-Oxley legislation, the CEO and CFO must certify in each annual and quarterly report submitted by the company that they have reviewed the report, and, based on their personal knowledge, that the report does not contain any untrue statements of material fact, or omit a material fact necessary to make the statements made not misleading, and that the financial statements in the report fairly present in all material respects the company's financial condition and results of operations.[80] Additionally these two senior officers must affirmatively state their responsibility for the company's internal controls and that they have in fact designed internal controls to ensure they receive material information relating to the company.[81] The report must further affirm that the CEO and CFO have evaluated the effectiveness of the company's internal controls and reported to the company's audit committee and outside auditors any deficiencies in internal controls that could adversely affect the company's ability to record and report financial information and any fraud, whether material or not, involving management or other employees with a significant role in the company's internal controls.[82]

As various commentators have observed, the senior management review obligations created by the Sarbanes-Oxley legislation can represent a heavy task.[83] Some companies, for instance, issue 10-K reports with dozens or even hundreds of pages of dense language and numbers, all of which, under Sarbanes-Oxley, require a personal review.[84] Moreover, the SEC has interpreted the "fair presentation" standard to which the senior officers must attest to be a standard of overall material accuracy and completeness broader than simply GAAP compliance.[85] As stated by the SEC:

> In our view, a "fair presentation" of an issuer's financial condition, results of operations and cash flows encompasses the selection of appropriate accounting policies, proper application of appropriate accounting policies, disclosure of financial information that is informative and reasonably reflects the underlying transactions and events and the inclusion of any additional disclosure necessary to provide investors with a materially accurate and complete picture of an issuer's financial condition, results of operations and cash flows.[86]

Regulations enacted by the SEC also make a distinction between "internal controls" and "disclosure controls and procedures." According to one treatise, "internal control refers to the controls that provide reasonable assurance regarding the reliability of financial reporting and preparation of the financial statements . . . [while] [d]isclosure controls and procedures are those that ensure that material information is made known to the [CEO and CFO] by others in the entity, on a timely basis."[87] Sarbanes-Oxley makes the senior management responsible for both.

Section 404 of Sarbanes-Oxley additionally mandates that the senior officers will provide an annual internal control report.[88] In the report, management must both acknowledge its responsibility for establishing and maintaining adequate internal control structure and procedures for the company's financial reporting, and assess the effectiveness of such internal controls.[89] While management can look to others to assist in the design, monitoring, and assessment of internal controls, such as outside contractors expert in the design and implementation of control systems, or internal auditors that regularly test controls, commentators note that management cannot avoid ultimate responsibility for the ensuring the implementation of an effective internal control environment.[90]

Much has been and continues to be written about the means by which management should design and evaluate a company's internal controls. A full discussion of alternative approaches is beyond the scope of this chapter. At a minimum, however, commentators make clear that management must undertake substantial analysis of its internal control environment, be cognizant of the various internal control procedures appropriate for their company's industry or business, reference professional standards for testing internal control frameworks, and document internal controls and evaluations sufficiently for auditor review.[91]

INTERNAL AUDITORS

Although not specifically mentioned by Sarbanes-Oxley, and while required but only generally referred to by the NYSE and Nasdaq governance standards, the role of internal auditors has received increased attention in the Sarbanes-Oxley era. Within their purview of internal control, internal auditors have the responsibility to examine and evaluate all of a company's systems, processes, operations, functions, and activities.[92] Given this access, expertise, and knowledge, internal audit can play an important role in ensuring the effectiveness of internal controls and in bringing any weaknesses noted to the attention of the appropriate parties.

Commentators explain that establishing the appropriate reporting structure is essential to an effective and objective internal audit function.[93] Internal auditors must have unrestricted access to a company's audit committee, which should review the scope of, and provide the resources for, their audit procedures.[94] While the corporate governance reforms require audit committees to have executive sessions with internal auditors, commentators have articulated that a company may enhance the value of internal audit's contribution to the internal control structure by taking the internal auditor's primary reporting responsibility away from the CFO, where it traditionally has resided, and move it to the audit committee.[95]

Some nationally prominent audit firms suggest that internal audit departments adopt an expansive view of their mission.[96] At a minimum, assert some commentators, the internal auditors of a company must understand the business of the company, the financial and control risks that it faces, and the corporate governance processes in place to ensure that corporate transactions are appropriately authorized and accurately reported.[97] Such auditors should also understand the fundamental accounting concepts employed by the company and examine significant financial transactions.[98] In that way, according to the commentators, the internal auditor can bring professional judgment to bear on the results of the audit tests performed and provide an objective set of eyes to the audit committee and management. Additionally, the internal auditors should undertake to assist corporate officers and the audit committee to reinvigorate the company's risk assessment and control processes over financial reporting.

Various commentators also advise that internal audit should view the audit committee as its primary client. This requires that internal auditors understand the risk and control objectives of the audit committee and align its work plan to respond to those objectives.[99] Internal auditors should also keep the audit committee focused on the most significant risks facing the company.[100] Additionally, the auditors should take the initiative to establish effective information systems that provide the audit committee with objective, comprehensive, and comprehensible information. As suggested by the Blue Ribbon Committee, that communication scheme should include regular meetings between internal auditors and the audit committee and the production of regular confidential memoranda or reports circulated only to the audit committee.

ENFORCEMENT

The Sarbanes-Oxley legislation provides that violations of the act or any rule or regulation issued under the act will be treated in the same manner as a violation under the Securities Exchange Act of 1934. While an in-depth discussion of the SEC enforcement powers is beyond the scope of this chapter, generally the SEC has the ability to seek civil money penalties and disgorgement, and injunctive relief against violators, and to bar individuals from being associated with the management of public companies. When a restatement of financial statements occurs, the SEC can also seek from a CEO or CFO return of incentive pay tied to a company's performance. The legislation also provides for more stringent criminal penalties for those who knowingly give false certifications or impede investigations of securities violations.

PROTECTIONS FOR DIRECTORS AND OFFICERS

The increased responsibility of corporate directors and officers under the Sarbanes-Oxley Act and related corporate governance rules makes attracting and retaining highly qualified individuals a key goal. Ironically, the establishment of these standards may have the effect of causing some qualified persons to shy away from such service, fearful of incurring personal liability. As two highly respected Delaware jurists, William B. Chandler III and Leo E. Strine, Jr., recently suggested, breach of fiduciary claims likely will arise from purported failures of corporate directors and officers to conform to the best practices requirements of Sarbanes-Oxley and the exchange governance rules.[101]

Three important mechanisms may offer directors and officers possible protection against personal loss resulting from their service to the corporation: statutory limited director liability; advancement and indemnification; and liability insurance.[102] The ability of such limited liability, indemnification, and insurance to protect directors and officers may vary depending on a company's state of incorporation. By way of example, Delaware—where many public companies are incorporated and which historically has been influential in the development of corporate law—allows a corporation to eliminate or limit a director's personal liability to the corporation or its shareholders for money damages for certain breaches of duty.[103] Directors can obtain this limitation on their personal liability only for actions taken in their capacities as directors, and cannot rely on this statutory protection to avoid liability for breaches of traditional duties of loyalty, failures to act in good faith, or certain other acts or omissions listed in the statute.[104] Recent Delaware court decisions, seemingly equating a lack of good faith with a director's failure to monitor and engage in proper oversight of corporate affairs, also have caused some to question the scope of the protection a corporation can provide its directors for a breach of their duties of care, noting the "good faith" exception set forth in the statute may eviscerate the duty of care exculpation.[105]

For those acts or omissions for which corporations cannot eliminate or limit personal liability of directors, corporations are permitted (and in some circumstances may be required) to protect directors, officers, employees, and agents by advancing defense expenses and providing indemnification for certain real or threatened litigation or investigations resulting from their service to the corporation.[106] Directors' and officers' liability (D&O) insurance potentially provides another degree of protection.[107] A primary purpose of D&O insurance is to protect directors and officers from personal loss resulting from their service to a corporation. D&O policies also commonly reimburse a corporation for indemnity amounts it pays in connection with claims made against directors and officers. D&O insurance also may protect directors and officers in the event the company is financially unable to meet its indemnification obligations or the corporation is prohibited from indemnifying directors and officers.[108] D&O insurance policies, in general, however, contain exclusions for dishonest conduct and unlawful profit or benefit. Companies may also purchase commercial crime or fidelity coverage to protect against loss or liability to third parties caused by employee dishonesty or other criminal or fraudulent acts. The terms and conditions of D&O insurance options and fidelity coverage vary considerably and should be negotiated.

CONCLUSION

This chapter has attempted to provide a survey of key legislative and regulatory reforms for corporate governance of public companies. The Sarbanes-Oxley Act and the NYSE and Nasdaq rules impose obligations on, or establish responsibilities for, board members, audit committees, management, and internal auditors that persons fulfilling each of these roles will need to know and follow. While each particular individual must gain a more in-depth understanding of these requirements, and consult with legal counsel where appropriate, it is hoped that this survey will alert the reader to the key regulatory provisions aimed at improving corporate governance and deterring future financial fraud.

NOTES

1. Sarbanes-Oxley Act of 2002 (Public Company Accounting Reform & Investor Protection Act), Pub. L. 107-204, 116 Stat. 745 (July 30, 2002).
2. Arthur Levitt, Chairman, United States Securities and Exchange Commission, "The Numbers Game," Remarks before the NYU Center for Law and Business, September 28, 1998.
3. Id.
4. Id.

5. N.Y Stock Exch. & Nat'l Assoc. of Sec. Dealers, *Report & Recommendations of the Blue Ribbon Committee on Improving the Effectiveness of Corporate Audit Committees,* at 10-12, 22-26 (1999), *available at* http://www.nasdaq.com/about/blue_ribbon_panel.pdf (last visited Aug. 16, 2006).
6. Id.
7. *In re Caremark Int'l Inc. Derivative Litig.*, 698 A. 2d 959 (Del. Ch. 1996).
8. J. Morrow, 2004 MCB UP Limited, Mar. 1, 2004; R. Wise, *Who Was Enron's & Worldcom's Ultimate Guardian of Investor Interest and Corporate Accountability? A New Paradigm for Director Liability*, Util. Indus. Litig. Rep. (Aug. 28, 2002).
9. *See, e.g., In re WorldCom, Inc. Sec. Litig.,* No. 02 Civ. 3288, 2003 U.S. Dist. LEXIS 21359 (S.D.N.Y. Dec. 1, 2003).
10. John T. Bostelman, *The Sarbanes-Oxley Deskbook* § 2:3, at 2-9, 2-10 (2006).
11. Id.
12. 15 U.S.C. § 78j-1m.
13. 15 U.S.C. § 7241(a).
14. 15 U.S.C. § 7262(a)-(b).
15. 15 U.S.C. § 7264(a).
16. 15 U.S.C. § 7265(a).
17. NYSE Listed Company Manual §§ 303A.01, 303A.02, 303A.03.
18. NYSE Listed Company Manual § 303A.04-.05; NASD Marketplace Rule 4350(c)(3)-(4).
19. NYSE Listed Company Manual § 303A.07; NASD Marketplace Rule 4350(d).
20. NYSE Listed Company Manual §303A.07(d).
21. NYSE Listed Company Manual § 303A.10; NASD Marketplace Rule 4350(n).
22. John J. Madden and Lisa E. Toporek, *New Directions for Corporate Governance in the United States,* The M&A Lawyer (August 2002).
23. Zabihollah Rezaee, *High Quality Financial Reporting: The Six-legged Stool,* Institute of Management Accountants (February 2003).
24. 15 U.S.C. § 78j-1(m)(3)(B); NYSE Listed Company Manual § 303A.01-.02; NASD Marketplace Rules 4200, 4350(c)(1).
25. Commentary to Rule 1 of NYSE Corporate Governance Rules (November 4, 2003).
26. 15 U.S.C. § 78j-1(m)(3)(A); NYSE Listed Company Manual §§ 303A.01, .04, .05; NASD Marketplace Rules 4350(c)(3)-(4), (d)(2); *see, e.g.,* Bart Schwartz and Jonathan Freedman, *Accounting Scandals: The New Rules & Board Culture,* 228 N.Y. L. J. 5 (2002).
27. *See* commentary to NYSE Listed Company Manual § 303A.02.
28. Id.
29. Id.
30. *See* commentary to NYSE Listed Company Manual § 303A.03.
31. *New Directions for Corporate Governance in the United States, supra* note 23; *see also* P. Atkins, Commissioner, United States Securities and Exchange Commission, *The Sarbanes-Oxley Act of 2002: Goals, Content and Status of Implementation,* Remarks at University of Cologne, Germany, February 5, 2003("[I]t is beyond debate that it is beneficial to have financially literate directors. Indeed, studies show that companies that have board members with significant financial knowledge need to restate the financial statements less than companies with less-experienced board members.").
32. Id.
33. Press Release, Houlihan Lokey Howard & Zukin, Corporate Board Member Measures Impact of New Rules & Regulations (Apr. 21, 2003), *available at* http://www.hlhz.com/main.asp?p=CORP_PRSearch-&pr=86 (last visited Aug. 16, 2006).
34. *New Directions for Corporate Governance in the United States, supra* note 22; *see also* USA Compliance With the ICGN's Recommended Best Practice, Int'l Corp. Governance Network (June 2004) ("An increasing number of U.S. companies are voluntarily adopting ownership requirements for executives and non-employee directors.").

35. *See* 15 U.S.C. § 7264(a); NYSE Listed Company Manual §§ 303A.09-.10; NASD Marketplace Rule 43509(n).
36. Paul Palmes and Sanford Liebesman, *Quality's Path to the Boardroom,* Quality Progress (October 2003).
37. Id.
38. Robert E. Bostrom, *Responding to the Evolving Roles and Responsibilities of Boards of Directors and Audit Committees: The Importance of a Compliance Risk Management,* The Metropolitan Corp. Counsel (November 2005).
39. *See Enterprise Risk Management—Integrated Framework,* Committee of Sponsoring Organizations of the Treadway Commission (COSO) (September 2004) ("Enterprise risk management is a process, effected by an entity's board of directors, management and other personnel, applied in strategy setting and across the enterprise, designed to identify potential events that may affect the entity, and manage risk to be within its risk appetite, to provide reasonable assurance regarding the achievement of entity objectives.").
40. *Responding to the Evolving Roles and Responsibilities of Boards of Directors and Audit Committees: The Importance of a Compliance Risk Assessment, supra* note 38.
41. *New Directions for Corporate Governance in the United States, supra* note 22.
42. Id.
43. Id.
44. *See* Joann S. Lublin, *Enron Audit Panel is Scrutinized for Cozy Ties with the Firm,* Wall St. J. (February 1, 2002).
45. *WorldCom, supra* note 9, 2003 U.S. Dist. LEXIS 21359.
46. *See, e.g.*, Richard Siklos, *SEC Puts 3 Hollinger Directors on Notice,* N.Y. Times (December 15, 2005); Stephen Taub, *Wells Notices for Hollinger Directors,* CFO.com (December 14, 2005).
47. Peter M. Collins, *Sarbanes-Oxley Act Creates a New Role for the Audit Committee,* 228 N.Y.L.J. 4 (2002).
48. Wm. F. Floyd and Andrew J. Surdykowski, *Sarbanes-Oxley Act; Corporate Reform: The Role of the Audit Committee,* The Corp. Counselor (December 2002).
49. 15 U.S.C. § 78j-1(m)(3)(B).
50. 15 U.S.C. §7265(b); NASD Marketplace Rule 4350(d)(2)(A); *see also* Commentary to NYSE Listed Company Manual §303A.07(a).
51. *Sarbanes-Oxley Act Creates a New Role for the Audit Committee, supra* note 47.
52. *See e.g.,* Frederick D. Lipman, *Six Common Mistakes of Audit Committees,* Directors and Boards (3d Quarter 2004); Stuart D. Buchalter & Kristin Yokomoto, *Audit Committees' Responsibilities and Liabilities,* The CPA Journal (2005).
53. NYSE Listed Company Manual § 303A.07(c)(iii)(E).
54. Matt T. Morley, Richard A. Steinwurtzel, Karl A. Groskaufmanis, Dixie L. Johnson, and Paul H. Pashkoff, Fried Frank Harris Shriver & Jacobson, *Questions Every Audit Committee Should Be Asking in the Wake of Enron,* SecMail (Feb. 2, 2002), available at http://www.ffhsj.com/secreg/pdf/sc020204.pdf (last visited Aug. 16, 2006).
55. 15 U.S.C. §§ 78j-1(k), 7262.
56. 15 U.S.C. §§ 78j-1(m)(4), 7241(a)(5).
57. *Sarbanes-Oxley Act Creates a New Role for the Audit Committee, supra* note 47.
58. Id.
59. Id.
60. Stephen A. Scarpati, *CPAs As Audit Committee Members,* Journal of Accountancy (Sept. 2003) ("Conscientious members arrive at audit committee meetings prepared to address key issues and to ask the right questions.").
61. *Six Common Mistakes of Audit Committees, supra* note 52.
62. Id.

63. Id.
64. Id.
65. NYSE Listing Company Manual § 303A.07(iii)(B).
66. NYSE Listing Company Manual § 303A.07(iii)(C).
67. Sarbanes-Oxley Compliance Journal (November 23, 2004) ("According to a poll of over 200 financial services audit committee members by PricewaterhouseCoopers LLP, their top focus is on their company's implementation of Sarbanes-Oxley Section 404.").
68. *See Financial Statements: How Audit Committees Are Working to Improve Financial Reporting,* Financial Analysis, Planning & Reporting (December 2004) ("'Section 404 has to be the number-one item on any corporate financial executive's priority list and the audit committee' said Dennis R. Beresford [accounting professor at the University of Georgia] . . . 'Audit committees want to make sure the company is getting ready, doing the right thing, and hopefully will not have any material weaknesses.'").
69. 15 U.S.C. § 78j-1(m)(2).
70. Id.
71. 15 U.S.C. § 78j-1(i)(1)(A).
72. NYSE Listed Company Manual § 303A.07(c)(iii)(A), (G).
73. 15 U.S.C. § 78j-1(m)(2); NYSE Listed Company Manual §303A.07(c)(iii).
74. Steve Klein and Mike Thronson, *Best Practices for Audit Committees After Enron,* Western Banking Magazine (December 2002/January 2003).
75. NYSE Listed Company Manual § 303A.07(c); NASD Marketplace Rule 4350(d)(1).
76. Id.
77. Id.
78. *Sarbanes-Oxley Act Creates a New Role for the Audit Committee, supra* note 47.
79. Id.
80. 15 U.S.C. § 7241(a). Additionally 18 U.S.C.§1350(a) provides that the CEO and CFO shall provide with each periodic report containing a financial statement a written statement that such financial statement complies with SEC reporting requirements and that information contained in the periodic report fairly presents, in all material respects, the financial condition and results of operations. This Section 906 reporting requirement is logically encompassed with the broader CEO and CFO certifications set forth in Section 302 but is subject to explicit criminal penalties.
81. 15 U.S.C. §7241(a)(4)(A)-(B).
82. 15 U.S.C. §7241(a)(5)(A)-(B).
83. David E. Hardesty, *Practical Guide to Corp. Governance and Acct'g: Implementing the Requirements of Sarbanes-Oxley Act* (2005 ed.) at ¶ 302.
84. Id.
85. *SEC Release No. 33-8124, II.B.3.*
86. Id.
87. *Practical Guide to Corp. Governance and Acct'g, supra* note 83.
88. 15 U.S.C. § 7262(a).
89. Id.
90. *Practical Guide to Corp. Governance and Acct'g, supra* note 83 at ¶ 1602.
91. Id.
92. J. Hamilton and T. Trautmann, *Responsibilities of Corporate Officers and Directors Under Federal Securities Law* (CCH) (October 2004) at ¶ 507.
93. L. Rittenberg, *Lessons for Internal Auditors,* Inst. of Internal Auditors (April 2002).
94. Id.
95. Eric Hespenheide, Deloitte & Touche LLP, *Optimizing the Role of Internal Audit in the Sarbanes-Oxley Era*, at 2 (2d ed. 2006), available at http://www.deloitte.com/dtt/cda/doc/content/US_IA_Optimizing%20The%20Role%20of%20Internal%20Audit_2ED.pdf (last visited Aug. 16, 2006).

96. *Optimizing the Role of Internal Audit in the Sarbanes-Oxley Era, supra* note 95.
97. Id.
98. Id.
99. Larry Rittenberg, *How Internal Audit & the Audit Committee Can Improve Their Relationship,* Institute of Management Administration (IOMA) PREVENTING BUSINESS FRAUD 02-4 (2002).
100. Id.
101. *See* Sarah R. Wolff, *The Evolving Definition of "Fiduciary Duty,"* The Corporate Board (January/February 2005).
102. *See* E. Norman Veasy, Jesse A. Finkelstein, and C. Stephen Bigler, *Delaware Supports Directors with a Three-Legged Stool of Limited Liability, Indemnification, and Insurance,* 42 Bus. Law. 399 (1987).
103. *See* Del. Code tit. 8 § 102(b)(7).
104. *See* id.
105. *The Evolving Definition of "Fiduciary Duty," supra* note 101.
106. *See* Del. Code tit. 8 § 145(a)-(f).
107. *See* Id. § 125(g).
108. *See Delaware Supports Directors with a Three-Legged Stool of Limited Liability, Indemnification, and Insurance, supra* note 102.

Chapter 11

Generation X Technologies and Information Assurance

Jagdish Pathak and Amelia A. Baldwin

OVERVIEW

This chapter addresses the enrichment of basic information systems assurance measures and models in the overall context of fraud deterrence in organizations. In addition, recent developments in enterprise technology are addressed and probable assurance measures are identified. The chapter will address these questions:

- What are the state-of-art technologies in the integrated enterprise-based information systems arena?
- Why is information systems integration considered such a challenge?
- Why does assured information emanate from assured systems?
- Is information assurance a function of strategic importance?
- What are the existing information assurance and control measures available to the professionals from the cross-sectional fields?

We describe the information integration challenge to "next-generation enterprises" by reviewing state-of-the-art technologies and platforms and describing the process of integration in terms of internal controls and assurance. Then we discuss the impact of information integration on both internal and external audit procedures. The strategic importance of information assurance in information systems-centric organizations is then addressed, along with measures of information assurance and controls devised by the enterprising entities. The chapter concludes by identifying future needs and directions for both basic and applied research.

DO WE NEED A PARADIGM SHIFT IN SYSTEMS ASSURANCE AND AUDITING?

Today's enterprise systems extend beyond the traditional corporate data center[1] to include customers, suppliers, partners, and electronic marketplaces. Because the adoption of e-business transaction models has significantly outpaced the development of tools and technologies to deal with the information explosion, many businesses find their systems breaking under the sheer volume and diversity of their data.[2] Enterprises that can quickly extract critical nuggets of information from the river of accessible data and transform them into valuable business assets are in a strong position to dominate their business environment. Such an undertaking is no small task.

GENERATION X ENTERPRISE TECHNOLOGIES: STATE OF THE ART

Data management systems have been at the core of enterprise software infrastructure for over three decades.[3] The introduction of the relational data model and the concept of data independence revolutionized the data management industry and quickly overtook network and hierarchical systems for large-scale data management.[4] Over the next two decades, the relational database is expected to be transformed into a high-performance, high-volume query processing engine, mainly through innovations in storage and retrieval techniques, concurrency control and recovery, and query processing technology, such as cost-based optimization.[5]

Distributed systems and parallel processing techniques enabled global enterprises to manage large volumes of distributed data. Extensible database architectures have allowed data types, access strategies, and indexing schemes to be introduced easily as new business needs arise.[6] Federated database technology provided a powerful and flexible means for transparent access to heterogeneous, distributed data sources.[7] As database management system (DBMS) technology evolved to manage business data, other important technologies evolved in parallel to make the tasks of managing business logic and business processes easier. Data warehouses, data mining, and online analytical processing technology added business intelligence, providing a means for discovery-driven and hypothesis-driven analysis over business data to identify trends and patterns and play out what-if scenarios.[8] Work-flow systems helped to automate business processes, providing the infrastructure to manage processes such as order fulfillment from step to step, assign tasks in the process to the right resources, and invoke automated steps at the appropriate times.

Business applications evolved alongside data management and enterprise management systems, exploiting the best features of both to create sophisticated software packages that form the foundation of nearly all of today's businesses. Significant development and computing resources are devoted to transporting data from one system to another and transforming data from one format to another. Likewise, data federation has a solid research foundation and several commercial implementations.

Databases deal quite naturally and robustly with the storage, retrieval, and reliability requirements for traditional business data and can easily accommodate a variety of data and access patterns. A platform that exploits and enhances the DBMS architecture at all levels is in the best position to provide robust end-to-end information integration. In a business environment, this translates into automatic cooperation between enterprises. Any enterprise requiring business interaction with another enterprise can automatically discover and select the appropriate optimal Web services relying on selection policies.[9]

Web services can be invoked automatically and payment processes can be initiated. Any necessary mediation is applied based on data and process ontology and the automatic translation of their concepts into each other. An example is supply chain relationships where an enterprise who manufactures short-lived goods must frequently seek suppliers as well as buyers dynamically. Instead of employees constantly searching for suppliers and buyers, the Web service infrastructure does it automatically within defined constraints. Still, more work needs to be done before the Web service infrastructure can make this vision come true.

The explosion of the World Wide Web (WWW) and e-business in recent years has caused a secondary explosion in the amounts and types of information available to enterprise applications. This abundance of information presents an exciting cross-industry business opportunity.[10] The prime challenge facing today's businesses is information integration.[11] Enterprise applications of today must interact with databases, application servers, content management systems, data warehouses, work-flow systems, search engines, message queues, Web crawlers, mining and analysis packages, and other enterprise integration applications. Similarly, these enterprise applications must use a variety of programming interfaces and understand a variety of languages and formats.[12] They should be enabled to extract and combine data in multiple formats generated by multiple delivery mechanisms.

Clearly, the boundaries that have traditionally existed among database management systems, content management systems, data warehouses, and other data management systems are blurring, and a great need has arisen for a platform that provides a unified view of all of these services and the data they deliver. More data will be generated in this decade, if the current trend continues, than in all of recorded history. The widespread adoption of the Internet has made most data just a URL (uniform resource locator) away. Information integration is a technology approach that combines core elements from data management systems, content management systems, data warehouses, and other enterprise applications into a common platform.[13] These systems combine data with different time properties, such as real time stock tickers, news wires, databases, slightly out-of-date mid-tier caches, database replicas), and data warehouses.[14] Stieren indicates that such data are generated by multiple delivery mechanisms in a variety of formats e.g. relational tables, XML documents, images, video, and sound.[15]

INFORMATION SYSTEMS INTEGRATION: A CHALLENGE

Clearly, the world is becoming more "wired." While all countries have become more connected over the last few decades, network proliferation has been concentrated in the most developed nations, especially in the United States and Canada. These countries continue to "computerize" the public and private infrastructures, which now run everything from telecommunications and banking services to electric power generation and distribution. The still-accelerating development, proliferation, and adoption of information and communications technologies have benefited the world enormously. The nations of North America have made huge strides in science and medicine, and have greatly increased productivity.

However, as computers and networks become more ubiquitous, we grow more dependent on them. Thus, we become more vulnerable to criminals and terrorists who would use these systems against us. Just as technology has improved the efficiency and effectiveness of business operations, it has also increased terrorists' abilities to launch sophisticated attacks against our increasingly interdependent infrastructures. Information today is worth more than ever. In the past, attackers could collect information only while it was being transmitted from place to place; today our data are vulnerable 24 hours a day, wherever they are located. Systems handling the various disaster scenarios must rely on data management systems and enterprise applications that come with their own set of application programming interfaces (APIs) and tools, and an enterprise must develop complex in-house integration and administration software to maintain them. Although these different scenarios come from a diverse set of industries, they indicate that the boundaries that have traditionally existed between database management systems (DBMSs), data warehouses, content management systems, and other data transformation and integration services are blurring. Various similarities between these scenarios illustrate a common set of requirements for robust information integration platform.

Enterprise applications require support for XML as a first-class data model. Although the relational data model has driven business applications over the past three decades, XML has become the lingua franca for portable data. Businesses rely heavily on it for enterprise integration. XML is more suitable for representing both semistructured and unstructured data, and, unlike the relational model, it also provides a standard representation of the metadata to describe those data. This flexibility allows financial services companies to receive reports from multiple publishers, provides a common language for a freight broker to negotiate bids with multiple carriers, and enables a telecommunications company to integrate the various customer support systems acquired through its mergers.

Clearly, businesses rely on multiple, diverse sources of data in their enterprise applications. A financial services company relies on real-time data feeds, databases, spreadsheets, and media servers. A freight broker depends on real-time access to external flight scheduling systems and carriers. A telecommunications application requires access to multiple autonomous vertical applications. These scenarios make use of information consolidation, where data are both collected from multiple sources and consolidated in a central repository and federation, in which data from multiple autonomous sources are accessed as part of a search but are not moved from their original sources. Some sources of data conform to a schema, whereas other sources, such as information portals, do not.

Because an enterprise receives information from so many sources, metadata to describe the data available from a source are as important as the data. Today's enterprise systems require sophisticated search and data transformation services with increasingly demanding performance requirements. Such scenarios require parametric search, full-text search, mining, and digital asset management services over data stored in a variety of systems and in a variety of formats. Although specialized systems with different APIs exist today to handle each kind of search, a single system that provides access to all data and services through a unified interface would simplify application development and provide better performance.

One scenario also demonstrates that business processes are inherently asynchronous. Customers reporting problems are satisfied with a confirmation number and do not need to remain on the phone while the problem is repaired. Busy stock traders may not want to poll for information, but instead prefer to be notified when events of interest occur. Furthermore, continuous availability requirements mean that applications must continue running in the face of failures. Data sources and applications come up and go down on a regular basis, and data feeds may be interrupted by hardware or network failures. If the telecommunications customer service system goes down, field technicians should continue to work on repairs assigned to them. If a particular carrier is not available, the freight broker should negotiate bids from the carriers that are available. A single system that provides access to all data and services through a unified interface would simplify development and provide better performance.

Finally, the complexity of the applications in these scenarios illustrates an essential requirement for open standards. Such applications weave together a host of data sources, management systems, and applications. Without standards governing their interfaces and a consistent programming model, the effort to integrate and administer new sources in this dynamic environment could be astronomical, and the cost to recruit and retain staff with the skills necessary to develop the integration software might quickly overtake the value of the system itself.

A layered architecture for a robust technology platform that addresses the information integration challenge is depicted in the Exhibit 11.1. The base layer supports storage, retrieval, and transformation of data in different formats from different sources. A second layer of integration built on top of the base layer draws from enterprise integration applications to provide the infrastructure to transparently embed data access services into enterprise applications and business processes. The layer at the top provides standards-based programming models and flexible query language support to access the rich set of services and data provided by the base and integration layers.

As shown in the exhibit, the base layer is at the heart of the information integration platform and provides a core set of services to store and retrieve heterogeneous data. The base layer is dependent on a high-performance DBMS engine extended at all levels with data integration functionality. These extensions include support for XML as a native data store, XQuery as a native data interrogation language, and a federated data access component that provides access to external data and applications as if the data and applications were natively managed by the engine. The convergence of communications networks with the systems, however, also increases business susceptibility to cyber attacks. Indeed, by the end of the twentieth century, businesses had become more vulnerable than any other segment of the society to cyber attacks aiming to interrupt, degrade, or destroy vital services such as electrical power, banking, or stock trading. Current trends indicate that information integration is a cross-industry challenge. Industries from financial services to manufacturing have all been touched by the volumes and diversity of data and continual demands introduced by a Web-based business model. Securing the business networks is a huge task, though the discussion on security is not within the scope of this chapter. However, the basic understanding of security shall be the mainstay of identifying the assurance provided by the information systems. Such assured systems in turn will be essential for obtaining assured information for decision making by all levels including the stakeholders.

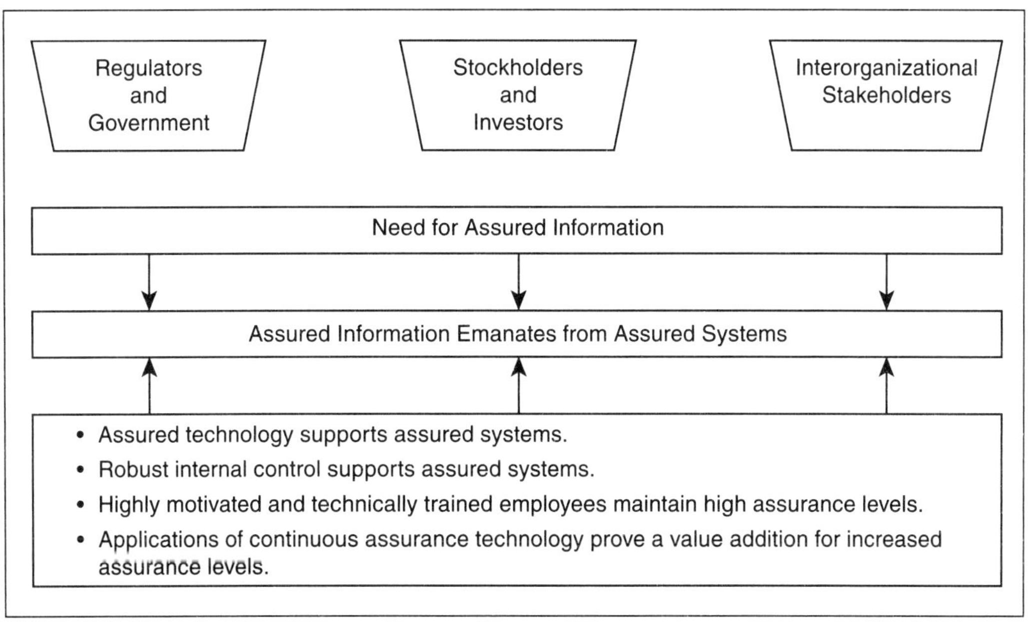

Exhibit 11.1 Generation X Integrated Information Systems Technologies

ASSURED INFORMATION EMANATES FROM ASSURED SYSTEMS

Strickland and Willard stated that it is the assured and trusted information systems that carry the integrity element in the information provided for decision making.[16] What matters most is the quality of information and data retrieved from the databases whose integrity is neither assured nor trustworthy. The assurance starts from the data-gathering stage. They further boost their point by citing the case of the issuance of a U.S. visa to a known terrorist, who ultimately masterminded the World Trade Center (WTC) garage bombing in 1993 or the issuance of student visa after his death to the terrorist who took active part in the 9/11 plane crash. This viewpoint reiterates that assured information can emanate only from an assured information system. The assurance aspect of complex information technology (IT) should not be limited to the IT knowledgeable people but should percolate down to the level of end users, particularly the external and internal auditors, who are the users in the form of verifiers of internal controls to determine their opinions for statutory or operational purposes. And, to other stakeholders who must trust in the systems providing information and data for policy and decision making. Ultimately, the assurance aspect extends to all layers of the IT architecture, as shown in Exhibit 11.2.

Electronic dependencies and interconnections create vulnerabilities that are rapidly exploited by criminals. A substantial growth has been reported in the number of known electronic breaches of information security over the past few years. The business community has, however, begun recognizing the potentially catastrophic costs related to information infrastructure vulnerabilities. The level of private sector motivation and resources devoted to information assurance is increasing, and stakeholders have begun to understand the strategic importance of the information assurance function.

The time is right for government, industry, and academia to engage in a strong, long-term collaborative effort to create the methods, technologies, and means for generating information assurance. Progress requires careful consideration of the equities of all the parties involved and focused efforts to transcend cultural and national boundaries and minimize or eliminate legal boundaries on cooperation.[17]

INFORMATION ASSURANCE: A FUNCTION OF STRATEGIC IMPORTANCE

The IT resources in the entity and the optimal utilization of these scarce resources have become an issue for devising a competitive strategy in globalized businesses. In the current dynamic and competitive markets, management is placing increasing demands on IT resources to operate as a major component of market strategy. Thus, increased quality standards, decreased throughput time, and continuously evolving service levels on both the hardware and software fronts are being demanded.

Several factors point to an expanding IT universe and are placing greater demands on the IT control environment: increasing system complexity due to increasing use of Web technologies, constantly decreasing cost of hardware, effective and efficient end-user computing due to graphic user interfaces (GUIs) in applications, and also a trend toward open and decentralized architecture in computing. The greater emphasis on applications and system resources outsourcing, demand for reduced system development time, and tendency of entities toward the enterprise-wide computing adoption are some other factors in the same direction. Therefore, the importance of maintaining and monitoring controls over this expanding universe must also be treated as a strategic issue.

Strategy for any entity is knowledge driven, which in turn is information dependent. Data generate information if presented in a cohesive and coherent format to the right person at the

Database Technologies	• XML • Structured • Meta • External data amd applications
Base Technologies	• Storage • Retrieval and search functions • Federation
Various Integration Technologies	• Metadata • Data mining • Messaging • Indexing • Work flow • Data warehousing
Application Interfaces	• Java database connectivity • Open database connectivity • Simple object access protocol • Extensible Mark-Up Language • SGL • SQL • X-Query • Web services • Universal description, discovery, and integration
Enabling	• B2B and B2C • eCRM • eBusiness • EDI and VANs

Exhibit 11.2 Need for Information Assurance

right time. Data are of paramount importance, and the quality of data impacts the ultimate quality of strategy formulated by the entity. Internal control systems in place in organizations affect the quality of data. Poor internal controls have serious ramifications on the end product, and, in this case, poor-quality data (low integrity and reliability) will result in equally poor strategy for the entity. In a similar vein, the failure to optimally implement strategic initiatives into operational modules can also have equally serious impact on the organizational results. It is at this point that management utilizes IT/IS (information systems) auditing as a tool for ensuring: the reliability and integrity of information, compliance with IT policies and procedures, the safeguarding of IT assets, the economical and efficient use of the IT resources, and the accomplishment of established IT objectives and goals.[18]

Information technology is also used to facilitate the shrinkage and collapsing of the organizational structures and enterprise-wide resource planning (ERP) applications are coincidentally handy to all the strategic managers in fulfilling this desire. Services are being demanded under the increasing cost constraints. These cost constraints involve not only the deployment of cost-effective strategic information technologies but also often involve the smart sizing or delayering of organizations. Many of these layers originated in the infrastructure of organizational internal control systems. The control functions performed by these layers are either overlooked or not replaced by suitable alternatives during and after the delayering process.

These cited deficiencies are indicative of an inadequate internal control environment and imply that, with respect to end-user computing, we may still be in Nolan's contagion phase of IT assimilation.[19] Therefore, not only do the IT resources need to respond to increased functional demands, they also need to respond to the need to replace or enhance internal controls, which stem from changes in the organizational structure and objectives. In order to ensure that the business requirements for information are met, adequate control measures need to be defined, implemented, and monitored to ensure the stakeholders that controls exist, that they are working, and that they are adequate given the risk involved.

Ratliff et al. indicate that activities within the management structure are subject to established policies, standards, and procedures which can be thought of as a pervasive network of system controls, generally called internal controls.[20] These controls are employed to maintain effective vigil over activities and operations. Auditors (both IT/IS and internal) are used by the management and stakeholders to assist in monitoring the control environment, including testing compliance with management directives and evaluating the efficiency, effectiveness, and economy of internal controls and operations.

As demands on IT resources mount and their complexity increases exponentially, the need for IS/IT audit expertise should increase correspondingly. In this context, we can easily define the IS/IT audit's basic or primary mission as providing stakeholders with a level of assurance that the entity's IT resources are being efficiently, effectively, and economically deployed to support the organization's strategic objectives. Therefore, a major dilemma faced by many organizations is how to adequately, efficiently, effectively, and economically control IT resources while at the same time allocating and balancing audit activities under existing constraints in a way that maximises the added value of internal audit resources. Although a good amount of empirical research has been done in the area of management information systems (MIS) and in auditing, no such body of knowledge or theory addresses the unique needs of the IT/IS audit community.

Internal controls constitute the policies and procedures adopted by management to assist in achieving the entity's objective of ensuring the orderly and efficient conduct of its operations, including adherence to management policies, safeguarding of assets, the prevention and detection of fraud and error, the accuracy and completeness of records, and the timely preparation of information.[21] The primary objective of internal auditing is to provide an appraisal of the entity's controls to ensure that business risk or uncertainty—variety—is addressed and that the entity's goals and objectives are achieved efficiently, effectively and economically. Internal controls provide a road map to navigate the organization's internal network. This assertion is better explained in visual schema as shown in Exhibit 11.3. Management enacts internal controls to reduce variety, ambiguity, risk, and uncertainty in the decision-making process. Management employs internal auditors to evaluate the existence, functioning, and adequacy of these internal controls.

What is the role of internal auditing in such a network? Internal auditing has an important role to perform in the form of patrolling this complicated network and act as a constable "on the beat" by directing those who have strayed back onto the course. Here the role implies issuing tickets to the defaulters in the form of audit reports to the most serious kind of offenders.

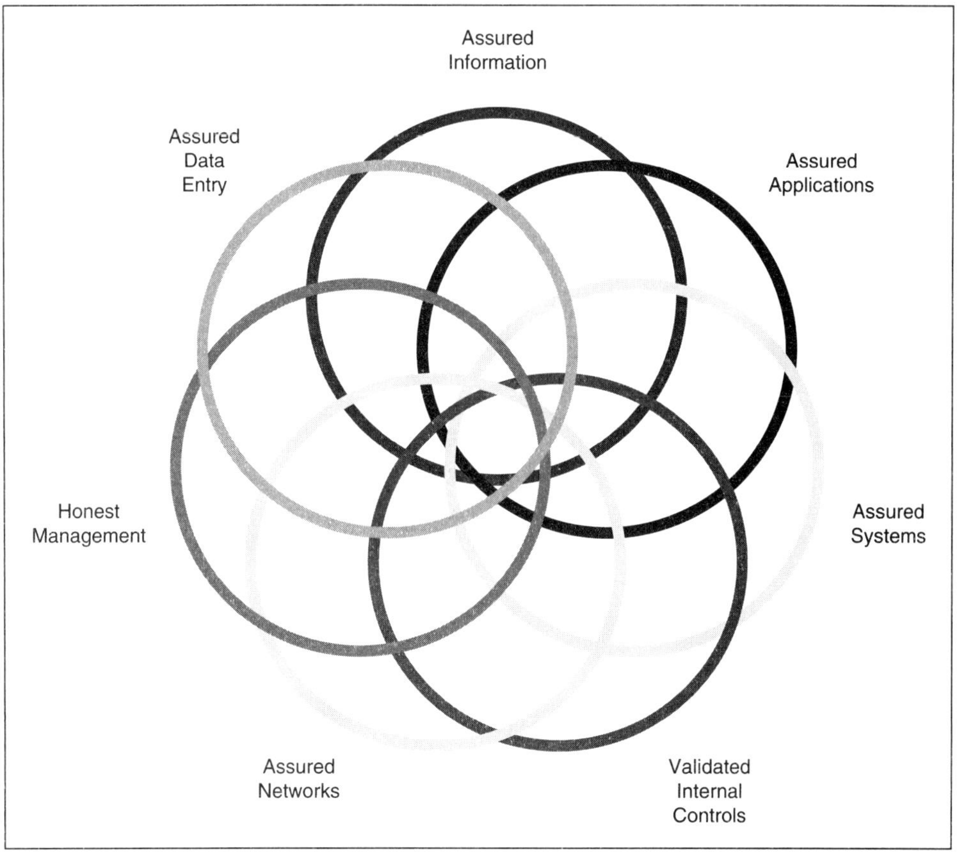

Exhibit 11.3 Information Assurance Is Intertwined with Assurances of All the Segments

The relative variety, uncertainty, or risk of various activities is the single most critical factor in directing the activities of the internal audit function.[22] It is important to note that Beer mistakenly identifies management auditors, whose primary responsibility is evaluating the state of internal controls, as variety reducers, when in fact it is the internal controls created by management and imposed on the organization that reduces variety.[23]

However, the role of the external auditor is to attest to the fair presentation of the financial statements. As such, the external auditor's role can be described as attesting to the state of the organization at a given point of time. The external auditor is not directly part of the internal organization's feedback loop, but instead is part of a larger feedback loop that includes stakeholders, governmental agencies, and other external parties, who are often more concerned with states and outcomes than with the processes that generate those states and outcomes. Internal auditors, including IT/IS auditors, act as a part of the internal feedback control system of an organization. A historical role for auditors was to act as detectors in first order feedback systems.

This traditional role of an auditor was to detect deviations from goals and to provide negative feedback in the form of audit reports. The auditee or the client management was expected to correct the deviation restoring the equilibrium, irrespective of changes in the environment and/or the materiality of the events. As intelligent entities evolve, memories of prior experiences are maintained and used for the best alternative course of action. The ability to store and recall information, allowing the system to choose alternative courses of action, is called learning.[24] In second-order feedback systems, the entities have the ability to change its goals by changing the behavior of the system. Thus, goal changing becomes the part of the feedback process.

Simultaneously, auditors also evolved from solely being both detectors and comparators. Auditors began weighing the significance of departures in the context of the auditee's environment (significance and materiality) rather than merely reporting departures from the established norms. Auditors in the 1980s and 1990s also became part of the third-order feedback systems by participation in the early stages of system development, participating in information systems planning functions, and developing applications that are utilized to better control the entities' activities, such as continuous and self-audits. Third-order systems not only have the ability to learn from the previous errors, but also incorporate a feed-forward system, which provides information on the projected future environment.

As a player in the third-order feedback systems, auditors play a significant role in the implementation of anticipatory controls (controls that anticipate future problems and make adjustments before departures from normality occur). Auditors intelligently scan the environment to detect conditions that could lead to future departures. Auditors often embed modules within information systems that log specified transactions into a system control audit review file. Most of the large systems manufacturers have started embedding such audit modules in their application systems.

The mere fact that the auditors are publicly known to be monitoring a specific situation may be adequate in itself to deter some from inappropriate behavior. Today's auditors are being utilized to provide guidance early in the system development life cycle. Their participation in the life cycle and IT planning activities provides a higher level of assurance that future system control problems are actively anticipated and that changes are designed into systems early along in the development process in order to avoid expensive mistakes, repairs, and interruptions once the system has gone into operations.

VARIOUS INFORMATION ASSURANCE AND CONTROL MEASURES

These measures are the measures to be implemented at the Web level and the measures to be followed in their entirety. The first type of measures is developed by enterprising entities, including two most prominent accounting bodies, to extend the assurance of the Web-based information to the end users. Similarly, the second type—the measures to be followed in their entirety—are in fact, frameworks designed and developed by another set of professional bodies, the Information Systems Audit and Control Association (ISACA), the Institute of Internal Auditors (IIA), British Standards (Directorate of Trade & Industry), and one of the International Systems Security Engineering Association (ISSEA). These measures are described in brief and the related Web addresses are given for further information.

Web-Level Assurance Measures

The area of extending information assurance to the end users in the last 10 years has seen development at various levels. Professional accountants' bodies of the United States and Canada have made a good beginning by introducing SysTrust and WebTrust seals of assurance. These seals of assurance have their inherent limitations as they cannot extend a blanket assurance. If followed in letter and spirit, these seals of assurance can help extend the horizon of e-commerce. Even though research has shown that WebTrust may influence consumer's behavior, it has had very limited success in the marketplace for B2C (business to commerce) assurance seals, with less than 30 implementations since its inception.[25] Competitor seals, such as Better Business Bureau On-Line (BBB On-Line), TrustE, and VeriSign, have been much more successful while providing a more limited scope of assurance.

The cause for lesser implementations of WebTrust seal might lie in its cost and its scope. Because of the scope of assurance, the cost to acquire a WebTrust seal is significantly higher than alternative seals. Most consumers are likely to be unable to differentiate between the information content of alternative seals.[26] Most probably, a combination of these two factors and perhaps others have contributed to the lack of success of WebTrust assurance. Of particular interest in this study, however, is the second issue in terms of the impact of varying levels of information quality (i.e., information content and reliability) on Internet consumers' purchasing choices.

The focus on information quality is particularly important; if consumers cannot differentiate among different seals' quality, then acquiring WebTrust assurance with its greater expense would not be an economically prudent decision. If consumers can differentiate among seals and are influenced by the assurance provided by a CPA/CIA, acquiring a WebTrust seal may be a sound investment for some companies. WebTrust is a different type of venture for CPAs/CAs in that it is a CPA service that is sold to a company's marketing department rather than its finance department.

WebTrust provides assurance in four areas:

1. Business practices and disclosures
2. Transaction integrity
3. Information protection
4. Information privacy (ca. 2001)

As Primoff noted, WebTrust was proposed as a potential solution to consumers' concerns with regard to the risk of transacting business over the Internet. Other assurance seals focus on a subset of these dimensions.[27] For instance, VeriSign focuses on transaction integrity and information protection, while TrustE focuses on information privacy. The assurance offered by BBB On-Line is even more limited. An organization pays a relatively small fee to register with the BBB and acquire seal usage rights based on documentation of practices; the organization continues to display the seal unless a certain number of complaints are lodged with the Better Business Bureau by consumers regarding the actual business practices. Nonetheless, if consumers tend to focus simply on the presence or the absence of a seal, then assurance seals that offer low information quality may be equally desirable and cost may be the most significant differentiator in assurance seal acquisition decisions.

Control Objectives and System Assurance

IT resources are critical to management's successful accomplishment of the objectives of creating value through effective, efficient, and economical use of resources.[28] The American Institute of Certified Public Accountants (AICPA) Statement on Auditing Standards No. 1 provides guidance to external auditors, whose primary responsibility is the fair presentation of the financial statements. It states that an internal control should have four fundamental control objectives[29]:

1. To encourage adherence to management's prescribed policies and procedures
2. To promote efficiency in all of the firm's operations
3. To safeguard the assets of the firm
4. To ensure the accuracy and reliability of the accounting data and information

The Institute of Internal Auditors in their General Standard 300 provide guidance to internal auditors, whose primary responsibility is the efficient, effective, and economic utilization of organizational resources. They expand on the AICPA's definition and define a set of five control objectives:[30]

1. The reliability and integrity of information
2. Compliance with policies, plans, procedures, laws, and regulations
3. The safeguarding of assets
4. The economical and efficient use of resources
5. The accomplishment of objectives and goals for operations and programs

In 1991(revised in 1994), the IIA issued the Systems Auditability and Control (SAC) report, which provided one of the first attempts to codify control in the IT context.[31] SAC stressed the need to assess risk and weigh the cost and benefits of controls and the economic benefits of building controls into systems rather than adding them after implementation. SAC identified risks including fraud, errors, business interruptions, and inefficient and ineffective use of IT resources. It further set forth a set of control objectives to mitigate these risks and ensure information integrity, security, and compliance. The report concluded that the system of internal control consisted of three components: the control environment, manual and automated systems, and control procedures. The control environment includes the organizational structure, control frame work, policies and procedures, and external influences. Automated systems consist of system application software. Control procedures consist of general, application, and compensating controls. Within these controls, SAC provided five classifications:

1. Preventive, detective, and corrective
2. Discretionary and nondiscretionary
3. Voluntary and mandated
4. Manual and automated
5. Application and general controls

In 1996, in order to provide a comprehensive and detailed framework for establishing and refining control objectives in an IT context, the Information Systems Audit and Control Foundation (ISACA/F) issued its Control Objectives for Information and Related Technology (COBIT).[32] Starting the analysis from broad quality, fiduciary, and security requirements, seven distinct control categories were extracted. COBIT defines the IT control objectives as:

1. *Effectiveness* deals with information being relevant and pertinent to the business process as well as being delivered in a timely, correct, consistent, and usable manner.
2. *Efficiency* concerns the provision of information through the optimal (most productive and economical) use of resources.

3. *Confidentiality* concerns the protection of sensitive information from unauthorized disclosure.
4. *Integrity* relates to the accuracy and completeness of information as well as to its validity in accordance with business values and expectations.
5. *Availability* relates to information being available when required by the business process now and in the future. It also concerns the safeguarding of necessary resources and associated capabilities.
6. *Compliance* deals with complying with those laws, regulations, and contractual arrangements to which the business process is subject (i.e., externally imposed business criteria).
7. *Reliability of information* relates to the provision of appropriate information for management to operate the entity and to exercise its financial and compliance reporting responsibilities.

COBIT, Parker and Benson, and others have emphasized the importance of linking IT strategy with business objectives.[33] A busy IT manager working in isolation from the business environment will have difficulty identifying the relationships between investments in technology and improved results. Decisions to invest in technologies solely for the sake of the technology itself tend not to support improved business performance. In the same regard, a business manager working in isolation from the technology environment will also have difficulty making this same link. The optimum solution is a partnership between strategy and IT investments. In this perspective and armed with the COBIT framework, IS audit plays a crucial role in establishing and reinforcing the link between business and technology by ensuring stakeholders that the organization is making the most effective and economical use of the organization's IT resources in the context of the organization's business strategy.

BRITISH STANDARDS: BS7799 AND BS 7799-2:2002

BS7799 is the most widely recognized systems security standard in the world. Although it was originally published in the mid-1990s, it was the May 1999 revision that really catapulted it onto the world stage. Ultimately, it evolved into BS EN ISO17799 in December 2000. BS 7799 (ISO17799) is comprehensive in its coverage of security issues, containing a significant number of control requirements. Compliance with it is consequently a far from trivial task, even for the most security conscious of organizations. British Standard 7799: Part 2: 1998 Specification for Information Security Management Systems provides a series of mandatory controls that a company must implement successfully before obtaining certification. The controls cover these areas in a significant level of detail:

- Information security policy
- Security organization
- Assets classification and control
- Personnel security
- Physical and environmental security
- Computer and network management
- System access control
- Business continuity planning
- Compliance

The development of BS 7799-2:2002 is now complete. This new edition has been produced to harmonize it with other management system standards, such as BS EN ISO 9001:2000 and BS EN ISO 14001:1996, to provide consistent and integrated implementation and operation of management systems. It also introduces a Plan-Do-Check-Act (PDCA) model as part of a management system approach to developing, implementing, and improving the effectiveness of an organization's information security management system. The implementation of the PDCA model will also reflect the principles as set out in the Organization for Economic Cooperation and Development guidance governing the security of information systems and networks.[34] In particular, this new edition gives a robust model for implementing the principles in those guidelines governing risk assessment, security design and implementation, and security management and reassessment.

SYSTEM SECURITY ENGINEERING CAPABILITY MATURITY MODEL: SSE-CMM

The SSE-CMM is a tool for making analysis of security needs of an entity. This tool is both a model and a process. This model is owned by a community of 50 companies and agencies led by the U.S. National Security Agency (NSA) and the Canadian Communication Security Establishment (CSE). The model presents security engineering as defined, mature, and measurable discipline. The model and appraisal method enable capability-based assurance, focused investment in security engineering tools, and qualifying vendors, suppliers, and organizations connecting to a system. (For a brief overview, visit www.theiia.org.)

This particular model has five maturity levels defined from lowest to highest levels. It also includes 22 separate process areas. According to the approach advocated by the ISSEA, the maturity level for each of these process areas is a separate decision. (For detailed discussion, please visit www.issea.org.)

CONCLUSION

The recent and ongoing developments in the field of information technology with a focus on enterprise technology and its convergence with communication technology have a tendency to put many of our age-old auditing practices in jeopardy, particularly in relation to the electronic evidence and its acceptability by stakeholders and especially regulators. The complexity of enterprise information technology-based systems makes all of us sit up and make efforts to update auditing techniques, methods, and auditing processes because the technology-oriented people may not be able to appreciate the importance of internal control mechanisms put in place by accounting people.

With the increase in the complexity of the systems assured by them not only from the accounting and auditing practices point of view but also from the infrastructure security viewpoint, the assurance providers are also expected to update their relevant methodologies. Assurance area researchers must find out the best practices from established practitioners and also involve those who design such complicated systems. In the end, one must remember that information assurance is intertwined with assurances of all the segments pertaining to the operation, maintenance, and governance of the information systems.

NOTES

1. Steven Marlin, "Enterprise Systems Management: Banks Look to Get a Grip on IT," *Bank Systems & Technology* 36, no. 11 (1999): 42–48. Danica Pravica, "Centralized Systems Help Reduce Risks," *Computing Canada* 25, no. 30 (1999): 23–24. Teri Robinson, "Think Big Picture: Incorporating e-Commerce Sites into Core Business Systems Has Made Processing More Important Than Ever," *Internet Week* 772 (1999): 37.
2. Tefko Saracevic, "Information Science," *Journal of the American Society for the Information Science* 50, no. 12 (1999): 1051–1063. Victor Lessor et al., "BIG: An Agent for Resource-bounded Information Gathering & Decision Making," *Artificial Intelligence* 118 (2000): 197–244.
3. Nicholas Petrely, "Open Rules for e-Business," *Computer World* 36, no. 25 (2002): 48.
4. Stephen Ferg, "Data Independence & the Relational DBMS," *Datamation* 32, no. 21 (1986): 103–105.
5. Liu Ling, Calton Piu, and Han Wei, "An XML Enabled Data Extraction Toolkit for Web Sources," *Information Systems* 26, no. 8 (2001): 563–583.
6. M. Brian Blake, Gail Hamilton, and Hoyt Jaffery, "Using Component-based Development & Web Technologies to Support a Distributed Data Management System," *Annals of Software Engineering* 13, no. 1 (2002): 13–34.
7. Amitabh Saran et al., "Scientific Modelling Using Distributed Resources," Proceedings of the 4th ACM Workshop on Advances in Geographic Information Systems, 1996, pp. 68–75.
8. W. F. Cody et al., "The Integration of Business Intelligence & Knowledge Management," *IBM Systems Research Journal* 41, no. 4 (2002): 697–713.
9. Christoph Bussler, Dieter Fensol, and Alexander Maedche, "A Conceptual Architecture for Semantic Web-enabled Web Services," *ACM SIGMOD,* Special Issue: Special Section on Semantic Web & Data Management, 31, no. 4 (2002): 24–29. Available at: www.doi.acm.org/10.1145/637. 411-.637415.
10. Simpson 2001, Dykstra 2002, Bansal 2002, Paul Simpson, "The International e-Commerce Evolution," *World Trade* 14, no. 6 (2001): 66–68. Gail Dykstra, "2002 SIIA Annual Conference," *Information Today* 19, no. 6 (2002): 1, 46. Praveen Bansal, "Smart Cards Spread Across Europe," *The Banker* 152, no. 913 (2002): 122–123.
11. Bin Liu, Chen Songting, and Elke A. Rundensteiner, "Data Warehousing & OLAP: Batch Data Warehouse Maintenance in Dynamic Environments," Proceedings of the 11th International Con-ference on Information and Knowledge Management, November 2002. pp. 68–75. Available at: http://doi-.acm.org/10.1145/584792.584807. Anderson et al. 2002?
12. D. G. Waddington and H Hutchison, "Resource Partitioning in General Purpose Operating Systems: Experimental Results in Windows NT," *ACM SIGOPS Operating Systems Review* 33, no. 4 (1999): 52–74.
13. Milan Merher, "Evolving Storage Integration Opportunities," *Computer Technology Review* 21, no. 10 (2001): 30–31. Barry P. Arlinghaus, "Information Gathering, Technology and Enterprise Systems," *Tax Executive* 53, no. 5 (2001): 354–364. "Business Software Solutions-CRM Update," *Accountancy* (London), 128, no. 1300 (2001): 1. Mark Heidorn, "The Importance of Design Data Management," *Printed Circuit Design* (San Francisco), 19, no. 7 (2002): 8–10+. Michael J. Hennel, "Forecasting Demands Begin with Integration," *B to B* (Chicago), 87, no. 11 (2002): 9.
14. Bettina Kemme and Gustavo Alonso, "A New Approach to Developing and Implementing Eager Database Replication Protocols," *ACM Transactions on Database Systems* 25, no. 3 (2000): 333–379. Craig McGuire, "Internet Financial Networks Sign with First Call," *Wall Street & Technology* 17, no. 8 (1999): 62. "BTOB Web Price Index," *B to B* 85, no. 6 (2000): 24.
15. Carl Stieren, "Add One Egg, a Cup of Milk, and Stir: Single Source Documentation for Today," Proceedings of the 15th Annual International Conference on Computer Documentation, 1999, pp. 255–262. Available at: http://doi.acm.org/10.1145/263367.263400.
16. Lee Willard Strickland and Jennifer Willard, "Re-Engineering the Immigration Systems: A Case for Data mining & Information Assurance to Enhance Home land Security: Part 1: Identifying the

Current Problems," *Bulletin of the American Society of Information Science & Technology* (October/November 2002): 16–21.

17. Allan Berg, "Can Information Assurance Efforts Be United," *Security Management* 45, no. 3 (2001): 160–162.
18. Institute of Internal Auditors, *Standards for the Professional Practice of Internal Auditing* (Altamonte Springs, FL: Author, 1978).
19. R. L. Nolan, "Managing the Crisis in Data Processing," *Harvard Business Review* (March-April 1979): 115–123.
20. Richard L. Ratliff et al., *Internal Auditing: Principles & Techniques* (Altamonte Springs, FL: Institute of Internal Auditors, 1996).
21. AICPA, 1996.
22. Ratliff et al., *Internal Auditing.*
23. Stafford Beer, *The Brain of the Firm,* 2nd ed. (New York: John Wiley & Sons, 1995).
24. Peter P. Schoderbek, Charles G, Schoderbek, and Asterios G. Kefalas, *Management Systems: Conceptual Considerations* (Homewood, IL: Irwin, 1990).
25. S. E. Kovar, K. G. Burke, and B. R. Kovar, "Consumer Responses to the CPA WebTrust Assurance," *Journal of Information Systems* 14, no. 1 (2000):17–36. J. L. Craig Jr., "AICPA Modifies WebTrust to Respond to Marketplace," *The Trusted Professional* (June 2000)." Available at: www.nysscpa.org/trusteprof/archive/0600/6Tp8a.htm.
26. "WebTrust: A Progress Report," *CPA Journal* (July1999): 13–14.
27. W. M. Primoff, "Electronic Commerce and WebTrust," *CPA Journal* (November 1998). Available at: www.nysscpa.org/cpajournal/1998/1198/Features/f141198.html.
28. John W. Lainhart, "Arrival of COBIT Helps Refine the Valuable Role of IS Audit and Control in the Enterprise," *Information Systems Control Journal* 4 (1996): 20–23.
29. American Institute of Certified Public Accountants, Committee on Auditing Procedure, Statement of Auditing Standards No. 1, "Internal Control—Elements of a Coordinated System and Its Importance to Management and the Independent Public Accountants" (New York: Author, 1973).
30. IIA, *Standards for the Professional Practice of Internal Auditing.*
31. Institute of Internal Auditing, *Systems Auditability and Control* (Altamonte Springs, FL: Author, 1991). Institute of Internal Auditing, *Systems Auditability and* Control (Altamonte Springs, FL: Author, 1994).
32. Information Systems Audit and Control Foundation, *Control Objectives for Information and Related Technologies* (Rolling Meadows, IL: Author, 1996).
33. Marilyn M. Parker and Robert J. Benson, *Information Economics: Linking Business Performance to Information Technology* (Englewood Cliffs, NJ: Prentice-Hall, 1988).
34. OECD Guidelines for the Security of Information Systems and Networks 2002.

Chapter 12

The Impact of Communications Infrastructure on Fraud Detection and Deterrence

Sandy Kronenberg

INTRODUCTION

E-commerce allows the transaction of business at incredible speeds. Unfortunately, this same technology allows businesses to be defrauded at that same rate.

This chapter delivers an organized understanding of currently available security technologies. These security technologies provide protection to the communication flowing throughout the organization. Although many of these security technologies were not developed with fraud detection and deterrence in mind, if properly deployed, these solutions can provide instant or near-instant reporting of possible fraud attempts. At the very least, these solutions can yield in-depth information allowing forensic investigation to shed light on both the scope and the identities of those involved in fraud.

FRAUD AND TECHNOLOGY

Fraud deterrence focuses primarily on the controls used in order to prevent the behavior. But it is the behavior of the individual willing to commit the fraud that must be analyzed to understand the best technology to combat fraud and detect its occurrence.

This chapter does not serve to help change the behavior of employees or improve morale—there are many books on business management well suited for that discussion. Rather the object of this chapter is to provide information technology (IT) staff, executives, and auditors with information about the security technologies available and known behaviors that can be detected by these technologies.

Fraud is often committed by those without loyalty, those who have been scorned, those who are financially compromised, and/or those who are simply greedy. When we analyze these symptoms to understand the root causes, patterns emerge to describe the methods that many people use to commit fraud.

Some view this categorization of all people as a Draconian harshness, but this approach serves many criminal investigations. Furthermore, understanding these behaviors allows us to create observation infrastructures that can correlate information from a multitude of sources in order to help identify fraud as it is occurring (or shortly thereafter).

COMMUNICATION SECURITY SOLUTIONS

Firewalls

Technology. Firewalls are synonymous with computer security. Many individuals who do not have daily interaction with IT often feel that if they have a firewall and virus protection, they have sufficient security. After reviewing this chapter, you will come to realize that there are many different facets of security. To secure any computing environment, a combination of the methodologies is required. A firewall is just one of those many layers.

The firewall, while being an effective security device filtering or blocking traffic that flows through it, has its flaws, as much of the internal network traffic never flows through it. Therefore, it primarily identifies Internet traffic. This traffic very often is masked by a technology known as Network Address Translation (NAT). NAT is employed simply because the Internet protocol (IP) address space in use today is limited. In order to avoid running out of IP addresses, computers and laptops within an organization often appear to other devices on the Internet as the same IP address. While this solves the problem with limited IP address space (essentially buying time until the world standardizes on a new protocol known as IPV6), it has created a problem with identifying the true source or destination of the traffic. Therefore, the logs from the firewall become important to tracing internet activity.

Implications to Fraud Detection and Deterrence. According to the Federal Bureau of Investigation (FBI) and the Computer Security Institute (CSI) 2001 survey, twice as many respondents cited their Internet connection as a more frequent point of attack as those who said assaults came from within their internal systems.[1]

Since the firewall is often used to provide protection from external attack, it may be used to serve risk management personnel and auditors. All of the traffic that traverses the firewall can be logged. Although the traffic is often masked by using NAT, the real source and destination computers can be rebuilt (when using the right tools).

Messaging: E-mail

Technology. In many organizations, e-mail messages consume more bandwidth than all other communication types (especially when factoring in unwanted mail such as spam). As this is the case, there is a heavy burden to sort and index all of the e-mail messages sent or received. Therefore, many groupware solutions that most organizations use are optimized for the sending and receiving of e-mail, not on the monitoring and logging of message content. This is the case with Microsoft Exchange, Lotus Notes, Novel Groupwise, Mirapoint and the various forms of Unix/Linux-based Sendmail. In my opinion, these solutions do not have advanced monitoring capabilities nor do they have detailed logging of message content. Furthermore, these e-mail solutions do not have sufficient compliance and/or auditing considerations.

A wide range of e-mail management tools have been created to address these limitations. Many of these are third-party tools, but some features can be purchased as options to existing packages (i.e., Microsoft Exchange 2007). One type of e-mail management tool focuses on the ability to monitor specific e-mails with certain content or attachments. For instance, a corporate word list can be created where either a single word or a combination of words found anywhere within the message would trigger notification to the proper staff and/or log the activity. Other e-mail management tools feature the ability to store every sent or received e-mail message. Once every e-mail message has been stored, the full content and attachments can be indexed in a database. Often this database resides on a different server. Therefore, an e-mail message can be retrieved even if has been deleted. Furthermore, queries can be made against a wide range of search parameters.

Implications to Fraud Detection and Deterrence. Informing employees that they should have no expectation of privacy with regard to e-mail or any other use of the corporate network and computer system can act as an excellent deterrent to fraudulent activity. Often the computer usage policy or security policy is published in the employee handbook or new hire documentation. These policies must be reinforced with the actual ability to audit and/or block e-mail messages. Risk management staff and auditors must be able to access this data.

Messaging: Instant Messaging

Technology. According to a study by ComScore MediaMetrix, more than 250 million people use instant messaging (IM) regularly.[2] And International Data Corporation (IDC) estimates that more than 7 billion instant messages are sent every day.[3] Many of these instant messages are sent by people at work but without the consent of their employers.

The IM program can either be a stand-alone program, or it can be a Web-enabled (i.e., an application launched within a Web browser, such as Microsoft Internet Explorer or Mozilla Firefox).

Since the instant messages can be sent without installing an application but by simply accessing a Web page, corporate IT staffs have been playing leapfrog with the IM service providers, trying to control, manage, or block instant messages. Since many IM programs use the same communication ports that web browsers use (TCP port 80), IM traffic cannot not be blocked without making significant changes to security policies or with the use of other technologies.

Implications to Fraud Detection and Deterrence. The most popular IM services are AOL, Yahoo, MSN, and ICQ. Since these IM services are hosted by their respective providers, many users mistakenly assume that their employers have no ability to log this traffic. In fact, there are a number of solutions available. Some solutions can identify the IM traffic from other Web traffic using the same TCP ports. Once this traffic is identified, it can be blocked outright or controlled to allow only certain IP addresses or users to have access to instant messaging. Furthermore, the content of the instant message can be stored along with any files that are transferred during the IM session. By storing the IM traffic in a database, the corporation can leverage the potential productivity of instant messaging with the assurance that message content can be scanned for abnormal behavior just like e-mail.

Messaging: Voice/Video/Interactive Communication

Technology. There have been solutions for recording voice communication for many years, but with the advent of new technologies have come new challenges and new enhancements.

Some of the new challenges with recording voice have been the widespread use of Voice over IP (VOIP) and IP Telephony. While I will not address the various laws related to the recording of telephone calls, there exists an ability to monitor and record voice traffic by using a methodology similar to "sniffing" data streams. However, a new challenge emerges with the requirement of securing voice communication with encryption.

Solutions available today can allow authorized voice recording as well as the actual information on the screen of the employee.

Implications to Fraud Detection and Deterrence. While the knowledge of voice recording can assist with fraud deterrence, to be truly effective, the recordings must all be reviewed for abnormal behavior. Hiring people as watchdogs can become prohibitively expensive. The typical result is that compromises are made and only small samples of voice conversations are actually reviewed. A new approach has been to use speech recognition technology to continually monitor all voice communication to identify key words or phrases. Furthermore, the actual keyboard, video, and mouse activity can be logged and correlated to the voice recording to help with abnormal behavior determination and alerting.

Content Filtering

Technology. Content filtering solutions are used primarily to limit and or log access to specific Web sites on the internet. These solutions are usually located just inside the corporate firewall and can either be placed in-line or are "queried." Both of these strategies have their pros and cons.

The in-line variety content filter acts as a bridge whereby all communication traversing the Internet will be mirrored to a processor that will analyze all the traffic and identify specific content such as:

- Instant messaging
- http/https Web URLs and content
- Online gaming traffic

The in-line content filter can present a warning to a user, block the traffic, and/or log the entire "conversation."

The "queried" content filter is one that may be centrally located and can allow many different egress points throughout the corporation to access the Internet yet all of the Web traffic is authorized and/or logged. The advantage to this type of content filter is that there is only one server/appliance to manage while still maintaining a complete report of all Web traffic. The disadvantage to this method is that the in-line content filter can monitor many other types of traffic, not just http. Regardless of the solution implemented, the logging and recording capabilities of these systems can be leveraged to provide detailed understanding of the employee activity.

Implications to Fraud Detection and Deterrence. Content filtering solutions were originally designed to address the needs of corporations that want to give Internet access to employees without sacrificing productivity. An additional benefit was discovered by human resource (HR) departments eager to mitigate the possibility of employees accessing certain Web content while using corporate communication systems. While employee handbooks have had sexual harassment policies for decades, only recently can Internet usage policies strictly adhere to these policies with the use of content filters. HR departments continually urge IT staffs to leverage content filters to block employee access to pornographic Web images of or other nonacceptable content.

An organization must contemplate and identify business goals while paying attention to employee concerns before deploying any filters. For many years employees have had free access to the Internet; the introduction of a filter may cause negative morale and feelings of invasion of privacy—it is like trying to close Pandora's Box. Communicating the policy and the presence of filtering solutions to employees is critical. A secret deployment could cause serious repercussions.

Beyond productivity and HR considerations, content filters naturally began to fit the needs of emerging compliance standards. Content filters can assist with:

- Sarbanes-Oxley (SOX)
- Health Insurance Portability and Accountability Act (HIPAA)
- Gramm-Leach-Bliley (GLBA)
- ISO17799 (BS17799)
- PCI Data Security Standard
- California Senate Bill No. 1386
- NERC Cyber Security Standards
- American Express Data Security Standards
- MasterCard Site Data Protection Program
- Visa Cardholder Information Security Program

Some companies are drawn to Web-filtering solutions by a lack of perceived control, especially in the wake of these new regulations, which are meant to protect privacy and oversee transactions.

Because organizations are keepers of vast amounts of sensitive data, including credit card numbers and Social Security numbers, there is no room for error. That means they simply cannot rely upon antivirus or antispyware blocking products for Internet security. Employees, too, can put organizations in financial and legal jeopardy when they disclose sensitive information through unauthorized Internet access by e-mail or instant messaging. And with the Sarbanes-Oxley Act and Gramm-Leach-Bliley pushing to protect nonpublic client data, financial organizations cannot afford to have less than the best in internet security solutions.

Network Admission Control

Technology. Many are familiar with the process by which a user supplies credentials (whether it is a basic username and password or a more advanced strong schema of either two-factor or certificate—see the "Centralized Authentication" section) to access a resource (much like using a key to open a lock in a door). This "authorization" to the computer and/or network can have another layer of protection added. This additional layer of protection incorporates a decision as to whether the user and the device he or she is using should be "admitted" onto the network. This is referred to as admission control. An analogy can be drawn to a bouncer at a nightclub: If you do not have the proper attire, then you are not allowed in even if you have an invitation (the invitation being the authorization credentials). Admission control can check a device and confirm if it meets the predefined security policy of the organization. These admission control policies can be very flexible to meet the needs of the organization and may include requirements such as:

- Operating system updates
- Security patches
- Virus protection
- Spyware protection
- Host-based intrusion detection
- Registry keys
- Organization-specific software

The Network Admission Control (NAC) software can not only distinguish whether the required software is installed on the system but also confirm that the software is running and operating properly. If the admission policy is not met, then the user can be placed in a "dirty VLAN"—a segmented area of the network that only allows remediation of the policy violation. Once the admission policy is met (perhaps the latest patches needed to be applied or the latest virus definitions needed to be downloaded), then the device is allowed onto either the internal network or some other network segment (perhaps multiple admission and/or access levels have been established —i.e., an auditor network or guest network with access only to the Internet).

Implications to Fraud Detection and Deterrence. Once admission control has been implemented, the monitoring and management of network resources can be dramatically increased. This reveals a double-edged sword. Unknown threats can be thwarted more easily; there is an added layer of protection against Trojan horses and other tools that would provide access or information about a secure network since a device that has not properly been admitted is sectioned off in a "walled garden." All activity on this network can be carefully monitored. But, on the flip side, now that these invisible barriers exist, a new concern has arisen: Unbeknownst to the auditor/analyst, only limited access is given to the network, possibly preventing full investigation or disclosure.

Centralized Authentication

Technology. In our security-conscious society, we use a wide range of programs, each with its own security systems. The reason each program has its own security is essentially due to a lack of a good trust system that can universally verify the identity of a user across diverse systems. The result is users who are forced to remember a wide range of user names and passwords. These users invariably cause IT staff to fail security audits identifying social engineering flaws when passwords are discovered written down on a note under the keyboard or in a desk drawer. One solution is Single-Sign-On. Another solution is called Federated Identity Systems. Solutions that have been around for decades are Kerberos and RADIUS. Many of these solutions can give the user the appearance that their programs are integrated by using the same credentials.

Regardless of the technology chosen or the underlying security schema, the desired goal is centralized authentication systems that provide detailed reports of user activity.

Implications to Fraud Detection and Deterrence. Many IT directors report security breaches that occur from within the network. The security breach may be due in part to a careless user not logging out of their terminal or it may be a directed attack with a Trojan used to gain unauthorized access. One method of combating these breaches is through the use of centralized authentication. The centralization of authentication can ease the management of authentication to many systems while providing comfort that the corporate security is being met and that credentials can be revoked in a consistent manner. Finally, centralized authentication can provide detailed reporting of access to all hosts and/or network infrastructure. This reporting can yield rapid results during forensic investigation of fraud across one or more systems.

Network and Host-based Intrusion Detection Systems (NIDS & HIDS)

Technology. Intrusion detection systems (IDSs) are designed to monitor the activity of one or more network resources. This monitoring is designed to determine if there is abnormal activity. In order to detect abnormal behavior throughout the corporate network, often multiple IDSs need to be deployed. The multiple IDSs can determine the exact abnormal behavior via a signature (many are familiar with virus signatures that need to be regularly updated) or via heuristic analysis. The first generation of IDSs only had the ability to report and notify on abnormal behavior. Subsequent generations have added abilities to mitigate the anomalous behavior by shutting down threads or ports (often referred to as "shunning traffic"); therefore, some manufacturers are referring to these products as intrusion prevention systems (IPSs). IDS/IPS security solutions can be further divided into hostbased (server and/or workstation) or network based. Network-based IDS/IPS deployment can either be in-line with the communication operating in a transparent fashion or reconfiguration of switches to send all traffic on the network segment to the out-of-band IDS/IPS.

Implications to Fraud Detection and Deterrence. Intrusion detection systems are often invisible to users. Therefore, concerns around "entrapment" and privacy often are cited. Neither of these factors is a concern to the key stakeholders in an organization who are looking to help secure an organization or to the auditor who is looking to confirm the validity of financial or compliance statements. Entrapment is a legal defense only from law enforcement prosecution of a crime. Privacy would be concern if the Federal Wiretap Act did not have an exemption that allows security technologies to collect information about people as long as it is protecting their environment.

Some forms of anomalous behavior are difficult to detect with IDSs alone. One way to help determine if fraudulent activity is being attempted is through the use of a honey pot. (Honey pots are used for the sole purpose of securing an organization; they are legal especially if a login banner is used that states only authorized personnel are permitted and the user consents to having all activity monitored and shared with third parties.) A honey pot is an attractive target designed to help detect or deflect unauthorized attempts at gaining access to information. The honey pot could simply be a server that should never be logged into or one with limited defenses that an IDS can easily determine is abnormal.

Another enhancement available to IDSs is incident response. "Incident response" traditionally has referred to the group of individuals responsible for carrying out a specific "playbook" when a new security threat has been discovered. Today incident response is an automatic change of network behavior based on elevated threat levels. Incident response is still a newer technology and although there is not an industry standard term for this technology; each manufacturer has similar capabilities. These capabilities include the ability for the network to respond to anomalous behavior beyond just shunning an IP address or port. The response can include dynamic segmentation of user traffic into secure areas (virtual LAN) changes in access to users or groups of users, and traffic/speed limitations. Essentially, incident response technologies provide a higher security level until the source of the escalated threat level has been addressed. The source could be a virus that has been wreaking havoc on computer networks throughout the globe, so an automated incident response could be in effect until the virus signature has been written and incorporated into the virus scanners. Note that incident response could be triggered by a multitude of network resources automatically or by an IT staff member manually. Manual intervention could be mandated when a business event occurs (examples include the termination of an employee or the unconfirmed report of a security breach).

ANTI-"X": Virus, Spam, Trojans, and Other Malware Detection

Technology. Network infrastructure as well as computer workstations are susceptible to attacks from virus, spam, Trojans, and other malware. "Malware" is a term used to describe any software that would have a negative impact on a system. The software used to combat malware is often referred to as anti-X: antivirus, antispam, and so on. These anti-X solutions can be deployed on hosts (servers or workstations) and/or deployed on gateways to the network. Often a combination of both host and gateway deployment of anti-X solutions provides the best protection from spam and malware.

Implications to Fraud Detection and Deterrence. Viruses, spam, Trojans, bots, worms . . . the list goes on and on. This general categorization of malware has a dramatic impact on fraud detection and deterrence. These programs are now available to a wide range of computer users, not just a few advanced programmers. Malware is not just a threat to business continuity; it is a threat to national security, so much so that many government organizations publish security recommendations. Even the typically secretive National Security Agency publishes comprehensive security configuration guidelines (www.nsa.gov/ia/index.cfm). Malware and spam are now the dominant source of traffic on the Internet. While much of this negative traffic is random, nearly anyone can launch very precise attacks. This sort of information warfare need not be launched just by terrorists or foreign nations. Attacks can be from disgruntled employees, those looking to lower valuations/stock prices, competitors, those looking to hide fraudulent activities, and the like. It is recommended that organizations use both gateway and host deployments of anti-X solutions and that they use more than one manufacturer's solution.

Vulnerability Scanners

Technology. All communication devices have services to allow other devices to connect to and utilize resources. The connection is typically made on a "port." Just as a physical port has size and dimension limitations to its interface to allow something to plug into it, virtual ports will restrict the type of connections made to it based on a number of parameters or protocols. These protocols can apply to industry standards. This connection type may be widely adopted, or proprietary/customized protocols can be created. The connection to a port is often initiated by a "handshake"— a very specific set of communiqués and acknowledgments. Programs scan these sets of protocols and handshakes to see if they are behaving normally. Furthermore, a secured machine is one that has all of its ports turned off (and therefore they will not respond) for services not being used by that device. While this may seem obvious, the default setting for many network devices is set to permit traffic (the port is turned "on"). Often, if devices are shipped secure (with the default setting "off") then those programs will not "work" right out of the box. Therefore, security must often take a backseat to functionality since manufacturers are often appealing to customers looking for a "turn-key" solution.

IT staff should turn off services (ports, etc.) that are not in use before deploying any new technology solution; the problem is that often many services are active without the knowledge of the IT staff. A vulnerability scanner can help here, by providing insight into each device and possible problems associated with them. First the vulnerability scanner scans a segment of the network and identifies any devices that respond to it. Next it checks the open ports on that device. Finally it attempts to communicate to those open ports and learn information about the device. The output of a vulnerability scan is a report that will define the "potential" sources of vulnerability on the device, and it typically ranks those in order of priority or potential risk.

Implications to Fraud Detection and Deterrence. While the IT staff members typically use vulnerability scanners to protect the device or network, others may use the vulnerability scanners to identify exploits. These exploits can be used to gather information, gain a "foothold" (in order to control a system or set of systems), or launch an attack. While this might sound severe, it is exactly what occurs in many instances of computer fraud. Financial information is often the primary target but any information is vulnerable.

Content Addressable Storage

Technology. Data retention policies associated with many compliance standards have driven a new wave of IT products that securely index and archive computer files and database records. These solutions often "journal" all content created into a separate system that has vast storage capability. Vast storage is required since every instance of data, regardless if it has been deleted, is retained. Therefore, no space is reclaimed until certain conditions have been met. Whole transactions can be re-created or whole directories of files can be restored even after the originator of the files deleted them and destroyed the system they were created on.

Implications to Fraud Detection and Deterrence. Obviously the implications to fraud detection and deterrence are vast when considering content addressable storage. Every bit of data can be retained as deemed necessary by the organization compliance or security policy. While this retention is useful for forensic investigation, it can also be used in real-time detection. Software can be tied into these content-addressable storage solutions that can trigger notifications to proper staff when abnormal behavior arises. Examples of such behavior could be specific words or phrases, types of transactions in a database, or the addition or deletion of files.

Access Control, Surveillance, and Real-time Location Systems

Technology. Physical security solutions in the past have used analog signaling and often proprietary protocols. Separate access-control and surveillance networks needed to be supported. Recent developments have provided for advancements in physical security systems to allow their "convergence" onto the TCP/IP—Ethernet network. "Convergence" is the term often used when multiple technologies, cable plants, and monitoring/management platforms are collapsed into one network. A single network is cheaper to install and operate. Since many organizations can leverage their existing copper, fiber, and wireless technologies, the largest investment is the replacement of the legacy end point with a TCP/IP device. The legacy end point could either be a camera for surveillance or perhaps a proximity or biometric sensor used for access control.

Further leveraging of existing technology can allow for a new type of physical security system: Real-Time Location Systems (RTLS). The existing wireless network can be used to triangulate people and/or resources in real time. Widely available today, 802.11 wireless technology allows an organization to cost-effectively reap some benefits from RTLS. Soon more cost-effective tags and sensors will allow other Radio Frequency Identification (RFID) technologies to become ubiquitous. With RTLS (using 802.11 or RFID), a map can display people and/or resources as they move throughout a facility. Furthermore, this information can be stored in a database and/or compared to rule sets that check for anomalous behavior. Real-time RTLSs allow for the integration of the physical and virtual security needs of an organization. Further integration of the physical and virtual worlds can be gained by monitoring access control and user logins to the network. If a user used her badge at the building entrance, then remote access to the network over the Internet should not be occurring. And if a user logged in remotely over the Internet, then no one should be using that badge to access the building.

Essentially, technology has allowed the integration of many physical security technologies as well as network authentication and other "data security" technologies to have consolidated reporting.

Implications to Fraud Detection and Deterrence. Access control systems are now IP-based, and systems from many corporate sites can be linked using the corporate wide area network (WAN) to provide centralized credential and access management. This limits the number of personnel who need access to such systems and allows for centralized logging of ingress (and possibly egress) to corporate facilities and/or restricted areas. Often video surveillance systems are coupled to access control systems. New IP-based video surveillance systems can provide centralized image and event capture. These images and events can be matched to access control logs of facilities and/or restricted areas. The centralization of these data can provide much more control than legacy tape systems can provide. IP surveillance removes the need for swapping tapes and automates the transfer of surveillance logs back to centralized secure servers. Furthermore, some of the new video surveillance systems have images that are stored in encrypted and unalterable formats that are admissible as evidence in legal proceedings. In addition to access control and IP surveillance, new systems leveraging RFID and 802.11 wireless technologies have the ability to track people and/or resources in real time. In fact, this tracking information can be compared to virtual security systems to provide a comprehensive view of the activity of any individual.

The convergence of these physical security technologies to IP yields wide-sweeping capabilities in the distribution, search, video analytics and information sharing that greatly increases accessibility to captured security information.

These "smart building" technologies provide real-time fraud detection since for the first time both physical and virtual security can be truly integrated.

CORRELATION

Many of the security technology solutions described in this chapter can provide sufficient detection and deterrence of fraudulent activity (or at least identification of abnormal activity that should be investigated further by human eyes), but they are not enough. Many of the aforementioned security solutions can generate hundreds if not thousands of log entries per second. The sheer volume of data that must be reviewed is often impossible to accomplish by a single or even small group of dedicated security professionals. Even if these security professionals focus just on reports from these various solutions, they would be buried by insurmountable task of comparing one security log with another to identify any abnormal behaviors. The comparison of one log entry with another from a different security solution is crucial to identifying anomalous behavior. This comparison of logs or "correlation" is the highest level of security any organization can attain. It represents the culmination of security technologies in order to provide a holistic overview.

This holistic overview is helpful in fraud detection and deterrence. Monitoring comprehensive logs from all of the aforementioned security technologies can yield a wide variety of network abnormalities that can be tracked back to criminal activities. For instance, high network utilization in off hours, communication to competitors, and transactions from improper sources can all be monitored. Monitored abnormalities over one or more aspects of the converged network can be reassembled automatically. Reassembled sessions from a multitude of devices can then be analyzed by a correlation engine to process the data and determine if anomalous behavior is occurring. Finally, triggers can block the traffic and/or notify the proper staff for incident response.

The incidence of this type of activity is higher than most expect. During a six-month period at a small Internet service provider (ISP), I recall three separate incidents that eventually involved the FBI or cybercrimes divisions of city police departments. In one case an entire corporate database was transmitted over the Internet.

While there is no perfect protection schema, the use of all of these technologies and the correlation of their logging information can help provide some of the tightest security practices available.

NOTES

1. Securitystats.com—Infosec Stats, <http://www.securitystats.com/infosec.html>.
2. Wired News: Instant Messaging goes Graphical, <http://www.wired.com/news/technology/0,1282,649-69,00.html>.
3. Ibid.

Chapter 13

Process and Information Validation

David E. Zulawski, Douglas E. Wicklander, and Marion E. Briggs

PART I: INTERVIEW AND INTERROGATION PROCESS

The aims of this chapter are to:

- Establish the difference between the interview and interrogation process.
- Recognize five different forms of lying.
- Understand the various question types and their uses.
- Obtain and evaluate the subject's untainted story.
- Recognize the different forms of interviews.
- Explain the structure of the non-confrontational interrogation.

Unfortunately, the process of interview and interrogation is applicable most often when the fraud deterrence efforts of the organization have failed. The company controls have been breached from the inside or outside, allowing a fraud to take place.

Still, the most productive component of an investigation is the effective use of interview and interrogation. Many frauds are revealed as only the tip of the iceberg and the interviews and interrogation uncover the full scope of the problem. A suspect's confession is the crown jewel of the investigation, substantiating the method of theft, flow and location of proceeds and individuals involved.[1] It is the interview and interrogation skills of the investigator that give true meaning to the documents and evidence recovered during the investigation.

Contrary to what is seen on television, the cooperation of witnesses and the confessions of suspects are usually obtained through persuasion and skilled well-thought-out approaches. Once understood and carefully applied, the process of interview and interrogation becomes a productive avenue for case resolution. The problem for the new interviewer/interrogator is that what works in one case may be absolutely wrong for the next. Interviewers/interrogators must be flexible in their approach in dealing with people from different backgrounds, financial means, and cultures.

While remaining flexible in their approach, skilled interviewers and interrogators know that the best techniques are those that work most often with most people. However, flexibility does not mean a random unplanned rambling. There is an underlying structure to the process that provides a road map for dealing with witnesses, victims and suspects.

DIFFERENCE BETWEEN INTERVIEW AND INTERROGATION

The dynamics of interview and interrogation are very different. Although most people understand the difference between interviews and interrogation, when it comes to putting the processes into practice, there is often confusion. Some of the confusion is caused by avoiding the word "interrogation" because it does not sound "friendly" and having investigators substitute the word "interview." This renaming does not change the desired outcome; it merely makes the process sound more politically correct.

By clearly defining the desired outcome, investigators must choose a course that complements the investigation strategy. If they seek facts or are looking to confirm information, they interview; if the end result is a confession, they must interrogate. This is like a north-south highway leading to different cities. If you turn north, the road always takes you to that city, and south to the other. If you turn the wrong direction, you will not get to where you want to go, unless you take a considerable amount of time to do so. Interviews and interrogations are very much the same; if investigators interview, often the process will not lead to a confession; and if it does, plan on a long trip.

The two processes are different, as are the actions of the investigators. The terms "interview," "interrogation," and "subject" and "suspect" are used to tell the reader what the investigator is doing in the encounter, gathering facts or attempting to gain an admission.

Interview

An interview is a non-accusatory fact-gathering or behavior-provoking conversation to determine facts, sequence of events, or alibis or to confirm information with a victim, witness, or suspect. The interviewer allows the subject to do the majority of the talking by asking open-ended questions to encourage a narrative response. In the latter stages of the interview, the investigator may use closed-ended questions to clearly establish or confirm details. Because of the dynamics of interviewing, the investigator should not expect a confession, but only for the subject to confirm or deny information.

Interrogation

An interrogation is conducted when a suspect is believed to be guilty. It is a search for the truth to obtain admissions or confession from the suspect that independently confirms the investigative findings. The suspect's admissions or confession should support the details of the investigation and establish the individual's participation in the act. In an interrogation, the interrogator seeks information that establishes the suspect's culpability and mental state, which will provide sufficient cause to prosecute, discipline, or discharge the individual.

PREPARATION AND ROOM SETTING

Regardless of whether the individual is to be interviewed or interrogated, the investigator must prepare for the encounter. Understanding what information the individual may have, how he or she fits into the investigation, and the way he or she may respond to the encounter are just a few of the considerations the investigator must analyze before beginning an interview or interrogation.

First and foremost, the investigator must determine what company policy and procedures are relevant to interviewing an employee. Are there any specific notifications that must be made prior to the interview to obtain permission to speak with the associate? Depending on the organization and position of the employee, this might require the notification of legal, human resources, or senior management.

The interviewer should also review the investigation with supervisors to double check its thoroughness. During this review the interviewer is selected. The primary investigator may or may not ultimately be assigned the interview. The selection of the interviewer should be based on skill, knowledge of the investigation, and personal compatibility with the subject. For example, asking a woman to confront a male who believes that women are inferior is only adding an unnecessary hurdle to the conversation. Planning for personality differences often allows the interviewer to establish and maintain rapport with the subject more easily than if this aspect of the encounter is ignored.

Witness selection should also be considered in conjunction with the selection of the interviewer. Many organizations, by policy, use a witness for any interviews or interrogations. The witness selected should generally be a trustworthy member of management who will be able to observe the process and testify fully to what was observed. Careful selection of the witness is important to avoid personality conflicts with the subject or potential embarrassment issues.

Another consideration in preparing for the interview/interrogation is the subject's likely response to being questioned. Anticipating the individual's reaction to the encounter allows the investigator to prepare a contingency plan to deal with problems so he or she does not have to improvise a solution. If, for example, it appears likely the subject will respond with anger, the investigator should have a plan in place to control the anger or avoid it completely. This control might be established by selection of location, style of accusation, the interviewer, or even the witness who will be present during the encounter.

The subject's schedule should also be taken into account when determining the timing of the encounter. The investigator should allow sufficient time to obtain the necessary information. On occasion uncooperative subjects will use a previous appointment, lunch, or quitting time to avoid the conversation. Planning for the subject's possible excuses will allow the interview or interrogation to proceed unhindered.

The investigator also must consider what evidence is available and whether it can be revealed to the subject. The evidence may be either direct or circumstantial, but it should be considered in two ways.

1. Will revealing the evidence to the subject compromise an informant or reveal the investigation to other targets?
2. What possible explanations might the subject use to explain away the incriminating evidence?

The evidence evaluation will enable the investigator to anticipate potential subject explanations and use questioning techniques to minimize the individual's ability to deflect the evidence.

The interviewer may also need to satisfy personal or corporate needs. Establishing what information is necessary to make the decision to terminate or prosecute tends to make both the investigator's and decision maker's lives easier. The legal department may also have specific information needs to file lawsuits against the alleged participants or to protect the company. Recognizing these disparate needs allows the investigator to do a more comprehensive interview since the necessary questions are asked the first time, reducing the need for re-interviewing.

For example, in one case a human resource executive wanted to know if the employee knew when he was stealing from the company that it was wrong. The interrogator confirmed with the suspect that he knew stealing from the company was a crime and had the suspect include this in his written statement. Knowing that the employee was aware that his actions were wrong made it easier for the executive to make the decision to terminate the individual. While the crime was confirmed by the investigation, it was expressly stated by the suspect in his confession, relieving the executive of his anxiety over how to handle the situation.

Many interviewers audio- or videotape their interviews. The recording provides an accurate copy of the conversation, much more comprehensive than note taking, although less convenient to review. If the interviewer decides to record the interview, the equipment needs to be in working order with sufficient tapes and batteries to accomplish the task. Many of the new investigative case management systems allow audio and video retention as an integral part of the electronic investigative file. This makes it easy to store and share the interview results with other investigators. Another benefit of recording the interview is that doing so makes it more difficult for subjects to change their story or alibi. However, it is still useful for the interviewer to make contemporaneous notes to aid in conducting the interview and locating relevant portions of the recording to review. Also, if the recording is going to be used in some form of a hearing, it will likely have to be transcribed, adding some expense.

If the investigator plans on recording the interview/interrogation, there are three major factors to consider. The first factor is the legality of recording the conversation. Many states have enacted laws prohibiting the surreptitious recording of others without their permission. In general, the eavesdropping laws, absent a court order, fall into two basic categories: those that require only one party's consent and those that require all the parties to consent to the recording. While a number of states require only one-party consent, the investigator's, most organizations take a more conservative approach and obtain consent from all parties.

The second factor to consider is the policy of the organization regarding recordings. Some organizations prohibit the audiovisual recording of any interview or interrogation; others use it as a matter of course. Many states are currently passing legislation requiring public law enforcement to record interrogations of serious crimes or those involving juveniles. Currently there is no legal mandate for the private sector to record interviews or interrogations, and it remains a matter of company policy or personal preference.

The third consideration is the quality of the recording. Unless the microphone is carefully placed, the placement of equipment and background noise can distort or miss much of the conversation. Barely audible background noise can have a dramatic impact on the clarity of the recording even when it is not a distraction to the interviewer. Some recorders also can be used in a voice-activated mode; they may miss portions of the conversation while returning to operation. Careful preparation will increase the quality of the recording obtained.

One final consideration affecting both the interview and interrogation is establishing the desired end result. Knowing the desired outcome helps all involved assess whether the objective of the interview or interrogation has been achieved. For each outcome, there will be thresholds of information that must be obtained from the individual. Investigators who fail to clarify these thresholds of information may be disappointed when the decision maker fails to act in the desired manner. For example, if the investigator fails to establish the individual's intent, management may not authorize termination or prosecution of the individual.

Room Setting

The investigator's primary concern in room setting is establishing a private location for the conversation. A public distraction-filled environment often increases the individual's reluctance to cooperate. People are much more likely to provide information in private than in front of a group. Consider what it would feel like to be under the watchful eyes of others as they considered and critiqued each piece of information being provided. The path of least resistance for the subject is to give no or very limited information to preserve his or her self-image.

Investigators may find themselves conducting interviews in a variety of locations depending on the circumstances. In fraud investigations, the interviews are often conducted in a business environment that will have private offices or conference rooms available. However, if the investigation leads out of the company, the investigator will have much less control over the location, timing, and privacy of the interview. Depending on the importance of the interview, careful thought should be given to the location chosen.

Once the decision is made to interrogate a suspect, a more controlled location is desirable for the encounter. The interrogator should take into account the availability of evidence, witnesses, timing, and general control of the process when selecting a room.

Unless no other options exist, it is generally inadvisable to select the suspect's office or department to conduct the interrogation. For example, investigations in specialty stores offer very limited options within the store for interview space. It may be useful to use a mall office, hotel conference room, or some other space that is convenient and private rather than suffer the interruptions of the store.

While the room setting will vary based on the location, certain furniture arrangements are preferable. There should be sufficient chairs for the subject, witness, and investigator. The witness's and investigator's chairs should not block the individual's exit to the door. With neither the witness nor the interviewer blocking the subject's exit to the door, it makes it less plausible for a subject to claim he was held against his will. To avoid being a distraction, the witness should be placed to one side and slightly out of the line of sight of the subject. This gives the impression of privacy even with the witness in the room.

If possible, there should be a desk or table available to write on, although it should not be placed between the investigator and subject. In most instances, it is desirable to have the investigator and subject face one another with no barrier between. This allows the investigator to have an unobstructed view of the individual to make behavioral observations and establish rapport.

The room should have been prepared in advance to remove distractions and position the chairs. Drawing the blinds, turning off the phone, and putting up a do-not-disturb sign minimize the possibility of interruptions that might distract the participants from the conversation. Interruptions and distractions can impede the flow of the conversation and jeopardize the element of privacy.

INTERVIEWER/INTERROGATOR DEMEANOR

Unlike the gruff abrasive interviewers of television and the movies, real-life investigators are more likely to be successful when they are able to establish strong rapport with the subject. The aggressive personality rarely puts people at ease or truly opens the lines of communication. People who have a natural curiosity about others and are capable of establishing rapport quickly generally prove to be most successful in the job.

An element of understanding human behavior also is important in talking with subjects. For example, an interviewer who expresses interest in a particular piece of information may have actually increased the subject's resistance by focusing on the item directly. Once a seller discovers the buyer's need for something, the price always goes up. In the same way, once the subject discovers the importance of the information he or she possesses, the subject may be more resistant to sharing it.

Rapport

No discussion of interview and interrogation is ever complete without a discussion of establishing rapport. The problem with discussing rapport is there is no clear structure to how it is to be achieved. Almost everyone has had the experience of meeting someone for the first time and feeling like they had known the individual for years. This level of "comfort" is how the investigator attempts to connect with the subject. The question is what causes this rapport and how can the investigator consistently connect with people in this fashion.

When two people are in rapport, their bodies naturally began to match one another in body position, breathing, and even speech patterns. Many people suggest that intentionally mimicking or mirroring the other person's body position, breathing, and speech pattern will cause rapport to occur. However, the mirroring of behavior is the effect of rapport, not its cause. Some anecdotal research suggests that intentionally mirroring another's behavior may actually irritate the other person.

Rapport is achieved by finding something in common with the other person, a mutual experience shared. This may be as simple as beginning a discussion of the current weather, which is common experience. The investigator is unlikely to develop deep rapport with the subject easily, but should strive for a neutral to slightly positive relationship. It may be that over time a deeper rapport will develop, but to obtain the cooperation of the subject, being neutral and non-threatening is sufficient.

The investigator who tries too hard to establish this connection with the subject will appear forced and unnatural. People often distrust the motives of another person when he or she is overly friendly. This overt friendliness may actually cause the person to become more guarded instead of open. The investigator must be aware of the other person's response to the rapport-building attempt and be flexible in what he or she says and does. Some subjects are no-nonsense, get-to-the-point people, while others want to talk and connect before getting down to business. Observation, flexibility, and an interest in people will go a long way in opening the lines of communication.

Appearance

The investigator's appearance may also influence rapport and the cooperation of the subject. The investigator's manner should be professional, and he or she should be dressed appropriately for the context of the interview. The manner of dress is generally dictated by the practice of the location. If the individual's normal dress is more formal, it would be inappropriate for the investigator to dress in polo shirt and slacks. Conversely, the investigator dressing in a $1,500 suit while talking to an hourly employee may not achieve the desired results either. An investigator will never go wrong by at least matching the clothing of the subject. People more easily trust someone who is like them, and clothing is certainly a representation of similarity. The desired result is a competent professional appearance and manner that adds, not distracts, from the task at hand.

Together the location, demeanor, rapport, and appearance combine to create a sense of confidence in the investigator, confidence that the investigator knows what he or she is doing and can be trusted. Expressing trust in another means a freer expression of facts, opinions, and perhaps secrets.

DETECTING DECEPTION

One of the most difficult tasks that an investigator undertakes during an interview or interrogation is determining the truthfulness of the individual's statements. The easiest way to detect a person's deception is to compare what he or she has said against verified investigative findings. Contradictions help locate likely deceptions. Determining deception becomes much more difficult when the investigation is incomplete or there is no information against which to compare the individual's story. The investigator must now rely on the person's behavior to give an indication of truthfulness.

A number of factors influence whether a deception will be discovered. The first of these is the investigator him- or herself. Is the investigator a careful observer of human nature? Is he or she biased for or against the subject? Does the investigator have a clear behavioral norm for the subject?

Before any interview or interrogation, the investigator must establish a behavioral norm for the individual. Without a behavioral norm, the investigator may observe the normal verbal and physical behavior of the person but misinterpret it as deceptive because it appears unusual. The investigator's observations may also be tainted if he or she is biased for or against the person. This bias can lead to a self-fulfilling prophecy where the individual's behavior is used to confirm the investigator's beliefs.

Establishing a behavioral norm requires the investigator to observe the subject's verbal and physical responses to non-threatening questions. The investigator begins by asking questions that the person will likely tell the truth to, such as current address or date of birth. The investigator leads the individual through a series of seemingly innocent background questions, which require the person to use short- or long-term memories plus to create information. The person's responses to these questions provides the investigator with a snapshot of how the individual reacts when retrieving a memory or creating an answer. The investigator then compares these patterns to responses during the interview to assist in the evaluation of the reply.

To observe the individual's short-term memory, the interviewer asks questions that explores information that is used all the time. For example:

- What is your current address?
- What is your current position with the company?
- What is your date of birth?

Because these answers are used so often, they are kept in the short-term memory for repeated use. There is little delay in the response because the answer is on the tip of the tongue. What might a delay suggest to the investigator? It could be a new address, change of job, or perhaps a deception about the individual's age.

The next area to be explored is the individual's long-term memory. For example:

- What was your first real full-time job after graduating?
- What were your responsibilities in that first job?
- When did you first visit that location?
- When was the first time your supervisor accompanied you on a business trip?

Here the individual has to search his or her memory for the answer, so a delay in the response is appropriate. It may take a moment or two to estimate when that first visit or trip occurred. But if the person gives an answer immediately, the interviewer must ask why that information would be on the tip of the subject's tongue? Had the subject prepared the answer in anticipation of the question, or did the subject respond immediately to this question for some other reason? It may be that the person had recently been asked the question or anticipated it might be asked. People attempting deceptions often try to anticipate questions they may be asked and are prepared with answers.

The third area that needs to be considered is how the person looks and acts when creating an answer to a question that was not anticipated or experienced. For example:

- What is the one thing you would change about your job?
- If someone was going to take away part of your job responsibilities, what is the one area that you would not want to give up?
- How do you think a person would feel if they had done that?

Because the subject has not anticipated a question like this, likely he or she will require a delay while considering an answer. The investigator should carefully observe what the person does physically while constructing this answer. Remember, the answer may or may not be true, but it was newly created in response to a question. Not every created answer is an attempt at deception, but when there is a creative response to a question that should be coming from memory, perhaps the answer requires closer examination. It is also worth noting that once an answer has been created, it is relegated to long- and short-term memory, thus becoming less reliable as a clue, since now it just must be recalled accurately.

The investigator's careful observation of the subject's responses provides a pattern that can be used to evaluate questions where the subject may or may not be telling the truth. A change in the behavioral pattern after a question or a deviation in the timeliness of response may give the investigator an indication that the individual is attempting deception. If nothing else, the investigator should purse additional questions in this area to test the subject's consistency of answers and behavior.

Another factor affecting whether an individual's deception will be identified is the interviewer's personal bias. An investigator who trusts the subject is less likely to identify deceptive behavior because he or she is not suspicious of the individual's answers. Conversely, investigators who distrust the subject are likely to interpret even innocent behavior as deceptive because it confirms their predisposition of the individual's truthfulness.

The investigator's personal bias really addresses the question of whether it is easier to identify deception with someone who is well known to the investigator or someone who has just been met. While the investigator has a clear behavioral norm of someone who is well known, he or she may trust the individual, which will cause the investigator to overlook deceptive behavioral clues. In situations where the investigator has no previous relationship with the individual, there will be no bias for or against the person. The investigator should be able to evaluate the subject's behavior and facts as a neutral party. Most investigators can recall instances where the fact giver was baffled about the crime, but the investigator was able to easily identify the suspect because he or she was not biased toward the individual.

Another factor that may affect an investigator's ability to detect deception is when the subject has successfully lied to the investigator previously. A subject who has a fear of detection will likely alter behavior, either verbally or physically. The greater the individual's fear of detection, the greater the behavioral changes are likely to be. However, if the individual has successfully lied to the investigator previously, his or her fear of detection would diminish, resulting in less observable behavioral changes.

Emotion

The leakage of deceptive behavior may also result from the individual's emotional state. When subjects know or can anticipate that an interview or interrogation is going to occur, they may be able to suppress their emotions and control their behavioral responses. For example, when suspects are first contacted by an investigator regarding the incident, they literally explode internally, both physiologically and psychologically. Subjects will undergo physiological changes, such as increased heart rate, dilation of the pupils, and paling or flushing of the skin, that are readily observable. Psychologically suspects are panicked and momentarily confused as the fear of detection mounts. If interviewed immediately at that point, it is expected that subjects would find it more difficult to control their answers under this psychological and physiological. This would likely result in verbal and physical clues that the subjects are under extreme stress. For this reason, the investigator might consider not scheduling an appointment with a guilty party but rather just show up. If the subjects were alerted to come in later for an interview, they would be much more in control physically and psychologically. Obviously, just showing up for an interview without an appointment also presents some obvious problems for the investigator, so the benefits must be weighed against possible consequences.

The six basic emotions—fear, happiness, anger, sadness, surprise, and disgust—may be observed during the interview. Some emotions can be used to cover the real emotion. For example, a suspect may cover fear of detection by pretending to be angry or disgusted by the interviewer's questions. Careful observation of the individual may lead to the observation of what are called micro-expressions. These micro-expressions represent the six basic emotions shown for a fraction of the second before the individual can consciously suppress them. An observant investigator may see the momentary expression of fear before the individual covers it with a forced smile. These observations can assist the investigator in assessing an individual's truthfulness.

Subjects themselves can also present some difficulties to the investigator attempting to determine the truth. If subjects are inventive, smooth talkers, with a good memory, they will be less likely to trip over their own words. Plus, if subjects are skilled, practiced liars, they will have less fear of detection because they have successfully gotten away with their deceptions time and time again. In essence, the subjects are actors who are playing the role of a truthful individual with prepared lines and the mask of innocence.

Types of Lies

The way in which subjects choose to lie may also have some impact on the investigator's ability to detect the deception. When subjects can anticipate a need to lie, not only will their fear of detection diminish, but their ability to practice their deception will increase their confidence in carrying out their lies. The more people know about the investigation, the more likely they will be able to successfully defend their deceptions. This knowledge reduces their fear of detection and allows them to be much more rational responders capable of controlling their behavior.

The types of questions asked by the investigator will also determine what type of lie the subjects will use. There are five common types of lie:

1. Simple denial
2. Lie of omission

3. Fabrication
4. Minimization
5. Exaggeration

The first type of lie is a simple denial: "No, I didn't." In this type of why, subjects simply say no. On its surface this would seem to be the simplest lie to tell; however, it creates an internal conflict, or dissonance, that can make subjects uncomfortable. Think of this as a good versus evil struggle in a subject's mind. To avoid this discomfort, many people will go to great lengths simply not to say "No, I didn't do it."

The second type of lie is the most common, the lie of omission. The lie of omission relies on a simple recitation of the truth, omitting only those areas that do not benefit the individual. The bank teller acknowledges he came to work at 8 A.M., left for lunch at noon, then returned and stayed until the end of the business day. This is a true recounting of events; however, the teller omitted the fact that he stole $10,000 from his funds just before he left for lunch. To detect a lie of omission, the interviewer must carefully question and account for the individual's time in great detail. Hearing words such as "later on," "about," "probably," and "basically" often indicates there is additional information to be gleaned.

The third type of lie is fabrication. This is the most difficult type of lie to tell because it requires individuals to make up a story about what happened. Suspects are under increased stress, constantly having to be on the lookout for contradictions and inconsistencies in their stories. Through careful questioning, the interviewer will force deceptive individuals into fabrications that can be later disproved through investigation. For example, initially the suspect claimed she was at home using her cell phone at 8 A.M. on the day of the incident. However, later investigation of the suspect's phone records place that cell phone 50 miles away from her home. The suspect's own words will now come back to haunt her since where she claimed to be when making the call is impossible. When the investigation can disprove the subject's fabrication, it is almost as powerful as the subject's confession.

The fourth type of a lie is minimization. In a lie of minimization, the subject acknowledges a small portion of the incident but minimizes its seriousness. Statements such as "I might have just brushed against her" or "I was just borrowing it" are common examples. Each example acknowledges a portion of the action while minimizing the seriousness of what was done. Minimization also reduces the suspect's stress level since he or she is acknowledging a portion of the act while rationalizing its seriousness.

The fifth type of a lie an investigator may encounter is exaggeration. People may exaggerate their job history, salary, or even military heroics for a variety of reasons. In fraud investigations, it is not unusual to uncover exaggerated job histories or inflated stories of success while conducting background investigations on target individuals.

Detecting Deception

When the investigator assesses the subject's behavior, he or she does so by first comparing the individual against the population as a whole. Essentially, the investigator compares the subject against what most people would do under the given set of circumstances. For example, when the investigator introduced him- or herself to the subject for the first time and was met with insulting angry statements, the investigator must ask whether this is the typical way most people would react upon meeting someone for the first time. The subject's unusual response to the introduction certainly did not match how most people react to meeting someone new.

While this response is unusual, the investigator must also consider the context of the situation to determine if there is some other reason why the subject might act this way. It could be his fear of detection or real anger over embarrassing rumors that a subject attributed to the investigator.

The second step in evaluating the subject's behavior is for the inteviewer to compare the individual to the individual him- or herself. What is the person's normal behavior and speech pattern in his or her day-to-day world? Certainly the individual may be nervous about being interviewed, but this nervousness will normally diminish over time as the interview progressed. Behavior that is outside the subject's norm, either verbally or physically, may be an indication of an attempt at deception. The problem for the investigator attempting to identify deception is that there is no single behavior, either verbal or physical, that will always indicate that an individual is attempting to lie. Some people may not look at others because of an attempt at deception, or it could be caused by differing social status. Another problem for the investigator is a liar who may on one occasion fold her arms across her chest and at a later deception leave her arms unfolded and look away. Behavioral clues may change in even a single individual. It is not *the* behavioral clue but the consistent appearance of *a* clue that may alert the investigator to the deception.

Other factors will alter an interviewer's ability to detect deception. An individual's medical condition, drug or alcohol usage, or mental capacity could all alter his or her behavioral responses. These alterations are not necessarily the result of deception but could be artifacts of a physical condition. There may also be behavioral differences unrelated to deception because of cultural, racial, geographic, and economic differences between people. For instance, people will stand farther apart or even smile more often depending on their geographic location in the United States. These differences have nothing to do with deception but are simply behaviors related to location.

For a behavior to be relevant in detecting deception, the response must be both on time and consistent. An on-time behavior occurs at the conclusion of the investigator's question and may last throughout the subject's answer. For example, the investigator asks, "Do you know who falsified these documents?" and the subject immediately crosses his legs and looks away replying "No, I don't." The crossing of the legs and breaking of eye contact were on-time behaviors since they occurred immediately after the investigator's question while the individual was beginning the response. The subject who crosses his legs 10 seconds after he finished denying knowledge is not on time and thus the behavior is not likely related to the stress of the question. The second aspect making behavior relevant is consistency. This is not to say that every time suspects lie they will do exactly the same thing behaviorally, but rather that there is some type of behavior consistently occurring at each question. Hypothetically, a suspect might cross his legs while answering the first question, uncross them at the second question, and cross arms while responding to the third. To each question the subject responded with a different physical behavior, but they were all on-time and consistent.

CONDUCTING THE INTERVIEW

When deciding whether to conduct an interview during an audit or fraud investigation, the interviewer must consider the implications of each interview. Many investigations have been derailed because of interviewing decisions made early in the investigation. The interview subject, who may be the victim, witness, or suspect, will learn much about the investigation based on the questions asked by the interviewer. Especially in these early interviews when the full scope of the investigation is not yet apparent, the decision to interview should be carefully decided.

During routine audits, the interviewer should be aware of the behaviors of associates in the department being audited. It is not unusual for individuals involved in a fraud to give themselves away by changes in their behavior prior to the investigation targeting them. Currently, most frauds are not uncovered by audits, but by tips from former employees, current associates, or vendors. Once the tip has been received, the investigation can be much more focused and the likelihood of success increases dramatically. Experience has shown that typically only a portion of the fraud scheme will come to light through these tips. It is not unusual to have multiple parallel frauds in place as dishonest associates look to increase their flow of cash. The difficulty of identifying an unknown fraud scheme without knowing where to look is clearly a problem; however, people's behavior may be another tip-off.

As mentioned, many investigations have been seriously hampered as a result of suspects learning they are under investigation. This knowledge allows individuals to cover their tracks, alert co-conspirators, or destroy incriminating evidence before being questioned. If they become aware of the investigation, suspects may also become much more resistant to making admissions when it comes time to confront them with their scheme.

Establishing the Case Facts

The interviewer's first task upon becoming aware of a possible fraud is to establish the case facts and parameters. Often this begins by interviewing the tipster who is making the allegations of misconduct against the target. It is unusual for informants to possess clear direct evidence of wrongdoing against a suspect. More often the information will be circumstantial relating to business practices or rumors. The interviewer must determine what parts of the informant's story are fact, speculation, biased, or tainted by personal dislike or just plain inaccurate.

The interview with the informant is generally best accomplished off-site where privacy and secrecy can be maintained. Bringing the informant into the corporate office to meet for hours behind closed doors may start the rumor mill that will reach the suspect's ears only hours later. This opening interview is likely to be wide-ranging and provide information on the organization's business practices, vendors, lifestyle of the associate, and detailed examination of the allegations being brought. It may be necessary to arrange additional interviews with the informant to clarify and expand on information uncovered during the investigation. Keeping the informant's identity secret may also provide a continuing flow of information as the investigation progresses.

Following the initial interview with the informant, the interviewer must identify what laws or company policies may have been violated. This examination effectively identifies what must be proved and provides some direction for the forthcoming interviews. It is also useful to begin to create a list of possible individuals who may have information or may need to be interviewed as the investigation progresses. This list might also include former employees who have worked with the organization.

It is at this early stage that the interviewer begins to develop background information on the potential target that may be useful during later interviews or interrogations. It may be useful to add to the witness list people who may provide information relating to business practices or organization procedure that might clarify or corroborate information provided by the informant. These interviews may also contribute to the background and lifestyle information relating to the potential target of the investigation.

Once the decision has been made to begin interviews with former employees, vendors, and associates, there is a possibility that suspects may learn that an active investigation of them is beginning. If it is necessary to conduct interviews relating to business practices, these interviews should be broad-based to conceal the actual targets of the inquiry. If the interviewer needs to examine phone records, for example, a sufficient number should be requested to conceal those records he or she actually is interested in reviewing. Likewise, if the interview relates to some aspect of business practice, the investigator should also conceal the primary interest. The investigator should consider likely excuses the suspect could give for his or her actions and inquire about their plausibility while determining the organization's business practices. It is possible that there is a less sinister explanation than that the individuals are involved in fraud. Often the targets actions, when examined from a different perspective, are readily explainable as a standard business practice.

The interviewer should also conduct sufficient preliminary interviews to become familiar with the terminology used, ordinary operating procedures, and documents produced in the area where suspects are employed. It may be useful to select as a witness a person with this knowledge or at least have such a person available for consultation during the interview with suspects. Suspects who are expert in the workings of the department may be able to bluff the investigator based on knowledge of the area's inner workings.

Purpose of the Interview

The most difficult interview to conduct is one where there is no clearly defined outcome. Not knowing what is important leaves the interviewer with a broad range of questions that may or may not reveal the information that subjects possess. The obvious problem is that subjects may or may not be forthcoming during the interview. Some subjects will not intentionally lie, but neither will they offer information unless they are specifically asked. When an investigator can clearly define the information subjects have, it helps to formulate questions and test subjects' candidness.

The interviewer should recover any evidence that may be relevant to the investigation during the interview. It may be difficult or impossible at a later point to recover evidence relating to the fraud inquiry easily. As the investigation becomes public, evidence may be altered or destroyed if it was not secured by the interviewer when it was first identified. It is easier for an interviewer to recognize possible evidence when he or she has established a clear understanding of the possible elements of the crime, its scope, and the needs of the decision makers.

The interviewer should be prepared to persuade reluctant subjects to cooperate. Really, what benefit do subjects derive from cooperating? Some people will cooperate motivated only by the idea that it is a citizen's responsibility to solve crimes. However, many will find the interview an intrusion and even be concerned that cooperation may result in their being drawn into the case.

The interviewer should consider resistance to the interview and probable concerns when determining what method of persuasion might be most effective. Sometimes rapport and a please is all that is needed to achieve cooperation; other times a direct request from a supervisor may provide the information.

Types of Questions

Interviewers use a variety of questions to produce the information during interviews. The best interview is one where subjects do the majority of the talking while the interviewer simply listens. The interviewer's use of silence encourages subjects to continue talking and expand on the information already provided or point to additional areas of inquiry. It is not unusual for subjects to offer new information or infer its existence as they continue to talk. People are uncomfortable with silence, especially with a relative stranger, so they talk to fill awkward pauses.

Open-Ended Questions. The most useful of all interview questions is the open-ended question. By and large, these questions will provide the interviewer with the most facts and more behavioral observations than any other type. The interviewer uses open-ended questions to encourage a narrative response from subjects. These questions allow subjects to provide an untainted story, selecting or omitting what they believe is important to the response. An open-ended question, such as "Tell me what happened when Mark arrived at the warehouse?" provides subjects an opportunity to relate the story without contamination from the interviewer. Subjects tell their pure untainted version of the event, choosing their own words, selecting and omitting details based on what they believe is important.

The interviewer can now evaluate and expand subjects' untainted story using additional questions. The interviewer examines the story looking for changes in the level of detail, missing time or facts, analyzing subjects; word choice, and considering behavioral changes that occurred during this first telling. This is the pure version of the story, untainted by questions from the interviewer. Here subjects themselves have made the decision what to include and how to describe the event. The interviewer will undoubtedly ask additional questions to draw out the pertinent details; however, the questions should do so without contaminating the story.

Expansion Questions. After subjects have provided a framework for the event using their words in the untainted story, the interviewer now expands the story using subjects' own words in the expansion question. By using subjects' own words, the interviewer does not influence the story by either adding or directing the person's responses. For example, a subject may have said, "After he paid for dinner, he took us out to a club for drinks and then we headed to the game." An expansion question might be: "Now, you said, 'He took us out to a club for drinks.' What happened during that time?" The interviewer has correctly identified that there must be more details available about what happened in the club before heading to the game. Repeating the subjects' own words maintains the pure version of the story while allowing them to add details of what occurred. The interviewer also in no way misinterprets the subjects' words since the question mirrors their response.

Closed-Ended Questions. Closed-ended questions are best saved until the end of the interview since they interrupt the flow of the story that subjects are recalling. Once the interviewer has the basic story and then has expanded it using subjects' own words, there may be specific details to be determined. Closed-ended questions are used to obtain that very specific information. For example, the interviewer might ask the cost of the dinner: "How much was the dinner for all of you?" or "What was the name of the club you went to after dinner?"

A closed-ended question generally should not provide or assume information, but should target specific details of the incident. It is much better to ask "What was the name of the club?" than "Was the club you went to Winners?" By asking subjects to confirm the name of the club, the interviewer may have inadvertently tainted their recall or encouraged them to provide faulty information. In addition, including the name of the club in the question might give subjects information about the investigation's progress and scope.

Closed-ended questions can also test subjects' answers against information known from the investigation. If the individual claimed that the club was called Code Blue instead of Winners, the interviewer must now consider if other information might be faulty or wonder if the subject is attempting to deceive. Every question provides some information to the person who is being interviewed; if interviewers are not careful, subjects may learn as much from the questions as interviewers learn from the responses.

The interviewer may periodically summarize the story using the subjects' words and ask for confirmation that the information is correct. Once the entire story or sequence of events have been covered and confirmed, it is time to use closed-ended questions to make sure that the details are correct. Using closed-ended questions at the conclusion of the interview is less likely to contaminate subjects' stories because the majority of the information has already been retrieved.

The closed-ended question can also assist the interviewer in confirming the meaning of words or a phrase. Subjects may use a word or slang that needs clarification: "You said you felt 'blitzed.' What did you mean by that?" Witnesses define their actual level of intoxication after they left the club for the game.

Leading Questions. In most instances, interviewers should avoid using leading questions with victims or witnesses, since many people are extremely suggestible. This is especially true with young people and small children. Asking a question such as "Was the shirt blue?" may actually encourage individuals to confirm the information when in fact they really were unsure of its exact color. These types of questions have the capacity to contaminate individuals' responses by allowing them to agree with the faulty information provided by the interviewer.

As a general rule, an interviewer should avoid using leading questions; however, they do have some utility in certain situations. A leading question may be used when the investigator has a good understanding of the case and knows the correct answer. The interviewer in this case uses a leading question to encourage a truthful response from subjects. "So from there you went on to the restaurant, correct?" This question plants the seed that the investigator may actually know the correct answer to many of the questions being asked. This encourages individuals to be truthful since they do not know what the investigator has discovered in the investigation. Leading questions also allow the investigator to move subjects' recollection to another portion of the story while omitting details that may be irrelevant to the investigation.

Leading questions also may be used during reinterviews with victims or witnesses. These leading questions are phrased using the individual's exact wording to confirm information and move through the story, collecting additional details in relevant areas. Sometimes using leading questions to move into different areas of the story will encourage additional recollection details by the witness.

Compound Questions. Interviewers should avoid using compound questions unless they are absolutely sure that both parts of the question are correct. A compound question asserts two actions, both of which must be correct or faulty information will be obtained. For example, asking subjects "Did you run to the car and drop the bag?" requires that they both ran to the car and dropped the bag. If one part of the compound question contains faulty details, then witness agreement to it would have retrieved inaccurate information.

The interviewer should also ask questions that are appropriate to subjects' educational level. Using sophisticated language with an uneducated individual can only result in confusion and perhaps a loss of rapport. People will never be offended when questions are asked simply and clearly. In addition, the interviewer should avoid terms of art or slang that subjects may be unfamiliar with.

Final Question. The final question in an interview should ask subjects if there is anything else relevant to talk about. Some witnesses will not volunteer information, but only respond to questions that they are specifically asked. Specifically asking witnesses if there is anything else that should be discussed or was missed by the interviewer allows them to offer information or be put into the position of having to actively lie to the investigator. People can rationalize their failure to provide information because "I wasn't asked that," but it is much more difficult for them to actively withhold information they have been asked about.

The interviewer should consider subjects' behavioral responses during the interview to determine if they may be withholding additional information. Lingering at the conclusion of the interview may prompt subjects to provide additional information. If the interviewer believes there may be more information than was revealed, it may be useful to offer a rationalization to subjects. Saying something like "You know, sometimes people aren't sure whether they should or shouldn't say something. Sometimes it is because they are not sure if it is true and they do not want to offer incorrect information, but if it is just speculation, that is something that is obviously kept confidential. We then know it is just speculation and we view it only as something to be confirmed or disproved by the investigation." Rationalizations like this encourage people to cooperate and minimize the seriousness of withholding information. The rationalization is then followed by an assumptive question: "What else do we need to talk about?" This question assumes that there are additional areas that need to be discussed and encourages subjects to resume talking.

There also may be instances where subjects will need to be persuaded to cooperate with the interviewer. Many subjects think, "What's in it for me if I cooperate?" People do not generally want to become involved in situations not of their making, since it may require that they testify or perhaps have some liability as a result of cooperating. The interviewer uses rationalization and persuasion to encourage the reluctant witnesses' cooperation. After all, the interviewer is asking them to give up their time while getting nothing in return. Just as suspects have to overcome hurdles of resistance before confessing, witnesses are often concerned about losing time from work having to testify or even potential retaliation for their cooperation.

An interviewer who is able to establish rapport with subjects often finds that they will go to considerable lengths to help. Only rarely does an aggressive, harsh approach elicit complete cooperation.

Obtaining the Untainted Story

Subjects' first telling of story, alibi, or sequence of events contains a treasure trove of information. It contains clues to the story's truthfulness and offers tantalizing glimpses where additional concealed information may lie. As people recount their story over and over, they include more information from questions they were asked during its previous telling. However, the first telling of the story includes those points that subjects considered to be important. As questions are asked and details provided, subjects include them in each retelling of the story until it becomes a compilation of information both subjects and questioner felt was important.

Every account of events deletes some information that tellers considered irrelevant or felt was in some way threatening. For example, "I had breakfast with my wife and later went to work." In this statement the husband acknowledges being with his wife for breakfast and later going to work, but omits all the details between these two events. This could be done for two reasons: The events between breakfast and the husband's leaving are irrelevant, adding nothing to the listener's understanding of the story, or the husband is intentionally concealing information he finds threatening and does not want the listener to know. As discussed previously, the lie of omission is the easiest one to tell. Subjects tell the truth, leaving out only those details that may be incriminating. In this case the truthful statement would have been "I had breakfast with my wife, shredded all of the Peterson contracts, and went to work."

After asking subjects to recount the untainted story, the interviewer should just listen and avoid interrupting the flow of details. This allows the subjects to tell the story from their perspective without interruption. Listening to the subjects' stories, the interviewer may identify gaps in time, qualifying statements, the inclusion of extraneous information, or unusual sentence structure. Gaps of time may be indicated by phrases such as "later on," "shortly after," or something similar. Qualifiers are words that indicate estimates or uncertainty, such as "about," "maybe," and "basically that's all." Such words need to be explored more fully with additional questions. Changes in descriptions of individuals may also indicate a change in relationships. There is a significant difference in the relationship indicated when a father says "my daughter" versus "that girl." There is also a difference between someone's relationship to an action when he says "I went to the store" versus "Then went to the store." In the second sentence, "Then went to the store," the subject has omitted the pronoun "I." This is often an indication that the individual does not want to be associated with the action.

These types of assessments of the untainted story may lead the interviewer to more effective questioning of individuals. As mentioned, the interviewer will enlarge a subject's story using questions that contain the subject's own words, expanding it without contaminating it.

The interviewer also examines the untainted story for changes in the amount of detail contained within it. Individuals attempting to withhold information often become vague and less definitive in portions of the story they are reluctant to talk about. The interviewer should also examine the untainted story for the inclusion of irrelevant information. Why would subjects include this seemingly irrelevant information that has no real linkage to the story? It may be that the irrelevant information was included to provide a reason for doing something later or being present at a particular location. "I like pink lemonade, and the only place I know I can get it is the gas station at Grant and Beverly Roads." By mentioning pink lemonade, the subject has now given a reason to be near the gas station at Grant and Beverly. The interviewer should ask him- or herself is there something special about that location that would require a subject to explain his presence there. The untainted story may provide additional investigative leads or direct the interviewer's questioning to valuable sources of information.

Some interviewers actually have subjects write out the untainted story and then conduct an extensive evaluation of their word choice, level of details, and structure of the story. This more systematic evaluation may provide additional areas of inquiry that would have been missed if the interviewer had just listened to an oral presentation.

Types of Interviews

A variety of different interviews may be used when developing information during an investigation. The purpose of the interview may differ from collecting and confirming facts, to encouraging recollection or to identification of deception, depending on the situation.

Each interview has a clearly defined purpose that corresponds to the overall investigative strategy. In almost every interview, the investigator will establish rapport and provide persuasive support for individuals to cooperate in the inquiry.

Fact-Gathering Interview. Probably the most common of all interviews is the fact-gathering interview. In the fact-gathering interview, the investigator attempts to confirm specific information regarding a particular component of the investigation. This interview answers the questions who, what, where, when, how, and why. In some cases the fact-gathering interview is extremely focused, while on other occasions it may be much more wide-ranging. For example, the fraud investigator may be required to establish exactly how a particular document is prepared and under what circumstances. In this case the inquiry is narrowly targeted on a particular piece of information, the preparation of a single document. However, a fact-gathering interview's scope could be much broader, perhaps to understand the flow of business in a particular department.

The fact-gathering interview is also used to establish an alibi or the sequence of events, or to confirm a witness recollection. When dealing with suspects, the fact-gathering interview is designed to lock individuals into their stories, establishing as many relevant details as possible. These details are then subject to verification during the inquiry. Disproving a suspect's story by investigation can become powerful evidence of the individual's guilt. In essence, the investigator can question the individual's truthfulness using the suspect's own words. A disproved story can be as powerful as a suspect's confession. If the suspect elects to testify at some point, his or her credibility can be easily challenged using his or her own words and the contradictory facts.

The fact-gathering interview can also be used to challenge the truthfulness of multiple suspects. Often individuals will attempt to support one another's story by providing an alibi. Suspects often construct alibis in a fragmentary fashion: "All right, if anybody asks we'll tell them we went to the movie and then over to Bobby's house." Unfortunately for the suspects, this fragmentary construction of an alibi provides interviewers everything they need to break the story. Detailed questioning of each suspect will provide numerous inconsistencies in the alibi. For example:

- What movie did you go to?
- What time did the movie start?
- Where was the movie playing?
- Where did you sit in the theater?
- Who sat next to you on your right?
- How did you get to the theater?

The suspects neglected to prepare their alibi in enough detail to stand up to the investigator's detailed questioning. Even if they did attempt to construct their alibi in detail, they will have a difficult time remembering what was agreed on. Normally during the preparation of an alibi, one would expect the suspects to discuss a number of possible options before coming to an agreement. The problem for the suspects is remembering which of the details were agreed to by the group.

During the development of a suspect's story, the investigator should look for details that may be confirmed or repudiated by investigation. A simple statement, such as "As we were buying tickets for the movie I called my brother" may prove a clue. Through phone records the investigator may be able to confirm that the call was not made or was made from a different location, or confirm a fact supporting the subject's alibi. The phone records would reveal the cell tower, number called, and time of the phone call, but not necessarily who made the call.

The fact-gathering interview may also be used to follow-up details or inconsistencies in previous interviews. It is generally preferable to conduct a single thorough interview than have to repeatedly return to requestion subjects. However, there may be a need to contact witnesses again for clarifications or with additional questions as the investigation develops. It is useful to ask at the close of the interview if subjects would mind being contacted again if it became necessary as part of the investigation. When individuals have agreed to be reinterviewed, they are much more likely to cooperate later if the investigator must return.

Lifestyle Interviews. In cases where extensive fraud is uncovered, a lifestyle interview may be useful. Since most cases involving extensive fraud or kickbacks involve the significant transfer of money, there may be lifestyle indicators of this excessive cash. In many ways, a fraud investigation is like a drug inquiry where large amounts of cash are either being concealed or spent. The lifestyle interview focuses on how targets spend their money, their likes and dislikes, their personality and overall general demeanor. People fall into patterns of behavior, which, when understood, may assist the investigator in two ways.

1. The investigator may identify additional investigative leads because of the lifestyle investigation. For example, a wine connoisseur who purchases expensive wines with meals may also be spending significant amounts of cash purchasing wine for a home cellar.
2. The lifestyle interview may assist the investigator in understanding how subjects are likely to respond when interviewed or interrogated. Subjects' interaction with people will help determine the investigator's approach when interviewing or interrogating them. Subjects prone to arrogance and dominance need to be approached in a different fashion from much more compliant individuals.

The lifestyle interview's scope of inquiry is much broader than the very targeted fact-gathering interview. The investigator asks questions that will reveal how individuals live their lives, their interests, how they spend their money, and how they deal with people. This interview may prove to be an integral part of a fraud case that follows the money. For example, a suspect has a salary of $60,000 per year, yet she is spending over $100,000 per year. Where does this extra money come from? The fact that witnesses continually report that the suspect has large amounts of cash in her purse may provide a significant clue. One can imagine the suspect's difficulty in attempting to explain how she came to have this extra money that far exceeds her salary. What are her options? Say nothing or construct some explanation for the cash. Many times subjects attempt to lie their way out of the situation by claiming a source for the cash. She might claim the money came from an inheritance, gambling winnings, or some type of legal settlement. The suspect's problem is that her explanation must stand up to the scrutiny of the investigation.

Interviewers make a number of common errors. Probably the most common error is interrupting subjects while they are talking. This interruption breaks people's train of thought and may result in details being omitted. The interviewer should allow subjects to finish talking before asking the next question.

Another error is having a preconceived notion of what an individual knows. Many interviewers who mistakenly believe that they know exactly what subjects are going to say move to using closed-end questions too early in the interview. Using closed-ended questions early in the interview may limit the information ultimately obtained from individuals. It is much better to have people independently confirm information already revealed in the investigation; this helps establish the information's credibility while concealing the investigation's scope and progress. Sometimes witnesses may contradict previous information, necessitating additional interviewing or reinvestigation to confirm who is telling the truth.

Asking rapid-fire questions is another common problem. Interviewers who attempt to use the rapid-fire questioning approach may actually confuse subjects or miss potential information. Silence is a much more effective means of gaining information since it allows subjects time to talk and the interviewer time to consider what was said.

A final problem is the interviewer's failure to summarize the subjects' statements and obtain a confirmation of their accuracy. Using the summarization technique allows subjects to correct any misconceptions and confirm the accuracy of the information. This technique usually results in additional details being obtained from subjects.

Remember, the questions asked may reveal what the investigator knows or suspects. The interviewer's body language and focus of the questions can reveal much to the subject. Investigators should carefully consider the way they ask questions as well as their timing so as not to reveal investigative findings.

Diagrams

It can be useful for the investigator to use diagrams to understand subjects' stories. Having subjects draw a diagram to assist in the explanation of their story can add clarity to complicated explanations. This diagram becomes an integral piece of evidence to support the information in the interview. The drawing may reveal details that contradict or confirm the individuals' stories. For example, a subject claims he walked a particular path through the warehouse and arrived at the loading dock in less than a minute. However, the only way he could have arrived within his time frame is to have sprinted the entire distance. The diagram can also reveal subjects' lines of sight and generally provide a visual context for the interviewer.

Subjects should sign and date the diagram, indicating when it was prepared. The diagram should be maintained as evidence and referenced in the investigator's report. Since the diagram could be important evidence, it should be protected. The original document should be maintained in a secure location with a copy kept in the case file for reference.

Depending on the complexity of the investigation, it can be useful to maintain a witness list of people who need to be interviewed. As each witness or lead is identified, the person can be assigned to a lead sheet for follow-up. Organizing the investigation in this fashion allows the investigator to know at a glance who has been interviewed and what tasks are yet to be completed. The lead sheets control the interviews and leads, ensuring that the assigned investigator completes each step.

INTERROGATION

Once the investigation has been completed, with all interviews and evidence documented, it is time to confront suspects. In most investigations, the encounter with subjects can be planned and conducted at a time and location of the investigator's choosing. However, there may be instances where suspects are confronted due to circumstances beyond the investigator's control. This could occur when the investigation becomes public knowledge or suspects decide to leave the organization's employ.

An early case closure presents some obvious difficulties for the interrogator since not all details have been confirmed or evidence obtained. Even in cases where the investigation has been completed, successful closure may require a subject's confession. This is especially true in cases where the evidence of guilt is circumstantial. An interrogator may choose to confront guilty suspects in a number of different ways. The investigator chooses the actual method based on the type of case, personality of the individual, and the evidence available.

Because many cases will hinge on whether suspects confess, the most experienced and effective interrogator should be chosen to conduct the conversation. Unlike an interview, an interrogation has an entirely different set of dynamics. Bringing an interrogation to successful closure requires experience and skill.

Preparation to Interrogate

The first step is to select the interrogator, which may or may not be the primary investigator. The interrogator's style and personality should complement the suspect's demeanor. Just because an investigator led the investigation does not necessarily mean that he or she is the correct person to close the case.

The second step is to clearly identify the evidentiary thresholds that will allow certain actions to take place. For example, if the suspect says this, the organization will then be able to do one of these steps: transfer, terminate, file a civil suit, or criminally prosecute the suspect. Each course of action will be dependent on the suspect's statement and the elements necessary to prove the crime or policy violation. Clearly identifying what must be proved will assist the interrogator in developing the suspect's statements and confession.

Some cases will result in the development of a confession that will be sufficient to terminate the individual's employment, but not to file either civil or criminal charges. The interrogator must clearly understand the violation and the elements necessary to prove that the violation took place. To prove a case of theft, for example, the interrogator must obtain a statement from suspects that they took something of value from the organization without permission and intended to permanently deprive it of the asset. If suspects' statements contain each of these elements, the confession will support a criminal charge of theft; however, if the statement lacks these elements, the subjects' behavior may constitute a policy violation.

The interrogator should also consider the location and timing for the interrogation. The interrogator must insure there is sufficient time to talk with suspects without interruption. Considerations relating to the location of the interview, such as privacy, sufficient space, and investigative resources, may dictate the best location to select for the interrogation.

In addition, the interrogator should consider possible difficulties that may arise as a result of the conversation. Preparing contingencies in anticipation of difficulties arising allows for a seamless response to the problem. For example, what is the interrogator's response going to be if a suspect attempts to leave or becomes angry? Having a plan in place allows the interrogator to make the correct decision, rather than having to improvise in the heat of the moment.

The interrogator should also have access to management to assist in the decision-making. Depending on the case, it may be useful to have access to legal, human resources, or senior management in the event a specific decision needs to be authorized. Some situations may require supplemental manpower to conduct follow-up investigations, searches, or additional interviews as the interrogation progresses. Without a plan in place to handle the contingencies, an appropriate response might be impossible.

A final point worth noting is that each company likely has policies and procedures regarding the conduct of an employee interview. The interviewer may be required to make specific notifications before conducting a dishonest employee interview. Communicating with the management ensures the interrogator is conforming to policy while determining the decision makers' criteria for terminating an individual.

Decision to Confess

The interrogator must also consider the suspect's decision to confess. Typically people who make a confession do so for one of three reasons.

1. They believe that their guilt is known.
2. They want to make some form of explanation or offer an excuse that minimizes the seriousness of their actions.
3. Some confess to relieve their sense of guilt over having participated in dishonest activity.

Clearly guilt alone or the desire to offer an explanation will not cause individuals to confess unless it is combined with the belief that they have been caught. The investigator's action, as he investigates and begins the interrogation, conveys information to suspects. An improper approach can convey that individuals are suspected but their guilt is uncertain. This will result in an increase in resistance and a more difficult interrogation.

Once the interrogation of suspects begins, the interrogator, through body language and words, must communicate to the individuals that their guilt is known. This is critical in establishing suspects' belief that they have been caught. In general, this alone is not sufficient to obtain a confession. The interrogator must also overcome suspects' fears or hurdles before they will ever confess. Most suspects are afraid of one or more of these hurdles:

- Loss of employment
- Embarrassment
- Arrest, prosecution, or civil lawsuit
- Restitution
- Retaliation

For most employees, the first and foremost fear is loss of employment, closely followed by embarrassment. Many times being arrested is not even a consideration.

People are more likely to confess, which greatly overcomes many of the hurdles associated with the investigation, when they believe their guilt is certain. The interrogator supports suspects' self-image by offering explanations that mitigate the situation. These rationalizations minimize the seriousness of what suspects have done and preserve their self-image. Interrogators who do not allow suspects to rationalize are asking them to confess both to the crime and to being a bad person.

Rationalization

An emotional interrogation is driven by the interrogator's use of rationalization. The interrogator uses rationalization to minimize the seriousness of suspects' actions without removing the elements of the crime or the policy violation. People, and especially criminals, use rationalization to justify their actions. The rationalization may be as simple as justifying going a few miles an hour over the speed limit or as sinister as justifying the theft of millions of dollars. Regardless, the use of rationalization is the same: to allow individuals to live with their actions and avoid guilt.

Embezzlers may justify their theft because they are not being paid enough, they deserve fine things, or perhaps they are just working too hard. While these rationalizations may or may not be true, they allow individuals to preserve their self-image and relieve guilt while satisfying their need for money.

The interrogator uses this same process of rationalization to focus individuals' attention on the resolution of the problem and away from the consequences of their actions. Rationalization provides two important psychological benefits: It minimizes the seriousness of what the individual has done, and it continues the process of rapport begun at the onset of the encounter. The interrogator, using rationalization, shifts the blame for the criminal events to life circumstances, financial problems, peer pressure, or some other justification that makes the individual's actions more understandable. In essence, the interrogator uses the same process of rationalization as the suspect to justify the person's actions. However, the interrogator's rationalizations may or may not be the real reason the subject became involved; they simply make it easier for an individual to confess by providing an understandable context for his or her actions.

Method of Interrogation

The most effective means of interrogating a suspect is an emotional appeal combined with an accusation that does not allow any room for the suspect to deny involvement in the incident. An interrogator can confront suspects in a number of ways when attempting to obtain an admission. The selection of the confrontation method is dependent on the circumstances of the case, the personality of the suspect, and the ultimate objective of the interrogation. In certain cases the interrogator may be required to obtain an admission to a specific issue before he or she can open the interrogation to areas where the individual's guilt is less certain. Regardless of which accusation is chosen, the interrogator should work from a plan that encourages truthfulness while reducing the suspect's level of resistance.

In situations where there are multiple suspects, it is often useful to confront them simultaneously. This requires planning to arrange for sufficient manpower and space for the task. The plan must consider how the suspects will arrive, where they will go after the interrogation, and perhaps even how they will be fed.

Confronting the members of the group simultaneously allows the interrogators to compare stories, effectively providing themselves a means to detect lies and confirm truthful information. The interrogators know that until all the suspects, who have separately confessed, are telling the same story and confirmed the evidence, they have not told the whole truth. Confronting the suspects with information obtained during other interrogations can be a useful wedge to encourage truthful responses and to expand the scope of the group's admissions.

Factual Method. In cases where extensive evidence exists indicating an individual's guilt, the factual approach may be used. This approach is best used when there is direct evidence linking the suspect to the crime. However, in most cases this extensive evidence will be circumstantial in nature rather than direct proof of an individual's guilt. When interrogators simply present evidence to a suspect, they must remember that they are asking the suspect to confess not only to the incident(s) but also to confess that he or she has been a "bad person." With the factual approach, interrogators do not include the rationalizations that support the individual's self-image, so even in the face of strong evidence, the suspect may deny involvement.

Prior to presenting any evidence, the interrogator should lock suspects into their story or the sequence of events. If this is not done, suspects may be able to offer excuses or plausible reasons for the evidence at hand. However, when suspects have committed to their stories before they know what evidence is available to investigators, their own words contradict them and the evidence appears even more formidable.

One final problem with using a factual attack is the amount of information it provides to suspects. Once aware of the evidence against them, suspects can deduce the scope of the investigation, identify informants and investigative methods, and know with some certainty whether they need to divulge any other schemes that might be in place. In addition, suspects may conclude that the evidence presented to them is not sufficient to prove their guilt. Once suspects doubt the thoroughness of the investigation, they are likely to deny their guilt and stand their ground.

Presenting evidence alone, without a structured approach or rationalization, will cause some suspects to confess. However, by using this approach, an interrogator often makes the job more difficult for both him- or herself and the suspect. On a final note, interrogators who rely on a wealth of evidence alone to close cases will find that their ability to obtain admissions in less successful investigations is diminished.

Wicklander-Zulawski Non-confrontational Method. The Wicklander-Zulawski (WZ) Non-confrontational Method uses a structured emotional approach that avoids forcing suspects into a position where they have to deny their guilt. When suspects have not directly denied their guilt, they are less likely to protect their position and are more open to persuasion. While a structured approach, the method allows sufficient flexibility to deal with a variety of different suspects and cases.

For fraud cases, the WZ non-confrontational interview and interrogation structure obtains timely admissions from suspects, while avoiding the necessity of revealing evidence. A more detailed discussion of the method can be found in the book by Zulawski and Wicklander.[2]

STRUCTURED APPROACH TO THE INTERVIEW AND INTERROGATION OF A SUSPECT IN A FRAUD INVESTIGATION

Establish Rapport

In the opening part of the interview or interrogation, the investigator establishes the individual's behavioral norm by asking a series of biographical questions. The investigator notes the person's verbal and physical behavioral responses to these non-threatening questions. This allows the investigator to establish a baseline of truthful behavior for the individual that can be contrasted to the person's behavior when questioned about the incident.

Following the biographical questions, the investigator begins to establish rapport with the person by asking open-ended questions. Rapport is often accomplished by showing interest in the individual or finding common interests. One simple way to begin this task is by asking about the person's job and responsibilities. Discussing the individual's job plays two important roles in the process.

1. It establishes rapport since the interviewer is asking about an important part of the person's life, his or her work.
2. It allows the investigator to confirm how the person fits within the organization and the scope of his or her responsibilities.

The investigator is now free to discuss reporting relationships and flow of work and documents. The understanding of the organization's operation will lead logically to the participatory portion of the approach, and will help the investigator develop likely subject excuses for the events suggested by the evidence discovered.

Participatory Approach

The participatory approach is a natural extension of the rapport-building inquiries and is designed to conceal investigative evidence while locking individuals into their stories. The interrogator has already evaluated the existing evidence and anticipated suspects' possible explanations for any incriminating evidence before beginning this portion of the conversation. For example, having subjects detail their understanding and compliance with a particular policy precludes them from later saying they did not know or understand the policy. Suspect are prevented from claiming the incident was a misunderstanding or a training issue and are left with only the single option that the action was done intentionally. The existing evidence is more powerful now since any other explanation besides dishonesty has been removed.

Selective Interview

The selective interview is an optional component that can be used when the interviewer is uncertain whether a person is involved in dishonest activity. This interview can also be used to identify suspect excuses and measure resistance when there is evidence of the person's involvement in dishonesty.

The selective interview can take place before or after the participatory piece of the interrogation, or it may be used as a means of backing out when no confession has been obtained. The selective interview is a non-accusatory behavior-provoking series of questions that elicit responses from subjects that help eliminate or focus the investigation on them. Each of the questions used in the selective interview is governed by a general principle that allows it to be scored. For example, "What should happen to a person who is stealing money from the company?" is one question from the interview. The general principle governing this question is that truthful people tend to suggest harsher punishment, while the guilty are more lenient. By evaluating the questions using the principle and suspects' behavior, the investigator can eliminate the innocent and focus on the guilty.

The selective interview can also be used during a fact-gathering interview to evaluate subjects' truthfulness. It can take place immediately after subjects provide their untainted story as a spacer before the interviewer asks them to recount the story again. This allows some time to pass before recounting the story again, making a fabricated story more difficult to tell.

Introductory Statement

The interrogator now uses the non-confrontational introductory statement to indirectly accuse suspects. The introductory statement is the interrogator's monologue that introduces the idea of internal theft into the conversation. The introductory statement consists of three parts:

1. *Who we are/What we do.* Since the interrogator has allowed suspects to talk about their jobs, it is only natural that the interrogator now have an opportunity to talk about him- or herself. This allows the interrogator to take control and direct the conversation in a very structured fashion, introducing the idea of internal theft and beginning the process of rationalization.
2. *How losses occur.* The interrogator next discusses methods that are used by employees to steal from companies. The theft methods are presented, grouping cash and merchandise losses separately, with a slight verbal emphasis on the one suspects are using to steal. While listing the theft methods, the interrogator is also watching for behavioral indications from suspects that may indicate other methods that are being used to steal, but were not revealed by the investigation.
3. *How we investigate.* The final part of the introductory statement discusses ways in which investigations are conducted. The interrogator discusses a variety of investigative and evidence techniques that, if used, would have resulted in the suspects' theft activity being discovered. When these three parts are combined properly, they indirectly convey to suspects that their guilt is known.

Rationalization

The interrogator now shifts to rationalization to minimize the seriousness of the crime and focus suspects' attention away from the consequences of their actions. Through the use of stories and anecdotes, the interrogator shows how good people make poor judgments and do things that are wrong.

Rationalization continues the rapport between interrogator and suspect, building a bond of understanding. The interrogator may blame pressure from financial problems or friends for causing suspects to become involved in the fraud. However, the rationalization does not absolve suspects of the crime; it simply reframes their actions. It really makes no difference to the case if suspects used the money to pay bills or bought drugs, but it does make a difference to their self-image. They are good people who were put into a difficult situation to which they reacted improperly, but now they are doing the right thing. Suspects' behavior will tell the interrogator whether the rationalizations are effective and help determine when the assumptive question should be used.

Assumptive Questions

The interrogator now uses an assumptive question directly related to what is known from the investigation. For example, if the investigation had revealed a subject was stealing money, the question would be: "Let me ask you, what would you say would be the most amount of money you took in any single week?" If the investigation had revealed gifts from vendors, the interviewer might ask, "What would you say is the most expensive gift you've received from a vendor in the last 12 months?"

Each of these assumptive questions directly focuses on what is known from the investigation. While the interviewer might know that associates received gifts in excess of the policy, he or she might not know of all the gifts received by them. The assumptive question allows associates to make an admission to either what is known or what they believe is known by the interviewer.

The assumptive question could also be formulated as a choice question related to the last rationalization used. If the rationalization revolved around peer pressure, a choice question might be "Was it your idea to do this or was it theirs?" Suspects' selection of either choice is their first admission to the incident that logically progresses to developing the admission.

Development of the Admission

The interrogator develops suspects' admission and substantiates the details of the confession. Returning to the basic investigative questions who, what, where, when, how, and why, the interrogator obtains the details of the wrongdoing and identifies evidence that corroborates it.

The development may also discover new leads that need follow-up or areas of dishonesty not revealed by the investigation thus far. Depending on the case, suspects may identify evidence or other people involved in the scheme. The interrogator may have suspects draw sketches to clarify points or obtain the whereabouts of stolen property.

Summary Statement

The final component of the interrogation should be a detailed summary statement in which associates clearly summarize their admission. This summary should substantiate in as much detail as possible each of the admissions made by the individuals. If evidence was discussed, it should be dated, initialed, and discussed during the statement. The statement should be witnessed, then dated and signed by suspect, interrogator, and witness.

The statement is a critical document that summarizes a suspect's admissions. It may take several forms, from handwritten, to typed, to audiovisual recording. Regardless of its form, the statement must contain the elements of the crime committed by the suspect and the details of admission that conform to the confession.

CONCLUSION

The process of interview and interrogation is critical to the success of the investigation. To be successful, there must be a plan reflective of the needs of the organization, investigation, and suspect. The investigator who masters the structured yet flexible approach to the process will be a valuable asset to any investigation.

PART II: FORENSIC DOCUMENT AND HANDWRITING EXAMINATION

WHAT IS A "DOCUMENT"?

A document is any material that carries a communication, explicit or implied.[3] It may be a written message (handwritten, hand-printed, typewritten, painted, carved, etc.) on paper (ruled, unruled, tissue, parchment, check stock, laser, bond, etc.), canvas, cardboard, a wall, box, truck, or even a cucumber. Anything. Attention becomes focused on document authenticity when something is noticed to have been:

- Added
- Omitted
- Substituted
- Eradicated

Critical examination is conducted to determine whether a questioned document is or is not:

- An original
- A computer-generated printout
- A copy machine printout
- A fax transmission printout
- Comprised of out-of-sequence entries and/or assembly of multiple pages

When a document is in dispute and it has been determined that examination by a forensic document examiner is needed, a number of examination protocols may be required. However, a full range of available testing procedures may not be needed. For example, determination of sequence, writer identification or writing instrument continuity, ink analysis or indentation development may or may not be required.

Preliminary examination is usually conducted with the handheld magnifier and the stereomicroscope. Ultraviolet lighting may be helpful to determine difference in paper stock, and inconsistencies within a multiple-page document and infrared examination may disclose evidence that different inks have been used. Whenever the original questioned document is available, indentations of miscellaneous writings or markings of other documents that were written when placed on top of the one in question can often be revealed. Laboratory equipment for this testing is usually the ESDA (Electrostatic Detection Apparatus) or an IMED (Indentation Materializer Electrostatic Device). However, examination with a stereomicroscope, or even a hand-held magnifier, and oblique lighting can frequently reveal indentations. These testing procedures are all non-destructive. The document is not altered in any way.

There are occasions when more extensive testing is required; such as ink dating and removal of upper layer of writing or miscellaneous obliterations. Ink dating involves extraction of small plugs from the writing, which are then inserted into a chemical solution and applied to a test plate. While the punctures are minute and easily overlooked, the procedure is classified as "destructive" because the document has been altered. It is no longer in its original form.

A new and highly efficient atomic oxygen testing procedure has been developed at the NASA Glenn Research Center, Electro-Physics Branch, in Cleveland, Ohio. Miscellaneous writings on a variety of paper stocks and concealed by overwriting and miscellaneous obliterations were revealed by an atomic oxygen beam directed toward specified areas. Substances that covered lower layers of previous writings were quickly and effectively removed. The research is continuing and being expanded as budget conditions allow.[4] This testing can be scheduled for forensic document examiners, if needed.

Note: Client permission must be obtained before any destructive testing procedures are to be conducted.

FORGERY

Just writing someone else's name, *with no attempt to simulate or imitate the valid signature writing of that person* in a notebook or on a chalkboard, for example, is not forgery. However, if that name is written as a check endorsement, signed on a quit claim deed, or a recommendation for promotion, for example, and monetary or other benefit is expected to be gained, that signature is then classified as "spurious" and charges of fraud can be expected.

> A person is guilty of forgery if, with purpose to defraud or injure anyone, or with knowledge that he is facilitating a fraud or injury to be perpetrated by anyone, the actor: (a) alters any writing of another without his authority; or (b) makes, completes, executes, authenticates, issues or transfers any writing so that it purports to be the act of another who did not authorize that act, or to have been executed at a time or place or in a numbered sequence other than was in fact the case, or to be a copy of an original when no such original existed; or (c) utters by writing which he knows to be forged in a manner specified in paragraph (a) or (b) Model Penal Code 224.1.[5]

Further examination of questioned documents is conducted to determine whether evidence of any of these activities is present:

- Alteration or modification
- Simulation or imitation
- Copying, duplicating or reproducing
- Counterfeiting
- Plagiarizing

Manipulation of documents and their content has been an enterprising activity or "business" since the beginning of human interchange and trade. Procedures that produce the desired results, and the instruments employed, continue to become more and more sophisticated, and it is highly unlikely the list will stop expanding.

The most simple and basic "tools" used for document manipulation remain viable. Those commonly used are:

- Pen
- Pencil
- Toothpick
- White-Out (correction fluid)
- Transparent tape
- Window, or other source of backlight
- Carbon paper

- Tracing paper
- Scissors
- Signature stamp
- Correctable typewriter ribbon
- Typewriting correction tape
- Paste or Post-it glue
- Photocopy machine
- Color copy machine
- Digital camera
- Scanner
- Computer
- Printer
- Disappearing ink
- Erasable ink
- Ego

Note: A document, or any portion of it, such as a signature, can be scanned into a computer, repositioned or added to any kind of document, downloaded, and printed out. It can be printed 1, 10, 100, 1000 (or more) times, and all printouts will be considered "original." Confirmation as to whether the print and miscellaneous writings are original ink or the product of a printing system is highly recommended. This can usually be determined with stereomicroscopic examination.

RED FLAGS OF DOCUMENT EXAMINATION

- The document origin is suspicious.
  - Where was it "found"?
- Chronological dates are out of sequence.
- There are repeated errors and corrections in date entries.
- There are different folds of a page or pages within a multiple-page document.
- A different font is used within miscellaneous typed or printed entries or narrative text.
- There is evidence of different stapling within a multiple-page document.
- There is evidence of erasure(s), obliterations, or correction fluid use.
- Writing is done with a soft-tip pen.
  - Extra caution: Use of a soft-tip pen with purple ink. (Such an ink formula may be one that disappears in two to three days.)
- Different ink colors are used within same entry.
- Handwriting characteristics change within individual entries.
- Smaller writing is crowded into existing entries.
- Entries allegedly done on different dates are precisely aligned.

- Entries allegedly done at one sitting are misaligned.
- Check documents have no perforated edges.
- Check paper has rough, dull surface, limp consistency, and ink "bleeds" into the fibers.
- There are horizontal and/or vertical lines in the signature area of a machine-copy document.
- Anonymous notes:
    - How was it "delivered"? Save the envelope if available.

CAUTION

- Promptly place the *original* document(s) in a protective sleeve (plastic).
- *Do not* fold, staple, paper clip, puncture, cut, or tear the document(s).
- *Do not remove* staples from any documents in question without permission.
- *Do not* write anything on the document in question: no initials, arrows, underlining, circles, exclamation marks, numerals. *Nothing.*
- *Do not* write or mark anything on another document page that has been placed on top of the document in question.
- Keep all beverages away from the vicinity of the document in question.

The most prevalent feature of documents that become an issue, in both civil and criminal matters, is the handwriting, and it has many forms. Some of them are:

- Signatures
- Narrative text
- Numerals
- Symbols (#, %, &, $, etc.)
- Cursive
- Manuscript (hand-printing/lettering)
- Shorthand
- Punctuation
- Printscript
    - Cursive/print combinations
- Ideographs
    - Chinese, Hebrew, Arabic, Greek, and so on

All writings, sketches, drawings, and the like are comprised of four elements: dot, straight line, curve, and hook. Yet no two persons write exactly the same and no one writes exactly the same twice.[6]

Most forgeries are poorly executed. The imitator must be acutely knowledgeable of how the target writer incorporates a very wide range of components into the final writing specimen.

> . . . each person's writing, like each person's fingerprints, contains certain individual characteristics. This is the fundamental principle on which handwriting comparisons are based and on which testimony is given in and accepted by courts of law.[7]

Some of the writer's habits and handwriting characteristics that must be accurately, and without hesitation, incorporated into the attempted simulation are: slant, size, spacing, height ratios, proportion, line intersections, t-crossing length/direction/placement, i-dots and j-dots formation/placement/direction, penmanship, skill.

Obviously, this is not easily accomplished. Therefore, some individuals just trace an authentic signature or other desired writing. That is another poorly executed method. Pen movement is slow, hesitation is probable, and ability to stay on course is extremely difficult. Evidence of outlining is then present in various areas along the line of writing. In addition to attempts of signature simulation, some cases may involve an attempt to distort or disguise one's handwriting characteristics and then claim it to be a forgery. One of the most common methods employed is writing with the opposite hand. However, the writer's unconscious habits remain and with a good quantity of the suspect's known writing, identification of the writer is possible.

Ability to accurately identify an individual writer's habits and natural variations, such as changes in handwriting characteristics resulting from time span, writing conditions, environment, and circumstances, is imperative. The primary requirement for accurate comparison results is high-level visual acuity. It can be cultivated with practice and knowing what to look for, and where.

Comparing a currently written signature with those written several years earlier, or vice versa, can present authentication problems. Handwriting characteristics can change considerably over time, for various reasons. Comparison of the questioned signature with a quantity of known signature writings that are contemporaneous to the date of the questioned signature is of utmost importance. Canceled checks, if available, are an excellent source of standards for comparison. They are usually kept in quantity, for an extended period of time. However, if they are provided as standards, or known writings, it is recommended they be in numerical sequence, to preclude possible accusation that only those that are supportive of the subject's position are being used.

Formal or request-writing standards are not preferred *unless* accompanied by those that were previously written, such as a course of business documents. To request the subject to be seated and write his or her name 10 times provides opportunity to distort or attempt to disguise that writing, if the subject chooses to do so.

Note: Joint account signature cards taken home for signing by another party should be viewed with caution. They may or may not be returned with an authentic signature or one voluntarily written by that party. In the event a signature of an account holder becomes an issue of dispute, comparison of both signatures on the joint account signature card with that of the questioned document is important.

RED FLAGS OF HANDWRITING IDENTIFICATION

- Is the signature authentic?
    - Are all writer habits and handwriting characteristics consistent with those of known signature writings?
- Is the signature, or other disputed writing, in original ink . . . OR

  Is it a computer printout? . . . OR

  Is it a fax printout? . . . OR

  Is it a copier printout? A color copier printout?

- Is the signature a simulation, or imitation, of an original signature writing?
- Is it a tracing of an original signature?
- Is it a spurious signature—a "simple forgery"— written with no attempt to imitate an authentic signature writing?

There is no simple formula or process for identification of the writer of a particular signature or writing specimen. Primarily this is due to the fact that no two things in nature are exactly the same. Similar, yes. Identical, no. Professional, critical comparison of the handwriting will usually reveal subtle characteristics that distinguish individual writers.

Opinion regarding validity, or authenticity, of a questioned signature or other writing(s) can vary. It is based on the "evidence available, to date." Therefore, additional evidence received at a later date can result in opinion revision. There are also occasions when the available evidence, such as lack of sufficient quantity of standards for comparison, or receipt of poor quality copies, can result only in an opinion that is inconclusive.

When determination has been reached that a signature is not authentic, answering the question "Who did it?" may or may not be possible. The answer could be "I don't know."

SUGGESTED READING

Eckman, Paul. *Emotions Revealed* (New York: Henry Holt, 2003).

Eckman, Paul. *Telling Lies* (New York: Berkley Books, 1985).

Ekman, Paul, and Richard J. Davidson. *The Nature of Emotion/Fundamental Questions* (New York: Oxford University Press, 1994).

Ekman, Paul, and Erika Rosenburg. *What the Face Reveals* (New York: Oxford University Press, 1997).

Gudjonsson, Gisli H. *The Psychology of Interrogations and Confessions: A Handbook* (Hoboken, NJ: John Wiley & Sons, 2003).

Hagen, David M., and Ed Hagen. *Law of Confessions* (Clark, Boardman Callaghan, 2004).

Zulawski, David E., and Douglas E. Wicklander. *Practical Aspects of Interview and Interrogation* 2nd ed. (CRC Press, 2002).

NOTES

1. In this chapter the term "subject" refers to someone who is a victim, witness, or suspect. The "interviewer" is attempting to obtain or confirm information but not a confession from the individual. The term "suspect" is used when the investigation has focused on an individual who is believed to be responsible for the incident. The "interrogator" is attempting to obtain an admission or confession from that person. These definitions are the same as those used by the Center for Interviewer Standards and Assessment in its examination to receive the Certified Forensic Interviewer (CFI) designation. The term "investigator" is used to describe the work of either an interviewer or interrogator where the context of gaining information or a confession is not relevant.
2. David E. Zulawski and Douglas E. Wicklander, *Practical Aspects of Interview and Interrogation,* 2nd ed.
3. Roy A. Huber and A. M. Headrick, *Handwriting Identification: Facts and Fundamentals* (Boca Raton, FL: CRC Press, Boca Raton; New York, 1999).
4. Lynda Taylor-Hartwick, "Rocket Science and Document Restoration." Presentation, before the Independent Association of Questioned Document Examiners Educational Seminar, Sarasota, FL, 2002.

5. *Black's Law Dictionary, with Pronunciation,* Fifth Edition 5th ed. (St. Paul, MN: West Publ. Co., St. Paul, MN Publishing, 1979).
6. Edna W. Robertson, *Fundamentals of Document Examination* (Chicago: Nelson-Hall, Publ., Chicago, 1991).
7. FBI Laboratory, Documents Section, *They Write Their Own Sentences* (reprinted from the *FBI Law Enforcement Bulletin,* Rev. 4/73), April 1973.

Chapter 14

Data Analysis and Monitoring: How Effective Data Analysis Can Identify Fraud Risk Indicators and Promote Business Intelligence

Brieh Guevara and James Martin

INTRODUCTION

High-Level View of the Devil in the Details

Data analysis is not a "techie" subject. The domain expertise for creating a data analysis program should not rest solely with an information technology (IT) department. In fact, the need for a data analysis and monitoring program must first be recognized by the highest-level thinkers in an organization: the board and executive management. They are collectively responsible for establishing the standards for how an organization conducts business and ensuring that those standards are met. In controls parlance, this oversight involves ensuring operations are effective, financial reporting is accurate, and regulations and laws are complied with. This group therefore, should appreciate the ability to reach deep into the corporate trenches, pick out the bytes and bits flowing through the company, and transform that data into decision-grade information. As described by David Coderre in his writings on fraud and data analysis, such monitoring rightly relies on the entity's transactional data as it is the "fundamental measure and record of the organization's activity."

Historically, such high-level monitoring has been performed by asking tough questions or by asking the right questions—think "quarterly review meeting." Then direct reports would go forth, seeking satisfactory answers to those questions by pulling the information out of subordinates, running existing business reports again, or creating new queries that pull information out of a business system with new fields or processing logic added to an old report. Such monitoring activities are highly manual and ineffective over the long term due to the one-time nature of the analysis used to address the original oversight question. Furthermore, the method for creating an irregular report to, for example, identify inappropriate cost center charges may be too subjective to rely on. What cost center charges are inappropriate? How should cost center charges be calculated and applied? What systems and tables were used to create this new report?

If questions from the board and from executives are worth answering once, they may be worth answering regularly and automatically.

As a further introduction to the central themes of this chapter, let us examine how question-based monitoring played out in an example:

In the fall of 2001 an audit committee chair, seeking to determine the validity of the financial statements, focused all of his questions on the reasons behind and evidence for the company's sustained sales growth. The continued increase in sales booked by the company over the last eight quarters was nice, but the company's competitors were struggling, their customers were struggling, and the company's product just did not seem to be all that hot in the market. On top of that, rumors of accounting liberties had been circulating ever since one of the company's vice presidents had been rotated out of a line position due to conflicts that escalated during a management budgeting and forecasting meeting six months earlier. The audit committee chair suspected that the company was "stealing" sales from future quarters to book in the current quarter.

As it turned out, the question opened up a can of worms, or investigators, as it were. Once the direct reports came back to the audit committee with their sample of large customer contracts and supporting sales documentation, it soon became obvious that the company was playing a dangerous game of catch-up as it stuffed massive loads of product into the distribution channels in order to book possible future revenue today.

In this example, it is laudable that the audit committee member helped identify the accounting scandal before an outside regulator had to step in. However, the risk of improper revenue recognition should not have been a "tough" area to address. According to the Report Pursuant to Section 704 of the Sarbanes-Oxley Act of 2002 by the Securities and Exchange Commission (SEC), of 515 SEC enforcement actions reviewed, 126 actions related to improper revenue recognition—more than in any other category. Of those 126 actions, 81 related to improperly timed revenue recognition, 80 related to fictitious revenue, and 21 related to improper valuation issues. The risk of improper revenue recognition at the manufacturing company just described should have been known. Furthermore, it is precisely this scenario, and numerous others like it, that can be more effectively monitored using automated data analysis techniques.

Imagine sitting on an audit committee, being privy to periodic reports illustrating information such as current total sales by customer as compared to that customer's historical average purchasing pattern and that customer's product return, discount, and other incentive activity.

Such a report in the example would have made it clear that the company's three largest customers were eroding all purchases in excess of their historical purchasing pattern by returning large quantities of product and by taking discounts that were more than triple the industry average.

Imagine another report that includes graphs of customer returns by product versus customer sales forecasts by product, and the rate of increase in purchasing raw materials for the production of that product.

Such a report would be able to show that for the last eight quarters, the net product used by customers had been falling while the rates of production for the product were increasing.

This is the nature and power of data analysis. From the highest levels in the organization, this discipline requires persons with a view of the various and diverse activities taking place in the business to realize that every aspect of how transactions are initiated, authorized, recorded, processed, and reported generates a trail of data in both hard copy and digital formats. This data trail can be exploited. Doing so starts by determining what information, if collected, would provide insight as to whether business is executing in line with policy and in support of management's objectives.

Before an effective data analysis and monitoring program can be developed, one must thoroughly understand the business. Gaining this understanding begins at the top of the organization cascading down to the lowest level of procedural detail and to the data generated by the simplest of activities.

Certain data analysis and monitoring can be designed for the board and for executives. The board may primarily be concerned with ensuring business is conducted according to the parameters set forth in the policies and procedures, seeking notifications and alerts to nonconforming activity. Executives may be most interested in creating operationally useful views of the enterprise, seeking "dashboards" (see Chapter 15) and balanced scorecard information (see Chapter 1) that aids in big-picture decision making. If one moves deeper into the organization, it is easy to see that still other groups, such as internal audit and procurement, might need a mix of specific data alerts and operational information.

Chapter Objectives

Effective data analysis and monitoring has a place in almost every corner of the organization. With the information provided in this chapter, you will be equipped to:

- Apply the four tenets of a useful data analysis and monitoring program
- Discuss the need for and uses of data analysis and monitoring in the area of your business that needs it most
- Discuss specific methods for understanding large and diverse populations of data
- Develop specific analytical plans
- Assess data analysis tools by comparing key functional characteristics to your analytical needs

The fundamentals of data analysis and monitoring covered in this chapter can be used by a lone auditor or analyst with nothing more than a computer and one of many analytical tools available on the market for between $200 and $2,000. The fundamentals covered in this chapter can be used at a company with a single information system or at a company with numerous systems, data warehouses, and on-line analytical processing (OLAP) initiatives.

Establishing effective data analysis and monitoring begins with data basics.

DATA BASICS

No Shortage of Raw Material and Reason

Technology advances continue to increase the volume of electronic data businesses collect. A study by Keenan Vision estimates online business-to-business transactions occurred 1.1 trillion times in 2004 alone. Each of these transactions likely flowed through to individual companies, generating exponentially more data as ledgers were updated, inventory levels adjusted, accounts reconciled, and descriptive data (e.g., dates, locations, prices) was captured.

By understanding and viewing this electronic record in aggregate, specific analyses can be applied to gain new insights from data. These insights will help identify fraud indicators and promote business intelligence.

A sound governance structure should provide assurance that business transactions comply with management objectives. To be effective, policies and procedures must provide appropriate coverage and an appropriate level of detailed instruction to employees who then execute business activities "on their own" on a day-to-day basis. Organizations are thus faced with inherent risk as individual judgment, miscommunication, and other intentional or unintentional deviations can lead to business activity in violation of the policies and procedures. Preventive controls might be designed and implemented flawlessly; however, there always exists such threats as a management override of internal controls—an area the American Institute of Certified Public Accountants (AICPA) has called "the Achilles' heel of fraud prevention." Because controls cannot prevent all fraud, after-the-fact monitoring for fraud is a must.

As legislation such as Sarbanes-Oxley and general public sentiment encourage auditors and management to fight fraud, the need for comprehensive fraud detection is greater than ever. Identifying what information, if collected, would help detect fraud is the first step in a data monitoring project. In most cases, this information will be generated by various business transactions that create electronic and paper-based records of the transaction. Historical and ongoing analysis of this record is the essence of monitoring, allowing auditors and managers to begin to detect numerous types of activity that indicate possible violations or issues in the business.

Useful Data Analysis and Monitoring Systems

The challenges associated with effectively monitoring enterprise-wide data should not be underestimated. For starters, data stores are enormous. According to Experian, companies double the amount of data they collect each year—this from a position paper in 2003 titled "Data gridlock: the costs and risks of data proliferation to your business." To minimize the risk of data analysis and monitoring project failure, auditors and management should utilize proven methods in their monitoring system; these methods depend on three steps:

1. Designing a useful data analysis and monitoring system
2. Developing a standard and cost-effective rollout process for that system
3. Capturing business intelligence from collected data

Good execution of these methods will ensure that monitoring efforts can be sized appropriately for various business areas, will maximize coverage by automating assessments, and will add value by efficiently providing business information that was not previously available.

In developing a data monitoring program, four criteria should be satisfied; useful data analysis and monitoring systems should be:

1. *Independent.* Information should be analyzed outside of its native system.

   Data should be extracted and analyzed with a "sterile" application. Data queried with report writers in their original environment are subject to filters and other database relationships that may have been corrupted, intentionally or not, long ago. In those cases, attempts to tie out financial statement account amounts or to get at all of the data in a table may inappropriately indicate that data reconciled, when in fact it should not have.

   By extracting data as of a specific date and time, it is also possible to allow others to easily verify results, share the data with other business units, and track changes within specific fields at a later date that may indicate an attempted cover-up by employees. When time is invested in acquiring, importing, and analyzing data, business intelligence analyses should also be run. These might include sourcing and sales analyses or customer relationship management routines that segment and summarize customer data in new ways.

2. *Powerful.* Large volumes of data, spanning entities and time periods, should be analyzed, not just samples.

   The keys here are processing power and storage space. Query and data manipulation speed are normally very important because the end users of such monitoring systems will invariably see results that prompt them to dig deeper or to cross-check data in new areas on the fly. The ability to execute such commands and not have to wait too long for results depends on processing power. The storage aspect is significant because comprehensive monitoring can quickly require manipulation of data with over 1 million records and 100 or more fields per record.

3. *Unifying.* Diverse sources of information should be integrated and validated against the business rules.

   Once the initial data monitoring project is successful, additional analyses can be added in bolt-on fashion by integrating data from disparate sources, such as Word documents, e-mail, Internet click streams, PC directories, and accounting, operational, and other enterprise resource planning (ERP) modules. For example, by comparing disbursement, vendor, and general ledger data, you can identify fraud indicators such as *high-dollar payments* made to *newly created vendors* with *a name similar to an existing vendor* that result in *charge-offs* when entered by *the same user ID.*

4. *Programmable.* Standard, complex, and ad hoc analysis should be readily available.

   Effective monitoring programs should strive to isolate individually dubious transactions and to provide valuable high-level analyses, such as trend information on specific ledger accounts, network usage patterns, or metrics that can be used to benchmark performance over time. Certain executive users may only need summary information, while other "power" users may wish to advance monitoring efforts with complex statistical tests and artificial intelligence. Standard techniques for fraud detection that can be run on many types of data include regression analysis, minimum-maximum and outlier identification, Benford's Law, joining related data from multiple systems, identifying gaps in sequential data, and graphing to represent relationships between data fields. These techniques make large populations of data easier to understand by subsetting data into small groups of records or fields.

Adherence to the criteria discussed in this chapter will support the creation of a data analysis and monitoring program that grows with the organization, provides auditors and managers with good information, and leverages the up-front investment in data acquisition and understanding by addressing business needs that include and go beyond fraud deterrence and detection.

Master Data

Before picking apart complex information systems, one must examine the building blocks of those systems: master data and transactional data. Other types of data exist, but understanding these two types first is a prerequisite to conducting any useful analysis. As the "independent" facet of an effective data analysis and monitoring program is based on removing data from their native system, our approach to monitoring is more continual than continuous for now.

Assume you have targeted purchasing-related data from three business areas that you would like to analyze. You extract the data as of a point in time, in this case, the calendar year-end. The data would include one group of information that has remained relatively unchanged for a long period of time and one group of information that changes regularly. Lists of data such as vendor names and vendor addresses that you buy goods from are two examples of data that have probably not been updated recently. Other unchanged information in the data would include things like the descriptions of the goods being purchased or the list of subledger accounts that such purchases can be attributed to.

Data that are used but not created or updated in the course of routine business transactions can generally be considered master data.

For example, specific master vendor data might include rows of information listed beneath these fields: Vendor Code, Vendor Name, Vendor Address 1, Contact Name, Contact Phone Number, Vendor Type Code, Subject to 1099 Code, Active/Inactive Code, Purchase Discount Code (see Exhibit 14.1).

Exhibit 14.1 makes several aspects of master data immediately clear. The first characteristic to note is that some data in each row are intelligible on their face. Take the Vendor Name and Contact Phone Number fields. Any person viewing the data in these fields can immediately understand the information and use it because the content and field name is written in "plain English." Other data looks significant based on the field names (e.g., Active/Inactive Code, Purchase Discount Code) but in its current form remains meaningless. To interpret data in the Purchase Discount Code field, an additional table is necessary. Without regard to how the system makes data clear to a person in the purchasing department, the snapshot of the Purchasing Discounts Master Table (see Exhibit 14.2) helps us now.

Comparing the discount code for Gatherall, YL4, to the additional data about that code in Exhibit 14.2 gives further meaning to the Vendor Master Table. Gatherall's discount percentage, now known to be 15 percent, may be applied to certain orders.

Another characteristic to note about master data is that not all rows and fields will necessarily be populated. The Gatherall vendor does not list a contact phone number, while the e-Chips vendor does not list a purchase discount code. This may be because the design of those fields does not require data to establish a valid business record. Alternatively, the design of those fields may require data but for some reason, as in the last case, has none. In the latter scenario you have identified an invalid vendor record. Preserving the data you extracted as of December 31 would then become very important. It contains missing required data—your key evidence of a corrupt table or of inappropriate tampering by employees or other persons.

Missing data, even if permitted by the system, are one fraud risk indicator. For instance, without vendor contact information, it is much more difficult to verify orders that may need to be scrutinized during an internal audit or fraud investigation.

Exhibit 14.1 Vendor Master Table

Vendor Master Table (Select Fields Shown)

Vendor Code	Vendor Name	Vendor Address 1	Contact Name	Contact Phone Number	Vendor Type Code	Subject to 1099 Code	Active/ Inactive Code	Purchase Discount Code
44433	JTM Parts	123 Main	J.T. Marlin	555.4343	1A	Y	A	YL2
34999	Gatherall	207 Wixom Rd.	B. Johnson		1A	Y	A	YL4
334ADE3	e-Chips	43 Software Ln.	N. Stutz	555.0330	1T	Y	I	

Exhibit 14.2 Purchasing Discounts Master Table

Purchasing Discounts Master Table (Select Fields Shown)

Purchase Discount Code	Discount Percentage	Authorization Required	Date Last Updated
Y	.5	N	9/22/02
YL1	1	N	9/22/02
YL2	5	N	9/22/02
YL4	15	Y	9/22/02

A final characteristic worth noting about the data in Exhibits 14.1 and 14.2 is that they come in several main types and formats. The primary types of data include numeric, character, and alpha-numeric definitions. Fields with a numeric data type contain values that are numbers or behave like numbers (i.e., they are subject to standard mathematical handling, such as addition and subtraction). Character data types contain values best thought of as symbols. Usually these symbols take the form of the letters of the alphabet, but they may also include dollar signs, asterisks, and dashes and the like. Alpha-numeric data types (actually a subset of the character data type) primarily display strings of both alphabetic and numeric data. The e-Chips Vendor Code contains a good example of alpha-numeric data: 334ADE3.

The format of data gets at what data types and characteristics are valid for specific fields. The variety of data formats you may encounter while conducting data analysis is vast. In some cases, a data format will limit the length of permissible data in a field to 12 characters (or some other prespecified length). In other cases, valid data formats may be limited to calendar dates. Understanding the types and formats of data you plan to analyze is important. It will prevent erroneous alteration of data as you handle it and ensure that you communicate your analysis results without misinterpreting the reports you produce.

Data critical to the analysis you wish to conduct or the business areas most in need of monitoring will likely come from more than one system. Different systems and even different users of the same system have different naming conventions for referring to the table view of master data provided. Other names virtually synonymous with the "table" moniker include: file, object, list, entity, directory, or data set. However, differences in naming conventions and other data layout nuances do not stop there. Prior to conducting any analysis of your master and transactional data, always obtain and review an up-to-date data dictionary for the system area you are looking at. Reference information on data dictionaries can be found in the "Appendix" section (at the end of the "Data Basics" section of this chapter). The data dictionary will help you comprehend the important characteristics of data covered thus far.

Master data are used by information systems and people with high frequency but are created and updated with zero to low frequency. Because master data will factor into so many unique transactions, they must always be complete, accurate, valid, and protected from unauthorized access and corruption. Master data are sacred and often underestimated building blocks in an information system.

An effective data analysis and monitoring program should begin with an assessment of the master data. Once their status is known, the analysis can expand to include assessments of transactional data.

Transactional Data

At a glance, transactional data looks very similar to master data. However, confusing the two could be detrimental to your data analysis.

Staying with the purchasing-related data extraction example used to introduce master data, look carefully at the transactional records in Exhibit 14.3. In narrative form, the table shows that of three transactions recorded in the not-too-distant past, two originated in the United States, one in Europe, and two took advantage of purchasing discounts. Also, it is safe to assume (just this once) that the Payee Vendor Code field identifies the recipient of the Net Amount Paid. To learn more about that recipient, you must refer back to the Vendor Code field in the Vendor Master Table (Exhibit 14.1). Codes from the Vendor Code field that match the Payee Vendor Code in the Purchasing Transaction Table offer a more complete view of the vendors selling goods to your company.

In Exhibit 14.3, it is impossible to tell who vendor 34999 is, but by referring back to the Vendor Master Table it should be clear that this vendor's name is Gatherall.

Each row of data in Exhibit 14.3 table was created as transactions were executed, processed, and recorded. The particulars of each transaction dictated what information would appear in each field. The transaction table will grow by one or more rows every time a purchasing transaction occurs. Because transactional tables primarily capture data necessary to reflect the obligations, circumstances, timing, and nature of some executed event, they will not show additional detail, such as the address or name of the vendor to be paid for purchased goods or services.

Data that are created or updated in the course of routine business transactions can generally be considered transactional data.

Even with the limited information in Exhibit 14.3, two issues are readily apparent. The first involves the date of the invoice for invoice number FABR.12XY. Unlike the other invoices in the table, FABR.12XY was paid and posted within three days of the invoice date. Generally, such prompt payments are made only with discount incentives, yet no discount was taken. That much information might lead you to suspect there were inefficiencies or a lack of procedural know-how and oversight in the purchasing department. Note: Invoice Date is in Year, Day, Month order (YYYYDDMM); Invoice Posting Date is in Month, Day, Year order (MMDDYY).

The second issue can be gleaned from the Purchasing Transaction Table only if we incorporate what we know about the Vendor Master Table: Vendor Code 334ADE3 is inactive (as noted by the 'I' in the Active/Inactive Code field). This suggests that the payment to e-Chips for $25,000 is a nonconforming transaction; it is a good indicator of possible fraud or of some other serious process and control failure.

Exhibit 14.3 Purchasing Transaction Table

Purchasing Transaction Table (Select Fields Shown)

Originating Purchasing Division	Subledger Account Number	Invoice Number	Invoice Date	Payee Vendor Code	Gross Amount	Net Amount Paid	Invoice Posting Date	Journal Number
Purchasing-USA	AP13144	RAW.AB44	20053003	44433	20,000	19,000	05/01/05	3444
Purchasing-USA	AP13144	COMP.AAAA	20053103	34999	50,000	42,500	05/01/05	3445
Purchasing-EU	AP13131	FABR.12XY	20052904	334ADE3	25,000	25,000	05/01/05	3446

Transactional data captures detail about the business activities and events of the organization. If analyzed appropriately, transactional data can offer tremendous insight into what the organization will do next (predictive analysis) and what the organization should do next (business intelligence and fraud deterrence and detection).

Normalized Data

To understand how data coming out of one or more information systems are organized, it is important to understand the concept of data normalization. Data normalization is a major component of relational database theory and is one of the key design concepts that almost every enterprise wide system utilizes.

Additionally, you will be manipulating data and tables extensively as you progress with your data analysis. As you do, you should use the principles of data normalization to ensure that you do not inadvertently corrupt data while working with it. Allowing data corruption to go undetected in the course of your analysis will likely cause you to produce erroneous results, causing more harm than good.

According to www.webopedia.com, "normalization" can be defined as:

> The process of organizing data to minimize redundancy. Normalization usually involves dividing a database into two or more tables and defining relationships between the tables. The objective is to isolate data so that additions, deletions, and modifications of a field can be made in just one table and then propagated through the rest of the database via the defined relationships.

Therefore, if seeking to discover or confirm a fact, there should be only one way (read "one database relationship") to get at that fact. While there are more than three levels of normalization, most practitioners consider a database normalized once the third level has been achieved. Technically, though, relationships in either the first or second level can also be considered normalized. Validating business logic embedded in systems and portrayed by records of data at specific points in time can be more efficient if you know what form of normalization you are dealing with.

By revisiting a simplified version of the purchasing-related information described earlier—prior to normalizing any of the data related to it—it is easy to imagine a table that was set up as shown in Exhibit 14.4.

Exhibit 14.4 Purchasing Master Table (Prior to Normalization)

Purchasing Related Table (Prior to Normalization; Select Fields Shown)

Vendor ID	Vendor Name	Product Name
1	JTM Parts	Dowel, Screws, Fasteners
2	Gatherall	Fasteners, Binding
3	e-Chips	Microprocessors
4	Tuff Goods	
5	Spartan U	Pencils, Fasteners
6	MFG, Inc.	Paper, Pencils, File Folders

This is not a useful way to store information. For instance, if you needed to find out who sold Fasteners, you would have to skim the list and look for each vendor with Fasteners included in their product section. In order to make the data in Exhibit 14.4 more user and database friendly, you must move these data through the three levels of normalization: First Normal Form, Second Normal Form, and Third Normal Form.

Getting to First Normal Form requires you to eliminate repeating groups of data. To do this, create a separate table for each set of related fields. The same data in First Normal Form are depicted in Exhibit 14.5.

Now if you want to see which vendors sell Fasteners, simply look up "Fasteners" in the Product Table. A query on "Fasteners" in the Product Table would identify three vendors (as associated to the Vendor Table through the Vendor ID): JTM Parts, Gatherall, Spartan U.

Getting to Second Normal Form requires you to eliminate redundant data. Currently, certain products are associated with multiple Product ID values. For instance, pencils are associated with Product ID 8 and 9. This is redundant. Fixing the Product Table requires us to again create two tables from one. One table will be the normalized Product Table; the other will be the newly created Vendor Product ID Table. The Second Normal Form tables are depicted in Exhibit 14.6.

The last thing required to get these data into Third Normal Form involves eliminating columns that are not dependent on the Primary Key. In the vendors' case the Vendor ID is the Primary Key. Returning to the original master data table (Exhibit 14.1), think of the discount information related to the vendors. This information was once in our Second Normal Form table

Exhibit 14.5 Vendor Table and Product Table (First Normal Form)

Vendor Table

Vendor ID	Vendor Name
1	JTM Parts
2	Gatherall
3	e-Chips
4	Tuff Goods
5	Spartan U
6	MFG, Inc.

Product Table

Product ID	Vendor ID	Product Name
1	1	Dowel
2	1	Fasteners
3	1	Screws
4	2	Fasteners
5	2	Binding
6	3	Microprocessors
7	5	Fasteners
8	5	Pencils
9	6	Pencils
10	6	Paper
11	6	File Folders

Exhibit 14.6 Vendor Table, Product Table, and Vendor Product ID Table (Second Normal Form)

Vendor Table

Vendor ID	Vendor Name
1	JTM Parts
2	Gatherall
3	e-Chips
4	Tuff Goods
5	Spartan U
6	MFG, Inc.

Product Table

Product ID	Product Name
1	Dowel
2	Fasteners
3	Screws
4	Binding
5	Microprocessors
6	Pencils
7	Paper
8	File Folders

Vendor Product ID Table

Vendor ID	Product ID
1	1
1	2
1	3
2	2
2	3
3	5
5	2
5	6
6	6
6	7
6	8

below (see Exhibit 14.7). Note: A Primary Key uniquely identifies each record in a table, similar to the uniqueness of your Social Security Number as it identifies you.

The Vendor ID in Exhibit 14.7 describes only the Vendor Name, not the discount related data. To achieve Third Normal Form, the fields related to purchasing discounts should be moved into a separate table. This is why the Exhibit 14.2 information was not included in the table in Exhibit 14.1. If this information was not separated from the Vendor Table, think about what would happen if Vendor ID 6 (MFG, Inc.) was deleted. All record of the "1" Discount Percentage would be lost!

Exhibit 14.7 Vendor Table (with Key Independent Fields)

Vendor Table

Vendor ID	Vendor Name	Discount Percentage	Authorization Required
1	JTM Parts	5	N
2	Gatherall	15	Y
3	e-Chips		
4	Tuff Goods	.5	N
5	Spartan U	5	N
6	MFG, Inc.	1	N

With normalized data, you substantially reduce the risk of experiencing so-called delete and update anomalies. In other words, you can modify data in one location without erroneously modifying (or not modifying) the same data elsewhere in the database. For instance, if you need to change the address in the database associated with the Gatherall vendor, you would want to be sure that the new address was entered and that Gatherall was no longer associated with the old address in any part of the system.

In summary, normalized data helps maintain the overall integrity of the information stored and retrieved from the company's information systems. Attention to the key elements of the normalization process through the first three forms will also help you maintain integrity in the analysis you use to analyze and monitor the business.

Appendix

Data Dictionary. A data dictionary defines the basic components and logical arrangement of a database. A complete data dictionary contains: a list of all tables in a database; the names, types, and formats of data in each field; and the beginning and ending position of each field. Depending on the table and system you are working with, you may be need to refer to the data dictionary extensively.

Data dictionaries are, for the most part, system specific. The content and format from one data dictionary to the next will not be uniform; however, the information relayed in the data dictionary will generally include:

- *Plain English data translations.* System names for tables and fields are usually different from the user or common names for tables and fields. For example, the system name for a table might be APABSHP, while the common name translates to Master Vendor Table.
- *Data definitions.* Given the types of data and numerous formats they can come in, descriptive information on how tables, fields, primary keys, and relationships have been defined takes the guesswork out of your analysis.
- *Programming elements.* Certain procedures written in programming code are often put in place to move data about or to manipulate them in some way. Understanding how stored programs (if any are used) logically handle data will help you plan your analysis. This understanding will also help you account for differences in similar data over time. For example,

a stored program that updates customer billing rate information may only run once per month. Work using that customer billing rate data that spans months would need a way to update the billing detail in a similar fashion.

- *Control totals.* Because the data dictionary can often be created dynamically by querying the system for a point-in-time data dictionary, you may be able to obtain control totals. Control totals provide basic summary information, such as the total number of records in each table or the summed amount of the general ledger debits, for instance. You should always try to produce the same summary information with the data you plan to analyze. If there is a discrepancy between the data dictionary's control totals and the totals you come up with, something is wrong. Either you have more or less data than you should, or there is a misunderstanding in how to produce your summary information.
- *Entity relationship diagrams.* Entity relationship diagrams (E-R diagrams), or ERD for short, are a data modeling tool; these help by organizing data into entities (e.g., store, department, employee) and by defining the relationships between those entities. Think of an entity as anything real or abstract about which you want to store data. As data is collected about an entity, such as the "department" entity, that information is further organized into the fields and other attributes that describe a department. Once the key data are captured for a group of entities, the E-R diagrams help by representing the relationships permitted between those entities. For instance, one store may have more than one department, one department may be assigned multiple employees, and one employee may be assigned to work in only one department but at many stores (as long as the employee works in that department at those stores). Such real-life relationships must be reflected within the system(s). In analyzing data, you will often need to run tests that confirm that the system logic and business logic associated with relationships between entities are in sync.
- *System process descriptions.* Maintaining, analyzing, and monitoring complex information systems require a good understanding of each process performed by the system. System process descriptions should clarify:
  - Where and how data enter the system
  - What processing is done to the data and why
  - The outputs of such processing from the system
  - The business rules driving these points

Any assessment you are planning to perform should include an assessment of the data dictionary. Data dictionaries that are incomplete, out of date, or nonexistent pose inherent risks to businesses. System updates and maintenance may be impossible or inefficient, while growth or loss prevention efforts may be difficult to support. These risks are sometimes mitigated by managers who rely heavily on knowledgeable staff or stagnant business processes. However, it is not hard to see that deficient data dictionaries in those cases still pose a great risk over the long term.

Table Relationship Diagrams. Most databases store records of data in a table. For example, all the records for customers of a company might be stored by one table, the customer table. A table is a tabular arrangement of data, similar to a spreadsheet. Tables consist of vertical columns and horizontal rows. The columns are usually referred to as fields or elements. The rows are usually referred to as records (see Exhibit 14.8).

Exhibit 14.8 Table Structure

Table			
Field (Element)	**Field (Element)**	**Field (Element)**	**Field (Element)**
Record 1	(data)	(data)	(data)
Record 2	(data)	(data)	(data)
Record 3	(data)	(data)	(data)

One table has many records. The field names within each record in one table do not change, although the values in those fields may differ. For example, every customer record has a payment type field. The values in the payment type field might be Cash, Credit Card, Voucher, or Gift Card.

Each record in the customer table contains information for a specific customer. Each record must be unique and independent of any other record in the table. Uniqueness of each record is maintained by a field or a combination of fields that identify each record in the table. The unique identifier for a record is called the *primary key,* or the key. The primary key allows you to distinguish one record from all of the others in a table.

Once a primary key has been established, there should never be more than one record in a table with the same primary key.

When a field or combination of fields in one table matches the primary key of another table, the field(s) is referred to as a foreign key.

Exhibit 14.9 depicts two tables that are related to one another. In the Department table, the primary key is the Dept. ID field. The Dept. ID identifies the department description and employee ID associated with each record in the Department table. As the primary key, each record's Dept. ID field in the Department table is and will be unique. The Department table also contains a foreign key called Employee ID. The foreign key does not have to be unique. In the example, it allows you to see which employees work in a given department. However, the Employee ID field in the Employee table is that table's primary key. Within the Employee table, the Employee ID will always be unique.

One way to describe the relationship between the two tables in Exhibit 14.9 is to say that "one employee may be assigned to one or more departments" (e.g., Jane Smith is assigned to Home Goods and Outdoor Supplies).

Table relationship diagrams increase in value as the number of relationships they are able to describe goes up. Other relationships you would likely want to see addressed between the Department and Employee tables involve answering questions such as:

- Must an employee be assigned a department?
- Can a department be assigned more than one employee?

Knowledge of such detailed relationships between tables will become increasingly important as you move from a data analysis pilot project to an analysis set that includes multiple systems and business areas. For instance, appropriately integrating data across tables from payroll and human resources requires an accurate reflection of the business rules in the data analysis program you create.

Primary Key — Foreign Key — Primary Key

Department		
Department ID	Department Description	Employee ID
AA	Home Goods	22
BB	Outdoor Supplies	22
CC	Evening Wear	33

Employee		
Employee ID	Name	Position
22	Jane Smith	Sales Clerk
33	Cameron Dean	Sales Clerk
44	David Rosenberg	Finance

Exhibit 14.9 Table Relationships

INFORMATION SYSTEMS

Relation to Business Processes

Deciphering the business processes and their relation to information systems in any business should be universal. There are five main steps for conducting data analysis for a fraud or controls-related engagement:

1. Understand the design and operation of the business activities first.
2. Identify those activities that inherently pose the greatest risk of fraud.
3. Understand what information, if collected, would provide assurance that business is executing in line with policy.
4. Write a brief narrative of the tests and analysis you may wish to perform.
5. Then dive into the data:
   - Use a generic approach first:
     - Assess basic data quality.
     - Profile the data population to quickly understand it and describe it to others.
     - Identify available data in the tables you are working with; there are almost always more data in the tables (e.g., date of entry time stamps, user identification logs, last date of change fields) than on your standard business reports.
   - Integrate your understanding of the business activities with your new understanding of the actual data within your systems.

Understand the design and operation of the business activities. It is often best to think about specific data analysis and monitoring initiatives as a series of exercises in scoping. You should generally start by thinking big picture: Determine or confirm what business entity you are conducting analyses for and then narrow your scope from there. (Any data gathered that relates to out of scope entities can be discarded—no small point as you attempt to manipulate large data sets.) The scoping effort must then look at those business processes using or generating data associated with the information you seek. This step is critical; it will help you create a catalog of all processes directly and peripherally impacting the business question(s) you are trying to address. Building out this catalog includes understanding the discreet business activities within processes so that you can identify all information systems supporting those activities. What you will typically find is that like information can come from a variety of sources, including formal systems, such as the accounting system and customer-facing systems, or from informal sources, such as one department's custom-built database. Navigating the interconnectedness of business activities and information systems to identify your authoritative source for the data you must analyze requires detailed understanding of how business events are initiated, processed, recorded, and reported.

Identify those activities that inherently pose the greatest risk of fraud. Both fraudulent financial reporting schemes and assets misappropriation result in fictitious entries to the financial statements. For financial statements, it is the direct action to create the fraud; for asset misappropriation, the entries are made to conceal the removal of the asset.

That being said, data analysis can help detect anomalies indicating potential fraud for both types of fraud. But like most audit or monitoring programs, targeted monitoring based on a thorough understanding of the business process is required. Since 80 percent of frauds involve asset misappropriations and cash is the targeted asset 90 percent of the time, a good place to devote your energy is to identifying all conceivable cash outlets, such as:

- Payroll
- Expense reimbursement
- Special arrangements, such as housing reimbursement
- Petty cash
- Check disbursements
- Wire transfers
- Cash receipts that may be intercepted before making it to the company accounts

Once the primary cash outlets are defined, you have to look into each major class of potential outlet. For example, if you are interested in disbursements made to vendors, you would want to profile this disbursement population to get a feel for how many checks are manually written versus batch run, or how many payments are made to vendors on a "one-time" basis versus on a recurring basis. If vendors are repeatedly being paid on a "one-time" basis, this may be because the staff is lazy and does not want to properly qualify the vendor or the worst-case scenario, the staff is intentionally inappropriately disbursing funds for personal gain. Also, many frauds involving cash go undetected because the reports needed to spot the wrongdoing exist in two separate locations. Rather than spend time and money in the short term on system integrations, you can extract the source data for those reports and analyze them in a single location—a highly effective and cost-efficient method for combining two reports that do not talk to each other.

At this stage in the game, we should offer a warning: Y data analysis plan thus far stalls if the (hypothetical) risk scenarios you intend to analyze are not married to actual business operations.

Understand what information, if collected, would provide assurance that business is executing in line with policy. With a well-defined set of policies and procedures that begin at the highest levels of the organization, you can drill down and monitor detailed activity that provides data quality and processing assurance. Consider the fact that individual judgments (that may or may not conform to the boundaries of permissible activities defined in a company's procedures and control design) never fail to generate a trail throughout business functions and processes within the organization. Furthermore, preventive controls might be designed and implemented flawlessly; however, in addition to threats such as a management override of internal controls, the personnel responsible for operating a control may not be available, as in the case of a company that implemented major downsizing of its staff. Thus, using current and appropriately detailed work-flow information, in narrative and/or flowchart format, you can pinpoint the points at which data monitoring will be worthwhile and identify data points across the business that should be integrated for monitoring purposes.

If we look at the process and subprocess example in Exhibit 14.10, we have defined such business components as: Purchasing, Work-flow Management, Information Technology, Client Intake, Human Resources, Marketing, and Billing.

Note: Even at a subprocess level, the business components are at too high a level and too encompassing to attach specific analyses to. You must drill down to a "Task-Level" of detail. Drilling through the "Ordering" subprocess beneath "Purchasing"—where tasks include: Setting Up a Purchase Order for Processing, Submitting the PO to a Purchasing Review Manager, and Management Monitoring of Executed PO—brings us to an appropriate level of detail (see Exhibit 14.11).

At the task level, you can confirm whether various specific procedures and controls are executing. It is within these procedures and controls that you should embed data analysis routines.

Processes

Purchasing	Work Flow Management	Information Technology	Client Intake	Human Resources	Marketing	Billing
Subprocesses						
Approvals and Authorizations	Assign Staff	Personal Computer	Initial Client Acceptance	Recruiting	External Communications	Setup Validation
Ordering	Establish Budgets	Internet Browsing	Proposals	Interviewing	Messaging	Time and Expense Monitoring
Recurring Orders	Perform Work	Electronic Communications	Conflicts Check	Hiring	Design and Content	Pass-through Costs
Receiving	Monitor Project Status	Remote Access	Engagement Letters	Performance Evaluation	Review and Authorization	Approvals and Authorizations
Disbursements	Time and Expense	Security	Client Setup	Training	Cost-Benefit Analysis	Final Bill
Emergency Purchases	Archiving	Access Control	Manage Contacts	Separation		Late Payment/ No Payment
Prohibited Purchases	Continuity Planning	Administration				

Exhibit 14.10 Sample Process and Control Matrix

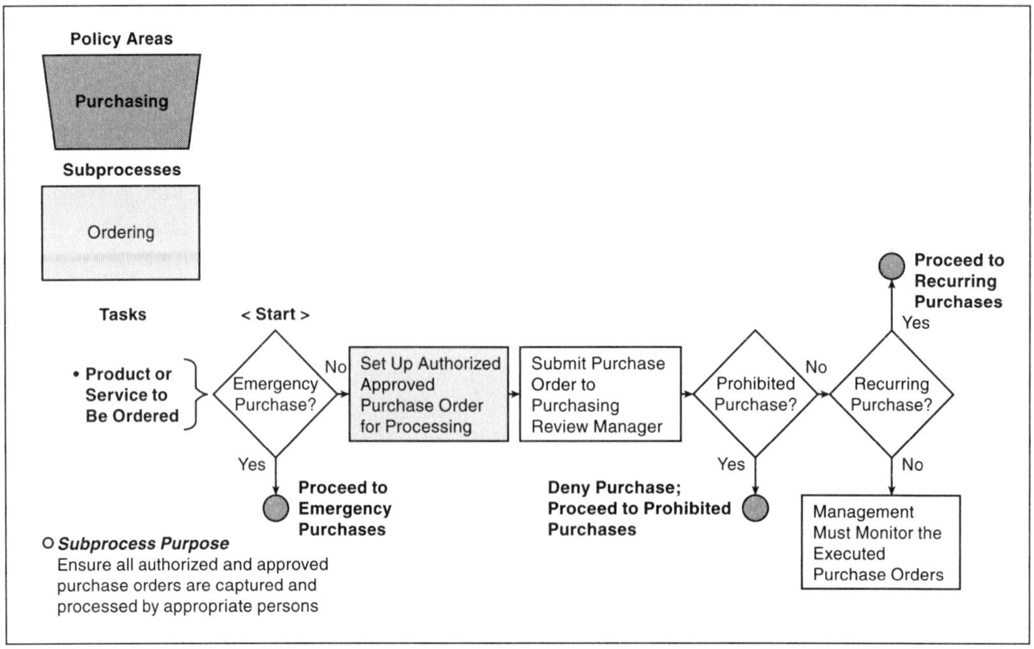

Exhibit 14.11 Sample Process and Control Flow

In Exhibit 14.12 we look at the key procedure and control information related to management's purchase order monitoring. By periodically extracting entire populations of source data (not samples), management is able to identify irregularities (or problems in the data that are problems on their face, such as duplicate PO numbers and orders executed for the same product on different days) and is also able to integrate tests to reconcile and compare Purchasing data to other system modules, such as the General Ledger or the Cash Management module.

Write a brief narrative of the tests and analysis you may wish to perform. Typically, it is through the coordinated performance of multiple techniques that clusters of telltale anomalies develop, for example, each underlined item (below) alone is just interesting. When a number of these are found together (clustered finding), noteworthy items include:

- Out-of-range payments to newly created vendors with name similar to an existing vendor
- Repeated charge-offs or reversals by the same person in a department with a known lack of separation of duties

Writing plain English descriptions of the tests you will perform will help you communicate your plans to other business units and to superiors. Examples of various plain English test statements include:

Sourcing analysis:

- Analyze procurement dollars by major categories and services
- Isolate spend categories for savings opportunities, e.g. high numbers of suppliers, variable procurement practices across divisions
- Identify accelerated payments to vendors where early payment discounts were not taken

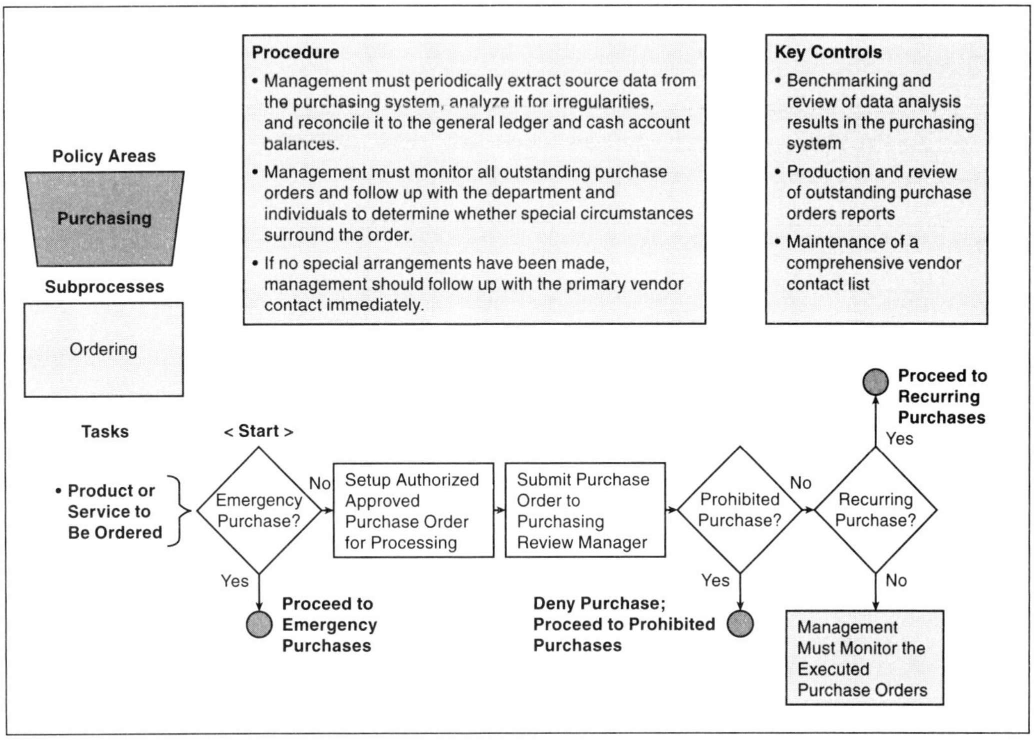

Exhibit 14.12 Sample Process and Control Procedures

Sales analysis:

- Establish regular monitoring of sales trends by region, division, product, etc. over any interval of time
- Track key ratios, e.g. sales to accounts receivables, costs per sales dollar, sales force compensation versus sales force performance
- Calculate profitability ratios by sales person

Customer relationship management:

- Segment customers by profit margin, cost, frequency of purchase, etc.
- Identify customer acquisition and retention costs
- Sample and aggregate customer information via internet, POS data, surveys, etc.

Then dive into the data.

Data Acquisition Data acquisition requires well thought out and specific data requests, especially when the data is requested as part of litigation. The data request specifies the data to be produced and the format of such production, and therefore should be a written, detailed document, rather than an informal email or off-handed request in a meeting. The request should be created by the data analysis and monitoring team, with input from the client or attorney, and responded to by data owners or IT in general.

Data requests typically include areas that address:

- Scope
- Extract detail

- Format
- Media
- Additional/miscellaneous

Sample Data Request

A sample data request follows.

Scope

This data request is for all account transactional and header records associated with ABC Subentity.

Extract

Data should be extracted from source system master and transactional tables—that is, processed and filtered reports should not be used. Please do not merge or join tables where they reside separately in the system.

Please name extracted files using the following sample naming convention: SS_TTTTT_MMDDYY, 'SS' denotes the system/module, 'TTTTT' denotes the table/ report from the system, and 'MMDDYY' denotes the date of the extraction in month-day-year format.

Format

Data should be provided in a text file in one of these formats:

As a delimited file where valid delimiters include:

- Pipe: '|'
- Tab

As a fixed-width field layout. Single-record format is preferable; however, multiple-record formats are acceptable with an appropriately detailed data dictionary.

For all extractions, please provide a "data dictionary." This should list the fields included in the extraction, describe those fields, and list their order or position in the file. If multiple tables are provided, please also list the relevant descriptive portion from the table-relationship diagram, including primary and foreign key information per table.

Media

Please save all data extracts to either an external hard drive or CD.

If you are unable to provide data to the above specifications, let us know and we can discuss alternative solutions.

Additional

In addition to the above requests, please provide:

An overview memo describing

- The information system(s) for the data provided
- Extract procedures used for the data provided, including a copy of the query instructions used to extract the data

Data Profiling Data profiling involves getting accurate counts of all table and system parameter information available. Profiling in general provides for a wide range of options when trying to determine the best way to view information. If you think along both categorical and numeric lines, you will be able to tailor your profiles to your audience. For instance, if you are on an audit team, a profile dimension that identifies materiality by department, customer, unique transaction, or account will quickly guide the rest of the team to decisions about where to focus their detail testing efforts.

Data Integrity Based on the information covered in the "Data Basics" section, the first test set you run should go to data integrity. Understand what the data dictionary specifies in terms of field types and data formats. Query all fields and take note of any anomalies identified. Tracking such anomalies may put your analytical findings in context later in the project.

Exception and Threshold Analysis With executive management and functional representatives, develop and validate the business rules that, when violated, qualify as exceptions. This list should drive the analytical tests you ultimately perform on your data. Thresholds can be derived from laws that the company must comply with (e.g., not charging over a certain interest rate on loans) or may derive from company policies designed to manage risk and efficiencies. Knowing the purpose of the business rule you test will help your case when it comes time to escalate your findings and create action items.

In many cases, the techniques used to monitor the business will drive the need for certain additional tactical analysis. The very nature of such tactical analysis requires creativity to be applied to the analytical needs of each situation. Consider the case example below that involved nontraditional uses of the data analysis tool:

Background Challenge:

- The client produced multiple external hard drives with between 389 and 3,000 unique folders each.
- ~500 files spread across those 3,000 folders needed to be analyzed.
- ~60,000 report pages included in the 500 files: 3.2 million rows of data.
- ~85% of all the files were discovered to be duplicate.

Process:

- With SAS, a program was designed to seek and import all relevant files.
- Every file was combined into a single master file.
- SAS was used to delete header information, blank rows, and garbage data.
- Based on dates and names, duplicate files were identified and deleted.
- Note: Developing this process took about 20 hours; repeating this process on multiple hard drives took about 20 minutes per hard drive.
- Repeat the process on additional hard drives.

Results and Deliverables:

- A single table with 319,732 rows of "good" data
- Data available to produce rapid, tactical queries, subsetting, and other analyses to support areas under review.
- Detailed logs that show all steps executed.

GENERATING BUSINESS INTELLIGENCE

Overview

Five general types of data analysis can be used to promote your capabilities throughout the organization:

1. *Audit support.* Verify information integrity by validating financial statements at their source. For instance, recalculate and foot complex system and reporting logic with raw source data. If performed in a sterile operating environment, you can mitigate the risk that critical system feeds or reporting logic is still valid. Additionally, you can quickly narrow and understand the population of information you must follow-up with for procedures such as SAS99 (which requires consideration and examination of potential fraud in the general ledger).
2. *Data mining.* Focus on large data stores throughout the company and find out what information managers are operating without. Utilizing flexible data analysis tools, you can integrate various types of data, including any mix of databases, free text search, e-mails, and Internet click streams. The goal of the data mining effort is to identify sources of and final information to enhance decision making in the company.
3. *Business intelligence.* This is the ability to derive knowledge from data and to process volumes of information, identify patterns, trends, rules, and relationships that are too large to be handled through simple human analysis.
4. *Data migration, conversion, and implementation.* Mitigate the risk of downtime and processing error proliferation by validating critical IT activities. For instance, validating the data en route to populating a new IT system will help you avoid go-live delays, data rejection, and inappropriate field, table, and system relationships.
5. *Data integrity.* Monitor data as they are stored, processed, and transferred to systems. Over time, all systems, and the data they hold, experience some degree of deterioration. Attention you pay in terms of regular maintenance to data quality will lower the need for future expensive comprehensive analyses of data.

Modern data analysis tools allow tremendous creativity and flexibility; these tools can be deployed in a number of situations to provide new insight and to reduce work previously performed manually.

Audit and Assurance

Recalculation and footing of 100 percent of key information system data does not have to be on a sample basis, nor does it require enormous investments in time. Data analysis can add value through "re-directed" audits that emphasize the integrity and mechanics of financial reporting-related systems. For example, income recognition module analyses can validate these types of key calculations:

- Recalculating earned and unearned income
- Validating principal balance via reamortization
- Recalculating finance charges and origination fees
- Validating payment application rules

- Validating feeds to other key areas (e.g., general ledger)

Additional sample areas for recalculations and footing include:

- Loan portfolio valuation
- Securitization of receivables
- Accounts payable and disbursement validation
- Re-create query logic in "bolt-on" report writers

If management or the auditors need specific support to address standards such as SAS99, you can review 100 percent of the general ledger and related tables. Begin by developing analytical routines that apply to all data, utilizing microlevel analytical procedures to isolate transactions of interest. (Note: Certain populations of data, for example, 'ALL GL Data', should be analyzed with higher level procedures. Other populations, for example, 'Non-Standard GL' data, that could be made up of manual GL entries or some other non-standard indicator, should be put through a more rigorous set of procedures, see Exhibit 14.13.)

Business Intelligence

Consulting initiatives aimed at increasing profitability or decreasing costs typically begin with detailed analysis of the primary profit and loss levers. As three business activities that get a lot of attention during such analysis, sourcing, sales and marketing, and customer relationship management, each depend on vast and disparate data stores. Key views into the business provided by data analysis in these areas include:

In strategic sourcing, you:

- Analyze procurement dollars by major categories and services.
- Isolate spend categories for savings opportunities (e.g., high numbers of suppliers, variable procurement practices across divisions).

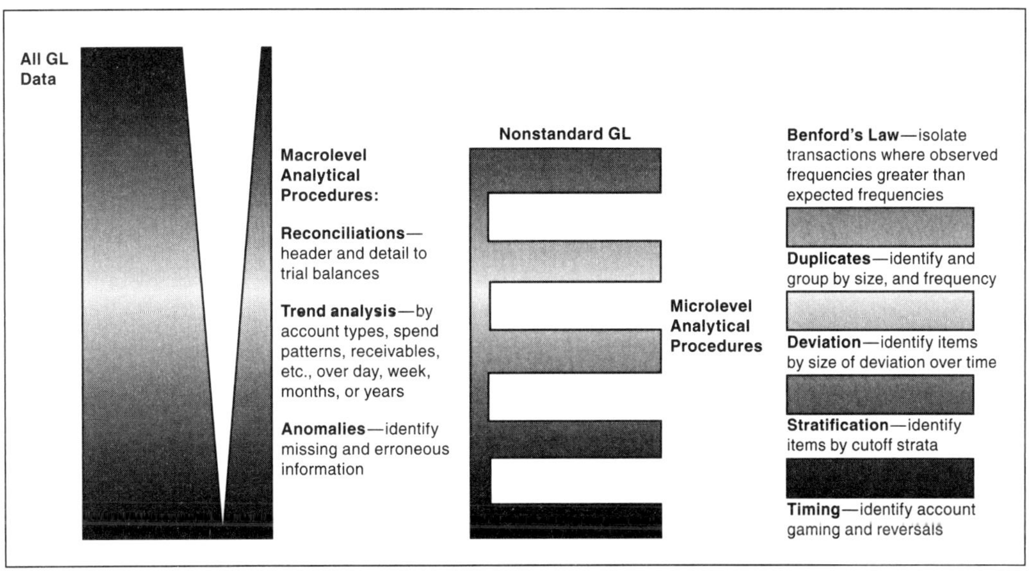

Exhibit 14.13 Macro and Micro Level Analysis

- Identify accelerated payments to vendors where early payment discounts were not taken.

For sales and marketing, you:

- Establish regular monitoring of sales trends by region, division, product, and so on over any interval of time.
- Track key ratios (e.g., sales to accounts receivables, costs per sales dollar, sales force compensation versus sales force performance).
- Generate profitability reports by salesperson.

In customer relationship management, you:

- Segment customers by profit margin, cost, frequency of purchase, and so on.
- Identify customer acquisition and retention costs.
- Perform regression analysis to monitor complex purchasing trends.
- Sample and aggregate customer information via Internet, point-of-sale data, surveys, and the like.

Systems Implementations and Conversions

Populating and re-populating databases, processing data with new application logic, and presenting data with new reports or through new web page layouts are aspects of systems implementations and conversions that should focus a great deal of attention on data quality. With the proper methodology, the data quality aspects associated with implementations and conversions can run smoothly. Business-side personnel affected by implementations and conversions should be able to validate the data related activities of the migration team. Doing so requires a basic understanding of Migration and Conversion Analysis concepts that include:

- The inherent complexities in a data migration process can cause delays in go-live dates and cause these types of population errors in the new system:
    - Missing data
    - Invalid data per field
    - Invalid intrafile relationships per table
    - Invalid interfile relationships across tables
- Additionally, erroneous data may be generated if system interfaces and batch transaction processing design are not managed.
- Understanding of data normalization and standardization methodologies allows you to help in two ways:
    1. Through active participation in the migration
    2. Through post implementation validation of a successful migration
- Your approach should be based on linking the criteria for migration with a normalization and standardization assessment model. (See Exhibit 14.14.)

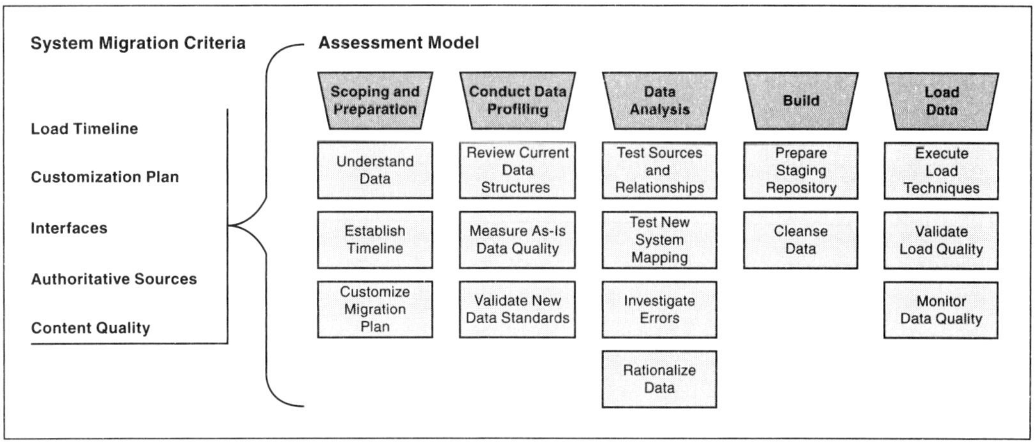

Exhibit 14.14 Systems Migration Criteria and Assessment Model

WHAT TO LOOK FOR IN DATA ANALYSIS TECHNOLOGY

Depending on your project needs, the specific tools you use while conducting data analysis can vary. At all times, you should have an understanding of the tools available for a given project and the pros and cons associated with selecting each tool. Here we provide a sample software strength comparison; it may not be complete due to the changes at data analysis tool provider companies. The points that follow will serve as a useful template as you begin planning your data analysis initiative.

Software Strength Comparison

ACL. ACL is excellent for analyzing individual, large files quickly. It provides you with a nice starter kit of preprogrammed queries and tests. ACL is not efficient or thorough in analyses requiring complex, adaptable, or numerous steps.

SAS. SAS is a best-in-class product. It is designed for analyses requiring numerous, large files with any level of import, processing, and reporting complexity.

IDEA. Idea is billed as "Excel on steroids." It is strong in providing quick summary information on large files—if processing logic is not complex. Logical steps must pass through the database one at a time; this is inefficient.

Access. Access is useful for storing, querying, and displaying relatively static data. For data analysis purposes, it requires use of wizards and complex VBA coding, while not providing a history or log of your activities.

i2 Analyst. The i2 suite was designed with governmental and law enforcement agencies in mind. It is good for visually representing relational data; however, it is weak in handling complex logic and requires piecemeal upgrades for powerful analyses.

PUTTING IT ALL TOGETHER

Take a fresh look at your current approach to data analysis and monitoring. If this program is not formalized or is virtually nonexistent in your organization, set up a meeting with senior management or owners and walkthrough an assessment of where your organization stands in six pivotal areas:

1. Formal and informal experience with data analysis, including experience brought in from previous careers or isolated projects
2. Understanding of data stores and data flows through the company, including personnel understanding and clarity and accuracy of related documentation
3. Status of current data quality
4. Staffing and technology resources
5. Exposure to risks within business activities due to fraud and other process breakdowns
6. Opportunities to enhance decision making based on creating new views of the organization

A discussion of these areas may generate multiple project ideas or one giant initiative, but it is wise to start small. Identify a manageable business area in which to implement a pilot project. The tasks and key steps of that pilot project should be straightforward and should require application of the principles you learned in this chapter.

The primary tasks and key steps of such a pilot project might resemble the plan shown in Exhibit 14.15.

Exhibit 14.15 Sample Project Plan

Tasks	Key Steps
Analyze cross-section of company data to identify useful benchmarking, trending, and exception testing information	1. **Understand data.** Coordinate extraction, identify layout and complexity of data within systems, and measure basic data quality and integrity. 2. **Develop analysis objectives.** Prioritize list of analysis objectives, including trending, benchmarking, and exception testing. 3. **Identify available data analysis tool(s) based on data volume, format, and test complexity.** Compare tools based on such characteristics as power, coding, scalability, price, learning curve, and business need. 4. **Execute analyses and track performance.** Using the available data, execute analyses and produce reports, then determine what additional data would be needed to enhance procedures.
Identify current and new analytical/monitoring procedures that may be automated	1. **Review current analytical/monitoring procedures.** Determine ease and impact of automating various existing procedures. 2. **Identify additional analytical/monitoring procedures.** Identify process review and data analysis procedures to enhance analyses.

Chapter 15

Reporting

Harry Cendrowski and James Martin

INTRODUCTION

Fraud deterrence engagements and Sarbanes-Oxley Section 404 compliance reports typically generate a plethora of data on the intimate details of an organization and its internal control system. While such information is normally viewed and analyzed with respect to the safeguarding of assets, much additional value can be gleaned from these reports.

Specifically, fraud deterrence reports should be viewed as process improvement enablers that guide the organization to increased effectiveness and efficiency. These reports should provide an organization with the information it needs to standardize tasks and increase employee efficiency. Standards from the Institute of Internal Auditors (IIA) and the American Institute of Certified Public Accountants (AICPA) provide general guidance for the fraud deterrence practitioner. It is important to remember, however, that the internal control structure of an organization can vary greatly based on the size and needs of the organization. The report must be tailored to address those needs.

With respect to a fraud investigation, reports that are generated by examiners must be prepared in a way such that they are usable in a litigation setting: They should be free of opinion and errors, impartial, and presented in a timely manner.

This chapter details the function of fraud deterrence reports, a methodology for reporting on internal controls, and the intricacies associated with reporting in investigations.

FUNCTION OF FRAUD DETERRENCE REPORTS

Fraud deterrence engagements are a comprehensive analysis of an organization's internal control processes and an assessment of the readiness of those processes to help safeguard assets and achieve organizational objectives. Given that internal control procedures need to evolve over time to meet new organizational objectives and changing risks, a fraud deterrence engagement report should document the current state of internal control procedures within the organization and provide the road map for process improvement. These engagements should not be viewed as external to an organization's central objectives, but rather as a vehicle that provides a means to achieve such objectives.

While internal controls have historically been responsible for safeguarding assets and minimizing the risks of fraud within a corporation, they are also responsible for defining metrics to achieve business objectives. As such, effective definition of internal controls, and an assessment thereof, is essential in steering the ship toward both financial and operational success.

Fraud deterrence engagements are not only responsible for tracking the effectiveness of internal controls as they relate to the safeguarding of assets, but they also should seek to understand and critically evaluate a firm's internal controls as an overall business best practice. In this manner, fraud deterrence engagements should be performed in lockstep with other corporate-wide initiatives to ensure that the tone at the top, set by management, is communicated and followed by all throughout the organization. In this sense, a fraud deterrence engagement is not another cog in the machine of corporate projects—not a flavor of the month—but rather a holistic, probing process improvement initiative that seeks to benefit the mission and values of a corporation.

In accordance with this objective, it is essential that the reports generated by a fraud deterrence engagement be both easy to understand and actionable. More specifically, reports should provide status-at-a-glance information that the individual who receives the report can affect directly.

In order for an organization to run efficiently, all employees and managers must possess the ability to constantly monitor metrics with ease and celerity. Such a belief is the basis for the Lean Manufacturing concept of the *andon* board and visual management in the manufacturing discipline. Indeed, the Balanced Scorecard movement of the mid-1990s also placed a heavy emphasis on this tenet by guiding managers in producing accurate reports that quickly assessed the organizational health of the firm.

Lean also places a heavy emphasis on the creation of employee-understandable metrics at all levels of the organization. For example, while the chief financial officer of a corporation may pay particular attention to a division's return on assets (ROA), such a metric has no tangible meaning for an equipment operator working in one of the division's plants. However, ROA can effectively be translated to the shop floor through the creation of a series of metrics, such as first-time-through quality rate and equipment changeover time, that the employee can directly effect.

In a similar manner, the control procedures identified in a fraud deterrence engagement must be captured in a way to provide value and direction to the organization at all levels. This model is a guide for the modern view of internal controls and sets a challenge for the reporting process.

When a fraud deterrence engagement is initiated, it is essential that the service provider clearly define its scope and future deliverables to senior management. If an engagement is to focus solely on a division of a corporation, or a particular entity, this should be explicitly outlined in the engagement letter. Such a practice will safeguard the deterrence analyst from litigation in the event that fraudulent activity occurs in an area of the organization not defined in the project scope.

Moreover, when an engagement is first kicked off to the organization, it is essential that both senior and midlevel management be present at this preliminary meeting. Adherence to this protocol will serve to ease tension between deterrence analysts and employees of the contracting organization and allow midlevel managers to better understand the importance of the engagement.

In a high percentage of engagements, an analyst typically finds many discrepancies between corporate policies and the actual, daily practices followed by employees. For this reason, the kickoff meeting must address the fact that the fraud deterrence engagement is designed for the betterment of the organization and that thoughts should be shared candidly with those performing the assessment. Meeting participants should also state that there will be no backlash for voicing honest opinions and that individuals will not be "called out" in any communications with management.

While the high-level management of an organization is responsible for setting the tone at the top, midlevel managers must play a key role in defining control procedures and activities that mitigate risks facing individual business units. Such a practice often proves quite challenging for many businesses because these midlevel managers are frequently individuals who are already overloaded with the daily grind of their jobs. They may view a fraud deterrence initiative as unworthy of their time unless an evaluation of their job performance is tied specifically to this issue.

Nonetheless, midlevel managers are essential in effecting changes recommended by a fraud deterrence analysis. For example, the manager of the accounts payable department is in the best position within the organization to understand the risks facing that unit and the control procedures best suited to minimizing those risks and achieving the department's objectives. He or she is also the most qualified individual to institute and monitor recommendations elaborated in a fraud deterrence report.

While much microlevel detail is contained within a report, it is important to remember that this document presents only a static image of a dynamic process: As business processes and procedures change over time, so too should the internal controls utilized by the organization. After the conclusion of a fraud deterrence analysis, it is ultimately the organization's midlevel managers who will be responsible for ensuring that appropriate changes are made to the internal control system and that these changes are tracked in a satisfactory manner.

Many employees throughout the reaches of an organization do not see their jobs as an amalgamation of standardized processes that need to be optimized for the benefit of the corporation. However, a fraud deterrence engagement documents the tasks and performance levels required to achieve an objective and the performance gaps that could allow an undesirable outcome.

Indeed, both fraud deterrence engagements and Section 404 compliance necessitate the creation of detailed databases that are brimming with knowledge about the current state of standardized practices within an organization. Rather than let this valuable information go to waste, organizations should use these reports, and their electronic counterparts, as a basis for the measurement of all jobs and tasks throughout the firm.

This information could also be used as a training manual for new employees who will replace other individuals, providing them with guidance on the current procedures employed within the department. In this manner, the unwritten, "tribal knowledge" each employee solely possesses is minimized by the wealth of information generated by the fraud deterrence analysis.

REPORTING ON INTERNAL CONTROL

Reports generated by fraud deterrence and Section 404 compliance engagements are comprehensive and often quite lengthy. It is therefore imperative that the author develop a coding scheme to convey key information in a status-at-a-glance manner, so that a reader may quickly assess the current status of an internal control system.

At the inception of a fraud deterrence engagement, process flowcharts should be created for all areas of the organization included within the scope of the engagement. Flowcharts are complex tools that convey large amounts of information in an easy-to-read format.

The first step in the creation of a flowchart is to identify key tasks within a given corporate process. Flowcharts should pictorially detail all steps within this process and include task-level detail on the roles and responsibilities each staff member has for every task. Once a flowchart has been created, a practitioner can move to analyzing the current status of the internal control system within each unit of the organization.

When evaluating a business entity's internal controls, it is important to first define the risks, control objectives, current control status, and recommendations associated with control improvements to management in a detailed manner. This information should be recorded for each task within a given corporate process. Exhibit 15.1 presents an example of the information that should be included in a fraud deterrence report. (Note that this example pertains to an analysis of internal controls within a financial reporting process.)

In this example, FR-020-010 corresponds to a specific task associated with the input of journal transactions, process FR-020. With respect to this task within a process, the current status of the control is documented, along with a detailed recommendation for improvement.

Over the course of a fraud deterrence engagement, hundreds of such records on control objectives, current control status, and recommendations will be documented. This assimilated data provides a valuable, paper-based microcosm of the organization itself.

Once all data have been compiled, it is the responsibility of the practitioner to assemble a report that largely focuses on the control gaps present within an organization.

The creation of such a report facilitates the implementation of standardized procedures within the organization, as detailed, task-level information is created and analyzed by the practitioner. While the responsibility for implementing recommendations ultimately rests with corporate officials, a report on internal controls should be prepared in a manner (such as that shown in Exhibit 15.1) that permits simple and immediate implementation of outlined recommendations.

When preparing a report, it is often best to parse the document into sections tailored directly to specific audiences: senior managers, midlevel managers, supervisors, and employees. A detailed executive summary that highlights all pertinent findings and conclusions should also be provided.

Exhibit 15.1 Sample Information for Inclusion in a Fraud Deterrence Report

Reference	Task	Risk	Control Objective	Current Control	Recommendation
FR-020	Input journal transactions	Unauthorized or inappropriate transactions may be posted and not detected.			
FR-020.1			Journals are reviewed by management and approved prior to entry to the system.	Discrete journal entries are not actually prepared; accounting clerks enter activity directly into general journal for posting. When all the current month activity has been accumulated, the journal is posted.	Develop procedures to document discrete journal entries and obtain management approval prior to posting ledger.

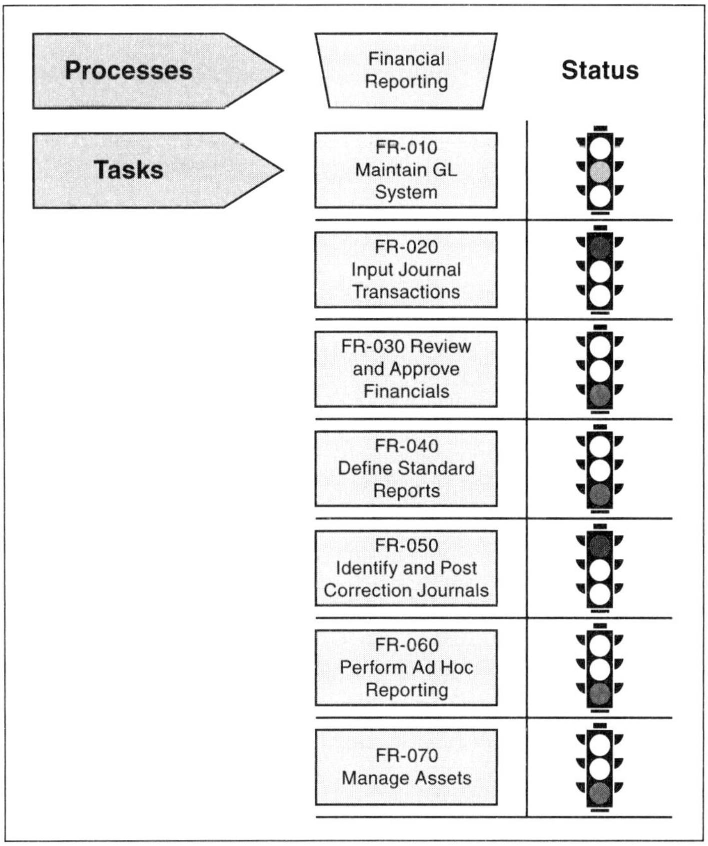

Exhibit 15.2 Sample Report on Overall Process Internal Control Status

After all tasks for a given process have been analyzed in detail, a practitioner should then comment on the status of internal controls for each task. Exhibit 15.2 presents a simple method for reporting the aggregate status of internal controls for each task.

The "traffic light" method allows readers to easily see areas that require: immediate attention (denoted by red lights), eventual attention (denoted by yellow lights), and little attention (denoted by green lights). The use of this methodology allows managers within the organization to visually determine which areas contain large deficiencies in the internal control system that require immediate focus. Note that an analyst should not state that an area requires "no attention." Such a practice would provide easy ammunition for a prosecuting attorney should an opportunity for fraud be exploited in a "green light" area.

Furthermore, when preparing a report, the practitioner should remember to employ a coding method that preserves a desired message when the document is faxed or photocopied—that is, use of color alone is not a sufficient coding method. For this reason, a redundant scheme should be employed that conveys information in at least two different ways. For example, the traffic light methodology uses both color and position to accurately depict meaning.

AICPA Standard AT Section 501, "Reporting on an Entity's Internal Control over Financial Reporting," specifies content that should be included in reports speaking to the effectiveness of an entity's internal control over financial reporting. This standard provides guidance for the fraud deterrence practitioner, as it reiterates several important points about management's responsibility and the limits of a practitioner. These points include:

- Indications about the independence of the practitioner
- An identification of the subject matter (internal control over financial reporting) and the scope of the engagement together with any limitations
- A statement that management is responsible for maintaining effective internal control over financial reporting
- A paragraph stating that, because of the inherent limitations present in any internal control system, misstatements due to errors or fraud may occur and without detection (The paragraph also should state that projections of any evaluation of internal control over financial reporting to future periods are subject to the risk that internal control may become inadequate because of changes in conditions or because the degree of compliance with the policies or procedures may deteriorate.)
- The manual or printed signature of the practitioner's firm
- The date of the examination report

The standard also indicates that management eventually must conclude that the system of internal controls is either adequate or inadequate, while the practitioner, in the case of an AT 501 engagement, only issues an opinion on management's conclusion.

To reiterate, the practitioner should not reach a conclusion about the adequacy of controls in a report: This is purely a management responsibility. If a practitioner chooses to opine on this issue, he or she is assuming tremendous liability.

REPORTING IN AN INVESTIGATION

Reports generated at the conclusion of an investigation should provide the reader with information on the evidence gathered by the examiner. The report must convey all facts of possible relevance to the investigation including information on: interviews, dates, names, and supporting information for findings, while showing no bias either toward or against the subject of a fraudulent act.

A report must be checked ad nauseam for careless errors and inaccuracies, as the inclusion of either can render it effectively useless in a court of law: Such errors will introduce questions about the capability and qualification of the examiner and, moreover, the care with which the examiner follows his or her own investigative processes.

Furthermore, under no circumstances should the examiner prepare a communication with the idea that the information will not be disclosed to adverse third parties. A fraud report will be widely disseminated, especially in the event of litigation, with reviewers most likely including:

- Company insiders
- Internal legal counsel
- External legal counsel
- Insurance carriers
- Defendant

- Defendant's legal counsel
- Judge
- Mediator
- Jury
- Defendant's expert witness

To this end, a report must be authored in a clear, concise manner while at the same time being brief. To accomplish this goal, an examiner should try to limit the use of long sentences in his or her writing. An attempt should be made to curtail phrases that exceed 20 words in length. Use of the Flesch Reading Test may help the examiner in achieving this goal.[i]

Words that intensify sentence meaning (i.e.: obviously, reasonably, prudent, significant, etc.) should also be avoided. Use of such words may raise questions in litigation, such as "Who defines what is 'prudent'?" or "What is meant by 'significant'?"

In addition, reports prepared for litigation must not list any opinions of the examiner. Rather, they must elaborate on specific conclusions drawn from an analysis of the evidence. Failure to adhere to this guideline could allow an opposing attorney to demonstrate that an examiner was biased in his or her analysis and possibly lead to the dismissal of an expert witness.

If multiple interviews are performed within an investigation, it is essential that the notes from these activities be transcribed contemporaneously and that each interview proceed in a similar manner. Adherence to such a practice will show impartiality on the part of the examiner and illustrate the objective thought process employed in analyzing the case either for or against a fraudulent activity.

For instance, examiners should develop a list of questions, take frequent notes, and even use the same room, if possible, for all interviews. Notes from the interview should be transcribed quickly, in accordance with a set protocol—usually within 24 hours of the interview.

Furthermore, given the potential broad audience of a report, technical terms within the document should be explained in detail and industry jargon should be avoided.

Pictorial representations and schematics should be used throughout the report in order to clearly diagram situations to a reader unaccustomed with the situation or one who lacks knowledge of core business principles. Such representations will allow a reader to better understand the events that occurred up to that point to the examiner's conclusion.

Moreover, reports should not in any way contain editorial or judgmental information, as the report is a reflection of an *objective* assessment of historical information.

The concluding date of an examination should also be enumerated within the report, in the event that a fraudulent activity occurs between the time an engagement concludes and a report is presented.

Numerous professional standards outline procedures associated with the reporting of fraud investigation-related results. For instance, the Institute of Internal Auditors' Practice Advisory 1210.A2-2 highlights four key points with respect to reports centered on fraud[2]:

1. A draft of the proposed final communications on fraud should be submitted to legal counsel for review. In cases where the organization is able to invoke client privilege, and has chosen to do so, the report must be addressed to legal counsel.
2. When the incidents of significant fraud, or erosion of trust, have been established to a reasonable certainty, senior management and the board of directors should be notified immediately.
3. The results of a fraud investigation may indicate that fraud may have had a previously undiscovered adverse effect on the organization's financial position and its operational results for

one or more years for which financial statements have already been issued. Senior management and the board of directors should be informed of such a discovery.

4. A written report or other formal communication should be issued at the conclusion of the investigation phase. It should include the basis for beginning an investigation, time frames, observations, conclusions, resolution, and corrective action taken (or recommendations) to improve controls.

Depending on how the investigation was resolved, the report may need to be written in a manner that provides confidentiality to some of the people involved. The content of this report is sensitive, and it must meet the needs of the board of directors and management, while complying with legal requirements and restrictions and company policies and procedures.

In essence, this excerpt from the Practice Advisory reiterates points that are somewhat obvious to a seasoned fraud examiner, but nonetheless, highly important. In particular, it is imperative that, should "incidents of significant fraud" be "established to a reasonable certainty," these results must be promptly communicated to senior management and the board of directors. As these individuals are ultimately responsible for setting the tone of the organization, such findings require immediate reporting in order for remediation to begin. Furthermore, this advisory reminds the examiner that fraud may have wide-ranging, adverse implications for historical financial statements. Hence, senior management and the board of directors should be promptly alerted of fraud.

Beyond this, the advisory simply states that a formal report "should be issued at the conclusion of the investigation phase" and that a copy of this proposed, final communication should be submitted to "legal counsel for review." This last point raises the natural question of what to include in a fraud deterrence report and how to format it. Unfortunately, there is no ubiquitous answer to this question. Instead, when preparing a final report on fraud deterrence, one must first address the needs and wants of the client in order for it to be of utmost value to the organization.

There are also several AICPA standards that provide guidance to examiners in preparing fraud-related reports for investigations. These are, most notably, AICPA Consulting Services Special Reports 93-1 and 93-2 and Consulting Services Practice Aid 96-3 and 97-1.

Consulting Services Special Report 93-1 lays forth these essential points for CPAs involved in reporting results of a fraud investigation:

- In attestation engagements, the opinion of the CPA firm is expressed. In litigation engagements, the individual practitioner is the expert expressing an opinion.
- This naturally limits the degree of leverage that can be used in the engagement, and the preparation of the report.
- Depending on the understanding (agreement) between the CPA and client, the CPA may or may not need to provide a conclusion or written report at the end of the engagement. Standard reporting formats are impractical and unrealistic because of the diversity of those engagements.
- As discussed, however, a report should still be prepared for the practitioner's records.

Consulting Services Special Report 93-2 states that a CPA who is engaged as an expert witness does not serve as an advocate for the client. Instead, the CPA is presented to the trier of fact (i.e., the judge or jury) as someone with specialized knowledge, training, and experience in a particular area who will represent positions in an objective manner.

Consulting Services Practice Aid 96-3 discusses the minimum elements that must be included in a report submitted under Rule 26 (a)(2)(B) of the Federal Rules of Civil Procedure. It also includes a discussion of these report elements for experts to consider: table of contents, executive summary, introduction and background, objectives of the engagement, assumptions, and references.

Perhaps the most important and crucial piece of a written report is the executive summary, as it succinctly details the overall motivations, findings, results, and conclusion presented in the report in a brief format.

Consulting Services Practice Aid 97-1 enumerates these essential points regarding the presentation of results from fraud investigations:

- The information included in a report may vary depending on the needs of the client and the client's attorney.
- The format of the report can vary from a short letter or memorandum to the client to an affidavit or similar written declaration to a very detailed report.
- Besides the items commonly included in any litigation services report, a fraud investigation report may include a statement of predication, a list of the interviews conducted, and a summary of interview information.
- The CPA should avoid stating any conclusions about the presence or absence of fraud.

Aside from the formal reports prepared for an investigation, it is also essential that an expert be well versed in the techniques of witnessing and forensic accounting, should an investigation end in litigation.

There are five Federal Rules of Evidence (FRE) that an examiner should keep in mind when preparing for a fraud litigation, FRE 702 through 706. However, FRE 702 is particularly important, as it effectively permits judges to act as "gatekeepers" for expert testimony. More specifically, this rule allows judges to exclude expert testimony should they find it does not adhere to this specification: a "witness qualified as an expert . . . may testify thereto in the form of an opinion or otherwise, if (1) the testimony is based upon sufficient facts or data, (2) the testimony is the product of reliable principles and methods, and (3) the witness has applied the principles and methods reliably to the facts of the case."[3]

Rule 702 requires that expert testimony must provide insight on subjects outside the understanding of the average layperson and that the witness testifying to the evidence must possess significant knowledge, skill, experience, training, or education in the subject of testimony.

In the 1993 United States Supreme Court decision *Daubert v. Merrell Dow Pharmaceuticals, Inc.,* the Court mandated that, prior to a trial, a judge must determine whether expert testimony will be admitted. It is important to note that many experts are denied admission based on a judge's pretrial decision. According to *Daubert on the Web,* experts had an admissibility rate of 60 percent through June 2006, when the trial was classified by the Web site as pertaining to "Accountants and Economists."[4]

It is therefore, extremely important that experts consider these four *Daubert* factors when analyzing evidence:

1. Whether the theory or technique in question can be (and has been) tested
2. Whether it has been subjected to peer review and publication
3. Its known or potential error rate
4. Whether it has attracted "widespread acceptance within a relevant scientific community"[5]

If experts do not adhere to these guidelines in formulating an opinion with respect to a fraud litigation, they run the risk of being denied admission or legally challenged by the opposing attorney. To this end, Figlewicz and Sprohge outline 10 guidelines aimed at helping experts avoid legal challenges[6]:

1. Know the relevant professional standards.
2. Apply the relevant professional standards.
3. Know the relevant professional literature.
4. Know the relevant professional organizations.
5. Use generally accepted analytical methods.
6. Use multiple analytical methods.
7. Synthesize the conclusions of multiple analytical methods.
8. Disclose all significant analytical assumptions and variables.
9. Subject the analysis to peer review.
10. Test the analysis—and the conclusions—for reasonableness.

Aside from these guidelines, an expert witness must remember to refrain from the use of words such as "always," and "never" in both testimony and reports, as such a practice could leave portions of testimony vulnerable to cross examination.

IMPORTANCE OF DOCUMENTATION

While in most instances an examiner will be asked to prepare a report that summarizes key conclusions and activities he or she performed, this is sometimes not the case. Occasionally those who request a fraud deterrence assessment will state that the generation of a report is outside of the scope of the engagement. Even though this may be stated to the examiner, it is nonetheless imperative for him or her to prepare a report, complete with all work papers, in the event that litigation arises in the future. The examiner does not need to disseminate this report, but it should be kept in a safe, accessible place should the activities of the engagement ever come into question.

Within this report should be specific details on the scope of the engagement, the services performed, and the conclusions reported to management. All transcripts from interviews, information on evidence collected, and conclusions based on the evidence should be thoroughly discussed within this document. This information should be based on facts and not opinions.

This internal document is important for two reasons:

1. It provides the examiner with a record of the engagement to refer to should the client request additional information.
2. It serves as a legal document in the event that litigation arises against the examiner

Let us suppose that a fraud deterrence engagement was performed and the client did not request a formal report detailing the engagement's activities. If a fraudulent activity were to occur after the engagement concluded, the examiner could be held legally responsible if the prosecuting attorney was able to show that an examiner failed to identify an opportunity for fraud—even if the fraudulent activity occurred in an area outside of the engagement's scope. Without thorough documentation of the services requested and performed, an examiner leaves him- or herself open to significant liability. This problem can be remedied simply by authoring a report that includes the aforementioned information.

CONCLUSION

In sum, the information generated by fraud deterrence and Section 404 compliance engagements provides an organization with a wealth of information. If used effectively, this information can serve to improve the operational efficiency of the organization.

When preparing a report, the practitioner should attempt to convey information in a status-at-a-glance manner. Adherence to such a practice will allow time-constrained managers to quickly glean information from the report and effect changes based on its recommendations.

With respect to reporting in an investigation, an examiner must ensure that his or her report presents an *objective* assessment of historical information and contains no bias. To this end, several IIA and AICPA standards provide guidance for the creation of reports centered on investigation.

Furthermore, even though a client may deem a formal report to be outside the scope of an engagement, the creation of such a document is necessary to protect the examiner from liability.

NOTES

1. Rudolf Flesch, "How to Write in Plain English." Available at:www.mang.canterbury.ac.nz/writing_guide/writing/flesch.shtml.
2. Institute of Internal Auditors' Practice Advisory 1210.A2-2. Available at: www.theiia.org/index.cfm-?doc_id=73.
3. Federal Rules of Evidence 702. Available at: www.law.cornell.edu/rules/fre/rules.htm#Rule702.
4. www.daubertontheweb.com/accountants.htm.
5 .509 U.S. 579, 113 SCt 2786 (1993).
6. R. E. Figlewicz. and H. D. Sprohge. "The CPA's Expert Witness Role in Litigation Services: A Maze of Legal and Accounting Standards," *Ohio CPA Journal* (July-September 2002): 35.

Section III

Applications of Fraud Deterrence

Chapter 16

Deterring Fraudulent Financial Reporting and Asset Misappropriation

Harry Cendrowski and Louis W. Petro

INTRODUCTION

Deterrence is the first step in the eight-step fraud management life cycle described by Wesley Kenneth Wilhelm, Strategic Planning Manager at Fair Isaac Company.[1] Wilhelm defines deterrence as "the stopping of fraud before it happens." He notes: "[D]eterrence is characterized by actions and activities intended to stop or prevent fraud before it is attempted; to turn aside or discourage even the attempt at fraud through, for example, card activation programs."

Asset misappropriation, often referred to as employee fraud, consists of theft and/or embezzlement. The most common theft target is cash. Other targets are inventories, property, plant and equipment, and investments. Misappropriation involves such things as billing, accounts receivable, and disbursement manipulations, and payroll frauds (ghost employees and ghost time). This type of fraud results in a direct gain; the perpetrator receives cash or some other asset of value that can be used to satisfy their motive for fraud.

Fraudulent financial reporting, a type of management fraud, involves the intentional misstatement of financial position, results of operations, cash flows, or financial statement footnotes for the purpose of misleading financial statement users. These misstatements typically result in an indirect gain, such as a raise, bonus, or perquisite based on the rosy, yet fictional performance. For this reason, the compelling reason to misstate the financials is often described as an "incentive" or "pressure."

Deterrence of fraudulent financial and asset misappropriation reporting involves four different types of policies and procedures:

1. Organizational (corporate) culture
2. Organizational (corporate) governance
3. Internal controls for deterrence
4. Deterrence monitoring

ORGANIZATIONAL (CORPORATE) CULTURE

Corporate culture, beginning with the tone at the top, is the primary ingredient in the deterrence of fraudulent financial reporting. It provides the umbrella under which all financial reporting activities take place. The corporate culture consists of:

- The ethical environment
- Realistic goals and objectives
- Corporate policies and procedures
- Communication procedures
- Internal controls

Ethical Environment

The ethical environment for an organization begins with the publication of a corporate code of ethics. An effective code of ethics should cover four areas:

1. Competence
2. Objectivity
3. Integrity
4. Confidentiality

Competence. Competence means that all personnel have the skill levels and expertise needed to effectively and efficiently handle their job responsibilities. Management must be familiar with relevant laws, regulations, and professional reporting standards relevant to their organization. Competence requires management to recognize their professional limitations and constraints on their judgment that might hinder effective performance. They need to know when outside expertise may be required.

Employees must be familiar with the policies and procedures needed to carry out their job responsibilities.

Objectivity. Objectivity requires an independent mental attitude. It is the ability to handle facts or conditions without perceptual distortions caused by prejudices, feelings, or preconceived ideas.

Integrity. Integrity, or trustworthiness, consists primarily of the avoidance of any conflicts of interest, both real and apparent. Both employees and management should avoid conduct that might prevent them from acting ethically as well as conduct that might discredit the organization. Integrity should be a concern in external relationships with customers, suppliers, investors, creditors, insurers, and auditors as well as in internal relationships.

Confidentiality. Organizational information and data should, in general, be kept confidential. Confidence should be breached only when authorized as appropriate by management or by law. Management and employees should not use confidential information for illegal or unethical purposes.

The corporate code of ethics should be publicly displayed in the organization. Its importance should be communicated to all personnel. A confidential ethics hotline should be available to all personnel in the organization. Personnel should be able to anonymously report any ethical concerns, including those related to accounting, internal controls, and financial reporting, as well as theft and embezzlement, through the hotline. The hotline should be either to the organization's board-level audit committee or to an outside organization. The audit committee should be independent of the organization's management.

Realistic Goals and Objectives

The fraud triangle discussed in Chapter 5 consists of motive, opportunity, and rationalization. The motives and rationalizations for fraudulent financial reporting are directly affected by organizational goals and objectives. If management perceives financial reporting goals as unreasonable, it may be motivated to distort financial records and reports so as to attain them. The motivation is particularly strong if management's evaluation and pay are based on meeting financial targets, such as income or earnings per share (EPS). Management rationalizes fraudulent behavior by saying things as:

- "We are so close to the target."
- "Our actions will increase shareholder value."
- "This company would be nothing without me. I built it."
- "The financial reports are merely 'window dressing.' We have a solid business."

The setting, by participative management or by some version of management by objectives (MBO), would ease the motivation to alter financial records and reports.

The motives and rationalizations for asset misappropriation are different from those for fraudulent financial reporting. The primary motive is a compelling need for funds. The need is usually driven by family problems, lifestyle desires, substance and/or gambling addiction, or some short-term cash need. These motives are not affected by the goals and objectives placed on employees. Pay for performance programs, however, if not properly designed and monitored, can motivate employee fraud. For example, a piecework, or piece-rate, production worker payment scheme may encourage employees to falsify production counts and/or attempt to include defective output with good output. Piecework systems require careful design, implementation, and monitoring to prevent employee abuse. Pay for performance systems based on group efforts and outputs tend to be less prone to fraud.

Corporate Policies and Procedures

Corporate policies and procedures should include a code of ethics or professional conduct, as noted earlier, as well as an anonymous issue reporting channel (hotline) and an effective internal control system base on the Committee of Sponsoring Organizations (COSO) model. The COSO model is mandated for publicly held corporations by the 2002 Sarbanes-Oxley Act (SOX). The COSO model is covered in Chapter 9.

Communication Procedures

As noted earlier, public companies are required to maintain an anonymous reporting facility that protects the identity of the person reporting the issue. Tips from internal and external sources are an excellent way to reveal fraud and misconduct within an organization, and the anonymity of the reporting channel should help potential tipsters come forward. An effective hotline requires:

- Anonymity for users
- A culture encouraging its use
- Policies regarding acceptable and unacceptable behavior
- Policies regarding the handling and retaining of hotline submissions
- Accessibility

Effective hotlines are an important tool in the deterrence of fraudulent financial reporting. Additionally, Section 806 of the Sarbanes-Oxley act defined "whistleblower protection" that prohibits any adverse action against anyone for performing a lawful act. This section of Sarbanes-Oxley covers all employees, officers, contractors, subcontractors of any organization, not just employees of public companies. This was included in Sarbanes-Oxley to allow employees to feel comfortable in revealing a situation of fraud or misstatement within their company.

Internal Controls

The control environment, the first component of the COSO model covered in Chapter 9, is the most effective deterrent to fraudulent financial reporting. The control environment deals with the tone at the top. In particular, it covers:

- Management philosophy and style
- Employee competence and integrity
- A code of ethics or professional conduct
- Personnel policies and procedures
- An independent board-level audit committee
- An internal audit function reporting to the audit committee

The control environment is the most important internal control deterrence of fraudulent financial reporting.

ORGANIZATIONAL (CORPORATE) GOVERNANCE

Corporate governance requirements that help deter fraudulent financial reporting include:

- Audit committees
- Chief executive officer (CEO)/chief financial officer (CFO) certifications
- Insider trading rules
- Codes of ethics

These requirements are included in Sarbanes-Oxley.

Audit Committees

SOX mandates an audit committee for publicly held corporations. The SOX requirements have been proposed for not-for-profit organizations by the United States Senate Finance Committee. The audit committee is to be made up of financially literate nonmanagement directors. At least one of the directors is to be a designated financial expert. The criteria for the designated financial expert are that he or she:

- Understands generally accepted accounting principles (GAAP) and financial statements
- Is an expert in the preparation and audit of financial statements for a comparable organization
- Is an expert in internal controls
- Understands audit committee functions

The audit committee functions consist of:

- Approving the selection of the external auditor (certified public accountant [CPA])
- Interacting with the external auditor
- Determining external auditor compensation
- Overseeing the external auditor's work
- Resolving audit disputes and disagreements
- Overseeing the internal audit function

The external auditor is required to report to the audit committee. The director of the organization's internal audit function should report to the audit committee. These standards of audit committee makeup and role – required for public companies -are considered by many to be the "best practice" standard for all organizations, not just public companies. These standards have been shown to be an effective deterrent of fraudulent financial reporting

CEO/CFO Certifications

Sarbanes-Oxley mandates the CEO and CFO of publicly held corporations certify two things.

1. They certify that the financial statements have been reviewed and, that to the best of their knowledge, the financial statements are free from material misstatement and that the financial statements fairly present in accordance with GAAP or other appropriate reporting criteria.
2. The CEO and CFO certify management's responsibility for establishing and maintaining the internal control system and that the internal control system has been evaluated within 90 days and whether the system is effective.

Effectiveness is compromised if there are one or more material weaknesses in the internal control system. Failure to certify or false certification may result in criminal penalties—fines and/or imprisonment.

Insider Trading Rules

SOX has shortened to 48 hours the time allowed between the execution of and reporting to the Securities and Exchange Commission (SEC) of an insider stock trade made by the management of a publicly held company. The pre-SOX rules allowed the trader to delay reporting of the sale or purchase until the 10th of the month following the month in which the sale or purchase occurred. This would allow as many as 41 days between execution and reporting. In addition, the act generally prohibits insider trading during a corporation's pension plan blackout periods. Blackout periods, also called lockdown or transition periods, occur when the plan participant's ability to take certain actions is temporarily curtailed.

Codes of Ethics

The Sarbanes Oxley Act requires publicly held corporations to have a code of ethics for senior financial officers. The corporation is required to disclose whether, and if not, the reason why not, that the corporation has adopted such a code. The act also requires immediate disclosure to the SEC of any change in or waiver of the code of ethics for senior financial officers.

INTERNAL CONTROLS FOR DETERRENCE

Since the upper levels of management can override the internal control system, normal internal controls are not a very effective deterrent of fraudulent financial reporting. What is required is a proper tone at the top, as discussed earlier organizational/corporate governance. It is imperative that the board of directors and the audit committee be reasonably sure that such a tone exists. The considerations discussed under governance, if implemented and monitored, would help provide for the proper tone, a tone that is conducive to the deterrence of fraudulent financial reporting.

Internal controls to help deter asset misappropriation should follow the COSO model. The COSO model describes six control activities relating to the safeguarding of assets and authorized, complete, accurate, and timely financial reporting:

1. The assignment of authority and responsibility
2. A system of management authorizations
3. The maintenance of adequate accounting records
4. A system of independent verifications
5. The limiting of access to assets
6. The proper separation of the incompatible duties.

There are four incompatible duties:

1. Transaction authorization
2. Transaction execution
3. Transaction recording
4. Custody of assets

DETERRENCE MONITORING

There are two critical elements to the effective monitoring of fraudulent financial reporting: an effective board of directors and an effective internal audit function.

An effective board of directors is one made up primarily of competent, involved, active, nonmanagement directors. The chair of the board should not be the CEO. The board should meet regularly and be aware of the financial and reporting issues facing the organization. There should be a board-level audit committee structured and operating as described in the Sarbanes-Oxley Act and discussed earlier in the chapter.

Internal audit is an independent, objective assurance and consulting activity designed to add value to and to improve an organization's operations. It helps the organization accomplish its objectives by evaluating and helping to improve the effectiveness and efficiency of risk management, internal control, and organization governance processes. The internal audit department reporting to the audit committee should be staffed with competent internal auditors. Competence is often evidenced by certification as a Certified Internal Auditor (CIA), Certified Information Systems Auditor (CISA), Certified Fraud Examiner (CFE), or CPA. In addition, internal auditors should have relevant organizational auditing experience.

The internal audit department should have a charter covering:

- The scope and authority of the internal audit function
- The needs and desires of the audit committee
- The establishment of objectivity and organizational independence
- The operation of the internal audit function

The internal audit function should have the authority to access the assets, records, and personnel needed to carry out its responsibility. Internal audit responsibility is defined by the scope articulated in the internal audit charter. The scope defines the areas within the bounds of internal audit responsibility. The areas to be considered in the scope are:

- Risk management
- Compliance with laws, regulations, contracts, policies, and procedures
- Financial reporting integrity
- Safeguarding assets
- Effective and efficient use of resources

The internal audit function should be accountable to the audit committee. If the audit committee is composed of nonmanagement directors, such accountability provides the organizational independence needed for objectivity. Accountability should cover items such as the costs and quality of internal audits as well as the quantity of audits and the time spent on them. Regarding the deterrence of fraudulent financial reporting, the internal audit function should, in effect, be, through the audit committee, the eyes and ears of the board of directors.

NOTE

1. Wesley Kenneth Wilhelm, "The Fraud Management Lifecycle Theory: A Holistic Approach to Fraud Management," *Journal of Economic Crime Management* 2, no. 2 (Spring 2004).

Chapter 17

Fraud and the Bankruptcy Code

Robert A. Weisberg, Lawrence A. Lichtman, Christopher A. Grosman, and Patrick J. Kukla

INTRODUCTION

President George W. Bush commented when signing the Bankruptcy Abuse Prevention and Consumer Protection Act of 2005 ("Bankruptcy Abuse Act") that, in part, this new law was designed to stop those who "try to commit fraud" and to "clamp down on bankruptcy mills" that advise abusers on how to "game the system."[1] The United States Bankruptcy Code (the "Bankruptcy Code") and related statutes have historically included numerous devices for punishment and prevention of fraud. The Bankruptcy Abuse Act added provisions to address how claims of fraud may be treated in bankruptcy as well as expanded liability for fraud in the context of a bankruptcy filing. Because bankruptcy often is used as a device to escape liability, it is critical to understand its workings when seeking recompense for fraudulent acts. This chapter discusses and analyzes both new and historical provisions of the Bankruptcy Code that are designed to identify and prevent fraud.

There is a perception, in the mind of the general public, that many debtors are abusing the bankruptcy process through criminally fraudulent activity. Evidently this perception is shared by both the Unites States Congress, which in 2005 passed the Bankruptcy Abuse Act, and by President Bush, who signed the act into law. The Bankruptcy Abuse Act represented government's attempt to eliminate a perceived abuse of the Bankruptcy Code, fraudulent or otherwise.[2]

In the public's mind, corporate "crooks" are abusing the bankruptcy laws at the expense of innocent creditors, investors, employees, and retirees. This belief has been fueled by the media coverage of recent bankruptcy filings of several large, billion-dollar corporations, including Enron and WorldCom.

This intense media focus and the unfortunate and dire consequences of these large corporate bankruptcy cases have fostered the public's negative perception of both corporate America and the bankruptcy process. "Enron-type" bankruptcies and the attendant criminal prosecutions provide the public, which is largely uninformed as to the intricacies of bankruptcy fraud and the bankruptcy process in general, with the impression that abuses are rampant and that the bankruptcy courts protect the perpetrators of bad acts.

In 2001, "Enron ranked seventh on the Fortune 500 list of America's largest corporations in 2001, and was, by all appearances, an immensely successful and profitable company."[3] By

Note: The authors gratefully acknowledge the invaluable contribution of Jason C. Seewer, Esq., without whose assistance the successful completion of this chapter would not have been possible.

December 2001, however, Enron had dramatically and quite unexpectedly filed for bankruptcy protection. How could a billion-dollar, publicly traded corporation, which showed a prosperous balance sheet, be reduced to bankruptcy in less than one year? During the bankruptcy case, it was revealed that Enron had concealed tens of billions of dollars in debt through the use of "off–balance sheet" partnerships and other accounting irregularities.[4] The Enron bankruptcy had a devastating effect on countless groups of people, including the company's creditors, shareholders, and employees (whose retirement plans consisted largely of Enron stock, which was rendered worthless).

What impact did Enron's bankruptcy case have on any claims against Enron of fraud? Fraud claims against corporations in bankruptcy do not receive preferred treatment over general trade claims. Presumably, without a bankruptcy filing, any value in Enron's business and assets may have been lost to the detriment of various creditor groups. The public may have been left with the impression that somehow a bankruptcy filing is a device used to protect wrongful acts. Bankruptcy, however, does not facilitate fraud. In fact, it protects against a "feeding frenzy" on a fixed asset pool available to pay claims. It may also make it easier to recover damages due to fraud.

As provided in the Bankruptcy Code, bankruptcy proceedings can be in the form of a reorganization for either businesses or individuals (Chapter 11), a repayment plan for individuals limited by debt and asset ceilings (Chapter 13), or a straight liquidation of nonexempt assets for businesses or individuals (Chapter 7). Each of these chapters incorporates various provisions relating to acts of fraud committed both prior to and in conjunction with the bankruptcy filing.

Bankruptcy is often thought of as a device to escape or reduce one's financial obligations, and in some instances this view is accurate. The Bankruptcy Code, however, also enhances the prospect of recovery for victims of fraud, while substantially limiting the ability of debtors to discharge liability for fraudulent conduct. The Bankruptcy Code affects perpetrators, beneficiaries, and victims of fraudulent acts that occur prior to the commencement of bankruptcy proceedings (i.e., common law and statutory fraud). Related statutes also create their own codified construct for fraudulent acts undertaken in connection with an actual bankruptcy proceeding.

While various types of fraud will be discussed, this chapter is not intended to describe or define all types of fraud. Fraud is a state or federal law cause of action, and only in limited circumstances is it unique to the Bankruptcy Code. This chapter includes a review of how the Bankruptcy Code may permit perpetrators of fraudulent acts to escape from liability and what steps can be taken to prevent such an outcome. Fraud, as a part of actual bankruptcy proceedings, is also explored so as to illuminate the traps, including criminal statutes, set for those who use the Bankruptcy Code in a fraudulent manner. The Bankruptcy Code further creates vehicles to enhance the opportunities to pursue and obtain redress for fraud. Additionally, the recent amendments to the Bankruptcy Code, through the Bankruptcy Abuse Act, are addressed, including the increased scope of the law as it relates to a larger potential population of "bad" actors and "bad" acts. Finally, available alternate remedies for fraud actions against certain third parties are reviewed and discussed.

BANKRUPTCY REFUGE FOR FRAUDULENT ACTORS

Once fraud has occurred, the next logical step is to pursue the fraudulent party to recover damages suffered as a result of the fraud. There are a number of avenues available to creditors that have been defrauded. There are, however, also steps that individuals and businesses can take to frustrate collection efforts. Creditors need to be aware of what debtors can and cannot legally do to frustrate remedial efforts.

Frequently, in an attempt to avoid their financial responsibility, perpetrators of fraud will file for bankruptcy protection. For actions based on fraud committed outside of a bankruptcy proceeding, however, only certain limited benefits are available in bankruptcy to fraudulent actors. Despite what may be portrayed in the media, or by legislators, the Bankruptcy Code has traditionally offered less protection to perpetrators of fraud than to other debtors.

Discharge

Bankruptcy is designed to permit debtors, to one degree or another, to begin their financial life anew. Central to the goal of a "fresh start" for debtors through bankruptcy is the concept of discharge. By filing for bankruptcy protection under Chapter 7 of the Bankruptcy Code, an individual debtor (as opposed to a corporate debtor) can obtain a discharge of most debts incurred prior to the bankruptcy filing. A discharge in bankruptcy relieves an individual debtor from all debts that arose before the petition date, regardless of whether a proof of claim based on any such debt has been filed.[5]

Only debtors who are individuals may obtain a discharge.[6] A corporation is, however, effectively discharged once all of its assets have been distributed through a Chapter 7 liquidation. At that point, there is no remaining ability to collect from the corporation. Additionally, if the corporation is in a Chapter 11 reorganization proceeding and is able to confirm a plan, the corporate debtor would be discharged as to liability for any debts that arose prior to confirmation.[7] Individual debtors in a Chapter 13 bankruptcy are also entitled to a discharge once their repayment plans are consummated.[8]

No Discharge for Fraud. Despite the availability of a discharge, the Bankruptcy Code provides no shelter to an individual that has committed fraud or is liable to a creditor for fraud. While claims of fraud enjoy no greater "priority" as against other claims, they may be treated more favorably as they are eligible to survive the bankruptcy. The Bankruptcy Code provides specific exceptions to discharge for debtors that have acted fraudulently. Specifically, the Bankruptcy Code contains two Sections pursuant to which a debtor that has committed fraud can be denied a discharge. Under Section 727, a debtor can be denied a discharge as to all of his or her debts. Section 523 precludes the discharge of specific debts, including those arising from fraud.

- 11 U.S.C. § 727(a)(2)

  Section 727(a)(2) of the Bankruptcy Code provides that an individual debtor will not be granted a discharge if the debtor acted fraudulently during the bankruptcy case or within one year before the petition date.[9] Under this Section, if applicable, the debtor would be denied a discharge as to *all* of his or her debts. Specifically, Section 727(a)(2) provides that the court shall not grant the debtor a discharge if:

  > (2) the debtor, with intent to hinder, delay or defraud has transferred, removed, destroyed, mutilated or concealed—
  >
  > (A) property of the debtor, within one year before the date of the filing of the petition; or
  >
  > (B) property of the estate, after the date of the filing of the petition.

  Individual debtors who abuse the bankruptcy process by committing fraud while the bankruptcy case is pending will not receive the potential benefit from filing bankruptcy (i.e., a discharge of prefiling or prepetition debts). Those individual debtors who have fraudulently transferred property belonging to the debtor prior to the bankruptcy filing will be similarly disadvantaged. In the case of *In re Womble,*[10] the debtor was denied a discharge based on his fraudulent transfer or concealment of assets prior to filing bankruptcy. Specifically, on the eve of bankruptcy, Womble transferred approximately $72,000 into closely held corporate entities purportedly for grazing rights for cattle owned by Womble.

In denying discharge, the court looked at several factors when determining if the money transferred was for a legitimate purpose, including whether: (1) the transfer was pursuant to a standard business practice; (2) the transfer was an arm's-length transaction; (3) the debtor transferred the funds voluntarily, or whether the situation effectively forced the transfer upon the debtor; and (4) the debtor received proper consideration for the transfer. The debtor in *Womble* maintained no records to substantiate his claim that the transfer was to pay for grazing rights. The transfer was not at arm's length, and the debtor was in dire financial condition at the time of the transfer. The debtor also introduced no evidence that he was required to pay the closely held entities (e.g., invoices to the debtor, bills that such entities had to pay for expenses associated with grazing, or evidence of consideration). As a result, the court denied the debtor a discharge pursuant to Section 727(a)(2).

A denial of discharge precludes release of all of the debtor's prepetition debts, and a creditor can pursue the prepetition obligations after discharge is denied. The creditor, however, can only seek satisfaction from nonexempt assets.[11]

- 11 U.S.C. § 727(a)(3)

  A debtor can also be denied a discharge if the debtor has concealed or destroyed financial records. Specifically, Section 727(a)(3) of the Bankruptcy Code provides that the court shall not grant the debtor a discharge if:

  > (3) the debtor has concealed, destroyed, mutilated, falsified, or failed to keep or preserve any recorded information, including books, documents, records, and papers, from which the debtor's financial condition or business transactions might be ascertained, unless such act or failure to act was justified under all of the circumstances of the case.

  A debtor was denied a discharge pursuant to Section 727(a)(3) in the case of *In re Vetri.*[12] In *Vetri,* the debtor was a principal in nine corporations, owning and operating restaurants located in shopping malls throughout the United States. The debtor was unable to identify the location of the corporations' business records and claimed the records may either be at his parents' houses in Pennsylvania or Florida, or the records may have been lost when his home was burglarized and vandalized in 1987. In the end, the debtor failed to produce the records.

  The only records the debtor did produce were bank statements, canceled checks, and federal income tax forms. The debtor did not, however, provide any records relevant to his income for the period during which the bulk of large deposits and withdrawals occurred. The court held that due to the debtor's unjustified failure to keep adequate books and records from which his financial condition could be ascertained, the debtor should be denied a discharge under Section 727(a)(3).

- 11 U.S.C. § 523(a)(2)

  Pursuant to Section 523 of the Bankruptcy Code, certain specific debts can be found to be nondischargeable, even though the debtor might be entitled to a general discharge of prepetition debts. One such exception to discharge under Section 523(a) is for debts owed by the debtor resulting from fraud.[13] Simply put, if a debtor defrauds a creditor, the debtor will not be able to use the Bankruptcy Code to discharge this specific debt, even if the debtor is otherwise entitled to a discharge.

Specifically, Section 523(a)(2) provides:

> (a) A discharge under Section 727, 1141, 1228(a), 1228(b), or 1328(b) of this title does not discharge an individual debtor from any debt—
>
> (2) for money, property, services, or an extension, renewal, or refinancing of credit, to the extent obtained by—
>
> (A) false pretenses, a false representation, or actual fraud, other than a statement respecting the debtor's or an insider's financial condition;
>
> (B) use of a statement in writing—
>
> (i) that is materially false;
>
> (ii) respecting the debtor's or an insider's financial condition;
>
> (iii) on which the creditor to whom the debtor is liable for such money, property, services, or credit reasonably relied; and
>
> (iv) that the debtor caused to be made or published with intent to deceive.

To prevail under the discharge exception for debts obtained through false pretenses or false representation,[14] the creditor must establish that: (1) the debtor obtained money from the creditor by making a false representation or a false pretense; (2) the debtor knew that the representation or pretense was false when the debtor made it; (3) the debtor made the representation or pretense with intention to deceive the creditor; (4) the creditor relied on the false representation or pretense; and (5) the creditor suffered a loss as a proximate result.[15]

If it is established that the debt is nondischargeable, Section 523(a)(2) prevents the discharge of all liability arising from fraud, not merely amounts exacted from the creditor by the debtor.[16] In practical terms, this renders nondischargeable indebtedness arising from payments the creditor was required to make to third parties due to the debtor's fraud.[17] An objection to discharge pursuant to Section 523(a)(2) was illustrated in the case of *In re Ledet*.[18] In *Ledet,* the federal district court affirmed the bankruptcy court's decision to hold the debt to a bank nondischargeable under Section 523(a)(2). The bankruptcy court found that loans from the bank were obtained by false pretenses and false representations through the knowing submission of false borrowing reports to the bank for at least four contracts on which the debtor was not yet entitled to payment. The court also held that the bank justifiably relied on these false reports in extending credit.

The court relied on the testimony of the bank's loan officer and expert accountant that a valid receivable is one that has been earned under the terms of the contract and that reports which include receivables before the relevant account debtor could have been obligated for payment constituted clear misrepresentations.[19]

The court noted that nothing on the face of the borrowing base reports indicated that the supporting invoices were false and that the bank had performed a cursory examination of the reports without discovering any abnormality. Therefore, the court held the bank's reliance was justifiable. The debtor was denied discharge of the debt owed to the bank, pursuant to Section 523(a)(2).[20]

Nondischargeable debt based on fraud can also occur in the context of credit card transactions. In the case of *In re Van Dyke,*[21] the debtor opened a MasterCard account with a $5,000 credit limit with AT&T on December 30, 1995, at or about the time he became unemployed.

During the ensuing months of January and February 1996, the debtor obtained numerous cash advances on the credit card and quickly accumulated a debt of $2,900. The debtor became employed during the month of February, and his salary provided him with $1,800 per month. The debtor made minimal payments on the card, but he continued to increase the debt until finally reaching the $5,000 limit. At the time the debtor filed for bankruptcy, the credit card balance was $5,065.69.

The bankruptcy court stated that the general rule is that credit card charges made or cash advances received by individuals, who never intended to repay the charges, can be held to be nondischargeable under Section 523(a)(2). Fraudulent intent under this Section may be inferred from the surrounding circumstances. The court held that the charges the debtor incurred on the credit card during January and February were incurred while the debtor was clearly relying on the existence of future income. By the end of February, however, it was clear that the charges the debtor continued to incur were made while he was both already insolvent and lacking any reasonable belief of being able to repay his debts. The court further concluded that the debtor knew he was without such ability to repay the debt, and, as a result, he intended to deceive AT&T. The court decided, therefore, that the amount of the credit card debt incurred on and after March 1, 1996, was nondischargeable under Section 523(a)(2)(A).

Notably, Section 523(a)(2)(C) provides that certain debts are presumed to be non-dischargeable. Consumer debts for more than $500 for luxury goods and services that are incurred within ninety days of the bankruptcy filing are presumed nondischargeable.[22] Similarly, cash advances for more than $750 under an open ended credit plan within seventy days of the bankruptcy filing are also presumed nondischargeable.[23] Congress, in the Bankruptcy Abuse Act, amended the former, similar provisions of the Bankruptcy Code, extending the time limit and lowering the dollar amounts. These provisions indicate the disfavor that Congress has with those debts that are incurred so close to the filing of a bankruptcy. Indeed, Congress presumes these debts to be incurred on a fraudulent basis, thereby placing the burden on the debtor to prove that these debts were not incurred through fraud.

- 11 U.S.C. § 523(a)(4)

Section 523 also sets forth additional exceptions to discharge that involve, or may potentially involve, some element of fraud. Section 523(a)(4) provides an exception to discharge for debt from fraud or defalcation while acting in a fiduciary capacity.[24] Thus, for example, if a director incurs a debt to a creditor based on a breach of fiduciary duty claim, the director might not be able to use the Bankruptcy Code to discharge this debt.

Specifically, Section 523(a)(4) provides:

> (a) A discharge under Section 727, 1141, 1228(a), 1228(b), or 1328(b) of this title does not discharge an individual debtor from any debt—
>
> (4) for fraud or defalcation while acting in a fiduciary capacity, embezzlement, or larceny.

In the case of *In re West,*[25] the debtor was a clergyman who advertised a program at the church to assist people with "financial difficulty," offering budget counseling and assistance with mortgage refinancing. The plaintiffs were an elderly couple who owned two inherited homes and struggled with their mortgage payments. At the first meeting, West requested a power of attorney from the plaintiffs, so that he could make arrangements for them to receive "favorable financing," and the couple agreed. West also convinced them to transfer the titles in their homes to the church in order to secure this "favorable financing."

West told them to make mortgage payments to the church in order to regain ownership and that those payments would be the same amount as before. The plaintiffs began receiving invoices for mortgage payments that were substantially higher than promised. The couple stopped making payments at the advice of an attorney, and the properties were foreclosed. The plaintiffs obtained a judgment against West for approximately $510,000.

West subsequently filed a Chapter 7 bankruptcy, and the plaintiffs sought to have West's debt to them determined to be nondischargeable under Section 523(a)(4) as a breach of fiduciary duty. A fiduciary duty is imposed upon an individual when he is in a position of confidence or trust whereby others rely on him to act on their behalf.[26] The court held that West acted in an agency and a fiduciary capacity pursuant to the granting of the power of attorney. West was in a position of dominance, for the plaintiffs were unsophisticated retirees who simply sought assistance in refinancing their homes. As opposed to Section 523(a)(2), a breach of fiduciary duty under Section 523(a)(4) does not require an actual intent or motive to commit fraud; rather, Section 523(a)(4) may also consider whether a party neglected his duties to act as a fiduciary for another.[27] West's actions constituted defalcation since he was acting in a fiduciary capacity pursuant to the power of attorney, and he did not discharge his fiduciary duty.

In a further effort to prevent perceived abuse of the bankruptcy laws and to limit protection for fraudulent acts, the Bankruptcy Abuse Act revised Chapter 13 of the Bankruptcy Code. Chapter 13 permits individuals with a regular income to propose a plan for repayment, as opposed to facing liquidation under Chapter 7. Under prior law, upon completion of all payments under a Chapter 13 plan, if debts based on fraud were addressed under the plan, any amounts of such claims remaining unpaid would be discharged. Pursuant to the latest amendments to Section 1328 of the Bankruptcy Code under the Bankruptcy Abuse Act, discharge for fraud claims articulated in Sections 523(a)(2) and (4) is no longer available.[28]

Both Section 523(a)(2)(A) and Section 523(a)(4) provide exceptions to discharge for the occurrence of fraud, yet each may be distinguished based on several factors. For example, Section 523(a)(2)(A) requires some actual reliance on the debtor's conduct, while Section 523(a)(4) does not require such reliance.[29] Most notably, however, Section 523(a)(2)(A) provides for a nondischarge for debts incurred through *actual* fraud. Section 523(a)(4) does not have such similar limiting language, instead providing simply for the nondischarge of fraud that occurs through a fiduciary relationship. Although the case law has not directly addressed this distinction, Section 523(a)(4) arguably precludes a discharge for debt incurred through actual *or* constructive fraud in a fiduciary relationship. This expansive definition of fraud covers both intentional fraud (actual) and fraud that may be implied based on the circumstances (constructive).

Preclusion of a discharge for fraud is not automatic. Procedurally, if a creditor seeks to have a debt determined to be nondischargeable, or seeks to have a general discharge denied, the creditor must commence an adversary proceeding against the debtor seeking such relief. An adversary proceeding is essentially a lawsuit brought in the Bankruptcy Court and in the larger bankruptcy case.

Exempt Assets

Even if a creditor is successful in having a debt determined to be nondischargeable, a debtor can still frustrate a creditor's collection efforts by taking full advantage of the legal right to exempt certain property from being available to satisfy allowed creditor claims, even claims resulting from fraud. If property is exempt, it cannot be seized by creditors or liquidated in order to satisfy a debt owed. Thus, debtors who are subject to claims for fraud can still protect themselves to a limited degree by claiming certain assets to be exempt. Each state provides its own exemptions from collection for certain property, at least to the extent of certain dollar amounts.

The Bankruptcy Code also provides similar, but distinct, exemptions to those provided by state law. Like state exemptions, the Bankruptcy Code permits the debtor to retain the value of certain assets post–bankruptcy filing, free of any claims of unsecured (as opposed to lien or other secured) creditors. Section 522 is the principal Bankruptcy Code Section governing exemptions in bankruptcy cases.[30] It provides that debtors must file with their bankruptcy petitions lists of their exempt property. Section 522(b) also permits the use of either state or federal exemptions, unless the debtor's state does not allow the debtor to choose the federal exemptions.

States that prohibit debtors in bankruptcy from using the federal exemptions are often referred to as opt-out states. Debtors residing in opt-out states *must* utilize the exemptions that exist under the law of their particular state. Currently 34 states have opted out of the federal exemption system.[31] If a state has not opted out of the federal exemption system, then the debtor is free to choose either the exemptions provided for under Section 522(d) or under state law. Certain state statutes, such as Florida's, frequently provide greater and broader exemptions than the federal exemptions contained in Section 522(d). Debtors will frequently elect the state exemptions in these liberal states.

Federal or state exemptions can benefit the debtor and frustrate creditors. State exemptions are available to debtors in and out of bankruptcy to protect exempted assets from attachment by creditors. Federal exemptions under Section 522(d) are available only in bankruptcy and preclude those assets from being administered by a trustee for the benefit of creditors. Exemptions divide the estate into property reserved for the debtor, up to certain dollar limits, and property that will be available for the creditor's benefit. The exemptions assist the debtor in having some assets available after bankruptcy, so the person is not completely destitute.

Debtors often use pre–bankruptcy planning to take full advantage of the exemptions. To a limited degree, one may convert nonexempt property into exempt property prior to a bankruptcy filing. For instance, one could attempt to sell nonexempt property and use it to increase the amount of property owned in an exempt category. Further, and as discussed in more detail later, the debtor may attempt to move from one jurisdiction to another to take advantage of that jurisdiction's more favorable exemptions. The Bankruptcy Abuse Act, however, has substantially limited debtors' ability to undertake such bankruptcy planning by, among other things, placing lengthy time requirements on residency in certain jurisdictions before taking advantage of real estate exemptions.[32] Specifically, in order to take advantage of a particular state's exemptions, Section 522 (b)(3)(A) requires domicile for 730 days in a single state prior to filing. If such domicile does not exist for such period, then the domicile for the period of 180 days (or the longest period of such 180 days) prior to the 730-day period will govern which state's exemptions apply.[33]

Federal and State Exemptions

Section 522(d) provides the specific federal exemptions along with their corresponding dollar amounts.[34] State law exemptions may vary substantially from the federal exemptions. Whether a debtor should opt to use state law exemptions depends on the person's specific needs. For instance, certain state exemptions, because of their broad protection, are very appealing to debtors. Debtors, therefore, must carefully examine their asset portfolios to determine which exemptions will provide them the maximum protection. Assuming that debtors are not in an opt-out state, they must choose one or the other; they cannot pick and choose from both federal and state law exemptions.[35] Michigan is an example of a state that has not opted out of the federal exemptions. Therefore, debtors in Michigan can choose either the state or federal exemptions, but not some combination of the two.

Michigan is typical in that it provides for greater monetary exemptions than the federal exemptions as to certain property. For example, wearing apparel and burial plots have unlimited exemptions.[36] Prior to January 2005, Michigan only provided a homestead exemption of $3,500 to individuals inside and outside of bankruptcy, as opposed to the $18,450 under the federal exemptions, thereby dissuading many from even considering the use of the Michigan exemptions.[37] Notably, however, Michigan statutory changes in January 2005 now provide different exemptions for debtors who file for bankruptcy. While debtors outside of bankruptcy may still only take advantage of the $3,500 homestead exemption, a debtor in bankruptcy may exempt up to $30,000 for his or her homestead and up to $45,000 if the individual is elderly or disabled. These exemptions coincide more closely with the federal bankruptcy exemptions.[38] The new Michigan homestead exemption remains subject to interpretation by the courts. For example, in *In re Lindstrom,*[39] the court held that joint debtors may only exempt $30,000 in their homestead; they cannot each use the exemption for an aggregate of $60,000.

In addition, Michigan does provide extensive homestead protection for those who own property as husband and wife in a tenancy by the entirety.[40] Real or personal property owned in a tenancy by the entirety may be exempt if the cotenant does not also file for bankruptcy.[41] Other states also provide much more lucrative exemptions than the federal exemptions. For example, Texas provides an overall personal property exemption of $30,000.[42] In West Virginia, debtors may exempt 80 percent of their wages.[43]

Aside from some of these more lucrative state exemptions, the majority of exemptions provided for under either state law or Section 522(d) of the Bankruptcy Code are for relatively small amounts and provide minimal assistance to debtors who are attempting to prevent a creditor's collection efforts. For example, under the federal exemptions, a debtor may protect only $2,950 in value of a motor vehicle[44] and only $9,850 in total for household furnishings and clothing.[45] It should be noted, however, that these amounts double in value for a household if both spouses file for bankruptcy protection.

The ability of debtors to perform bankruptcy "planning" depends to a large degree on the language of the exemptions. For example, Section 522(d)(10)(E) provides an exemption to the debtor for payments from a pension plan.[46] Additionally, the Bankruptcy Abuse Act amended the Bankruptcy Code to provide that a debtor can exempt retirement funds in a 401(k) plan.[47] While these two exemptions might provide protection for assets with substantial value, they provide only minimal assistance in bankruptcy planning because a debtor will not be able to immediately convert nonexempt assets into pension funds or a 401(k). Furthermore, there are various restrictions limiting the timing of the use of funds in these plans.

Pursuant to Section 522(c), unless the bankruptcy case is dismissed, property exempted under Section 522(d) cannot be used to satisfy any debts that arose prior to the petition date, other than certain limited exceptions such as tax, alimony, maintenance, and support claims that are exempt from discharge. Significantly, Section 522(c) does not provide an exception for debt that was found to be nondischargeable pursuant to Section 523(a)(2).

Property of the Estate. Certain property may not even be considered to be part of the bankruptcy estate. Like exempt property, this property may not be sold to satisfy the claims of creditors. Pursuant to Section 541(c)(2) of the Bankruptcy Code, a debtor's interest in a spendthrift trust is not considered property of the debtor's estate and cannot be used to satisfy claims. A spendthrift trust is "a trust in which by the terms of the trust or by statute a valid restraint on the voluntary and involuntary transfer of the interest of the beneficiary is imposed."[48] With a spendthrift trust, trust beneficiaries cannot voluntarily transfer their interest in the trust.[49] Because certain pension plans have a spendthrift trust provision, they may not be considered estate property. Similarly, because of the nature of Employee Retirement Income Security Act ("ERISA") qualified plans, providing that the benefits cannot be assigned or alienated, the U.S. Supreme Court has held a debtor's interest in an ERISA-qualified pension plan may be excluded from estate property pursuant to Section 541(c)(2).[50]

Homestead Exemption. One exemption that does provide a great deal of benefit to debtors is the homestead exemption. A homestead exemption allows debtors to shield from creditors, at least in part, the equity interest debtors have in their residences. The right of a homestead exemption is available pursuant to the law of many states and can be utilized in connection with a bankruptcy filing. A federal bankruptcy homestead exemption is available, but it is significantly more limited in comparison to some of the state homestead exemptions.[51]

Yet although some states have very favorable homestead exemptions, these favorable exemptions may now be limited by the revised Bankruptcy Code, as discussed later. For example, debtors who establish residences in Florida can shield from their creditors all of their equity in their homes, subject to certain minimal limitations. Article X, Section 4 of the Florida Constitution prevents an attempt to seize a Florida homestead to satisfy the claims of a creditor.[52] While the Florida homestead exemption is extremely broad, the Florida Constitution provides three exceptions to this exemption: (1) for taxes owed by the homesteader; (2) for obligations incurred by the owner which created the lien on the property by consent (i.e., a home mortgage); and (3) for claims of laborers and material men who contributed to the repair and improvement of the homestead.[53]

Despite these exceptions to the exemption, the liberal provisions of Florida's homestead exemption have been perceived as a source of abuse. The Florida homestead exemption had permitted debtors to protect the homestead even if it was acquired on the eve of, or immediately after, a judgment or if the debtor only recently obtained Florida residency. The ability to exempt the homestead in Florida was available even if a debtor's claims were based on fraud. In theory, this permitted a debtor who had committed fraud to liquidate her assets, take the proceeds, and move to Florida. If she invested those proceeds in an expensive house and filed for bankruptcy protection, she essentially protected all of her assets. This is commonly referred to as the mansion loophole,[54] and it can provide a safe haven for fraudulent actors.

The ramifications of the mansion loophole are illustrated in the litigation between Kevin Adell ("Adell") and John Richards Homes Building Co., LLC ("JRH"). The dispute between Adell and JRH included litigation in two states, Michigan and Florida, and involved fraud, dischargeability, and the Florida homestead exemption.

The Adell-JRH dispute began as a civil action in the Michigan state courts based on alleged breaches of a contract for the construction of a "high-end" home. Subsequently, Adell filed an involuntary bankruptcy petition (the "Involuntary Bankruptcy Case") against JRH in the Bankruptcy Court for the Eastern District of Michigan (the "Michigan Bankruptcy Court"), asserting claims arising under the contract.

The Involuntary Bankruptcy Case was defended by JRH, which sought dismissal and compensatory and punitive damages, based on a "bad faith" filing under Section 303(i) of the Bankruptcy Code.[55] On July 15, 2002, the Michigan Bankruptcy Court dismissed the Involuntary Bankruptcy Case and, thereafter, on April 25, 2003, awarded JRH compensatory damages in the amount of $4,100,000, punitive damages in the amount of $2,000,000, and attorneys' fees and costs in the amount of $313,230.68, plus interest at the statutory rate (the "Sanctions Order").[56]

Following entry of the Sanctions Order, Adell liquidated certain of his assets and moved to Florida. Specifically, Adell sold 13 vintage cars for $536,000, cashed in treasury bills in the amount of $1,700,000, withdrew $300,000 from his checking account, and wired all of these funds to his attorney in Florida.[57] Adell arrived in Florida on May 5, 2003, and began looking to purchase a home. Immediately upon his arrival, Adell took steps to establish his residency in Florida, including registering to vote, registering his car, and obtaining a fishing license.[58] On May 7, 2003, Adell signed a contract to purchase a residence in Naples, Florida, for $2,800,000. The purchase of the Florida residence closed on May 8, 2003.[59]

Following the purchase of the Florida residence, Adell filed a declaratory complaint in the Florida state court, seeking a determination that the Florida residence was entitled to the homestead exemption granted by the Florida Constitution.[60] JRH was able to get the complaint removed to the Michigan Bankruptcy Court. On September 17, 2003, the Michigan Bankruptcy Court entered an order (the "Homestead Order") providing that the Florida residence did not qualify for the Florida homestead exemption because (1) the Florida homestead exemption is trumped by Section 303(i) of the Bankruptcy Code (providing for sanctions for filing an involuntary petition), and (2) Adell was not a bona fide resident of Florida.[61]

Based on the Homestead Order, JRH was entitled to foreclose on the Florida residence. Adell then filed a bankruptcy petition under Chapter 11 on November 14, 2003, in the Bankruptcy Court for the Middle District of Florida (the "Florida Bankruptcy Court") immediately triggering the automatic stay provision of Section 362 of the Bankruptcy Code and preventing any foreclosure action by JRH.[62] Despite the bankruptcy filing, JRH contended that Adell's right to claim the Florida residence as a homestead had already been resolved by the Michigan Bankruptcy Court. Notwithstanding the Michigan Bankruptcy Court's Order, the Florida Bankruptcy Court held that Adell was entitled to a homestead exemption for his Florida residence.[63]

The Florida Bankruptcy Court noted that the purpose of Bankruptcy Code Section 303(i) is to compensate an entity that suffered damages as a result of an involuntary petition that had been improperly filed.[64] The Florida Bankruptcy Court reasoned that an award pursuant to Section 303(i) was similar to any other type of money judgment entered in a civil action based on an intentional tort.[65] The Florida Bankruptcy Court stated that such a judgment would not trump the homestead exemption under Florida law. While the Florida Bankruptcy Court noted that the Florida homestead exemption had been preempted by Section 1955(d) of Title 18 of the United States Code relating to a gambling forfeiture,[66] it did not believe that a preemption based on a federal gambling violation (or other criminal violations such as federal drug charges) should be applied in connection with a sanction order. It reasoned that the Sanctions Order was not akin to a violation of a criminal statute. The Florida Bankruptcy Court held thereby that the issuance of the Sanctions Order did not preempt the Florida homestead exemption.[67]

In examining the results of the homestead exemption, the Florida Bankruptcy Court concluded that Adell was a Florida resident entitled to the homestead exemption. The Florida

Constitution requires satisfaction of these criteria in order to avail oneself of the Florida homestead exemption: "(1) the debtor is a 'natural person'; (2) the debtor is a Florida resident and has established that he made, or intended to make the homestead at issue, his or her permanent residence; (3) the debtor is the owner of the homestead; and (4) the property claimed as a homestead is not in excess of acreage permitted by the Florida Constitution i.e., one-half acre within the boundary of a municipality or one hundred sixty acres of contiguous land located in the unincorporated areas of the municipality."[68]

The Florida Bankruptcy Court held that Adell owned his Florida residence, resided and continued to reside in Florida, and developed a new business venture in Florida. Based on these and other factors, the court concluded that Adell had the intent to become a bona fide resident of Florida and as such was entitled to the Florida homestead exemption.[69]

The *Adell* case provides an illustration of the breadth of protection which laws such as the Florida homestead exemption provide. Through the Florida homestead exemption, Adell was able to legally prevent JRH's collection of indebtedness by converting nonexempt assets into exempt assets through the purchase of the Florida residence. Had Adell not availed himself of this option, the vintage cars, cash, treasury bills, and other nonexempt assets could all have been seized by JRH to satisfy the indebtedness he owed. The homestead exemption in Florida makes no distinction in protecting a debtor's property from claims arising in the ordinary course based on fraud. Importantly, this exemption will not permit perpetrators of fraud to protect proceeds obtained through fraud via the mansion loophole. [70]

In Adell's bankruptcy case, JRH, as alternative relief, sought to have the Florida Bankruptcy Court impose either a constructive trust or equitable lien on Adell's Florida residence. The court recognized that it had the power to impose such a lien or trust if the proceeds of fraud were used to purchase the homestead.[71] The Florida Bankruptcy Court declined, however, to apply either a constructive trust or equitable lien because there was no evidence that Adell had purchased the Florida residence with proceeds obtained by fraud. Specifically, the Florida Bankruptcy Court stated:

> This Court has no difficulty to accept the proposition that if it is established by competent proof that the debtor who is claiming the homestead exemption acquired the homestead by fraudulently obtained funds or by embezzlement, it is appropriate to impose an equitable lien and possibly, in the alternative, a constructive trust. However, the record in this case is totally devoid of any evidence that would warrant the conclusion that the Debtor in the instant case purchased his Naples, Florida residence with embezzled funds or obtained funds through fraud. For this reason none of these alternative remedies sought by JRH have any merit.[72]

While debtors who create the homestead as an attempt to avoid creditors may protect the homestead, they may not be entitled to a discharge. In the *Adell* bankruptcy case, JRH objected to both the dischargeability of the Sanctions Order debt as well as Adell's general discharge. The Florida Bankruptcy Court found that Adell was not entitled to a discharge pursuant to Section 727(a)(2)(A) of the Bankruptcy Code because the homestead was purchased with intent to hinder, delay, or defraud within one year of the date of the bankruptcy filing. The Florida Bankruptcy Court found that:

> The record in this case leaves no doubt that the Debtor converted nonexempt assets into exempt assets, namely his Naples, Florida, homestead; that the transfer took place within one year before the date of the filing of the petition; and, based on the circumstances and events surrounding the sudden move to Florida, the transfer was made with the intent to hinder, delay or defraud a creditor, JRH. While the Debtor's homestead exemption is protected by the Florida Constitution

> and are [sic] not subject to attack under these circumstances, *Havoco of America, Ltd. v. Hill*, 790 So.2d 1018 (Fla. 2001), his discharge is vulnerable.[73]

Thus, while the Florida residence was exempt and protected from seizure, JRH could continue to pursue collection efforts against Adell's other nonexempt present and future assets. The homestead exemption is "designed to promote the stability and welfare of the state by encouraging property ownership and independence on the part of its citizens, but most importantly, by preserving a home where the family may be sheltered and live behind reach of economic misfortune."[74] Whether consistent with this purpose or not, the homestead exemption enables debtors to protect significant assets from being subject to creditor attacks and, importantly, can even do so where fraud exists and in the shadow of the creditor obtaining a judgment.

New Limitations on Homestead Exemption. Statutes like the Florida homestead exemption have resulted in changes to the Bankruptcy Code. Through the addition of Bankruptcy Code Sections 522(o), (p), and (q), the Bankruptcy Abuse Act has limited a debtor's ability to take advantage of state homestead exemptions.

Section 522(o) states that the value of a property claimed as a homestead must be reduced by the amount of value that was generated through disposition of nonexempt property, with the intent to hinder, delay, or defraud creditors, and made within 10 years before the bankruptcy was filed.[75] Essentially, a debtor must refrain from infusing into the homestead any proceeds of nonexempt assets disposed of for the purpose of frustrating creditors. Furthermore, a court may circumstantially infer that any prepetition asset transfers made within 10 years before the bankruptcy and that created homestead equity were made with the intent to hinder, delay, or defraud creditors.[76] For example, in one case, the bankruptcy court rejected a homestead claim after it was revealed that the debtor had sold his truck days before filing for bankruptcy and then applied the proceeds to his home equity line of credit.[77] The debtor would not have been able to exempt his truck, so he sold it and used the proceeds to pay down his home equity line of credit. Before this amendment, debtors could effectively conduct exemption planning by converting nonexempt assets to exempt assets. The Bankruptcy Code now prevents such conversion of assets from enhancing the homestead exemption.

Section 522(p) provides that a debtor may not exempt an interest in a homestead that was acquired within 1215 days (three years and four months) preceding the bankruptcy filing and that exceeds the aggregate amount of $125,000 in real or personal property that the debtor claims as a homestead exemption.[78] Congress specifically stated that it wants to require debtors to reside in a state for a certain period of time before that person can take advantage of that state's homestead exemptions. This has effectively frustrated debtors who might otherwise engage in bankruptcy planning and move to states like Florida simply to take advantage of the state's favorable homestead provisions.[79]

Like Section 522(o), Section 522(q) seeks to limit the homestead exemption in the circumstance of bad acts by the debtor. Section 522(q) provides that a debtor may not claim a homestead exemption in excess of $125,000 if:

(1) The debtor was convicted of a felony which demonstrates that the filing of the bankruptcy case was an abuse of the Bankruptcy Code; or

(2) The debtor owes a debt arising from

   (a) A violation of the federal or state securities laws

(b) Fraud in a fiduciary capacity or in connection with the purchase of registered securities; or

(c) Any criminal act, intentional tort, or willful or reckless misconduct that caused serious physical injury or death to another individual in the preceding five years.[80]

These provisions seek to prevent the escape from debt for those individuals who have engaged in certain types of conduct that is wrongful, and, in some instances, criminal. Congress effectively deemed certain individuals to be less worthy of full bankruptcy protection and thus precluded their ability to take complete advantage of the Bankruptcy Code.

The impact of these amendments to the Bankruptcy Code remains in flux. One issue that has arisen is whether the \$125,000 statutory homestead exemption cap of Section 522(p) (and, by extension, Section 522(q) as well) applies to debtors with homesteads located in states that have elected to opt out of the federal exemptions.

The breadth of the homestead cap was first addressed by the United States Bankruptcy Court in Arizona. Arizona, like Florida, is an opt-out state. In the case of *In re McNabb,*[81] the Arizona Bankruptcy Court determined that the \$125,000 homestead exemption cap applies only to debtors who live in states that allow debtors in bankruptcy to utilize either state or federal exemptions.[82] The court in *McNabb* focused on the phrase "*as a result of electing* under subsection (b)(3)(A) to exempt property *under state or local law,* a debtor may not exempt . . . ";[83] and, therefore, the court concluded that these sections can apply only to debtors who live in states that allow election of either state or federal exemptions in bankruptcy cases.[84]

Since Arizona is an opt-out state, the court in *McNabb* concluded that Section 522(q)'s statutory cap did not apply. The Arizona Bankruptcy Court acknowledged that its interpretation would result in the homestead exemption cap being applicable in the only two states, Texas and Minnesota, that allow debtors to choose between federal and state exemptions and also allow homestead exemptions in excess of \$125,000.[85]

Following the decision in *McNabb,* the same issue arose in Florida, another opt-out state. Contrary to the decision in *McNabb,* the United States Bankruptcy Court for the Southern District of Florida, in the case of *In re Kaplan,*[86] concluded that the \$125,000 homestead exemption cap applied to all states, regardless of whether they have opted out of the federal system of exemptions.[87] The *Kaplan* court addressed the *McNabb* decision, finding that the decision was only supportable based on narrow rules of statutory construction.[88] The *Kaplan* court rejected such a construction and instead relied on the legislative intent of Section 522, finding that the legislative intent was for the homestead exemption cap to apply to all states.[89] The court recognized the confusing language in Section 522(p) and (q), which references an election under state or local law, but it also noted how highly unlikely it would be for Congress to codify law that would only apply to two states.[90]

Based on the decisions in *McNabb* and *Kaplan,* there is currently a split of authority as to whether the \$125,000 homestead exemption cap applies to opt-out states. There are several reasons why other courts addressing the issue may be persuaded to follow *Kaplan*. First, Florida is the state most commonly associated with the homestead exemption and the mansion loophole. By default, therefore, the Florida court's opinion may have the most impact on any asset protection analysis. Second, the Florida court's opinion appears to be better reasoned in light of the legislative history evidencing the purpose and intent behind this provision in the Bankruptcy Abuse Act.

Importantly, the mansion loophole is affected only by the statutory cap if debtors file bankruptcy. Should debtors not file bankruptcy, then they would be entitled to avail themselves of all debtor-friendly state laws including, in Florida, a homestead exemption in excess of $125,000. In this scenario, however, with no bankruptcy filing, other collection efforts would not be stayed.

New Deterrents to Fraudulent Actors

The Bankruptcy Abuse Act has imposed other procedural requirements on debtors in an attempt to limit manipulation by fraud within the bankruptcy system. The "honor system" has been discarded, and individual debtors are now required to submit copies of their tax returns and pay stubs with the bankruptcy petition. In connection with a bankruptcy case, a debtor is required to file a sworn statement containing an oath, under penalty of perjury, swearing to the authenticity of a statement of facts. Attorneys filing bankruptcy petitions are also now expressly required to make an effort to verify the accuracy of the debtor's sworn statement.

The Bankruptcy Abuse Act also provides a "means test" in order to determine if a debtor is eligible to file a Chapter 7 bankruptcy petition, such that only certain debtors in lower income levels are now able to file a Chapter 7 bankruptcy as opposed to a Chapter 13.[91] Debtors also must attend an approved financial management course in order to receive a discharge. Debtors who have the ability to do so will now be required to pay back at least a portion of their debts. Furthermore, the permissible time period for repeat bankruptcy filings has been increased from six years to eight years. The Bankruptcy Abuse Act is a further effort to ensure that the Bankruptcy Courts are not refuges for fraudulent actors.

BANKRUPTCY FRAUD

Dating back to the first American bankruptcy statute in 1800 and continuing through to the present day, Congress has enacted legislation that provides for criminal punishment to persons who abuse the bankruptcy process through fraud and falsification.[92] Violation of these statutes is commonly referred to as bankruptcy fraud. While these criminal statutes have been revised and expanded over time, the intent of the criminal statutes has remained consistent: Bankruptcy fraud interferes with the goals and purpose of the Bankruptcy Code and must be deterred. The current criminal statutes enacted by Congress to address bankruptcy fraud are found in Title 18, Sections 152 through 157 of the United States Code, and the types of acts that these statutes address are known as the bankruptcy crimes.[93] Also, as part of the Sarbanes-Oxley Act of 2002,[94] an additional statute dealing with obstruction of justice, in circumstances including bankruptcy, was added.[95]

The issue of bankruptcy fraud is increasingly becoming a hot topic. Some form of bankruptcy crime statute has been in existence for over 200 years. For the vast majority of that time period, however, prosecutions for bankruptcy crimes were rare. This is no longer the case.

Debtors and their attorneys, creditors of bankrupt debtors, the courts, and various federal law enforcement agencies, such as the United States Trustee's Office and the United States Department of Justice, have a strong interest in preserving, protecting, and defending the integrity of the bankruptcy system.[96] Over the past decade, the United States Department of Justice has placed an increased emphasis on the prosecution of persons committing bankruptcy fraud.[97] This fact, along with the U.S. sentencing guidelines (which govern sentencing of defendants convicted of bankruptcy crimes), has meant that persons who commit bankruptcy fraud are now frequently sentenced to prison.[98] No longer is bankruptcy fraud viewed as a semi-harmless white-collar crime. Bankruptcy fraud is a serious crime with serious consequences.

The bankruptcy crimes statutes identify several situations that can subject a person to significant consequences, including fines, imprisonment up to five years, or both. Importantly, the bankruptcy crimes not only apply to debtors but, with certain limited exceptions, also apply to any person committing one of the various prohibited acts. Although the vast majority of bankruptcy prosecutions focus on either the debtors or creditors, professionals advising the debtors, including attorneys, can face criminal prosecution as well.[99] Imposing a high level of scrutiny on debtors, creditors, and professionals helps to keep them honest, which ultimately deters illegal manipulation of the bankruptcy system and enhances the prospects for creditor recovery.

Concealment of Assets; False Oaths and Claims; Bribery—18 U.S.C. §§ 152–158

Introduction. The key bankruptcy crime statute for purposes of detecting and preventing fraudulent conduct in connection with a bankruptcy case is Section 152 of Title 18 of the United States Code ("U.S.C."). Section 152 is a broad provision "attempting to cover all of the possible methods by which a debtor . . . may attempt to defeat the Bankruptcy Act through any type of effort to keep assets from being equitably distributed among creditors."[100] Section 152 makes it a crime for a person to conceal assets,[101] provide a false oath or account,[102] make a false declaration,[103] file a false proof of claim,[104] destroy or conceal the debtor's financial records,[105] or give or accept a bribe in connection with a bankruptcy case.[106] Each of these actions, if not detected, would substantially interfere with the purposes and goals of the Bankruptcy Code by ultimately depleting recovery to creditors. These criminal acts are discussed next.

Section 152(1) Fraudulent Concealment. Section 152(1) makes it a criminal offense for a person to fraudulently conceal assets of the debtor's estate in connection with a bankruptcy case. Fraudulent concealment is the most commonly prosecuted bankruptcy crime.[107]

- *Disclosure of assets.* In addition to providing a fresh start to debtors, the Bankruptcy Code's intent is to provide a fair and equitable distribution of a debtor's assets to creditors.[108] In order to assure disclosure of the debtor's assets and liabilities to the court, any appointed trustee, and the creditors, the Bankruptcy Code and the Bankruptcy Rules impose certain obligations upon a debtor after filing for bankruptcy protection. The Bankruptcy Rules specifically require that every person who files bankruptcy must truthfully complete: a list of creditors; a schedule of all assets, liabilities, current income, and current expenditures; and a statement of financial affairs.[109] The Bankruptcy Rules also require every debtor to appear under oath at the beginning of each bankruptcy case and to answer questions about his or her financial affairs at the first meeting of creditors.[110] The debtor's disclosure requirement includes disclosure of *all* assets, even if their status is uncertain.[111] Failure to comply with the Bankruptcy Rules may constitute a violation of Section 152(1).

  Property of the debtor is defined in broad terms, and a debtor must disclose all assets, including equitable interests.[112] Disclosure of the debtor's equitable interests was discussed in *United States v. Moynagh.*[113] In *Moynagh,* the defendant maintained a power boat and a sailboat and subsequently transferred legal title to the boats to Marlin Boat Company, which was owned by the defendant's mother and son. Later the defendant paid off some of the debt and maintenance costs for the boats. When the defendant subsequently filed bankruptcy and filed his schedules of assets, he failed to list an interest in the boats. The court held that even though legal title to the boats had been transferred to and registered in the name of Marlin Boat Company, the defendant retained an equitable interest in the boats because he still owed money pursuant to liens on the boats.[114] A failure to list that equitable interest can support a charge of concealment of assets. In this case the court concluded that there was sufficient evidence to establish the defendant had an equitable interest in the boats. Even assets that are considered exempt assets and not subject to administration by the debtor's estate, either pursuant to state law exemptions or the Bankruptcy Code, need to be disclosed.[115]

As in *Moynagh,* the Seventh Circuit in the case of *In the Matter of Kaiser*[116] reviewed whether the debtor retained an equitable interest in certain property and whether it was part of the bankruptcy estate.[117] In *Kaiser*, the shareholders of the debtor corporation owned land used by the debtor. The shareholders never leased or sold the land to the corporation, but the corporation paid the loans and real estate taxes on the land. Because of this seemingly dual ownership of the land, the court scrutinized whether the corporation truly owned the land or whether the individual shareholders owned it and were merely using taking advantage of bankruptcy laws.[118] The disclosure statement of the corporation stated that the land was an asset of the bankruptcy estate of the debtor corporation. This permitted the corporation to obtain an extension of credit during bankruptcy. The court held that the debtor corporation properly disclosed its equitable interest in the land, for it paid all expenses on the land and both the corporation and its shareholders held it out as property of the corporation. The debtor retained an equitable interest despite the fact that legal title was still in the individual's name and was never transferred to the debtor.[119]

While Section 152(1) aims to prevent the fraudulent subversion of the bankruptcy process by providing a specific statute making such fraudulent concealment of assets a criminal act, it is important to keep in mind that the statute criminalizes fraudulent concealment and not negligent disclosure. Thus, in order for a person to be in criminal violation of Section 152(1), it is necessary for the concealment to have been committed knowingly and fraudulently.[120]

- *Elements of fraudulent concealment.* The elements of fraudulent concealment of assets generally consist of:
    - The existence of a bankruptcy case;
    - Concealment of property of the debtor's estate; and
    - Concealment of the property knowingly and fraudulently with the intent to circumvent the bankruptcy process[121]

In light of the criminal nature of the action, in order to convict a person of fraudulent concealment of assets, all of the above elements must be established beyond a reasonable doubt.

- *Existence of a bankruptcy case.* Of the preceding elements, the first is the simplest to prove. In order for a bankruptcy crime to have been committed, there must first be a pending bankruptcy case. Thus, a prosecution under Section 152(1) "clearly requires that bankruptcy proceedings have commenced, and proceeded sufficiently far for a Trustee, Marshall or other Court officer to have been appointed."[122] The remaining two elements, however, have proven more difficult to establish.
- *Concealment of property of the debtor's estate.* Before determining if an asset was concealed, courts must first establish that the asset in question was actually property of the

estate. Courts have broadly interpreted what qualifies as "property" and "assets."[123] Property and assets include all legal or equitable interests the debtor has in property existing on the date that the bankruptcy case is filed or that the debtor acquires after the commencement of the bankruptcy case. A broad definition of the terms "property" and "assets" is consistent with the stated purpose of providing a fair and equitable distribution of assets.

In connection with Section 152(1), the term "concealment" includes any act that hides the existence of property or assets belonging to the debtor's estate from persons entitled to know about such property or assets, including creditors, the court, and other interested parties.[124]

The element of concealment has been in this way defined:

> Concealment means, not only secreting, falsifying and mutilating . . . but also includes preventing discovery, fraudulently transferring or withholding knowledge or information required by law to be made known.
>
> . . . Clearly concealment means more than "secreting"; one does not have to put something in a hidden compartment, a safe, or a hole in the backyard in order to "conceal" it. It is enough that one "withholds knowledge," or "prevents disclosure or recognition."[125]

Concealment can take many shapes and forms. One particularly egregious case occurred in *United States v. Kubick.*[126] In *Kubick,* the defendant was a successful real estate developer in Anchorage, Alaska. Following the collapse of the Alaskan oil market in the mid-1980s, the value of Kubick's real estate holdings decreased, and he began to experience financial difficulties. As a result, Kubick conceived a plan whereby he would conceal his assets and attempt to discharge his debts through a bankruptcy proceeding.[127]

Kubick enlisted the assistance of various people, including family members, friends, accountants, and his attorneys, William Herron and Carol Birdwell. Kubick filed for Chapter 7 bankruptcy. Assets not disclosed in the bankruptcy case included $150,000 that was laundered through Herron's firm in anticipation of filing bankruptcy, a Range Rover that was purchased for $48,000 with money in Herron's trust account, his big-game trophy collection, jewelry, furs, buried money, and various other properties totaling a value in excess of $4.6 million. Kubick also failed to disclose his controlling interest in several corporations and partnerships that continued to hold or participate in various real estate developments in Alaska and Wyoming.

Kubick was criminally indicted for conspiracy to commit bankruptcy fraud, among other charges. Ultimately, Kubick pleaded guilty to one count of conspiracy to commit bankruptcy fraud and one count of conspiracy to impede and impair the IRS. The court sentenced Kubick to 58 months in prison.[128]

In addition to Kubick, his attorneys, Herron and Birdwell, were also indicted. Herron pleaded guilty to one count of conspiracy to commit bankruptcy fraud and was sentenced to 36 months in prison.[129] Herron appealed his sentence to the Ninth Circuit Court of Appeals. The court upheld Herron's sentence. On appeal, Herron contended that the court considered "non-fraudulent" conduct in determining the sentence. The court disagreed and noted that the $48,000 used to buy the Range Rover came from Herron's trust account and the $150,000 was wired from Herron to his attorneys in Anchorage, Alaska. The court determined that these matters were properly considered in determining Herron's sentence. Furthermore, the Ninth Circuit held that federal sentencing guidelines may be applied to bankruptcy proceedings and used to "increase the offense level of a defendant who conceals assets in violation of the bankruptcy process."[130]

While Kubick's conduct was particularly egregious, concealment can take a more subtle form, such as fraudulent accounting. This was evident in the case of *United States v. Turner.*[131] In *Turner,* the defendant owned most of the stock in and was employed by a car dealership. The dealership experienced financial difficulties and filed for bankruptcy under Chapter 11. Following the bankruptcy filing, the defendant sold a car to another dealership. The sale, however, was not recorded in the debtor's records.[132] After an investigation by the FBI, the defendant was indicted for fraudulently concealing assets in violation of Section 152. The court, in upholding the defendant's conviction, noted that possessing the proceeds from the sale of the car was not an element of the crime of concealment: "Turner's crime was not in selling the car, possessing the proceeds, or using the proceeds to pay debts, but rather in preventing the discovery, by the trustee or the corporate debtor, of what he had done with the money."[133]

Intentional undervaluing of assets can also amount to fraudulent concealment. In *United States v. Walker,*[134] the defendant and his wife filed for bankruptcy protection. In the bankruptcy case, the debtors' statement of financial affairs specifically undervalued their personal property by over $245,000.[135] The defendant was ultimately charged with fraudulent concealment of assets pursuant to Section 152 and pleaded guilty.

- *Knowing and fraudulent concealment.* In order for one to be guilty of a criminal violation, the perpetrator must act with *mens rea,* or a guilty mind. For the concealment to be criminal, it must be both knowing and fraudulent. As seen in the *Turner* case above, concealment means more than merely secreting assets. It is sufficient that a person withholds knowledge of an asset or prevents disclosure or recognition of an asset or fails to list several bank accounts.[136] Thus, Section 152 is not intended to punish inadvertent, innocent, or unknowing actions. Because the onus is broad for disclosure of assets, if a person is uncertain as to whether an asset should be disclosed, the debtor should err on the side of caution and report the asset.

  In addition to concealment, Section 152(1) also requires that the concealment is made fraudulently. A fraudulent act in this context requires a false representation of material fact made with knowledge of its falsity and with the intent to deceive.[137]

  The distinction between knowing and fraudulent concealment is illustrated in *United States v. Yasser.*[138] In Yasser, the defendant was employed by Crawfords, Inc. ("Crawfords"). Prior to Crawfords filing for bankruptcy, the defendant removed merchandise from Crawfords and sold portions of the merchandise.[139] After Crawfords filed bankruptcy, the defendant continued to retain either the merchandise or the proceeds of the sale of the merchandise.[140] Subsequently, the defendant was charged with and convicted of fraudulent concealment of Crawfords' assets.

  On appeal, the court overturned the defendant's conviction. The evidence indicated that while the defendant may have been familiar with the books and records of Crawfords, the defendant was not informed of the bankruptcy. The evidence indicated that the defendant was not aware of any bankruptcy proceeding until the commencement of the criminal action against him. In overturning the conviction, the court stated that with respect to fraudulent concealment, "the essence of the crime is knowingly and fraudulently to conceal from the receiver or trustee in bankruptcy. It must, therefore, appear that the defendant had actual knowledge of the existence of a receiver or trustee in bankruptcy or that he willfully closed his eyes to facts which made the existence of such an officer obvious."[141] The prosecution did not offer any evidence that the defendant knew of the existence of the bankruptcy case.[142]

Thus, the defendant lacked the requisite willful conduct necessary to establish fraudulent intent.

Section 152(7) Concealment in Contemplation of Bankruptcy. In addition to the prohibition against concealing of assets during a pending bankruptcy case, Section 152(7) criminalizes the concealment of assets in contemplation of filing bankruptcy. Specifically, Section 152(7) prohibits a person in either a personal capacity or as an agent or officer of a person or corporation, while contemplating filing bankruptcy, from fraudulently concealing or transferring their property with the intent to defeat the provisions of the Bankruptcy Code:

> The purpose of criminalizing a transfer or concealment of assets, if done with the requisite *mens rea,* and in contemplation of bankruptcy or to defeat the provisions of Title 11, is to prevent and punish efforts to circumvent the provisions of Title 11, including the "priorities among creditors . . . and the rule that claimants within a class share pro rata.[143]

The application of Section 152(7) was illustrated in the case of *United States v. Sabbeth.*[144] In *Sabbeth,* the defendant was the sole shareholder and president of Sabbeth Industries, Ltd. The defendant was also the landlord for the corporate headquarters and occasionally lent money to the corporation. The corporation filed for bankruptcy protection on December 28, 1990. The corporation owed the defendant approximately $2 million for past due obligations; however, this debt was subordinated to the indebtedness owed to the corporation's secured lender. The secured lender discovered that the defendant had been withdrawing money in the form of company checks in an amount exceeding $1 million, with approximately $750,000 of this amount having been withdrawn between June 1, 1990, and December 28, 1990.

The defendant claimed that the money he took from the corporation during the contemplation of bankruptcy did not violate Section 152(7), since the money was in satisfaction of antecedent debts. The court, nonetheless, held that the money was taken in contemplation of bankruptcy and for the purpose of receiving more money from the company than other creditors. It was, therefore, "property" of the corporation and taken in violation of Section 152(7). The court concluded that the receipt of each corporation check in payment of an antecedent debt was criminal at the moment of transfer.

Section 152(2) and (3) False Oath or Statement. Section 152 also makes it a crime to make a false oath[145] or a false statement[146] in connection with a bankruptcy proceeding. In prosecuting such a charge, four things must be established:

1. A bankruptcy case was in existence.
2. A false statement or oath was made.
3. The statement related to a material fact.
4. The statement was made knowingly and fraudulently.[147]

The threshold issue is a determination as to whether the oath or statement was false. A false statement is generally defined as "a statement or assertion which is known to be untrue when made or when used."[148] False statement prosecutions frequently involve the debtor's failure to disclose an interest in certain corporate assets, misrepresentation regarding the number of bank accounts, or a false statement concerning the highest bid for property[149] in connection with a bankruptcy sale.

The false statement also must be material. A false statement or oath with respect to a matter that is inconsequential to the bankruptcy proceeding would not violate the statute: "Materiality does not require a showing that creditors are harmed by the false statements. Matters are material if pertinent to the extent and nature of the bankrupt's assets, including the history of a bankrupt's financial transactions."[150]

In the case *United States v. Center,*[151] the defendant was an attorney representing debtors in a Chapter 11 bankruptcy case and assisting them in preparing and filing their schedules of assets and liabilities. The defendant failed to list a debt owed to the debtor on the asset schedule.[152] After the defendant discovered that the asset had been omitted, the defendant did not take any action to notify the bankruptcy court of the omitted asset. Instead, the defendant had documents executed and book entries backdated for the purpose of creating a setoff.[153] At trial, the defendant was convicted of falsifying and making false entries in a document affecting or relating to the affairs of a debtor. The appellate court upheld his conviction.[154]

The court noted that "the purpose of [Section] 152 is to proscribe the concealment of a bankrupt's assets (with false book entries being one of the possible vehicles available to affect a concealment)."[155] In upholding the conviction, the court found that the book entry was fraudulent since it misrepresented the date of the transaction.[156]

Section 152(4) False Claims. Section 152(4) makes it a criminal offense for a person to knowingly and fraudulently file a false proof of claim against the debtor's estate. The elements for filing a false proof of claim under Section 152(4) are:

1. A bankruptcy case was in existence.
2. A proof of claim was willfully presented in the bankruptcy proceeding.
3. The proof of claim was false as to a material matter.
4. The defendant knew the proof of claim was false at the time it was made and thus made it knowingly and fraudulently.[157]

Good faith is a defense to a charge of filing a false proof of claim.[158] This bankruptcy crime is similar to the offenses prohibited by Sections 152(2) and (3), with the distinction that statements under the latter statutes are made under oath, while a false proof of claim can be criminal without the claim being made under oath.[159]

Section 152(6) Bribery. Section 152(6) essentially criminalizes bribery in the context of a bankruptcy proceeding. Section 152(6) prohibits a person connected with a bankruptcy proceeding from offering or accepting money or property in exchange for acting or forbearing to act in a bankruptcy case. Prosecutions under this act are extremely rare and as a result published cases are equally rare.[160] In *United States v. Weiss,*[161] the defendant attempted to obtain $500 by promising to refrain from bidding at the sale of debtor's assets. The defendant advised that if he were not paid the $500, he would attempt to outbid the other party.[162] The defendant was convicted of violating Section 152. The defendant attempted to argue that he did not violate the statute because his actions were only preparatory in nature and not an actual attempt to bribe. In essence, the court found that the defendant did exactly what he promised he would do if not paid the money, which was to bid on the assets.[163]

Section 152(5) Fraudulent Receipt of Debtor's Property. In addition to the prohibition against bribery contained in Section 152(6), Section 152(5) makes it a crime for a person to knowingly and fraudulently receive any material amount of property from a debtor after the filing of a bankruptcy proceeding.

Sections 152(8) and (9) Concealment, Destruction, and Withholding of Documents. Section 152 contemplates that wrongdoers, in an attempt to cover-up their fraudulent acts, will "destroy the evidence." Accordingly, Sections 152(8) and (9) make any attempt by a person to falsify, destroy, or withhold records of the debtors a separate criminal offense. In the case of *In the Matter of Orenduff,*[164] the court concluded that the debtor had access to certain records and did not reveal them to the trustee.[165] As a result, the court denied the debtor a discharge.[166]

Aiding and Abetting Notably, Section 152 punishes any "person" who commits one of the enumerated crimes in the statute. Thus, it is not only the debtor who can face criminal liability under Section 152, but also the professionals who assist the debtor, including the debtor's attorneys. In *United States v. Dolan,*[167] the debtor's attorney was convicted of aiding and abetting in the concealment of property from the bankruptcy estate. Gary Dolan, an attorney, represented David Anderson in several business litigation matters. On September 16, 1987, an involuntary Chapter 7 bankruptcy case was filed against Anderson.[168] Dolan represented Anderson in the case, which was converted to one under Chapter 11. Dolan also assisted Anderson in filing his schedules of assets and liabilities.[169] The schedules included several omissions, including the omission of Anderson's ownership of a Ferrari valued at $85,000.[170]

Also omitted was reference to a lawsuit filed by Anderson against Intermedics, Inc. during the bankruptcy case (the "Intermedics Lawsuit").[171] The Intermedics Lawsuit was filed during the course of the bankruptcy case. While Dolan was not the lead attorney, he was listed as additional counsel and was aware of the existence of the Intermedics Lawsuit.[172] A settlement was reached with Intermedics, Inc. whereby Anderson received two checks totaling approximately $1.9 million.[173] Dolan was aware of the settlement.[174] The settlement agreement also provided that Dolan was to receive $50,000 as a personal bonus.[175]

Despite knowledge of the existence of the settlement proceeds and the Ferrari, neither Dolan nor Anderson ever amended the schedules to include these items.[176] While Anderson amended the schedules in other respects, he failed to list either the Ferrari or the settlement proceeds.[177]

Dolan repeatedly told Anderson's creditors that Anderson was unable to pay them.[178] Dolan did not mention the ownership of the Ferrari or the receipt of the settlement proceeds during settlement negotiations with various creditors.[179] Specifically, at Dolan's trial, a number of attorneys testified that Dolan explicitly advised them that Anderson did not have sufficient funds to pay claims. This misrepresentation resulted in a creditor settling a $21,245.81 claim for $5,000. This creditor's attorney testified that if she had known of the existence of the settlement proceeds, she would not have settled for such a small amount.[180]

In upholding Dolan's conviction, the court noted that Dolan was aware of Anderson's ownership of the Ferrari and the $1.9 million settlement proceeds, and Dolan signed an acknowledgment that authorized the payment of the settlement proceeds directly to Dolan. Based on Dolan's knowledge and his failure to disclose the existence of the assets, the court concluded that Dolan's actions were criminal.

An attorney was similarly convicted of aiding and abetting her client's fraudulent concealment in *United States v. Webster.*[181] Steven Deiss purchased a tavern and retained the services of attorney Leslie Webster to incorporate his ownership of the business.[182] The attorney advised Deiss and his wife to consider filing for bankruptcy in order to discharge their debts.[183] The attorney incorporated a new entity that acquired the tavern and its assets.[184] Following the incorporation of the tavern, Deiss and his wife followed the defendant's advice and filed for Chapter 7 bankruptcy. The defendant represented the Deisses in the bankruptcy case and in this capacity drafted the debtors' bankruptcy schedules and statement of financial affairs.[185]

The schedules and statement of financial affairs contained two significant false representations. First, the Deisses' schedules stated that Steven Deiss had voluntarily surrendered ownership of the tavern in exchange for release of an unpaid balance of a land contract.[186] Deiss failed to identify in the schedules that his tavern had been conveyed to a corporation on the eve of the bankruptcy filing.[187] Additionally, on the debtors' list of personal property, the defendant failed to report any stock ownership Deiss had in the new corporation and represented to the bankruptcy trustee that this was a "no asset case."[188] Approximately one year after Deiss was discharged, an investigation by an insurance company regarding a fire at the tavern uncovered the debtors' bankruptcy filing, which indicated that Deiss had no interest in the tavern. Deiss was subsequently charged with fraudulent concealment of assets to which he pleaded guilty. Deiss's cooperation with the government investigation led to the defendant, his attorney, being indicted and convicted on the charge of aiding and abetting the fraudulent concealment of assets.[189] On appeal, the court noted that there was ample evidence to convict Deiss including participation in the incorporation; backdating stock certificates; and with this knowledge, preparing the schedules and statement of financial affairs of the debtor.[190]

The reasoning of these cases may also apply to other professionals, such as accountants. Consequently, no group of professionals is immune to the provisions of Section 152.

Embezzlement—18 U.S.C. § 153

Title 18, Section 153 of the United States Code makes it a criminal offense for a person to knowingly and fraudulently misappropriate, for his own use, embezzle, spend, or transfer property of the debtor's estate. Additionally, Section 153 makes it a criminal offense for a person to knowingly and fraudulently secrete and destroy any documents belonging to the debtor's estate.

Section 153 is not as far reaching as Section 152, since Section 153 applies only to persons in a fiduciary relationship with respect to the debtor's assets and property. A person in a fiduciary relationship has an obligation of trust with respect to the assets of another. Section 153 also applies to persons participating in the administration of the bankruptcy estate as a trustee, custodian, marshal, or an attorney. Courts have defined a "custodian" under Section 153 as a person other than a trustee or receiver (but including the trustee's attorney) who takes custody of any property belonging to a bankrupt estate.[191] This offense carries a penalty of up to five years imprisonment and/or a fine.

The bankruptcy crimes of "fraudulent concealment" and "embezzlement" are similar but distinct criminal offenses. Oftentimes related activities may give rise to violations of both statutes. Such was the scenario in the case of *United States v. Atiyeh*.[192]

Atiyeh was the president and controlling shareholder of Quality Realty Construction, Inc. ("QRCI"). In 1996, QRCI sold a building to Regional Realty Holding, Inc. ("RRHI"), subject to a purchase money mortgage. On February 7, 1997, QRCI filed for bankruptcy under Chapter 11.

The bankruptcy court entered an order that required the debtor to deposit all mortgage payments received from RRHI in a debtor-in-possession ("DIP") account. The bankruptcy court expressly prohibited the debtor from disbursing any of the funds received from RRHI unless the court authorized the disbursement. The debtor established four DIP accounts.

Between March 1997 and August 2000, the defendant, without authorization, wrote checks and made withdrawals from the DIP accounts totaling approximately $280,000. Compounding his wrongdoing, the defendant proceeded to submit false monthly operating reports to the bankruptcy court in an effort to conceal these transfers of estate assets. Additionally, the defendant deposited checks, drawn on accounts with insufficient funds that he controlled, into the DIP account in order to create falsely inflated DIP account balances to further conceal his embezzlement. The defendant was indicted under Sections 152 and 153.

The *Atiyeh* defendant attempted to have the criminal indictment dismissed, arguing that the counts were multiplicative, charged the same offense in two or more counts, and violated the double jeopardy clause of the United States Constitution.[193]

The court noted that embezzlement under Section 153 requires that a person knowingly and fraudulently appropriate or embezzle property belonging to the debtor's estate.[194] In contrast, fraudulent concealment requires that a person knowingly and fraudulently conceal, in connection with a bankruptcy case, any property belonging to the debtor's estate. The latter does not require that the person be in a fiduciary relationship or that the property be misappropriated for the person's own use. The court noted that Section 153 requires proof of embezzlement, whereas Section 152 does not, and, similarly, Section 152 requires concealment, while Section 153 does not. Therefore, the *Atiyeh* court found that the two counts addressed two different and separate criminal offenses, and thus the defendant may be convicted of both crimes.[195]

Bankruptcy Fraud—18 U.S.C. § 157

Pursuant to Section 157 of title 18 of the United States Code,[196] it is a bankruptcy crime for a person to utilize a bankruptcy filing or related document for the purpose of carrying out or concealing a fraudulent scheme. While Sections 152 and 153 criminalize certain actions or inactions of a person involved in a bankruptcy proceeding, Section 157 aims to prevent a person from utilizing the Bankruptcy Code to commit fraud or conceal fraud.

Section 157 was passed as part of the Bankruptcy Reform Act of 1994[197] and represented the first bankruptcy crime statute passed since 1898.[198] At the time of its passage, there had been increased evidence of individuals using the Bankruptcy Code and, in particular, the protection provided for by the automatic stay of Section 362(a), in unanticipated ways. Congress enacted Section 157 in an attempt to prevent the use of the Bankruptcy Code to advance or conceal a fraudulent scheme.

To be in violation of Section 157(1), a bankruptcy petition in furtherance of a plan to defraud or conceal fraud is required to be filed.[199] Under Section 157(2), a violation occurs when one also files a pleading in a bankruptcy case in furtherance of a plan to defraud or in an effort to conceal such fraud.[200] The distinction between Sections 157(1) and 157(2) is that in the latter, a bankruptcy proceeding already exists, and the ongoing bankruptcy process is used to advance or conceal a fraudulent scheme. Finally, under Section 157(3), making a false or fraudulent representation related to a bankruptcy proceeding constitutes a violation under the statute.[201] A written pleading is not required; rather, any false representation, whether made in writing or filed in court is sufficient. This includes false testimony or a false declaration and commonly arises when a person fraudulently represents the existence of a bankruptcy case.[202]

Courts have recognized these elements for bankruptcy fraud under Section 157:

> 1) the existence of a scheme to defraud or intent to later formulate a scheme to defraud and 2) the filing of a bankruptcy petition 3) for the purpose of executing or attempting to execute the scheme.[203]

In *United States v. Brown,*[204] the court found that the defendant met all of these elements.[205] The defendant devised a scheme to defraud homeowners and lenders by working with debtors to file falsified real estate deeds in the bankruptcy petitions of the debtors in an effort to frustrate foreclosure proceedings.[206] The defendant argued that debtors may legitimately file for bankruptcy in order to delay foreclosure proceedings, and thus her scheme was not an effort to defraud.[207] The court, however, pointed out that unlike legitimate bankruptcy petitions, the petitions here were based on fictitious deeds of trust that were created by the defendant. Based on this evidence, the court concluded that there was sufficient evidence to find that the defendant had a scheme to defraud, and the defendant assisted debtors in the filing of bankruptcy petitions in furtherance of a scheme to defraud the homeowners and lenders. The defendant's conviction was upheld.

Miscellaneous Bankruptcy Crimes—18 U.S.C. §§ 154, 155, and 156

Sections 152, 153, and 157 of Title 18 of the United States Code are the most relevant bankruptcy crime statutes for purposes of detecting and/or preventing fraud. There are, however, three other bankruptcy crime statutes, Sections 154, 155, and 156 of Title 18, that should also be of concern to professionals assisting individuals or corporations in bankruptcy. While these sections are more specific and, therefore, more limited in their application, they are equally important.

Section 154 provides that dishonest officers of the bankruptcy court (including trustees) can be criminally punished for (1) knowingly purchasing any property of the bankruptcy estate to which the person is an officer; (2) knowingly refusing to permit an interested party from having a reasonable opportunity to inspect the documents of the estate which are in the officer's possession when such interested party has court authority to inspect such documents; and (3) knowingly refusing to permit the United States Trustee from having a reasonable opportunity to inspect the estate documents within the officer's control.[208]

Section 155 makes it a criminal offense to knowingly and fraudulently enter into an arrangement to fix the fees or compensation to be paid from the estate.[209] Under Section 155, "attorneys may not knowingly and fraudulently enter into agreements, express or implied, for the purpose of fixing compensation to be paid in a bankruptcy case."[210] Compensation and reimbursement of professional persons is allowed after notice and a hearing and judicial review pursuant to Section 330 of the Bankruptcy Code. In *Lutheran Hospitals & Homes v. Duecy,*[211] the Ninth Circuit Court of Appeals held that the purpose of Section 155 "is to keep the fees under the control of the court to prevent trustees, creditors and others, and their counsel, from playing fast and loose with other people's money in courts of bankruptcy."[212]

Finally, Section 156 makes it a criminal offense to knowingly disregard a bankruptcy law or rule.[213] Unlike the other bankruptcy crimes, Section 156 applies only to a "bankruptcy petition preparer."[214] Essentially, Section 156 makes it unlawful in certain situations for a non-attorney bankruptcy preparer to intentionally disobey the Bankruptcy Rules or Bankruptcy Code.[215] The Bankruptcy Code defines a bankruptcy petition preparer as a person, other than an attorney, who prepares for compensation a document for filing.[216] The type of services, however, that a bankruptcy petition preparer can provide are limited. Some services a bankruptcy petitioner may provide include meeting with a prospective debtor and providing forms for the debtor to complete, without any assistance from the bankruptcy petition preparer. The bankruptcy petition preparer can also transcribe information provided by the debtor. The bankruptcy petition preparer cannot give legal advice or otherwise assist the debtor in completing the forms other than providing secretarial-type services. Also, pursuant to Section 110 of the Bankruptcy Code, the petition preparer is required to sign a debtor's petition or schedules and statement of financial affairs. If the bankruptcy petition preparer fails to comply with this requirement, the bankruptcy petition preparer can face a fine, imprisonment, or both, pursuant to Section 156 of the United States Code.[217]

Punishment

Violations of Sections 152, 153, and 157 are subject to fines up to $250,000 and/or an imprisonment up to five years. Violations of Section 154 are subject to fines up to $250,000 and forfeiture of office. Violations of Sections 155 and 156 are subject to fines up to $250,000 and/or imprisonment of up to five years.

Obstruction of Justice—18 U.S.C. § 1519

Section 1519 of Title 18 of the United States Code was passed as part of the Sarbanes-Oxley Act of 2002 and provides enhanced punishments for alteration, falsification, or destruction of records designed to impede investigations of federal agencies or in connection with bankruptcy proceedings. There has not yet been any significant interpretation of this section by the courts;[218] therefore, the meaning of this broad statutory language is unclear.[219] The language of Section 1519 indicates that this section applies to Title 11 of the United States Code, which includes the Bankruptcy Code. Although this section is sometimes referred to as an anti-shredding provision (presumably it addresses the excesses alleged to have occurred within the Arthur Andersen accounting firm in connection with the Enron debacle), its language certainly goes beyond that characterization. Section 1519 also appears duplicative of the statutory language already found in Sections 152(8), 152(9), and 157 of title 18.

A violation of Section 1519 provides for punishment of up to 20 years imprisonment, while Section 157 provides for not more than 5 years imprisonment. Commentators have criticized the statutory language of Section 1519 for being undefined, unspecific, and vague.[220] Nonetheless, given its broad provisions and significant punishment, Section 1519 could act as a powerful tool to deter and punish fraud in a bankruptcy context.

FRAUDULENT TRANSFER STATUTES

While the Bankruptcy Code presents certain obstacles to all creditors, it can also enhance prospects for recovery, particularly concerning fraudulent transfers of property. Certain remedies are unique to the Bankruptcy Code, while others are creatures of state law that may also be enforced through a bankruptcy proceeding.

For centuries, debtors in financial distress have employed fraudulent devices in an effort to avoid having to pay or otherwise satisfy obligations owed to their creditors. At the same time, lawmakers have sought to enact legislation, and courts have endeavored to decide cases, so as to deter and/or set aside such fraudulent transactions. Both federal and state laws include provisions designed to remedy debtors' attempts to defraud creditors. Modern fraudulent conveyance law focuses on both traditional *actual fraud,* where the transferor acts with the intent to hinder, defraud, or delay creditors, and *constructive fraud,* where the financially distressed transferor engages in a transaction, or a series of transactions, resulting in a transfer of some or all of the transferor's assets (i) in exchange for something worth less than its reasonably equivalent value, or (ii) without receiving fair consideration.

All 50 states have adopted either the Uniform Fraudulent Conveyance Act ("UFCA") or the Uniform Fraudulent Transfer Act ("UFTA").[221] Under these state statutes, a creditor can attack a transfer made fraudulently as to creditors based on the actual or constructive fraud of the transferor. If the transferor becomes a debtor under the Bankruptcy Code, the trustee or debtor-in-possession may institute a proceeding on behalf of creditors pursuant to similar provisions contained in Section 548 of the Bankruptcy Code. This section permits avoidance of fraudulent transfers that were made within two years[222] prior to the date that the bankruptcy petition was filed. Additionally, under the trustee's "strong-arm powers" of Section 544(b) of the Bankruptcy Code, the trustee or debtor-in-possession may also institute a proceeding to avoid any transfer that is voidable under applicable non-bankruptcy law (e.g., applicable state UFCA or UFTA laws). This ability to employ state law for the benefit of the bankruptcy estate may extend the so-called look-back period well beyond two years and enable the trustee or debtor in possession to avoid certain transactions that would otherwise be unassailable under Section 548.

State Law

Modern fraudulent conveyance law can be traced back to England's Statute of 13 Elizabeth, enacted in 1571. Many American jurisdictions either wholly adopted or relied on some form of the Statute of 13 Elizabeth.[223] Under Chapter 5 of the Statute of 13 Elizabeth, any conveyance of property made with the intent to "delay, hinder or defraud creditors" was deemed void.[224] The intent to delay, hinder, or defraud creditors is, however, rarely capable of direct proof.[225] Therefore, in an effort to achieve fair and just results, courts began to recognize certain "signs and marks of fraud" from which a court can infer the requisite intent.[226] These commonly referred to "badges of fraud" include transfers to friends or relatives, transfers for no consideration, secret transfers, transfers where the debtor remains in possession of and continues to use the property, and transfers made when creditors have already commenced collection activity.[227]

Twyne's Case, the seminal English case on fraudulent conveyance law that is still cited and relied on by modern courts, provides a typical fact pattern to which fraudulent conveyance laws would apply. In *Twyne's Case,* the debtor, Pierce, owed "C" £200 and owed Twyne £400. Pierce secretly transferred his property, including his sheep, to Twyne. Pierce, however, retained use and possession of the sheep, including selling certain sheep, shearing and marking others, and generally behaving as if the sheep were still Pierce's property. In an effort to collect his £200, C sent a sheriff to levy on the sheep that C thought were Pierce's property. Friends of Twyne prevented the sheriff from seizing the property, indicating that the sheep no longer belonged to Pierce, but were instead owned by Twyne. In reaching its conclusion that Pierce's transfer to Twyne was fraudulent as against Pierce's creditors, the court noted six "signs and marks of fraud" (now generally referred to as badges of fraud), namely:

1. The "gift" was a general transfer of all of Pierce's property, including necessities.
2. Pierce retained possession of the property and continued to use it as if it were his own.
3. The transaction was secret.
4. The transfer was made while C was pursuing collection activity against Pierce.
5. There was a friendship between Pierce and Twyne.
6. The transfer document explicitly recited the transfer was made "honestly, truly, and bona fide."[228]

Twyne's Case illustrates that courts first presented with fraudulent transfer cases were focused on debtors' bad conduct to protect their interest in their property at the expense of their creditors.

Uniform Fraudulent Conveyance Act.[229] In 1918, in an effort to modernize and make uniform fraudulent conveyance laws, the National Conference of Commissioners on Uniform State Laws ("NCCUSL") promulgated the Uniform Fraudulent Conveyance Act.

The UFCA proved successful in reducing confusion, inconsistencies, and uncertainty in the law. The UFCA not only codified established common law principles, it also clarified substantive issues and simplified procedures. For example, in addition to continuing to invalidate transfers made with "actual fraudulent intent," the UFCA introduced the concept of "constructive fraud," by including provisions to invalidate conveyances without regard to the party's actual intent. In analyzing actual fraud cases under the UFCA, courts continued to rely on the traditional badges of fraud that had developed at common law to establish a party's subjective intent. In the case of *In re Reed's Estate,*[230] the court explained that:

> Since it is impractical to look into a person's mind to ascertain his intention, it is necessary to consider surrounding circumstances. Since it is most difficult to prove intent by direct evidence, circumstantial evidence is necessary. The issue of actual fraud is commonly determined by recognized indicia, demonstrated badges of fraud, which are circumstances so frequently attending fraud; a concurrence of several will make out a strong case and be the circumstantial evidence sufficient to sustain a court's finding.[231]

As explained in greater detail later, the badges of fraud commonly relied on by courts include: the relationship between the debtor and the transferee; the consideration for the conveyance; any insolvency or indebtedness of the debtor; how much of the debtor's estate was transferred; a reservation of benefits, control, or dominion by the debtor; and any secrecy or concealment of the transaction.[232]

The UFCA identifies several situations involving "constructive fraud" that may be attacked based on certain objective criteria. Specifically, a conveyance may be deemed "constructively fraudulent" as to creditors if it is not supported by "fair consideration" and one of these three conditions is met:

1. The transferor is insolvent or rendered insolvent by the transfer.[233]
2. The transferor is engaged or about to engage in a business or transaction for which the property remaining in his hands after the conveyance is unreasonably small.[234]
3. The transferor intends or believes that he will incur debts beyond his ability to pay as they mature.[235]

An essential element of a "constructive fraud" claim is lack of "fair consideration." Section 3 of the UFCA provides that:

> Fair consideration is given for property, or [an] obligation, (a) [w]hen in exchange for such property, or obligation, as a fair equivalent therefor, and in good faith, property is conveyed or an antecedent debt is satisfied, or (b) [w]hen such property, or obligation is received in good faith to secure a present advance or antecedent debt in amount not disproportionately small as compared with the value of the property, or obligation obtained.[236]

What is fair consideration must be determined by the facts of each case.[237] Courts agree, however, that a promise of future support is not fair consideration.[238]

Uniform Fraudulent Transfer Act.[239] The Uniform Fraudulent Transfer Act was proposed by the NCCUSL in 1984 as a replacement for the UFCA and to update fraudulent conveyance law to reflect changes incorporated into the Bankruptcy Code in 1978 and certain provisions of the Uniform Commercial Code.

The UFTA continued the long-standing rule prohibiting transactions consummated with an actual, subjective intent to hinder, delay, or defraud creditors.[240] In contrast to the UFCA (which failed to provide courts with any guidelines for establishing actual intent), Section 4(b) of the UFTA acknowledges the usefulness of objective criteria by listing a number of factors that courts *may* consider in assessing the transferor's and transferee's subjective intent.[241] The factors listed in Section 4(b) of the UFTA correspond closely to the badges of fraud that had developed under the common law to create a presumption of fraudulent intent. Comment 5 to the UFTA makes clear that the factors listed in Section 4(b) should be considered as mere relevant evidence and do not constitute presumptions of fraud.[242] The comments to the UFTA also encourage courts to consider any circumstantial evidence that may negate a conclusion of fraudulent conduct.[243]

Similar to the UFCA, under the UFTA certain transactions may be challenged as fraudulent solely because objective factors indicate that the rights of unsecured creditors are affected by the transaction.[244] Both the UFCA and the UFTA consider these "constructively fraudulent" transfers sufficiently harmful to creditors to justify avoidance of the transfer, regardless of the actual intent of the parties.[245] Under the UFTA, a transaction may be set aside as "constructively fraudulent" if: (i) the transfer was made or the obligation incurred for less than "reasonably equivalent value,"[246] and (ii) one of these three situations exists:

1. The transferor is insolvent.[247]
2. The transferor's business is left with "unreasonably small capital" or "unreasonably small assets."[248]
3. The transferor intended to incur or believed, or reasonably should have believed, that it was incurring debts beyond its ability to pay them as they came due.[249]

In contrast to the UFCA's "fair consideration" definition that considers the value received by the transferor *and* the good faith of the transferee,[250] the UFTA removes the issue of the transferee's good faith from the constructive fraud analysis. Instead, the UFTA focuses on the transferor's receipt of "reasonably equivalent value" and ignores the good faith of the transferee.[252] Under the UFTA, however, a transferee may assert its good faith as a defense to the action.[252]

The UFTA fails to define "reasonably equivalent value," instead adopting the Bankruptcy Code's general approach to the concept.[253] The determination of "reasonably equivalent value" generally involves simply comparing the value of what was transferred with what was received.[254] For example, the court for *In re Shape* explained that a payment of $70,000 for stock worth more than $1.5 million lacks reasonably equivalent value.[255] Similarly, the court in *BFP v. Resolution Trust Corporation* explained that, in most cases, the traditional common law notion of fair market value is the benchmark for determining reasonably equivalent value.[256] Decisions interpreting the bankruptcy definition of value do not, however, offer certainty or predictability because courts have concluded that the fact finder must have considerable discretion in determining whether reasonably equivalent value was exchanged.[257] Moreover, the case law does not establish a fixed percentage or safe harbor, but it does indicate that courts will consider all the facts and circumstances surrounding the particular transaction, including the type of value exchanged.[258]

Who May Commence an Action. Under the UFCA and the UFTA, creditors whose claims have matured at the time a suspect transaction occurs (i.e., present creditors), *and* creditors whose claims arise after the transaction but before the action to avoid the transfer is commenced (i.e., future creditors) may challenge transfers constituting actual fraud.[259] Only *present* creditors may challenge constructively fraudulent transfers made for inadequate consideration when the transferor is insolvent.[260] Both present *and* future creditors, however, may challenge constructively fraudulent transfers made for less than adequate consideration where the debtor (i) is left with unreasonably small assets and (ii) intends to incur debts beyond its ability to pay.[261]

Federal Law

Bankruptcy Code Section 548.[262] Section 548 of the Bankruptcy Code provides a vehicle to attack fraudulent transfers made by a person or entity that subsequently becomes a debtor under the Bankruptcy Code. Section 548 is based, in large part, on the UFCA. Similar to the UFCA and the UFTA, Section 548 provides that a trustee or debtor-in-possession can avoid certain transfers made by the debtor within two years[263] of the filing of a bankruptcy petition (i) if certain financial tests are met (i.e., constructive fraud)[264] or (ii) if actual intent to hinder, delay, or defraud creditors is established (i.e., actual fraud).[265]

Application of UFCA and UFTA under the Bankruptcy Code. Notwithstanding the existence of the fraudulent transfer provisions of Section 548 of the Bankruptcy Code, the UFCA and the UFTA continue to play an integral role in fraudulent transfer avoidance under the Bankruptcy Code. Given the similarities in the statutes, cases decided under the UFCA and UFTA are considered persuasive authority for similar issues arising under Section 548 of the Bankruptcy Code.[266] Additionally, under Section 544 of the Bankruptcy Code, trustees and debtors-in-possession are given the status of a hypothetical lien creditor, thereby allowing trustees (or debtors-in-possession) to step into the shoes of a creditor of the debtor and utilize applicable state law (i.e., UFCA or UFTA) to seek to avoid a transaction that a creditor would have been able to attack but for the debtor's bankruptcy filing.[267]

Section 544's "strong arm" power provides the trustee (or debtor-in-possession) with, minimally, two advantages over using Section 548 of the Bankruptcy Code or the UFCA or UFTA outside of bankruptcy. First, utilizing the UFCA or the UFTA significantly expands the trustee's (or debtor-in-possession's) avoiding powers by allowing the trustee to utilize the significantly longer statutory "reachback" periods of the UFTA and the UFCA (which typically provide for a four- to six-year reachback period depending on the state), rather than the two-year time frame permitted under Section 548 of the Bankruptcy Code. Second, by utilizing the UFCA and the UFTA pursuant to Section 544(b) of the Bankruptcy Code, the trustee is able to pursue a claim on behalf of all creditors. As long as there is one creditor in existence at the commencement of the case who can challenge the transfer under applicable state law, the trustee can bring the action on behalf of all creditors of the debtor. By contrast, absent the benefit of Section 544, an individual creditor might not be economically motivated to bring an action to avoid a transfer under the UFCA or UFTA because the legal expense involved with the action might be cost prohibitive. Additionally, it would be left to each creditor to bring an action against the transferee for each such creditor's own individual benefit.

Recent Amendments to the Bankruptcy Code. The Bankruptcy Abuse Act, which went into effect on October 17, 2005, substantially amended the Bankruptcy Code, specifically as it relates to fraudulent activity. A driving force behind the Bankruptcy Abuse Act was the belief that the bankruptcy laws were being abused by undeserving debtors.[268] The recent amendments to the Bankruptcy Code were designed to prevent this perceived abuse. Several of the amendments to the Bankruptcy Code, promulgated by the Bankruptcy Abuse Act, address issues of fraud and fraud avoidance.

- *Fraudulent transfer "look-back" period.* Prior to enactment of the Bankruptcy Abuse Act, Bankruptcy Code Section 548 provided that a trustee (or debtor-in-possession) may avoid any transfers of an interest of the debtor in property that were made or which occurred within *one year* before the date of the filing of the bankruptcy petition. The Bankruptcy Abuse Act amended this Section to increase the "look-back" period from one year to two years.

  This amendment applies only to cases that are commenced one year after the effective date of the Bankruptcy Abuse Act (October 17, 2005). Thus, for any bankruptcy case commenced prior to October 17, 2005, the debtor will only have the ability to avoid fraudulent transfers made within one year of the bankruptcy filing.

  The expansion of the "look-back" period from one year to two years represents a significant change and brings the Bankruptcy Code current and consistent with the provisions of state law regarding fraudulent transfers as articulated in the UFTA and the UFCA. The delayed enactment feature is also significant as it gives debtors fair warning that the fraudulent transfer period has been expanded. Professionals advising debtors should be aware of the revised Section 548 and its ramifications.
- *Avoidance of insider compensation.* In addition to extending the "look-back" period for the avoidance of fraudulent transfers from one year to two years, the Bankruptcy Abuse Act also amended Section 548 to expand the types of transfers that can be avoided. Under amended Section 548, there is now an express provision for a debtor to avoid a transfer, or the incurrence of an obligation, to or for the benefit of an "insider" under an employment contract which is not made in the ordinary course of business.[269]

  Moreover, a review of illustrative cases decided under Section 101(31) provides some further insight as to the meaning of the term "person in control" for purposes of determining who might be an insider. An attorney can be an insider if he or she exercises such control or influence over the debtor as to render their transactions not at arm's length.[270] A voting arrangement between all stockholders of the debtor and individual members of a limited partnership, effectively giving the members control over the corporation, resulted in all parties being considered "persons in control" for purposes of Section 101(31).[271]

  This revision to the Bankruptcy Code means that debtors will not be allowed to fraudulently transfer assets to or for the benefit of "insiders" by creatively structuring the transfers as part of an employment compensation package. Unless the employment contract was made in the ordinary course of the debtor's business, any transfer, or incurrence of an obligation, to or for the benefit of an insider will be subject to avoidance and recovery for the benefit of the debtor's creditors.
- *Ten-year bankruptcy planning reachback.* The Bankruptcy Abuse Act also amends Section 548(e)(1) of the Bankruptcy Code to provide that a transfer can be avoided if:

  (a) A debtor transfers property to a trust

  (b) Of which the debtor is a beneficiary

  (c) Within 10 years of the bankruptcy filing

  (d) With the intent to hinder, delay or defraud creditors.

  This change is significant in that the prior reachback provision under Section 548 was limited to one year.

INTENTIONALLY FRAUDULENT TRANSFERS

As discussed earlier, modern fraudulent transfer statutes are designed to address both actual (i.e., intentional) fraud and constructive fraud. To prove that a transfer was intentionally fraudulent under the UFCA, UFTA, or Section 548 of the Bankruptcy Code, a plaintiff must demonstrate that the transfer was perpetrated "with actual intent to hinder, delay, or defraud" creditors.[272] As noted, however, direct evidence of a fraudulent intent is often unavailable. Therefore, under the UFCA and the Bankruptcy Code, courts generally rely on circumstantial evidence to infer fraudulent intent.[273] When evaluating the circumstances of a transaction, courts have often relied on badges of fraud that include:

- The relationship between the debtor and the transferee
- The consideration for the conveyance
- Any insolvency or indebtedness of the debtors
- How much of the debtor's estate was transferred
- A reservation of benefits, control, or dominion by the debtor
- Any secrecy or concealment of the transaction[274]

Rather than relying exclusively on the courts to develop this evidence of fraud, the drafters of the UFTA provided a nonexclusive list of the indicia of actual fraudulent intent. This list includes, among other things, the debtor (i) transferring property or incurring an obligation to an insider; (ii) not disclosing, or concealing, a transfer or obligation; or (iii) retaining possession or control of property after its transfer by the debtor.[275] The factors listed in the UFTA are those that courts have historically relied on when determining the existence of actual fraud.

The court in *Huennekens v. Gilcom Corp. of Va. (In re Sunsport, Inc.)*[276] explained that a prima facie intentional fraud case may be established under Section 548 of the Bankruptcy Code and the UFTA by showing the presence of indicators of fraud.[277] In reaching its conclusion that an alleged prepetition "sale transaction" involving all of the debtor's assets constituted an intentional fraudulent transfer, the *Sunsport* court relied on these facts as evidence that several of the badges of fraud were present:

- The sale "transaction was obviously constructed very hastily and with hardly any regard for formalities" and with only minimal involvement of accountants and lawyers even though the principal of the "buyer" was found to be a "shrewd businessman."[278]
- Two officers and directors of the selling debtors stayed on as officers and directors of the "buyer."[279]
- The consideration paid was grossly inadequate.[280]
- The creditors of the selling debtors were "pressing very hard against the company at the time it transferred its assets to" the defendant.[281]
- The debtor's "principals were evasive, uncooperative, and actually concealed the asset transfer on [debtor's] bankruptcy schedules."[282]

As noted by the Fourth Circuit in *Tavenner v. Smoot,*[283] any transfer between related parties will be closely scrutinized by courts and, if made without adequate consideration, will create a presumption of actual fraudulent intent.[284] In *Smoot,* the defendant, Ken Smoot, received $217,059.25 in settlement of a personal injury action. Smoot promptly (the same day) transferred the settlement proceeds to Glass Apple Corporation, a family corporation of which he was the president, his wife was the vice president, and his son was the secretary and treasurer. Smoot's wife held 50 percent of Glass Apple's stock, and his children held the rest. Glass Apple then distributed such proceeds out to Smoot and his family in the form of loans, "wages," a car for his wife, and a motorcycle for his son.

Two months after receipt of the settlement proceeds, and at a time when Smoot was otherwise experiencing personal financial problems, Smoot was ordered to pay approximately $350,000 in connection with a federal wiretapping action that had been commenced against him by his former employer and a union. After filing a personal Chapter 7 bankruptcy proceeding, wherein Smoot claimed an exemption for the settlement funds pursuant to a Virginia law creating an exemption for money recovered in personal injury actions, Smoot's Chapter 7 Trustee sued Smoot and his family members that had received the benefit of the transfers made by Glass Apple.[285] The court of appeals noted that because the transfers were made between related parties, there was a presumption of actual fraudulent intent on the part of Smoot to hinder, delay, or defraud his creditors.[286] The court explained that this presumption established the trustee's prima facie case and shifted the burden of proof to the debtor to establish the absence of fraudulent intent.[287] Since Smoot had not rebutted the presumption of actual fraud raised after he transferred the proceeds to a corporation owned entirely by members of his immediate family without consideration, the trustee was entitled to avoid the transfer.[288]

CONSTRUCTIVELY FRAUDULENT TRANSFERS

Even absent evidence of actual intent on the part of the transferor to hinder, delay, or defraud creditors, a transfer can still be challenged as fraudulent by establishing "constructive fraud." A constructively fraudulent transfer is one in which: (1) a transferor does not receive "fair consideration" or "reasonably equivalent value" in exchange for the transfer, *and* (2) in which the transferor: (a) is insolvent at the time of the transfer or is rendered insolvent because of the transfer; (b) retains unreasonably small capital with which to operate its business; *or* (c) intends to incur debts beyond its ability to pay as those debts mature.[289] There is no requirement to show ill intent on the part of the transferor; the focus is on the net effect of the transfer on the debtor's estate rather than on the intent of the transferor.[290]

"Fair Consideration" or "Reasonably Equivalent Value"

The outcome in many constructive fraud cases under the UFCA turns on the question of "fair consideration," which is defined as a fair equivalent given in good faith.[291] By including a good faith requirement under the UFCA, the drafters directed the inquiry into the nature of the exchange attacked. Therefore, even when a conveyance is challenged without regard to actual intent to defraud, a court must consider the good faith of the transferee. [292]

In determining whether the value received by the transferor was reasonably equivalent (the standard utilized under the UFTA and Section 548 of the Bankruptcy Code), the focus is on the quantifiable economic consideration received by the transferor in exchange for the transfer, rather than on the value given up by the transferee.[293]

Neither the Bankruptcy Code nor the UFTA provides a definition of "reasonably equivalent value." As noted by the Supreme Court in *BFP v. Resolution Trust Corp.*,[294] "of the three critical terms 'reasonably equivalent value,' only the last is defined: 'value' means, for purposes of [Section] 548, 'property, or satisfaction or securing of a . . . debt of the debtor.'"[295] Accordingly,

"Congress left to the courts the obligation of marking the scope and meaning of [reasonably equivalent value]."[296] The lack of a precise definition presents an especially difficult task for courts in cases where a debtor exchanges cash for intangibles, the values of which are difficult, if not impossible, to ascertain.[297]

The court in *Mellon Bank, N.A. v. The Official Committee of Unsecured Creditors of R.M.L., Inc.* (*In re R.M.L., Inc.*)[298] was presented with the task of valuing an intangible asset.[299] In *Mellon*, the debtor paid Mellon Bank $515,000 in loan commitment fees in connection with a formal loan commitment letter (that was subject to numerous closing conditions) issued by it.[300] After the loan failed to close, the debtor filed a Chapter 11 bankruptcy proceeding, and the Committee sued the bank to recover the $515,000 as a fraudulent transfer under the Bankruptcy Code. In defense of the action, Mellon argued, among other things, that the commitment letter conferred "reasonably equivalent value" on the debtor (i) measured by the fair market value of the services it provided and (ii) because the letter provided a financially troubled company with the "chance" of obtaining financing that could save it from bankruptcy.[301] The court agreed with Mellon that the mere opportunity to receive an economic benefit in the future may constitute "value" under the Bankruptcy Code.[302] The court, however, ultimately concluded that, based on the numerous conditions in the loan, it was unlikely that the debtor could have ever closed the loan and, therefore, the debtor had exchanged "substantial fees for an extremely remote opportunity to receive value in the future."[303] The court concluded that this minimal "value" was not reasonably equivalent to the fees the debtor had remitted to Mellon and ordered Mellon to return the portion of the fees not related to true out of pocket expenses incurred by Mellon.[304]

Transfers Made When the Transferor Was Insolvent, and Transfers that Made the Transferor Insolvent

UFCA. The UFCA uses a "balance sheet test" for determining insolvency.[305] Under Section 2(1) of the UFCA, "[a] person is insolvent when the present fair salable value of his assets is less than the amount that will be required to pay his probable liability on his existing debts as they become absolute and matured."[306] Courts have made clear that insolvency is determined "as of the time of the conveyance."[307] "Present fair salable value" means the value that can be obtained if the assets are sold with reasonable promptness in an existing (not theoretical) market.[308]

When a bankruptcy filing is not "clearly imminent" on the date of the challenged conveyance, the weight of authority holds that assets should be valued on a going concern basis.[309] When an entity is determined to be on its "deathbed" at the time of the conveyance, a liquidation value should be used.[310] Under this complicated calculation, debtors may be insolvent (for UFCA purposes) even when the value of their assets exceeds the amount of their debts, if the assets are illiquid and the debts are short term.[311]

UFTA and 11 U.S.C. § 548. Both the UFTA and Section 548 of the Bankruptcy Code use a simplified version of the UFCA "balance sheet" test for insolvency. Under the UFTA and Section 548, debtors are insolvent if the sum of their debts is greater than that of their assets "at a fair valuation."[312] The definition of assets is expansive and includes unliquidated and contingent claims.[313] Contingent assets and liabilities should not be considered at face value but rather must be discounted by the probability that the contingency will materialize.[314] Both the UFTA and Section 548 exclude any property that was transferred, concealed, or removed with the intent to hinder, delay, or defraud creditors when valuing the debtor's assets.[315] Additionally, under the UFTA, the debtor is presumed to be insolvent if the debtor is not paying debts as they come due.[316]

In attempting to value a debtor's guarantee of its parent corporation's debt (i.e., a contingent liability), the court in *Covey v. Commercial National Bank*[317] concluded that the liability must be discounted by the probability that the contingency will materialize.[318] The court determined that the proper method of valuing the guarantee was to multiply the total guaranteed debt by the probability that the guarantor would be called upon to satisfy the obligation.[319]

In *Official Committee of Former Partners v. Michael G. Brennan* (*In re Labram & Kuak, LLP*),[320] the court was faced with the issue of the proper valuation of a stream of future liabilities in determining the solvency of the debtor law firm.[321] In *Labram*, the official committee of former partners[322] of the dissolved debtor law firm and the official committee of unsecured creditors brought a fraudulent transfer action against a former partner of the debtor law firm to recover distributions made by the debtor prior to the bankruptcy case. In attempting to demonstrate that the debtor was insolvent at the time of the distributions, the plaintiffs' expert designated the entire amount of the debtor's "contingent lease payables" (i.e., its future monthly rent obligations under leases extending for several years) as liabilities. In reaching its decision not to include the entire amount of the "contingent lease payables" as a liability in the insolvency analysis, the court explained that "it is logical not to include all of the future rent as liabilities because this calculation miscategorizes the future rent liabilities as an obligation presently due in full, while, if the debtor remained a going concern, would have consisted of making installment payments in the future during the tenancy."[323] The court went on to explain that "if accounting to render all future rents immediately payable could be done as to rent, it could be so done with respect to any projectable future expense. Again, this would render any business with substantial projectable future expenses artificially deemed insolvent."[324]

Unreasonably Small Capital or Inability to Pay Debts

With a debtor-transferor situation, the fraudulent transfer acts allow a creditor, the trustee, or the debtor-in-possession to attack a constructively fraudulent transfer by establishing that the transfer left the debtor with (i) unreasonably small capital or (ii) an inability to pay its debts, rather than proving that the debtor was insolvent at the time of the transfer.[325]

Unreasonably Small Capital. Section 548(a)(1)(B)(i) to (ii)(II), UFCA Section 5, and UFTA Section 4 apply to transfers and obligations for less than a reasonably equivalent value that leave the debtor with unreasonably small capital for the continuance of a business or transaction. The debtor does not need to be insolvent at the time of the transfer or rendered insolvent as a consequence of the transfer.[326] The critical inquiry in determining whether a transfer or conveyance has left a company with unreasonably small capital involves weighing the raw financial data against both the nature of the enterprise itself and the extent of the enterprise's need for capital during the period in question.[327]

In the context of a UFCA Section 5 challenge, the court in *Barrett v. Continental Ill. Bank and Trust Co.*[328] explained the importance of considering the nature and extent of the transferor's business subsequent to the transfers.[329] In *Barrett,* the record demonstrated that the transferor, Eastern Capital Corporation ("Eastern"), was "perennially short of cash."[330] Two former owners and creditors of Eastern commenced an action against the defendant Continental to recover a $2 million transfer from Eastern to Continental, claiming that subsequent to the transfer, Eastern was left with unreasonably small capital. The $2 million transfer to Continental at issue in the case existed initially in the form of certificates of deposit issued by Continental.[331] The owner of Eastern transferred these certificates to Eastern to cover its capital requirements when he purchased the commodities brokerage.[332] When the certificates matured, the sole shareholder of Eastern caused Eastern to transfer the $2 million back to Continental.[333] The court initially noted the "somewhat unusual" situation, "for the challenged transfer was made by a company that was indisputably going out of business at the time the transfer was made."[334] The court explained that other courts have observed "that the basic purpose of [Section] 5 [of the UFCA] is to 'prevent an undercapitalized company from being thrust into the market place to attract unwary creditors to inevitable loss.'"[335] In reaching its conclusion that the debtor was not left with unreasonably small capital, the court acknowledged that, viewed in isolation, the $2 million transfer clearly left Eastern insolvent or nearly insolvent. The court held that "when the transfer is placed in the broader context of the operations Eastern contemplated during the spring of 1984 [when Eastern was essentially winding down its operation], the $2 million payment to Continental does not appear to us to have left the company with an 'unreasonably small capital.'"[336]

Inability to Pay Debts. Bankruptcy Code Section 548(a)(1)(B)(i) to (ii)(III), UFCA Section 6, and UFTA Section 4 apply to transfers and obligations for less than a *reasonably equivalent value* at a time when the debtor intended to incur or believed that the debtor would incur debts beyond the debtor's ability to pay as they came due. Solvency at or around the time of the transfer is not a defense to an attack under these provisions. It is unnecessary to prove particular debts have been contemplated; a general intention is enough.[337] Existence of an intent or belief concerning a debtor's ability to pay debts is a question of fact to be decided by the court.[338]

While there has not been a significant amount of case discussion on this subject, the court for *In the Matter of Farmers Federal Cooperative, Inc.*[339] was asked to decide whether the debtor intended to incur debts beyond its ability to pay when it issued chattel mortgages to its lender, McMillen Federal Finance ("McMillen").[340] The debtor issued three chattel mortgages to McMillen in exchange for three separate loans that the debtor used to purchase livestock. Based on testimony of an employee of the debtor that, prior to the granting of the first mortgage, McMillen was "experiencing difficulties in meeting its debts as they matured" and that he believed that the debts existing as of the date of the granting of the first mortgage, as well as subsequently incurred debts, "were beyond the Company's ability to pay as they matured," the court concluded that the debtor intended to incur debts beyond its ability to pay.[341] Accordingly, the court voided the mortgages granted to McMillen as fraudulent conveyances.[342]

APPLICATION OF FRAUDULENT TRANSFER LAWS

As debtors began to engage in more sophisticated commercial transactions, fraudulent transfer law and, specifically, the constructive fraud aspect of it evolved to address modern realities.

Leveraged Buyouts

One type of transaction that has engendered a significant amount of fraudulent transfer litigation is the leveraged buyout ("LBO"). In general terms, an LBO is a method of purchasing a company whereby the acquirer leverages (i.e., borrows against) the assets of the target company to finance the purchase of the target company's shares or assets.[343] An LBO can be thought of as three separate transactions:

1. The buyer's lender advances funds to the buyer, usually through an entity formed solely for the purpose of making the acquisition.
2. The acquirer uses the funds to purchase the target's assets or stock.
3. The acquirer causes the target to collateralize the original loan by granting liens on its assets and/or payment guaranties to the lender.

Given their structure, LBOs can be detrimental to creditors of the target company. The proceeds of the loans obtained by the acquiring company from the lender (which are now collateralized by the assets of the new company) pass through to the target's shareholders. Therefore, unsecured creditors of the target, who normally would have been repaid ahead of equity holders in the event of a bankruptcy, typically find themselves subordinated to a significant amount of LBO secured debt.

Initially, courts struggled with the application of fraudulent transfer law to LBOs.[344] For example, the court in *Kupetz v. Wolf*[345] explained that fraudulent conveyance laws were designed to prevent collusive transfers between debtors and their families and should not be applied to LBO transactions because the "debtor-creditor relationship is essentially contractual."[346] Commentators also initially questioned the applicability of fraudulent transfer law to LBOs.[347] In their article entitled "Fraudulent Conveyance Law and Its Proper Domain," Douglas G. Baird and Thomas H. Jackson explained that "a firm that incurs obligations in the course of a buyout does not seem at all like the Elizabethan deadbeat who sells his sheep to his brother for a pittance."[348] Notwithstanding the initial struggle to apply fraudulent conveyance law to LBOs, the vulnerability of the typical LBO to fraudulent transfer attack has now been confirmed nearly unanimously by the courts.[349]

The District Court for the Middle District of Pennsylvania in *United States v. Gleneagles Investment Co.*[350] was the first court to recognize the applicability of fraudulent conveyance law to LBOs.[351] The district court's opinion was affirmed by the Third Circuit and has become the seminal case in this area. In *Gleneagles,* the LBO was structured such that the target company and its affiliates received loan proceeds from a lender in exchange for a mortgage on their assets. The target companies then loaned the loan proceeds to the acquirer, which paid the money to the target's shareholders in exchange for the stock of the target. The Third Circuit expressly held that fraudulent conveyance laws are applicable to LBOs.[352] In reliance on the broad language of Pennsylvania's fraudulent conveyance statute, the Third Circuit explained that "this broad sweep does not justify exclusion of a particular transaction such as a leveraged buyout simply because it is innovative or complicated."[353]

The cornerstone of challenging an LBO transaction as a fraudulent conveyance is the idea that, as first recognized by the *Gleneagles* court, the series of transactions involved in an LBO should be "collapsed" and viewed as a single transaction to determine whether sufficient consideration has been given, rather than reviewing the effect of each discrete transaction.[354] Once the series of transactions has been collapsed, it is nearly impossible for a lender to show that the target company received fair consideration when it collateralized the LBO loans because, in the end, substantially all of the cash has been distributed out to the shareholders of the target rather than remaining in the company.

The bankruptcy case of *In re Hechinger Investment Company of Delaware*[355] provides a more recent example of a relatively large LBO that survived a challenge as to certain of the involved parties after the target company commenced a bankruptcy proceeding.[356] Prior to September 1997, Hechinger owned and operated stores under the Hechinger's and Home Quarters' trademarks. Until the Hechinger LBO, Hechinger and the England Family defendants retained control over the company with 70 percent of the voting power. From 1983 to 1996, Hechinger added 84 stores to the 34 stores that already existed. Due to intense competition in the industry, many of the stores were forced to close, and the corporation was left with a loss of $206 million for the seven-month period immediately preceding the LBO. Simultaneously, Builder's Square ("BSQ") was suffering from similar losses. Defendant Leonard Green & Partners ("Green") decided to acquire BSQ and merge it with Hechinger through an LBO.

After acquiring BSQ, the defendant acquired Hechinger through a triangular merger.[357] The Chase Bank Group financed both the BSQ acquisition and the Hechinger LBO with a loan amounting to $160.8 million in capital, after deducting fees and expenses. The loan was secured by all of BSQ's inventory, accounts receivable, and equipment. At this time, Chase Bank Group also loaned Hechinger $112 million, which, in relatively small part, paid off Hechinger's former capital lenders. The remaining $100 million was paid out to the shareholders, including Hechinger and the England Family. The inventory owned by Hechinger and BSQ was transferred in a series of steps to Hechinger Investment Company of Delaware ("HICD"), which became the permanent borrower under a $600 million secured loan made by the Chase Bank Group. A $243 million portion of the loan was used to pay off the BSQ loan, and $127 million of the loan was used to pay fees and to cash out the Hechinger shareholders. Hechinger emerged from the transaction with a 71.9 percent debt to capital ratio.

Shortly after the LBO, the ratings on Hechinger's senior notes and debentures dropped to poor standing. In the next 18 months, BSQ and Hechinger continued to lose money. By December 1998 Hechinger was in a severe liquidity crisis. Finally, after closing 34 BSQ stores, Hechinger and its affiliates voluntarily filed for Chapter 11 protection. Shortly after the filing and the closing of 89 additional stores, liquidation became inevitable.

The Official Committee of Unsecured Creditors of Hechinger Investment Company of Delaware (the "Hechinger Committee") and its affiliate debtors filed suit against various former directors and officers, as well as the controlling shareholders of Hechinger and certain lenders and investors who financed the Hechinger LBO. The plaintiff contended that Hechinger received less than reasonably equivalent value in exchange for the BSQ acquisition, including the payments to Hechinger's stockholders and the payment of transaction fees to Green and the Bank.

The court initially noted that the Third Circuit recognizes that multistep transactions can be collapsed when the steps of the transaction are part of one integrated transaction.[358] The court concluded that the steps of the transaction should be collapsed and considered as a single transaction because the directors, Green, and the bank all knew about the multiple steps of the transaction, and each step would not have occurred on its own.[359]

After rejecting the Hechinger Committee's intentional fraud claim as to the bank and Green, the court concluded that there was sufficient evidence in the record to imply fraudulent intent with respect to the directors:[360]

- The transaction may not have been completely disclosed to all of the directors.[361]
- The majority of the directors may have been "interested" directors, as the transaction was approved without a formal, uninterested director committee.[362]
- The directors that were also officers of Hechinger benefited substantially from the transaction, since prior to the transaction the board of directors increased their severance packages.[363]

Therefore, the court denied the directors' motion for summary judgment with respect to the plaintiff's intentional fraudulent conveyance claims.[364]

As to the Hechinger Committee's constructive fraud claims against the shareholders, the court concluded that the plaintiff did not satisfy its burden of proving that Hechinger had not received equivalent value through the transaction.[365] When determining the value of the transaction, the court here considered the fact that the merger of BSQ and Hechinger created a larger company which was more capable of competing in the current market.[366] Further, once the two companies were combined, the overhead costs of running both businesses were reduced.[367] The court also factored in the line of credit Hechinger produced as a result of the transaction and the newly combined accumulated assets from both companies that were valued at $260 million.[368] The fact that neither company was performing particularly well before or after the transaction had no bearing on the court's determination of value.[369] Furthermore, the $127 million paid out to the shareholders was far less than the value of assets acquired in the merger.[370] According to the court, this expressly defeated the plaintiff's argument that the money paid out to the shareholders in exchange for their shares was lost and never compensated.[371]

Similarly, the court concluded that the plaintiff failed to prove that Hechinger did not receive equivalent value for the fees paid out to Green.[372] An expert provided by Green testified that based on Green's work performance and industry standards, Hechinger received reasonably equivalent value for the payment of the management fees.[373] The court concluded that it was clear from the record that Green expended a significant amount of effort throughout the course of the transaction.[374] Obviously, this conclusion was tied to the court's determination that no actual or constructive fraud existed. Accordingly, the court granted defendant Green's motion for summary judgment with respect to the alleged constructively fraudulent transfers.[375]

Intercompany Guaranties

Lenders to one member of a corporate group will often require a guaranty of the debt from other members of the corporate group. Accordingly, creditors of a "stronger" member may be adversely affected if such member guarantees the bank debt of another "weaker" member of the corporate group.

A subsidiary's guaranty of a parent's obligation (an "upstream guaranty") frequently creates fraudulent transfer risk, as the court analyzes whether the subsidiary received "fair consideration" for its guaranty.[376] By contrast, when a parent company issues a guaranty for a subsidiary's obligations (a "downstream guaranty"), the fraudulent transfer risk is significantly lower since the parent (as the owner of the subsidiary) likely receives value from the additional credit obtained by the subsidiary.[377] A sister affiliate's guaranty of another affiliate's obligations (a "cross-stream guaranty") is likely to create the same fraudulent transfer risk associated with an upstream guaranty and will be subjected to the same scrutiny by the courts in determining whether an affiliate received "fair consideration" in guaranteeing the obligations of a sister company.[378]

Equivalent value will almost always be raised as a defense to a fraudulent transfer attack on a corporate guaranty. Equivalent value has been found to exist when a parent and subsidiary are part of an enterprise where each of their businesses benefits from the operations of the other and, therefore, access to additional credit can be said to benefit both group members.[379]

In *Tryit Enterprises v. General Electric Capital Corp. (In re Tryit Enterprises)*,[380] the plaintiffs were four related companies in the business of owning and operating rent-to-own franchises that leased home furnishings, electronics, and appliances. Prior to filing their Chapter 11 cases, the plaintiffs and another non-debtor affiliate entered into a loan agreement with General Electric

Capital Corporation ("GECC") pursuant to which GECC made approximately $7 million in financing available to the related entities to consolidate all of the outstanding obligations of the plaintiff and their nondebtor affiliates into one credit facility and provide funding to finance their daily operations. While each entity had guaranteed the entire obligation and each provided GECC with a security interest in their respective assets, each entity only received a portion of the loan proceeds.

In the ensuing bankruptcy case, the debtors-in-possession commenced an action against GECC to set aside the cross-collateralization and cross-guaranty provisions of the lending facility with GECC as fraudulent transfers under Texas law, contending that there was no fair consideration for the joint liability incurred by each plaintiff for the amount of the loan. The court ruled that the loan transactions were *not* voidable because they were made for fair consideration under the "single business enterprise" theory. As mentioned by the court, factors relevant to the "single business enterprise" analysis include a "single corporate" office that pays the bills for its affiliates, and each affiliate is charged with its proportional share of the main office expense, overlapping ownership among the business entities, centralized accounts, and where all entities are referred to by a single name.[381] In reaching its decision that the plaintiffs operated as a "single business enterprise," the court relied on, among other factors, the fact that the plaintiffs, as a group, were able to enter into the GECC facility, thereby providing them funding to continue to acquire inventory, finance their daily operations, pay off their existing obligations, and work with only one major secured creditor.[382] Separately, the plaintiffs would not have qualified for such financing.[383] Under these circumstances, the court found that the consideration given for the loans (i.e., the cross-guaranties of the plaintiffs) was "fair," and therefore the guaranties were not avoidable.[384]

Ponzi or Pyramid Schemes

Another transaction that has resulted in a significant amount of fraudulent transfer litigation is that of the pyramid or "Ponzi" scheme. As explained by one court:

> A "Ponzi" scheme is a term generally used to describe an investment scheme which is not really supported by any underlying business venture. The investors are paid profits from the principal sums paid in by newly attracted investors. Usually those who invest in the scheme are promised large returns on their principal investments. The initial investors are indeed paid the sizable promised returns. This attracts additional investors. More and more investors need to be attracted into the scheme so that the growing number of investors on top can get paid. The person who runs this scheme typically uses some of the money invested for personal use. Usually, this pyramid collapses and most investors not only do not get paid their profits, but also lose their principal investments.[385]

When a Ponzi enterprise fails and enters bankruptcy, the trustee is generally left with very few physical assets from which to pay creditors or investors that lost money. Often the only assets of the failed Ponzi enterprise are fraudulent transfer claims against those investors who received "returns" on their "investments." For example, in the Bennett Funding Group bankruptcy case,[386] the trustee filed over 10,000 fraudulent transfer lawsuits against former investors seeking recovery of over $100 million in transfers to investors.

The case of Bennett Funding Group, one of the largest bankruptcies involving a pyramid or Ponzi scheme, provides a typical example of the workings of this scheme. For years, Bennett Funding (and a number of related companies) leased office equipment and sold various interests in those leases to third-party investors. By early 1996, Bennett Funding had sold approximately 7,400 different investment products with a stated value of over $2 billion to over 220 banks and other financial institutions and to thousands of individual investors. In March 1996, as a result of a lawsuit filed by the Securities and Exchange Commission alleging investor fraud, certain of the Bennett Funding companies filed for bankruptcy protection. As revealed by the schedules of assets and liabilities filed by the trustee in the bankruptcy case, Bennett Funding owed, on a consolidated basis, approximately 11,500 individual investors in excess of $674 million and owed banks and other financial institutions another $215 million. The structure of the scheme was best described by the bankruptcy trustee:

> Using the proceeds of sales to new investors and bank borrowing to make payments on earlier investments, more and more cash was consumed in maintaining a massive pyramid scheme.
>
> Cash from banks and investors alike in all of the Bennett entities was commingled in a "honey pot" account. Cash was moved from the honey pot through a maze of transactions, often with affiliates or an inner ring of business associates. Cash transfers resembled a pinball machine, bouncing from company to company and creating the appearance of economic activity. When the music stopped, the collective debts of the group exceeded $1 billion, much of which will never be repaid.[387]

In addition to the Bennett Funding situation, numerous other bankruptcy cases have been filed in recent times involving fraudulent transfer attacks in connection with failed Ponzi schemes.[388]

Defendant-investors have raised several defenses to a fraudulent transfer claim with varying degrees of success. For example, some investors have argued that the trustee cannot establish that the transfer was "of an interest of the debtor in property," one of the elements necessary to establish a fraudulent transfer claim. The argument by these investors is that the property transferred by the debtor to the investor was obtained by the debtor through a fraud on other investors, and therefore, the debtor never actually obtained title to the funds.[389] Courts have generally held that the debtor has an interest in funds obtained from investors in a Ponzi scheme, and thus such a defense is not available.[390] The few courts that have allowed the defense have done so *only* when the Ponzi-investor can establish that the funds he received were the same funds that the Ponzi-investor invested in the debtor.[391]

Another defense raised by investor-defendants is based on the fact that the transfers received from the debtor generally come in one of two forms: Transfers can be a return of principal or a profit on the initial investment. Most courts have held that a debtor does receive equivalent value for the return of an investor's original principal investment, and therefore, such a transfer cannot be recovered as a fraudulent transfer.[392] Courts have almost unanimously held that the debtor does *not* receive reasonably equivalent value for any amount received in excess of the original investment thereby subjecting such amounts to fraudulent transfer attack.[393]

REMEDIES FOR THE RECOVERY OF FRAUDULENT TRANSFERS

Once a transfer has been determined to be fraudulent, the property that was transferred or the value of it can be recovered from the recipient. Section 550(a) of the Bankruptcy Code covers the liability for avoided transfers and, in pertinent part, provides:

> the trustee may recover, for the benefit of the estate, the property transferred, or, if the court so orders, the value of such property, from—

(1) the initial transferee of such transfer or the entity for whose benefit such transfer was made; or

(2) any immediate or mediate transferee of such initial transferee.[394]

The Bankruptcy Code does not define the terms "initial transferee," "immediate transferee," or "mediate transferee." In general, the party that receives the transfer or property *directly* from the debtor is the initial transferee.[395] Courts have used the "dominion or control" test to determine whether a recipient of funds is an "initial transferee" under Section 550.[396] Under the dominion or control test, a party is not considered an initial transferee of a transfer received directly from the debtor unless that party gains actual dominion or control over the funds.[397] When an intermediary party receives but does not gain actual dominion or control over the funds, that party is considered a mere conduit or agent for one of the real parties to the transaction.[398] Dominion or control over money or an asset means having the right to put the money to one's own use for whatever purpose the recipient so desires.[399] As explained by the Eleventh Circuit Court of Appeals, the application of the dominion or control test requires the court to "step back and evaluate a transaction in its entirety to make sure that their conclusions are logical and equitable."[400]

Fraudulent transfer defendants have been found to be an "initial transferee" when:

- The entity, a lender, received transfers from a corporate debtor guarantor upon instructions by insiders to apply the transfers to reduce the insider's debt to the lender because the lender was the only party to exercise control over funds immediately after they were transferred by the debtor.[401]
- The entity was the beneficiary of the trust fund which received the initial transfer.[402]
- The entity was the lessor of the debtor who received payment for rent arrearage as a precondition to giving a new lease to the purchaser of the debtor's business.[403]
- The entity retained a portion of the payment as its fee (at least as to the portion of the property transferred).[404]
- The entity was a shell corporation through which selling shareholders in a leveraged buyout were paid.[405]

The court in *Bonded Financial Services, Inc. v. European American Bank*[406] held that the defendant bank acted as a "mere conduit" when it handled the debtor's check, payable to the defendant's order with a note directing the defendant bank to deposit the check into another account.[407] The court explained that, even though the bank was the payee on the check, it acted only as a financial intermediary and received no benefit.[408] Similarly, a law firm holding its client's funds in escrow has been held to be a mere conduit.[409] Several other courts, however, have adopted a slightly different approach from that of the *Bonded Financial* court. These other courts have relied on equitable factors, such as good faith and lack of knowledge, in addition to lack of benefit received, to determine if an initial transferee is liable or just a conduit.[410]

The UFCA, UFTA, and Section 548 of the Bankruptcy Code provide some protection to good faith purchasers for value. Section 550(b) of the Bankruptcy Code provides that if an immediate or mediate transferee takes "for value, . . . in good faith, and without knowledge of the voidablity of the transfer," the trustee or debtor-in-possession may not recover the property or its value from such immediate or mediate "good faith transferee."[411] The trustee also may not recover the property or its value from a subsequent good faith transferee.[412] Congress has explained that the "good faith" requirement of Section 550 is intended to preclude a transferee (from whom the trustee can recover the property) from "laundering" or "washing" the property through an innocent third party.[413]

In *Davis v. Cook Construction Co.* (*In re SLF News Distributors, Inc.*),[414] the court held that a fraudulent transfer defendant, who had released a mechanic's lien in exchange for a $10,000 certified check without knowledge that the funds actually came from an insolvent debtor rather than from the entity who actually owed the money, was a protected, good faith, secondary transferee. Accordingly, the trustee could not recover the $10,000 from the defendant.

Sometimes courts will give a good faith transferee credit for amounts previously paid if the court determines that the good faith transferee did not pay "full" value. In *Burtrum v. Laughlin* (*In re Laughlin*),[415] the Laughlins transferred a piece of real property valued at $40,000 to their son for $1, and he then sold the property, subject to a $12,000 lien, to the Millers for $5,000. The court explained that the transfer from the Laughlins to their son for $1 was unquestionably an avoidable fraudulent conveyance.[416] Yet because the Millers took the property in good faith for value, they qualified as good faith transferees. Accordingly, the court gave the Millers the option either to (i) return the property to the trustee, subject to a lien for the $5,000 they paid for the property, or (ii) pay the trustee the fair market value of the property, less the $5,000 they had previously paid.

CORPORATE ACTORS/INDIVIDUAL LIABILITY

Once a defrauded creditor has exhausted its remedies in bankruptcy and remains unpaid, it still may have options available to it. While fraud claims have no greater priority in bankruptcy than general unsecured claims, individual debtors may be denied a discharge in bankruptcy as to some or all of their debts where fraud exists. A corporation only gets a discharge by confirmation of a plan of reorganization. Notwithstanding the lack of a discharge in bankruptcy, actual collection from individuals or corporations is another story. An insolvent corporation, in or out of bankruptcy, may simply liquidate its assets and cease to exist. Individuals may attempt to make themselves "judgment proof" by refusing to accumulate assets postbankruptcy (at least none that can be used to satisfy claims). In either situation, fraud victims may need to look to other solvent third parties to obtain payment. Transferees (or advisors of transferees) of fraudulent transfers, as discussed, are in such a group. In a corporate context, there may be the ability to pursue shareholders, officers, or directors, on a variety of theories. These theories may provide alternate avenues for recovery where the debtor has insufficient assets to satisfy fraud claims.

Personal Liability for Fraud

If a creditor has been defrauded, one obvious and direct avenue of recovery is to sue the individual person who committed the fraud. Persons are liable for their own fraudulent behavior.[417] As a general rule, officers and directors "are personally liable for these torts which they personally commit . . . even though performed in the name of an artificial body."[418] Since fraud is a tort, officers and directors will face personal liability for fraudulent actions that they commit, even if the actions are made on behalf of a corporation.[419] This may provide creditors with a direct avenue of recovery where, as often is the case, the corporation does not have sufficient assets to satisfy the claim.

Piercing the Corporate Veil

Creditors of a corporation may also seek to "pierce the corporate veil." Under this method of recovery, a creditor can pursue a claim directly against the shareholders normally protected from liability by the corporation for any claims against the corporation, including fraud claims. A claim to pierce the corporate veil is akin to a claim of fraud, as it is an allegation that the corporate shell is being used to hide or disguise the real identity of the debtor and its activities to defraud creditors.

In order to successfully pierce the corporate veil, a creditor must show that the shareholder abused the legal separation of corporation from owner and that the shareholder abused the corporation for illegitimate purposes:[420]

> In determining whether to pierce the corporate veil and find an alter ego, the court considers: (1) gross undercapitalization; (2) failure to observe corporate formalities; (3) non-payment of dividends; (4) insolvency of the debtor corporation; (5) siphoning of funds by the dominant shareholder; (6) non-functioning of other officers and directors; (7) absence of corporate records; and (8) the fact that the corporation is a mere façade for the operations of the dominant stockholder.[421]

The plaintiff has the burden of showing liability by "clear and convincing evidence."[422]

One example of a case where a defrauded creditor was able to pierce the corporate veil successfully was *Cantiere DiPortovenere Piesse S.p.A. v. Kerwin*.[423] In *Kerwin,* the plaintiff/creditor previously obtained a judgment against NRG in the amount of $190,981.33. Jerome Kerwin was the sole shareholder of NRG, and his wife, Helen Kerwin, was an officer of NRG. The plaintiff, after discovering that NRG was insolvent, sought to pierce the corporate veil and hold the Kerwins liable for the debt of NRG. The plaintiff alleged that NRG was a sham corporation, that the Kerwins exercised total control over NRG, and that they had rendered NRG insolvent by plundering and converting corporate assets. On a motion for new trial, the district court found that expert testimony established that the Kerwins had disregarded the corporate formalities of NRG. The court also ruled that proof of fraud was not required in order to pierce the corporate veil.[424]

Breach of Fiduciary Duty

Breach of fiduciary actions also often arise in the context of fraudulent transfers. Officers and directors of a corporation need to be aware that they may potentially be exposed to individual liability for actions that are undertaken when the corporation is insolvent or operating in the zone of insolvency.

In the event that the corporation fraudulently transfers assets, the directors may also be exposed to a claim for breach of fiduciary duty. Courts that have addressed this issue have found that personal liability extends for breach of fiduciary duty to directors, officers, and even to those individuals (i.e., lower-level corporate employees) who aid, abet, or conspire to commit the fraudulent transfer.[425]

Insolvency for a corporation is defined under the Bankruptcy Code as a financial condition such that the sum of an entity's debts is greater than all of its assets.[426] Under general corporate law, in a solvent corporation, directors owe a fiduciary duty to the shareholders of the corporation. Courts have taken the position, however, that the directors of an insolvent corporation owe a fiduciary duty to the corporation's *creditors*.[427] The rationale for this change is that the business decisions made by the officers and directors of an insolvent corporation directly affect the creditors.[428]

> The general rule is that directors do not owe creditors duties beyond the relevant contractual terms absent "special circumstances . . . e.g., . . . insolvency . . . ." When the insolvency exception does arise, it creates fiduciary duties for directors for the benefit of creditors.
>
> * * * *
>
> The economic rationale for the "insolvency exception" is that the value of creditors' contract claims against an insolvent corporation may be affected by the business decisions of managers. At the same time, the claims of the shareholders are (at least temporarily) worthless. As a result it is the creditors who "now occupy the position of residual owners."[429]

If the corporation is insolvent, the directors essentially become trustees for the corporation's creditors and hold the corporate assets in trust for the benefit of the corporation's creditors.[430] The directors owe a fiduciary duty not to deplete the corporate assets to the disadvantage of creditors. Thus, directors face broadened duties when a corporation is operating in the vicinity of insolvency that may expose them personally.[431]

In *Flegel v. Burt & Assoc., P.C. (In re Kallmeyer)*,[432] the debtor was a physician who formed a corporation, NIM, that provided patient and billing services. The debtor was the sole director, officer, and shareholder of NIM. A creditor sued NIM for unpaid legal fees. Following NIM's entry into insolvency, the debtor filed for bankruptcy, and the creditor sought to have the debt owed to it declared nondischargeable pursuant to Section 523(a)(4). The creditor alleged that the debtor breached her fiduciary duty to it after NIM transferred $71,800 to the debtor as a shareholder.

The court found that the debtor, as a director of NIM, owed a fiduciary duty to the creditor.[433] Thus, the debtor, as a director, had a shifting fiduciary duty to preserve NIM's assets for the benefit of its creditors. By facilitating the transfer of money from NIM to its shareholders while NIM was insolvent, the debtor breached her fiduciary duty to the creditor and committed a defalcation, rendering the debt nondischargeable under Section 523(a)(4).

Aiding and Abetting Fraudulent Transfers

Courts have recognized a cause of action for aiding and abetting a fraudulent transfer. Thus, in addition to pursuing fraudulent transfer claims, creditors who have been defrauded have also attempted to collect from a debtor's professionals, such as attorneys and accountants, under a theory that they aided and abetted the corporation in making a fraudulent transfer. This is a powerful tool for creditors. Currently it is not clear whether attorneys or accountants may be liable for aiding and abetting their clients to commit fraud based on their counsel and advice. Regardless of any potential liability under an aiding and abetting claim, attorneys and accountants would still be liable for any personal acts of fraud which they commit.

The issue of whether a cause of action exists for aiding and abetting a fraudulent transfer arose recently in the Illinois case of *Coleman v. Greenfield.*[434] In *Coleman,* the court concluded that under Illinois law a cause of action for aiding and abetting a fraudulent transfer does exist.[435]

In *Coleman,* the plaintiff filed a 10-count complaint seeking to enforce a judgment obtained against affiliates of the defendant. The plaintiff had previously obtained a $954,028.60 judgment against Bar Louie Tempe, Inc. and a $488,604.20 judgment against Restaurant Development Group ("RDG"). Roger Greenfield and Theodore Kasemir were the officers, directors and sole shareholders of both RDG and Bar Louis Tempe. In the complaint, the plaintiff alleged that Greenfield and Kasemir, in an effort to avoid paying the judgment, caused RDG to transfer certain of the defendants' assets for no consideration. Subsequently, RDG ceased its business operations. In the complaint the plaintiff sought to avoid the alleged fraudulent transfers. Additionally, one count of the 10-count complaint alleged a charge of aiding and abetting a fraudulent transfer. The defendants sought to dismiss the aiding and abetting count asserting that under Illinois law there was no separate count for aiding and abetting. The *Coleman* court noted that the United States Seventh Circuit Court of Appeals previously stated that aiding and abetting was essentially the basis for imposing liability for the tort and was not in and of itself a separate tort.[436] The *Coleman* court went on to acknowledge that since the Seventh Circuit's holding in *Eastern Trading Co. v. Lefco, Inc.*,[437] courts have recognized a separate cause of action for aiding and abetting.[438] Specifically, the court cited *Thornwood, Inc. v. Jenner & Block*,[439] which recognized a claim for aiding and abetting fraud and aiding and abetting a breach of fiduciary duty.[440] The court also noted the recent opinion from *In re Parmalat Security Litigation*,[441] in which the court recognized a separate claim for aiding and abetting.[442] The *Coleman* court elected to follow this decision and stated that there was a separate claim for aiding and abetting and, thus, denied the defendant's motion to dismiss the count.[443]

Significantly, the court went on to state that it believed that any discussion of this issue was essentially academic because the:

> Seventh Circuit and the intermediate Illinois courts agree that knowingly assisting another to commit fraud gives rise to civil liability under Illinois law; they simply disagree as to whether such count should be called "fraud" or "aiding and abetting fraud."[444]

The Florida Supreme Court, however, reached a different conclusion on the aiding and abetting issue. In *Freeman v. First Union National Bank*,[445] the Florida Supreme Court unanimously ruled that there is not a cause of action for aiding and abetting a fraudulent transfer when the alleged aider and abettor was not the transferee.[446]

In *Freeman*, creditors brought suit against First Union National Bank ("First Union") for First Union's role in an alleged Ponzi scheme conducted by Unique Gems ("Unique").[447] Following the commencement of the lawsuit, a court order freezing Unique's assets, including certain funds in its account with First Union, was entered by the court.[448]

After the freeze, Unique allegedly wire-transferred approximately $6.6 million from its First Union account to a third party. Following the wire transfer, the plaintiffs sued First Union, alleging that First Union was liable for money damages on the legal theory that it aided and abetted a fraudulent transfer by allowing Unique to transfer the funds from its First Union account. The district court dismissed the claim with prejudice, citing the failure to state a cause of action under Florida law for the aiding and abetting claim.[449]

On appeal, the United States Eleventh Circuit Court of Appeals held that the Florida UFTA differs from Section 548 of the Bankruptcy Code because it includes a "catch-all" phrase providing for any other relief the circumstances may require.[450] Thus, the Eleventh Circuit certified a question for Florida's Supreme Court regarding whether the Florida UFTA created a cause of action for damages in favor of a creditor against an aider or abettor to a fraudulent transaction.[451]

The issue posed to the Florida Supreme Court was whether the Florida UFTA remedies, like the remedies available under Section 548, include only equitable powers to avoid the fraudulent transfer or whether the additional language of "any other relief the circumstances require" gives rise to a common law claim against a third party who aided or abetted the fraudulent transfer. In its opinion, the Florida Supreme Court concluded:

> On the face of the statute, there is no ambiguity with respect to whether FUFTA creates an independent cause of action for aiding and abetting liability. There is simply no language in FUFTA that suggests the creation of a distinct cause of action for aiding-abetting claims against non-transferees. Rather, it appears that FUFTA was intended to codify an existing but imprecise system whereby transfers that were intended to defraud creditors be set aside.
>
> * * * *
>
> To adopt the appellants' position in this case would be to expand the FUFTA beyond its facial application and in a manner that is outside the purpose and plain language of the statute. Consistent with this analysis we conclude that the FUFTA was not intended to serve as a vehicle by which a creditor may bring a suit against a non-transferee party (like First Union in this case) for monetary damages arising from the non-transferee party's alleged aiding and abetting of a fraudulent money transfer.[452]

Based on the recent decisions from *Coleman* and *Freeman,* the resolution of the issue of whether a claim can exist for aiding and abetting a fraudulent transfer is unclear. Attorneys, accountants, and other professionals advising corporations and individuals need to be aware of potential exposure for fraudulent transfers and understand that even though they may not have personally committed fraud, they can be held liable. While the facts in neither *Coleman* nor *Freeman* involved attorneys or accountants, the legal arguments raised by the defrauded creditors can similarly be asserted by a defrauded creditor against an attorney or accountant that facilitated a fraudulent transfer of assets. Professionals should be aware of potential personal liability with respect to the advice and counsel they provide their clients.

CONCLUSION

The advent of the Bankruptcy Abuse Act represents the latest significant effort to deter and remedy fraudulent acts, whether occurring prior to or in connection with the bankruptcy process. Even absent the promulgation of this act, modern business practices, the evolution of transaction structures, and heightened media attention on high-profile bankruptcy cases have all caused increased scrutiny of conduct that may be challenged as fraudulent.

While not involving bankruptcy fraud per se, the legacy of recent major Chapter 11 cases, such as Enron and WorldCom, is that the improper business practices exposed by those cases, and related investigations and proceedings, have fostered an unprecedented cynical view of corporate America and the ethics of modern American businesspeople. As a result, the scope of legislation and court activism to address fraudulent conduct has reached a new zenith.

For businesses, businesspeople, and their professional advisors, it is more essential than ever to be vigilant in knowing the legal parameters that circumscribe appropriate conduct. Nowhere is this truer than in bankruptcy, where the net has been cast to a wider extent than ever to address perceived fraud, both actual and constructive. In an increasingly aggressive and litigious American business community, no one is immune from attack. Two things, however, appear clear:

1. There have never existed better legal tools to pursue claims in bankruptcy against bad actors who have engaged in fraudulent acts and transactions.
2. Even businesses and businesspeople who act in good faith may find themselves subject to claims if they are ignorant of the laws and legal theories that govern their conduct and transactions.

APPENDIX 17A

Uniform Fraudulent Conveyance Act and Uniform Fraudulent Transfer Act

Uniform Fraudulent Conveyance Act	
State	**Statutory Reference**
Maryland	Code, Commercial Law, §§ 15-201 to 15-214
New York	McKinney's Debtor and Creditor Law, §§ 270 to 281
Virgin Islands	28 V.I.C. §§ 201 to 212
Wyoming	Wyo. Stat. Ann. §§ 34-14-101 to 34-14-113

Uniform Fraudulent Transfer Act	
State	**Statutory Reference**
Alabama	Code 1975, §§ 8–9A–1 to 8–9A–12
Arizona	A.R.S. §§ 44–1001 to 44–1010
Arkansas	A.C.A. §§ 4–59–201 to 4–59–213
California	West's Ann. Cal. Civ. Code, §§ 3439 to 3439.12
Colorado	West's C.R.S.A. §§ 38–8–101 38–8–112
Connecticut	C.G.S.A. §§ 52–552a to 52-5521
Delaware	6 Del. C. §§ 1301 to 1311
District of Columbia	D.C. Official Code, 2001 Ed. §§ 11–160
Florida	West's F.S.A. §§ 726.101 to 726–112
Georgia	O.C.G.A. §§ 18–2–70 to 18–2–80
Hawaii	HRS §§ 651C–1 to 651C–10
Idaho I.C.	§§ 55–910 to 55–921
Illinois	S.H.A. 740 ILCS 160/1 to 160/12.86–814
Indiana	West's A.I.C. 32-18-2-1 to 32-18-2-21
Iowa	I.C.A. §§ 684.1 to 684.12
Kansas	K.S.A. 33–201 to 33–212
Maine	14 M.R.S.A. §§ 3571 to 3582
Massachusetts	M.G.L.A. c. 109A, §§ 1 to 12
Michigan	M.C.L.A. §§ 566.31 to 566.43
Minnesota	M.S.A. §§ 513.41 to 513.51
Missouri	V.A.M.S. §§ 428.005 to 428.059
Montana	MCA 31–2–326 to 31–2-342

Uniform Fraudulent Transfer Act *(Continued)*	
State	**Statutory Reference**
Nebraska	R.R.S. 1943, §§ 36-701 to 36-712
Nevada	N.R.S. 112.140 to 112.250
New Hampshire	RSA 545-A:1 to 545-A:12. 215
New Jersey	N.J.S.A. 25:2-20 to 25:2-34
New Mexico	NMSA 1978, §§ 56-10-14 to 56-10-25
North Carolina	G.S. §§ 39-23.1 to 39-23.12
North Dakota	NDCC 13-02.1-01 to 13-02.1-10
Ohio	R.C. §§ 1336.01 to 1336.11
Oklahoma	24 Okl. St. Ann. §§ 112 to 123
Oregon	ORS 95.200 to 95.310
Pennsylvania	12 Pa. C.S.A. §§ 5101 to 5110
Rhode Island	Gen. Laws 1956, §§ 6-16-1 to 6-16-12
South Dakota	SDCL 54-8A-1 to 54-8A-12
Tennessee	T.C.A. §§ 66-3-301 to 66-3-313
Texas	V.T.C.A. Bus. & C. §§ 24.001 to 24.013
Utah	U.C.A. 1953, 25-6-1 to 25-6-14
Vermont	9 V.S.A. §§ 2285 to 2295
Washington	West's RCWA 19.40.011 to 19.40.903
West Virginia	Code, 40-1A-1 to 40-1A-12
Wisconsin	W.S.A. 242.01 to 242.11

APPENDIX 17B

Uniform Fraudulent Conveyance Act

§ 1. **Definition of Terms**

In this act "Assets" of a debtor means property not exempt from liability for his debts. To the extent that any property is liable for any debts of the debtor, such property shall be included in his assets.

"Conveyance" includes every payment of money, assignment, release, transfer, lease, mortgage or pledge of tangible or intangible property, and also the creation of any lien or encumbrance.

"Creditor" is a person having any claim, whether matured or unmatured, liquidated or unliquidated, absolute, fixed or contingent.

"Debt" includes any legal liability, whether matured or unmatured, liquidated or unliquidated, absolute, fixed or contingent.

§ 2. **Insolvency.**

(1) A person is insolvent when the present fair salable value of his assets is less than the amount that will be required to pay his probable liability on his existing debts as they become absolute and matured.

(2) In determining whether a partnership is insolvent there shall be added to the partnership property the present fair salable value of the separate assets of each general partner in excess of the amount probably sufficient to meet the claims of his separate creditors, and also the amount of any unpaid subscription to the partnership of each limited partner, provided the present fair salable value of the assets of such limited partner is probably sufficient to pay his debts, including such unpaid subscription.

§ 3. **Fair Consideration.**

Fair consideration is given for property, or obligation:

(a) When in exchange for such property, or obligation, as a fair equivalent therefor, and in good faith, property is conveyed or an antecedent debt is satisfied, or

(b) When such property, or obligation is received in good faith to secure a present advance or antecedent debt in amount not disproportionately small as compared with the value of the property, or obligation obtained.

§ 4. **Conveyances by Insolvent.**

Every conveyance made and every obligation incurred by a person who is or will be thereby rendered insolvent is fraudulent as to creditors without regard to his actual intent if the conveyance is made or the obligation is incurred without a fair consideration.

§ 5. **Conveyances by Persons in Business.**

Every conveyance made without fair consideration when the person making it is engaged or is about to engage in a business or transaction for which the property remaining in his hands after the conveyance is an unreasonably small capital, is fraudulent as to creditors and as to other persons who become creditors during the continuance of such business or transaction without regard to his actual intent.

§ 6. Conveyances by a Person about to Incur Debts.

Every conveyance made and every obligation incurred without fair consideration when the person making the conveyance or entering into the obligation intends or believes that he will incur debts beyond his ability to pay as they mature, is fraudulent as to both present and future creditors.

§ 7. Conveyance Made with Intent to Defraud.

Every conveyance made and every obligation incurred with actual intent, as distinguished from intent presumed in law, to hinder, delay, or defraud either present or future creditors, is fraudulent as to both present and future creditors.

§ 8. Conveyance of Partnership Property.

Every conveyance of partnership property and every partnership obligation incurred when the partnership is or will be thereby rendered insolvent, is fraudulent as to partnership creditors, if the conveyance is made or obligation is incurred:

(a) To a partner, whether with or without a promise by him to pay partnership debts, or

(b) To a person not a partner without fair consideration to the partnership as distinguished from consideration to the individual partners.

§ 9. Rights of Creditors Whose Claims Have Matured.

(1) Where a conveyance or obligation is fraudulent as to a creditor, such creditor, when his claim has matured, may, as against any person except a purchaser for fair consideration without knowledge of the fraud at the time of the purchase, or one who has derived title immediately or mediately from such a purchaser:

 (a) Have the conveyance set aside or obligation annulled to the extent necessary to satisfy his claim, or

 (b) Disregard the conveyance and attach or levy execution upon the property conveyed.

(2) A purchaser who without actual fraudulent intent has given less than a fair consideration for the conveyance or obligation, may retain the property or obligation as security for repayment.

§ 10. Rights of Creditors Whose Claims Have Not Matured.

Where a conveyance made or obligation incurred is fraudulent as to a creditor whose claim has not matured he may proceed in a court of competent jurisdiction against any person against whom he could have proceeded had his claim matured, and the court may:

(a) Restrain the defendant from disposing of his property,

(b) Appoint a receiver to take charge of the property.

(c) Set aside the conveyance or annul the obligation, or

(d) Make any order which the circumstances of the case may require.

APPENDIX 17C

Uniform Fraudulent Transfer Act

§ 1 Definitions

As used in this [Act]:

(1) "Affiliate" means:

(i) a person who directly or indirectly owns, controls, or holds with power to vote, 20 percent or more of the outstanding voting securities of the debtor, other than a person who holds the securities,

(A) as a fiduciary or agent without sole discretionary power to vote the securities; or

(B) solely to secure a debt, if the person has not exercised the power to vote;

(ii) a corporation 20 percent or more of whose outstanding voting securities are directly or indirectly owned, controlled, or held with power to vote, by the debtor or a person who directly or indirectly owns, controls, or holds, with power to vote, 20 percent or more of the outstanding voting securities of the debtor, other than a person who holds the securities,

(A) as a fiduciary or agent without sole power to vote the securities; or

(B) solely to secure a debt, if the person has not in fact exercised the power to vote;

(iii) a person whose business is operated by the debtor under a lease or other agreement, or a person substantially all of whose assets are controlled by the debtor; or

(iv) a person who operates the debtor's business under a lease or other agreement or controls substantially all of the debtor's assets.

(2) "Asset" means property of a debtor, but the term does not include:

(i) property to the extent it is encumbered by a valid lien;

(ii) property to the extent it is generally exempt under nonbankruptcy law; or

(iii) an interest in property held in tenancy by the entireties to the extent it is not subject to process by a creditor holding a claim against only one tenant.

(3) "Claim" means a right to payment, whether or not the right is reduced to judgment, liquidated, unliquidated, fixed, contingent, matured, unmatured, disputed, undisputed, legal, equitable, secured, or unsecured.

(4) "Creditor" means a person who has a claim.

(5) "Debt" means liability on a claim.

(6) "Debtor" means a person who is liable on a claim.

(7) "Insider" includes:

(i) if the debtor is an individual,

(A) a relative of the debtor or of a general partner of the debtor;

(B) a partnership in which the debtor is a general partner;

(C) a general partner in a partnership described in clause (B); or

(D) a corporation of which the debtor is a director, officer, or person in control;

(ii) if the debtor is a corporation,

(A) a director of the debtor;

(B) an officer of the debtor;

(C) a person in control of the debtor;

(D) a partnership in which the debtor is a general partner;

(E) a general partner in a partnership described in clause (D); or

(F) a relative of a general partner, director, officer, or person in control of the debtor;

(iii) if the debtor is a partnership,

(A) a general partner in the debtor;

(B) a relative of a general partner in, a general partner of, or a person in control of the debtor;

(C) another partnership in which the debtor is a general partner;

(D) a general partner in a partnership described in clause (C); or

(E) a person in control of the debtor;

(iv) an affiliate, or an insider of an affiliate as if the affiliate were the debtor; and

(v) a managing agent of the debtor.

(8) "Lien" means a charge against or an interest in property to secure payment of a debt or performance of an obligation, and includes a security interest created by agreement, a judicial lien obtained by legal or equitable process or proceedings, a common-law lien, or a statutory lien.

(9) "Person" means an individual, partnership, corporation, association, organization, government or governmental subdivision or agency, business trust, estate, trust, or any other legal or commercial entity.

(10) "Property" means anything that may be the subject of ownership.

(11) "Relative" means an individual related by consanguinity within the third degree as determined by the common law, a spouse, or an individual related to a spouse within the third degree as so determined, and includes an individual in an adoptive relationship within the third degree.

(12) "Transfer" means every mode, direct or indirect, absolute or conditional, voluntary or involuntary, of disposing of or parting with an asset or an interest in an asset, and includes payment of money, release, lease, and creation of a lien or other encumbrance.

(13) "Valid lien" means a lien that is effective against the holder of a judicial lien subsequently obtained by legal or equitable process or proceedings.

§ 2. Insolvency.

(a) A debtor is insolvent if the sum of the debtor's debts is greater than all of the debtor's assets at a fair valuation.

(b) A debtor who is generally not paying his [or her] debts as they become due is presumed to be insolvent.

(c) A partnership is insolvent under subsection (a) if the sum of the partnership's debts is greater than the aggregate, at a fair valuation, of all of the partnership's assets and the sum of the excess of the value of each general partner's nonpartnership assets over the partner's nonpartnership debts.

(d) Assets under this section do not include property that has been transferred, concealed, or removed with intent to hinder, delay, or defraud creditors or that has been transferred in a manner making the transfer voidable under this [Act].

(e) Debts under this section do not include an obligation to the extent it is secured by a valid lien on property of the debtor not included as an asset.

§ 3. **Value.**

(a) Value is given for a transfer or an obligation if, in exchange for the transfer or obligation, property is transferred or an antecedent debt is secured or satisfied, but value does not include an unperformed promise made otherwise than in the ordinary course of the promisor's business to furnish support to the debtor or another person.

(b) For the purposes of Sections 4(a)(2) and 5, a person gives a reasonably equivalent value if the person acquires an interest of the debtor in an asset pursuant to regularly conducted, noncollusive foreclosure sale or execution of a power of sale for the acquisition or disposition of the interest of the debtor upon default under a mortgage, deed of trust, or security agreement.

(c) A transfer is made for present value if the exchange between the debtor and the transferee is intended by them to be contemporaneous and is in fact substantially contemporaneous.

§ 4. **Transfers Fraudulent as to Present and Future Creditors.**

(a) A transfer made or obligation incurred by a debtor is fraudulent as to a creditor, whether the creditor's claim arose before or after the transfer was made or the obligation was incurred, if the debtor made the transfer or incurred the obligation:

(1) with actual intent to hinder, delay, or defraud any creditor of the debtor; or

(2) without receiving a reasonably equivalent value in exchange for the transfer or obligation, and the debtor:

(i) was engaged or was about to engage in a business or a transaction for which the remaining assets of the debtor were unreasonably small in relation to the business or transaction; or

(ii) intended to incur, or believed or reasonably should have believed that he [or she] would incur, debts beyond his [or her] ability to pay as they became due.

(b) In determining actual intent under subsection (a)(1), consideration may be given, among other factors, to whether:

(1) the transfer or obligation was to an insider;

(2) the debtor retained possession or control of the property transferred after the transfer;

(3) the transfer or obligation was disclosed or concealed;

(4) before the transfer was made or obligation was incurred, the debtor had been sued or threatened with suit;

(5) the transfer was of substantially all the debtor's assets;

(6) the debtor absconded;

(7) the debtor removed or concealed assets;

(8) the value of the consideration received by the debtor was reasonably equivalent to the value of the asset transferred or the amount of the obligation incurred;

(9) the debtor was insolvent or became insolvent shortly after the transfer was made or the obligation was incurred;

(10) the transfer occurred shortly before or shortly after a substantial debt was incurred; and

(11) the debtor transferred the essential assets of the business to a lienor who transferred the assets to an insider of the debtor.

§ 5. Transfers Fraudulent as to Present Creditors.

(a) A transfer made or obligation incurred by a debtor is fraudulent as to a creditor whose claim arose before the transfer was made or the obligation was incurred if the debtor made the transfer or incurred the obligation without receiving a reasonably equivalent value in exchange for the transfer or obligation and the debtor was insolvent at that time or the debtor became insolvent as a result of the transfer or obligation.

(b) A transfer made by a debtor is fraudulent as to a creditor whose claim arose before the transfer was made if the transfer was made to an insider for an antecedent debt, the debtor was insolvent at that time, and the insider had reasonable cause to believe that the debtor was insolvent.

§ 6. When Transfer is Made or Obligation Is Incurred.

For the purposes of this [Act]:

(1) a transfer is made:

(i) with respect to an asset that is real property other than a fixture, but including the interest of a seller or purchaser under a contract for the sale of the asset, when the transfer is so far perfected that a good-faith purchaser of the asset from the debtor against whom applicable law permits the transfer to be perfected cannot acquire an interest in the asset that is superior to the interest of the transferee; and

(ii) with respect to an asset that is not real property or that is a fixture, when the transfer is so far perfected that a creditor on a simple contract cannot acquire a judicial lien otherwise than under this [Act] that is superior to the interest of the transferee;

(2) if applicable law permits the transfer to be perfected as provided in paragraph (1) and the transfer is not so perfected before the commencement of an action for relief under this [Act], the transfer is deemed made immediately before the commencement of the action;

(3) if applicable law does not permit the transfer to be perfected as provided in paragraph (1), the transfer is made when it becomes effective between the debtor and the transferee;

(4) a transfer is not made until the debtor has acquired rights in the asset transferred;

(5) an obligation is incurred:

(i) if oral, when it becomes effective between the parties; or

(ii) if evidenced by a writing, when the writing executed by the obligor is delivered to or for the benefit of the obligee.

§ 7. Remedies of Creditors.

(a) In an action for relief against a transfer or obligation under this [Act], a creditor, subject to the limitations in Section 8, may obtain:

(1) avoidance of the transfer or obligation to the extent necessary to satisfy the creditor's claim;

(2) an attachment or other provisional remedy against the asset transferred or other property of the transferee in accordance with the procedure prescribed by [ ]

(3) subject to applicable principles of equity and in accordance with applicable rules of civil procedure,

(i) an injunction against further disposition by the debtor or a transferee, or both, of the asset transferred or of other property;

(ii) appointment of a receiver to take charge of the asset transferred or of other property of the transferee; or

(iii) any other relief the circumstances may require.

(b) If a creditor has obtained a judgment on a claim against the debtor, the creditor, if the court so orders, may levy execution on the asset transferred or its proceeds.

§ 8. Defenses, Liability, and Protection of Transferee.

(a) A transfer or obligation is not voidable under Section 4(a)(1) against a person who took in good faith and for a reasonably equivalent value or against any subsequent transferee or obligee.

(b) Except as otherwise provided in this section, to the extent a transfer is voidable in an action by a creditor under Section 7(a)(1), the creditor may recover judgment for the value of the asset transferred, as adjusted under subsection (c), or the amount necessary to satisfy the creditor's claim, whichever is less. The judgment may be entered against:

(1) the first transferee of the asset or the person for whose benefit the transfer was made; or

(2) any subsequent transferee other than a good faith transferee who took for value or from any subsequent transferee.

(c) If the judgment under subsection (b) is based upon the value of the asset transferred, the judgment must be for an amount equal to the value of the asset at the time of the transfer, subject to adjustment as the equities may require.

(d) Notwithstanding voidability of a transfer or an obligation under this [Act], a good-faith transferee or obligee is entitled, to the extent of the value given the debtor for the transfer or obligation, to

(1) a lien on or a right to retain any interest in the asset transferred;

(2) enforcement of any obligation incurred; or

(3) a reduction in the amount of the liability on the judgment.

(e) A transfer is not voidable under Section 4(a)(2) or Section 5 if the transfer results from:

(1) termination of a lease upon default by the debtor when the termination is pursuant to the lease and applicable law; or

(2) enforcement of a security interest in compliance with Article 9 of the Uniform Commercial Code.

(f) A transfer is not voidable under Section 5(b):

(1) to the extent the insider gave new value to or for the benefit of the debtor after the transfer was made unless the new value was secured by a valid lien;

(2) if made in the ordinary course of business or financial affairs of the debtor and the insider; or

(3) if made pursuant to a good-faith effort to rehabilitate the debtor and the transfer secured present value given for that purpose as well as an antecedent debt of the debtor.

§ 9. Extinguishment of [Claim for Relief] [Cause of Action].

A [claim for relief] [cause of action] with respect to a fraudulent transfer or obligation under this [Act] is extinguished unless action is brought:

(a) under Section 4(a)(1), within 4 years after the transfer was made or the obligation was incurred or, if later, within one year after the transfer or obligation was or could reasonably have been discovered by the claimant;

(b) under Section 4(a)(2) or 5(a), within 4 years after the transfer was made or the obligation was incurred; or

(c) under Section 5(b), within one year after the transfer was made or the obligation was incurred.

§ 10. Supplementary Provisions.

Unless displaced by the provisions of this [Act], the principles of law and equity, including the law merchant and the law relating to principal and agent, estoppel, laches, fraud, misrepresentation, duress, coercion, mistake, insolvency, or other validating or invalidating cause, supplement its provisions.

Appendix 17D

18 U.S.C. §§ 152–157

18 U.S.C. § 152. Concealment of Assets; False Oaths and Claims; Bribery.

A person who—

(1) knowingly and fraudulently conceals from a custodian, trustee, marshal, or other officer of the court charged with the control or custody of property, or, in connection with a case under title 11, from creditors or the United States Trustee, any property belonging to the estate of a debtor;

(2) knowingly and fraudulently makes a false oath or account in or in relation to any case under title 11;

(3) knowingly and fraudulently makes a false declaration, certificate, verification, or statement under penalty of perjury as permitted under Section 1746 of title 28, in or in relation to any case under title 11;

(4) knowingly and fraudulently presents any false claim for proof against the estate of a debtor, or uses any such claim in any case under title 11, in a personal capacity or as or through an agent, proxy, or attorney;

(5) knowingly and fraudulently receives any material amount of property from a debtor after the filing of a case under title 11, with intent to defeat the provisions of title 11;

(6) knowingly and fraudulently gives, offers, receives, or attempts to obtain any money or property, remuneration, compensation, reward, advantage, or promise thereof for acting or forbearing to act in any case under title 11;

(7) in a personal capacity or as an agent or officer of any person or corporation, in contemplation of a case under title 11 by or against the person or any other person or corporation, or with intent to defeat the provisions of title 11, knowingly and fraudulently transfers or conceals any of his property or the property of such other person or corporation;

(8) after the filing of a case under title 11 or in contemplation thereof, knowingly and fraudulently conceals, destroys, mutilates, falsifies, or makes a false entry in any recorded information (including books, documents, records, and papers) relating to the property or financial affairs of a debtor; or

(9) after the filing of a case under title 11, knowingly and fraudulently withholds from a custodian, trustee, marshal, or other officer of the court or a United States Trustees entitled to its possession, any recorded information (including books, documents, records, and papers) relating to the property or financial affairs of a debtor,

shall be fined under this title, imprisoned not more than 5 years, or both.

18 U.S.C. § 153. Embezzlement against estate.

(a) OFFENSE. A person described in subsection (b) who knowingly and fraudulently appropriates to the person's own use, embezzles, spends, or transfers any property or secretes or destroys any document belonging to the estate of a debtor shall be fined under this title, imprisoned not more than 5 years, or both.

(b) PERSON TO WHOM SECTION APPLIES. A person described in this subsection is one who has access to property or documents belonging to an estate by virtue of the person's participation in the administration of the estate as a trustee, custodian, marshal, attorney, or other officer of the court or as an agent, employee, or other person engaged by such an officer to perform a service with respect to the estate.

18 U.S.C. § 154. Adverse interest and conduct of officers.

A person who, being a custodian, trustee, marshal, or other officer of the court—

knowingly purchases, directly or indirectly, any property of the estate of which the person is such an officer in a case under title 11;

knowingly refuses to permit a reasonable opportunity for the inspection by parties in interest of the documents and accounts relating to the affairs of estates in the person's charge by parties when directed by the court to do so; or

knowingly refuses to permit a reasonable opportunity for the inspection by the United States Trustee of the documents and accounts relating to the affairs of an estate in the person's charge, shall be fined under this title and shall forfeit the person's office, which shall thereupon become vacant.

18 U.S.C. § 155. Fee agreements in cases under title 11 and receiverships.

Whoever, being a party in interest, whether as a debtor, creditor, receiver, trustee or representative of any of them, or attorney for any such party in interest, in any receivership or case under Title 11 in any United States court or under its supervision, knowingly and fraudulently enters into any agreement, express or implied, with another such party in interest or attorney for another such party in interest, for the purpose of fixing the fees or other compensation to be paid to any party in interest or to any attorney for any party in interest for services rendered in connection therewith, from the assets of the estate shall be fined under this title or imprisoned not more than one year, or both.

18 U.S.C. § 156. Knowing disregard of bankruptcy law or rule.

DEFINITIONS. In this section—

(1) the term "bankruptcy petition preparer" means a person, other than the debtor's attorney or any employee of such an attorney, who prepares for compensation a document for filing; and

(2) the term "document for filing" means a petition or any other documents prepared for filing by a debtor in the United States bankruptcy court or a United States district court in connection with a case under Title 11.

(b) OFFENSE. If a bankruptcy case or related proceeding is dismissed because of a knowing attempt by a bankruptcy petition preparer in any manner to disregard the requirements of Title 11, United States Code, or the Federal Rules of Bankruptcy Procedure, the bankruptcy petition preparer shall be fined under this title, imprisoned not more than 1 year, or both.

18 U.S.C. § 157. Bankruptcy fraud.

A person who, having devised or intending to devise a scheme or artifice to defraud and for the purpose of executing or concealing such a scheme or artifice or attempting to do so—

(1) files a petition under Title 11, including a fraudulent involuntary bankruptcy petition under Section 303 of such title;

(2) files a document in a proceeding under Title 11, including a fraudulent involuntary bankruptcy petition under Section 303 of such title; or

(3) makes a false or fraudulent representation, claim, or promise concerning or in relation to a proceeding under Title 11, including a fraudulent involuntary bankruptcy petition under Section 303 of such title, at any time before or after the filing of the petition, or in relation to a proceeding falsely asserted to be pending under such title,

shall be fined under this title, imprisoned not more than 5 years, or both

Appendix 17E

11 U.S.C. § 548. Fraudulent Transfers and Obligations

(a) (1) The trustee may avoid any transfer (including any transfer to or for the benefit of an insider under an employment contract) of an interest of the debtor in property, or any obligation (including any obligation to or for the benefit of an insider under an employment contract) incurred by the debtor, that was made or incurred on or within 2 years before the date of the filing of the petition, if the debtor voluntarily or involuntarily—

(A) made such transfer or incurred such obligation with actual intent to hinder, delay, or defraud any entity to which the debtor was or became, on or after the date that such transfer was made or such obligation was incurred, indebted; or

(B) (i) received less than a reasonably equivalent value in exchange for such transfer or obligation; and

(ii) (I) was insolvent on the date that such transfer was made or such obligation was incurred, or became insolvent as a result of such transfer or obligation;

(II) was engaged in business or a transaction, or was about to engage in business or a transaction, for which any property remaining with the debtor was an unreasonably small capital;

(III) intended to incur, or believed that the debtor would incur, debts that would be beyond the debtor's ability to pay as such debts matured; or

(IV) made such transfer to or for the benefit of an insider, or incurred such obligation to or for the benefit of an insider, under an employment contract and not in the ordinary course of business.

(2) A transfer of a charitable contribution to a qualified religious or charitable entity or organization shall not be considered to be a transfer covered under paragraph (1)(B) in any case in which—

(A) the amount of that contribution does not exceed 15 percent of the gross annual income of the debtor for the year in which the transfer of the contribution is made; or

(B) the contribution made by a debtor exceeded the percentage amount of gross annual income specified in subparagraph (A), if the transfer was consistent with the practices of the debtor in making charitable contributions.

(b) The trustee of a partnership debtor may avoid any transfer of an interest of the debtor in property, or any obligation incurred by the debtor, that was made or incurred on or within 2 years before the date of the filing of the petition, to a general partner in the debtor, if the debtor was insolvent on the date such transfer was made or such obligation was incurred, or became insolvent as a result of such transfer or obligation.

(c) Except to the extent that a transfer or obligation voidable under this section is voidable under Section 544, 545, or 547 of this title, a transferee or obligee of such a transfer or obligation that takes for value and in good faith has a lien on or may retain any interest transferred or may enforce any obligation incurred, as the case may be, to the extent that such transferee or obligee gave value to the debtor in exchange for such transfer or obligation.

(d) (1) For the purposes of this section, a transfer is made when such transfer is so perfected that a bona fide purchaser from the debtor against whom applicable law permits such transfer to be perfected cannot acquire an interest in the property transferred that is superior to the interest in such property of the transferee, but if such transfer is not so perfected before the commencement of the case, such transfer is made immediately before the date of the filing of the petition.

(2) In this section—

(A) "value" means property, or satisfaction or securing of a present or antecedent debt of the debtor, but does not include an unperformed promise to furnish support to the debtor or to a relative of the debtor;

(B) a commodity broker, forward contract merchant, stockbroker, financial institution, financial participant, or securities clearing agency that receives a margin payment, as defined in Section 101, 741, or 761 of this title, or settlement payment, as defined in Section 101 or 741 of this title, takes for value to the extent of such payment;

(C) a repo participant or financial participant that receives a margin payment, as defined in Section 741 or 761 of this title, or settlement payment, as defined in Section 741 of this title, in connection with a repurchase agreement, takes for value to the extent of such payment;

(D) a swap participant or financial participant that receives a transfer in connection with a swap agreement takes for value to the extent of such transfer; and

(E) a master netting agreement participant that receives a transfer in connection with a master netting agreement or any individual contract covered thereby takes for value to the extent of such transfer, except that, with respect to a transfer under any individual contract covered thereby, to the extent that such master netting agreement participant otherwise did not take (or is otherwise not deemed to have taken) such transfer for value.

(3) In this section, the term "charitable contribution" means a charitable contribution, as that term is defined in Section 170(c) of the Internal Revenue Code of 1986, if that contribution—

(A) is made by a natural person; and

(B) consists of—

(i) a financial instrument (as that term is defined in Section 731(c)(2)(C) of the Internal Revenue Code of 1986); or

(ii) cash.

(4) In this section, the term "qualified religious or charitable entity or organization" means—

(A) an entity described in Section 170(c)(1) of the Internal Revenue Code of 1986; or

(B) an entity or organization described in Section 170(c)(2) of the Internal Revenue Code of 1986.

(e) (1) In addition to any transfer that the trustee may otherwise avoid, the trustee may avoid any transfer of an interest of the debtor in property that was made on or within 10 years before the date of the filing of the petition if—

(A) such transfer was made to a self-settled trust or similar device;

(B) such transfer was by the debtor;

(C) the debtor is a beneficiary of such trust or similar device; and

(D) the debtor made such transfer with actual intent to hinder, delay, or defraud any entity to which the debtor was or became, on or after the date that such transfer was made, indebted.

(2) For the purposes of this subsection, a transfer includes a transfer made in anticipation of any money judgment, settlement, civil penalty, equitable order, or criminal fine incurred by, or which the debtor believed would be incurred by—

(A) any violation of the securities laws (as defined in Section 3(a)(47) of the Securities Exchange Act of 1934 (15 U.S.C. 78c(a)(47))), any State securities laws, or any regulation or order issued under Federal securities laws or State securities laws; or

(B) fraud, deceit, or manipulation in a fiduciary capacity or in connection with the purchase or sale of any security registered under Section 12 or 15(d) of the Securities Exchange Act of 1934 (15 U.S.C. 78l and 78o(d)) or under Section 6 of the Securities Act of 1933 (15 U.S.C. 77f).

11 U.S.C. § 522 Exemptions

11 U.S.C. § 522(d).

The following property may be exempted under subsection (b)(2) of this section:

(1) The debtor's aggregate interest, not to exceed $18,450 in value, in real property or personal property that the debtor or a dependent of the debtor uses as a residence, in a cooperative that owns property that the debtor or a dependent of the debtor uses as a residence, or in a burial plot for the debtor or a dependent of the debtor.

(2) The debtor's interest, not to exceed $2,950 in value, in one motor vehicle.

(3) The debtor's interest, not to exceed $475 in value in any particular item or $9,850 in aggregate value, in household furnishings, household goods, wearing apparel, appliances, books, animals, crops, or musical instruments, that are held primarily for the personal, family, or household use of the debtor or a dependent of the debtor.

(4) The debtor's aggregate interest, not to exceed $1,225 in value, in jewelry held primarily for the personal, family, or household use of the debtor or a dependent of the debtor.

(5) The debtor's aggregate interest in any property, not to exceed in value $975 plus up to $9,250 of any unused amount of the exemption provided under paragraph (1) of this subsection.

(6) The debtor's aggregate interest, not to exceed $1,850 in value, in any implements, professional books, or tools, of the trade of the debtor or the trade of a dependent of the debtor.

(7) Any unmatured life insurance contract owned by the debtor, other than a credit life insurance contract.

(8) The debtor's aggregate interest, not to exceed in value $9,850 less any amount of property of the estate transferred in the manner specified in Section 542(d) of this title, in any accrued dividend or interest under, or loan value of, any unmatured life insurance contract owned by the debtor under which the insured is the debtor or an individual of whom the debtor is a dependent.

(9) Professionally prescribed health aids for the debtor or a dependent of the debtor.

(10) The debtor's right to receive—

- (A) a social security benefit, unemployment compensation, or a local public assistance benefit;
- (B) a veterans' benefit;
- (C) a disability, illness, or unemployment benefit;
- (D) alimony, support, or separate maintenance, to the extent reasonably necessary for the support of the debtor and any dependent of the debtor;
- (E) a payment under a stock bonus, pension, profitsharing, annuity, or similar plan or contract on account of illness, disability, death, age, or length of service, to the extend reasonably necessary for the support of the debtor and any dependent of the debtor, unless -
  - (i) such plan or contract was established by or under the auspices of an insider that employed the debtor at the time the debtor's rights under such plan or contract arose;
  - (ii) such payment is on account of age or length of service; and
  - (iii) such plan or contract does not qualify under Section 401(a), 403(a), 403(b), or 408 of the Internal Revenue Code of 1986.

(11) The debtor's right to receive, or property that is traceable to—

(A) an award under a crime victim's reparation law;

(B) a payment on account of the wrongful death of an individual of whom the debtor was a dependent, to the extent reasonably necessary for the support of the debtor and any dependent of the debtor;

(C) a payment under a life insurance contract that insured the life of an individual of whom the debtor was a dependent on the date of such individual's death, to the extent reasonably necessary for the support of the debtor and any dependent of the debtor;

(D) a payment, not to exceed $18,450, on account of personal bodily injury, not including pain and suffering or compensation for actual pecuniary loss, of the debtor or an individual of whom the debtor is a dependent; or

(E) a payment in compensation of loss of future earnings of the debtor or an individual of whom the debtor is or was a dependent, to the extent reasonably necessary for the support of the debtor and any dependent of the debtor.

(12) Retirement funds to the extent that those funds are in a fund or account that is exempt from taxation under Section 401, 403, 408, 408A, 414, 457, or 501(a) of the Internal Revenue Code of 1986.

11 U.S.C. § 522(o).

For purposes of subjection (b)(3)(A), and notwithstanding subsection (a), the value of an interest in—

(1) real or personal property that the debtor or a dependent of the debtor uses as a residence;

(2) a cooperative that owns property that the debtor or a dependent of the debtor uses as a residence;

(3) a burial plot for the debtor or a dependent of the debtor; or

real or personal property that the debtor or a dependent of the debtor claims as a homestead,

shall be reduced to the extend that such value is attributable to any portion of any property that the debtor disposed of in the 10-year period ending on the date of the filing of the petition with the intent to hinder, delay, or defraud a creditor and that the debtor could not exempt, or that portion that the debtor could not exempt, under subsection (b), if on such date the debtor had held the property so disposed of.

11 U.S.C. § 522(p).

(1) Except as provided in paragraph (2) of this subsection and Sections 544 and 548, as a result of electing under subsection (b)(3)(A) to exempt property under State or local law, a debtor may not exempt any amount of interest that was acquired by the debtor during the 1215-day period preceding the date of the filing of the petition that exceeds in the aggregate $125,000 in value in—

(A) real or personal property that the debtor or a dependent of the debtor uses as a residence;

(B) a cooperative that owns property that the debtor or a dependent of the debtor uses as a residence;

(C) a burial plot for the debtor or a dependent of the debtor; or

(D) real or personal property that the debtor or dependent of the debtor claims as a homestead.

(2) (A) The limitation under paragraph (1) shall not apply to an exemption claimed under subsection (b)(3)(A) by a family farmer for the principal residence of such farmer.

For purposes of paragraph (1), any amount of such interest does not include any interest transferred from a debtor's previous principal residence (which was acquired prior to the beginning of such 1215-day period) into the debtor's current principal residence, if the debtor's previous and current residences are located in the same State.

11 U.S.C. § 522(q).

(1) As a result of electing under subsection (b)(3)(A) to exempt property under State of local law, a debtor may not exempt any amount of an interest in property described in subparagraphs (A), (B), (C), and (D) of subsection (p)(1) which exceeds in the aggregate $125,000 if—

(A) the court determines, after notice and a hearing, that the debtor has been convicted of a felony (as defined in Section 3156 of title 18), which under the circumstances, demonstrates that the filing of the case was an abuse of the provisions of this title; or

(B) the debtor owes a debt arising from—

any violation of the Federal securities laws (as defined in Section 3(a)(47) of the Securities Exchange Act of 1934), any State securities laws, or any regulation or order issued under Federal securities laws or State securities laws;

fraud, deceit, or manipulation in a fiduciary capacity or in connection with the purchase or sale of any security registered under Section 12 or 15(d) of the Securities Exchange Act of 1934 or under Section 6 of the Securities Act of 1933;

any civil remedy under Section 1964 of title 18; or

any criminal act, intentional tort, or willful or reckless misconduct that caused serious physical injury or death to another individual in the preceding 5 years.

(2) Paragraph (1) shall not apply to the extent the amount of an interest in property described in subparagraphs (A), (B), (C), and (D) of subsection (p)(1) is reasonably necessary for the support of the debtor and any dependent of the debtor.

APPENDIX 17G

11 U.S.C. § 101(31). Definitions

The term "insider" includes—

(A) if the debtor is an individual—

(i) relative of the debtor or of a general partner of the debtor;

(ii) partnership in which the debtor is a general partner;

(iii) general partner of the debtor; or

(iv) corporation of which the debtor is a director, officer, or person in control;

(B) if the debtor is a corporation—

(i) director of the debtor;

(ii) officer of the debtor;

(iii) person in control of the debtor;

(iv) partnership in which the debtor is a general partner;

(v) general partner of the debtor; or

(vi) relative of a general partner, director, officer, or person in control of the debtor;

(C) if the debtor is a partnership—

(i) general partner in the debtor;

(ii) relative of a general partner in, general partner of, or person in control of the debtor;

(iii) partnership in which the debtor is a general partner;

(iv) general partner of the debtor; or

(v) person in control of the debtor;

(D) if the debtor is a municipality, elected official of the debtor or relative of an elected official of the debtor;

(E) affiliate, or insider of an affiliate as if such affiliate were the debtor [defined in 11 U.S.C. § 101 (2)]; and

(F) managing agent of the debtor.

NOTES

1. White House Press Release (April 20, 2005).
2. The intent of the Bankruptcy Reform Act is evidenced right from the title, which is "The Bankruptcy Abuse and Prevention Act of 2005."
3. Martin H. Pritikin, "Toward Coherence in Civil Conspiracy Law: A Proposal to Abolish the Agent's Immunity Rule." *84 Neb. L. Rev. 1* (2005): 2 (*citing* "Second Interim Report of Neal Batson, Court-Appointed Examiner," *In re Enron Corp.,* No. 01-16034, 5 (Bankr. S.D. N.Y. 2003)).
4. Id.
5. 11 U.S.C. § 727(b). "A proof of claim is a written statement setting forth a creditor's claim." Fed. R. Bankr. P. § 3001(a).
6. 11 U.S.C. § 727(a)(1).
7. 11 U.S.C. § 1141.
8. 11 U.S.C. § 1328.
9. 11 U.S.C. § 727(a)(2).
10. 289 B.R. 836 (Bankr. N.D. Tex. 2003).
11. *In re Montana,* 185 B.R. 650 (Bankr. S.D. Fla. 1995).
12. 155 B.R. 782 (Bankr. M.D. Fla. 1993).
13. 11 U.S.C. § 523(a)(2).
14. False pretenses and false representation are different for purposes of exception to discharge. Money obtained by false pretenses involves an *implied* misrepresentation that is meant to create and foster a false impression, whereas a false representation involves an *express* misrepresentation. *In re Bruce,* 242 B.R. 492 (Bankr. W.D. Pa. 2001).
15. Id.
16. *In re Pleasants,* 219 F.3d 372, 375 (4th Cir. 2000).
17. *See* id.
18. 2000 U.S. Dist. LEXIS 3334 (E.D. La. 2000).
19. Id. at 12.
20. Id. at 13–14.
21. 205 B.R. 587 (Bankr. W.D. Mo. 1997).
22. 11 U.S.C. § 523(a)(2)(C)(i)(I).
23. 11 U.S.C. § 523(a)(2)(C)(i)(II).
24. 11 U.S.C. § 523(a)(4).
25. 2006 WL 771609 (Bankr. E.D. N.Y. 2006).
26. *See* "Breach of Fiduciary Duty," p. 46.
27. *Matter of Felt,* 255 F.3d 220 (5th Cir. 2001).
28. 11 U.S.C. § 1328(a)(2).
29. *St. Paul Fire & Marine Ins. Co. v. Alford* (*In re Alford*), 2003 Bankr. LEXIS 1985 (Bankr. N.D. Fla. 2003).
30. *See* Appendix 17F for the complete statutory language for 11 U.S.C. § 522.
31. *See* Collier on Bankruptcy ¶ 522.01. These states have opted out of the federal exemption system: Alabama, Arizona, California, Colorado, Delaware, Florida, Georgia, Idaho, Illinois, Indiana, Iowa, Kansas, Kentucky, Louisiana, Maine, Maryland, Mississippi, Missouri, Montana, Nebraska, Nevada, New York, North Carolina, North Dakota, Ohio, Oklahoma, Oregon, South Carolina, South Dakota, Tennessee, Utah, Virginia, West Virginia, and Wyoming.
32. 11 U.S.C. § 522(b) and (o).
33. Id.
34. The federal exemptions are: (1) the debtor's interest, up to $18,450, in real property that the debtor uses as a homestead or a burial plot; (2) the debtor's interest, up to $2,950, in a motor vehicle; (3)

the debtor's interest, up to $475 per item and $9,850 total, in household furnishings, wearing apparel, appliances, books, animals, crops, or musical instruments; (4) the debtor's interest, up to $1,225, in jewelry; (5) the debtor's interest, up to $9,250, of any unused amount from the residence exemption under (1); (6) the debtor's interest, up to $1,850, in professional books or tools of the trade of the debtor; (7) an unmatured life insurance contract; (8) the debtor's interest, up to $9,850, in accrued interest or dividends from a life insurance contract; (9) prescribed health aids; (10) the right to social security, unemployment compensation, veterans' benefits, disability, alimony, support, or a payment from a stock bonus, pension, annuity, or similar plan; (11) the right to a crime victim award, a wrongful death payment, a life insurance payment, or a bodily injury payment; and (12) the debtor's interest in a retirement fund that is exempt from taxation.

35. 11 U.S.C. § 522(b).
36. M.C.L.A. § 600.6023(1).
37. M.C.L.A. § 600.6023(1)(h).
38. William P. Boylan and Melanie R. Beyers, "The Trek of Michigan Exemptions in the Universe of Bankruptcy," *Michigan Real Property Review* (Summer 2006).
39. 331 B.R. 267 (Bankr. E.D. Mich. 2005).
40. M.C.L.A. § 600.6023a.
41. M.C.L.A. § 600.6023a.
42. Tex. Prop. Code §§ 42.001, 42.002, and 42.003.
43. W. Va. Code §§ 38-5A-3, -9, and 38-5B-12.
44. 11 U.S.C. § 522(d)(2)
45. 11 U.S.C. § 522(d)(3).
46. 11 U.S.C. § 522(d)(10)(E).
47. 11 U.S.C. § 522(d)(12).
48. *8 Nevada Lawyer 9* (April 2000): 19 (*quoting* Restatement (Second) of Trusts § 152(2)).
49. Id.
50. *Patterson v. Shumate,* 504 U.S. 753 (1992).
51. *Compare* 11 U.S.C. § 522(d) *with* Fla. Const. art. X § 4(a)(1).
52. Fla. Const. art. X § 4(a)(1).
53. *In re Adell,* 321 B.R. 562, 572 (Bankr. M.D. Fla. 2005).
54. 151 Cong. Rec. H1993-01, 2048 § 2415-02 (2005).
55. *Adell,* 321 B.R. at 564. A bad faith bankruptcy filing is determined by the court pursuant to one of several tests: (1) the improper use test, which looks at whether the creditor used an involuntary bankruptcy to gain an unfair advantage; (2) the improper purpose test, which looks at whether the creditor sought the involuntary bankruptcy because of ill will toward the debtor; (3) the objective test, which looks at whether the creditor acted as a reasonable creditor in the situation; or (4) a test applying the Bankruptcy Rule 9011 standards. *In re Bayshore Wire Products Co.,* 209 F.3d 100 (2d Cir. 2000).
56. *Adell,* 321 B.R. at 564.
57. *In re Adell,* 310 B.R. 460, 463 (Bankr. M.D. Fl. 2004).
58. Id.
59. Id.
60. *Adell,* 321 B.R. at 565.
61. Id. at 566.
62. Id.
63. Id. at 569.
64. Id.
65. Id.
66. Id. (*citing United States v. 18755 N. Bay Rd.,* 13 F.3d 1493, 1498 (11th Cir. 1994)).
67. Id.

68. Id. at 572.
69. Id.
70. Id. at 569–70.
71. Id.
72. Id.
73. *See In re Adell,* 332 B.R. 844, 849 (Bankr. M.D. Fl. 2005).
74. *Adell,* 321 B.R. at 570.
75. *In re Maronde,* 332 B.R. 593, 597 (Bankr. D. Minn. 2005).
76. Id. at 600.
77. Id. at 598.
78. 11 U.S.C. § 522(p).
79. H.R. Rep. No. 109-31, 15–16 (2005).
80. 11 U.S.C. § 522(q).
81. 326 B.R. 785 (Bankr. D. Ariz. 2005).
82. Id. at 791.
83. Id. (emphasis added).
84. Id.
85. Id.
86. 331 B.R. 483, 488 (Bankr. S.D. Fla. 2005).
87. Id. at 487.
88. Id. at 486.
89. Id. *See also In re Virissimo,* 332 B.R. 201, 205-06 (Bankr. D. Nev. 2005) (agreeing with the *McNabb* court, finding a defect within Section 522 which created an ambiguity, and holding that the legislative history clearly demonstrated an intent for Section 522(p)(1) to apply to debtors in all states).
90. Id. at 488.
91. There are several elements to the means test. The first step is to determine if the debtor's current monthly income is greater than the median income in the debtor's state. If the answer to this threshold question is no, then the debtor can file for Chapter 7 bankruptcy protection. If the debtor's current monthly income is greater than the median income in the debtor's state, then the means test must be employed. The means test provides that *X* is equal to the debtor's current monthly income less the debtor's expenses, multiplied by 60. If *X* is $6,000.00 or less, the debtor can file a Chapter 7 bankruptcy. If *X* is 25 percent or less of unsecured debt, the debtor can file a Chapter 7 bankruptcy. If *X* is more than 25 percent of unsecured debt or is $10,000.00 or more, the debtor must file a Chapter 13 bankruptcy.
92. *6 Am. Bankr. Inst. L. Rev. 317* (Winter 1998): 320.
93. *See* Appendix 17D for the complete statutory language for 18 U.S.C. §§ 152 to 157.
94. Pub. L. 107-204 (July 30, 2002); 116 Stat. 745.
95. 18 U.S.C. § 1519.
96. *18-6 American Bankruptcy Institute Journal* (July/August 1999): 10.
97. Craig Peyton Gaumer, "Bankruptcy Fraud: Crime and Punishment." *43 S.D. L. Rev. 527* (1998): 527–28.
98. Id. at 528.
99. Id.
100. *United States v. Novak,* 217 F.3d 566, 575 (8th Cir. 2000) (*quoting United States v. Goodstein,* 883 F.2d 1362, 1369 (7th Cir. 1989); *In re May,* 12 B.R. 618, 625 (N.D. Fla. 1980).
101. 18 U.S.C. § 152(1).
102. 18 U.S.C. § 152(2).
103. 18 U.S.C. § 152(3).

104. 18 U.S.C. § 152(4).
105. 18 U.S.C. § 152(8).
106. 18 U.S.C. § 152(6).
107. *6 Am. Bankr. Inst. L. Rev. 271* (Winter 1998): 271.
108. *Beigier v. IRS,* 496 U.S. 53, 58 (1989).
109. *See* Fed. R. Bankr. P. 1007 and 1008.
110. *See* 11 U.S.C. §§ 341 and 343.
111. *United States v. Cherek,* 734 F.2d 1248, 1254 (7th Cir. 1985) (stating that 18 U.S.C. § 152 requires a debtor to discuss the existence of assets even if the immediate status of the assets is unknown).
112. *United States v. Weinstein,* 834 F.2d 1454, 1461 (9th Cir. 1987) ("The bankruptcy estate includes equitable as well as legal interests.").
113. *United States v. Moynagh,* 566 F.2d 799 (1st Cir. 1997).
114. Id. at 802–03.
115. Id. (*citing United States v. West,* 22 F.3d 586 (5th Cir. 1994)).
116. 791 F.2d 73 (7th Cir. 1986).
117. Id. at 74.
118. Id. at 75.
119. Id. at 77.
120. *United States v. Beery,* 678 F.2d 856 (10th Cir. 1982).
121. *6 Am. Bankr. Inst. L. Rev. 317* (Winter 1998): 331 (*citing United States v. Shadduck,* 112 F.3d 523, 526 (1st Cir. 1997) (using concealment of a bank account to define the elements of a Section 152 violation); *United States v. Cherek,* 734 F.2d 1248, 1252 (7th Cir. 1984) (using concealment and fraudulent intent as elements of a Section 152 violation); and *United States v. Guiliano,* 644 F.2d 85, 87 (2nd Cir. 1981) (listing a case under title 11, concealment, knowledge, and intent to defraud as the elements of a Section 152 violation)).
122. *Burke v. Dowling,* 944 F. Supp. 1036, 1065 (E.D. N.Y. 1995).
123. *6 Am. Bankr. Inst. L. Rev. 317* (Winter 1998): 331.
124. Id. at 332.
125. Id. at 336 (*citing United States v. Turner,* 725 F.2d 1154, 1157 (8th Cir. 1984) (analyzing the district court's definition and stating that one "withholds knowledge" or "prevents disclosure or recognition")).
126. 205 F.3d 1117 (9th Cir. 1999).
127. Id. at 1120.
128. Id. at 1121.
129. Id.
130. Id. at 1120.
131. 725 F.2d 1154 (8th Cir. 1984).
132. Id. at 1156.
133. Id. at 1158–59.
134. 29 F.3d 908 (4th Cir. 1994).
135. Id. at 910.
136. Id.
137. *American Bankruptcy Institute Journal* (Spring 1997): 2.
138. 114 F.2d 558 (3rd Cir. 1940).
139. Id. at 560.
140. Id.
141. Id.
142. Id.

143. *United States v. Sabbeth,* 125 F. Supp. 2d 33, 37 (E.D. N.Y. 2000) (*citing United States v. Shapiro*, 101 F.2d 375, 379 (7th Cir. 1939)).
144. 125 F. Supp. 2d 33 (E.D. N.Y. 2000).
145. 18 U.S.C. § 152(2).
146. 18 U.S.C. § 152(3).
147. *6 Am. Bankr. Inst. L. Rev. 409* (Winter 1998): 425 (*citing Metheany v. United States,* 390 F.2d 559, 561 (9th Cir. 1968) (referring to the essential element of fraud charge in a bankruptcy proceeding)).
148. Id. (*citing United States v. Young,* 339 F.2d 1003, 1004 (7th Cir. 1964) (stating that the offense of making a false oath is completed at the time the false schedule is sworn to and filed, regardless of any subsequent disclosure)).
149. Id. at 425–26 (*citing United States v. Diorio,* 451 F.2d 21 (2nd Cir. 1971) (affirming conviction for failure to disclose corporate assets)).
150. *United States v. O'Donnell,* 539 F.2d 1233, 1237-38 (9th Cir. 1972).
151. 853 F.2d 568 (7th Cir. 1988).
152. Id. at 570.
153. Id.
154. Id. at 569.
155. Id. at 571.
156. Id.
157. Id. (*citing United States v. Overmeyer,* 867 F.2d 937, 949 (6th Cir. 1989)).
158. *United States v. Connery,* 867 F.2d 929, 934 (6th Cir. 1989).
159. *6 Am. Bankr. Inst. L. Rev. 409* (Winter 1998): 427.
160. Id. at 428.
161. 168 F. Supp. 728 (W.D. Pa. 1958).
162. Id. at 729.
163. Id. at 730.
164. 226 F. Supp. 312 (N.D. Ok. 1964).
165. Id. at 314.
166. Id.
167. 120 F.3d 856 (8th Cir. 1997).
168. Id. at 860.
169. Id.
170. Id.
171. Id. at 861.
172. Id.
173. Id.
174. Id.
175. Id.
176. Id.
177. Id.
178. Id. at 862.
179. Id.
180. Id. at 862–63.
181. 125 F.3d 1024 (7th Cir. 1997).
182. Id. at 1026.
183. Id.
184. Id. at 1026–27.

185. Id. at 1027.
186. Id.
187. Id.
188. Id.
189. Id. at 1028.
190. Id. at 1035.
191. *Jackson v. United States,* 72 F.2d 764 (3rd Cir. 1934).
192. 330 F. Supp. 2d 499 (E.D. Pa. 2004).
193. Id. at 504 (*citing United States v. Pollen,* 978 F.2d 78, 83 (3rd Cir. 1992)).
194. Id.
195. Id. at 504–05.
196. 18 U.S.C. § 157.
197. *6 Am. Bankr. Inst. L. Rev. 409* (Winter 1998): 431.
198. Id.
199. 18 U.S.C. § 157(1).
200. 18 U.S.C. § 157(2).
201. 18 U.S.C. § 157(3).
202. *See United States v. Daniels,* 247 F.3d 598 (5th Cir. 2001) (holding that filing of bankruptcy to prevent foreclosures on properties of shell corporation constituted bankruptcy fraud).
203. *United States v. McBride,* 362 F.3d 360, 373 (6th Cir. 2004) (*quoting United States v. DeSantis,* 237 F.3d 607, 613 (6th Cir. 2001)).
204. 4 Fed. Appx. 420 (9th Cir. 2001).
205. Id.
206. *6 Am. Bankr. Inst. L. Rev. 409* (Winter 1998): 421.
207. Id. at 423.
208. 18 U.S.C. § 154.
209. 18 U.S.C. § 155.
210. *In re Gianulias,* 111 B.R. 807, 870 (E.D. Cal. 1989).
211. 422 F.2d 200 (9th Cir. 1970).
212. Id. at 207.
213. Id.
214. 18 U.S.C. § 156.
215. Id.
216. 11 U.S.C. § 110(a)(1).
217. *In re Merriam,* 250 B.R. 724 (Bankr. D. Co. 2000).
218. The only case citing this statute is an unreported decision in *Thrower v. U.S.,* 2005 WL 1460128 (N.D. Ohio 2005).
219. Keith Palfin and Sandhya Prabhu, "Obstruction of Justice." *Am. Crim. L. Rev. 873* (2003): 874.
220. Jonathan D. Polkes, "Obstruction of Justice Nexus Requirement Unclear in New Statutes." *N.Y. L.J.* (July 7, 2003): 7 (criticizing the language as "undefined and unspecific" and alluding to notice problems that would accompany a vagueness criticism).
221. Maryland, New York, Wyoming, and the U.S. Territory of the Virgin Islands continue to retain the UFCA, while all others states have adopted the UFTA. *See* Appendix 17A for a listing of statutory references by state.
222. The two-year lookback applies to cases filed one year *after* the effectiveness of the Bankruptcy Abuse Act. The period is one year for all other cases. 11 U.S.C. § 548.
223. Peter M.Alces and Luther M. Dorr, "A Critical Analysis of the New Uniform Fraudulent Transfer Act." *U. Ill. L. Rev. 527* (1985): 530. Collier on Bankruptcy ¶ 548.01[2] (15th Edition Rev. 2006).

224. 13 Eliz., ch. 5 (1570) (Eng.) (providing text of statute).
225. *See Breitenstine v. Breitenstine,* 62 P.3d 587, 592 (Wyo. 2003).
226. *Twyne's Case,* 76 Eng. Rep. 809 (Star Chamber 1601).
227. *Breitenstine,* 62 P.3d at 593 (listing some of the more common badges of fraud).
228. *Twyne's Case,* 76 Eng. Rep. at 812–14.
229. *See* Appendix 17B for full text of Uniform Fraudulent Conveyance Act.
230. *In re Reed's Estate,* 566 P.2d 587 (Wyo. 1977).
231. Id. at 590–91.
232. *In re Otis & Edwards, P.C.,* 115 B.R. 900, 913 (Bankr. E.D. Mich. 1990).
233. UFCA § 4.
234. UFCA § 5.
235. UFCA § 6.
236. UFCA § 3.
237. *Halsey v. Winant,* 258 N.Y. 512, 513 (N.Y. 1932).
238. Id.; *see also Matter of Oppenheim,* 269 App. Div. 1040 (N.Y. 1945).
239. *See* Appendix 17C for full text of the Uniform Fraudulent Transfer Act.
240. UFCA § 4(a)(1).
241. UFTA § 4(b).
242. UFTA § 4, comment 5.
243. UFTA § 4, comment 6.
244. Alces and Dorr, *U. Ill. L. Rev. 527* (1985).
245. Id.
246. *Compare* UFCA §§ 4-6 (requiring proof of less than "fair consideration") *with* UFTA §§ 4(a)(2) and 5 (requiring proof of less than "reasonably equivalent value").
247. UFTA § 5(a).
248. UFTA § 4(a)(2)(i).
249. UFTA § 4(a)(2)(ii).
250. UFCA § 3. "Fair consideration is given for property, or obligation, (a) When in exchange for such property, or obligation, as a fair equivalent therefore, and in good faith, property is conveyed or an antecedent debt is satisfied . . . ." Id.
251. UFTA §§ 4(a)(2) and 5(a).
252. UFTA § 8(a).
253. Alces and Dorr, *U. Ill. L. Rev. 527* (1985). The UFTA provides a general, nonexclusive definition of "value," adopted from 11 U.S.C. § 548(d)(2). UFTA § 3, comment 2.
254. *Shape, Inc. v. Midwest Engineering* (*In re Shape, Inc.*), 176 B.R. 1 (Bankr. D. Me. 1994).
255. Id.
256. *BFP v. Resolution Trust Corporation,* 511 U.S. 531 (1994).
257. Alces and Dorr, *U. Ill. L. Rev. 527. See also* Collier on Bankruptcy ¶ 548.05[1][b] (15th Ed. Rev. 2006). *See Klein v. Tabatchnick,* 610 F.2d 1043 (2d Cir. 1979) (allowing consideration of the debtor's need for the challenged loan and the ability to obtain a loan elsewhere as well as the value of the securities transferred in exchange for the loan); *accord, Roth v. Fabrikant Bros.,* 175 F.2d 665 (2d Cir. 1949); *Security Discount Co. v. Wesner* (*In re Peoria Braumeister Co.*), 138 F.2d 520 (7th Cir. 1943); *Pennsylvania Trust Co. v. Schenecker,* 289 Pa. 277 (1927).
258. Alces and Dorr, *1985 U. Ill. L. Rev. 527. See also* Collier on Bankruptcy ¶ 548.05[1][b] (15th Ed. Rev. 2006).
259. UFCA § 7; UFTA § 4(C)(1).
260. UFCA § 4; UFTA § 5.
261. UFCA §§ 5 and 6; UFTA §§ 4(a)(2)(i) and (ii).

262. *See* Appendix 17E for full text of 11 U.S.C. § 548.
263. The two-year look-back applies to cases filed one year *after* the effectiveness of the Bankruptcy Amendments. The period is one year for all other cases. 11 U.S.C. § 548.
264. 11 U.S.C. § 548(a)(1). Like the UFTA, the Bankruptcy Code applies the "reasonably equivalent value" standard rather than the "fair consideration" standard used by the UFCA, thereby shifting the inquiry from the debtor's thoughts at the time of the transfer to the impact of the transfer upon the creditors.
265. 11 U.S.C. § 548(a)(2).
266. Collier on Bankruptcy, ¶ 548.01[4] (15th Ed. Rev. 2006).
267. 11 U.S.C. § 544.
268. White House Press Release (April 20, 2005).
269. *See* Appendix 17G for 11 U.S.C. § 101(31) of the Bankruptcy Code (providing a definition of an "insider").
270. *In re Lemanski,* 56 B.R. 981 (Bankr. W.D. Wis. 1986).
271. *In re Colesville Medical Center Ltd. Partnership,* 20 B.R. 87 (Bankr. D. Md. 1982); *See also In re Missionary Baptist Foundation, Inc.,* 712 F.2d 206 (5th Cir. 1983); *Butler v. David Shaw, Inc.,* 72 F.3d 437, 438 (4th Cir. 1996) (explaining that the definition of an insider is not exhaustive; rather, an insider may be any person or entity whose relations with debtor is sufficiently close so as to subject the relationship to close scrutiny; in order to satisfy this standard, the alleged insider must exercise sufficient authority over debtor so as to unqualifiedly dictate corporate policy on a disposition of corporate assets.); *Mishkin v. Siclari* (*In re Adler, Coleman Clearing Corp.*), 277 B.R. 520 (Bankr. S.D.N.Y 2002) (holding that an investor who held an account with a broker was found to be an insider, where the investor had close, personal relationship with the head trader at broker, the investor benefited from fraud and broker in ways that were not materially different from ways insider would, and investor's relations with the broker was not arm's length); and *In re Babcock Dairy Co.,* 70 B.R. 657 (Bankr. N.D. Ohio 1986) (finding that an allegation that a party that only had a superior bargaining position in contractual relationships with debtor was insufficient to qualify that party as an insider).
272. 11 U.S.C. § 548 (a)(1); UFCA § 7; and UFTA § 4(a)(1).
273. *Liquidation Trust of Hechinger Inv. Co. of Del., Inc. v. Fleet Retail Finance Group* (*In re Hechinger Investment Company of Delaware*), 327 B.R. 537, 550-51 (D. Del. 2005); *In re Victor Int'l, Inc.,* 97 Fed. Appx. 365, 369 (3d Cir. 2004); *Moody v. Sec. Pacific Bus. Credit, Inc.,* 971 F.2d 1056, 1064 (3d Cir. 1992), *affirming Moody v. Sec. Pacific Bus. Credit, Inc.,* 127 B.R. 958, 991 (Bankr. W.D. Pa. 1991).
274. *Moody,* 127 B.R. at 991; *In re Otis & Edwards, P.C.,* 115 B.R. 900, 913 (Bankr. E.D. Mich. 1990).
275. UFTA § 4(b).
276. 260 B.R. 88 (Bankr. E.D. Va. 2000), *aff'd* 43 Fed. Appx. 562 (4th Cir. 2002).
277. Id. at 111.
278. Id. at 116.
279. Id.
280. Id. at 113.
281. Id. at 114.
282. Id.
283. 257 F.3d 401 (4th Cir. 2001).
284. Id. *See also Hyman v. Porter* (*In re Porter*), 37 B.R. 56, 60–61 (Bankr E.D. Va. 1984); *Pauy v. Chastant* (*In re Chastant*), 873 F.2d 89, 91 (5th Cir. 1989).
285. Since the personal injury settlement proceeds would have been exempt under Virginia law, the court initially addressed the issue of whether transfers of property that would have been exempt from the bankruptcy estate under state law can be the subject of an avoidance and recovery action by the bankruptcy trustee on the ground that the debtor transferred the property with the intent to hinder,

delay, or defraud his creditors. Id. at 406. The court explained that "[in]disputably, had Smoot left the proceeds from the settlement of his FELA suit against CSX in his account, he could have exempted those proceeds from his bankruptcy estate." Id. After noting the split of authority on the issue, the court concluded that the majority position, "that transfers of exemptible property are amenable to avoidance and recovery actions by bankruptcy trustees," was better reasoned. Id. at 406–07. Therefore, the court held that Smoot's transfer of his personal injury settlement proceeds was subject to attack by his bankruptcy trustee. Id.

286. Id. at 408. *See also Hyman,* 37 B.R. at 60–61; and *Chastant,* 873 F.2d at 91.

287. *Smoot,* 257 F.3d at 408. *See also Porter*, 37 B.R. at 61.

288. *Smoot,* 257 F.3d at 408. The court also held that, in addition to avoiding the transfer on the basis of actual fraud under 11 U.S.C. § 548(a)(1)(A), the trustee was entitled to avoid the transfer under 11 U.S.C. § 548(a)(1)(B) because Smoot transferred the settlement proceeds without receiving any consideration and while he was insolvent. Id. at 409.

289. UFCA §§ 4, 5, and 6; UFTA §§ 4(a)(2) and 5; and 11 U.S.C. § 548(a).

290. *See In re Jeffrey Bigelow Design Group,* 956 F.2d 479 (4th Cir. 1992).

291. UFCA § 3(a).

292. *Sharp International Corporation v. State Street Bank and Trust Company* (*In re Sharp International Corporation*), 403 F.3d 43, 53–54 (2nd Cir. 2004).

293. *Consove v. Cohen* (*In re Roco Corp.*), 701 F.2d 978, 982 (1st Cir. 1993) ("[T]he value to be considered is that received by the [transferor] and not that forfeited by the transferee."); *SPC Plastics Corp. v. Griffith* (*In re Structurlite Plastics Corp.*), 193 B.R. 451, 456 (Bankr. S.D. Ohio 1995) ("[W]hether consideration in a transfer alleged to be fraudulent is 'fair' must be viewed from the standpoint of the [transferor]."). Neither the Bankruptcy Code nor the UFTA defines "reasonably equivalent value."

294. 511 U.S. 531 (1994).

295. Id.

296. *In re Morris Communications NC, Inc.*, 914 F.2d 458, 466 (4th Cir. 1990).

297. Among others, these courts have struggled to develop a workable test for reasonably equivalent value: *In re Young,* 82 F.3d 1407 (8th Cir. 1996) (determining whether the debtors obtained value in exchange for charitable contributions to a church); *In re Chomakos,* 69 F.3d 769 (6th Cir. 1995) (examining whether the debtors obtained value in exchange for $7,710 in gambling losses); *Morris,* 914 F.2d at 458 (attempting to determine the value of shares in a corporation whose only asset was a license application pending before the FCC that had a 1 in 22 chance of approval); *In re Fairchild Aircraft Corp.*, 6 F.3d 1119, 1125–26 (5th Cir. 1993) (deciding whether the money the debtor spent in a failed attempt to keep a commuter airline afloat conferred value on the debtor).

298. 92 F.3d 139 (4th Cir. 1996).

299. Id.

300. Id.

301. Id. at 148.

302. Id. at 153.

303. Id. at 148.

304. Id. at 153–54.

305. UFCA § 2(1).

306. Id.

307. *In re Moody,* 971 F.2d 1056, 1067 (*quoting Angier v. Worrell,* 31 A.2d 87, 89 (Pa. 1943)).

308. *United States v. Gleneagles Inv. Co.,* 565 F. Supp. 556, 578 (M.D. Pa. 1983).

309. *Moody,* 971 F.2d at 1067. *See also In re Taxman Clothing Co.*, 905 F.2d 166, 169–70 (7th Cir. 1990).

310. Collier on Bankruptcy, ¶ 101.32[4] (15th Ed. Rev. 2006).

311. *Moody v. Security Pac. Business Credit, Inc.*, 971 F.2d 1056, 1067 (3d Cir. 1992) (following the majority rule of going concern assets valuation when a bankruptcy is not clearly imminent).

312. UFTA § 2(a); 11 U.S.C. § 101(32).
313. *In re Smoot,* 265 B.R. 128 (Bankr. E.D. Va. 1999).
314. *Nordberg v. Arab Banking Corp.* (*In re Chase & Sanborn Corp.*), 904 F.2d 588, 594 (11th Cir. 1990); *In re Xonics Photochemical, Inc.,* 841 F.2d 198, 200 (7th Cir. 1988); *Covey v. Commercial National Bank of Peoria,* 960 F.2d 657 (7th Cir. 1992) (holding that contingent liability should be determined by multiplying total debt guaranteed by the probability that the debtor would be required to make good on a guarantee).
315. UFTA § 2(d); 11 U.S.C. § 32(A)(i).
316. UFTA § 2(b).
317. 960 F.2d 657 (7th Cir. 1992).
318. Id.
319. Id.
320. 227 B.R. 383 (Bankr. E.D. Pa. 1998).
321. Id.
322. Prior to commencing the action, the official committee of former partners of the debtor law firm obtained court authority to commence the action on behalf of the debtor's estate. Id. at 385.
323. Id. at 389.
324. Id.
325. *See* 11 U.S.C. 548(a)(1)(B)(ii); UFCA § 5; UFTA § 4(a)(2)(i).
326. *Steph v. Branch,* 255 F. Supp. 526 (E.D. Okla. 1966); *In re Atlas Foundry Co.,* 155 F. Supp. 615 (D. N.J. 1957) (describing how a purchaser of a business gave a mortgage on realty to the selling shareholders and used most of the company's cash to pay the selling shareholders for their shares, resulting in the corporation having an unreasonably small amount of capital to carry on its business, resulting in the mortgage being void as against the trustee).
327. *Matter of Atkinson,* 63 B.R. 266, 269 (Bankr. W.D. Wisc. 1986) (holding that for a violation of Section 5 of the UFCA, capital must be unreasonably small "relative to the nature of the venture").
328. 882 F.2d 1 (1st Cir. 1989).
329. Id. at 2.
330. Id.
331. Id. at 3.
332. Id.
333. Id.
334. Id. at 5.
335. Id. (*quoting Wells Fargo Bank v. Desert View Building Supplies,* 475 F. Supp. 693, 696 (D. Nev. 1978)).
336. Id.
337. *Harnett v. Doyle,* 16 Tenn. App. 302 (1932).
338. Id.
339. 242 F. Supp. 400 (W.D. N.C. 1965).
340. Id. at 401.
341. Id.
342. Id. In light of the court's decision in *Farmers Federal Cooperative,* lenders should use caution when making secured loans to financially distressed borrowers.
343. *Official Committee of Unsecured Creditors of Hechinger Investment Company of Delaware Inc. v. Fleet Retail Finance Group* (*In re Hechinger Investment Company*), 274 B.R. 71 (D. Del. 2002).
344. *Kupetz v. Wolf,* 845 F.2d 842 (9th Cir. 1988) (expressing doubt that "above board" LBOs are voidable as fraudulent conveyances). *See also Credit Managers Assoc. of Cal. v. The Federal Co.,* 629 F. Supp. 175, 179 (C.D. Cal. 1985) (stating that a court might hold that LBOs are exempt from fraudulent conveyance law).

345. 845 F.2d 842 (9th Cir. 1988).

346. Id.

347. Baird, Douglas G., and Jackson, Thomas H. "Fraudulent Conveyance Law and Its Proper Domain." *38 Vand. L. Rev. 829* (1985) (arguing that because fraudulent conveyance laws arose out of a simplistic and outdated sixteenth-century setting, applying such laws to transactions as modern and complex as an LBO is inappropriate).

348. Id. at 852.

349. *See, e.g. Lippi v. City Bank,* 955 F.2d 599 (9th Cir. 1992); *Mellon Bank v. Metro Communications,* 945 F.2d 635, 645–46 (3d Cir. 1991); *Kupetz v. Wolf,* 845 F.2d 842, 847 (9th Cir. 1988); *Aluminum Mills Corp. v. Citicorp (In re Aluminum Mills)*, 132 B.R. 869, 885 (Bankr. N.D. Ill. 1991); *Crowthers McCall Pattern, Inc. v. Lewis,* 129 B.R. 992, 997–98 (S.D.N.Y. 1991); *Moody,* 127 B.R. at 989, n. 7; *Murphy,* 126 B.R. at 392; *Ferrari v. Barclay's Business Credit (In re Morse Tool)*, 108 B.R. 389, 391 (Bankr. D. Mass. 1989); *Vadnais Lumber Supply v. Byrne (In re Vadnais Lumber Supply)*, 100 B.R. 127, 134–35 (Bankr. D. Mass. 1989); *Wieboldt Stores v. Schottenstein,* 94 B.R. 488, 499 (N.D. Ill. 1988); *Ohio Corrugating Co. v. DPAC, Inc. (In re The Ohio Corrugating Co.)* (Ohio Corrugating II), 91 B.R. 430, 434–35 (Bankr. N.D. Ohio 1988); *Kaiser Steel v. Jacobs (In re Kaiser Steel)*, 87 B.R. 154, 160–61 (Bankr. D. Colo. 1988); *Credit Managers Ass'n of Southern Cal. v. Federal Co.,* 629 F. Supp. 175, 179 (C.D. Cal. 1985); *Anderson Indus. v. Anderson (In re Anderson Indus.)*, 55 B.R. 922, 926 (Bankr. W.D. Mich. 1985).

350. 565 F. Supp. 556 (M.D. Pa. 1983).

351. Id.

352. *United States v. Tabor Court Realty Corp.,* 803 F.2d 1288, 1297 (3rd Cir. 1986).

353. Id.

354. *See, e.g., Vadnais Lumber Supply v. Byrne (In re Vadnais Lumber Supply)*, 100 B.R. 127 (Bankr. D. Mass 1989).

355. 327 B.R. 537 (D. Del. 2005).

356. Id.

357. A "triangular merger" is a method of amalgamation of two corporations by which the disappearing corporation is merged into a subsidiary of the acquiring corporation, and the shareholders of the disappearing corporation receive shares of the surviving corporation. *Black's Law Dictionary,* Abridged Sixth Edition.

358. *Hechinger,* 327 B.R. at 546.

359. Id. at 546–47.

360. Id. at 550–52.

361. Id. at 552.

362. Id.

363. Id.

364. Id.

365. Id.

366. Id.

367. Id.

368. Id.

369. Id. at 553.

370. Id.

371. Id.

372. Id.

373. Id.

374. Id.

375. Id.

376. *Hall v. Arthur Young & Co.* (*In re Computer Universe, Inc.*), 58 B.R. 28 (Bankr. M.D. Fla. 1986).
377. *See, e.g., Garrett v. Faulkner* (*In re Royal Crown Bottlers of N. Ala., Inc.*), 23 B.R. 28, 30 (Bankr. N.D. Ala. 1982); *Lawrence Paperboard Corp. v. Arlington Trust Co.* (*In re Lawrence Paperboard Corp.*), 76 B.R. 866, 874 (Bankr. D. Mass. 1987).
378. *Rubin v. Manufacturers Hanover Trust Co.,* 661 F.2d 979 (2d Cir. 1981).
379. *Tryit Enterprises v. General Electric Capital Corp.* (*In re Tryit Enterprises*), 121 B.R. 217 (Bankr. S.D. Tex. 1990).
380. Id.
381. Id. at 223.
382. Id. at 224.
383. Id.
384. Id. at 223.
385. *Martino v. Edison Worldwide Capital* (*In re Randy*), 189 B.R. 425, 437, n. 17 (Bankr. N.D. Ill. 1995).
386. *In re Bennett Funding Group, Inc.,* Ch. 11, Case Nos. 96-61376, 96-61377, 96-61378, 96-61379, jointly administered.
387. Mark A. McDermott, "Ponzi Schemes and the Law of Fraudulent and Preferential Transfers." *72 Am. Bankr. L.J. 157* (Spring 1998).
388. *See Sender v. Johnson* (*In re Hedged-Invs. Assocs., Inc.*), 84 F.3d 1267 (10th Cir. 1996) (stock options; approximately 1,400 investors ultimately lost $ 200 million in the scheme); *Jobin v. Youth Benefits Unlimited, Inc.* (*In re M&L Bus. Mach. Co.*), 59 F.3d 1078 (10th Cir. 1995) (computer leasing companies); *Wyle v. C.H. Rider & Family* (*In re United Energy Corp.*), 944 F.2d 589 (9th Cir. 1991) (energy modules); *Hayes v. Palm Seedlings Partners* (*In re Agricultural Research and Tech. Group*), 916 F.2d 528 (9th Cir. 1990) (seed-germination facilities); *Apostolou v. Fisher,* 188 B.R. 958 (N.D. Ill. 1995) (commodities); *Brandt v. American Nat'l Bank & Trust Co.* (*In re Foos*), 188 B.R. 239 (Bankr. N.D. Ill. 1995) (radio stations); *In re Lake States Commodities, Inc.,* 253 B.R. 866 (Bankr. N.D. Ill. 2000) (commodity futures trading and participation in commodity pools); *In re Carrozzella & Richardson,* 286 B.R. 480 (D. Conn. 2002) (deposit funds for fraudulent annual rate of return between 8 to15 percent); *In re Financial Federated Title & Trust, Inc.,* 309 F.3d 1325 (11th Cir. 2002) (life insurance policies); *U.S. v. Grasso,* 173 F. Supp. 2d 353 (E.D. Pa. 2001) (work-at-home scheme); *Bald Eagle Area School Dist. v. Keystone Financial, Inc.,* 189 F.3d 321 (3rd Cir. 1999) (investment in school bonds for construction); *S.E.C. v. SG Ltd.,* 265 F.3d 42 (1st Cir. 2001) (investment game for personal entertainment and Internet users); *U.S. v. Deavours,* 219 F.3d 400 (5th Cir. 2000) (wire transfers); *Chosnek v. Rolley,* 688 N.E.2d 202 (Ind. App. 1997) (fraudulent investment scheme); *In re Unified Commercial Capital, Inc.,* 260 B.R. 343 (Bankr. W.D. N.Y. 2001) (debentures and certificates of deposits); *In re Ramirez Rodriguez,* 209 B.R. 424 (Bankr. S.D. Tex. 1997) (equipment service procurement contracts); *U.S. v. Benson,* 79 Fed. Appx. 813 (6th Cir. 2003) (gasoline marketing scheme); *U.S. v. Gold Unlimited, Inc.,* 177 F.3d 472 (6th Cir. 1999) (cosmetic anti-saturation policies).
389. McDermott, *72 Am. Bankr. L.J. 157.*
390. *Jobin v. Lalan* (*In re M&L Business Machine Co.*), 160 B.R. 851, 857 (Bankr. D. Colo. 1993), aff'd, 167 B.R. 219 (D. Colo. 1994). *See also In re Taubman,* 160 B.R. 964, 982 (Bankr. S.D. Ohio 1993) (holding that funds obtained from Ponzi scheme investors are property of the debtor's estate); and *Dicello v. Jenkins* (*In re International Loan Network, Inc.*), 160 B.R. 1, 11 (Bankr. D. D.C. 1993) (noting the unanimous position of the courts that the debtor has an interest in property transferred through a Ponzi scheme).
391. *Jobin,* 160 B.R. at 857 (stating that "a claimant must be able to identify and trace the fraudulently deprived funds or property to which he claims ownership"); *Danning v. Bozek* (*In re Bullion Reserve of North America*), 836 F.2d 1214, 1217 (9th Cir. 1988).
392. *Merrill v. Abbott* (*In re Independent Clearing House Co.*), 77 B.R. 843, 857 (D. Utah 1987) (concluding that "the debtors received a 'reasonably equivalent value' in exchange for all transfers to a defendant that did not exceed the defendant's principal undertaking").

393. *Sender v. Buchanan* (*In re Hedged-Invs. Assocs., Inc.*), 84 F.3d 1286, 1290 (10th Cir. 1996) (holding that a Ponzi debtor does not receive reasonably equivalent value in exchange for any amounts it transfers to an investor in excess of the investor's principal investment); *Scholes v. Lehmann,* 56 F.3d 750, 757 (7th Cir. 1995) (holding that, under the Illinois version of the UFCA, a debtor does not receive fair consideration for transfers of fictitious profits paid pursuant to a Ponzi scheme); *Scholes v. Ames,* 850 F. Supp. 707, 715 (N.D. Ill. 1994) (holding that payments received in good faith by investors in a fraudulent investment scheme in excess of the principal invested were "voluntary gifts" and hence fraudulent conveyances that could be recovered by receiver), *aff'd sub nom.,* 56 F.3d 750 (7th Cir. 1995).
394. 11 U.S.C. § 550(a).
395. Collier on Bankruptcy ¶ 550.02[4][a] (15th Ed. Rev. 2006).
396. *Southmark Corporation v. Schulte, Roth & Zabel, L.L.P.,* 242 B.R. 330 (5th Cir. 2000); *Security First National Bank v. Brunson* (*In re Coutee*), 984 F.2d 138, 141 (5th Cir. 1993); *Liebersohn v. IRS* (*In re C.F. Foods, L.P.*), 265 B.R. 71 (Bankr. E.D. Pa. 2001).
397. Collier on Bankruptcy ¶ 550.02[4][a] (15th Ed. Rev. 2006).
398. *Nordberg v. Societe Generale* (*In re Chase & Sanborn Corp.*), 848 F.2d 1196, 1200 (11th Cir. 1988).
399. *Southmark Corporation,* 242 B.R. at 338; *Danning v. Miller* (*In re Bullion Reserve of North America*), 922 F.2d 544, 548 (9th Cir. 1991).
400. *Nordberg,* 848 F.2d at 1199.
401. Collier on Bankruptcy ¶ 550.02[4][b] (15th Ed. Rev. 2006) (*citing Nordberg,* 848 F.2d at 1196).
402. Collier on Bankruptcy ¶ 550.02[4][b] (15th Ed. Rev. 2006) (*citing Kupetz v. United States* (*In re California Trade Technical Schools, Inc.*), 923 F.2d 641 (9th Cir. 1991)).
403. *In re Queen City Grain, Inc.,* 51 B.R. 722 (Bankr. S.D. Ohio 1985).
404. Collier on Bankruptcy ¶ 550.02[4][b] (15th Ed. Rev. 2006) (*citing Commercial Recovery, Inc. v. Mill Street, Inc.* (*In re Mill Street, Inc.*), 96 B.R. 268 (9th Cir. B.A.P. 1989)).
405. Collier on Bankruptcy ¶ 550.02[4][b] (15th Ed. Rev. 2006) (*citing Lippi v. City Bank,* 955 F.2d 599 (9th Cir. 1992)).
406. 838 F.2d 890 (7th Cir. 1988).
407. Id. at 893.
408. Id.
409. *Gropper v. Unitrac, S.A.* (*In re Fabric Buys of Jerico, Inc.*), 33 B.R. 334 (Bankr. S.D.N.Y. 1983).
410. *DuVoisin v. Kennerly, Montgomery, Howard & Finley* (*In re Southern Industrial Banking Corp.*), 126 B.R. 294, 299 (E.D. Tenn. 1991). *See also Nordberg v. Societe Generale* (*In re Chase & Sanborn Corp.*), 848 F.2d 1196 (11th Cir. 1988); *Gropper v. Unitrac* (*In re Fabric Buys of Jericho, Inc.*), 33 Bankr. 334 (Bankr. S.D. N.Y. 1983).
411. 11 U.S.C. § 550(b)(1).
412. Id.
413. H.R. Rep. No. 595, 95th Cong., 2d Sess. 376.
414. *Davis v. Cook Construction Co.* (*In re: SLF News Distribs., Inc.*), 649 F.2d 613 (8th Cir. 1981).
415. 18 B.R. 778 (Bankr. W.D. Mo. 1982).
416. *See* Missouri's version of the Uniform Fraudulent Conveyance Act.
417. *Ohio Cellular Prods. Corp. v. Adams USA, Inc.,* 175 F.3d 1343, 1350 (Fed. Cir. 1999).
418. *Nizam's Institute of Medical Sciences v. Exchange Technologies, Inc.,* 1994 U.S. App LEXIS 16552, *11 (4th Cir. 1994) (*quoting Tedrow v. Deskin,* 290 A.2d 799, 802 (Md. 1972)).
419. Id.
420. Id.
421. *Teamsters Health and Welfare Fund of Philadelphia v. World Transportation, Inc.,* 241 F. Supp. 2d 499, 503 (E.D. Pa. 2003).

422. Id. (*quoting Kaplan v. First Options of Chicago, Inc.,* 19 F.3d 1503, 1522 (3rd Cir. 1994)).
423. 739 F.Supp. 231 (E.D. Pa. 1990).
424. Id. at 237.
425. *In re Healthco Int'l, Inc.*, 208 B.R. 288 (Bankr. D. Mass 1997).
426. 11 U.S.C. § 101(32).
427. Christopher W. Frost, "The Theory, Reality and Pragmatism of Corporate Governance in Bankruptcy Reorganizations." *72 Am. Bankr. L.J. 103* (1998): 107.
428. Id.
429. *In re Ben Franklin Retail Stores, Inc.,* 225 B.R. 646, 653 (Bankr. N.D. Ill. 1998) (*citing Geyer v. Ingersall Publications Co.,* 621 A.2d 784, 787 (Del. Ch. 1992)).
430. *Clarkson Co. Ltd. v. Shaheen,* 660 F.2d 506 (2nd Cir. 1991).
431. *Credit Lyonnais Bank Nederland, N.V. v. Pathe Communications Corp.,* 1996 Del. Ch. LEXIS 157 (1996).
432. 242 B.R. 492 (B.A.P. 9th Cir. 1999).
433. Id. at 495.
434. 2005 U.S. Dist. LEXIS 23498 (N.D. Ill. 2005).
435. Id.
436. Id. at *4–5.
437. 229 F.3d 617, 623 (7th Cir. 2000).
438. *Coleman,* 2005 U.S. Dist. LEXIS at *4–5.
439. 344 Ill. App. 3d 15 (Ill. App. Ct. 2003).
440. *Coleman,* 2005 U.S. Dist. LEXIS at *5–6.
441. 377 F. Supp. 2d. 390, 412-14 (S.D.N.Y. 2005).
442. *Coleman,* 2005 U.S. Dist. LEXIS at *6–8.
443. Id. at *17.
444. Id. at *7.
445. 865 So. 2d 1272 (Fla. 2004).
446. Id.
447. Id. at 1273–74.
448. Id. at 1274.
449. Id.
450. Id. at 1275.
451. Id.
452. Id. at 1277.

Chapter 18

Discovery and Preventing Fraud in Business Formation and Dissolution

Samuel C. Damren

INTRODUCTION

Analyzing the various techniques to prevent or detect constituent fraud necessitates considering the provisions contained in the business's organizational documents. This is because many of the statutory and legal rights accorded the constituents of business entities (whether corporations, partnerships, trusts, limited liability companies, or other entities) can be expanded or restricted by the provisions of the organizational documents. Constituent rights that are central to the prevention and detection of constituent fraud in the formation, operation, and dissolution of a business include access to information regarding actions that the entity or constituent has or taken or is considering undertaking and approval rights with respect to specific activities or conduct.

FUNDAMENTAL ASSESSMENTS

The business professional must undertake certain fundamental assessments to prudently and effectively negotiate constituent informational and approval rights in a business's organizational documents and to advise constituents with respect to their obligations, rights, and business alternatives after formation.

Constituents

Before entering into a significant business relationship, it is always wise to conduct a thorough background check on each prospective constituent to the relationship. In addition to obvious information and credit issues, the background check should include a search of local court records for litigation that a constituent has been a party to and a check of relevant state and county records for all business entities that the constituent has been associated with. Prospective business associates should also be encouraged to disclose all of their past and present relationships in the same or related fields of business. It should also be determined through appropriate means if a constituent has been a good or bad partner, employee, or associate with others in the past and whether the constituent has a good reputation in the business or relevant community.

After assuring oneself of the integrity of each constituent to a prospective business relationship, the next step is to assess the competency of each constituent for his or her particular role in the conduct and success of the prospective business. This determination will directly affect the negotiation and application of the terms in the organizational documents and requires answering three questions.

1. What is the constituent's role?
2. How are other constituents able to assess whether the constituent has fulfilled or failed to satisfy his or her responsibilities?
3. What rewards are available to the constituent for meeting those responsibilities, and conversely, what remedies are available to other constituents if the constituent fails to meet his or her responsibilities?

The types of provisions that might be negotiated as part of the organizational documents to deal with these particular role issues are subject to innumerable permutations given the spectrum of possible roles—for example, provider of capital, sweat equity, specific professional competence, intellectual property, sales, manufacturer—and the unique combination of these roles in each particular business.

Risks and Rewards Inherent to the Business

Every category of business has different inherent risks and rewards. These risks and rewards can change over time in a particular industry and profession and often differ depending on regional locations, the size of the business, and its position in the hierarchy of competitors, suppliers, and customers. Once again, countless combinations can result from these various differing factors. Nevertheless, understanding the interplay of these permutations is essential to identifying situations in which a potential "risk" or "reward" to a business entity might become an "opportunity" for a constituent to fraudulently "profit" at the expense of the business and the other constituents.

Part of this analysis involves determining whether differing "risks" and "rewards" have conflicting purposes or favor short-term success for certain constituents at the expense of long-term success for others. Although these type of tensions always exist in business where the roles and talents of the various constituents differ, the degree to which these tensions may be unduly highlighted in "good" times as opposed to "bad" times, or vice versa, must also be carefully considered. If these tensions weigh too heavily for or against a particular constituent, that person may be encouraged to commit fraud as a way of avoiding a particularly difficult, and from his or her perspective, unfair circumstance.

Risk of Third-Party Fraud in Dissolution

When a business dissolves and is required to wind up its affairs, third parties often view this circumstance as an opportunity to acquire potentially valuable business assets at a discount. While taking advantage of these opportunities is not necessarily fraudulent, problems may arise where a constituent of a failing business acts in conjunction with a third party to fraudulently acquire assets at a discounted value and unfairly profits at the expense of other constituents from the undervalued sale of these assets.

FACTORS AFFECTING WHETHER THE FRAUD WILL SUCCEED

From the constituent's perspective, the integrity and success of a business relationship with another depends on the free flow of accurate and complete information. Fraudulent conduct interferes with unfettered communication either through deception or as a result of one constituent's failure to disclose certain information on a timely basis in the face of an obligation to do so. In preventing, detecting, and addressing fraud that is premised on deception, it is critical to ascertain the "shelf life" of the deception that is employed to accomplish the fraud (i.e., how long does the deception have to be maintained in order for the fraud to work and the victim to be left without an effective remedy?). In contrast, preventing, detecting, and addressing fraud based on a failure to disclose information requires determining the likelihood that the victim will acquire the information from another source, and, if so, how quickly the undisclosed information may become known.

In addition to shelf life, another factor critical to the success or failure of a fraudulent scheme is the expertise required to discover it. This factor, of course, also involves time, but where special expertise (forensic accounting, attorney investigation, or other expertise) is required to unravel the scheme, these substantial expenses can be additional impediments to discovering the fraud.

Those who engage in fraudulent conduct span the spectrum of sophistication. The least sophisticated purveyors of fraud simply hope to be out of reach by the time the fraud is discovered. More sophisticated practitioners may create a circumstance where they can plausibly deny that the fraud occurred, through a he-said-she-said denial, by a false paper trail, or by destroying evidence. Masters of fraud include in their overall scheme a plan to frame someone else for their wrongdoing or place the victim of the fraud in a situation where disclosure and any steps to remedy the fraud will either co-opt the victim or expose him or her to otherwise avoidable harm from third parties.

INFORMATIONAL RIGHTS AND FRAUD

While the various categories of fiduciary obligations that trustees, partners, shareholders, directors, officers, members, and managers have toward their respective constituencies are similar, the statutory rights of beneficiaries, partners, shareholders, and members to information regarding the affairs of the business vary considerably. These statutory rights can be expanded through the entity's organizational documents or agreements among the constituents and the entity. In the context of constituent fraud, the issue is not breach of contract in failing to provide required information; rather, the inquiry focuses on whether the misrepresentation of facts or failure to disclose critical facts is part of a constituent's larger scheme to defraud the business and other constituents. Except in cases of outright embezzlement or theft, another important consideration to this issue involves whether the information that a constituent needs to expose a fraud committed by another constituent is in the possession of third parties.

The particular variety of constituent informational fraud that might occur in the life of a business varies depending on the stage the business is in (formation, operation, or dissolution).

At the time of formation, constituents may fraudulently misrepresent the status of assets that they will contribute to the business, their expertise, or their relationship with important business associates. During the shelf life of this deception, constituents' relationships to the business may enable them to acquire profits or other business opportunities that they would otherwise not receive. While the business is operating, constituent informational fraud typically involves the diversion of funds or opportunities through some sort of scheme with or without a third-party accomplice. At the time of dissolution, constituent informational fraud often involves directing undervalued business assets or opportunities to a constituent or an accomplice. Informational fraud, of course, can be the basis for a court-ordered dissolution and a court-supervised winding up of the business.

APPROVAL RIGHTS AND GOVERNANCE

In organizational documents and as provided by statute, constituents are accorded various approval rights over certain business actions. These approval rights may require majority vote, supermajority vote, or the approval of disinterested constituents. The increase in constituent approval requirements generally parallels decisions that are increasingly fundamental to the operation of the business, such as merger, the sale of all or substantially all of the assets, and dissolution. Constituent fraud involving these types of transactions is generally rare where the potential purchaser or purchasers have no relationship to any of the constituents and where negotiations are conducted at arm's length.

Other transactions that involve less fundamental business decisions, but may nevertheless be subject to increased constituent approval rights, do not enjoy this intrinsic buffer to possible constituent fraud. Typical of these types of transactions are relationships between the business and another business in which a manager and/or constituent of the former has an interest. Fraud in these types of transactions can occur in three different fashions. First, managers or constituents who are required to seek constituent approval of such a transaction can misrepresent or omit the fact that they have an interest in the other business. Second, despite disclosing their relationship to the other business, managers or constituents can misrepresent the nature or extent of that interest, including indirect benefits that they might receive in a variety of different forms as a result of the approval of the transaction by the other constituents. Third, the other business can conduct its business in a fraudulent manner with managers or constituents thereby improperly profiting from the relationship at the expense of the business and its other constituents.

In contrast to nearly all other circumstances in a business's existence, when a business is formed, it requires the approval of all constituents. During formation, the constituents' primary concern is that each of the constituents brings to the table what has been promised. The organizing documents for the business can provide that if one constituent fails to do what she has committed to doing, then the other constituents can void the formation, dissolve the business, or treat the failure as a breach and continue the business with various remedies against the responsible constituent. These types of options can also apply to breaches by constituents that occur at other times in the business life of the entity. The provision of these types of remedies in the organizational documents complements approval rights because it gives rights that cannot be blocked by the offending constituent to constituents who are the victims of fraud.

Fraudulent conduct by a constituent also raises a more fundamental concern for the other constituents: whether they should remain in business with this person. These constituents should recognize that anyone who will defraud partners is certainly capable of defrauding others and may have done so while representing the business. The business and all of its constituents are placed at risk by this circumstance. In fact, if it becomes generally known that your partner cheated you and that you let it go, individuals across the business community are going to wonder about you just as much as they will wonder about your partner and your business.

In addition to damages to compensate the business and its other constituents for the harm caused, separate remedies in the organizing documents to restructure the business upon the occurrence of constituent fraud should include the ability to remove the defrauding party from management, to force a buyout of the defrauding party's equity interest at substantial discount, or to dissolve the business and bar the defrauding party from having any major role in the dissolution process. The fact that a business's organizing documents provide sure and certain remedies against any constituent who defrauds the business will certainly deter one who may be tempted to step across the line. Similarly, a constituent's objection to including such provisions in an organizing document should be a red flag to other potential constituents.

Anyone who has even modest experience in business knows that there is no one-size-fits-all approach for addressing these types of issues. From the onset of a business relationship through its conclusion, if your trust in your business constituents' commitment and integrity is justified and your assessment of their capabilities is accurate, then fraud is not likely to ever be an issue. However, trust can be misplaced, assessments can be inaccurate, and people do change. In approaching these issues at the time of formation, it is often useful with less experienced businesspersons to first discuss what will happen if a constituent becomes incapacitated during the existence of the business and is unable to perform his or her obligations. A discussion of remedies for fraud is the logical next step since both involve the constituent's failure to perform his or her obligations, albeit for decidedly different reasons. However, because of these differences, the remedies for constituent fraud must be more robust than those for constituent incapacity.

The selection of professionals is another matter that may properly be subject to constituents' approval rights as professionals are potentially another obstacle to prevent, and an early warning system in the detection of, fraud. When selecting legal counsel and accountants, for example, the relationships other constituents may have to these firms should be carefully evaluated. Clearly, if a business has failed or is forced into dissolution, it may be appropriate to engage new counsel and accountants to handle that process.

ADDITIONAL DRAFTING SOLUTIONS

The drafting solutions described below for privately held companies can minimize the possibility of constituent fraud, increase the discovery of fraud, and provide remedies that enhance the ability of other constituents to make themselves whole. Publicly held companies are subject to regulatory agencies that provide a separate set of protections.

MINIMIZING THE OCCURRENCE OF FRAUD

Where self-dealing in some measure is permitted as part of the operation of a business, supermajority or disinterested constituent approval rights of these relations are often appropriate to minimize the possibility that fraud may arise out of these relations. These same devices typically are often utilized with respect to certain transactions that the business may contemplate entering into, whether the transaction involves direct self-dealing or not.

Conversely, restrictions or limitations on allowing constituents to compete with the business are also appropriate to limit constituents from engaging in competitive practices with the company that may, in the view of other constituents, suggest or encourage fraud.

DISCOVERY OF FRAUD

Permitting constituents to have informational rights beyond those required by statute is useful in discovering fraud. These additional informational rights can vary greatly but must balance the costs of undue intrusion into the operation of the business with the benefits of increased transparency. The drafting solution appropriate to a particular business is idiosyncratic given the type of business, the relationship of the parties, and a host of other factors previously identified in this chapter. Other devices that aid in the detection of fraud include the requirement of certifications by specified officers of various transactions or financial statements that include the types of certification now required from officers of publicly held companies: the CEO and CFO certify that the financial statements of the organization are both accurate and complete.

A requirement for independent accountants or counsel to periodically review or audit certain matters or particular transactions may also be appropriate, where the expense of these reviews is justified. Similarly, where the expense is warranted, the inclusion of independent directors or business advisors for certain business decisions and transactions may also be appropriate.

REMEDIES

The dissolution or a forced buyout by the company of a constituent based on a fraud is a drastic remedy that courts rarely impose. But the court's decision on these matters often depends on whether other remedies are available. It is often appropriate to provide for these types of remedies in the company's organizational documents upon the occurrence of certain benchmark events. While the term of the company can be one, earlier events are also appropriate. Financial performance, the percentage of distributions from profits, and the ability of dissenting constituents who cannot prevent the occurrence of certain transactions are often useful benchmarks that can be employed to provide constituents with an option to withdraw from a business organization in the face of disagreement, whether that disagreement arises from fraud or not. These types of devices promote constituent harmony by requiring majority constituents to take into account the concerns of the minority in a wide variety of circumstances. By so doing, they provide safety valves to business disagreements that often lead to accusations of fraud. The percentage amount that a constituent might be paid for his or her interest can also be appropriately discounted in these circumstances, since the exercise of these rights provides liquidity for one constituent that is not available to other constituents and places short-term financial stress on the company.

Establishing the value of the company and the constituent's percentage discounted interest is typically based on a set formula, appraisals, or a combination of such factors coupled with an arbitration provision to enforce these determinations. In refining these provisions, floors and a ceiling to the purchase/sale price and terms for payment can also be provided, as well as provisions for only the partial withdrawal of a constituent's equity interest. These options can be further refined by providing nonwithdrawing constituents with their own set of options, should they wish to avoid the financial burden of a buyout of another constituent's interest (e.g., dissolving the company in lieu of paying the discounted amount or requiring payments over a specified period of time). "Puts" and "calls" between constituents at specified times or under specified circumstances are often appropriate devices to secure similar benefits.

The methodology for dissolution available under business formation documents can also provide similar benefits. These devices include Dutch auctions, actual auctions conducted by third parties, either between constituents or involving nonconstituents with limitations on constituent participation in the purchase.

Chapter 19

Identity Theft and Privacy Protection

Brian Sommariva and James Martin

INTRODUCTION

Identity theft has become a problem for which technology providers and law enforcement officials are still struggling to find an adequate solution. In 2005 the Federal Trade Commission (FTC)received over 685,000 fraud complaints with consumers reporting losses of over $680 million. Identity thefts comprise 37 percent of overall fraud complaints made to the FTC in 2005. In previous years, identity theft was found mostly in the 20- to 29-year age category, but in 2005, identity theft affected each age category—20 to 29, 30 to 39 and 40 to 49—equally at approximately 25 percent.[1] Surprisingly, less than 10% of reported identity thefts were in the 60+ category.

Currently there are some misconceptions surrounding identity theft. Perhaps the most common misconception is that identity theft is a newer phenomenon. Furthermore, many believe that the Internet and related technology are the reasons for the recent rapid ascent of identity theft. Many also believe that most identity thieves are unknown perpetrators—people with whom the victim has never had contact or personally known—and that identity theft victims are generally randomly targeted.

The truth is that identity theft is not a new crime; identity theft landed on the radar of some public agencies as early as 1992. However, crime such as check and credit fraud extend to the roots of the U.S. Banking and Financial systems.[2] Frank W. Abagnale—on whose life the motion picture *Catch Me If You Can* is based—successfully assumed at least four identities before he was 21 years old.[3] Although it is believed that Abagnale never assumed the identities of any actual people, he mastered the concept in the late 1960s, well before the development of even the earliest personal computers.

Additionally, the Internet and other electronic sources are not the main facilitators to stealing one's identity; most current data indicates that offline methods, such as mail theft and Dumpster diving, are the predominant ways to commit an identity theft. According to a 2005 survey by the Javelin Research Group, an overwhelming majority—68.2 percent—of identity thefts occurred using offline methods. Only 11.6 percent of thefts were perpetrated using "online" methods, indicating computers do not currently serve as a major tool in perpetrating an identity theft.[4] Widespread use of personal computers and the interconnectivity of the

Internet is an extremely recent development, and many identity thieves and scammers seem to still be perfecting their craft. The complexity or magnitude of computer-based attacks aimed at extracting our personal information continues to grow. The Internet appears to be growing to be the new frontier for most white-collar crime like identity theft, especially with links to organized crime and drug rings.[5,6]

Last, in over half of identity theft cases reported, the perpetrators knew the victims, either as a family member, business associate or employee, or neighbor.[7] In some examples, parents have been caught stealing the identities of their children to obtain credit.[8] Another common instance of identity theft occurs when the manager of an apartment complex improperly uses the tremendous amounts of personal information available in the tenant files. Housekeepers, roommates, and college students in dormitory settings all can gain access to documents containing personal information of others. As efforts to increase the security of our personal information both offline and online, we must not forget to guard that information from misuse by those in our circle of trust.

Similar to most frauds, absolute prevention of identity theft is unlikely, but following several recommendations can limit the possibility of becoming a victim. Since much of our private and identifiable information generally never changes, such as name, date of birth, and Social Security number (SSN), early detection of an identity theft requires constant monitoring. And after this nonchanging personal data are compromised once, a combination of fraud alerts or other monitoring methods may be required for a lifetime. Like other frauds, as public awareness of the scam grows and the fraud tactic becomes more difficult to perform, another easier method to commit fraud will appear. The public's growing awareness of the identity theft issue, and well-known advice to shred documents with personally identifying information, has pushed identity thieves to resort to more sophisticated attacks than dumpster-diving. Similarly, as people become aware of more common "offline" methods to safeguard their personal information, identity thieves will resort to more complicated technology-based attacks if those methods provide greater opportunity. The action-reaction relationship between fraud perpetrators and victims places additional imperatives on businesses and consumers to become better educated on common identity theft schemes.

DEFINITION

> "I did not use a gun. I did not use a knife. Call my lawyer and I will plead guilty and they will put me on probation."[9]

Identity theft is a fraud committed using the identifying information of another person.[10] Identity theft may also be referred to as an identity fraud, since the possession of another person's identifiable information is not necessarily a crime, but the subsequent frauds committed using that information are.

Identity theft, though not a new crime, has gained massive public attention recently, especially in June/July of 2005. During this short span, a security breach at CardSystems, a credit card processing company, exposed 40 million credit card numbers, the card security codes and some personal information of their respective cardholders. Furthermore, the Fair and Accurate Credit Transactions Act (FACTA) went into full effect impacting businesses and individuals and their data collection and disposal procedures.

Prior to 2005, the issue of identity theft was notably absent from the public eye, but identity theft was an issue that first appeared before the federal government as early as 1993 in one form or another.[11] Identity theft became an easy method for criminals to finance other illegal activities and easily escape prosecution as damages to victims usually failed to meet prosecution thresholds.

DEVELOPMENT OF AN EPIDEMIC

"If [identity theft] was a medical problem, it would be considered The Plague."[12]

A May 1998 General Accounting Office (GAO) report titled "Identity Theft: Information on Prevalence, Cost, and Internet Impact Is Limited" was one of the first government publications on the issue. Findings included information obtained through law enforcement investigations as well as discussion with private sector companies affected by identity fraud.

The May 1998 GAO report concluded that statistics on instances and losses were difficult to accurately track since identity theft usually involved other crimes. Aggregate statistics from other crimes, such as mail fraud, bank fraud, and credit card fraud, were used to estimate the impact of identity theft. These data were compiled from the U.S. Attorneys Office and other law enforcement databases, specifically criminal conviction data, but plea bargains may have skewed results on the actual occurrence of identity theft. In essence, the GAO report recognized the problem of identity theft and the need for more information on the issue. Furthermore, the GAO report concluded that no federal laws addressed identity theft as a separate crime. Crimes resulting from an identity theft fell under the jurisdiction of various federal laws, such as: identification document fraud (18 U.S.C. 1028), fraud in connection with access devices (i.e., credit cards), and misuse of social security numbers (42 U.S.C. 408 (a) (7)).

Similarly, the May 1998 GAO report found that it was difficult to investigate and prosecute identity theft criminals because "no one federal agency has primary jurisdiction regarding identity theft." However, two federal agencies—the Postal Inspection Service and Secret Service—tracked "certain types of identity fraud" as early as 1995. Despite this, no data were compiled and made accessible to all federal agencies with a stake in identity theft and related crimes.

At the time the May 1998 GAO report was authored, Arizona and California had already enacted legislation criminalizing identity theft, even before the federal government enacted its own identity theft laws. By 1998 Arizona had filed 89 court cases in response to 142 investigations, and California had yet to prosecute any criminals under California statute.

The May 1998 GAO report outlined the efforts of various government organizations to fight identity theft, but also detailed many failures from both the public and private sectors. The Identity Theft and Assumption Deterrence Act of 1998, [13] a federal law that made identity theft a federal crime, also failed to authorize a single federal agency to investigate and prosecute identity theft criminals. The 1998 Identity Theft Act instructed the Federal Trade Commission (FTC) to maintain a database of identity theft complaints so that the pervasiveness of identity theft could be accurately assessed; this database became known as the Consumer Sentinel, and it is still used today to track identity theft incidence rates. The FTC was also empowered to inform consumers and businesses of ways to deter and remediate identity thefts, and to refer identity theft complaints to "appropriate law enforcement agencies for potential law enforcement action."[14] By 2000 the FTC processed over 40,000 entries from victims of identity theft.[15]

In 2000, and in anticipation of the Identity Theft Prevention Act of 2000,[16] a House committee on Banking and Financial Services discussed identity theft. The committee sought updates and statistics from law enforcement and other federal agencies tracking identity theft, such as the FTC and the Secret Service Financial Crimes Division, and heard testimony from members of the private sector, including representatives from companies, special interest organizations, and individuals directly affected by related identity theft crimes. Associations representing credit reporting agencies, banks, research firms, investigative firms, and consumer privacy groups were all represented, and many testified that some provisions proposed for the 2000 Identity Theft Prevention Act would not necessarily reduce identity theft crimes. Additionally, those testifying observed a lack of enforcement of the 1998 act.[17]

A representative from the Secret Service Financial Crimes Division argued that much of the data used to commit an identity theft originated from online information repositories—or "data brokers" that buy, store, and sell personal information on millions of Americans. The Secret Service felt that the data, which was made available "via the Internet," aided organized crime from numerous countries, and that significant improvements would be made in the fight against identity theft if these data brokers were forced to comply with privacy acts such as the Gramm-Leach-Bliley (GLB) Act. The Secret Service representative testified that enforcement efforts from his agency had increased in response to criminal activity on the Internet that crossed national boundary lines; his agency was pursuing identity thieves that were creating risk to the community, and would offer the assistance of his 2,800 special agents to local, state, or federal prosecutors when asked. He also discussed a federal prosecution threshold, meaning U.S. Attorneys rarely pursued prosecution when losses to a victim failed to exceed approximately $100,000.

FTC testimony in 2000 stated they were in compliance with their obligation as defined by the 1998 Identity Theft Act but noted limitations in their authority to prosecute criminals. The FTC mentioned that over 280 law enforcement agencies were using a secure online database within the Consumer Sentinel designed for law enforcement officials to search for information compiled from FTC investigations. The Consumer Sentinel, established in 1999, also provided statistics to the FTC's Identity Theft Clearinghouse, which provided statistics on the state of identity theft. Some of the information in the Consumer Sentinel included victims' personal information and accounts affected by the identity theft. But the Consumer Sentinel was intended to be a resource to be used during an investigation rather than a notification tool informing law enforcement of trends or outbreaks in their jurisdiction. Additionally, the Consumer Sentinel stored information on remediation efforts by victims to clear their credit history. During the remediation process, inappropriate purchase history on the compromised accounts generally revealed information about the perpetrator. Oftentimes the steps a victim needed to take to remediate an identity theft provided most information that could be used to prosecute the perpetrator(s). A GAO report published two years after the testimony to the House Committee reported that the Consumer Sentinel system was not being used to its fullest capabilities in fighting identity theft and was leading to very few identity theft prosecutions.

Congressman Leach also revealed that unscrupulous businesses and individuals in the investigative industry placed advertisements that they could obtain data from various third-party databases that collect information on millions of Americans. An informal sting conducted by Leach's office was successful in demonstrating the willingness of those advertising such investigative services to reveal personal information on other individuals despite the GLB Act. For example, a female member of Leach's staff contacted several of the data companies and claimed her boyfriend had run off with her money, and she needed information on his whereabouts and account information. She never provided the necessary court orders as provisioned in the GLB Act to obtain confidential information on another person. In three hours, she placed calls to 26 firms; 11 firms completely provided the unauthorized personal information sought by the sting operators, demonstrating the little regard for personal privacy and the GLB Act.

Representatives from various consumer and individual privacy groups were also present, claiming that credit industry practices of issuing instant credit and the widespread sale of credit headers—the demographic and personal information, including Social Security Number, located directly above the credit history on a consumer credit report—were likely reasons for sudden rises in identity theft. Similar to the testimony of Leach and the Secret Service representative, privacy groups felt provisions of the GLB Act were not being followed and that enforcement lacked the resources to force creditors, banks, and third-party data miners to comply with the act. Testimony revealed that special exemptions in the GLB Act provided identity theft criminals the latitude to explore various methods of illicitly extracting personal information. One special exemption allowed those investigating parents in violation of child support commitments to avoid procedures in the GLB Act such as obtaining the proper court orders. Identity theft criminals quickly learned of this exploit, which led to the popularization of techniques such as phone pretexting, unauthorized account queries or takeovers, and change-of-address schemes.

Phone pretexting occurs when a criminal calls an organization, such as the victim's phone company, with a piece of the victim's personal information. The criminal supplies information known about a victim to the organization in order to gain additional information that he or she did not know. One example provided in testimony was that an identity theft perpetrator would call the phone company and supply the victim's name, address, and phone number—all of which was readily available in the public phone listings. Acting under the identity of the victim, the fraudster would "play stupid" and inquire if the victim had a second line listed. The second line could be used as an identifier to gain additional credit and circumvent detection efforts. The fraudster could also add another address to the account or change the billing address.

Most groups that testified saw a need for limiting who could compile, store, and retrieve personal information on millions of Americans, but each group argued that its industry should be among those permitted to access the information. Specifically, representatives from bank and credit associations felt that the restrictions proposed in the 2000 Identity Theft Act on the sale of consumer credit headers would negatively impact their business operations to offer their customers the instant credit that consumers demanded. Testimony from research groups (e.g., Lexis-Nexis) and private investigators demonstrated their opposition to provisions of the 2000 Identity Theft Prevention Act that limited access to personal information contained in credit headers as well as information stored in third-party databases used for research purposes. A representative from a private investigators' association testified that their ability to research an individual through various databases and credit history actually assisted victims of identity theft since they were able to track addresses, accounts, and personal information of the perpetrators.

The most well-received and insightful testimony came from Robert Douglas, chief executive officer of American Privacy Consultants, Inc. His testimony centered on four points to deter identity theft:

1. Financial service and credit industries need to understand the threat and form loss prevention strategies.
2. Tough legislation is needed at the federal and state level.
3. Establish or delegate authority of identity theft issues to a federal agency.
4. Investigate and prosecute criminals aggressively, regardless of prosecution thresholds.

Furthermore, Douglas testified that the federal prosecution threshold is often met if careful investigation is performed and efforts of all law enforcement agencies are compiled. He felt that conditions of steps 1 through 3 were met but that efforts to aggressively investigate and prosecute remained far behind.

Shon Boulden also testified before the committee on the challenges he faced as a victim of identity theft. As a victim, he testified that law enforcement was not helpful in remediation of his identity theft. His testimony also identified shortfalls by the credit reporting agencies to spot red flags in his case that he felt were common sense. In Boulden's situation, 12 people were using his Social Security number to obtain credit, which he felt the credit reporting agencies and creditors should have been able to spot. Boulden initially found out about the unauthorized use of his personal information when he tried to set up a new bank account and was denied. At the time of his testimony in 2000, he was still attempting to resolve effects of his identity theft, which he discovered approximately six months prior. However, frauds using his stolen identity dated back to as early as 1996 but had escaped detection by creditors and banks.

Data from the California Public-Interest Research Group showed that Boulden's efforts to remediate the theft of his identity were similar to other victims: approximately 175 hours and $808 in out-of-pocket costs. Boulden, who was 22 at the time, indicated that many of his attempts to clear his name were hindered by the fact that he did not have a subpoena from a law enforcement agency or judge and that no investigation was being conducted on the perpetrators that used his stolen identity.

Testimony from private investigators that assist other identity theft victims also mirrored Boulden's observations, especially if the victim's loss failed to meet federal prosecution thresholds. One witness testified that a client who was a victim of identity theft experienced losses around $80,000 and hoped for an additional $20,000 in losses so that his case could be considered for prosecution by a U.S. Attorney.

In the end, members from interested public and private organizations provided varied opinions to the Banking and Financial Services House Committee. Presenters cited various conclusions as to the contributing factors of identity theft, which seemed to conflict with other opinions presented. Many different perspectives on identity theft prevention were presented, as well as the specific effects that the pending 2000 Identity Theft Prevention Act would have on each organization. In the end, no set of recommendations or methodology to protect against identity theft was agreed on by all committee participants.

The GAO issued three additional reports on identity theft in 2002. In March 2002, "Identity Theft: Prevalence and Cost Appear to be Growing" informed Congress of the growing conditions of identity theft in the United States. The report echoed testimony at the 2000 Banking and Financial Services House Committee that while the FTC is authorized to collect and store victim complaints, the agency is not authorized to pursue criminal action against identity theft criminals. In the first two years, the FTC's Identity Theft Data Clearinghouse received 94,100 complaints, which included approximately 17,000 complaints transferred from the Social Security Administration (SSA) and Office of Inspector General (OIG).[18]

Despite the FTC's standardized collection of identity theft victim data through the Consumer Sentinel, various federal law enforcement agencies continued to police individual aspects related to identity theft. No one federal agency received centralized authority to investigate identity theft. Under this decentralized methodology, it is easy to see how the federal prosecution threshold was not attained, and identity thieves escaped prosecution. The FBI investigated bank frauds; the Secret Service investigated credit card frauds; and the Postal Inspection Service investigated mail fraud. Individually, crimes in each of these areas may have never reached

$100,000, but the collective impact of these various frauds was never aggregated or shared among federal agencies and presented to U.S. Attorneys.

As an indication of the rising epidemic, the March 2002 GAO report demonstrated that the Postal Inspection Service—one agency that began tracking identity theft on a more comprehensive basis—had increased investigation of identity thefts by 67 percent between 1999 and 2000.

The GAO also concluded in its March 2002 report that the use of e-commerce had grown steadily. One statistic cited was a Federal Deposit and Insurance Commission (FDIC) report that stated only one bank had a Web site that offered its users the ability to process financial transactions in 1995. In 2000, the FDIC reported that over 1,850 banks offered the same functionality. The GAO also deduced that an increased number of people had access to Internet technology, despite "security and privacy concerns" from consumers. The March 2002 GAO report never identified how most identity thefts occurred, specifically whether the perpetrators used offline or online methods.

The GAO issued two updates on identity theft in June 2002. The report was presented to a congressional terrorism and immigration committee and was titled "Identity Fraud: Prevalence and Links to Alien Illegal Activities." The GAO indicated that the FBI had noticed the increase in Web sites that combined computer hardware and software to make more authentic identification cards, including holograms and other artwork that can easily "resemble a state-issued driver's license," birth certificate, or law enforcement credentials.[19] Understandably, the focus of the congressional subcommittee was the relationship identity theft had on the "war on terror" that followed after the attacks on September 11, 2001.

In many instances, common offline frauds that required the change of an address, new credit applications, or account takeovers required criminals to possess falsified identification documents. New state and federal IDs were becoming more difficult to fake, but cunning criminals found ways to duplicate many of the security measures in government identification documents. At that time, the falsification of identification documents in the scope of terrorism posed a more grave threat to the nation's security than in the scope of identity theft.

Another June 2002 GAO report to a U.S Representative, titled "Identity Theft: Greater Awareness and Use of Existing Data Are Needed," found minimal data on enforcement of the 1998 and 2002 Identity Theft Acts. This report cited that few law enforcement agencies used the FTC's Consumer Sentinel information system. Furthermore, the GAO reported that the "cross-jurisdictional nature of identity theft" demonstrates the need for coordination of federal, state, and local law enforcement agencies in the fight against identity theft. The GAO recommended the use of task-forces, a joint operation of multiple law enforcement agencies, and to include private sector participants, such as banks and credit agencies.[20]

Almost every state had specific laws criminalizing identity theft by June 2002, and the Identity Theft Act of 1998 had been in effect for nearly four years. Yet the FBI's Uniform Crime Reporting Program did not record identity theft as a separate offense. According to the FTC, 59 percent of victims from November 1999 to October 2000 contacted the police, but approximately one in every three of these victims was unable to obtain a police report. Despite a resolution from the International Association of Chiefs of Police in late 2000 that encouraged law enforcement agencies to issue a police report to identity theft victims, many victims responded that law enforcement instructed them to contact their credit card company, bank, or other branches of law enforcement. In 2005 the FTC reported that 9 percent of victims that notified the police were unable to obtain a police report.

The GAO had provided examples of successful task-force operations in the "Greater Awareness and Use of Existing Data Are Needed" report. One example included in the report demonstrated the arrest of a Florida man "who assumed and lived under the identity of a California victim, who had lost his wallet while vacationing in Daytona Beach in 1987." The perpetrator was arrested in California based on a Florida warrant, executed by Florida county, state, and SSA/OIG officials. Widespread use of the Consumer Sentinel will enable more collaboration by various levels of local, state, and federal law enforcement officials.

THE OUTBREAK AND LAW ENFORCEMENT

From 1998 to 2002,the government passed four laws addressing identity theft and held numerous hearings on the issue, but the patchwork of laws illustrated many problems with fighting identity theft. Regulations were needed for both printed and electronic documents across many different private industries as well as public sector agencies. Finding a law that could encapsulate proper deterrence of identity theft across various institutions would be difficult, including one that dealt with personal privacy and data storage issues to satisfy all interested parties. From 2003 to 2006 the identity theft epidemic grew rapidly while other competing priorities captured law enforcement's attention.[21] As joint operations aimed at capturing identity thieves increased, examples of successful arrests increased, such as the one involving Florida officials just cited. As expected, though, the first enforcement efforts targeted the "big fish" and usually involved federal authorities. Arrests of "big fish" still entice law enforcement; for example, a postal inspector who investigates identity theft has stated that he does not touch "anything that does not get into the millions [of dollars in losses]."[22]

Arrest examples in 2002 and 2003 usually involved perpetrators of organized crime rings affecting numerous victims with high-value losses. Victims were often connected to other victims as employees or customers of the same company. An example of victim commonality was a 2002 Department of Justice Press Release in which a ring of six alleged identity theft perpetrators were arrested for the theft of personal information from employees of the same company. Investigators traced the perpetrators to obtaining official identification documents from Arkansas, which was later used to acquire money, property, and motor vehicles across the United States under the victims' identities.[23] The modus operandi of this fraud was the common method to commit identity theft: Steal personal information, obtain "valid" identification under the victim's name, and then purchase items under the victim's line of credit. Other identity theft arrests were piggybacked with arrests of high-profile spam operations.[24]

Given the large amounts of personal information stored, either as public record or made available cheaply through third-party research databases, scams such as phone pretexting usually can extract enough information to obtain a valid identification document, such as a driver's license. Obtaining valid state-issued driver's licenses under a falsified identity are relatively easy, and extremely realistic novelty driver's licenses are even easier to obtain. One scam involved the assumption of a deceased person's identity. Many times criminals use public death records to find victims that were of age to receive credit. From the death record, a criminal can obtain a valid birth certificate from the state or county, which includes a Social Security number. The birth certificate then is used as proof of identification when obtaining a driver's license under the deceased person's identity.

A 2003 GAO report detailed many inadequacies with the use of a Social Security number as an identifier. This GAO report to Congress was titled "Social Security Numbers: Improved

SSN Verification and Exchange of State's Driver Records Would Enhance Identity Verification." The GAO concluded in this report that only one-half of U.S. states used SSN verification offered through the Social Security Administration (SSA) to issue driver's licenses. The GAO found the SSA's computer system offering SSN verification to be costly, slow, and unreliable due to frequent system outages.[25]

In addition, the 2003 report found that no nationalized system was present to share personal information and the driving history found in all state information systems. State licensing agents had to rely on visual inspection of documents rather than a centralized information system that could verify license photos and perform checks for suspicious or conflicting activity. Only information on problem drivers and unsafe commercial drivers was centralized and made available to the states through the National Driver Registry and Commercial Drivers License Information System respectively.

The SSA offers two electronic methods for SSN verification, one online and one batch process. In essence, a non–real-time process only verifies that records already contained in a state's information system match SSA records, rather than during the issuance of a driver's license. Of the 25 states using the SSN verification system, 5 used the batch process. The 2003 GAO report disclosed a critical flaw with the batch method: It was unable to match death records against SSNs used in the licensing process. The online system contained this flaw initially, but it was later corrected. Therefore, 30 of the 50 states used a non–real-time system and relied heavily on visual inspection of documents to verify the identity of one seeking a driver's license. Criminals learned of states that were easy to obtain identification from and exploited this weakness.

The 2003 GAO report also identified a high failure rate during the process due to name changes, oftentimes due to marriage or divorce. Failures required manual verification by a state employee. With states experiencing mismatch rates near 30 percent, manual verification was timely and costly. The GAO concluded that "without a means to readily share all driver records, states face a greater risk for identity theft and fraud in the driver licensing process."

In many of the high-profile identity theft arrests detailed in media reports, most perpetrators possessed falsified identification documents of their victims.[26] Most creditors rely on a driver's license as a verification method, but few in the private sector realize the critical weaknesses behind obtaining a driver's license. Because there is no reason for concern, very few creditors take extra steps to verify an applicant's identity.

The federal government also passed legislation designed to force companies to properly dispose of sensitive consumer and business information in electronic and printed form. The Fair and Credit Transaction Act, or FACTA, was passed in 2003.[27] This disposal requirement took effect in 2005, but other provisions, such as increasing the rights of identity theft victims, took effect immediately. FACTA also standardized the concept of a fraud alert. A fraud alert informs creditors using reports from various credit reporting agencies, such as TransUnion, Experian, and Equifax, to use "reasonable" measures to verify the identity of the person applying for credit. FACTA enables individuals whose personal information is compromised or who are already victims of an identity theft to limit the damage before it occurred or before it caused further damages.

Another provision of FACTA limits credit and debit card receipts to display no more than five digits of the individual's card number, thus further limiting the number of documents containing personal information. FACTA also enables consumers to take a more proactive role in fighting identity theft by granting them free annual access to credit reports from all three credit reporting agencies (CRAs). FACTA gives consumers the right to opt out of lists and reports sold by CRAs to creditors, such as preapproved credit applications or home equity lines of credit. The opt-out enables consumers to reduce the amount of personal information shared with and stored by third-party creditors, mail or other printed material containing their personal information, and activity listed on their consumer credit report. Consumers who opt out in theory offer a reduced opportunity for Dumpster divers, mail thieves, and rogue creditors to obtain their personal information.

By the end of 2003, other major media topics still overshadowed the growing identity theft epidemic. However, coverage of identity theft arrests was beginning to increase, and the extent of the epidemic would soon be made public through media coverage of massive data releases. FACTA was intended to limit these data releases, but its scope applied in limited fashion to printed data, not data stored electronically.

On July 15, 2004, the federal government made another major stride in the fight against identity theft: the Identity Theft Penalty Enhancement Act.[28] The act added a mandatory two-year imprisonment to anyone who falsified his or her identity to commit various crimes, such as mail, bank, wire, firearm, or immigration fraud. The Penalty Enhancement Act ended the era of identity thieves receiving probation or concurrent sentences.

The act not only helped prosecutors put identity thieves behind bars, but also helped law enforcement officials investigate and arrest identity thieves. It appropriated $2 million per year to the Department of Justice from 2005 through 2009. With such a significant appropriation devoted to the issue, department agencies, such as the FBI and Secret Service, could devote more resources to combating identity theft.

Despite the appropriations of the 2004 Identity Theft Penalty Enhancement Act and increased media attention of high-profile identity theft arrests, law enforcement officials still do not publish statistics on identity theft arrests. In 2005 the FBI's Uniform Crime Reporting (UCR) system—a system that collects national statistics from participating law enforcement agencies—did not list identity theft as a crime.[29] The current FBI UCR handbook, which was published in 2004 and made available online to law enforcement officials, does not mention identity theft. Instead, a frequently asked questions (FAQ) supplement to the UCR, which dates back to 1992, currently instructs law enforcement officials investigating the various frauds and embezzlements common to an identity theft to file them in the UCR as separate crimes. One FAQ mentions an example of a criminal impersonating another person's identity to commit a fraud, but continues to instruct officials to file the crimes separately as credit card or mail fraud.[30]

Because of the lack of arrest statistics, it is very difficult to objectively assess the progress law enforcement agencies are making in the fight against identity theft. Media reports of arrests are increasing, and arrests made by local, county, and state officials are becoming more common when compared to early arrest examples, which primarily involved federal officials. More involvement by local law enforcement allows for a broadened effect on the fight against identity theft. Generally, federal law enforcement officials tend to pursue larger-profile criminals or those affiliated with organized crime. Increased enforcement by more local officials has generated arrests of smaller criminals. However, the fact that identity theft generally crosses state and national boundary lines usually limits the ability of smaller law enforcement divisions to track identity thieves efficiently.

Consumers and businesses need to understand the schemes identity thieves employ. The FBI and many local law enforcement communities are becoming more involved in educating consumers on how to protect themselves. Understanding our rights and obligation to protect the information that identity thieves seek vastly improves our chances of not becoming a statistic. Knowledge of how to quickly detect and defend against an identity theft also helps limit our losses. An executive order signed by President George W. Bush in 2006 that created a National Identity Theft Task Force shows increased commitment from law enforcement to protect individual consumers and the banking and financial communities, and increases public awareness on deterrence, detection, and defending against identity theft.[31]

However, the FTC reported in the 2005 Identity Theft Clearinghouse that 61 percent of identity theft victims never notified a police department, a statistic that has been consistent since 2003.

PROTECTING PERSONAL INFORMATION

Identity theft is a crime committed using the identifying information of a person, so naturally identity thieves seek your personal information. Additionally, the more criminals find out about the victim, the faster they can commit various crimes. The more identity thieves know about an individual, the more likely they are to use that person's identity to commit crimes compared to a person for whom the perpetrator has no information. A thief interested in stealing a car who finds one unlocked and running is more likely to steal that car than a locked one. Not only is the unlocked car faster to steal, but the element of detection is reduced if the thief does not need to smash a window to gain entry. Using this car theft analogy, it is also important to note that no car, and no person's identity, is completely theft-proof. But reasonable protection methods deter most criminals.

The same attitude found in car thieves can be found in identity thieves, especially in the sale of personal information between criminals. An individual's name, address and Social Security number is valuable, but it is not worth as much as the same information when combined with bank account numbers. The trade of personal information on the Internet is prevalent and continues to rise; consider this following message left on a Web site that enables trading of personal information:

> "Here is what I need. Decent Novs in any state, just decent. Not perfect but OK. eBay or any other auction account that can be sold from, and that has some decent feedback. The more FB the better."[32]

The Internet is becoming a conduit for the illegal trade of personal information, as evident by phishing and spoofing scams. Membership to Web sites that offer tutorials on identity theft as well as collaboration with other criminals can be purchased for less than $10 a month. Valid credit card numbers and Social Security numbers are sold on these Web sites for less than $200, sometimes as low as $50. Regardless of whether your personal information is stolen using online or offline methods, when it becomes available for sale or trade on the Internet, the severity of an identity theft can increase drastically. In this example, the potential criminal seeks a novelty identification card or driver's license, a "nov", and usernames and passwords to access an eBay or other online auction accounts with feedback, "FB". Online auction accounts use feedback, or a rating, from previous transactions to assist other users in determining whether a seller is legitimate, or a possible scam artist. An auction account with few or no feedback may alert other buyers and sellers that the account holder may be new or untrustworthy, and building feedback on an account would require more time and effort than most criminals care to invest into a fraud. This example illustrates how many criminals opt for the easiest route to commit a fraud, and it also demonstrations how criminals often use auction services to sell stolen merchandise or to sell merchandise without any intention to actually ship the goods. A compromised password to an account with high positive feedback rating is essentially an unlocked car for an identity thief. The more your personal information is exposed increases your chances of becoming a victim of identity theft and the likelihood that you will experience higher losses as your information may be used by multiple perpetrators.

What information do they seek? Again, the more criminals know, the more empowered they are. Identity thieves seek personal information such as:

- Name
- Address
- Social Security number
- Date of birth
- Phone
- ATM, debit, and credit card numbers
- Credit card security codes and personal identification numbers (PINs) for bank and credit accounts
- Bank account numbers and balances
- Income and credit history
- Driver's license number
- Passwords
- E-mail address
- Other personal information, such as maiden names, retirement accounts, citizenship and family/kin history

The more pieces of personal information criminals have, the more information they can extract. Criminals who already know a person's name, date of birth, and financial institution may be able to extract account balances and numbers if they call the bank and provide the information they know. Many banks use name, account number, and date of birth as an identifier during a phone call.

In most instances a credit card number alone is not enough to perform any transaction. But if the identity thief obtains a change of address on the account and then tricks the bank to issue a new card claiming that the card was either lost or stolen may allow the criminal to intercept the new card in the mail. At this point, the criminal will then have a valid card, account number, and card security code, located on the back of the credit card.

Another use of personal information by a thief concerns a personal check. Checks contain the account number, routing number (bank identifier), and the check number. Checks also print certain pieces of personal information that the consumer can control, such as name, address, phone, and sometimes a driver's license or Social Security number. When merchants accept checks, often the store clerk asks for personal identification. Additionally, employees may record the date of birth, telephone, or driver's license on the check. After such a transaction, your check contains nearly all the information necessary for a potential criminal to begin an identity theft. Despite methods to secure your check after it leaves your hands, the check processes a startling number of individuals which places you at considerable risk.

One common check scam is to steal the routing number and account number from a legitimate check and use those numbers on blank check stock, which is available at any office supply store, to falsify checks. Criminals use the provided software to quickly enter the same routing number, account number, and personal information found on the legitimate check and create multiples of new checks, all of which are ready to clear the banking system. In the age of automated check clearing systems, banks rarely verify the signature contained on checks. Instead, they rely on pattern recognition and consumer monitoring to protect against this type of check fraud.

Handing a credit card to a restaurant server or store clerk immediately reveals the name, account number, and card security code present on the card. When the credit card leaves sight of the rightful owner, an unethical employee may write down the personal information or run the card through a skimming device that can read and store information stored on the magnetic strip. Skimming devices can easily fit in the server's hand, on an employee's belt, or be fitted directly over the register. Skimming devices and fake ATMs can be found at unscrupulous businesses such as gas stations or party stores, or may be placed on top of existing ATMs found in common areas. Skimming devices may be used in conjunction with surveillance video cameras pointed at the ATM's keypad to capture PINs. In essence, everyday transactions, such as paying bills with check or credit card, reveal bits of personal information.

None of us can completely restrict exposure of our personal information, but we can limit, monitor and defend using these basic tips, some of which are compiled from the Department of Justice.

- *Share only pertinent information with necessary parties.* Never share information unless you initiate calls and can verify the identity of the person you are sharing information with, including door-to-door salespeople and those conducting surveys or petitions.
- *Beware of "shoulder surfers"*—people who observe you entering PIN or debit card numbers while at ATMs or store check-outs.
- *Avoid carrying unnecessary information in wallets or purses.* Passports, Social Security card, and health insurance cards are items that should be left at home. Most major medical providers do not need insurance to treat you, and most people hardly use Social Security cards and passports on a daily basis. Old IDs and old credit cards should be destroyed by shredder.
- *Make attempts to secure the mailbox at home and the office.* Avoid leaving mail unattended in your home mailbox for an extended period of time, especially a vacation. The post office can hold your mail while you are gone if you do not want your neighbors collecting your mail for you. Furthermore, try to limit mailing bills from your home, and if you must, do not put the red flag up. Doing so only alerts potential criminals that there may be a check or other important document in the mailbox. Corporate mailrooms and mailboxes are not as secure as the post office, and that should be taken accordingly when mailing sensitive documents from the office.
- *Secure information stored electronically.* Do not keep passwords or other highly sensitive information, such as Social Security and driver's license numbers, stored on the computer unless it is encrypted. Furthermore, limit access to your computer both physically and electronically. Care should be given to laptops and other storage devices. Refrain from leaving laptops or hard drives in your car, even when locked in the driveway of your own home or office. In addition, many PC makers are using chip-level security and fingerprint readers to further secure the information stored on a computer.
- *Set a password for all user accounts, including ones you do not use* (e.g., active accounts for children, spouse, or guest). If you are the only one using the computer, remove or disable any other accounts such as the guest account. Considering disabling remote access if you do not use it.

(Note: If your company issues you a computer, it is always prudent to discuss any change to hardware or software with management or the IT department to verify that the changes do not violate company policies and procedures.)

- *Use firewalls and protect home and corporate network equipment, servers, and computers with up-to-date antivirus/spy/crime software.* Intrusion detection systems may also detect attacks, both internally and from the Internet, that attempt to gain access to your personal information.
- *Limit e-mailing sensitive information.* Most e-mail systems are not encrypted and thus are not secure. Furthermore, most e-mails are stored on the server or in a mail file on a laptop or desktop computer, which an intruder may try to access.
- *Make copies of all information, identification, and credit cards carried in your wallet or purse, and note the toll-free numbers to call in case they are lost or stolen.* Store this copy in a safe location, such as a locked safe. Also store other personal identification documents not used everyday, such as birth certificates, Social Security cards and passports, in the safe.
- *Shred all personal documents, especially mail.* No matter how insignificant a credit card application or other financial document may be to you, it may be a huge key for a criminal interested in stealing your identity.
- *Opt out under your rights established by FACTA.* An opt-out will limit how much of your personal information gets sold and handled by others. To opt out from national credit reporting agencies, call 1-888-5-OPTOUT (1-888-567-8688).
- *Do not sign up for unnecessary credit accounts.* Saving 10 percent off a one-time purchase by establishing a store credit card may be a very short-lived benefit when you consider that store becomes another institution that stores your personal information. Furthermore, that becomes another account that you will need to monitor for unauthorized activity.
- *Review statements regularly for any unauthorized transactions or activity.* Usually banks and other credit providers must assume liability for any charges if the customer notifies them within 30 days. In an event of an identity theft, provisions of FACTA and the Fair Credit Reporting Act (FCRA) may supersede provisions such as these, but they require a police report or affidavit demonstrating the identity theft. However, reviewing statements regularly will help spot an identity theft faster, or before the criminal can fully exploit the benefits of assuming your identity.
- *Request copies of your credit report from all three credit reporting agencies on an annual basis.* Creditors report to different CRAs, and it may take a while for one agency to share data with another CRA. One FBI official suggested running a report from a different CRA every four months for continual coverage. For example, request a report from TransUnion in January, Experian in June, and Equifax in October.
- *Limit the use of checks to help reduce the amount of personal information.* Especially limit the information printed on a check. Financial institutions only require the amount, signature, account number, routing number, and check number to be printed. Printing a driver's license or SSN on a check is generally unnecessary and risky.
- *Practice safe computing.* Limiting the disclosure of your e-mail address can help reduce the number of spam, virus, and phishing e-mails that you receive. Read the privacy policy carefully when you sign up to receive e-newsletters, online services, or downloads. Avoid unsafe attachments, even from trusted sources. Some of these include file extensions such

as .exe, .vbs, .pf, .pif, .bat, .scr and many more. Many viruses and Trojans are guised as jokes, screensavers, and games, and viruses can be propagated unintentionally from friends and contacts. Other malicious computer viruses can be embedded in office documents or in compressed files (i.e. .zip and .rar files).

Stay up-to-date with operating system and other security updates for hardware and software. Specifically, make a point to use antivirus/spy/crime software that can detect viruses, Trojans, worms, and key-logging software. Key-logging software records anything that you type, such as passwords, account numbers and login details, as well as the online addresses to those accounts.

The overall concept of these general recommendations is to limit the exposure of personal information to unauthorized individuals. If you follow these recommendations, you make it considerably more difficult for a criminal to obtain the personal information commonly used to commit an identity crime.

DETECT UNAUTHORIZED USE

Detection of an identity theft relies on many of the proactive actions just illustrated. As stated earlier, the external use of personal information through checks, credits cards, wage and tax statements, and financial statements means complete deterrence of an identity theft is unlikely, no matter how vigilant you are. Therefore, emphasis on detection is equally important, including the ability to quickly identify a fraud and consequently limit further losses. Early detection can also be a deterrence method if identity thieves know that their gains will be limited when the affected individual takes measures such as fraud alerts or credit freezes.

Recently banks and other creditors, including credit card companies, have begun implementing substantial proactive measures to quickly deter identity theft–related frauds. But the scope of their detection efforts concerns only accounts and credit that they issue, in essence, to reduce their own losses. Banks issuing credit cards now call the account holder or temporarily disable the card from making additional transactions whenever unusual activity occurs on the account. Loss prevention strategies by the banks have had a major impact on the fight against identity theft related to credit transactions. The FTC reports in the 2005 Identity Theft Clearinghouse that victims that experienced a credit card fraud have decreased from 41 percent in 2002 to 26 percent in 2005. The FTC also reported a 1 percent decrease in loan fraud and a 1 percent increase in bank fraud from 2002 to 2005 despite nearly 90,000 additional identity theft complaints.

However, consumers should not rely solely on bank and credit detection systems for alerts of fraudulent account activity. Consumers also must become more aware of detection strategies, such as:

- *Review bank and credit card statements weekly.* Review all bills before paying them, and investigate the account detail if accounts with relatively similar monthly charges suddenly increase or decrease.
- *Evaluate whether it is most secure to receive statements from banks, financial or other providers in printed (mail) format or electronic (e-mail or secure Web site) format.*
- *Consider the use of a credit monitoring service.* The service will notify you by your choice of e-mail, cell phone or even text message to provide real-time updates should anyone run

your credit report. The notification also contains the name and phone number of the business that ran your credit so that you can contact it if you did not authorize the activity.

- *Review credit reports on an annual basis and from all three CRAs.* Look for any unauthorized accounts.

If you notice an unusual activity on your accounts, it might be wise to file a fraud alert by contacting each CRA. A fraud alert lasts for 90 days, and can be extended for seven years with a police report or affidavit of an identity theft submitted to a CRA in writing. When placing a fraud alert on your credit report, it may be wise to communicate the fraud alert to existing creditors with whom you have accounts since they may not query your credit report on a regular basis.

DEFEND AND REGAIN YOUR IDENTITY

Many victims of an identity theft did not know whom to contact or what to do when they first discovered that they were a victim. Some victims of identity theft described their reaction as fear similar to a burglary, assault, or rape, even though identity theft is a nonviolent crime. Numerous books and resources complete with remediation letters are available to a consumer. Here are some common remediation steps:

- *Report the incident to the police immediately, especially if it involved stolen identification.* File a report in each city where the fraud occurred. Also contact federal authorities, such as the FBI, Secret Service, or Postal Inspection Service. Obtain a copy of each incident report, as it may be necessary to show creditors of the identity theft. Also contact the FTC, and file a complaint through the Consumer Sentinel.
- *File an affidavit of forgery to establish your innocence to banks and creditors as well as recipients of fraudulent checks issued under your name.*
- *Contact all three credit reporting agencies in writing.* You may be asked to provide police reports and give additional affidavits. Monitor credit reports monthly for at least a year after the most recent occurrence of fraud, and consider whether a seven-year fraud alert or a credit freeze is best for you.
- *Report all stolen cards and identification documents to the issuers immediately.* Follow up each with a written notification.
- *Change all online account passwords over the telephone, or visit the branch in person.* Never use an old password as this may be among the information compromised.
- *Notify your bank if your checks were stolen.* Consider whether it is best to close your account at that bank completely or just change your account number. In the most severe cases, some experts recommend closing accounts, but your situation may cause you to have difficulty opening an account at a new bank.
- *Contact the Social Security Administration if you suspect someone may be using your SSN for employment purposes.* Social Security may issue you a new SSN, which may make it more difficult to obtain credit in the future. Also notify the Internal Revenue Service if you suspect employment fraud.
- *Save all records pertaining to an identity theft.* Save copies of all police reports, affidavits, and all written correspondence. Take notes of phone calls you make, including the name

of the person you talked to. Additionally, use certified mail for all mailed correspondence to CRAs, creditors, and law enforcement agencies involved in your identity theft case.

BULK DATA BREACHES

An individual can be as vigilant as possible in guarding personal information, follow all the recommendations, understand and know how to spot many of the schemes used to extract personal information, and yet still be at risk of becoming an identity theft victim through bulk data breaches or releases or thefts of personal information from commercial databases. Companies store a plethora of information on their customers and potential clients; no legislation exists governing an entity's ability to gather and store personal information. No set of information technology standards defines and enforces procedures designed to guard that personal information. Privacy groups have lobbied Congress regarding this issue, but as exemplified in testimony on identity theft to the 2000 Committee on Banking and Financial Services, numerous professional organizations insist that they need to store and access great volumes of personal information.

This section examines some of the recent major data thefts and releases and the consumer's right to be notified in the event of a data breach. These releases, which occur through no action or fault of the individual, highlight why constant vigilance and monitoring of credit records is essential. The previous tips designed to detect and defend against identity theft can help reduce the risk of loss following the release of personal information through a data breach. This section also describes for business owners the common procedures for the proper collection, storage, and disposal of personal information, their responsibility to notify the affected individuals, and ways to limit a data breach by an employee.

Imagine this public relations and ethics disaster: An employee of an organization loses a laptop containing the organization's customer database complete with personal information such as names, addresses, Social Security numbers, and purchasing history. This is the dilemma most businesses face in the event of a data release. Concerns over such an event frequently include:

- Should the organization notify those affected?
- Are we legally required to notify those affected?
- Are we willing to "roll the dice" and not notify the clients?
- If we choose not to disclose the breach, and a common thread of identity theft is found, are we willing to face civil penalties or lawsuits?
- What is the impact on the relationship with customers, as well as the negative press the business will receive if we notify those affected?
- Will we lose our clients?

If you are an individual affected by a bulk data release, of course you would want to know exactly what information was released. Some companies may choose not to inform those affected because fear of the impact on the business-client relationship or simply because laws in their state do not yet force them to do so. Because of this, there may be many instances of bulk data releases that the public may never hear about. Companies are also not required to disclose any data release that occurred prior to laws forcing companies to notify those affected. Here are some of the most egregious data releases reported, and how the breach occurred.

One of the most critical data releases occurred in 2000, and sparked not only a major change in how many companies handled data releases, but also led to a California law that helped bring massive media attention to the identity theft issue. In this release 265,000 California State employees had personal information exposed when a hacker exploited a payroll database. An investigation revealed high-level employees had personal information exposed. The hacker also employed a utility to automatically scan the computer for exploits, and the program e-mailed the hacker whenever it found a security exploit. The investigation revealed the hacker received 2,569 e-mails informing him of exploits. Many technology experts who followed the case felt that had the system administrators applied security updates regularly, many of the exploits would have been secured prior to the loss.[33]

This breach was a major contributing factor to the passage of California Senate Bill 1386 (SB1386), which mandated that all institutions that collect personal information must protect it against identity theft. If an incident occurs involving a compromise of that personal information, the institution must notify the affected individuals. This bill applied to any California government or educational institution as well as any business operating in the state.[34]

A second major data loss affected a California Health and Human Services Department database that contained names, addresses, and Social Security numbers of in-home healthcare recipients and their providers. Many of the 1.4 million affected were low-income elderly, blind, or disabled people. The database was improperly stored by a University of California–Berkley employee who failed to follow a policy requiring the removal of SSNs from database records.[35]

In 2005, many major data releases and thefts occurred and were subsequently reported to affected individuals as well as the national media. This was due largely to SB1386 and data breach notification laws that were being developed in other states.

In February 2005, ChoicePoint, Inc., a verification research database provider, exposed the personal information of 145,000 individuals.[36] A ring of identity thieves posing as small business owners deceived ChoicePoint into selling them information, which was in violation of the GLB Act. The FTC levied $15 million in fines against ChoicePoint in January 2006. Of the fine, $10 million was for punitive damages; $5 million was earmarked to assist those affected to monitor against identity theft. Class-action suits have also been filed against ChoicePoint. Originally ChoicePoint disclosed that only 32,000 individuals were affected.[37] This is a common thread in many data breaches: Time will reveal the number of actual individuals affected to be greater than originally reported.

Another data broker—LexisNexis, a division of Reed Elsevier Group PLC—disclosed a data breach affecting close to 310,000 people. Originally the company reported that 32,000 people had personal information such as names, addresses, SSNs, and driver's license number compromised by criminals who used methods similar to the ChoicePoint data breach to deceive LexisNexis into releasing the information.[38]

Another massive data breach affected Citigroup, Inc. in June 2005. According to media and company reports, Citigroup was transporting unencrypted computer backup tapes containing personal information and details on 3.9 million customers' loans. The backup tapes were lost during shipment and have not yet been recovered.[39]

DSW, Inc., a national footwear retailer, experienced a data breach when a hacker compromised the personal information and purchase preferences of 1.4 million customers. Names and credit card numbers were among the information stolen by criminals. DSW originally reported 100,000 individuals were affected.[40]

One of the largest data breaches ever reported occurred when nearly 22 million Visa and 14 million MasterCard account numbers were stolen from CardSystems, Inc., a credit card processor. The problem was revealed when investigators traced numerous fraudulent transactions back to credit cards processed by CardSystems, which allegedly violated Visa and MasterCard policies by storing the card numbers and card security codes.[41]

Businesses also must be aware of the rising trend of data theft by their employees. Employees often have considerable access to personal information and confidential company data. The sale of stolen data by an employee can be as lucrative as stealing physical company assets. Michigan State University professor Judith Collins, who conducted an investigative survey on 1,000 identity theft victims, estimates that approximately 70 percent of identity thefts start with the theft of data from an employer.[42] One former AOL employee pled guilty in July 2005 to the information theft of 92 million AOL customers. The perpetrator sold the data on at least two occasions for $52,000 and $32,500.[43] Another example of data theft by an employee occurred when a New Jersey cybercrime ring infiltrated at least four New Jersey banks, stealing information on over 676,000 consumer accounts. Nine people were charged in connection with the data theft, which included seven former bank employees. None of the people charged worked in the IT department; and they assembled stolen information in a database using information obtained while working as tellers or branch managers. The customer data was extracted using low-level methods, such as screen shots or printouts of customer databases, and data were later sold to more than 40 collection agencies and law firms.[44]

As of June 2006, 26 states have laws regulating data breaches, and federal laws are pending as well.[45] If your company does business or has customers located in one of the states that contain data breach laws, an organization may:

- Need to notify affected customers and businesses
- Be forced to inform credit reporting agencies of the data breach and the extent of the information compromised
- Be liable for credit-monitoring services, or the costs of other identity theft prevention services for those affected
- Be subject to fines levied by state and federal authorities as well as civil action

Protecting customer data is both a legal and customer relationship issue. With federal laws such as the Health Insurance Portability and Accountability Act (HIPPA), GLB, FACTA and FCRA, and the numerous state laws surrounding data breaches, each organization needs to assess how it collects, stores, and disposes of printed and electronic data. Note that electronic data breaches pose a more serious threat since 40 million electronic records can be stolen much easier by a computer CD, hard drive, or removable storage media than in hard-copy format.

Organizations can avoid the embarrassment and potential liability of experiencing a data breach in a number of ways.

Data Collection

- Only collect essential data.
- Obtain consent when data are collected.
- Understand all compliance issues and sensitivity to customers when providing data to third parties.

Data Security and Storage

- Do not store unnecessary data.
- Encrypt data on networks, laptops, and remote access devices.
- Update security software frequently.
- Save to networks, not hard drives.
- Beware of portable storage devices (MP3 players, USB key drives, external CD/DVD drives).
- Use locks, alarms, and video cameras to restrict and monitor physical access.
- Conduct employee background checks.
- Understand outsource relationships.
- Terminate network access when employees leave the organization.
- Limit access to sensitive data.

Data Disposal

- Use scrubbing software or physically destroy devices that store information: hard drives, CDs, or USB key hard drives. Current Department of Defense standards recommend that data is overwritten three times using a zero, one, and random character pass.
- Shred all sensitive documents,
- Maintain record retention and destruction policies.

THE ONLINE FRONTIER OF PHISHING AND SPOOFING

Phishing and spoofing are two ways identity thieves look to steal personal information "online." Phishing is the act of sending an e-mail claiming to be a legitimate enterprise with the intent to trick a user into revealing private information.[46] Phishers—or people who conduct phishing activities—may use the information for identity theft, but they also are heavily involved in the electronic trade of personal information to other phishers or identity thieves.

Phishing is not a new technique. The term extends back to the origins of the Internet, when hackers looked to steal usernames and passwords to dial-up Internet accounts, which allowed them to spend more time on the internet and under someone else's name. Phishing is also very similar to phreaking, an activity designed to steal local and long distance access that is often used for hacking. Hackers personalized the terms by removing the "f" from "fishing" and "freaking" and replacing it with "ph."

Phishing in its current form relies heavily on social engineering to scare the users into believing something bad will happen if they do not provide the information the e-mail seeks. Some of these social engineering tactics include deceiving users to believe that their account information has been compromised or that their access will be revoked. Victims of phishing attacks often follow the instructions because they do not want the bad event to happen.

The power of the Internet allows phishers to transmit an unlimited number of electronic messages and often remain anonymous during the process. Phishers are often well connected with illegal spam and e-mail address harvesting operations. Many of these phishers and spammers are experienced in using computers and networks that belong to others to conduct their fraudulent activities. Using the electronic resources of others allows criminals to remain anonymous and escape detection. These criminals can easily spoof the sender's field to deceive the user as to the identity of the sender.

The actual relationship between a user and the financial institution does not need to be known. In early phishing attempts, mass e-mails were sent to a large population of e-mail addresses, and criminals relied on blind luck that a user had an account at the institution described in the e-mail. This meant phishers can increase their chances of finding a victim by increasing the number of potential target e-mail accounts. Currently, even accounts at small community banks are being phished.

The phishing problem is a very fluid one. Recently an organization that tracks phishing—the Anti-Phishing Working Group (APWG)— has seen random trends both increasing and decreasing significantly. In March 2006, the APWG observed nearly 10,000 unique phishing Web sites in existence. The APWG also reported that March 2006 set a record in phishing complaints received. It was also the second highest month in the past year for the creation of phishing sites. The APWG reported that most scams were relatively low in complexity, but that trends of more complex attacks were rising. The financial services industry comprised 90 percent of phishing attacks detailed by the APWG in March 2006.[47]

A phishing e-mail looks to capture the following information:

- Name
- Credit card and account number, and card security code
- SSN
- Address
- Date of birth
- Passwords
- Other information such as mother's maiden name, and usernames and passwords for online auction accounts

The anonymity of the Internet and the difficulty in verifying the sending e-mail address is quite deceiving to most users. Therefore it is important to illustrate a few tips to help spot a phishing e-mail.

- E-mails from institutions where an individual does not have an account are generally phishing attempts.
- Account providers will never ask for information that they already or should know. E-mails asking for an update to personal information should be disregarded.
- Most phishing e-mails contain impersonal greetings, such as "Dear Account Holder." Many financial and other account providers provide a customer's name or another unique identifier in each e-mail.
- Phishing e-mails often contain spelling or grammatical errors.
- Threatening language is common in phishing e-mails to compel a person into releasing personal information. Phishing e-mails warn of fraudulent adverse action that may happen if the recipient does not follow the instructions contained in the e-mail.
- Phishing e-mails contain Web links (hyperlinks) containing IP addresses or incorrect domain names. Many times this Web link is falsified or displayed as an IP address. When users click on the link, they are directed to a fraudulent Web site.

As users are becoming more adept in spotting phishing e-mails, phishers and other cybercriminals are resorting to complex attacks, such as spoofing or DNS poisoning. The APWG detailed a financial institution Trojan attack that targeted over 100 financial institutions in Europe. A Trojan horse virus was installed on victims' computers that surreptitiously monitored the user's legitimate Internet activity. When users typed in the legitimate Web site address of one of the targeted financial institutions, the virus contacted a DNS computer located in Russia, which directed the users to an illegitimate Web site that simulated the legitimate Web site. The users did not receive any notification that they had been directed to the fraudulent Web site instead of the actual Web site. The only ways users would have observed the switch is if they had been accustomed to checking the security certificates and noticed the absence of one on the fraudulent Web site, or observed technical problems with the fraudulent site. However, most users would not notice these red flags until after they logged in, which meant that the attackers had the name of the financial institution as well as the username and password. The DNS server in Russia also allowed the scheme to continue if one site was taken offline.

Security software that includes antispam software can help bridge the technical gap between individuals and the cybercriminals. Most antispam software can filter for malicious code or attachments, verify the identity of the sender, and check for links to Web sites known to host phishing or spoofing sites. A proactive monitoring plan that continues to educate individuals while combining technology will help abate most online identity theft attacks.

IMPACT ON FRAUD DETERRENCE

Fighting identity theft requires constant monitoring by all individuals and businesses. Many lessons learned in the identity theft example can apply to other frauds that affect personal and business situations. Solving the identity theft problem, similar to other frauds, requires synergy by those affected by the issue to constantly assess the common schemes criminals employ and develop methods to reasonably deter those actions.

NOTES

1. Federal Trade Commission, "Identity Theft Victim Complaint Data, Figures and Trends: January 1–December 31, 2005."
2. Comptroller of the Currency, Administrator of National Banks, "Check Fraud: A Guide to Avoiding Losses," February 1999.
3. Abagnale & Associates, "About Frank Abagnale." Available at: www.abagnale.com/aboutfrank.htm.
4. "2005 Identity Fraud Survey Report." Javelin Strategy & Research and Better Business Bureau. Available at: www.javelinstrategy.com/reports/2005IdentityFraudSurveyReport.html.
5. Amanda J. Crawford, "2 Just Tip of Identity Theft Iceberg," *Arizona Republic*, February 6, 2005.
6. Byron Achohido and Jon Swartz, "Meth Addicts' Other Habit: Online Theft," *USA Today,* December 15, 2005.
7. "2005 Identity Fraud Survey Report."
8. FrankWitsil, "Ex-Senator Stole Son's ID, Cops Say," *Detroit Free Press,* May 17, 2006.
9. Steven C. LaTourette, Testimony at Committee on Banking and Financial Services, United States House of Representatives, Washington, DC, September 13, 2000.
10. § 602.q.3 Fair Credit Reporting Act of 2003. 15 U.S.C. § 1681, December 4, 2003.
11. United States General Accounting Office, "Identity Fraud: Information on Prevalence, Cost and Internet Impact Is Limited," May 1998. Available at: www.gao.gov/archive/1998/gg98100b.pdf.

12. Robert Douglas, Testimony at Committee on Banking and Financial Services, United States House of Representatives, Washington, DC,. September 13, 2000.
13. 18 U.S.C. 1028 (a)(7), Public Law 105-318.
14. 18 U.S.C. 1028 § (5)(a)(3)(b).
15. Federal Trade Commission, "Identity Theft Complaint Data: Figures and Trends on Identity Theft; January 2000 through December 2000."
16. H.R. 4311. 106th Congress, 2nd Session.
17. Testimony at Committee on Banking and Financial Services, United States House of Representatives, Washington, DC, September 13, 2000.
18. United States General Accounting Office, "Identity Fraud: Prevalence and Cost Appear to Be Growing," March 2002. Available at: www.gao.gov/new.items/d02363.pdf.
19. United States General Accounting Office, "Identity Fraud: Prevalence and Links to Alien Illegal Activities," June 2002. Available at: www.gao.gov/new.items/d02830t.pdf.
20. United States General Accounting Office, "Identity Fraud: Greater Awareness and Use of Existing Data Are Needed," June 2002. Available at: www.gao.gov/new.items/d02766.pdf.
21. Federal Trade Commission, "National and State Trends in Fraud & Identity Theft: January–December 2003."
22. Nadia Kounang, "Hunting Identity Thieves—Alone, One at a Time," CNN.com. May 21, 2006. Available at: www.cnn.com/2006/US/05/19/fraud.hunter/index.html.
23. United States Department of Justice, United States Attorney, Western District of Tennessee, "Identity Theft Arrests," Press Release, May2, 2002. Available at: www.usdoj.gov/usao/tnw/pressreleases/2002/2002MAY02_wisePRS.pdf.
24. New York Department of Law, Office of New York State Attorney General Eliot Spitzer. "'Buffalo Spammer' Arraigned on Identity Theft and Forgery Charges," Press Release, May14, 2003. Todd Weiss, "Fake PayPal, AOL Spam Operations Stopped by FTC, DOJ," ComputerWorld.com, March 24, 2004. Available at: www.computerworld.com/securitytopics/security/cybercrime/story/0,10801,91562,00.html.
25. United States General Accounting Office, "Social Security Numbers: Improved SSN Verification and Exchange of States' Driver Records Would Enhance Identity Verification," September 2003. Available at: www.gao.gov/new.items/d02766.pdf.
26. United States Department of Homeland Security, United States Secret Service, "U.S. Secret Service's Operation Firewall Nets 28 Arrests," Press Release, October 28, 2004. Available at: www-.secretservice.gov/press/pub2304.pdf. United States Department of Justice, "Houston Man Pleads Guilty to Federal Identity Theft Charges, Says Justice Department," Press Release, November 1, 2005. Lindsay Moyer, "A Picture Is Worth a Thousand Words, at Least to the Pottstown Police," *Pottstown Mercury*, May 19, 2006. Available at: www.pottstownmercury.com/site/news.cfm?newsid=166619-80&BRD=1674&PAG=461&dept_id=18041&rfi=6.
27. 15 U.S.C. 1681 (§§ 601–625), January 7, 2003.
28. 18 U.S.C. 47 § 1028, July 15, 2004.
29. Department of Justice, Federal Bureau of Investigation, *Uniform Crime Reports Online Database*. Available at: www.fbi.gov/ucr/ucr.htm.
30. Department of Justice, Federal Bureau of Investigation, *Uniform Crime Reports Summary Reporting: Frequently Asked Questions*. Available at: www.fbi.gov/ucr/ucrquest.htm.
31. Federal Trade Commission, "Deter-Detect-Defend: AvoID Theft." Available at: www.ftc.gov/bcp/edu/pubs/consumer/idtheft/idt01.pdf.
32. Beth Cox, "The Great Credit Card Bazaar," InternetNews.com, September 20, 2002. Available at: www.internetnews.com/ec-news/article.php/1467331.
33. Frank Hayes, "California Steamin'," ComputerWorld.com, June 3, 2002. Available at: www.computerworld.com/securitytopics/security/story/0,10801,71657,00.html.
34. California Civil Code 19 §1798.82, §1798.29, February 12, 2002.

35. Todd Weiss, "Update: California Lawmakers Rip Handling of Data Theft at University,"Computer-World.com, October 29, 2004. Available at: www.computerworld.com/securitytopics/security/privacy/story/0,10801,97042,00.html.

36. Bob Sullivan, "Data Theft Affects 145,000," MSNBC.com, February 18, 2005. Available at: www-.msnbc.msn.com/id/6979897/.

37. Bob Sullivan, "Database Giant Gives Access to Fake Firms," MSNBC.com February 14, 2005. Available at: www.msnbc.msn.com/id/6969799/.

38. "LexisNexis Theft Much Worse than Thought," MSNBC.com, April 12, 2005. Available at: www-.msnbc.msn.com/id/7475594/.

39. "Info on 3.9M Citigroup Customers Lost," CNN.com, June 6, 2005. Available at: http://money-.cnn.com/2005/06/06/news/fortune500/security_citigroup/.

40. "DSW Data Theft Much Worse than Predicted," USAToday.com, April 19, 2005. Available at: www.usatoday.com/tech/news/computersecurity/infotheft/2005-04-19-credit-card-dsw_x.htm.

41. Susanna Schrobsdorff, "Cyber-Insecurity," *Newsweek* and MSNBC.com, June 21, 2005. Available at: www.msnbc.msn.com/id/8306655/site/newsweek/.

42. Bob Sullivan, "Study: ID Theft Usually an Inside Job," MSNBC.com, May 21, 2004. Available at: http://msnbc.msn.com/id/5015565.

43. Bob Sullivan, "AOL Customer List Stolen, Sold to Spammer," MSNBC.com, June 24, 2004. Available at: www.msnbc.msn.com/id/5279826/.

44. Todd Weiss, "Scope of Bank Data Theft Grows to 676,000 Customers," ComputerWorld.com, May 20, 2005.Available at: www.computerworld.com/securitytopics/security/cybercrime/story/0,10801,101903,00.html.

45. Public Interest Research Group, Consumer Protection, "State Breach and Freeze Laws." Available at: www.pirg.org/consumer/credit/statelaws.htm.

46. Anti-Phishing Working Group, "Origins of the Word 'Phishing.'" Available at: www.antiphishing-.org/word_phish.htm.

47. Anti-Phishing Working Group, "Phishing Activity Trends Report." Available at: www.apwg.com/reports/apwg_report_mar_06.pdf.

Chapter 20

Intellectual Property

E. Leonard Rubin

INTRODUCTION

Many businesses have little or no idea of the intangible and sometimes unrecognizable intellectual property they have. While that property is identifiable most of the time if the trouble is taken to look for it, there is often an attitude that it is too insignificant, or too general, to warrant the attention that may be necessary to determine how, or even whether, to protect it from fraudulent use or theft by others. And where intellectual property is being used under a license agreement with another company, there is sometimes a laissez-faire attitude that, having taken a license for its use, no further thought should be given to whether there are implicit as well as explicit restrictions on that use. This chapter not only seeks to help in the identification of a company's intellectual property, but also offers ways that it may be protected, identifies methods used by those seeking to fraudulently steal or copy it, and the types of recourse that are available to those intellectual property owners that have taken steps to ensure that recourse is available. In this chapter, the terms "fraudulent use" and "theft" are almost synonymous, since the dangers and protections described here should operate easily for both transgressions.

What is intellectual property? The term "property" normally connotes something tangible, able to be felt, held, or observable as far as its size and shape are concerned. When the words "real property" are used, they are usually referring to land and improvements that have been made on it, such as houses, other buildings, fences, and structures and permanent improvements in the sense that they are not easily portable. Farms are real property; apartment buildings as well as the land on which they sit are real property; sheds, fences, roads, gardens are real property.

When the words "personal property" are used, they are usually referring to movable objects, also real and touchable, but portable and not anchored to the land. Automobiles are personal property; appliances are personal property; things that can be carried, moved, used with a person's hands are personal property.

What, then, is "intellectual property"? Actually, it is a term invented by the legal profession to mean property that may not necessarily be touched, felt, have specific dimensions or be transportable, although all of these descriptions are possible. It refers to products of the mind, and in the legal profession, those products, if they are to have any value, must have definitions and descriptions. They may be protectable by certain laws or customs, provided that some basic formalities are observed.

Intellectual property as it is thought of by lawyers consists of only a few categories of items. They are:

- Patents
- Trademarks
- Copyrights
- Trade secrets

These categories really reflect independent thought and the creation and implementation of ideas rather than simple descriptions of land or physical objects. The founders of this country, attempting to encourage creative thought and improvements in the quality of life, built into the U.S. Constitution incentives for this type of creation. Article I, Section 8, Clause 8 of the Constitution provides for the U.S. Congress:

> To promote the progress of science and useful arts, by securing for limited times to authors and inventors the exclusive rights to their inventions and writings.

This government granted monopoly is the basis for U.S. patent law (for inventors) and copyright law (for writers). It is intended to provide the possibility of monetary reward for the originator of the creative work by allowing recourse against those who only copy and do not originate.

Ideas themselves are not protectable; they must be reduced to some tangible expression, and even then, there must be some originality in them. When considering what constitutes fraudulent use of intellectual property, what must be taken into consideration is theft of that tangible expression, or unlicensed copying, or creation of a variation that is too close to the original, or attempts to assert unfounded claims of ownership. In each of these instances, the law provides some measure of protection or relief, although there will always be situations where the relief available cannot possibly compensate for what was really lost.

Patents

Of course, to prevent abuse of this monopoly power, the laws contain certain requirements before the protection is available. If the purpose of this incentive is to eventually enrich the public domain (which it is), these requirements should not be so loose that old inventions, or obvious writings, can continue to hide under a monopoly umbrella and thus be forever unavailable for the public to use. Therefore, not all inventions, and not all writings, may qualify for monopoly protection. It is important to note that where a patent is concerned, it is not necessarily the object in which the patent is embodied that is protectable, but rather the process by which the object is created. Protecting that process results in protection for the physical objects that may be manufactured using it.

For example, while a patent such as the process for developing film inside a camera immediately after a picture is taken may be embodied in a particular physical object or formula such as the camera, it is not the object itself, the actual camera, that is the patent; rather, the patent is the particular series of descriptions that allows a manufacturer to make the object. It is the process of manufacture that the patent protects. Consequently, the patent holder has a monopoly, and no one else may use the process to manufacture a camera that performs the same process. (This concept is not to be confused with rights to use or resell the physical object, such as legitimately purchasing it and then reselling it to another person.)

A patent, then, may be thought of simplistically as an invention that contains enough novelty, enough of an improvement over prior knowledge relating to the particular device, to warrant having the government grant a monopoly to the inventor for a period of years. In order for a patent to be protectable under U.S patent laws, an invention or a biological formula must be useful. This is different from rules relating to copyrights, as will be seen.

Inventing a new and useful device or formula does not automatically, without further action, confer upon the inventor a monopoly that allows the inventor to keep others from copying or otherwise taking the invention. The patent laws of the United States, as is true in most countries, contain requirements for eligibility that attempt to make certain that the public is not deprived of inventions that are not really novel, but merely obvious improvements of existing devices. A patent is granted by the U.S. government for only a "limited time"; in the case of a patent, it is for 20 years, after which the process falls into the public domain and may be freely copied by anyone. Until that time, however, the inventor or his or her assignee may control the exploitation of the patent and reap the rewards, if the invention fills a public need.

Trademarks

What is a trademark? A simplistic definition of a trademark is a name or symbol that identifies the source of goods or services. It is a brand or symbol that tells the public "This product or service is being offered by one source, and no one else may indicate that this product comes from the same source." Trademarks do not fall within the constitutional direction to Congress, but they are sufficiently important to the concept of interstate commerce that there is a federal law spelling out the requirements that must be followed before a trademark may be protected under that law.

A trademark is normally affixed to a particular product or service, so that again, it is not the individual product that is protected by this law, but the brand name or symbol used to assure the public that it is getting a product authorized by the one source and not an imitation that claims to be from the same source. The more a product is marketed using a trademark or symbol, the greater the value of that trademark may become, as the public becomes used to seeing the product, associating the name with it, and, if the product remains popular, asking for the product by that name. Where a purchaser uses a generic or descriptive name to purchase a product, a trademark owner could be losing that sale to a competitor.

Once again, the law imposes certain requirements on applicants for eligibility to duck under the law's umbrella. Failure to observe these requirements can result in serious losses to the trademark owner. For example, "Aspirin" was once a trademark of the Bayer Company, indicating its brand of the compound technically known as acetylsalicylic acid. Bayer's failure to properly police and protect its trademark led to the public using the word "Aspirin" to refer generally to anyone's brand of this product. The result was that the word "aspirin" has now become the generic word for acetylsalicylic acid, and asking for aspirin at a drugstore could result in the purchase of St. Joseph, Bayer, or any one of many brands of this product. Similar losses of valuable trademarks involve nylon (once a trademark of DuPont), escalator (belonging to the Otis Company), and a number of others.

Unlike patents and copyrights, trademark protection does not have a mandatory time limit. Registration of a trademark gives it protection for an initial 10-year period (subject to certain filing requirements between the fifth and sixth year after registration) and the possibility of further 10-year terms without limit. The main requirement for vitality of a trademark is use, and once a trademark has been legitimately registered, it may enjoy its statutory protection for as long as it is continuously used. Even with such continuing use, however, the law requires that certain formalities be observed in order for a trademark to maintain the law's protection. Among those formalities is notification to the U.S. Patent & Trademark Office (PTO) that the mark is still being used, along with evidence of that use.

A "service mark" is simply a trademark that denotes a service, rather than a product. Accountants, house cleaners, home decorators, and scavenger companies, for example, to name a few, render services; they do not normally have tangible products available on store shelves for consumers to buy. The law treats service marks the same as trademarks, except for the name.

Copyrights

The laws applicable to copyright protection differ substantially from those covering patents and trademarks, because the nature of the material being protected is quite different. Whereas patent protection is available only for processes that are useful, copyrights are limited to material that has no practical use by itself. Patents may protect ideas, but copyrights may not; they only protect the expression of those ideas, and even then, the expression must be original and creative. A greeting card may contain expression, words, and pictures that are original and protectable, but copyright protection cannot extend to the physical greeting card and thus grant a sort of monopoly that forecloses all others from creating their own greeting cards.

Copyright protection is available for most forms of artistic expression, including writings, painting, music, movies, television shows, architectural drawings, and computer programs. This protection is not available for the basic ideas that find expression in a creator's mind, however. As an example, an idea for a murder mystery might involve creating a private investigator, whose love interest turns out to be the guilty party. The author who converts this idea to expression may not appropriate that basic premise, but only the literary expression she gives to the idea; anyone else is free to use the same basic idea, giving it their own expression. For copyright purposes, it is not enough to have a cute, clever, or original idea; it must be reduced to some tangible means of expression before copyright law will grant it the monopoly that could result in financial or other benefit for the creator.

Certain forms of expression are not protectable by either copyright or patent laws. Because of the requirement of originality in copyright law, such expressions as calendars, timetables, and all facts do not qualify for copyright protection because the courts believe that from a technical point of view, facts exist by themselves. If someone discloses a fact not theretofore known, they have discovered something that existed before; discovery does not represent original thought. Discoveries, then, are not protectable. A theory might be the result of independent and original thought; facts cannot be original.

Similarly, formulas, processes, systems, methods of operation, concepts, and principles are not protectable by copyright. Neither does copyright protect minimal expressions, even if there is some originality in them. Titles, short expressions, even instructions are not protectable. The instructions for putting a toy, appliance, or series of parts together—"insert Tab A into Slot B"— are too minimal. Most recipes are not protectable because they are simply instructions for putting a culinary concoction together. Jokes are normally not copyrightable because their origins are always so uncertain.

Copyright law presents a creator of eligible material with a bundle of rights that are more extensive than simply prohibiting copying without permission. That bundle includes the right to control the creation of what are called "derivative works," which are other works that are based on the protected work. Easy examples of derivative works are movies based on books, paintings based on photographs, and theatrical works based on material from another medium. Other rights included in the "bundle" include the right to distribute, to publicly perform, and to publicly display protected works. In many instances these rights have an important value separate and apart from exploitation of the original form of the work, and should be carefully considered when appraising intellectual property assets.

Just as patent and trademark protection durations have their own terms, so copyright duration has its own term. For works created on and after January 1, 1978 (when the current copyright law went into effect) by persons in their individual capacities, the term of the copyright monopoly is the life of the author plus 70 years. For works created since the same date but as works made for hire for the benefit of companies, the term is 95 years from the date of first publication or 120 years from the date of creation, whichever is shorter.

Trade Secrets

A trade secret is unlike anything previously discussed. It may consist of material incapable of any protections previously discussed, and although it also has requirements, they normally do not deal with originality, creativity, or artistic expression. A trade secret is a business fact or set of facts, or a secret method, that gives a company a competitive edge and is not generally know to the competitors of that business.

There are other requirements in order for material to be considered a trade secret, such as the making of efforts by the owner of the secret to maintain secrecy, the informing of employees of the confidentiality of the secret, and often the requirement that employees sign what is usually called a "nondisclosure agreement" (NDA), in which the employee recognizes that confidential information will be disclosed to him or her, and he or she promises to maintain the confidentiality of it.

The principal virtue of having an NDA is the ability of a company to prevent a departed ex-employee from disclosing confidential information to a new employer who happens to be a competitor. All workers are presumed under the law to be able to take personal skills they learned on one job and use them in the next one, but job skills are vastly different from disclosure of confidential information, especially when such disclosure would cause the former company to lose a competitive edge with customers. Even such items as customer lists, if they contain names and titles not normally known or easily ascertainable to outsiders (e.g., from research into Google or the telephone directory), may be protectable as trade secrets.

HOW TO TELL WHEN YOUR COMPANY HAS INTELLECTUAL PROPERTY

What to Look For

Companies such as IBM, Microsoft, and General Motors understand their patent portfolio and also understand the extent of their trademark registrations. Companies that have not applied for patents, or trademarks, have less of a sense of whether they should make applications and whether they have material that is worth the expense of protecting; in some instances they have even less of an ability to recognize what it is they might want to protect.

Patentable devices or material may be difficult to discover. Patent law also makes it difficult to protect a patentable device if it has been somehow disclosed to the public more than a year before a decision is made to file a patent application. It is not generally known that a new software program may qualify for patent protection. What officers of a company must ask themselves is whether there are any new devices, formulas, or interesting inventions conceived by employees that could give the company some sort of competitive edge over rival companies. Specialized software programs developed to fulfill a company's special needs should also be closely examined.

The virtue of conducting an examination to determine what the company has that is different from what other companies have is not limited to protection for the discovered intellectual property. Sometimes a property worth protecting can be developed commercially, so that not only is the owner keeping the property away from competitors; the property might also turn out to be marketable and thus become an important new profit center.

Such an examination should include looking for written or photographed material that is original. Items such as brochures, advertising copy, training films, orientation material for new employees, and promotional videos prepared by or for the company may be copyrightable. Again, the virtue of applying for copyright registration lies in the ability to stop others from appropriating material that has some value. Many companies will commission outside experts to create sales materials, using copy that is designed to at least psychologically entice readers to think well of the company's products. Indifference to the possibility that a rival will take this material, fraudulently make insignificant changes, and compete more strongly as a result can be very costly for the commissioning company.

Inventory

The way to best determine whether a company has any intellectual property worth some investment in protecting is to first conduct, or have an intellectual property attorney conduct, an inventory of all of the creative material owned or used by the company. Many companies provide incentives to employees to come up with improved methods of performing the company's business, and it is entirely possible that those methods will qualify for a business method patent. Promotional material on a company's Web site often will casually create interesting names of various products or services to make the site more noticeable. These names, if they are not simply generic or descriptive words, might be capable of trademark registration, which would restrict other companies from using the same names for their competing products. An inventory conducted by a person knowledgeable about intellectual property can conceivably uncover assets a company never knew it had. Creating such an inventory is obviously the first step toward discovering the value of those assets.

Distinguishing between Owned and Licensed Intellectual Property

Virtually all businesses today operate with many kinds of software. In the modern world, computers are ubiquitous. Normally, the basic platforms on which specialized software programs run are purchased or leased, and title to those platform software programs rests with another company. Word is a word processing program, Excel is an accounting program, Outlook is an e-mail program. These are owned by others. Even though they may be purchased outright by a company to form the building blocks of specialized software programs, they come with restrictions.

Most of these basic software programs demand that a user click on an "I agree" button before the user can open the program. These are known in the legal profession as "clickwrap" agreements, in which the user, by clicking his or her agreement, commits to observe all of the conditions expressed in a license agreement spelled out above the "I agree" button. The most common condition found in these licenses is the restriction on copying, although there are usually many other restrictions as well.

But the restriction on copying creates a situation some companies ignore, and they do so at their peril. Purchasing one copy of this type of general software program, agreeing not to copy it, and then loading the program onto a number of computers is copying, for which the company can be held liable. That liability can result in a cost far greater than simply purchasing one copy of the software for each computer on which the program will be used.

It is for this reason that in conducting an intellectual property inventory, a distinction must be made between owned and leased software programs. For the leased programs, it is important for the company's employees to understand the limitations on use and to observe them. These programs are also already protected in some fashion by their originators, and so no consideration needs to be given as to whether and how to protect them. Rather, it is the add-ons, the specialized adaptations of them created by the company, that should be inspected for possible registration or other legal protection.

Determining Worth

Calculating the value of most intellectual property is extremely difficult. What is priceless to one company may be worthless to another. However, where the discovered intellectual property is intended to be used or kept by the company, its worth to the outside world may not be as important as its worth for purposes of obtaining legal protection. Some forms of property are protectable at a very reasonable cost, while others require some investment. Copyright registration is extremely cheap, while patent registration is expensive and time consuming. Trademark registration lies somewhere between these two, but still can run to several thousand dollars.

Consequently, a company must determine the worth of its intellectual property in terms of the cost of protecting it. Where it appears that failure to obtain protection could be more costly for the company, both financially and competitively, than spending the money for protection, the choice becomes obvious. Conversely, indifference to the possibility of copying or fraudulent use of the material makes the choice equally obvious. The point is that it is not the value for purposes of sale of the property that is important for these considerations, but the value for business purposes.

BASIC REASONS FOR PROTECTING

Competitive Edges

As has been seen, intellectual property may be worth much more than mere money. Something as seemingly basic as an employee manual may feature a management system in its contents that competitors would make marvelous use of. More important, perhaps, are specialized sales materials that have been prepared by sales experts at significant expense to a company. Failure to protect those materials can mean that a competing company may acquire the materials at no cost to them, and those companies may use the materials in such a way that they significantly cut into the original company's market share. Obviously, then, failure to protect can cost a company a lot more than the expense of preparing the materials.

Similarly, failure to protect a trademark can easily lead to imitation of the mark by a competitor. It is true that federal registration is not required for a trademark to have some validity, but such a failure means that the mark's effectiveness and enforceability will be much more limited. Imitations and creation of marks that are close in sound and appearance to the unregistered mark become much easier to originate, again offering competitors a free ride on a company's original effort.

Although patents are valid for only 20 years, the patent monopoly is the strongest protection available for intellectual property owners who have patentable material. It has been mentioned that copyright protection is not available for ideas, only for the tangible expression of them. But patent protection is available for ideas, as long as they otherwise qualify under the law and their implementation results in a useful product, plant, or chemical compound. Protecting the basic idea means that the only way others can use the idea is if they are able to invent around the entire patented process, and that is usually difficult to do.

Additional Asset Value

The preceding discussion concerns the nonmonetary value in intellectual property. Not to be disregarded, however, is the monetary value of those assets. Intellectual property may be valued for tax, inventory, and other purposes, and value may be assigned in the event of a sale of a company.

For example, copyrighted material may be licensed to others for a royalty payment. Patents, of course, are also capable of being licensed to others for royalties. Trademarks, in fact, cannot be transferred without assigning a value to their goodwill, and this value can be considerable. Attempting to calculate the value of a famous, long-standing trademark such as Budweiser for beer, Coca-Cola for a soft drink, and Cadillac for cars is a formidable task, but if the marks have been properly protected, they are worth a great deal of money by themselves, without worrying about product inventory, pending orders, owned real estate, and other assets.

Apart from considerations of assets for sale purposes, there is the prospect of licensing intellectual property to others for significant royalty payments. Cartoon characters that are also brand names have been licensed to food companies for use on packaging at exorbitant royalties. Personalities have licensed their images to cosmetic and apparel companies, again for important sums as royalties. Other examples of use of a famous name as a brand for products that the famous person does not manufacture or sell abound. And in each instance, fraudulent appropriation of these intellectual property items is punishable under the law.

ROUTINE PROTECTION

What the Laws Generally Provide

Each of the intellectual property laws discussed has its own statute; most are federal and some are state. Where patents and copyrights are concerned, there is federal law exclusively. Those federal patent and copyright laws preempt any state law that may be equivalent to the federal statutes. Trademarks are protected by the federal Lanham Act but may also have state law protection. Trade secrets are normally protected by state, not federal, laws. Some of the general provisions of these laws already have been discussed to a limited degree. It has already been noted, for example, that the duration of patent protection is 20 years; that trademarks and service marks, if used, may last virtually forever; that copyright protection exists for the life of the author plus 70 years (for works created on and after January 1, 1978); and that trade secrets may last for as long as they remain secret.

Generally, all of these laws effectively grant, to the owners of the intellectual property eligible for protection, a sort of monopoly over the control and exploitation of the property. Under most circumstances, the laws provide that an owner may use the court system to stop infringers from committing their acts of infringement. The laws also generally provide for the award of damages as well as confiscation or destruction of the infringing material. However, it is the responsibility of these owners to be vigilant and take whatever steps are necessary to maintain that monopoly. The special laws are not self-enforcing; one may not call the police because the protected property is being fraudulently mishandled or stolen. Failure to take these protective steps can lead to loss of the monopoly rights, as seen earlier in the discussion about trademarks, as well as loss of competitive advantages, sales, and future prospects. Those steps often begin with applications for registration.

Federal and State Registration

For obvious reasons, namely, forfeiture of secrecy, it is impossible to register trade secrets. For patents, trademarks, and copyrights, however, registration procedures are in place and under most circumstances give the property owner greater choices when it comes to enforcing rights.

Patents. For patents, the U.S. Patent & Trademark Office provides rules and regulations for submitting an application to them for registration. Those rules are complex, as are the eligibility requirements for registration. Because complete registration grants a kind of monopoly to the registrant, allowing that person to enforce rights and collect damages, certain basic standards must be met.

The material must be a new and useful process, machine, manufacture, or composition of matter, or any new and useful improvement thereof. (Note particularly that the material must be "useful.") No patent will be granted if the invention was known or used by others in the United States, or patented or described in a printed publication in the United States or a foreign country, before being invented by the applicant, or more than a year prior to the date of the U.S. application. The invention must be nonobvious; that is, if the differences between the subject matter sought to be patented and prior art are such that the subject matter as a whole would have been obvious at the time the invention was made to a person having ordinary skill in the art to which the subject matter pertains. Other restrictions present roadblocks that must be surmounted before a patent will issue. Material that for some reason is unpatentable becomes, unless protected by some other law such as copyright, freely available to the public without the necessity of asking permission or paying any royalty.

Once issued, as noted, the patent is effective for 20 years from the date the application was filed.

Trademarks. For trademarks, federal registration requires that the applicant has chosen a mark that ordinarily will not create confusion as to the origin of the product or service on which the mark will be applied. A number of categories of words and symbols are specifically excluded from protection, such as: immoral, deceptive or scandalous matter; flags or coats of arms or other insignia of the United States, or of any state or municipality, or of any foreign nation; proper names unless the consent of the person named has been obtained; or marks that so resemble another registered mark as to be likely to cause confusion, or mistake, or deceive.

As also noted, trademarks are valid for as long as they continue to be used. Use is an absolute requirement for trademark validity, and the cessation of use usually opens the door to use by anyone else, unless it can be convincingly shown to a court that there was no intention to abandon use, only to interrupt it for a short period. In the United States, it is possible to file an application on an intent-to-use basis. Assuming there are no objections raised by the PTO or by any other party once the application has cleared examination, what will issue is a notice of allowance, not a registration. The applicant then has six months within which to actually use the mark, after which, upon submitting proof of use, the PTO will issue that registration.

Registration in the PTO will give the registrant nationwide protection for the mark, but only in the classes of goods listed in the application. For trademarks, goods and services are listed in certain classes that are respected internationally. Acquiring a mark in one class does not mean the mark is unavailable to others who wish to use it in other unrelated classes of goods or services. For example, the mark "United" is used by an airline for travel-related services. But there is an unrelated company, United Van Lines, which uses the mark for furniture and household moving services, and United Insurance, which offers insurance-related products. Only where a mark has become so obvious, has been so widely used for a long time, will that mark be protectable for products outside its natural classification of goods. The mark Coca-Cola has been so pervasive a part of U.S. society for so long that, even though the mark is registered mainly in a class covering soft drinks and perhaps sporty apparel, it is likely that the owners of this mark could stop anyone who wanted to use it for some totally unrelated product, such as laundry soap.

Copyrights. For copyrights, all that is required is that an original idea has been reduced to some tangible means of expression, whether that is by a writing, capture on film or video, available on a compact disc or tape or other recorded device, or even scored on music or other note paper. Under current U.S. law, copyright protection begins the moment a new work is reduced to that tangible expression, whether the work is ever registered or not. Registration is an option, not an absolute requirement, and even if an eligible work is never registered, it is still protected by the copyright law.

However, there are certain benefits and requirements in order for an "author" (read this word as "creator") to enjoy the full benefits that the statute provides in the event that the work is fraudulently treated or stolen. Registration is an important part of the opportunities to realize those benefits.

To begin with, the law requires that in order for an author to have standing to sue for infringement (and any suit for copyright infringement must under the federal law be brought in a federal court), the author's claim of copyright must be registered. In most federal circuits, it is not enough to have filed an application for registration; the registration must have actually been issued, even though the registration process could take months. This is important because of the common situation where an author has not registered his or her claim and there is a fraudulent infringement taking place that the author wishes to stop immediately. Inability to have standing to ask a court to issue an injunction can be devastating in the immediate run, although perhaps the award of increased damages in the long run might make up for this defect.

Registration is considered by the courts to be prima facie evidence of the validity of the copyright and of the facts stated in the certificate of registration, but only if the application for registration has been made within the first five years after the first publication of the work.

Assuming the author has fulfilled this requirement, the burden of disproving the copyright automatically shifts to the accused infringer, who has a higher hurdle to overcome in order to contest a lawsuit.

Copyright registration does not involve the same sorts of obstacle that are found with attempts to register trademarks. The Copyright Office examiners usually are unable to tell whether a submitted work is original or copied from some other, perhaps obscure, source, unless the evidence is extremely clear. Quoting passages from the Bible, or from the works of Shakespeare, for example, could be flags that the examiner would notice. Otherwise, the examiner usually will simply try to determine whether the submitted work contains material that is protectable because it is not a set of facts, or a process, or is useful, or falls into any of the other categories of unprotectable works. Unlike patents, copyright cannot issue for useful articles unless their usefulness can be conceptually severable from their artistic elements. Even then, the issued copyright protects only those artistic elements and not the useful aspect of the work.

The law builds other advantages into the act of registration. Where a work has been registered before an infringing act has taken place, the author is entitled to choose between asking for statutory damages and for actual damages. Statutory damages are those that are determined by the court to be an amount that should compensate the author for the infringement, and can be a total that is much greater than an author's actual damages. That author may also ask for attorneys' fees, although an award for this latter claim rests in the discretion of the court.

Where registration has not taken place before the infringing act occurred, an author is limited to asking for actual damages, that is, the amount of lost profits of the author, plus any profits of the infringer attributable to the infringing act and that have not been measured in determining lost profits. It may well be that in certain situations, the author has had no actual damages, making this potential award very small. Where someone has taken an actionable portion of a book to use in an article, for which the infringer has been paid only a small amount, and the taking has not affected the sales of the book, actual damages are not much of a remedy, although the author may still obtain an injunction against further use and sales of the article and destruction of the infringing copies.

Notices

Formal notice of a claim of legal protection is only occasionally a statutory requirement, but it is almost always a psychological one. Patent notices should definitely be used, but the failure to use trademark and copyright notices does not result in forfeiture of protection. Notices are also persuasive to some degree in convincing a court to award more damages because an infringer was on notice that the work was protected. In other words, although a defense of innocent infringement may be available to an infringer ("we didn't know the work was protected"), that defense may be rendered totally ineffective because of the use of a notice. Notices need not be aesthetically intrusive, and usually may be placed in any location that a user of the work might reasonably be able to see.

For patents, the notice should read "Reg. U.S. Pat. Off." or an acceptable variation a patent attorney may prescribe. For trademarks, the notice for a registered mark may read "Reg. U.S. Pat. & TM Off." or by using the symbol ®. The latter symbol may not be used in situations where an application for registration is still pending or where there is an intent to apply but no application has been filed as yet. The letters ™ are often used beside a mark, but they have no official legal significance and normally are interpreted to mean simply that the owner of the mark is claiming trademark rights in it.

For copyrighted works, the notice consists of three elements: the international copyright symbol ©, the year date, and the name of the copyright proprietor. Thus, a proper notice for a work published in the year 2006 would read © 2006 ABC Corp.

Terms of License Agreements

Where a protected work is licensed to a user, as noted, the license agreement spells out the terms of the license. That agreement may have become binding on the licensee simply by clicking the "I Agree" button on the screen, necessary in order to open the software program, Of course, there are more explicit license agreements that are reduced to paper, negotiated between the parties, and accepted in a more formal manner. While in most instances the law allows a licensee to build on the licensed product in order to create something needed in the licensee's unique business, the terms spell out restrictions that a licensee should pay particular attention to. In some license agreements, as an example, the licensor demands that any improvement built onto the licensed product that has been developed by the licensee belongs to the licensor.

Another common feature in agreements licensing intellectual property is a waiver of warranties. State laws adopting some form of the Uniform Commercial Code place some limits on the ability of any company to completely disclaim any responsibility for whether a product works as it is intended to. But starting from that limitation, licensors will go as far as the law allows them to go in specifically stating as a term of the license that they are not responsible for failures of the licensed product.

These license terms are honored more often in the breach than in the acceptance. A licensor who does not pay attention to the uses actually being made by a licensee runs a large risk that all sorts of frauds are being committed against the licensor's property. Restrictions on the number of computers on which licensed software may be loaded are common license terms. However, it is difficult if not impossible for a licensor to enter onto a licensee's premises and inspect every computer in use, in order to determine whether the licensed product has been loaded onto more computers than authorized.

It is incumbent on both licensors and licensees to know and observe the terms of the license agreements. A dishonest employee of an honest employer can put that employer at great jeopardy by fraudulently using the licensed product. Since intent to infringe is not required in order to be found guilty of infringement, innocent supervisors may be held liable for the acts of guilty subordinates.

POLICING INTELLECTUAL PROPERTY RIGHTS

Cease and Desist Letters

Once an intellectual property owner gains knowledge that his or her property rights are being unlawfully used or copied, it is usually incumbent on that owner to take some sort of action. Failure to do so could provide the perpetrator of the fraud to claim that the owner sat on her rights for a sufficient time to mislead the perpetrator into believing that the owner was unconcerned about this misuse.

The simplest of the methods available to show the concern of the owner is what is called a "cease and desist" letter. This letter tells recipients that they are committing fraudulent acts for which they may be held responsible if those acts continue. The letter may be as strong or weak as the owner wishes: strong by threatening the possibility of legal action if the acts continue, or weak by stating that the owner will be watching the infringer. It is usually inadvisable to positively state that legal action will be brought if infringers fail to stop, because such a specific threat will give the infringers the right to begin the court action themselves by suing for a declaratory judgment that they are not infringing. This may be the route the owner planned to take eventually anyway, but the dispute is now proceeding as the infringers wish rather than as the owner wishes. Now it is too late for the owner to seek some alternative ways to settle the dispute.

Dispute Resolution

Arbitration and Mediation. Once an owner is satisfied that a fraudulent activity has definitely taken place, she has several choices available to her. She can, of course, file a lawsuit. However, lawsuits are very expensive propositions, and may not always provide either party with a satisfactory ruling. Going to arbitration or mediation is becoming an increasingly popular way of resolving these disputes. Either method involves the use of an impartial, independent arbitrator or mediator, who will listen carefully to both sides and then make a judgment as to which side has the better argument. Because court appearances are unnecessary, and complicated memoranda of law are not required (although written presentations are), the process is much less expensive. Both sides must agree to be bound by the decision of the mediator or arbitrator, of course.

Domain Name Proceedings through ICANN. An Internet domain name is generally accepted to be mainly an address, although it may also be a trademark. Use as an address, however, is normally not a trademark use, because that use is not as a brand name for a product, but rather as a location in order to get information about a company as well as a product. As addresses, domain names are treated differently from the intellectual property generally discussed in this chapter. It is possible for an early registrant of a domain name that acts as a trademark for another company to keep that domain name even though it may cause confusion among Internet browsers. As long as the purpose of registering the confusing name is not fraudulent, such as to trade on that confusion, or to divert customers, it is possible for a domain name owner to retain that name.

The international community has set up a procedure for settling disputes regarding domain names. An agency called ICANN, the Internet Corporation for Assigned Names and Numbers, by agreement among nations is the place to register complaints and disputes about domain names. Thanks to U.S. court decisions, domain names that use well-known trademarks but add derogatory words are considered to be protected by the First Amendment of the U.S. Constitution. The most popular add-on word is "sucks," so these gripe sites will register domain names such as "ABCCorpsucks.com," and there is nothing ABC Corporation can do about it. The public, of course, usually understands what these sites are and their bias, which dilutes their effectiveness.

Litigation

The U.S. court system is available for resolution of all intellectual property disputes. Unfortunately, this system is the most expensive method available for that resolution, although it also gives the most certain results. Once a court decision becomes final and appeals have either been exhausted or refused by the higher court, the final order is enforceable and puts an end to the dispute; there is no place else to go.

The expense of using this system can be and often is enormous. Because of the checks and balances built into it, the system is time consuming, complicated, and often subjective where the parties are looking for objectivity.

Because of the finality of a court order, litigation is sometimes a stimulus for settlement discussions between parties with legitimate disagreements over the extent of rights or interpretations of contract provisions. Where the property has been fraudulently used or taken, however, litigation is the best way to punish the infringer. Under most circumstances, a fraudulent misuse of intellectual property is not necessarily a crime, and so a civil judgment can impose fines as well as stop the fraudulent activity. There are exceptions to this concept, however.

The Copyright Law provides a section making certain types of infringement a criminal act. The punishment under this section can be fines and imprisonment. Several conditions must be weighed in determining whether a criminal prosecution should be pursued. In criminal cases, it is the governmental authority, whether state or federal, that is the plaintiff, and the intellectual property owner is relegated to the role of a complaining witness. Although fines as well as imprisonment may be the criminal penalties, money judgments in favor of that owner are not available.

POSSIBLE RECOVERIES THROUGH LITIGATION

Damages

It is true that litigation can take years to wind its way through the trial and appellate court systems. As noted, however, it is the surest solution to the problem of fraudulent misuse of intellectual property. Failure to obey a court judgment subjects the judgment's subject to being held in contempt of court, with further fines and even possible jail sentences as penalties. A final judgment awarding damages, which in intellectual property cases usually bears some relation to disgorging of profits of the entity committing the fraud as well as losses of the owner of the property, sometimes can be very substantial. Many patent cases result in an award in the millions of dollars because of the profits made by the patent infringer. In some instances, the court is given the power in the statute to make further awards in the nature of punitive damages for egregious conduct. Trademark infringement judgments also can be quite high. Under the Copyright Act, where registration occurred before the infringing act was committed, courts are allowed to render judgment for an amount of up to $150,000, but also in their discretion to award attorneys' fees. This latter possible award is often powerful incentive for defendants to agree to a settlement before trial.

Where an intellectual property owner can afford the time and the expense of pursuing a claim through the courts, and where the odds very much favor victory, litigation is the best of all possible choices. Most lawyers will advise that as a general rule, parties should stay out of court if at all possible, but it is very unlikely that an arbitrator or mediator will award the size of a judgment that a court will give. Going to court, of course, involves the diversion of resources to accommodate all of the discovery and tactical maneuvers each side will attempt to use on the other, so a decision to follow this path must be made very carefully and with full knowledge of all of the headaches lawsuits can bring.

But damages are not always sufficient to compensate the intellectual property owner whose property has been in effect vandalized. Theft and disclosure to others of a trade secret, as an example, can result in a loss of a competitive edge that is realistically immeasurable. There is no way to learn what customers might have done business with the secret's owner but for the disclosure of the secret and its use by others. Fraudulent taking of copyrighted material could also result in very little in the way of actual money damages, but the loss of the creative material could be critical. In such instances, other forms of relief imposable by a court could be of greater actual value.

Destruction of Infringing Material

At the election of the intellectual property owner, a court often has the power to order a losing infringer to destroy, or turn over to the owner, all copies of the work that contains the infringing material. This can result in an extraordinary expense for the infringer, since where the infringing product has been distributed, perhaps nationwide, there must be a recall of all of the unsold copies. This type of relief gives the owner control over those copies, to make certain they do not find their way into other marketplaces, legal or illicit.

CONCLUSION

The owner of any intellectual property also owns a sort of monopoly over its exploitation. When that monopoly expires, as it often does, the property passes into the public domain, which means that anyone may use it or any portion of it without asking for permission and without paying any royalties for that use. As a consequence of achieving public domain status, the property loses its financial value to the owner and perhaps becomes of financial value to other users. It thus becomes important for owners to determine what they have, assess its relative importance, and, if that assessment results in a determination that the property has value, take steps to protect it from fraudulent misuse. Failure to make these determinations can prove to be expensive missteps to any business, while observing them can mean the difference between survival and catastrophe. As stated in Proverbs 22:29, "Seest thou a man diligent in his business? He shall stand before kings."

Chapter 21

Fraud Deterrence in the U.S. Private Equity Finance System

David Brophy and Adam Wadecki

INTRODUCTION

The U.S. private equity system has achieved great success in recent decades with a minimum of direct regulatory oversight. However, it now participates in an environment in which the regulatory oversight of financial markets has intensified, due to recent incidences of egregious cases of financial fraud. This environment has significantly affected both the structure and activities of the private equity system. Private equity system managers are now subject to, both directly and indirectly, regulatory oversight originally crafted for application to public companies.

In this chapter we examine the structure of the U.S. private equity finance system, demonstrate its vulnerability to fraud, and recommend a framework for effective fraud deterrence within this system.

U.S. PRIVATE EQUITY SYSTEM AND ITS GOVERNANCE STRUCTURE

From its informal beginnings, private equity finance has become a well-established part of the U.S. institutional financial market system and is rapidly expanding throughout the developed and developing worlds. Unlike larger market participants (commercial and investment banks), its components follow a "cottage industry" model, with large volumes of capital managed by relatively small numbers of managers and staff in each firm. The privacy of the system and lack of transparency is viewed by participants as contributing to the system's exceptional risk-adjusted performance over time. In this chapter we discuss the ways in which those characteristics contribute to fraud vulnerability and the reasons why fraud deterrence is critically important in today's private equity system.

Private Equity System Components

The U.S. private equity (PE) system, presented in Exhibit 21.1, consists of three major categories of participants: investors, intermediaries and investee firms.

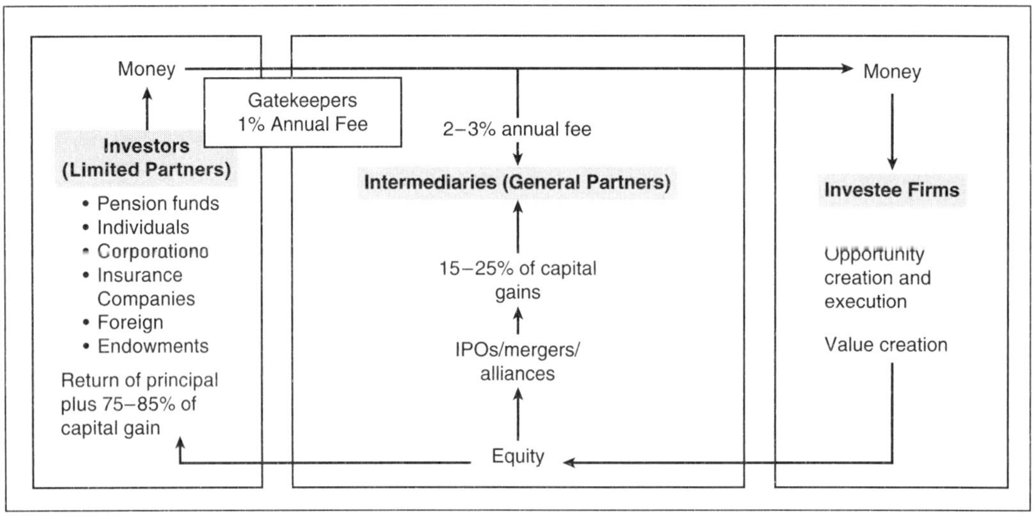

Exhibit 21.1 Private Equity Cycle

Investors and "Gatekeepers." Investors include high-net-worth individuals and the institutions (e,g., pension funds, insurance reserves, corporations, family offices, foreign investors) that represent major pools of investible savings and that have clear fiduciary and reporting responsibilities to their constituents. These institutions have been attracted to private equity over the past three decades as a means of achieving risk-adjusted returns superior to those available in the markets for publicly traded corporate securities.

As shown in Exhibit 21.1, investors commit amounts of liquid capital to intermediaries, also called general partners (GPs). Investors are typically organized as limited partnerships (LPs), under an agency and investment agreement carrying very specific and mutually accepted terms.

When an intermediary requires the funds of the limited partner for use in an investment, a "capital call" in which the LP provides the GP with liquid capital, is executed. This pool of funds is then drawn down for use in the investment.

Because of the complexity of the private equity business and the paucity of objective, published data on the quality and risk-adjusted performance of intermediaries, limited partners use the services of consulting firms (called "gatekeepers") that analyze and certify the quality and track record of intermediaries. Gatekeepers obtain and maintain pools of information on both LPs and GPs, and are tolerated and permitted to do so as a necessary market-making vehicle. Without the gatekeeper and the data, the LP would be hard-pressed to determine the track record of an intermediary seeking to raise capital for a new fund. Gatekeeper compensation is generally 1 percent of the corpus of funds under management.

Investors serve as the limited partners within the private equity limited partnership. The LP executive and management team oversee a portfolio of private equity funds, in each of which they have negotiated an investment contract, usually as a part of an institutional investment syndicate. While all syndicate members will have the same investment terms, each is responsible for performing due diligence investigation and determining that the investment terms are fair and appropriate for the proposed investment.

Portfolio Investee Firms. Investee firms are companies seeking growth capital and represent all stages of the business life cycle. Firms seeking venture capital are generally in a stage of operation that does not qualify for bank financing or funding through the market for publicly traded securities (unless they possess specific collateral to support project finance with public debt).

Because of youth, small scale, management "neglect," or project complexity, these firms represent a source of potentially attractive returns. Adding to their risk profile is the fact that they report no information publicly (aside from public-to-private transactions), so that the investment opportunity they represent is opaque except to insiders. As knowledge-based businesses, and because they often represent "disruptive" technologies or business plans (whether they are start-up companies or firms acquired in buyouts for restructuring or market realignment), their expected returns are seen as having a low correlation with the broader markets for publicly traded securities, thus promising to contribute desirable trade-offs of risk and return to institutional investment portfolios.

Firms sought by private equity buyout funds may be mature private or public companies, in either case having an established track record, and may have a more conventional mix of tangible and intangible assets than the venture capital private equity clientele. Such companies have audited records and established business systems and processes, usually with established product lines, markets and customers.

Intermediary Private Equity Funds. Unlike the public markets, where security trades are carried out in open communication among market participants, the private equity market is closed to outside view. As such, the market is incomplete and opaque, and therefore incapable of operation unless it has an entity to bring investor and investee together—a function similar to that of the stock exchange for public companies. The private equity investment fund serves this function.

Investee firms generally represent an array of specific industry and product domains that investors believe offer the return they seek over an investment horizon. To achieve portfolio diversification, and because they do not possess the breadth and depth of domain expertise required, investors empower the private equity firm as an investment intermediary and trust its managers with the task of finding investments, negotiating investment contracts with such firms, monitoring their progress, engaging in their management as board members, and successfully harvesting the investment through an initial public offering (IPO) or merger and acquisition (M&A) transaction.

The intermediary searches for investment opportunities within the framework of its agency charter and negotiates investment agreements with firms it believes will meet its internal rate of return (IRR) standards. This agreement sets the investment terms and the conditions under which the fund and the investee firm will work together to create value.

While debt instruments are sometimes used as part of complex capital structures in these transactions—particularly in buyout transactions where hard assets are normally present—the fund typically exchanges money and management services for a significant equity stake in the company, seeking investment return primarily from appreciation in equity value and its realization through a liquidity event (i.e., IPO or M&A) rather than solely through current return (i.e., interest or dividends usually paid in arrears after the liquidity event).

It is important to note that while the limited liability company (LLC) is occasionally used by the intermediary, our discussion will assume the use of a limited partnership.

Private Equity System Relationships and Major Economic Terms

The market participants interact according to the terms of investment agreements through which they bind their interests together at law. The investors become the limited partners in the intermediary limited partnership organization, surrendering control rights to the GP in exchange for the GP assuming all the partnership risk. The LP agrees to honor capital calls, under stated conditions, and to pay the GP a management fee, generally between 1.5 percent and 3.0 percent, depending on the investment focus involved. Upon realization of principal and gain through merger or sale of the company to a strategic or financial acquirer (M&A) or through an initial public offering (IPO), capital is returned to investors and the gain is divided between LP and GP according to a prearranged percentage (usually between 15 percent and 25 percent).

The compensation model in private equity is a major factor in the economics and governance of the total system. To assure sufficient operating funds to pursue opportunities in "inefficient" markets (in the sense of the Capital Asset Pricing Model), and to deter the agency risk involved, LPs agree to a GP compensation scheme that is unique in financial markets. The typical management fee (2 to 3 percent) is considerably higher than that usually found in the contracts of portfolio managers of publicly traded securities and hedge funds (1 to 1.5 percent).

In addition, to assure that the agent neither shirks her duty of loyalty and performance nor overconsumes assets through perquisites (perks), the LP agrees to a substantial "carried interest" in realized absolute gains on the investments, generally 15 percent to 20 percent, with extremes of 10 percent (scaled down for very large funds) and 35 percent (occasionally observed in cases of extremely successful GPs). This compensation formula has been sustained over the history of the institutional private equity market in the United States, which strongly suggests that it minimizes agency costs at a fee and profit-sharing price acceptable to LPs. This profit-sharing feature has been emulated in the hedge fund industry, but with slightly lower percentages.

Exhibit 21.2 Private Equity Investment Horizon Performance through December 31, 2005

Fund Type	1 Year	3 Years	5 Years	10 Years	20 Years
Early/Seed VC	8.3	3.1	−10.9	41.5	20.4
Balanced VC	24.3	11.7	−3.5	18.9	14.6
Later Stage VC	6.9	8.6	−4.1	11.3	13.5
All Venture	**15.6**	**7.5**	**−6.8**	**23.7**	**16.5**
Small Buyouts	11.5	7.8	2.1	7.9	25.4
Med Buyouts	33.8	10.0	2.9	10.9	16.5
Large Buyouts	18.2	16.0	4.0	10.2	12.7
Mega Buyouts	35.7	17.8	6.0	8.8	11.4
All Buyouts	**31.3**	**16.3**	**5.2**	**9.2**	**13.3**
Mezzanine	12.2	4.8	2.2	6.4	8.9
All Private Equity	**22.6**	**13.1**	**1.5**	**12.3**	**14.2**
Nasdaq	5.2	14.2	−2.2	7.7	12.4
S & P 500	6.3	10.1	−1.1	7.3	11.0

Source: Thomson Venture XPerts Database.

The private equity "model" has gradually found application to investee firms in many subfields of entrepreneurial finance, as shown in Exhibit 21.2, with wide-ranging implications for returns. These firms range all the way from start-up and early-stage companies, through expansion stage, to firms seeking "mezzanine" capital in advance of an initial public offering (IPO) or at harvest through merger or acquisition by a financial or strategic corporate buyer.

Exhibit 21.2 also shows the significance of returns experienced in the private equity industry, particularly by buyout funds. In examining the exhibit, one can clearly see that buyout funds have outperformed both the Standard & Poor's (S&P) 500 and the NASDAQ indices over a wide range of investment horizons. Venture capital funds, however, experienced a significant hit to their returns as many venture investments generated poor internal rates of return during the post-2000 market correction.

The ability to bring private equity investment to bear on diverse asset subclasses increases the power of the private equity organizational form to effect structural and economic change through buyouts, recapitalizations, turn-arounds, carve-in and carve-out investments, and purchase of distressed debt and private investments in public entities (PIPEs). In many ways, these are no less entrepreneurial than the start-up company that represented the "standard" traditional private equity investment.

Private Equity Capital Levels, Flows, and Investment Performance

While the private equity system has engendered great enthusiasm among investors, the market has shown high volatility in recent years. These characteristics are quite important from a governance and fraud deterrence viewpoint, inasmuch as volatility may be directly associated with vulnerability to fraud within any economic system, perhaps especially so in one with limited transparency such as that which occurs in private equity.

Long considered to provide superior, though cyclical, realized returns, with low correlation to returns on other asset classes, private equity is now being seen as an increasingly "efficient" marketplace with competition from many new sources. Such a phenomenon significantly increases the difficulty of achieving its hallmark "alpha" returns (i.e., the excess abnormal return above the rate predicted by its risk level).

The characteristics of PE returns over the long term may be best indicated by Exhibit 21.3 in which the aggregate Sand Hill Index values are shown from January 1989 to September 2005. Sand Hill Econometrics (www.sandhillecon.com) is a purveyor of analytical tools that describe the private equity industry.

Exhibit 21.3 illustrates that, in the decade prior to 1995 and the years since 2002, the level of investment in private equity grew at a rate of roughly 11 percent per annum. The period from 1995 to 2000, in contrast, saw a huge spike in the volume of private equity investment, followed by a "readjustment" that removed most of the apparent market value built up in the five-year period. Both the boom and the market decline that followed had disruptive effects on the market system, greatly depressing returns, dampening investor enthusiasm for the asset class, and stimulating a search for the causes of the observed condition.

As instances of sensational fraud and excess were discovered to exist in already highly regulated public companies, Congress sought to tighten existing regulations and add new ones through the Sarbanes-Oxley Act of 2002. Although the act is stated to apply to public companies, it has become clear that it indirectly affects the private equity system in ways that will be examined later in this chapter. Since the market nadir in 2001, private equity flows from LP to GP and investments by GP into portfolio companies have steadily increased and suggest

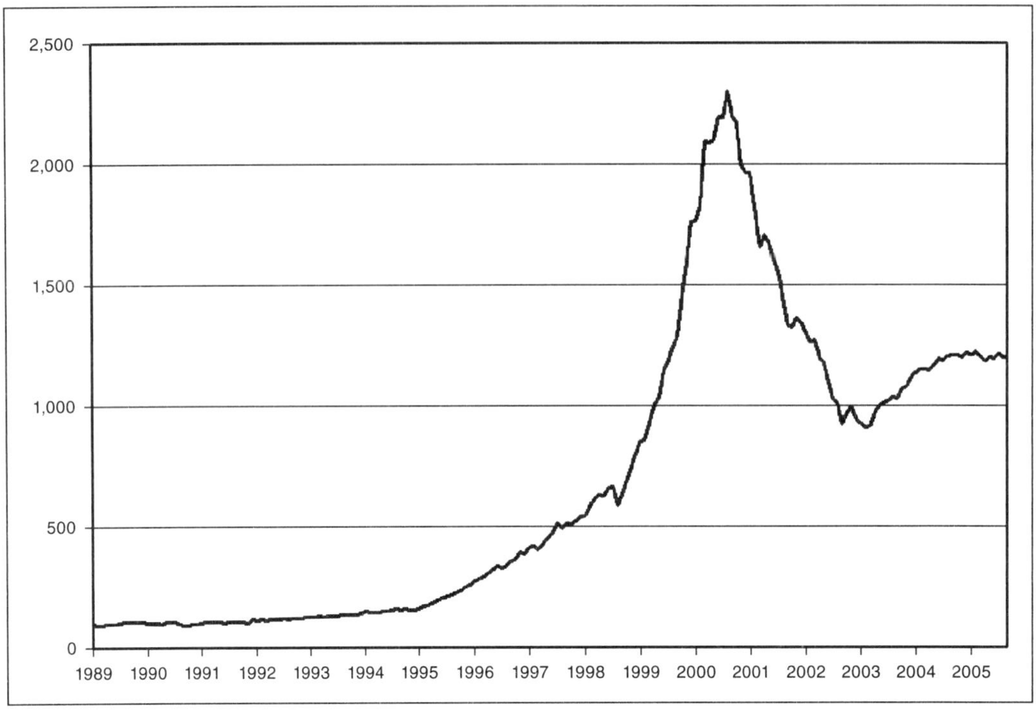

Exhibit 21.3 Sand Hill Index Values, January 1989 to September 2005

the possibility of another developing boom period. The sustainability of this recovery will affect and be affected by the extent to which improvements in governance and fraud deterrence continues to develop within the system.

Emerging Trends in the Private Equity System

The evolution of the private equity system is driven by its adaptability to new investment opportunities in industries and geographic regions heretofore less well served by the system. Already, the spread of the private equity model is evident in other countries. While historically most PE charters specifically prohibited PE funds and their portfolio of investee companies from investing outside the United States, in the current environment, every fund and investee target must have a global strategy when seeking funding at each level. The PE business has long been developed endogenously in western Europe and is now growing dramatically in eastern Europe. Similarly, PE has penetrated markets in Asia, with many U.S. PE funds establishing offices and relationships in both countries. These patterns offer challenges of a legal, regulatory, and cultural nature and demand new and improved governance and fraud deterrence programs from these firms. While PE firms native to these countries and regions have focused on opportunities in their domestic markets, they have begun to invest in U.S. and European spaces, thus pushing the envelope with respect to globalization of the PE system.

Similarly, PE investment is being channeled to opportunities in fields not previously believed attractive to PE investors and to institutional investment intermediaries (e.g., hedge funds) not historically active in PE. As well, the PE system faces co-optition (i.e., simultaneous cooperation and competition) with hedge funds and corporate strategic and financial PE investors.

In its most recent survey of tax-exempt institutional investment groups, Russell & Company found that such investors are investing large and growing portions of their "alternative investments" in hedge funds.[1] While hedge funds invest predominantly in publicly traded securities, most have discretionary set-aside ("side pocket") portions of their portfolio through which they invest in traditional private equity. This was calculated as 7 percent of total hedge fund assets in 2005. As a result, hedge funds participate directly with PE funds as co-investors of equity and providers of high-yield unsecured debt in PE buyout transactions. At the same time, they compete directly in bidding auctions for investment, potentially driving up the acquisition price to the disadvantage of "orthodox" PE firms. Large nonfinancial corporations have increased their presence in the PE market as well, similarly bidding up the price by paying the "strategic" premium for targets that can be melded into the operating process of the acquiring firm. Both of these represent new competitive dynamics for players in the PE system and extra pressure in the search for alpha.

FOUNDATIONS OF A FRAUD DETERRENCE SYSTEM IN PRIVATE EQUITY

The core of fraud deterrence within the U.S. private equity industry is the creation of a culture of integrity within the system at all levels (i.e., limited partner, general partner, and investee firm). Because individuals and collaborators dedicated to perpetrating fraudulent activity at any level of the system may continue such efforts, the culture must be backed up by a sound internal control system and an effective fraud reporting and sanctioning system.

This entire process must be subject to management and board oversight and audited both internally and externally. Where fraud is discovered, visible sanctions must be brought to bear, so that the message is clearly sent and the system's integrity is strengthened. In this section we discuss the foundations of fraud deterrence applied at all levels of the U.S. private equity system.

Argument for Fraud Deterrence: System Integrity and Long-Term Value Creation

In a recent presentation, Jensen argues that a firm's integrity is a necessary condition to the attainment of long-run value creation.[2] A firm or a system of firms, such as the U.S. private equity system, may be said to have integrity when it is whole, complete, and stable in its operations. As such, in Jensen's argument, nothing is hidden, there is no deception, no untruths, no violation of contract or property rights, and essentially no fraud in the market. As integrity declines, the workability of the system declines, and as workability declines, the likelihood of achieving long-run value maximization declines.

Jensen points to financial aspects of the firm as areas that are vulnerable to fraud. Specific among these is the implicit definition of the fiduciary duty of managers to only the current shareholders rather than to current and future debt holders and future shareholders as well. This leads to practices such as selling currently overvalued shares and paying out the proceeds to current shareholders, or acquiring a firm with overvalued shares, imposing the consequences on future shareholders.

Jensen specifies other financial reporting practices representative of those that destroy integrity and reduce the likelihood of achieving long-term value growth[3].

- Budget and target-based compensation plans that pay executives according to how closely they come to meeting their targets

- Managers choosing to treat the firm's relations with the capital markets "as a game" in which reporting is a strategy for managing and meeting analyst expectations
- Income smoothing, managing earnings, and manipulating analysts
- Making financial reporting choices that are strategic (i.e., made to manage to what "the Street" expects)
- Bankers misleading investors with fraudulent investment recommendations designed to serve client securities issuers

Each of these practices, and others like them, fits the definition of fraud, and all are targets of the fraud deterrence program that is the central theme of this chapter.

Corporate Governance Fundamentals within the U.S. Private Equity System: Pre–Sarbanes-Oxley

Commenting on the differences between the private equity organization and the public corporation, Jensen argued that at the time of his writing (1993), the private equity model had come to dominate the public company model with respect to the effectiveness of internal controls broadly construed.

> LBO associations and venture capital funds (i.e., private equity organizations) provide a blueprint for managers and boards who wish to revamp their top-level control systems to make them more efficient. They are, of course, the preeminent examples of active investors in recent U.S. history and they serve as excellent models that can be emulated in part or in total by virtually any corporation. The two have similar governance structures and have been successful in resolving the governance problems of both slow growth or declining firms (LBO associations) and high growth entrepreneurial firms (venture capital funds).[4]

Jensen ascribes these virtuous characteristics to the private equity organization[5]:

> Both . . . tend to be organized as limited partnerships. In effect, the institutions which contribute the funds to these organizations are delegating the task of being active investors to the general partners of the organizations. Both governance systems are characterized by:
>
> a. limited partnership agreements at the top level that prohibit headquarters from cross-subsidizing one division with cash from another;
> b. high equity ownership on the part of managers and board membership;
> c. board members (who are mostly PE firm members) who in their funds directly represent a large fraction of the equity owners of each portfolio company;
> d. small boards of directors (of the operating companies) typically consisting of no more than 8 people;
> e. CEOs who are typically the only insider on the board;
> f. CEOs who are seldom the chair of the board.

Along with Jensen's points, several other characteristics provide the private equity system with a governance edge over the public company system. Because of the compensation scheme in the private equity system, there is little free cash flow that is not committed by contract to specific stakeholders. Unlike the public company model, where dividends, stock repurchase programs, R&D expenditures, and other capital expenditures are made largely at the discretion of insiders, there is little choice over the disposition of cash flow in the contract-governed private equity system.

The limited life of the LP partnership establishes a cap on the duration of total risk exposure in the private equity system. Furthermore, virtually all intermediaries are now "commitment funds," in which committed capital is released upon formal capital calls. While public corporations can accumulate corporate slack and can move it around among projects with minimal discipline, the private equity system imposes discipline that reduces the amount of cash that is subject to insider discretion and potential fraud.

Perhaps the major comparative strength of the private equity system is the consistency of operating and financial reporting up the chain from portfolio company to intermediary to investor and the auditing and monitoring implicit in it.

Emerging Model of Corporate Governance within the U.S. Private Equity System: A Transition from the "Barefoot Days" to "SOX"

The standards outlined within the Sarbanes Oxley Act of 2002 (SOX) apply to financial reporting and internal controls in public corporations, and are comparable to those required under the Foreign Corrupt Practices Act of 1977 (amended in 1988 and 1998).

The Foreign Corrupt Practices Act was enacted principally to prevent corporate bribery of foreign officials. This act had three major parts:

1. It required the keeping by corporations of accurate books, records, and accounts.
2. It required issuers registered with the Securities and Exchange Commission (SEC) to maintain a responsible internal accounting control system.
3. It prohibited bribery by American corporations of foreign officials.

If we compare the characteristics claimed by Jensen to the summary objectives and requirements of SOX, we find a significant overlap. In an important sense, SOX seems to be an attempt to apply to regulated public companies those governance characteristics and attributes that seem to have formed spontaneously and without regulatory fiat in private equity organizations. This phenomenon begs the question of whether private equity system components should be required to comply with SOX, or if such a requirement would be redundant.

The governance standards just cited have existed to varying degrees of quality and completeness in the U.S. private equity system over the past five decades, while in many instances being honored in the breach. The Sarbanes-Oxley Act of 2002, and its application by the SEC, has brought standardization and consistency to corporate governance throughout the world of companies with publicly traded securities.

The U.S. private equity system in the pre-SOX—or to use a natural pun, the "barefoot" days—has been largely unregulated and, while subject to performance volatility over time, has made substantial contributions to the U.S. and global economies by executing an effective approach to funding the commercialization of innovative products and services. Given these contributions, the cry for regulation or system transparency has been muted until recently.

As the system has grown rapidly and become a larger part of the mainstream global financial system, the pressure for increased regulation, transparency, and standards of governance has increased. Corporate governance throughout the system has now become the watchword, and the provisions of SOX are becoming the de facto standard. While system members have resisted this development with claims that existing governance methods are more than adequate and that the benefits of SOX have not been shown to justify the cost, this resistance seems doomed to fail.

SOX has fast become the standard of governance among public corporations and not-for-profit institutions, including the institutions that are LP investors in PE firms. This, in turn, exerts SOX compliance pressure downward on PE firms to adopt governance measures consistent with those adopted by their LP investors. PE firms then impose governance rules on their portfolio companies, with the result that the new standard of governance is becoming applied in a consistent manner throughout the system. At least two factors are spontaneously accelerating this development:

1. The necessity that firms be SOX compliant at "harvest" and,
2. The impact of networking.

The first requirement speaks to the necessity that firms going public must comply on the date at which they file their S-1 with the SEC for an offering in the United States.

At the same time, a firm choosing to sell to another PE firm or to a strategic corporate investor must either be compliant or suffer an acquisition price discounted at least by the present value of the estimated cost SOX compliance.

In addition, PE buyout firms often use publicly issued debt in their transactions and are thereby required to be compliant. Because banks and other private lenders have standardized electronic reporting, SOX will become the standard of due diligence for them as well as for equity investors.

The only remedies for entities seeking to avoid the most immediate harvesting effects of SOX are to do an IPO outside the U.S. (e.g., England) or by sale of assets rather than sale of shares. These alternatives have their own implications and probably will not deter the widespread implications of SOX.

The second factor in this acceleration is the impact of networking at all levels of the system. Limited partners participate in private equity syndicates, and their investment interests in specific PE firms overlap. Increasingly, these investors exchange information both informally, through gatekeepers and in some cases as required by the Freedom of Information Act. PE firms also participate in syndicates and share information on processes and individual investments. Because syndicate members share the "SOX risk" when a portfolio company is harvested by IPO or M&A, any firm that wants to be a member of syndicates will need to conform to common standards. Clearly, this downward pressure is being felt by portfolio companies; the cost of compliance will be taken out of cash invested by PE firms and paid for in equity of the investee firm.

This rapid adoption of SOX as the standard of corporate governance may be viewed as a form of regulatory contagion and a dramatic ratchet in the strength of governance compliance in a heretofore lightly regulated part of the financial system. The strength and inevitability of this is reflected in the SEC's announcement that Section 404 governing internal control systems will ultimately apply to public firms of all sizes.

Whether SOX is ever applied directly to private companies or not, its indirect effect is sufficient to raise the standards of corporate governance within private companies and therefore within the U.S. private equity system. System participants may well believe that, along with specific values that SOX compliance brings, the pain and cost of such compliance may be worthwhile if it serves as a regulatory substitute for the SEC registration now required of hedge funds.

ADOPTION OF INTERNAL CONTROL SYSTEMS WITHIN THE U.S. PRIVATE EQUITY SYSTEM

The central technical requirement in the fraud deterrence system is the provision of an appropriate set of internal control mechanisms. In 1992, the Committee of Sponsoring Organizations of the Treadway Commission (COSO) prepared and made publicly available *Internal Control —Integrated Framework* as an aid for businesses and other entities in assessing and enhancing their internal control systems.

Sarbanes-Oxley's Section 404 now famously requires management to annually assess and report on the effectiveness of internal control over financial reporting. This independently audited report will be a regular and equally important part of financial reporting. Despite reaction from organizations representing the private equity community and small businesses, the SEC's position is that ultimately there will be no exemptions from this requirement. The private equity system and the operating companies in its portfolios must accommodate this requirement and find cost effective ways to comply.

Accordingly, the COSO framework has been modified to meet the 404 requirements and to provide consistency on an industry-neutral basis. Businesses and other entities are now turning to the framework as a standard of compliance, and this alternative is available to the private equity system and its components.

Fraud in Finance: The Context of This Analysis

A good place to start this discussion is with the opinion of Justice McKenna of the United States Supreme Court, in 1917. Justice McKenna wrote the Court's opinion in *Hall v. Geiger-Jones Co.,* encompassing three cases, all dealing with the constitutionality of state securities regulations. These regulations were generally referred to as the "blue sky" laws. Justice McKenna wrote:

> The name that is given to the law (i.e. "Blue Sky") indicates the evil at which it is aimed, that is, to use the language of a cited case, "speculative schemes which have no more basis than so many feet of 'blue sky'"; or, as stated by counsel in another case, "to stop the sale of stock in fly-by-night concerns, visionary oil wells, distant gold mines and other like fraudulent exploitations." Even if the descriptions be regarded as rhetorical, the existence of evil is indicated, and a belief of its detriment; and we shall not pause to do more than state that the prevention of deception is within the competency of government and that the appreciation of the consequences of it is not open for our review.[6]

Judge McKenna never disclosed the name of the "cited case," so we do not know the case in which the "blue sky" phrase was first used. However, the *Hall v. Geiger-Jones Co.* cases have become known as the blue sky cases, with Justice McKenna being known as the author of the phrase.

The constitutionality of state securities law was upheld in these cases,with many states thereafter adopting such laws. As such, securities law in the United States was exclusively a state-level matter until the stock market crash of 1929: No federal laws had yet been passed on the subject. In the aftermath of the crash, a stream of federal legislation was passed (the Bank Act of 1933, the Securities and Exchange Acts of 1934 and 1935, the Public Utility Holding Company Act of 1936, and the Investment Company Act of 1940) that added a strong federal dimension to securities law. In a sense, all of this legislation was aimed at the core issue captured in Judge McKenna's "blue sky" statement. Given the spate of recent federal law (the Foreign Corrupt Practices Act revision of 1996, the Sarbanes-Oxley Act of 2002), it appears as if many of the core issues first addressed by Judge McKenna remain with us today, continuing to defy complete solution.

The solution offered by the blue sky laws in many states was to empower the state securities commissioner to pass judgment on the merit of an investment proposal under review, based on which the investment would be permitted or barred from sale in the state. While this regulatory filter and accompanying sanctions doubtless scared off some fraudulent schemes, it caused its own problems of political bias, government corruption, and the preemption from state citizens of the right to buy shares in companies not favored by the commissioner—those largely in the "new economy" of the day. These laws still exist with varying degrees of severity (in some cases, "regulations in fee only") and must be adhered to in, for example, marketing initial public offerings in the particular state.

The "merit" aspect of these laws has been eliminated for the most part. Under the system in Michigan, for example, neither Apple Computer nor Genentech were found to have "merit," presumably "protecting" Michigan citizens from the capital gains taxes they would have paid had they been able to buy in at the IPO price of either company.

Fraud Deterrence in the Portfolio Company

Despite the long history of securities regulations in the United States, the business of private equity investment and finance is still especially susceptible to fraud. However, this particular type of finance is too important to prohibit or proscribe solely on the basis that fraud may be committed. The economic stakes are very high as the investment contracts largely involve "real options"—a financial term for the value assigned to the ability of an investor to "buy into" a subsequent round of financing, the value of which can only be estimated in a current context. Moreover, transparency is limited at all levels. The "privacy" in private equity is important and valuable for strategic competitive reasons, especially in the formative developmental stages of the firm and its projects.

We begin this analysis of the fraud deterrence in private equity with an analysis of the portfolio company because it is the fundamental seat of value in the PE system and because valuation is the most significant locus of fraud vulnerability. Because of their differences, we discuss separately the early-stage venture capital-backed company and the company acquired by a private equity buyout fund.

Valuation is a daunting task for the portfolio company in a private equity investment, even in the absence of intent to defraud. A typical private equity early-stage financing deal may have some of these (simplified) characteristics:

The entrepreneur has a technology-based project, the present value of which she claims to be quite high. To fund the project, she must convince one or more investors of this value. The higher and more certain the value the investors perceive, the more likely the receipt of the capital and the lower the cost of that capital (i.e., the higher equity stake the entrepreneur will retain). The investors have the opposite incentive: Believing in the high and relatively certain value, they make out better if they can convince the entrepreneur that the value is low and relatively uncertain. Ultimately, the haggle is about price, and each side has powerful incentives to maximize its position.

Since the future is murky, both sides concentrate on evaluating "assets in place." The spirit of the laws of "fraudulent conveyance" must apply here: No one would buy a pig in a poke without first checking into the intimate details of the deal. In essence, the value of this particular "pig," or the potential venture capital (VC) investment, is paramount. This value is what VC investors call the "premoney value" at which the new capital will be invested.

Let us suppose that our entrepreneur can convince the VC investor that her investment is currently worth $5 million. However, in order to take her idea to the next level, she requires an infusion of $5 million from a VC investor. If both parties mutually agree on the terms, then the entrepreneur will end up with a 50 percent equity stake in the company.

This example showcases the classical conflict, mentioned earlier, that is inherent in any VC deal. The entrepreneur would surely like to convince the VC that her investment is currently worth more than $5 million. If she only requires an additional $5 in capital, the entrepreneur is left with a larger piece of the corporate equity. However, the VC wishes to convince the entrepreneur that the premoney value is significantly lower than $5 million in order to obtain a larger equity stake in the business.

The VC investor's due diligence investigation is critically important in certifying the entrepreneur's ownership claims to the assets needed to support the desired premoney value. Postinvestment, continued diligence is required through monitoring all aspects of the firm's operations, especially as later rounds of funding are needed and particularly when new investors are brought into the deal.

This monitoring is provided, in part, by the phenomenon of staged capital that is employed by venture capitalists to encourage the entrepreneur to reach set goals in order to obtain future funding. It is also provided by the provisions set forth in the term sheet an entrepreneur signs that binds him or her to contractual obligations.

It is important to note that no valuation methodology can take the place of thorough due diligence investigation and provide complete confidence about truth in valuation. Both inputs to and outputs from discounted cash flow analyses or sophisticated real options models are estimates subject to optimism, pessimism, and outright fraud.

In certain types of buyout deals, the assets in place may be the only assets involved, and more objective appraisal methods may give results acceptable to all parties. Transactions involving companies with long operating histories typically may have greater transparency of data and bring less significant problems of asymmetric information. In the current environment, SOX regulations on internal controls probably have improved the accuracy of such valuations.

As shown in the recent case of *ABRY v. Providence Equity,* allegations of fraud involving valuation do occur in private equity.[7] In this case, ABRY claimed that Providence Equity fraudulently understated its earnings before interest, taxes, and depreciation and amortization (EBITDA) in a transaction involving an agreed-on valuation price multiple of 10 times EBITDA. The assertion is that the overestimation inflated the purchase price by a significant amount, suggesting that fraud went undetected by audits and the buyer's due diligence investigation.

It is not uncommon to see lawsuits brought between PE transactors under the doctrine of fraudulent conveyance. This type of suit charges that the seller conveyed less value in a transaction than he had "represented and warranted." It is often triggered by the failure of a purchased company to earn sufficient cash flow to cover the interest and principal on the purchase money used in the acquisition.

Hidden defects in assets or contracts, undisclosed agreements, forgery, and identity theft are potential areas of fraud in buyout transactions.

Since private equity funds (venture capital or buyout funds) typically harvest their investments by means of the sale of a company to another fund or to a strategic corporate buyer, or the sale of shares in an IPO, this type of fraudulent conveyance of value is a constant possibility in the private equity business.

Fraud Deterrence in the Private Equity Fund

Once the initial investment has been made at a value accepted by entrepreneur and GP, that valuation must be reported to the limited partners. Because the GP has assumed certain governance powers in the investee firm through ownership rights and board of director participation, he or she now has joint responsibility with the entrepreneur for the conduct, success, and reporting of value of the company to the LP. In this respect, the agency role is changed in an important way.

With the passage of time and the execution of business, the firm's value may increase, decrease, or stay unchanged. Both the company and the GP are dependent on success for future capital draws: the company from the GP and the GP from the LP. Success is expected to be accurately reflected in the periodic financial reports of the firm. Those reports are approved by management and the board (including the VC) and sent to the LP. Since PE portfolio companies are privately held, there is no public market pricing mechanism. Thus the LP is dependent on the GP's estimate of the value of the company.

U.S. generally accepted accounting principles (GAAP) require the GP to estimate the value of a PE company at its "fair market value"—the value at which two willing buyers would transact an exchange for the company in the absence of any need to buy or sell on either part. Unfortunately, this is unobservable, except in the case of an actual cash purchase of shares: It is by necessity an estimate, albeit one that can be transparently backed up by assumptions and understandings stated and recorded in footnotes to the financial statements.

On a continuing basis, due diligence investigation and oversight is required (by the GP of the company management, of the GP and management by the LP) through monitoring all aspects of the firm's operations, especially as later rounds of funding are needed and particularly when new investors are brought into the deal. While accounting transparency and clean audits are important, determined fraud perpetrators throughout history have successfully dodged fraud detection mechanisms.

The PE fund faces litigation for a variety of other aspects of the relationship with the portfolio company. Funds and partners have faced suits brought by portfolio companies for failing to provide promised financing, for passing on confidential information to another of their portfolio companies, or for assisting with the unlawful firing of a portfolio company executive. The fund must maintain formal procedures and meticulous records on how it deals at all times and in all matters with its portfolio companies and its employees.

The fund is a potential "deep pocket" when litigation is brought against a portfolio company by a third party. The fund managers must be trained and alert to handle fiduciary duty conflicts, bankruptcy-related conflicts, and employment-related statutory requirements.

Given the implications of SOX for public companies, the fund faces responsibilities for its going-public companies to be SOX compliant at the time of the filing of the S-1 with the Securities and Exchange Commission. These exposures to regulation and class-action lawsuits will increase should the fund maintain a board seat after the firm is a public company.

As an advisor to the portfolio company and as the agent of the investors, the general partners of the PE fund are exposed to fraud vulnerability from both sides. This vulnerability derives from the GP's fiduciary obligation and duty of care and loyalty in either direction, and because there is so much money involved in a situation where moral hazard abounds.

Fund managers must ensure that they are complying fully with the terms of their investment agreements—both with the LP and the portfolio company—and establishing a clear record of how they are fulfilling their fiduciary duties by diligently managing the fund's assets on behalf of the investors.

The fund also faces fraud allegations from its own partners and employees. The employment agreement and split of the management fee and the carried interest among partners can become contentious over issues of "who's doing the work" versus"who's getting the lion's share of the fee and carry." This can be related to generational change in the relatively small fund management company. Sound employment policies, practices, and legal services are essential to minimize and deter opportunities for fraud.

Fraud Deterrence at the Limited Partner Level

The limited partner faces pressures similar to and derived from those faced by the general partner and the portfolio firm.

LP performance is measured net of management fee and GP carried interest. Because the return levels of top-quartile GP performers are significantly higher than that of other GPs, there is intense competition among LPs to be invested with a top-tier GP. Top-tier GPs therefore have a strong bargaining position, and the LP may cave in to demands for lenient due diligence, easier investment terms, or even higher fees or carried interest if the LP is overly eager to invest in the fund. This could represent fraud on the LP's sponsor (i.e., the ultimate provider of the capital to the LP).

The wealth-creating (or, alternatively, the trouble-creating) performance of the portfolio companies assembled, managed, and monitored by the general partner (the hired and highly paid agent of the LP) is the main driver in the system. If good results are not forthcoming, the LP may sue the GP for cause. An example is the case brought by the State of Connecticut against Forstmann Little, alleging "style drift," in that Forstmann made "venture capital" investments in technology-based telecom companies despite an investment agreement that specified that the fund focus on buyouts.[8] The state won this case but was awarded no damages, largely because the judge ruled that the state had known about the investment and had not complained during the time when the investments were doing well. As with many other suits, it is sometimes difficult to tell the side on which the fraud exists.

CONCLUSIONS AND RECOMMENDATIONS

The U.S. private equity system plays a critically important role in the U.S. and global economic and financial system. Using unique methods and organizational characteristics, it provides an effective and fast-growing institutional conduit for the funding of venture capital and buyout transactions, while supplying a continuing stimulus for the creation of jobs, income, and wealth in the United States.

Institutional private equity has grown over the past five decades on the edge of the U.S. financial markets, soundly based in contract law but largely free of direct regulation and the requirement to report publicly on its activity. The investment agreements, reliance on reputation capital, and privacy of operations both bind and represent a valuable asset of the system, protecting transactions and the entities involved in them during their formative development phases.

The formalization of corporate governance requirements and the standardization of approach under Sarbanes-Oxley, ostensibly intended only for companies with publicly traded securities, now affects the private equity system and other parts of the financial markets at least indirectly. While the costs of compliance are seen as being impedingly high, the benefits of the act are not yet obvious, and praise for this regulatory innovation has been muted among those affected by it.

We have illustrated the nature and structural relationships that characterize the U.S. private equity system and have shown how the opaque nature of the system has contributed to certain vulnerabilities to fraudulent activity.

On the basis of our analysis, we conclude that the private equity system will benefit from formalizing and strengthening its fraud deterrence system and from the reporting requirements of Sarbanes-Oxley. The costs of improved internal controls at all levels of the system are being recognized as the price of reduction of operating risk and uncertainty and are being absorbed and offset by improved integrity in the system.

We recommend that the Congress and the Securities and Exchange Commission work positively with the legal and accounting professions to bring cost-effective transparency and quality of financial reporting to the U.S. private equity system. The goal is to strengthen the integrity of the system and its reporting mechanisms without impeding its ability to employ the privacy that enables it to allocate, monitor, and harvest the results of risk capital in this country and the world.

NOTES

1. Russell Survey, "Investing in Alternatives to Surge Worldwide" (2005). Available at:)www.russell-.com/WW/Press_Releases/PR20050912_ww_p.asp.
2. M. Jensen, (2006). "Putting Integrity into Finance Theory and Practice: A Positive Approach," Harvard NOM Working Paper 06-06, 2006.
3. Id.
4. M. Jensen, "The Modern Industrial Revolution, Exit, and the Failure of Internal Control Systems," *Journal of Finance* 48, no. 3 1993): 831–880.
5. Id.
6. *Hall v. Geiger-Jones Company,* 242 U.S. 539, 1917.
7. "Ruling in ABRY v. Providence Equity Partners Case Has Lessons for Buyers and Sellers." Available at: http://www.goodwinprocter.com/getfile.aspx?filepath=/Files/Publications/PE_ABRYProvidence_3_14_06.pdf.
8. "The Aftermath of Connecticut v. Forstmann Little: Lessons from Connecticut State Court." Available at: http://www.altassets.net/casefor/countries/2004/nz5362.php.

Glossary of Terms

Actual fraud With regard to bankruptcy proceedings, fraud occurs if the transferor acts with the intent to hinder, defraud, or delay creditors.

AICPA American Institute of Certified Public Accountants. This organization governs the practice of public accountancy except for standards related to the audit of public companies, which are defined by the Public Company Accounting Oversight Board (PCAOB). www.aicpa.org.

API Application programming interface.

ATF Bureau of Alcohol, Tobacco, Firearms and Explosives (also called BATF).

Balanced scorecard Measures a company's activities and progress by looking at four business perspectives: financial, customer, business process, and learning and growth.

Bankruptcy Abuse Act The Bankruptcy Abuse Prevention and Consumer Protection Act of 2005. This act enhanced the Bankruptcy Code by adding provisions that changed how claims of fraud are treated in bankruptcy and expanded liability for fraud in bankruptcy filing.

Bankruptcy Code The United States Bankruptcy Code. This law contains numerous provisions governing bankruptcy proceedings.

Benford's Law Logarithmic theory that states that in a random population of data, the leading digit '1' occurs with a frequency of about 30 percent, and it also states that the frequency declines as the leading digit of a number increases.

Blackout periods Time period in which the abilities of participants in a pension plan to carry out certain actions are temporarily reduced.

BS7799 British Standards 7799. They are the most widely recognized systems security standard in the world.

CFAA Computer Fraud and Abuse Act. This act allows the Secret Service to investigate alleged computer crimes.

Chapter 7 bankruptcy Involves the complete liquidation of the debtor's property with the proceeds used to pay creditors.

Chapter 11 bankruptcy Typically used for business bankruptcy and reorganization, it allows businesses to restructure themselves and continue to operate under the supervision of the bankruptcy court and their appointees.

Chapter 13 bankruptcy Bankruptcy in the form of reorganization for either business or individuals who work out a repayment plan with their creditors to pay off their debts.

CIA Certified Internal Auditor. A professional designation for the practice of internal auditing offered by the Institute of Internal Auditors.

Clayton Antitrust Act Passed in 1914, this act added restraints of trade to those specified in the Sherman Antitrust Act (1890) to limit monopolizing.

COBIT Control Objectives for Information and related Technology. The COBIT model for information technology control is published by the Information Systems Audit and Control Association (ISACA).

Constructive fraud Transferor engages in a transaction, or series of transactions, resulting in a transfer of some or all of transferor's assets in exchange for something worth less than its equivalent value or without receiving fair consideration.

Control environment The foundation of the internal control structure in an organization, including management's tone at the top. It is one of the five elements of the COSO model of control.

Control procedures Written policies and procedures that guide employees through the conduct of their daily tasks. It is one of the five elements of the COSO model of internal control.

Copyright The exclusive right of the creator of a literary or artistic work to publish, use, or transfer to another. As soon as a work is created in a tangible form, it automatically receives federal copyright protection. For any work created after 1978 to date, the protection period is for the life of the creator, plus 50 years, after which the work transfers to the public domain.

COSO Committee of Sponsoring Organizations of the Treadway Commission. An independent initiative formed in 1985 that focuses on causal factors of fraud and fraudulent financial reporting through recommendations on internal controls to enhance a business; www.coso.org.

CPA Certified Public Accountant. An accounting professional licensed by his or her respective state administrative board.

Custodian Under 11 U.S.C. Section 101, the term "custodian" means:

(A) receiver or trustee of any of the property of the debtor, appointed in a case or proceeding not under this title;

(B) assignee under a general assignment for the benefit of the debtor's creditors; or

(C) trustee, receiver, or agent under applicable law, or under a contract, that is appointed or authorized to take charge of property of the debtor for the purpose of enforcing a lien against such property, or for the purpose of general administration of such property for the benefit of the debtor's creditors;

D&O insurance Director's and officer's liability insurance. It offers protection to directors and officers from personal losses ensuing from their service to the company.

Discharge Occurs when a debtor who files for bankruptcy has all debts erased prior to filing date. Note that discharge is possible only for debtors who are individuals and have not engaged in any sort of a fraudulent scheme.

Document Any material that carries a communication: explicit or implied.

DOL United States Department of Labor.

Dutch auction	Auctions that are carried out by third parties during business dissolution, either between constituents or involving nonconstituents with limitations of constituent participation in the purchase.
Enterprise dashboard	A group of brief electronic reports that give the current status of business controls and metrics to management officials.
E-R diagrams	Entity relationship diagrams. A data modeling tool that organizes data into units and defines the relationships between the units.
ERISA	Employee Retirement Income Security Act of 1974. A federal law that sets minimum standards for most voluntarily established pension and health plans in private industry to provide investment protection for individuals in these plans.
ERM	Enterprise risk management. The analysis of all risks facing an organization, including financial, operational, and strategic risks.
ERP modules	Enterprise resource planning. An integrated information technology system that includes all basic business processes in a series of related databases.
Experian	One of the three major credit rating agencies.
FACTA	Fair and Credit Transaction Act. It is intended to force companies to dispose of confidential consumer and business information in electronic or printed form, primarily to help consumers fight the growing crime of identity theft. Accuracy, privacy, limits on information sharing, and new consumer rights to disclosure are included in FACTA.
FBI	Federal Bureau of Investigation. The chief investigative unit of the Department of Justice.
FCPA	Foreign Corrupt Practices Act. This act was passed in 1977 to attempt to put an end to bribery of foreign officials.
FCRA	Fair Credit Reporting Act. The act is intended to improve accuracy and fairness of credit reporting. Consumer reporting agencies are required to adopt reasonable procedures for meeting the needs of commerce for consumer credit, personnel, insurance, and other information in a manner that is fair and equitable to the consumer, with regard to the confidentiality, accuracy, relevancy, and proper utilization of such information. The FCRA was passed in 1970, but has been heavily amended and augmented by new laws reflecting computerized transactions.
FDA	Food and Drug Administration. This federal agency is responsible for the regulation of food, drugs, medical devices, biologics, animal feed and drugs, cosmetics, radiation-emitting products, and combination products.
FDICIA	Federal Deposit Insurance Corporation Improvement Act. This act was enacted in 1991 to make companies maintain sufficient internal controls following the COSO model.
Fraud deterrence	The proactive identification and removal of the causal and enabling factors of fraud.
Fraud triangle	Describes the three factors present in any fraud situation: motive, rationalization, and opportunity.

FRCP Federal Rules of Civil Procedure. These rules govern conduct in the federal court system.

FRE Federal Rules of Evidence. These rules govern the presentation of evidence in the federal court system. Many states have adopted FRE.

FTC Federal Trade Commission. The FTC was created in 1914; its purpose was to prevent unfair methods of competition in commerce as part of the battle to "bust the trusts." Over the years, Congress passed additional laws giving the agency greater authority to police anticompetitive practices. In 1938 Congress passed the Wheeler-Lea Amendment, which included a broad prohibition against "unfair and deceptive acts or practices." Since then the commission also has been directed to administer a wide variety of other consumer protection laws, including the Telemarketing Sales Rule, the Pay-Per-Call Rule, and the Equal Credit Opportunity Act. In 1975 Congress passed the Magnuson-Moss Act, which gave the FTC the authority to adopt trade regulation rules that define unfair or deceptive acts in particular industries.

GAAP Generally accepted accounting principles. These principles are defined for United States companies by the Financial Accounting Standards Board (FASB).

GAO Government Accountability Office. This independent, nonpartisan agency works for Congress. GAO is often called the congressional watchdog because it investigates how the federal government spends taxpayer dollars.

GLB Act The Financial Modernization Act of 1999, also known as the "Gramm-Leach-Bliley Act" or GLB Act. It includes provisions to protect consumers' personal financial information held by financial institutions. There are three principal parts to the privacy requirements: the Financial Privacy Rule, Safeguards Rule, and pretexting provisions.

GUI Graphical user interface. Interaction with a computer through the use of graphics and icons and a pointing device in addition to the keyboard.

GTAG Global Technology Audit Guides. These guides, introduced by the Institute of Internal Auditors (IIA), describe risks and needs related to the information technology control structure.

Hierarchy of needs An idea proposed by Abraham Maslow in which the needs a human attempts to satisfy in his or her life are demonstrated by a pyramid consisting of five layers: psychological, safety, love/being, esteem, and actualization.

HIPAA Health Insurance Portability and Accountability Act. This act, passed in 1996, is intended to improve portability and continuity of health insurance coverage in the group and individual markets; to combat waste, fraud, and abuse in health insurance and healthcare delivery; to promote the use of medical savings accounts; to improve access to long-term care services and coverage; to simplify the administration of health insurance; and for other purposes.

Homestead exemption One type of asset exemption that permits a debtor to safeguard from creditors the equity interest in a residence.

ICANN Internet Corporation for Assigned Names and Numbers. This internationally organized, nonprofit corporation has responsibility for Internet Protocol (IP) address space allocation, protocol identifier assignment, generic (gTLD) and country code (ccTLD) Top-Level Domain name system management, and root server system management functions. These services were originally performed under U.S. Government contract by the Internet Assigned Numbers Authority (IANA) and other entities. ICANN now performs the IANA function.

Identity theft Fraud committed using the identifying information of another person.

IDS Intrusion detection systems. These systems monitor the activity of one or more network resources for abnormal activity.

IIA Institute of Internal Auditors. This association is responsible for defining professional standards for the practice of internal auditing, risk assessment, and governance. www.theiia.org.

Incident response Improvement to intrusion detection systems. This newer technology is an automatic change of network behavior based on elevated threat levels.

Information and communication Describes the flow of information within an organization. First, information is provided to business units to adequately perform work functions; second, feedback information is provided to management. One of the five elements of the COSO model of internal control.

Intellectual property Term created by the legal profession meaning property that is intangible; it most likely cannot be felt, touched, or handled, although it is possible. Some categories are trademarks, patents, and trade secrets.

Internal Control—Integrated Framework One of the five major reports published by COSO since the mid-1980s; it is the COSO model of internal control and considered the gold standard of control for organizations.

Interrogation A search for the truth to obtain admissions or confession from the suspect that independently confirms the investigative findings. Interrogations may be both accusatory and confrontational.

Interview Nonaccusatory gathering or behavior- provoking conversation to determine facts, sequence of events, or alibis, or confirm information with a victim, witness, or suspect.

IP Internet protocol is used for communicating data across the internet. Devices are assigned an address; this address is used to route data packets to the appropriate device.

IPS Intrusion prevention systems. These systems shut down threads or ports after an intrusion detection system detects abnormal behavior.

ISACA Information Systems Audit and Control Association; www.isaca.org.

ISO International Organization for Standardization. This a global network: identifies what international standards are required by business, government, and society; develops them in partnership with the sectors that will put them to use; adopts them by transparent procedures based on national input; and delivers them to be implemented worldwide.

ISSEA International Systems Security Engineering Association; www.issea.org.

LBO Leveraged buyout. A transaction where a group or entity gains control of a target company's equity using debt or borrowed money.

Lanham Act Found in Title 15 of the U.S. Code. The act (also called the Trademark Act of 1946) contains the federal statutes governing trademark law in the United States. However, this act is not the exclusive law governing U.S. trademark law, since both common law and state statutes also control some aspects of trademark protection.

Lean Management tool that uses the standardization of processes to reach efficiency and organizational relevance.

Mansion loophole Scheme in which a debtor invests fraudulent earnings into an expensive residence and then files for bankruptcy protection. By doing so, the assets can be protected under the homestead exemption.

Master data Data that are normally used but not created or updated in the course of routine business transactions.

Mens Rea A guilty mind. For a perpetrator to be guilty of a criminal violation, this element must be present.

Monitoring Management efforts to positively establish the adequate performance of internal control procedures and assess organizational compliance. One of the five elements of the COSO model of internal control.

NAC Network Admission Control. This software verifies whether the required software is installed in a system and indicates that the software is running properly.

NACVA National Association of Certified Valuation Analysts; www.nacva.com.

Nasdaq National Association of Securities Dealers Automated Quotation. Nasdaq is the largest U.S. electronic stock market.

NAT Network address translation—a protocol that allows a single device to act as an agent between the Internet (or "public network") and a local (or "private") network. This means that only a single, unique IP address is required to represent an entire group of computers within the private network.

Normalization The process of organizing data to eliminate redundancy.

NYSE New York Stock Exchange.

Opt-out states States that prohibit debtors in bankruptcy from using federal exemptions.

OSHA Occupational Safety and Health Organization. This organization enforces safety and health regulations for most businesses and industries in the United States. It also is responsible for the evaluation of whistleblower protection claims.

Patent An invention that contains enough novelty to warrant the government to grant a monopoly to the inventor for 20 years.

PCAOB Public Company Accounting Oversight Board. This organization was created by the Sarbanes-Oxley Act of 2002, and is responsible for setting audit standards for public company audits.

Phishing Sending an e-mail claiming to represent a legitimate business to trick someone into revealing private information; this can also be called 'brand spoofing'. The bogus e-mail is referred to as a 'phish' or 'phish' e-mail. Phish is a variant on the word 'fish', i.e., the e-mail is a bait to attempt to retrieve information from a person. The 'ph' spelling derives from a long hacker tradition to change the letter 'f' to 'ph' to describe their deceptive actions.

Piercing the corporate veil To prove a corporation exists as a completely controlled front (alter ego) for an individual or group to allow the underlying persons to be held responsible for the actions of the corporation.

Ponzi scheme Also referred to as a pyramid scheme. In this investment scheme, investors are paid from funds of newly attracted investors who are promised lucrative returns.

Prima facie Latin for "at first look" or "on its face." The term describes a criminal prosecution or lawsuit in which the evidence before trial is sufficient to prove the case.

Private Equity (PE) Investment of capital by private individuals and companies.

Rapport Level of "comfort" an interviewer feels with a subject. If rapport is established, it can allow the interviewer to connect with the subject and obtain more accurate, in-depth information from the subject.

RFID Radio frequency Identification technologies. Such technologies are used by real-time location systems to show people and/or resources as they move throughout a facility.

Robinson-Patman Act An act passed by Congress in 1936 to supplement the Clayton Anti-Trust Act. The act prohibits charging a different price to different purchasers of the same commodity when the effect is to lessen competition or create a monopoly. The act was directly intended to protect the independent businesses from chain stores.

RTLS Real-time location system. This physical security system can triangulate people and/or resources in real time using 802.11 wireless technology or RFID.

Risk assessment An ongoing, proactive scan of the business environment to detect anything that could prevent the accomplishment of organizational objectives. One of the five elements of the COSO model of internal control.

Sarbanes-Oxley Act Momentous reform of corporate governance and reporting requirements for issuers of financial statements enacted in July 2002 due to numerous corporate scandals, such as Enron and WorldCom. It consists of many reforms and regulations to improve the corporate oversight process, including strengthening the role of the audit committee in corporate governance, management certification of financial results, and detailed reporting of internal controls for financial reporting.

SAS 99 Statement on Auditing Standards No. 99, published by the AICPA. This statement stresses that an auditor should consider distortion in the financial statements due to fraud in planning the financial statement audit.

SEC Securities and Exchange Commission. Congress passed the Securities Act of 1933 and the Securities Exchange Act of 1934 to restore investor confidence in capital markets by providing more structure and government oversight. Congress established this commission in 1934 to enforce the newly passed securities laws, to promote stability in the markets, and to protect investors.

Shelf life The amount of time deception must be maintained for a fraudulent scheme to be successful and leave the victim without an effective remedy.

Sherman Antitrust Act Passed in 1890 to prevent business practices leading to monopolies, e.g., horizontal price fixing, vertical price fixing, boycotts, and other anticompetitive schemes.

Spoofing Sending bogus messages with a falsified yet verifiable IP address indicating that the message is coming from a trusted host. Perpetrators looking to gain unauthorized access to computers send such messages.

SSE-CMM Tool Systems security engineering capability maturity model for making analysis of security needs for an entity. It is both a model and process.

TQM Total quality management. This management approach, which originated in Japan, centers on quality. Success is based on participation from all members of the company. The company's long-term success is recognized through customer satisfaction.

Trademark A distinctive design, picture, emblem, logo, or wording (or combination) affixed to goods for sale to identify the manufacturer as the source of the product. Words that just name the maker without particular wording or a generic product name are not trademarks.

Transactional data Data that are normally created or updated in the course of routine business transactions.

UFCA Uniform Fraudulent Conveyance Act. This act uses a "balance sheet test" for determining bankruptcy. It also introduced the idea of constructive fraud.

UFTA Uniform Fraudulent Transfer Act. This act was proposed in 1984 to enhance the UFCA by including new provisions that are incorporated in the Bankruptcy Code of 1978 and certain tenets of the Uniform Commercial Code.

Uniform Commercial Code A uniform act developed to harmonize the laws of sales and commercial transactions within the 50 states; it has been enacted by 49 states, with Louisiana as the sole holdout.

USDL U.S. Department of Labor. This department fosters and promotes the welfare of the job seekers, wage earners, and retirees of the United States.

Wicklander-Zulawski Non-confrontational Method Method of interrogation in which the interrogator does not put suspects in a position where they have to deny guilt.

Index

A

Access control, 186
Aiding and abetting fraudulent transfers, 313–315
Alpha (abnormal return), 10, 11
American Accounting Association, 119
American Institute of Certified Public Accountants (AICPA)
  accounting and review standards, 38
  Consulting Services Practice Aids, 254, 255
  Consulting Services Special Reports, 254
  and fraud triangle, 41
  as sponsor of Treadway Commission, 119
  Standard AT, reporting on internal control, 251, 252
  Statements on Auditing Standards (SAS), 30–37, 41, 45, 48–49, 171, 172
Anonymous reporting, 25, 27, 74, 123, 127, 262–264
Anti-Phishing Working Group (APWG), 377
Anti-X software, 184
Antitrust legislation, 19–21
Antivirus software, 184, 370, 371, 378
Arbitration, 71, 72, 393
Assets, misappropriation of, 48, 132, 261, 263
Association of Certified Fraud Examiners (ACFE), 39, 40
Assurance
  data analysis, 242, 243
  information systems. *See* Information systems
Attorneys
  ethics, 70, 73, 74
  and role of expert, 51, 52
  verification of debtor's sworn statement, 283
Audit committee
  accounting knowledge, 150
  communication, 150
  financial expert, 146, 147, 265
  independence, 144, 146, 150
  and internal audit function, 267
  internal auditor, role of, 154
  monitoring function, 137
  NASD Blue Ribbon Committee, 144, 145
  public companies, 146
  qualifications, 144
  responsibilities of, 149–152
  Sarbanes-Oxley requirements, 74, 123, 151, 152, 264, 265
  statutory and regulatory requirements, 149–152
  stock exchange listing standards, 147
Auditors
  certifications, 267
  communication, 37
  independence, 25, 26
  internal auditors, 153, 154, 267
  team discussions, 33, 49
Audits
  audit team discussions, 33, 49
  and data analysis, 242. *See also* Data analysis
  documentation, 31, 37
  evidence, evaluating, 36, 37
  external attest audits, purpose of, 49, 50
  and fraud deterrence, 47, 266, 267
  internal audit function, 139, 140, 147, 168–170, 266, 267
  internal control assessment, 49, 50

B

Background checks
  employees and job applicants, 79–84
  prospective business associates, 349, 350
Backups of data, 53, 54
Balanced Scorecard, 9–11, 223, 248
Bankruptcy
  Chapter 7 (liquidation), 270, 271, 275, 283, 286, 290, 301
  Chapter 11 (reorganization), 270, 271, 279, 287, 289–291, 302, 306, 307, 315
  Chapter 13 (repayment plan for individuals), 270, 271, 275, 283
  corporations, individual liability for fraud, 311–315
  deterrents to fraud, 283
  discharge of debts, 271
  Enron, 269, 270, 294, 315
  exempt property, 275–278, 331–333
  fraudulent transfers, 273, 275, 294–311, 315, 328–330
  homestead exemption, 277–283
  intent to defraud, 273–275, 280, 281, 285, 287, 288, 292, 294–301, 303
  means test, 283
  no discharge for fraud, 271–275, 311
  overview, 269, 270
  perpetrators of fraud, 270–275
  and spendthrift trusts, 278
Bankruptcy Abuse Prevention and Consumer Protection Act of 2005 (Bankruptcy Abuse Act), 269, 274–277, 281–283, 298, 299, 315
Bankruptcy Code, 269
  definitions, 334
  discharge, denial of, 271–274
  exemptions (11 U.S.C. § 522), 276, 277, 331–333
  fraudulent transfers and obligations (11 U.S.C. § 548), 328–330
Bankruptcy crimes, 283–294, 326, 327
Benchmarks, internal controls, 50
Better Business Bureau On-Line (BBB On-Line), 171
Bias, 52, 54, 55
Blue sky laws, 407, 408
Board of directors
  annual reviews, 149
  audit committee. *See* Audit committee
  and control environment, 123
  and deterrence of fraudulent financial reporting, 266
  fiduciary duties, breach of, 312, 313
  governance guidelines, establishing, 149

Board of directors *(Continued)*
indemnification, 154, 155
independence requirement, 147, 148
and monitoring process, 123
personal liability issues, 154, 311–315
qualifications of directors, 148, 149
statutory and regulatory requirements, 148, 149
Brainstorming, engagement team discussions, 33, 49
British Standards, 170, 173, 174
Budget, establishing, 52
Burden of proof, 51, 52, 71, 77–79, 312
Bureau of Alcohol, Tobacco, and Firearms (ATF), 17
Bush, George W., 269, 367
Business entities
advisers, selection of, 353
approval rights, 352–354
background checks, 349, 350
dissolution, 350, 351, 354, 355
factors affecting fraudulent conduct, 351
fiduciary duties, 351
financial statements, 354
formation of business and fraud opportunities, 351, 352
fraud, discovery of, 354
governance, 352, 353
organizational documents, 351–353
remedies, 354, 355
risk and reward analysis, 350
self-dealing, 353, 354
Business intelligence, 242–245
Business objectives and IT strategy, 173
Business processes
and control procedure objectives, 134, 135
and information systems, 164, 235–240
process improvement and fraud deterrence, 3–5, 11, 50
process walk-throughs, 138

C

Case development phase of investigation, 53, 54
Celler-Kefauver Anti-Merger Act, 19, 21
Cendrowski Corporate Advisors, LLC, 40, 52, 53
Centralized authentication systems, 182, 183
Certifications
internal auditors, 267
Sarbanes-Oxley requirements, 27, 123, 130, 143, 146, 147, 152, 153, 265
Certified Fraud Deterrence Analyst (CFD), 40
Certified Fraud Examiner (CFE), 39, 40, 42, 267
Certified Information Systems Auditor (CISA), 267
Certified Internal Auditor (CIA), 267
Certified Public Accountant (CPA), 267
Chain of custody, 54
Change management, 131, 132
Chief executive officers (CEOs), certifications under Sarbanes-Oxley, 27, 123, 143, 146, 147, 152, 153, 265
Chief financial officers (CFOs), certifications under Sarbanes-Oxley, 27, 123, 143, 146, 147, 152, 153, 265
Civil penalties
Fair Credit Reporting Act, 82
Sarbanes-Oxley, 28
SEC enforcement powers, 154
Class actions, whistleblower claims, 75, 76
Clayton Antitrust Act, 19, 20
Clean hands doctrine, 54
Clients, 48, 52, 54
COBIT, 126, 137, 172, 173
Code of ethics
components of, 262, 263
as part of corporate policy, 263
professional codes, 39, 40
SOX requirements, 146, 266
stock exchange listing standards, 147, 149
Code of Professional Ethics, Association of Certified Fraud Examiners, 39, 40
Code of Professional Standards, Association of Certified Fraud Examiners, 39, 40
Committee of Sponsoring Organizations of the Treadway Commission (COSO)
background, 119–122
boards of directors, responsibilities of, 149
control environment, 8, 121–126, 264
control procedures, 121, 131–136
enterprise risk management framework, 130, 131
information and communication, 121
Integrated Framework, 120–122
internal control activities, 266
internal control defined, 8
monitoring, 121, 123, 126, 137–140, 266, 267
and PCAOB Auditing Standard No. 2, 31
and private equity system, 407
reports of, 120
risk assessment. *See* Risk assessment
and SAS No. 78, 34
small public companies, 120
sponsoring organizations, 119
Web site, 120
Communication
accuracy, 126, 127
anonymous reporting, 25, 27, 74, 123, 127, 262–264
audit committee, 150
audit team, 33
auditors, 37, 154
and employees, 127, 128
expert witnesses, 54
and fraud deterrence, 128, 178–187
hotline, 262–264
openness of, 127, 128
as part of COSO framework for internal control, 121
security, 178–187
Communication Security Establishment (CSE), 174
Communications Assistance for Law Enforcement Act (CALEA), 18
Company Accounting Reform and Investor Protection Act of 2002. *See* Sarbanes-Oxley Act (SOX)
Compensation committee, 147
Compensation programs, 125, 263
Compliance programs, 124, 125
Computer crime, 18. *See also* Information systems
Computer Fraud and Abuse Act (CFAA), 18
Concealment
bankruptcy crimes. *See* Bankruptcy crimes
of fraud, 132
and routine audits, 48
Conflicts of interest, 48, 49
and control environment, 124, 125
and director independence, 147, 148, 150
whistleblower investigations, 72, 73
Consumer Credit Reporting Reform Act, 79
Consumer protection legislation, 21, 22, 79. *See also* Fair and Accurate Credit Transactions Act (FACTA); Fair Credit Reporting Act (FCRA)

Consumer reporting agencies, 80–82, 103, 104
Content addressable storage, 185
Content filters, 180, 181
Control environment, 8, 121–126, 264
  conflicts of interest. *See* Conflicts of interest
Control objectives, 172
Control Objectives for Information and Related Technology (COBIT), 126, 172, 173
Control procedures, 121, 131–136
Copyrights, 382, 384, 385, 387–392, 394
Corporate charter, 152
Corporate culture, 4, 14, 122, 123, 262–264
Corporate governance. *See* Governance
Corporate scandals, 69, 143–145, 149, 269, 270
Corporations
  bankruptcy. *See* Bankruptcy
  formation of. *See* Business entities
  piercing the corporate veil, 312
Correlation of log entries, 187
Corroboration, performance of procedures, 138
COSO. *See* Committee of Sponsoring Organizations of the Treadway Commission (COSO)
Credibility, expert witnesses, 59, 62
Credit and debit cards
  and discharge of debt in bankruptcy, 273, 274
  and identity theft, 368, 369
  Secret Service jurisdiction, 17, 362
Criminal liability
  bankruptcy crimes, 283, 284, 294
  burden of proof, 52
  copyright violations, 394
  Fair Credit Reporting Act, 82
  obstruction of justice, 294
  Sarbanes-Oxley, 28, 70
  SEC enforcement powers, 154

D

Damages
  and bankruptcy, 270, 271. *See also* Bankruptcy
  Fair Credit Reporting Act, 82
  intellectual property infringement, 389–391, 394, 395
  whistleblower cases, 72
Data analysis
  assessment, 246
  and business intelligence, 242–245
  data dictionary, 232, 233
  data request, sample, 240, 241
  and fraud detection, 224
  information systems, 235–241
  investigation phase, 53, 54
  master data, 225–227
  normalized data, 229–232
  overview, 221–223
  software comparison, 245
  systems, 224, 225
  table relationship diagrams, 233–235
  transactional data, 228, 229
Data management, 162, 163, 185, 375, 376. *See also* Information systems
Data mining, 242
Daubert v. Merrell Dow Pharmaceuticals, 55, 60, 61, 255
Depositions, 52, 53, 64, 65
Disaster planning, importance of, 50
Disclosure controls and procedures, 130, 153
Discovery
  and consulting experts, 64, 65
  depositions, 52, 53, 64, 65
  interrogatories, 52
Documents
  defined, 214
  destruction of, bankruptcy crime, 290, 291
  examination of, 214, 215
  forgery, 215, 216
  and fraud investigation reports, 256
  handling of, 217
  handwriting issues, 217–219
  red flags, 216, 217
  retention of, SOX requirements, 75
  testing, 214, 215
Domain names, 393
Duties, separation of, 132, 133

E

E-mail, 178, 179
Economic Espionage Act (EEA), 18
Electronic Communications Privacy Act (ECPA), 18
Electrostatic Detection Apparatus (ESDA), 214
Employee Retirement Insurance Security Act (ERISA), 74, 76, 278
  qualified plan exclusion from bankruptcy estate, 278
Employees
  anonymous reporting, 25, 27, 74, 123, 127, 262–264
  background checks, 79–84
  and compensation issues, 125
  control environment, 123, 124
  control procedures, 132–134
  data theft by, 375
  disclosure regarding consumer reports, 103, 104
  flowchart for obtaining consumer report on, 112, 113
  fraud, 33, 261
  job applicants, 79–82, 84, 103, 112
  and open communication, 127, 128
  qualifications of, 134
  and risk assessment, 123
  whistleblower protection. *See* Whistleblower protection
Energy Reorganization Act, 71
Enterprise-based information systems. *See* Information systems
Enterprise Dashboard (Executive Dashboard), 10, 223
Enterprise risk management (ERM), 130, 131
Equal Employment Opportunity Commission (EEOC), 86–98
Ethics
  attorneys, 70
  code of ethics. *See* Code of ethics
  conflicts of interest. *See* Conflicts of interest
  ethical environment and fraud deterrence, 262
  whistleblower compliance, 74, 75
Evidence
  destruction of, bankruptcy crimes, 290, 291
  Federal Rules of Evidence. *See* Federal Rules of Evidence (FRE)
  summaries of, 62, 63
Executive Dashboard, 10, 223
Expert testimony
  admissibility of, 58, 60–63, 255, 256
  credibility and trustworthiness, 62
  Daubert factors, 55, 60, 61, 255
  and fraud investigation reports, 255, 256
  functions of, 51, 52
  opinion, 57–65
  summaries of evidence, 62, 63
Expert witnesses
  credibility and trustworthiness, 62

Expert witnesses *(Continued)*
- depositions, 64, 65
- disclosure of, 64, 65
- fees, 65
- independent analysis and testing, 59, 60
- interrogatories, 64
- lay witness distinguished, 57, 58
- qualifications, 58–60
- reports required, 65
- testimony. *See* Expert testimony

Experts, consulting, 64, 65
External auditor, 265

F

Fair and Accurate Credit Transactions Act (FACTA), 358, 365, 366, 370, 375
Fair Credit Reporting Act (FCRA), 69, 370, 375
- adverse actions, 81–84, 111
- authorization form, 103, 104
- consumer reports, 80, 81, 83, 84, 105, 109, 112, 113
- and employee background checks, 79–84
- investigative consumer reports, 80, 81, 83, 105, 109
- job applicants, 79–82, 84, 103, 112
- medical information, 82
- pre-adverse action notice, sample, 110
- summary of rights under, 106–108
- types of reports covered, 80

Federal Bureau of Investigation (FBI), 18, 362, 363, 366
Federal Rules of Civil Procedure (FRCP), 57, 254
Federal Rules of Evidence (FRE), 57
- expert witness reports, 64
- fraud investigation reports, 255, 256
- Rule 702, expert witnesses, 59, 61
- Rule 1006, summaries, 62, 63

Federal Trade Commission Act, 19, 20
Federal Trade Commission (FTC), 19–22
- and consumer reporting agencies, 80
- and identity theft, 357, 360, 362, 363

Federal Wire Tap Act, 18
Fees
- expert witnesses, 65
- and first phase of investigation, 52

Fiduciary duties
- breach of in bankruptcy cases, 274, 275, 282, 291, 292, 312–314
- and private equity finance, 403

Financial Executives International (FEI), 119
Financial reporting, fraudulent, 7
- board of directors, 266
- control environment, 264
- deterrence of, 261, 262
- governance, 264
- hotlines, 25, 27, 74, 123, 127, 262–264
- internal audit function, 266, 267
- internal controls, 264, 266
- motives for, 45, 46, 48, 263
- and organizational goals and objectives, 261, 262

Financial reports, certification of, 27, 123, 130, 146, 147, 152, 153, 265, 267
Financial statements, disclosure requirements under Sarbanes-Oxley, 27, 28
Firewalls, 178, 370
Flowcharts, 249–251
Food, Drug, and Cosmetic Act, 19
Food and Drug Administration (FDA), 19
Food and Drugs Act, 19
Foreign Corrupt Practices Act, 22, 24, 405, 407
Forgery, 215–219
Fraud
- badges of, 295–297, 300
- and Bankruptcy Code, 270
- elements of, 51
- and piercing the corporate veil, 312
- prevention versus deterrence, 14
- types of, 33, 48

Fraud detection
- deterrence distinguished, 13
- and firewalls, 178

Fraud deterrence assessment, 4, 47
- investigation compared, 51
- need for, 49, 50
- and need for investigation, 50
- reasons for, 48–50

Fraud deterrence defined, 13, 14, 261
Fraud triangle, 7–9
- and control environment, 122
- and deterrence, 14, 41, 48
- elements of, 5, 41–45
- and external environment, 6
- and financial reporting fraud, 45, 46
- motive. *See* Motives for fraud
- opportunity, 41, 44–46
- and organizational goals and objectives, 263
- origin of, 41
- rationalization, 8, 14, 41, 43, 44

Fraudulent transfers
- actual fraud, 294
- aiding and abetting, 313–315
- bankruptcy law. *See* Bankruptcy
- constructive fraud, 294, 301–309
- federal law, 298, 299
- historical background, 295
- individual liability for corporations, 311–315
- intentional, 300, 301
- remedies, 309–311
- statutes, 294, 295
- Uniform Fraudulent Conveyance Act. *See* Uniform Fraudulent Conveyance Act (UFCA)
- Uniform Fraudulent Transfer Act. *See* Uniform Fraudulent Transfer Act (UFTA)

G

Geneen, Harold, 49
General Accounting Office (GAO), 359, 360, 362–364
Generally accepted accounting principles (GAAP), 33
Generally accepted audit standards (GAAS), 31
Gifts, conflicts of interest, 124
Global Technology Audit Guides (GTAG), 126, 127
Globalization
- and competition, 3, 11
- private equity finance, 402

Goals and objectives and fraud deterrence, 263
Governance
- board of directors. *See* Board of directors
- charter requirements, 152
- and fraud deterrence, 264–266
- private equity system, 397–399
- reform efforts, 144
- Sarbanes-Oxley provisions, 26, 27
- stock exchange listing standards, 143, 144
- and stock market performance, 10, 11

Governmental Accountability Office (GAO) Auditing Standards (Yellow Book), 37
Gramm-Leach-Bliley Act (GLB), 360, 361, 374, 375
Guidelines for Fraud Deterrence Engagements, 40

H

Handwriting, 217–219
Hart-Scott-Rodino Antitrust Improvement Act, 19
Health Insurance Portability and Accountability Act (HIPPA), 375
Hedge funds, 403
Hierarchy of Needs, 5, 6
Historical background, 15, 16
Homestead exemption, 277–283
Host-based intrusion detection systems (HIDS), 183, 184
Hotline for anonymous reporting, 262–264
Human resources policies and procedures. *See also* Employees
  and control environment, 125

I

I2 Analyst, 245
IDEA, 245
Identity theft
  bulk data breaches, 358, 373–376
  Consumer Sentinel, 359, 360, 362–364, 372
  defined, 358
  detection, 371, 372
  deterrence, 361
  enforcement efforts, 364–367
  extent of, 359–364
  GAO reports on, 359, 360, 362–365
  online methods, 357, 358, 360, 363, 365, 367, 370, 371, 376–378
  and organized crime, 364
  overview, 357, 358
  phishing, phreaking, and spoofing, 376–378
  phone pretexting, 361, 364
  protection of personal information, 367–371
  remediation, 372, 373
  and Social Security numbers, 358, 361, 362, 364, 365, 367–370, 372–374, 377
Identity Theft Act, 360, 361, 363
Identity Theft and Assumption Deterrence Act (ITADA), 18, 359
Identity Theft Penalty Enhancement Act, 366
Identity Theft Prevention Act, 359–362
Illicit activities and motive for fraud, 42, 48
Incentive or pressure to commit fraud, 45, 48, 261, 263
Indentation Materializer Electrostatic Device (IMED), 214
Independence of directors, 147, 148, 150
Information and communication. *See also* Communication
  assured information, 166. *See also* Information systems
  as part of COSO framework for internal control, 121
Information systems
  assurance, 166–173, 242, 243
  and business processes, 235–240
  data, increase in volume of, 161, 162, 223, 224
  and data analysis, 235–241
  data breaches, 375, 376
  integration challenges, 163–165
  security, 173–174
  state-of-the-art technologies, 162, 163
Information Systems Audit and Control Association (ISACA), 126, 137, 170, 172
Information technology (IT). *See also* Information systems
  assurance, 166–170, 242, 243
  and business objectives, 173
  COBIT, 126, 137, 172, 173
  and data analysis, 242. *See also* Data analysis
  monitoring, 137
  network admission control, 181, 182
  systems implementations and conversions, 244
Injunctive relief, SEC enforcement powers, 154
Insider trading, 265, 266
Insolvency, director liability issues, 312, 313. *See also* Bankruptcy
Instant messaging, 179
Institute of Internal Auditors (IIA), 170
  General Standard 300, control objectives, 172
  Global Technology Audit Guides (GTAG), 126, 127
  internal auditing defined, 139
  and IT control procedures, 172
  Practice Advisory 1210.A2-2, fraud reports, 253, 254
  as sponsor of Treadway Commission, 119
  standards, 38, 39
Institute of Management Accountants (IMA), 119
Insurance, officers and directors, 154, 155
Intellectual property
  arbitration and mediation, 393
  cease and desist letters, 392, 393
  copyrights, 382, 384, 385, 387–392, 394
  damages, 389–391, 394, 395
  defined, 381, 382
  destruction of infringing material, 395
  domain name proceedings, 393
  fraudulent appropriation of, 388
  inventory of, 386
  license agreements, 386–388, 392
  litigation, 393–395
  notices, 391, 392
  patents, 382–384, 386–389, 391, 394
  protection of, 387–395
  service marks, 384
  software, 385–387, 392
  trade secrets, 382, 385, 388, 389
  trademarks, 382–384, 387–391, 394
  value of, 381, 387, 388
Internal audit function. *See also* Audits
  and deterrence of fraudulent financial reporting, 266, 267
  information systems, 168–170
  listing standards, 147
  monitoring, 139, 140
Internal controls
  adequacy of, reporting on, 252
  annual report, 153
  assessment of, 49
  control environment, 8, 121–126, 264
  control objectives, 172
  control procedures, 121, 131–136
  and corporate objectives, 8
  COSO framework, 8, 31, 34, 118–140, 149, 263, 266, 407
  defined, 8
  and fraud deterrence, 4, 47, 247–249, 266
  historical background, 16
  importance of, 6, 7
  information and communication, 121
  information systems, 168–174. *See also* Information systems
  and internal auditors, 153, 154
  management assessment of, 146
  management responsibilities, 152, 153
  monitoring. *See* Monitoring
  and opportunity for fraud, 44, 45
  private equity system, 404–407
  as process improvement tool, 6, 7

Internal controls *(Continued)*
risk assessment. *See* Risk assessment
whistleblower compliance, 74, 75
Internal Revenue Service (IRS) Criminal Investigation Division (CID), 18, 19
International Standards Organization, 4
International Systems Security Engineering Association (ISSEA), 170
Internet
content filtering, 180, 181
domain names, 393
and identity theft, 357, 358, 360, 367, 376–378
Web assurance and control measures, 170, 171
Web services, 162, 163. *See also* Information systems
Internet Corporation for Assigned Names and Numbers (ICANN), 393
Interrogation
appearance and demeanor of interrogator, 191, 192
assumptive questions, 212
confessions, 208, 213
deception, detecting, 193–197
emotion, 195
interview distinguished, 188
introductory statement, 212
lies, types of, 195, 196
location for, 190, 191
methods, 209, 210
preparation for, 188–190, 207, 208
rapport, establishing, 192
rationalization, 209, 212
summary statement, 213
use of, 206, 207
Wicklander-Zulawski non-confrontational method, 210
Interrogatories, 52
Interviews
appearance and demeanor of interviewer, 191, 192
conducting, 197–206
deception, detecting, 193–197
diagrams, use of, 206
emotion, 195
facts, establishing, 198, 199
fraud deterrence versus formal investigation, 52, 53
interrogation distinguished, 188
lies, types of, 195, 196
location for, 190, 191
and monitoring performance of procedures, 138
notes, transcription of, 52, 54, 55
participatory approach, 211
passive, 52
preparation for, 188–190
purpose of, 199
questions, types of, 199–202
rapport, establishing, 192, 210, 211
selective, 211
types of, 203–206
untainted story, obtaining, 202, 203
Intrusion detection systems, 183, 184
Investigations
and fraud deterrence assessment, 47, 50–55
objectivity, 51
phases of, 52–54
reports, 252–256
seeking truth versus loyalty to client, 54
Investment Company Act, 22–24

J

Japanese management techniques, 4
Job applicants, 79–82, 84, 103, 112

K

Kaplan, Robert S., 9
Kickbacks, 124

L

Larceny. *See* Theft
Lean manufacturing, 4, 248
Legal and regulatory framework, 16–28
Levitt, Arthur, 144
Licensing, 386–388, 392
Life pressures and motive for fraud, 42, 48
Lifestyle needs and motive for fraud, 42
Limited liability companies (LLCs). *See also* Business entities
and private equity finance, 399

M

Malware, 184
Management
attitudes of and control environment, 122, 123
fraud, 33, 261. *See also* Financial reporting, fraudulent
motives and opportunity for fraud, 45, 46, 48
statutory and regulatory requirements, 152, 153
Management discussion and analysis (MD&A), 27, 28, 130
Manufacturing productivity, 6, 7
Maslow, Abraham, 5
MD&A. *See* Management discussion and analysis (MD&A)
Metrics and fraud deterrence, 10, 11, 248
Misappropriation of assets, 48, 132, 261, 263
Monitoring
audit committee function, 137
board of directors, 123
defined, 137
deterrence, 140, 266, 267
information technology controls, 126, 137
and internal audit function, 139, 140
as part of COSO framework for internal control, 121, 137–140
performance of procedures, 137, 138
transaction verification, 138, 139
Motives for fraud, 263
as element of fraud triangle, 41–43
and lack of internal controls, 7–9
managing, 43
and Maslow's Hierarchy of Needs, 5, 6
and need for professional skepticism, 48
and paradox of success, 5

N

Nasdaq listing standards, 143–145, 147–153
National Association of Accountants, 119
National Association of Certified Valuation Analysts (NACVA), 40
National Association of Securities Dealers (NASD), 144, 145
National Identity Theft Task Force, 367
National Information Infrastructure Protection Act, 18
National Security Agency (NSA), 174
Network admission control, 181, 182
Network intrusion detection systems (NIDS), 183, 184

New York Stock Exchange (NYSE), report on audit committees, 144, 145
New York Stock Exchange (NYSE) listing standards, 143–145, 147–153
Nominating committee, 147
Nondisclosure agreements, 385
Norton, David, 9
Not-for-profit organizations, 264

O

Obstruction of justice, 294
Occupational Safety and Health Administration (OSHA), 71
Officers
  CEO and CFO certifications under Sarbanes-Oxley, 27, 123, 143, 146, 147, 152, 153, 265
  liability insurance, 154, 155
  personal liability for fraud, 311–315
Opinion
  in fraud investigation reports, 253
  testimony. *See* Expert testimony
Opportunity for fraud, 41, 44–46
Organization for Economic Cooperation and Development, 174

P

Paradox of success, 5
Partnerships. *See also* Business entities
  private equity finance, 397–401
Patents, 382–384, 386–389, 391, 394
Patriot Act, 18
Pay for performance, 263
Payroll fraud, 261
PCAOB Auditing Standards, 29–31, 119
PCAOB (Public Company Accounting Oversight Board), 25
Piercing the corporate veil, 312
Pinkerton Detective Agency, 16–18
Plan-Do-Check-Act (PDCA), 174
Postal Inspection Service, mail fraud and identity theft, 362, 363
Private equity finance system
  components of, 397–399
  emerging trends, 402, 403
  Foreign Corrupt Practices Act, 405
  fraud deterrence, 403–411
  globalization, 402
  governance, 404–406
  and governance, 404–406
  intermediary private equity funds, 399
  internal controls, 404–407
  limited partnerships, 400, 401, 411
  overview, 397
  portfolio companies, 9, 408, 409
  private equity funds, 409–411
  Sand Hill Index, 401, 402
  and Sarbanes-Oxley, 401, 405–407, 412
  venture capital funds, 399, 401, 404, 408–409, 411
  volatility of market, 401, 402
Private portfolio companies, 9, 408, 409
Process improvement and fraud deterrence, 3–5, 11, 50
Productivity growth, 6, 7, 163
Professional skepticism, 33, 48
Public Company Accounting Oversight Board (PCAOB), 25
  auditing standards, 29–31, 119
Public Utility Holding Company Act, 22, 23

Q

Quality management tools, 3–5

R

Radio Frequency Identification (RFID), 186
Rationalization for fraud, 8, 14, 41, 43, 44
Real-time physical security systems, 186
Relevance, expert testimony, 55, 58, 60, 62
Reliability, expert testimony, 55, 58–62
Reports, 54
  documentation, 256
  expert witnesses, 64, 65
  fraud deterrence, 247–249
  on internal control system, 249–252
  investigation, 252–256
  objectivity, 253, 257
  standards, 247, 257
Retaliation, protection from, 76–79. *See also* Whistleblower protection
Revenue recognition and data analysis, 222
Risk assessment
  described, 128
  disclosure controls and procedures, 130
  employees, role of, 123
  enterprise risk management, 130, 131
  evaluation of risk, 129, 130
  financial statement audits, 33–35
  framework for internal control and fraud deterrence, 128–131
  and fraud deterrence, 131
  identification of risk, 34, 128, 129
  new businesses, 350
  as part of COSO framework for internal control, 121
Robinson-Patman Act, 19–21

S

Sarbanes-Oxley Act (SOX), 69
  annual internal control report, 153
  anonymous reporting, 127
  audit business, effect on, 49
  audit committees, 74, 123, 146, 147, 151, 152, 264, 265
  and Balanced Scorecard, 10
  board of directors, responsibilities, 148
  certifications by management, 27, 123, 130, 143, 146, 147, 265
  code of ethics requirement, 74, 75, 146
  disclosure controls and procedures, 130
  document retention policy, 75
  enactment of, 22
  enforcement, 154
  and financial statement fraud, 46
  and fraud triangle, 25
  insider trading rules, 265, 266
  internal audits, 139
  management responsibilities, 146, 152, 153
  obstruction of justice provisions, 283
  origins of, 69, 143
  and private equity finance system, 405–407
  provisions of, 8, 9, 11, 25–28, 121, 132, 136–139, 143–144, 146–147, 153, 247
  whistleblower protection, 69–76, 123
Schedules, 52
Scientific methods, admissibility of, *Daubert* factors, 55, 60, 61, 255

Secret Service, 17, 18, 360, 362, 366
Securities Act of 1933, 22, 23
Securities and Exchange Commission (SEC), 22–28
  "appearing and practicing" attorneys, 70, 73, 74
  and COSO framework for internal controls, 119
  enforcement powers, 154
  and ethics, 70
  insider trading rules, 265, 266
Securities Exchange Act of 1934, 22–24, 69, 134, 407
Security
  correlation of log entries, 187
  physical security, 186
  standards, 166, 172–174
Separation of duties, 132, 133
Service marks, 384
Sherman Antitrust Act, 19, 20
Small businesses, 133, 134
Software
  data analysis, 245
  intellectual property rights, 385–387, 392
  owned versus licensed, 386, 387
Spam, 184, 376, 378
Special audits, 49
Spendthrift trusts, 278
Standard of care, 52
Standards
  expert testimony on, 51, 52
  fraud investigation reports, 253–256
  listing standards, stock exchanges, 143–145, 147–152
  PCAOB Auditing Standards, 29–31, 119
  professional organizations, 29
  reporting, 247
  security standards, 166, 172–174
  Statements on Auditing Standards. *See* Statements on Auditing Standards (SAS)
  Statements on Internal Auditing Standards (SIAS), 38, 39
  Statements on Standards for Accounting and Review Services (SSARS), 38
State law
  exemptions from bankruptcy, 276, 277
  fraudulent transfers, 294–298
  homestead exemption, 278–283
  officer and director liability, 154, 155
  rules of procedure and evidence, 57
  securities regulation (blue sky laws), 407, 408
  whistleblower protection, 76–79
Statements on Auditing Standards (SAS), 30–37, 41, 45, 48–49, 171, 172
Statements on Internal Auditing Standards (SIAS), 38, 39
Statements on Standards for Accounting and Review Services (SSARS), 38
Subpoenas, 52
Surveillance networks, 186
System security engineering capability maturity model (SSE-CMM), 174
SysTrust, 170

T

Tax fraud, 19
Technology. *See also* Information technology (IT)
  and fraud, 177, 178
  and increase in volume of data, 161, 162, 223, 224
  and information systems. *See* Information systems
Telecommunications, 18
Telemarketing Fraud protection Act, 18
Theft, 132, 261
Total Quality Management (TQM), 4
Trade secrets, 18, 382, 385, 388, 389
Trademarks, 382–384, 387–391, 394
Transaction verification, 138, 139
Treadway, James C., Jr., 119
Treadway Commission, 119. *See also* Committee of Sponsoring Organizations of the Treadway Commission (COSO)
Trier of fact, 58
Trojans, 184, 371, 378
Trust Indenture Act, 22, 23
TrustE, 171

U

Uniform Fraudulent Conveyance Act (UFCA)
  overview, 296
  provisions of, 318, 319
  standing to bring action under, 297, 298
  state statutes, 294, 316
Uniform Fraudulent Transfer Act (UFTA)
  overview, 296, 297
  provisions of, 320–325
  standing to bring action under, 297, 298
  state statutes, 294, 316, 317

V

Venture capital. *See* Private equity finance system
VeriSign, 171
Viruses, 184
Voice messages, 179
Vulnerability scanners, 184, 185

W

WebTrust, 170, 171
Whistleblower protection
  and anonymous reporting, 25, 27, 74, 123, 127, 262–264
  and control environment, 123, 124
  federal law, 71, 77, 85
  Sarbanes-Oxley provisions, 69–76
  state law, 76–79
Whistleblower Protection Program of the Aviation Investment and Reform Act for the 21st Century (AIR21), 71
Wilhelm, Wesley Kenneth, 261
Wireless technology, 186
Witnesses
  experts. *See* Expert witnesses
  facts, knowledge of, 57

Y

Yellow Book, 37

Z

Zeune, Gary, 48